P9-EEO-041

By the same author:

Love At First Flight (with Charles Spalding)
When the Bough Breaks
Yesterday's Hero
Good Friday, 1963
The Paper Bullet
New Lease on Life
Chihuahua 1916
Welcome Back, Billy Rawls
The Fence Jumper
Eddie Bulwer's Ground
Throw the Rascals Out

FRONTIERS

THE DIARY OF PATRICK KELLY
1876–1944

A NOVEL BY
OTIS CARNEY

GENERAL PUBLISHING GROUP
Los Angeles

For information:
General Publishing Group, Inc.
2701 Ocean Park Boulevard, Suite 140
Santa Monica, CA 90405

Back cover photograph of Teddy Roosevelt
courtesy The Bettmann Archive.

Library of Congress Catalog Card Number: 95-077225
ISBN: 1-881649-05-9

Printed in the USA
10 9 8 7 6 5 4 3 2 1

General Publishing Group
Los Angeles

TABLE OF CONTENTS

ACKNOWLEDGMENTS

Patrick Kelly's diary is fiction, but the great events he lived through are historical facts. I couldn't have re-created them without the help of many individuals and original sources who shared with me their memories of what it was really like back then. I'm deeply indebted to them for the truth as they saw it, which is probably as much as we'll ever know.

For Patrick's Irish background, I drew on my own family's lore, particularly that of my grandfather, Will, and my great aunt Nora. Though they were reluctant to talk about their humble beginnings on the Other Side—the "No Irish Need Apply" opprobrium still stung—Nora lived with us until the age of 98, and couldn't help but wink out an occasional delicious tidbit from her past. A painter and a world traveler, she was a free spirit, a born gambler. When I'd sneak off to the racetrack—sinning against the work ethic—she'd slip me a fiver to bet for her, and mostly, bet on myself. At the bleakest times in my writing career, with my family and sensible friends begging me to give it up, Nora would whisper, "Go to it, lad. You've got but one life."

For Patrick's adventures in early Chicago, and then the Haymarket tragedy, I used Roger Butterfield's *The American Past,* and primarily Lloyd Wendt and Herman Kogan's excellent history, *Chicago.* Lloyd had been my patient editor when I wrote articles for his *Chicago Tribune* magazine. Later, when he reviewed my first novel and put it on the front page of the book section, he gave me some fatherly advice from the newsroom: "write it like you say it—and short!" Gratefully, and haltingly, I'm still trying.

Patrick's campaigns against the Sioux and Apaches have been my own lifelong obsession. As a boy traveling to Arizona, I'd peek out the windows of the Santa Fe Chief, longing for a glimpse of these fascinating creatures who lived in the desert. Since then, I've trudged a lot of mesquite and sagebrush looking for them. I've been to the old forts and battlegrounds, whether at Skeleton Canyon, Arizona, where Geronimo surrendered, or at Rosebud in Montana, where Crazy Horse, by defeating us so thoroughly, signed his own death warrant.

The classic source for this era is John G. Bourke's *On the Border with Crook.* As Crook's aide, this remarkable Irish Medal of Honor winner was not only an accomplished ethnologist but an accurate historian.

For the other side of the Crazy Horse and Wounded Knee stories, I turned to the Sioux themselves. The late Robert Burnette was a direct descendant of Crazy Horse. A former World War II Marine (unknowingly, we'd been present at the same Pacific battles), Robert later became chairman of the Rosebud Sioux Tribe and an author of national note. Generously, he spent days with my wife Teddy and me, revealing many truths about Crazy Horse that aren't in the white man's history books. According to Robert and another Sioux leader, Russell Means, most accounts have been doctored to preserve military reputations (how did so many of us get whipped by so few?), or desensitized so that we can live with the slaughter we perpetrated.

For example, my history lessons had never breathed more than a line or two about Wounded Knee. When I stumbled on the story shortly after VJ Day, I hurried out to that frozen hamlet in South Dakota, and learned of the tragedy first hand from an old and wounded Sioux survivor, Dewey Beard. Only many years later would I have a chance to tell it, first in a cringingly awful TV re-creation, peopled with the hoary likes of Lloyd Nolan and Joseph Cotten, and now, finally, hopefully with more truth, in the eyes of Patrick.

While filming the movie, *Cinerama Holiday,* I worked with a large crew of Apaches on their San Carlos Reservation in Arizona. At first inscrutable, they slowly accepted me and became a delight, spinning tales of the old Geronimo days.

For the Teddy Roosevelt story and our wars of empire, I'm indebted to many sources, including Stefan Lorant's *Life and Times of Theodore Roosevelt* and Edmund Morris' *The Rise of Theodore Roosevelt.* Particularly fascinating accounts of the Cuban and Philippine campaigns were found in G.J.A. O'Toole's *The Spanish War,* David Haward Bain's *Sitting in Darkness,* and Virgil Harrington Jones' *Roosevelt's Rough Riders.*

The accounts of General Pershing and Lt. George Patton in the Punitive Expedition of 1916 came to me first hand from two remarkable frontiersmen, both now dead. Lemuel Spilsbury, a giant of a ranchman when I interviewed him in Colonia Dublan, Chihuahua, had been Pershing's guide and almost a victim of the tragic fight at Carrizal.

Lem was at George Patton's side when the visionary young aide to Pershing launched the first automotive attack in U.S. history. Patton, a non-flyer, also *did* wreck one of Pershing's six precious air machines. Lem Spilsbury pulled him out, both of them grinning and sealing the secret between them all these years.

Harvey Taylor, a Mormon *éminence-grise* at Colonia Dublan, knew Pancho Villa as a boy, and told me of Pershing's fury after Carrizal that almost led to full-scale war between the U.S. and Mexico.

For World War I and the Earl Ellis adventure, I thank Colonel Robert Debs Heinl, Jr, USMC, for his *Soldiers of the Sea,* and the late

8

ACKNOWLEDGMENTS

Colonel John W. Thomason, USMC, for his epic "I-was-there" account, *Fix Bayonets.*

For an overview of American combat, Geoffrey Peret's *A Country Made by War* proved invaluable. I'm also indebted to my sister-in-law, Marina, for sharing her family memories of the Russian Revolution.

As for World War II, Patrick's adventures in the Pacific finally intersected with mine. His islands, Guadalcanal, Bougainville, Guam and the dreaded Carolines were all places I visited when people were shooting back.

My recollections of General Geiger were drawn from the 17 months I flew as co-pilot and navigator on his private aircraft. I was with him for the re-capture of Guam, then the horror of Pelelieu and the greater one, his last big command, the bloodbath of Okinawa. Though he was a gruff old warhorse, I admired him and he was awfully good to me, in the end trying to persuade me to sign on as a regular Marine. A fine career, he'd grunted, and why the hell go back to college with all the wars ahead?

The two night flights through the Carolines happened much as I wrote them for Patrick. The years have taken away the fear. Now it's just some excitement we had when we were kids, thank God never to have to do again.

My greatest gratitude goes to the patient friends who made *Frontiers* happen. Murray Fisher for his editing, and Quay Hays for his publishing.

Murray's skills contributed much to the success of Alex Haley's *Roots.* With me, he'd already sweated through thousands of pages of my earlier work, *Throw the Rascals Out,* a political satire published on blind faith by Quay Hays, and my non-fiction *Giving Up War,* which though unpublished expressed the same ideology as *Frontiers.* Murray's belief in what I was groping to say finally managed to wring it out of me in the form of Patrick.

None of it would have happened if it hadn't been for Quay Hays' untiring support from page one on. God knows how many drafts he's had to wade through. The happy ending was Quay's courage to plunge ahead with *Frontiers.*

In the end, Patrick's story is giving up war. For those who helped me so much in hope, and bringing it to life in peace, thanks for the memories.

To Will and Nora
Marie and Roy
and all of us who followed them
to The Other Side

"The things that will destroy America are:
prosperity at any price
peace at any price
safety first instead of duty first,
and the love of soft living and the get rich theory of life."

Theodore Roosevelt
January 10, 1917

EVE: Man need not always live by bread alone.
There is something else. We do not yet know what it is, but
someday we shall find out, and then we will live on that alone; and
there shall be no more digging or spinning, or fighting nor killing.

(She spins resignedly; he digs impatiently.)

Back to Methuselah
George Bernard Shaw

*"Uncle Sam, Uncle Sam,
won't you please come back to Guam!"*

*Song of Chamorro prisoners on Guam,
awaiting liberation by U.S. Marines, July, 1944*

PROLOGUE

JAKE
August, 1994

I've spent most of my life playing it safe. We were raised that way, avoid risk, control events, go for the sure thing. So we paid our dues to the system, and now at 72 I'm delighted to go coasting down the autumn river, watching the leaves turn scarlet and thanking my stars for the security and happiness I've known, indeed more than I deserve. Perhaps that's why I take it so much for granted. Oh, sure, there was adventure once. I had my bellyful of it in World War II and a nasty aperitif in Korea, but now those grisly places, the old comrades and terrors have long faded into shadows. For my generation and me, maybe our real game did end back then. Our job was done. We'd crossed every frontier that history and geography threw in our path. We'd put men on the moon, conquered the world, too, even though lately we seem to be having trouble digesting it.

So it was, with considerable shock that on the 12th of August 1994, a hand reached out to me from the grave and made me re-evaluate what all my years had been for.

Though I'm officially retired, I still keep a desk at my old investment firm of Castle, Dawes and Barrow. I'm not party to the decision-making anymore, but I do like the camaraderie of going in on the train with the fellows a few times a week. I read my *Wall Street Journal,* putter with a few securities. Then I take a stroll down LaSalle Street and have my familiar and usually convivial lunch at the Attic Club, hopefully with some of the young Turks who are still hard at the chase. After a brief nap and some more shuffling of papers, I catch the early train out to Lake Forest and try to get in a round of golf.

But on August 12th, there was no lunch at the Attic or golf. When I finally did come home, I would never again be the same man as the one who had left that morning.

Into my office, bowing politely, came two dignified gentlemen. Their calling cards, imprinted in English and Japanese, showed that they were tai-pans of one of the great Japanese conglomerates, Tanaka Group Ltd., with offices in Tokyo, Seoul, Singapore, Jakarta and Honolulu.

After the proper introduction formalities, they told me that they had learned of me, "Barrow-san," in the following way. Perhaps I hadn't realized, they said, but their company was adding to its worldwide chain of hotels. They already had several on Saipan and Guam, which were primarily destination resorts for Japanese honeymoon couples.

Their business had proved so lucrative that they'd decided to build still another honeymoon resort on the southerly cliffs of Guam. During their excavations to put down footings for the hotel, their laborers came on an old Japanese gun position, a sealed cave, with a buried entry port up to the cliff above.

As their blasting and bulldozing continued, they discovered a deep crevasse in the floor of the cave. Here, buried under rocks, lay a Japanese tin ammunition case. In it, wrapped in what appeared to be an Imperial Navy oilskin, was the partly handwritten and partly typed manuscript of a man's diary. His name was Patrick Kelly. I'm his grandson and namesake, John Patrick Kelly Barrow.

The moment was electric. In my office high above LaSalle street stood the erect and dignified Chairman Takeo Tanaka. Slowly, he opened an expensive leather suitcase, and from it drew out the battered ammunition tin. Wordlessly, he creaked it open and handed me the three ancient copy books in which my grandfather had recorded his life.

Takeo Tanaka bowed simply and said, in quite bad English, "Finding this, we have translation made. Reading Barrow family, Lake Forest, Illinois." He smiled. "From there, very easy. We have America offices, financial banks we trading with. One in Chicago, the Continental. They find you."

"My God," I said, fighting tears, "I can't believe this, sir. What do I say? How do I thank you?"

He bowed again and his close-cropped silver hair gleamed in the sunlight. "Is not necessary, thanking, Barrow-san. I am serving in the war, too. Air commander. Rabaul, Solomon Islands fighting. So few of us left. The shame of it, cause of Japan. But now, it is only friendship, yes? How it must be. From an old enemy, beg kind sir accept Japan gift of peace."

He came forward, stiff, shy. We embraced each other warmly, almost a clinging, I felt. A moment later, he and his associate bowed again, and left me holding Patrick Kelly in my hand.

What to say? I had no words and no one to say them to. The past swept over me. I could almost hear Patrick snorting, "So they call you Jake now, do they?" and he'd grab me by the nape of the neck and look me up and down. "Well, ain't ye the sissified little snot!" Feisty old bastard, how many times he'd lashed me with his truth. I fought him, I mocked him, but I always kept coming back to him for more, maybe for his strength. I stared dumbly at the three copybooks. I'd known that he'd kept a diary, in fact, I'd sneaked a brief look at it before World War II. But that was all so long ago.

Why had he never mentioned it again? Why had he just left it behind and buried the past? And yet, didn't I know the answer? He lived in the now, and never looked back.

I was almost afraid to open the first cover, for fear of what I'd find. Would I destroy these faded, yellowed pages if I dared touch them? Would it all drift away in dust? But thanks to the sensitivity of Chairman Tanaka, I noticed then that he'd left me a Xeroxed copy, bound in a tasteful cover, with the Tanaka Group logo—an opening flower with the sun rising from it—embossed discreetly in the bottom corner.

Yes, I could surely read the copy. It would be safer and easier. Yet I needed to touch the original. "Damn you, Grandpa," I whispered to him, "where have you been that I could never go!" His first notebook was crudely covered in animal hide, badly shrunken but still peppered with the brightly colored beadwork of some forgotten Indian.

Open it! I cried to myself. Yet the other books demanded a look as well. Leap to the end, bring him to me! Gingerly I touched them. My God, the sum of his diary was so heavy, I marveled that he could have carried it all those years. When I leafed the successive pages, they had the mustiness of the grave. The stains on them I imagined as splatters of the mud and blood and tears he'd known, and occasionally, I seemed to be smelling a sweetness, as if women wearing perfume had touched this before me. Faintly they remained, words of love dancing still in the elegant, cursive scrawl taught by nuns in Ireland, and later by Yankee schoolmistresses at Dobbs Ferry and Vassar. (My grandmother? I wondered. Even Mother?) Then machines began to chatter out the words, primitive Underwoods or Remingtons, their type faded and often overstruck as if the typist had not yet mastered the keys to their new world. And still more pages, typed now on the stationery of military headquarters, sometimes carbons, the originals apparently lost in the sweltering tents of far-off campaigns. A few pages toward the end were scrawled in pencil on Japanese rice paper, and smeared by the sweat of a last mourning and dogged survivor.

I was so disoriented that as I stood at the big window of my office, holding Patrick in my hand, my eyes were blurring across the great city of Chicago and the gleaming lake beyond. Hadn't he been here? Of course he had! Here with me and so long before me that there were still horse-drawn wagons churning the muddy streets, instead of sleek corporate jets whining in to land at the lakefront airport.

How much he knew that I never shall! I was almost resentful that he would throw it in my face, secure and complacent that I was, measured against him. And yet, what I had barely touched of him was a treasure. I knew that now.

Lately, I keep hearing people saying that every great nation needs a story, our own particular myth that binds us to our common past and gives us a star to steer by. A cry of survival, if you will.

This is us! "Warts and all, hell, yes, lad," Patrick would growl. "We've scarred our land with turrible wrongs, but who's perfect, anyhow?" So we suffered, died and were buried, yet new ones among us arose. William Faulkner called them the "strong loud voices unafraid." They rose to squall and scramble and shout in triumph until they were heard around the world. "This we are! We have prevailed! We shall prevail!"

My secretary was tapping me on the shoulder. "Mr. Barrow, you'll miss your train."

I turned to her with tears in my eyes she couldn't understand. "Yes, I'll miss it. No more calls. Lock my door."

"Sir?"

"Lock my damn door!"

Poor thing, did she think I was going to commit suicide?

Well, not anymore, I laughed to myself. These high-tech slabs of window glass were sealed in for the air conditioning. You couldn't open them if the building was burning down. The Crash of '29 and all the Black Fridays where men hurled themselves to death over scraps of paper were long behind me, with him in my hand.

Prevail. Prevailed.

Alexander Pope said, "They had no poets and they died."

But we didn't die. He showed me that.

We had a boisterous cacophony of poets. Nobody could shut us up! Kilroy was here! In my book, his name was Kelly!

This is us, still!

It is him.

Still ours.

Though he and we rest now in peace, lest we forget.

I can't forget.

Though I'm flawed and complacent and old, all my frontiers apparently crossed, no, this last one I must charge head-on.

Because I loved him. For all his bad-tempered truth, I loved him because he's more than me and our shared blood. He's what we are, his struggle so close in time to our struggles today that I'm ashamed when I complain about my losses, my petty ego failures. God help me, I thought, how dare I have anything but gratitude for this star he left me that I hold now in my hand.

Weakly, I sat down beside the window and opened the first diary, hoping against hope that it would be what I expected of him. I skimmed it, not really tracking or processing its import until I reached the last line. Here I heard him, and he shouted our myth.

"If you don't dream, me byes, you die!"

Sure, the words are illiterate, he could never shake his harsh Irish brogue that used to embarrass me so. But the language doesn't matter. To me, right then, his voice became the cries of uncounted thousands of immigrants, echoing in German, Polish, Scandinavian, black gullah or Jewish.

Us! That's what they're saying. This is our dream as much as his. Did we lose it along the way, or can we bring it back?

With a last glance at the hot sun searing Chicago, I whispered, "Take me home again, Patrick. Take us all." Then I turned the ancient page and began to read.

PATRICK

FIRST FRONTIER:
THE WILDERNESS
1876-1890

*WARNING to snoopers in
the barracks KEEP OUT!*

This copy book, my record of the events and the troubles, was bought by me, Private Patrick Kelly, 3rd U.S. Cavalry, at the sutler's store, Fort Fetterman, Wyoming Territory, New Year's Day, 1876.

Cost: 36 cents. In Chicago, it would have been a dime, the dirty robbers out here.

To protect this book from the harsh mountain weather, I had a half-breed post laundress stitch on a lovely elk-hide cover, with a pouch in it, to hold what the red savages would call "my Medicine." To wit:

St. Benedict's Medal, given to Patrick Malachy Kelly on the day of his birth, May 11, 1856, Laughrasheen Parish, County Mayo, Ireland, with instructions for use:

"1st. It drives from the human body every diabolical work, and where placed the infernal enemy cannot approach.

2nd. Preservation against plague.

3rd. Preservative against poison.

4th. Against lightning and storms.

5th. It brings consolation and strength to the tempted and desponding.

6th. Against the sickness of cattle (to be dipped in the drink of animals.)

Medal may be used by applying to the parts affected in case of illness, worn on the neck of the person, or placed on the door."

Well, lads, I still have the medal all right, but nary a door of my own to hang it from.

All these years building castles among the heathen, then pissing in the fire and moving on. Chasing the rainbow, I suppose. My mother always said, "You've got the wind at your back, and your hat on two hairs, Patrick."

Maybe that's why I took the wrong fork in the road so often, only to find the Divil Himself grinning at me from around the bend. But one day, God help me, I'll slip through his greedy fingers and make it all the way home.

If you don't dream, me byes, you die.

THE GIRLS I LEFT BEHIND ME

My tale begins with two women, one white, one red, and me such a greenhorn that they're in my heart, still.

They come into Fort Fetterman on the very same afternoon, March 10, 1876. A blizzard was raging so fierce that the snow didn't fall down straight, but whipped in sideways until it blinded us. Troopers were getting lost slogging from the barracks to the latrine.

Typical of the Army, for some reason we didn't know, dozens of us stiffs had been formed into ranks in front of the officers' quarters, stomping there with the frost stinging our faces. Pretty soon, I hear sounds rattling toward us, creaking wheels, the jangling of harnesses, and when teams of horses swirled out of the white mist, they were like ghosts, their bodies silvered with snow and their nostrils puffing steam.

Four Army ambulances had come racing in from the railhead which was miles away across the bleak prairie. What the ambulances carried wasn't wounded or dead men, but the wives of officers, rejoining their husbands in this hellhole.

"Wagonloads of hussies," grunts a soldier beside me. "Dangling their lace panties, daring us to look but dassent touch. Keep 'em east of the border, I says. Females and Army don't mix."

Most of them were the brides of junior lieutenants, crammed together until their knees were up under their chins and their booties resting on stacks of luggage. Happy to get there any way they could. But in the first ambulance rode one lady all by her lonesome. She was the wife of my captain, Cletus Bloxham.

He must have been expecting her, for he came charging out of his quarters, and when the back door of the ambulance opened, he bellowed at me, "Trumpeter Kelly!"

By the time I'd reached him, he'd already swooped her up in a bear hug. He was a stocky, powerful man, all the bigger in his buffalo coat and ear-muff cap. While he was stroking her, his gold spectacles got unhooked over one ear, and with the snow running down the lenses, he was blinking like he didn't know what he had his arms around.

God Almighty, I thinks, how did an old fart like him ever hook onto such a beauty? Ah, sure, she was showing some wear from the hard trip, and she had powdered herself up maybe to hide her age. Yet even at that, her features were delicate and had a high-bred look, her cheeks like ivory, and flushed pink from the fire in the ambulance stove. "Dear, dear Leah," Captain Bloxham kept whispering, "how I've dreamed of you." He was kissing her so hard and clumsy that he knocked off her hat and her hair spilled loose and golden.

Thinking it my place, being his trumpeter, I picks up her hat, whacks the snow off it and hands it to her. "Cold out here, ma'am."

Her eyes lifted to me and she smiled. "Why, thank you, soldier. I appreciate being so well cared for." She said it "kayd fo'." Her voice was soft and strange to me. Not being native-born, I wasn't used to accents from the South. She was Secesh, a soldier told me later. Rebel lady from Mississippi.

"Kelly's my new striker," said Captain Bloxham. "He'll attend your needs, my dear." He pointed me at the ambulance, and her first need weighed about two hundred pounds, a bulging steamer trunk that I had to heft on my back up the snowy path to officers' quarters.

By now the common soldiers had broken ranks and were swarming around the caravan, everybody wanting to baby the women and lug their baggage. We were starved for a female touch. Even if we couldn't do a damn thing about it, just to hear the laughter of white ladies, sniff their perfumes and watch their officers hugging their sweet flesh, God in heaven, it sure lifted our hearts.

Over near the headquarters log cabin, the post band was tootling away full swing, icy lips and frozen fingers blowing out "I Dream of Jeannie With the Light Brown Hair." And after it "The Girl I Left Behind Me." I felt sorry for the poor field musicians, standing there playing love songs with snow tears in their eyes.

The cabin door banged open and a tall man with a rusty beard stormed out. He was wearing raggedy hunting clothes, a civilian bum, I figures, until a nearby soldier hisses: "Watch your asses, boys. General Crook."

I hadn't seen the man before, but he sure come on like a general. "Dismiss!" he barked to his aides. "I'm not freezing my soldiers for this nonsense!" Then, shaking his head, he humped back into his log hut. From what the troopers said, he had a lot more important things on his mind right now.

There wasn't no secret to it. Crook was planning a winter campaign against the Sioux, and we were likely to get our marching orders pretty damn soon.

Fetterman had been thrown up in haste to prepare for a long war. The buildings were new frame Army style, and huddled beside them were some older adobes and log huts, probably from the trapper days. The whole shebang set on a high bluff below which the Platte River lay curled and frozen black. The fort was named for Captain Fetterman, killed by the Sioux and, so the lads said, by his own stupidity, charging into a swarming mess of heathen with only a handful of troopers. Most officers back then didn't have no fear of Injuns, figuring they'd licked hundreds of thousands of well-armed

Rebs in the War, compared to which these redskins was mangy coyotes, skedaddling at the first shot. Big talking it was, but I didn't say nothing until I'd seen for myself.

On a post as small as Fetterman, everybody knew everything. Even the Injuns could sniff out what lay ahead. For days now their drum tellygraph must have been humming. More and more bunches of Sioux were trailing across the prairie into the safety of the post. Hunt a hole before the bullets started flying. They come dragging travois, and their dogs and ponies were so starved down they could barely totter along. These Sioux stragglers were pretty much scorned by the wilder elements of the tribe. "Loafers around the fort," the warriors called them, and rightly so, for they were pitiful, snatching old bean cans from our mess or anything that shined and wasn't nailed down. General Crook probably figured that these were just less Indians we'd have to fight, so he let them pitch their teepees below our pickets along the frozen Platte. Their smoky, dirty camp was off limits, but soldiers being soldiers, a few of the lads skulked in there, hoping to bed a squaw. As for me, I wouldn't touch one. Lie in their greasy blankets and God knows what you'd get up with.

About then, I hear shouting over by the ambulances. Commotion of some sort, and I run toward it. Troopers with rifles were wading into a bunch of loafer Sioux. From what I could see, they were mostly squaws and kids wearing cast-off charity clothes and scraps of Civil War uniforms. They'd spotted a crate of officers' goods that had fallen from one of the ambulances and split open. Injuns figure, if a white man isn't using something, it's public property, help yourself and share it tribal style. So down they were in the snow, ripping out of the crate anything that caught their fancy.

A squaw run by me, stuffing a lace nightgown under her blanket. A pair of wiry, half-naked young bucks were getting away with pots and pans, and a limping grandpa had an umbrella opened and was pegging around beneath it. The soldiers come punching in, swinging rifle butts, and rescuing one trooper who was getting the tar licked out of him by a pack of Sioux lads.

In rushes a lieutenant, blowing a whistle. "Stop this! Break it up! Have the interpreter tell them to get back to their camp, or they'll be driven out of this post once and for all!"

"Sir!" a soldier cries. "Interpreter ain't around. They pretend they don't savvy."

The lieutenant grabs an Indian girl standing near him. "You! Tell them to clear out of here! No stealing will be tolerated!"

In the excitement, I might not have noticed that Sioux gal except for the way she acted. When the lieutenant touched her, she flung his arm off like it was a snake. Her eyes were hot black, her shoulders stiff, her head held high. This one sure wasn't no groveling charity case. She wore buckskin leggins fancied in bead-work, and had a blue blanket wrapped tight around her, covering everything but her eyes. "Watch that mean bitch," grunts a soldier beside me. "I seen 'em pack guns under them blankets."

The girl thrust past us like we wasn't there. Striding into the midst of the noisy, wrangling Injuns, all she had to do was jerk her head at them and snap out a word or two in Lakota. The brown faces whipped to her, fear maybe, respect, I don't know. But they stopped yammering and pulled their mitts out of the crate. With the snow blowing over her, she stood like a statue until the last of the Injuns were on their feet and drifting away.

It would have worked out just swell if a dumb, pimply-faced recruit hadn't started lording it over them, jabbing his Springfield muzzle into their bellies to hurry 'em along. The Sioux girl sprung at him and kicked the rifle out of his hands. He started to throw a punch at her but I grabs his mitt and like to break it off. "Leave her be, damn ye, or you'll start it all over again!"

After I'd shoved him aside, I noticed the Sioux gal kneeling in the snow. She was trying to fit the busted top back onto the wooden crate, but the nails were sprung and wouldn't slide into their proper holes. "Hell with that," I says, and squashes the thing down with my boot. When I reaches out to help her to her feet, she gives me not a whit of thanks, just a flash of her dark eyes, burning with hate.

"Good work," says the lieutenant, coming up to her. "You kept somebody from getting hurt, and that's how I expect it. Take your people back to their lodges and stay there, that clear?"

She twisted past him and started away, but he seized her. "I'm speaking to you, dammit! Answer me!"

Right then, Captain Bloxham comes huffing up, snow glistening on his short-cropped steely hair. Mrs. Bloxham was beside him, still in her brown traveling coat and clutching her fur collar tight against her neck. "Young man," Bloxham barked, "what the devil is all this ruckus? Can't you control these people?"

"Trying to, sir," the lieutenant said, "but it's the new bunch that drifted in from Fort Robinson. Spoiled Indians, sulkers, and I won't put up with it. This one, though," he jerked his head at the tall Sioux girl, "she's damn well going to learn better. I've made her responsible for order. She claims to have had schooling at Robinson, even done housework for whites."

"Oh, don't tell me!" Mrs. Bloxham exclaimed. "Really, Lieutenant, this is such luck. The Captain's quarters haven't had any care. They're a pigsty. You don't suppose the girl could help me out?"

"Well, I imagine so, ma'am. Most of 'em will do anything for a greenback."

Mrs. Bloxham gripped her husband's hand. "Clete, dear, please. You know we'll be entertaining, what with General Crook here and so many old friends. But I just can't do with that awful kitchen, if we have people in...."

Bloxham sighed. "Leah, the people will be gone very shortly. I've told you that."

"But I'll be here, the other wives, too. I want it nice for you when you come back. Remember Arizona, how cozy we were at Fort Grant? My little Lupe, was it? The Papago?"

"Pima," Bloxham grunted.

"Well, I couldn't have done it without her. And now this one." She turned and smiled at the Sioux girl. "She certainly looks strong enough. Do you think she's intelligent, Lieutenant? I mean, if she's already worked for whites or even been trained a bit?"

"Well, ma'am," the lieutenant said, "any of them can do the work, if they've got a mind to." Then he and the Bloxhams began eyeballing the girl from her leggins to her shiny black hair like she was livestock in a pen.

"She'll be fine, I can just tell," Mrs. Bloxham said. "Clete, can't we try her?"

Bloxham's heavy shoulders lifted and fell. "Whatever you wish, my dear." He turned to the lieutenant. "Tell her, young man, that we'll allow her to sleep in the kitchen, keep herself warm, but we shall tolerate no thieving of food for her relatives. I'm not feeding the tribe."

"Oh, Clete, bosh," Mrs. Bloxham said. "What's a little toting? I grew up with nigras taking things. These people have nothing else." Smiling, she approached the Sioux girl and patted her on the shoulder. "Dear, I'd like you to work at our quarters, no children to care for, just kitchen. Cook, clean?" She fluttered little hand signs about pots and scrubbing. "Do you understand ?" The girl remained silent, her eyes tracking over the powdery white face. "I pay well," Mrs. Bloxham added. "Twenty-five cents a day, how would that be?"

"Too much," Bloxham grunted. "Food is plenty."

"Clete, hush." Mrs. Bloxham turned back to the Sioux girl. "We'll take good care of you, I promise. What is your name, dear?"

The girl's black eyes didn't leave Mrs. Bloxham's.

"Tell the lady your name," snapped the lieutenant.

Slowly, the Sioux girl drew the blanket from her face. She sure wasn't no beauty by white man standards. She had a sharp Injun nose and eyes slanty enough for a Chinaman. Her skin was the color of dark bronze with purple tattoo marks pecked into it. But when snowflakes began dotting her high cheek bones and melting like tears, the savage look of her seemed to soften and a proud smile flickered across her lips. She took Mrs. Bloxham's left hand in both

27

of hers. "Injun say left hand come from heart," she murmured, then peeled back the lady's coat sleeve and touched a bracelet which was glittering there. "Pretty thing," she said. "Oh, you very fine, madam. Much monies." When Mrs. Bloxham started to draw her hand away, the girl gripped it. "Ah no, I don'· steal from waiscu. You surprise, fine madam? You say, Sioux girl intelligent? What you think? Yes? Oh, thank you, madam. Make cook, make bed, scrub floor. Keep white hands clean. Tell other fine madams, see my little Injun! Make me happy, keep my house. By'm'by girl tired, girl hungry, want sleep. No! No! Who you think you are! Injun sleep with dogs in barn. Injun eat bones. Lazy Injun! Whip her!!" She chopped her hand between them. "No more! Not for waiscu no more! Find black woman, slave woman! 'What is your name dear?'" she mimicked. "I am Walks Outside! Lakota woman. Where-I-stay. Outside!"

With a whisk of the blanket up over her mouth, she turned on her heel and strode back to her people who were shuffling off, disappearing into the snow.

"Oh my!" Mrs. Bloxham's hand flashed to her lips and she looked crestfallen. "Are they all like that? What did I do wrong?"

"Nothin', lady," grunted a soldier who'd been hanging around watching. "Spoilt, cocky. Put me under that one's blanket and I'd take her down a peg."

Captain Bloxham whirled. "Out!" he bellowed. "If you haven't any business better than a dirty mouth, I'll make some for you!"

"Just saying the truth, sir," the soldier muttered. "Sorry, Cap'n, no offense intended." He touched his cap in salute and hustled off.

Bloxham, red in the face by then, turned to his wife who was frowning as the Indian girl drifted away. "You've lost nothing, dear," he said. "Good riddance. Lately these Sioux are becoming more sullen and impudent than I can remember. But I'll find you a pair of hands, even if it has to be Kelly here."

As we slogged through the snow back to his quarters, he asks me how much cooking I'd ever done. "Corned beef and cabbage is about the extent, sir," I says, and tells him that on the Other Side, me Ma and sissies did the scullery.

"That just changed," he grunts. We hadn't but gotten back to the dark musty quarters before Mrs. Bloxham had stripped off her traveling coat and begins fussing in the dusty cupboards. I could see that she'd run help around plenty in her life, nagur slaves, I suppose, and I was the next in line. She was wearing a white, lacy blouse with puffy sleeves, didn't want to soil it, so she had me lay roaring fires in the cramped parlor and the kitchen stove. Next she sends me out in the blizzard to draw water from the post well, chop some ice while I was at it, all the time me thinking, "Chambermaiding dames sure ain't what I signed on for!"

When I come back in, stomping the snow off me, it was already dark and a new man was in the parlor, warming himself in front of the flames. A tall dandy he was, handlebar moustache and tailored cavalry boots that covered his knees. I'd seen him around the post, Major Scipio Shaw, 3rd Cavalry. The lads said that he was one of the roughest Injun fighters in the Army, but the way he was swanking around with Captain Bloxham's wife, he looked like a prissy lounger to me, and plenty stuck on himself. He and Mrs. Bloxham were tinking sherry glasses, her with soft laughter and him snaking his arm around her waist like they was going to dance or something.

Mrs. Bloxham was thirsting for gossip, so Shaw grins and says, "Well, Grant's brother Orville has his poker players in the White House basement. Now they're betting on this new game of baseball. They have leagues for it. But Sam's cigars are still first rate."

He tossed one to old Cap Bloxham who bit off the end. Then Mrs. Bloxham says, "Oh, give us the dirt, Cupe. That last ball at the White House. Who was there, who was dancing with who?"

"Or sleeping with," says Shaw with a wink.

"That's uncalled for, sir," Bloxham snapped. "And, I'm not sure I care."

They kept natterin' on, who was getting promoted or who cashiered out as a drunk. Social was a big thing to these regular Army families. Hell, they'd known each other since the Rebel war and had served together all over the plains, with not much else to do but gossip the lonely nights away.

Being out of it, just a common soldier, I clumps into the kitchen and rummages through the bean cans to see what I might feed the swells. Then, from the parlor, I hear Mrs. Bloxham laugh and say, "Oh Clete, tell him, turn him loose. Your striker, what's his name?"

With his blouse open and a sherry glass in his fist, Bloxham comes into the kitchen and says, "You won't be needed tonight, Kelly. Major Shaw insists on entertaining my wife."

He said it quiet, almost sour, and his eyes seemed tired behind his specs. "Yessir," I says, happy as a lark to get out of the scullery.

"But, Kelly, be here six a.m. sharp, fix breakfast. If you can find eggs at the sutler's store, buy some, charge my ticket."

"Yessir."

"Mrs. Bloxham is used to eggs."

We looked at each other, hearing from the parlor the light laughter of the lady and the major. "Anything else, Captain?"

"That will be all." Slowly, Bloxham turned and walked back to join them. On his way past the stove, he tossed in his dead cigar.

I never did fix that breakfast. About midnight, sergeants come barking into the barracks with orders from the headquarters log cabin. At 3 a.m. we'd break camp, heap our bedrolls into the wagons and go crunching off in the snow to find the hostiles. It wasn't a matter of roughing them up a bit and surrendering the rest. Them wild ones had a chance to come in with the friendlies, but they weren't about to. Daring us they were, holed up out in the mountains, ready to die before they'd quit. So we had no choice: Do what we had to, that was the order. Run 'em down and bury 'em.

When I dozed off again, a helluva nightmare come over me. A giant black horse, like one of the ambulance team wheelers, was charging in out of the snow, snorting fire from his nostrils. God Almighty, when he swept by me, astride him were two women, almost naked, the skin of one red and the other white. They didn't have faces on 'em that I could see, but I was shouting, warning 'em not to fall off or they'd freeze in the snow. I run after 'em, waving my arms, but never did find 'em. When I caught the horse, he'd turned snow white, and I rode him home alone, wherever home was. Never got to it. About then, reveille blew, and we was off to boots and saddles.

I don't know how many nights later, it was black as a whore's heart, and we were lying like corpses in the snow, huddled together, shivering, wondering if we'd die, and about half hoping we would, just to get the hell out of here.

Montana Territory, they called it, but for us bluebellies, it was a god-awful wilderness with the snow up to our horses' hocks, and not a track or a light or a human being to tell us we were still in the world.

We'd been following the Crazy Woman Fork of the Powder River, a long valley where black cottonwood trees stood like frozen skeletons. When we halted and lay in the snow, our officers passed the word that the Sioux camp was close by now. And not just any old camp, either. In it was the man we'd been sent to kill.

Crazy Horse. The name whispered through the ranks. Ah yes, I'd heard of the blackguard from some of the old timers at Fort Fetterman. Up and down the Bozeman Trail, Crazy Horse had struck terror into the frontier troops for years now. Many a miserable mother's son lay buried with the prairie dogs because of him. A charmed life he had, prancing his pony and playing the decoy, with an entire skirmish line blamming lead at him and failing to hit him even once. No question that he was a warrior of great renown, but he was also a holy man, possessed of powers that the other savages feared. T'was said he could foresee events before they happened. His medicine was so strong that a .45-70 Springfield couldn't knock him down, or so he believed.

"In a pig's eye," I says. Back at Fetterman, huddling in the troop quarters beside the roaring fire, I scoffed at my bunkies for spouting such rot. It was the stuff of hedge priests and leprechauns, all the goblins of simple folk that I thought I'd left back home. But still, the old timers would just stare at the snow piling up on the window frames and say: "You ain't been scared yet, sonny, until you hear the screaming of them reds, gouging their knives into your eyes."

So now the warm fires were gone, and we just had a few minutes left before we'd thunder down into the camp. Kill the savages while they slept. Kill Crazy Horse and all the rest of his pack. Gorge ourselves on the food they had, or sure as County Mayo is green, we would starve out here, and the wolves would be digging into the snow to gnaw our bones.

Ah, now, quit it, lad, I says to myself. But there was ice in my teeth, and I couldn't stop the shivering in my spine.

Cahoon, a big corporal from Texas, must have felt my flutterings because he was lying next to me. He whispers: "D'ye have any idea what day it is, Paddy?"

"Ah, hell, man, I wouldn't be knowing. I've lost track."

He grinned in the starlight, pulling off his buffalo gloves and giving me a chaw. "It's St. Patrick's Day, Kelly. Ain't that when you hod carriers do your praying?"

"Them that's pious does, I suppose. But with me, I'd play hell even getting into Purgatory, so my Momma says." I was thinking about her then, God help us, wouldn't she be working the beads for her lad if she could see him now!

"Yah, you better start prayin', recruit." says Severnson, a Swede private who was hunched up against his horse's forelegs. Severnson had a yellow beard, but it was all icicles now, glinting in the stars.

"Officer sonsofbitches!" somebody whispered. "Name of God, how long do we got to freeze here? Get us movin' one way or the other!"

Cahoon took out his chaw, lifted his ugly face to the sky and sniffed like a dog. "Smell 'em I do. That's Indian smoke, boys. They're down in that next coulee, sure as hell. They's layin' a bonfire to roast us on."

Then an officer hissed from someplace up on the snow bank. Or maybe it was a horse pissing, I couldn't tell. We were lying beside our horses, with their reins tied to our wrists. It was the only way to keep the beasts from running off on us, and there wasn't any way for a human to run off, much as I'd thought about it.

Severnson had deserted once, and they brigged him for six months after they hauled him back. They branded a D on his butt, and he was lucky at that. Some said that down in Kansas, a colonel named Custer had deserters flogged with steel whips, and then tied spread-eagled to wagon wheels. When the column moved out, the deserter would cartwheel along in the dust and heat and after a few miles, wish he was dead.

Severnson, trying to defend himself, told me that out of every three troopers in the rotten frontier army, at least one would head for the hills. And I thinks: How can you blame the poor clods if soldiering is like this?

We'd been days on the trail since leaving Fort Fetterman, slogging in snow, sliding on ice, up the frozen blue veins of the Tongue and then the Rosebud rivers. When it came time to leave the wagons, because they couldn't bust through the drifts, each of us carried a bedroll, meaning a blanket and a canvas, a Springfield weighing eight pounds, and 150 cartridges weighing ten.

Hell's fire, I hadn't even shot off my carbine, because they wouldn't give us target practice. Said it cost the guvmint too much money.

"Boys, you're beginning the Great Sioux War," a Mr. Strahorn says to us at our first night's campfire. He was a mournful-faced civilian who wrote stories for a newspaper in Denver. He was always scribbling in his pad, and trying to make us feel important by jotting down our names. But I must say, I listened to Strahorn as much as I could, because part of armying, I'd learned by now, was never telling us common soldiers one whit of where we were going or why. "We're no better than damn mules," I grunts to Strahorn.

"But tactically necessary, young man. Forced marching in the winter time is the only way we can catch the hostiles. They can't move their camps on us, they don't like to fight in the snow, because they lose the advantage of their swift ponies, which are much better in this country than our American ones. Trapped, they are. If this command can locate Crazy Horse and strike him down, mark my words—and General Crook has told exactly this to Sheridan—we will end the Sioux war before it begins. Burn their supplies, slaughter their ponies, and the stragglers that are left will have lost heart for fighting. They'll slink back into the agencies and you fine lads who did it can return to your posts and count the days till your discharge."

"Glory be," I says, a green recruit with pie in his eyes. But the old timers in the ranks just spat their chaws and turned away. They knew what we were up against. We hadn't but left Fetterman before a blizzard struck us. Winds came howling down across the gray, dead buttes, whipping the sagebrush first, and then the snow began burying the sagebrush until we couldn't see which direction was up or down. We were marching north along the Big Horn mountains, but when the clouds choked off the skyline, there was not a landmark to guide by except the butt of the trooper's horse ahead of you, and sometimes you couldn't even see that.

Making camp the second night out, we came into a grove of cottonwoods and found an Indian puppy, hung in a tree. It was like they were trying to tell us: Eat this, *waiscu* hairface, because it's the last vittles you'll get.

Third day, we were into big snow where you make a wrong step, you'd bury in a drift higher than the horse, and the fellers would have to put ropes on the floundering beast just to pull him out. Afternoon of that day, the half-breed scouts, Gruard, Pourrier and the Garnier boys started whooping like heathen. Something black was dragging toward us across the snow. The officers were trying to keep us from seeing it, but I saw it, up close too. It was an Army horse, nothing but bones and hair, stove up so bad you could push him over with your hand. Lashed across his back with thongs was a naked soldier, two big purple bullet holes in his frozen chest. When they cut him down and lay him in the snow, a sergeant recognized him as a recruit, 3rd Cavalry, who'd deserted the fall before. Story was, he'd been heading for the Black Hills to mine gold. The reds had stuck a wad of grass in his mouth, and when the surgeon pulled it loose, out flops the poor bugger's pecker, sliced off and stuffed down his throat.

Severnson, who was beside me, began puking. General Crook, who was leading this wild march, just sat on his horse with his sandy beard spiked with icicles and his eyes tracking across all of us. "The next man who plans to desert," Crook said, "let him come up here and bury this one."

By now there was a crowd of us flapping around in the snow like vultures, breathing steam that froze on our nostrils, and beating our arms on the sides of the St. Paul blanket coats most troopers wore. I was lucky to have a buffalo coat that Captain Bloxham had given me, and the hairy gloves to go with it, rather than the heavy felt ones that were issue.

I glanced up at Crook, who was a big man anyhow, and seemed about eight feet tall in the gray floppy hat he wore, and a collar of wolf fur wrapped up around his neck. He was riding a damn mule, of all things, and his greatcoat was greasy from campfire smoke and hanging in tatters. He didn't have one mark of U.S. on him. He could have been a tramp, slouching there on his mule, his gray eyes like gunsights beading across every one of our faces. He didn't say a word, just let the wind howl and riffle the dead soldier's long brown hair.

Nobody volunteered to touch the corpse. Finally, a pair of hospital stewards rolled out a rubber poncho to wrap the frozen remains. Crook says quietly, "Don't waste the poncho on him. Dig him into the snowbank. Mark the coordinates, Bourke," he says to his aide, who was a wiry Other Sider and a soldier so fierce they'd given him a Congressional Medal in the Rebellion. "Graves detail will come back for him when he thaws in the spring."

Then Crook booted his mule into a snowbank and began slogging out a new trail up onto higher ground. By dusk, he was on snowshoes near the camp, blasting into a covey of blue grouse, and dropping several on the wing with his repeating Winchester. A rifle, mind you, not a fowling piece like the lordships used back home to kill birds.

I thinks right then: I'm out here with different kind of men, all right. Hard faces, tough customers, only a step away from the animals, kill or be killed—living off the land, biting the blizzard in the teeth and daring it to try to put them down.

Surgeon Munn had a thermometer with the red bulb on it froze at 36 degrees below zero, and he says it was really about fifty below. Mother of God, I'd never seen so much as an icicle back in Mayo. Before daylight, the cook had to chop our bacon with an axe, and broke two axes doing it. We had to stuff our tin forks and knives into the embers before we used them, because if not they'd pull the skin off your tongue. The same for horses' bridles. You'd tear apart the beasts' mouths unless the iron was warm going in.

Days and days like this, ghosts a-horseback, drifting through snow-blown whiteouts where you couldn't see any direction or any sense in the madness of it. Worse were the nights, where we'd dig down deep into the snow, two men lying in each hole like rabbits and hoping that our miserable two blankets and pieces of canvas would be enough to keep us alive. You couldn't even get up to make water lest you'd freeze your precious little privates.

I began hating them reds, huddling in their snug teepees someplace we couldn't find. We hadn't seen a one of them. They knew better than to be outdoors. But Captain Bloxham would pull off his little gold-rimmed specs and say, "Bully luck for us, soldier. The hostiles don't suspect our presence. It'll be a shooting match when we find them."

We did just that, sometime in the dusk of St. Patrick's Day. Gruard, the head scout, came thundering in, kicking up snow. He'd spotted a small party of Sioux moving up the Crazy Woman canyon. General Crook and his officers spread their map out on the snow, and I was there with them, looking at it. Captain Bloxham had hooked onto me a couple of weeks before we'd left Fetterman. His battalion A was filled up with farriers, but he lacked a personal trumpeter, so I became it. They gave me a golden little bugle and all I had to learn was blow a couple of squeaks. Bugles were the only signal between the troops and, as Captain Bloxham said, "You ride a mount well, and you've got strong legs under you, Kelly. I guarantee you'll be doing some running to carry out my commands."

The officers jawed there a while, and then to most everybody's surprise, General Crook folded the map and said, "Reynolds, I'm giving you the camp. Don't fail me." The way I understood it, Crook broke the command in two. He and his troops would circle out northeast to block any possible retreat for the reds. The rest of us, three battalions under Colonel Reynolds, would move up the creek and swoop in on the hostiles while they slept.

So now, with a good 75 miles of marching behind us in just three days, we lay out on the snow, waiting for the orders to attack. The night was frozen chill, the stars glittering close. Beautiful, if you looked at it like the Lord Himself must have been doing. Black lumps of us lying in lines, and our horses stomping and nickering above us. My mount was a big-headed roan, government animal Number 117. I called him Freckles from the color of him. As I huddled in the snow, he was too tired even to fight the reins tied to my wrist. I reached up to his nose and pulled it against my neck. His breath was so warm it gave me a little shiver, or maybe it was just fright.

When I looked up again, the clouds were running low, and a silver-blue dawn was streaking them. "Trumpeter out," says Captain Bloxham, and I followed him over to a knot of officers, squatting on the hill.

Bloxham was breathing hard, just from the work of walking in the snow. Little wonder that he was showing his age. He'd fought in the Rebellion and had even been Army before that. When he overexerted, his face would get so puffy that his eyes were almost hidden in it. Unless he breathed into his rimmed specs and rubbed them clean, he had trouble seeing who he was talking to. Most of the old Army rankers figured him as kind of a joke. They called him Piggie, the way he'd huff around. Ah, he did have the pomp and bluster of those senior Armies, but underneath, he had a good soft heart. He took me under his wing, you might say, like a father to a son.

"Your first action," he grunted as we went up to join the others. "You will feel fear. I do. Every man who isn't a liar feels it. But do not be a coward, Kelly. The Sioux have a saying, It's a great day to die. At my age, any day is, with all the shot and shell I've seen. Consider yourself privileged to die like this if you have to."

"I ain't figuring on it, sir."

"Good. Then you will not play the coward, besides which I won't let you. I'd kill you first."

He was just big-talking, of course, fidgeting off his own nerves. I could see it the way his hands shook. Colonel Reynolds, another one too old to be doing this, was kneeling in the snow, drawing a map with his glove. A Battalion under Bloxham, and M Battalion under Major Scipio Shaw, would go into the village and do the killing. That's about all I got, except for seeing Shaw standing there, tall and erect, his handlebar moustache bristling with ice as he clicked cartridges into his revolver. Gone was the dandy who'd been tinking sherry glasses with Mrs. Bloxham. The fighter Shaw was a rough, fierce bastard that his men cursed one minute and loved the next. You couldn't give him too much kill. Cahoon used to sneer:

"That there Trojan, he'd bury the lot of us if it would give him a General's star."

Then Reynolds said the other battalion under Captains Moore and Dewees would be split to cover both sides of the village and prevent the hostiles from escaping. Major Shaw turns to Gruard, whom some said was a nagur and some said a kanaka from the Sandwich Islands. Anyhow, he had a black face and was head scout. "Are you certain this is Crazy Horse's village?"

"Figgers to be," Gruard answers. "I see three horses in the pony herd that come from his band. The rest, there's some Cheyenne, but I got a strong notion he's in there with 'em."

It wasn't but a minute or two later, we began to move. Poor old Captain Bloxham's fingers were so froze up, when he wanted to relieve himself he couldn't get his pants open. I stood there, wanting to help him, but then again, he was an officer and enlisted couldn't touch 'em. When he finally finished his squirts, he asked me to give him a leg-up and get him mounted. "Stay with me, Kelly. Within one yard of me at all times."

"There I'll be," I says.

"Thank you, son."

When we came over the crest, a big cottonwood bottom stretched below us, and hidden in it were the lodges of the reds. We couldn't make out any of the divils at this distance, but their campfire smoke was already curling up in the still air. Then as we slid down the slope into the canyon floor, the first soft light began rubbing the cliffs above the camp. Big boulders had rolled down here, and the sun turned them gray first, then red, then yellow. Cahoon whispers to me, "Let the Sioux get in them rocks, they'll make this our graveyard, you watch."

Captain Bloxham whirls to him. "Mind your tongue, soldier. Captains Moore and Dewees will be holding the high ground."

The Army way, I figured. Somebody's supposed to be here, and another somebody's supposed to be there. But they never are. Even then, I knew it was death's way, and I was riding right into it.

Ah, yes, t'was a grand thrill at first. "Troopers, two's into line," Captain Bloxham rasps, and beckons us with his gun barrel glinting in the dawn. Only then did I notice the piece he'd pulled out of his scabbard. It was a shotgun, an old fashioned fowling piece with twin hammers. I recalled then that he'd told me once: Long Tom rifles were for the enlisted marksmen. The only Indians the Captain worried about were the ones who got in too close, and he could rip them apart with shotgun slugs. The close ones were all he could see.

Then we started, rattling up, troopers abreast, first at a walk till we get in line. Cahoon grunts: "Too hot for fighting. Strip down, boys." He unbelts his blanket coat and flings it away, along with his felt gloves. Couldn't pull a trigger with those mitts on. Other troopers began tearing off their coats. Captain Bloxham swung to me, as if I could do something to stop it. "Damn you men!" he bellers. "You'll need your gear!"

Nobody was listening, the horses making too much racket, clopping on the icy ground. Then, over to our left, I hear a new commotion. Major Shaw, wearing a big buffalo hat and revolvers in both hands, spurs his horse into a gallop, and the gray horses of the rest of his troop fairly fly across the open ground toward the village.

We were running, too. I don't know how Number 117, my freckled roan, had any bottom left, but he sure showed it. He was flat out like a racehorse and I had to check him once because Captain Bloxham was huffing at me that he couldn't keep up.

Right then, in a great cloud of snow, we struck the first thing that wasn't supposed to happen. The open plain sheared off into a ravine, thirty foot deep and more than that wide. Gruard hadn't told 'em about that. A horse couldn't leap it, let alone get down the cliff. Major Shaw cries to the milling troops: "Here, this way!" He plunges into a cut in the bank, his horse butt down on his hocks and sliding bad. The second man to try it, his horse goes down and rolls on him. Then we're all swirling into the ravine, and the sheer weight of the horses is tearing down the bank.

I didn't know where anybody else was, or care either. I had my carbine up under my arm when the roan stopped and reared. Ten feet from me was an Indian, standing stony as a statue with a blanket wrapped up to his nose. I swung the carbine. "No!" Captain Bloxham struck it aside. "He's just a boy!"

I saw it then. He couldn't have been fifteen, his cheekbones bulging bronze and his black eyes never leaving mine. He just stood there waiting for the bullet, Captain Bloxham muttering: "He's out gathering ponies," and I saw some skittering ahead of us up the canyon. "Shoot, you'll wake the camp."

I couldn't believe it, but the reds were not awake. Sure, there were some mangy dogs beginning to yip, and calico Indian ponies running in all directions. But when Shaw's troopers came up over the rim, with us following, we weren't but fifty yards from the first teepees, enormous big cones of buffalo or elk skins, and scattered out in rocks and timber blowdowns were a hundred nasty places for reds to hide.

Rifles crashed, bullets ripping through the teepees, Major Shaw leaping over timber and firing with both hands. Then the troopers joined in, big Springfield slugs thocking wood and flesh and God knows what. Reds were spilling out howling on all sides. Some were naked, others had pulled on big, streaming war bonnets. Boom, flash! They were shooting back with heavy old guns. I felt the whiss of balls going past my face. God help us, I wanted to shoot somebody, but I couldn't pick one. They were scattering like grouse. Then close by, I catch sight of black hair and a deer hide shirt, painted with green circles. I fired into the center of it, and hit with a thuck and spray of blood. And moaning, too. When I come thundering past, I see it was a squaw with a bulging baby belly on her. She was lying on her back, bare feet kicking the ground and screaming in pain.

The troopers' volleys were ripping everywhere. You could hardly see for the powder smoke or hear above the roaring and screaming. Cahoon flashes past me. "Lodges, kill the lodges!" He flings himself off his horse and goes blasting his way into the entrance of a teepee. Other troopers dismount and run in with him. Kids screaming inside. Slash of a knife cuts the side of the teepee, and a naked little bugger runs out. "Kid!" I shout, but Severnson has already swung on him and fired. The bullet caught him in the back of the head and lifted him in the air.

"You goddamn murderer!" I screamed to Severnson, but more at myself for having killed that squaw. Severenson didn't answer. He was sitting erect on his horse and slowly his Springfield slid out of his hands and thumped to the ground. I'm thinking, He has a yellow beard, with icicles on it. But now they're red. He's making a gargle sound in his throat. One hand is lifting and plucking at his beard. He hasn't got a throat. Nothing but gushing blood, and it sprays hot in my face as he topples off his horse and crumbles to the snow.

"Swede?" I whispers.

"Keep the charge!" Captain Bloxham is howling. "Take the end of the village."

We're going again, carbines crashing in volleys. I see some reds, plenty of them now, scrambling up into the rocks. "Moore and Dewees!" Captain Bloxham shouts. He grabs me. "Blow the charge!"

My hands were so cold I could hardly fish out my bugle. I tooted a couple of notes, but hell, nobody could hear. My carbine breech was open, I was fumbling for another cartridge. Thunk! Freckles, Number 117, gives an awful shudder under me. He just stops and when I feel him falling over, I leap off, sliding on my face and elbows. When I crawled back to him, he was lying there with a bullet hole black in the center of his forehead. I turned away and wanted to puke. The force of the ball had blown both of his eyes out, and they were dangling like balls on little ropes.

"Sound dismount! Fight on foot!" Captain Bloxham was shaking me by the shoulder. "They're shooting the mounts."

Even as I looked, I saw two troopers cartwheel off their gut-shot beasts. One horse went end over end into a teepee which collapsed on him.

Cahoon come running by with a big slab of meat in his hand. Buffalo or venison, I couldn't tell. "Heap vittles in the lodges, boys!"

he hollered, and went plunging on into another one.

"We're in chaos," Captain Bloxham was crying to Major Shaw, who'd just galloped up. His reins were dangling down and had been clean cut by a bullet. Shaw dismounts and thrusts me the horse. "Tie these. Rig it some way." Then he turns on Bloxham and grips his arm. "I didn't hear what you just said, and don't say it again. We have the village, old man. We can hold it until Crook comes!"

Poor Captain Bloxham was flailing his arm at the rocky bluff just beyond us. "Idiocy, Shaw! We have no support! The hostiles have taken the high ground. Look in the rocks, man. They have us trapped!" He was blubbering so bad I could hardly understand him.

Then a lieutenant flashes by and Shaw cries: "Cooper. Take your troop and burn the camp!"

"No! You can't do it under fire!" Bloxham cried.

Shaw seized Bloxham's shoulders. "Don't be an old woman, Piggie. You're better than that!"

Shaw grabbed the reins I'd knotted, remounted and whirled off into the camp. Captain Bloxham was standing there, huffing hard, dabbing at his little scrunched-up eyes like he was weeping, and maybe he was, in the smoke of it. "Can't hold under fire," he kept muttering. "Madman, madman." Then he began patting around for his specs—they were hanging off one ear—and when he finally found them, he looked at me like he didn't even know me, or I was some soldier from some war far back. "Who's this?" he said. "Yes, Kelly. Of course. Bring Colonel Reynolds to me. On the double."

"I will that," I says, "but where would the Colonel be?"

"Coming up, all the reinforcements are coming." He was peering this way and that, and coughing in the smoke.

By now, Shaw's troopers were into the lodges, setting them afire with great torches. I went running through them, going back the way we'd come, toward the ravine. Lodges at the far end were already exploding in a great thundering whoosh of flame, lodgepoles thick as my arm whistling through the air.

Bullets from the reds in the rocks were kicking up around me, one so close it burned pebbles into my legs. As I fell, I toppled inside the mouth of a lodge the troopers hadn't got to yet.

I couldn't believe what I saw. Dark walls lined with big divans of buffalo robes. Finery and beaded dresses and headdresses of eagle feather tall as a man. There were bullet molds, powder kegs, all manner of pots and pans. Sides of buffalo and elk hanging from the lodge eaves. My mouth was watering for a gobble of such meat, thinking of the last frozen days when we'd been down to eating cracker crumbs left over in our pockets.

But no time to grab any of it. Troopers came rushing past me. "Get clear! Fire in the hole." I'd just barely run out before they touched this one off, too.

Racing toward the ravine, I heard some troopers shouting: "We've got the pony herd cut off on the south. Hundreds of 'em."

When I came plunging down into the ravine, more bluecoats were already there, sitting in the snow. Surgeon Munn, in his long white coat, catches sight of me. "Trooper! If you've got frozen limbs, in here."

I caught a glimpse of some barefoot men. They were dangling their feet and hands into a hole somebody had chopped in the ice. One poor bugger was sitting, moaning, and I wanted to strip off my buffalo coat and put it over him. "Circulation comes back this way," Munn was saying, and he was rubbing hard on a trooper's frozen feet with a rough old saddle blanket.

Hell, I couldn't stay, and wasn't frozen either, for I hadn't stripped for the fight like Cahoon and those who should have known better. With all the cavalry clattering into the ravine, I never could find Colonel Reynolds. Didn't matter anyhow. When I ran back to find Captain Bloxham in the center of the village, Reynolds was already with him.

The old gray-beard looked like a ghost. He was speaking to Bloxham in a low whisper. "Unforgivable," I heard him say. "Moore and Dewees weren't able to get around the bluffs. They held on top, why I'll never know. And the scouts were wrong. Crazy Horse is not in this camp."

Captain Bloxham blinked. "But Gruard told me he heard people calling his name."

"Best we can tell—Dewees has a squaw captive—mostly Cheyenne this camp, a few Minneconju. Crazy Horse and the Oglalas are upstream in another camp."

"In that case they'll hear the gunfire, Reynolds," Bloxham cried. "They'll be coming in on us."

"Damnation, I promised Crook a total victory!"

"Jack, in the name of God, man. You've destroyed the village, and you know we can't hold it. Let the hostiles regroup under Crazy Horse, they'll wipe out the command! I have eight hit or dead already, the rest frozen. You've done all you can, Colonel!"

Reynolds stared around at the great fiery camp, then at the scurrying shapes of reds. The sun was up by now, and I could see them darting around in the rocks above, a flash of a rifle and they'd go out of sight until they could find another one of us to put down.

"Sound recall," Reynolds says. "Come with me, Bloxham. I want all the battalions pulled out. We're going back down the canyon to Crook."

The two of them wheeled away from me, as if they'd never given the order, or in the excitement, forgot what it meant. Bloxham reined in and whirled. "Do it, Kelly! Recall. Keep sounding it until you've cleaned this place!"

Right then, a fresh rank of troopers gallops in. They had a sergeant I didn't know, big bearded face, and he pulls up short. I was already tooting recall, and he slaps the horn out of my mitts. "We ain't recalling nobody, soldier! We got this camp!" The men with him were muttering the same, dismounting and starting to run toward the rocks.

Next thing I know, Major Shaw rears up to me on his horse. His buffalo hat had fallen off, and there was a cut of some kind on his forehead, under his wet curly hair. "You were ordered to sound recall?"

"Yes, sir."

"Who gave the order?"

"Well sir, my officer. Captain Bloxham."

For just a flash of a second, Shaw grins. Handsome bugger, he might well have been dancing in a saloon for all the joy he was having in the fight. "Very well, soldier," he says. "You have your order. Sound recall and keep sounding it."

The other fresh troops heard that and let out a groan, some of them cursing at Shaw or me. Why quit? We were winning. We had the lodges, and we had wounded down at the edge of camp, too. Couldn't risk leaving them. Somebody hollered a couple of names nobody had been able to find.

Shaw let them jaw it all out. Then he stands in his stirrups. "You got this from me," he says. "We are taking those hostiles out of the rocks, and we will hold those bluffs all day and into the night, if need be! Into 'em, troopers!" and he lashes a wave with the one revolver he had left.

The troops cheered. That was the Scipio Shaw they loved, going for the kill, and maybe his general's star too.

Last thing I saw was Cahoon with him, and the rest of the blue-bellies scrambling around the burning lodges and firing their way up into the rocks.

I'm lifting my horn to keep sounding the recall, thinking: Now ain't this crazy mad? Here I'm blowing retreat for some of us, the way Captain Bloxham said. And the rest of us, under Shaw, are starting to fight again.

I hear a scream that's my own voice, and I'm blind, seeing stars, my right hand on fire, the trumpet slamming into my head, clanging, roaring, falling. Then, quiet and floating down a dark tunnel to the bottom of the world. I thinks, I know where I am, yes I do. I be dead and gone to hell for my sins. Ah, sweet Jesus, I cries. Then it just echoed away, and if He heard me at all, He never let on.

BLESS ME, FATHER, FOR I HAVE SINNED

On the night of May 12, 1875, I was nineteen years old, and working as a stable boy mucking out stalls for Himself, Francis His Lordship Cavan, on his great estate of Drogheda, overlooking the sea in County Mayo, Ireland.

What a glorious property it was, the Big House a castle dating from the time of Cromwell, when the invaders first speared their flags into our turf. The sea kept smashing the cliffs of the fortress, but could never bring it down, not with those gray stone turrets and gun ports cut in the walls. When there was trouble—and there had been much over the years—the Redcoats would clank up there with their rifles, and blast at the Irish rabble trying to destroy the damn eyesore. Perhaps that's why the mist from the sea made the dark windows of the castle weep. Yet that very same mist softened the air and greened the paddocks so that Himself's fine animals could gorge themselves. The moors, purple with flowers, lifted back into the highlands where the hedgerows made nests for the grouse and pheasant, salmon and trout in the streams, all the playthings and savories for the delicate palates of the English.

Like all of us on the grand estate, my family were servants of the Lord. There were seven of us whelps, but the closest and most beloved to me was my little sister, Nora. Ah, God, she was a saucy thing, hair as red as mine was black, freckles too, and skin like soft down. She was sixteen that summer, swelling into a womanhood so lovely that the lads in town couldn't help casting a glance down her shirtwaist. When it come time for her to start work in His Lordship's kitchen, I warned her: "Stay clear of that randy old goat. Mind ye never be alone with him."

Francis His Lordship Cavan had been a gallant officer of the King, to hear the boys tell it in town. And perhaps true. When he would dress up in his full uniform, his bulging chest sparkled with ribbons from the Empire, and his great bald head had a scar in it from some heathen's sword. His left hand had been blown off in one of those damn English wars in India, so they fixed him up with a hook. Ah, what a grand contraption, rigged for him to hold a shotgun in it, or strip in a fly line. That's all he did in his later years, hunt and fish and drink brandy. A lonely, cantankerous tyrant, living in dreams of the blackamoors he'd slaughtered in distant lands. His wife, Her Ladyship, a graceful person, I do say, had long sickened of him, and we landless peasants of County Mayo were too brothy for

42

her tastes. So she spent her days in the perfumed houses of London, and only came home to his bed for Christmas. Himself had constables, English scum, watching the lands of Drogheda for him, cutting the turf and grazing the beasts. Mostly what he'd watch were the girlies from the moors, coming and going into the Big House.

Well, now, on Nora's first day, Himself falls asleep in his leather throne where he could look across the lands and the crashing sea beyond. Knocks his damn brandy all over his pants. In comes Nora with her mop and pail to clean him up. Wouldn't you know, he'd be watching her close, then sweet-like, he reaches over with his hook and pulls the cover off a box of London chocolates. He says: "Go ahead. Eat some in front of me so you don't steal them behind my back."

Nora had a proud streak. "I will like hell!"

"You what?" He came bellering up out of his chair and cuffed her with his hook. "Address me as Your Lordship!"

"My Lord is my Lord," she says. "The real one." Then she curls her little lip proud: "Anyhow, I wouldn't be eatin' your damn chocolate. It makes me fart." With that, she slaps the mop into the pail and leaves.

I don't know how the rest happened. My father Brendan, who was Himself's gamekeeper, had gone up the road to Windy Gap so he could set weirs in the salmon stream there. My mother Bridget was off to Castlebar, reading tea leaves. She earned a pence or two from the townspeople in this superstitious work. She had a talent for it. The rest of the kiddies had gone with her in the jaunting cart, so it was just Nora and me, alone on the estate.

Six o'clock it was, the sun already dying. I came into the stable to prepare a sour mash for a blooded horse Himself had just imported from Epsom Downs. A racetrack animal with a head so thin, bred so fine, there was no room for brain between his eyes. "Settle yourself, you stupid poppycock," I says, entering the stall with the steaming bucket of wet grain. But the horse was rearing and making a crying sound. I'm thinking: what kind of a horse cries like a baby? Then, in a flash, I knew that it wasn't him at all.

Nora was huddling and sobbing just beyond the barn window, in the great hay pile I'd put in for winter. "God help us," I cries, running out there. "What is it, baby?"

Her dress, the gray kitchen maid's uniform she wore, was rumpled and torn, and a trickle of blood was running down toward her knee. She was gripping her female place with both tiny hands, and just weeping her heart away.

Somewhere in those dark, gloomy halls, Himself had run her down, stripped her and ravished her. Ah, God burn his blackguard soul! I went blind in the rage of it. But what could we do? He owned us. We were beasts, like those in the barn, to be saddled or jumped or put down under the sod when we could serve Himself no more.

I lay in the hay pile trying to comfort my little sister. Presently she quit sobbing and began cursing him, which was a good sign. Then I took her down the lane to the cottage. "Clean yourself up," I said, "get the stain of him off you." I made her some porridge and tea, and put her in her bed. "Don't tell them," she begged me, meaning our Ma and Pa. I thought: well, what would they do anyhow? Brendan was a good man. I loved him. But he was a soft man, too. Gentle. All he really cared for was his fish and birds. He'd suck his pipe all day long, in a stupor of calming himself, so that he could plod along like a dray horse, obeying the orders of the swine who employed him.

And Bridget, if she knew of her soiled daughter, she'd just offer her to God. "Life is a Cross."

"Ah, sweet Jesus, Momma," I cried to her once, "We ain't as good as Himself's grouse that would shit in our eye if we ever took one for our own pot! Serfs, we are, like what they got in Russia. Slaves without chains!"

"Patrick Malachy Kelly, divil take your ungrateful tongue! Get down on your knees and thank God for what He give us!"

Praying and starving. Ah no, not for this one, I thinks. And not knowing where to go or what to do, I left Nora sniffling in her bed and went back down to the barn.

What do I find but the narrow-headed horse escaped from his stall, because I left the door open when I went out to Nora. There he was now, thundering up and down the stable aisle, snorting and prancing as if he'd strike me with his hoof. "Ay, you bastard son," I cried. "Are you daring me, is that it?"

I snatched up a padded rope we had for schooling colts. When he raced past me on his next run, I threw the loop end of it over his neck, caught him and reeled him in like a salmon. He stood there, trembling, sweating. Would have bit me if I give him the chance. "All right, me fine boy," I says, "you just met your master!"

I knew better, of course. Knew my place. Oh yes, Himself would allow me to exercise the made horses, the plugs used by the English ladies for leaping fences. But I was forbidden to touch the fresh colts that would wear Himself's colors in the race meets. The breaking of these wild costly things, Himself gave to his English stable manager, Milo Perkins. But Milo was at Ascot now, racing the string, nor did the cowardly Cockney have the courage to take on this untamed colt.

So I says I will, by God!

No plan in it. Nineteen-year-old whelp putting his heedless young balls up into the saddle, one hand gripping the bridle reins, the other, Milo's breaking whip. "You rear," I cries, "and I'll cut you in half." The horse lifted skyward, and I lashed him. He gave a yelp and a long leap, thundered down the aisle and struck the stable door. Blew it open, lucky I hadn't shut it firm.

Then we were out in the paddock racing, a smear of fog and pitch dark now, the sun gone. Lamps were going on in the big house up on the hill, the horse flat out, flying through the streams of light, I so busy holding on I didn't know how fast or how far.

But I loved the going. Fleeing out the far end of the paddock and reaching the black cliffs, pounded with the spray of the sea. The horse stopped short, front feet planted wide, and stared at the roaring waves. Something he'd never seen before, or was too stupid to figure out. I says, smoothing my hand down the side of his neck, "Ay, lad, you've done everything you can do to me, and I'm still here. You didn't win this time, but maybe now you'll get some sense, and you'll make a horse someday."

Himself, and Milo Perkins neither, never talked to horses. Said they didn't understand the human voice, were only conquered by fear. But I know different, being raised with the beasts. God Almighty, I loved them wild things.

Well, this bold steed twisted his neck around, as if he had to see me on top of him to believe it. Sometimes the fierce studs will bite your foot, if you don't mind your wits. But when I stroked him again, he just gave a little shiver and nickered at me. I says then, "We're done for now, lad," and I rode him at a walk, shuffling through the wet, sweet turf back to the barn.

In the peaceful darkness there, with the smell of manure, I was just pulling the saddle off when a lamp flames up, and a thudding of feet. "In here, Lordship. Thief!"

First in was Grogan, Himself's constable from the slums of London, his shotgun glinting in his lamp. "Thief, me eye," I says. "Put the piece down, Grogan. It's Patrick!"

Wishing right then that it wasn't. "You!" bellers Himself, storming in, "You rode that horse!"

"I did indeed. He needed it, goin' stall-mad, he was."

A flash. My eyes went black, my cheek screaming pain. I was laying in the stall aisle with the horse whirling to get away from me. Francis His Lordship Cavan had struck me with his Hook, the flat side of it. I felt my stinging cheek. He didn't puncture me anyhow, or draw blood as he had on my sister.

"No stable boy tells me what my horses need! Spoil that animal in one ride. Get up, you rotter!"

I starts to get up, still dizzy from the blow. Maybe not fast enough for him. Still on all fours like a dog, I see the black of his army riding boot, see all of him coming at me, that drum of a bald head, and his arms drooping like wings in his baggy greatcoat. He lashes a kick at me. I twist and roll away, trying to get loose of him.

His eyes are flashing gray and green in the lamp. "You want a lesson, do you? Hold him, Grogan."

The constable butts into me, whirls me, trying to pin my arms behind my back. A lifetime, I thinks, right here and now. It's the last time I take this, so help me God. I have done nothing wrong.

Grogan was twice my weight and size, and used to handcuffing scum. But I was not scum, never would be. I kneed Grogan in the crotch, him letting out a groan and sinking away from me. That's when Himself struck me across the eyes with the horse-training whip. But not this Irish slave, by God. I fisted Himself in the belly, tearing the whip away from him because I was half blinded. "Leave me alone!" I cried. "I done nothin' wrong to you or your bloody horse! Not near what you done to me sister!"

"You," Himself thundered, "you will never touch me again!" Here was a man who'd wear a silk glove if he ever had to shake the hand of an Irishman. His shirt was pulled out in the force of my blow, silk underwear showing above his fly, and his belly hairs too. The belly that was on poor little Nora. Foul bastard, I thinks, he means to kill me now.

He'd snatched the shotgun from Grogan, his fat fingers cocking the first hammer. "Don't!" I cries, jumping out of the road of the barrel. But they'd kill an Irish whelp like a dog, and no court would try them for it.

The world exploded, first barrel roaring so close I could feel the shot, smell the powder. No place to run, the terrified colt thundering past me out of the barn. Again the shotgun, this time the mean bastard wouldn't miss.

It come to me that I had to do it, that the sweet Jesus, if there was one up there watching, was daring me to. Trying to get away, I had tripped and almost fallen over a pitchfork I'd left standing against the horse's stall.

Seizing it, I threw it at the gun. It clanged up the barrel, steel sparking steel, and plunged into the belly of Himself. "Oh, my God," I cries. He was gasping, falling to his knees. Blood was spurting out over his silk underwear, down his pants and into the tops of his black boots. "Murderer!" Grogan was screaming, lunging at me. I grabbed the gun, fired it at his feet, hoping to stop his rush. But when he crashed into me, his hands trying to rip out my throat, I knew I was done for. They'd have me hanging by the neck in the tree in front of St. Gregory's church like all the other Irish rebels who'd dared to fight back. I says, oh no, not me yet, you English pig! I kneed him again in the crotch, then swung the stock of the gun and broke it clean in two against the side of his head.

When I ran out of the barn, the wild horse was standing there in the wet darkness. He even made a move to come to me. I flung my arms around his neck, and shed tears, too, buried in the sweetness of his mane. Then I had to run, and run far, out into the night, blubbering for the life I'd thrown away.

I was fleeing, a common criminal you might say. From the bloody barn, I'd run along the cliffs to the cove where old Kelleher, the doryman, lived. I says: "Kelleher, I have murdered someone. Maybe two."

Kelleher was a cousin of my Mother, a smuggler and Irish patriot before there was even a Clan NaGael. "Did they need killing?" he asks, and I says, "They did."

Right then and there, he puts on his oilskins and takes me in his dory down the shore. In Galway Bay, he knew the sailing crowd, and shipmaster Daniel Candy, too, for Candy's mother was a Dunn. Long ago, the Dunns had left Mayo for Boston, and now, as luck would have it, the Amboy Princess was making up for a trip out there, with a hold full of hod carriers from Cork, some with wives and kiddies. Tight scared faces wrapped in shawls, filled with tears and dreams. The rest of the cargo was Irish linen and tweed, to be cut and tailored by the more skilled Americans.

When Candy said he had no room for me, except as a deckhand slop boy, I said I'd take that work for passage. Old Kelleher of my mother's blood give me five pounds out of his own pocket. "That's to start you," he says, "on the Other Side. God help you."

So it was that this poor greenhorn followed the path of thousands before him. I headed west to the new, free life in the US of A.

Poundin' the streets of gold, I'd be, chasin' the American Dream, and finally ending up in the great city of Chicago. With the big Depression on, people was getting fired, not hired. When I was about starved out and couldn't hook onto a respectable trade, I heads for the stockyards. The stink of the place made few want to work there. I wasn't fussy, though, and hung around until an opening come up at Armour's Meats, killing steers in their lanes with an old buffalo gun. It was cold and bloody but it paid a small fortune, three dollars and a half dime a week. Perhaps I'd be there yet if it wasn't for the Hand of God reachin' in, or, to be honest, the Divil himself.

One night, driving Armour's meat wagon along South Water Street, I sees a proud chestnut carriage horse down on the bricks, thrashin' his forelegs. Damn if he don't belong to General Philip Sheridan, a little red-faced pouter-pigeon, all be-medaled from the great wars he'd won. He was takin' his fine lady-friend to the Opera, and now with the horse stove up, they'd be late. I had some shoein' tools in the Armour wagon, so I tells the General I'll tack one on and get him to his entertainment. He stood over me, hands on his hips, watchin' me shoe and asks me where my brogue is from. I says, "Mayo, God help us." Well, he laughs, genial-like and says he's from the Other Side himself, born on the boat coming over. For my trouble, he give me a silver dollar tip and his personal calling card, should I ever need assistance in my new land.

Next day at the Yards I mentioned my good fortune to the lads—ah, them wickeds. They talks me into spendin' my dollar with 'em in a lousy whorehouse, an old frame shack that Mrs. O'Leary's cow should have burned down in the Great Fire of '71.

My girl was a blonde named Alma. That's all I remember as I plunged into the deadly sin of fornication.

Well, like my dear momma Bridget would say, "The Lord forgets nothing, lad." Two days later, He must have got together a new crew to do the killin' in the lanes. A shakeup, the foreman tells me, men from another plant who had seniority.

I had but a few quarters saved, and couldn't pay my rent in the man-house where I'd been living, so that night I went with the other fired stiffs to a shelter on Wabash. Big barn of a place, so cold that the bums were out on the street, warming their mitts over flaming barrels. "Partake of the wondrous charity of America," one bearded geezer says to me. Then a Salvation lady tinks her bell and we come inside and get dished some apples and broth.

Day after day, I trudged the streets of the dark, gritty Loop, looking for work. Do anything. Shoe horses, slop kitchens or carry hod. Nothing at all. There were signs in the windows. "No Irish Need Apply." Another said: "Jobs Are Too Scarce for Foreign Born. This is an American Enterprise. Dagos, Micks, Bohunks and Nagurs Keep Out." The bums were saying: It was General Grant's fault. He and his cronies were squandering millions pacifying wild redskins, and letting red-blood Americans starve.

There wasn't public toilets around on those dark streets. You'd just go in a back lot and make your water against a fence. Mine, though, was burning, and little Johnny Devil starting to drool. Now I was tough of constitution, I stood six foot four and strong as a mule. The cold didn't bother me like the geezers, or even the scant charity food. Never been sick a day in my life, but Johnny Devil says, You got some foreign ague now, lad, something you and me don't ken.

Next morning, I waited hours in line at the Sanitary shelter with lungers, drunks and old street harridans. When I finally got to the doctor in the shelter office, he says: "You've been lying down with dogs, and got up with fleas. You're clapped, fella."

"I ain't getting you."

"Gonohorrea. A venereal disease. Ah come on," he laughs, looking at me going pale. "It never killed anybody yet, just hangs around indefinitely."

"But ain't there a pill or something?"

"Salversan. Go outside, sign up for the treatment. But we have so many patients, I don't know when we'll get to you."

I was mad by then. "Mary and Joseph, it hurts me to piss, man. Ain't there some other hospital for us bums?"

He smiles. "Well, I suppose you could try the Army. They cure it as well as anybody. Pretty much have to. Can't have the pride of America walking around with their peckers leaking."

That very night, I pulls General Sheridan's card out of my brogan and strolls into headquarters. I expected it to be officey and stiff, but not at all. There were a few desks and fellers in shirtsleeves lounging around. Big maps on the wall and great paintings of General Grant and George Washington, too, who never told a lie, the saying goes.

Nor will I, I thinks, when I meet Corporal Daniel Drennan, the General's clerk. He was a wistful little gent with horn-rimmed glasses, didn't resemble a fierce soldier at all, but more like a hedge priest back home. Ah yes, he says, the General had told him of my quick work as a farrier. The chestnut horse was one of the General's favorites. Then we talked horses we'd both known on the Other Side. "I can see you're the authentic coin, boy," he said and smiled. "What might we do for you?"

I felt like blubbering. "Cure me of the damn clap, God help us. I'm bumming and broke, and can't find work with my parts on fire."

Well now, didn't they have just the remedy! But not, of course, for civilians. Because of the Depression, the Army was swamped with bums trying to get in, for the starting pay was a miracle for the needy: $12.35 a month, food and shelter courtesy of Uncle Sam. Even warm clothes. It was better than jail. "And right now, you're in luck, Patrick Kelly. Our troops are short of farriers out on the border. We could make a place for you."

I liked the place where I was, Chicago, all going grand for me before the Divil come in. But Drennan puts his arm around me and walks me up to the U.S. flag. With the stars winking down, I repeats after him the Pledge of Allegiance. Then I signs a paper saying where my belongings and my corpse could be sent in case I croaked. "Well," I says, "why not just ship 'em home to the Other Side?"

He looks at me strange. "You're in the army now, mister. There ain't no Other Side."

Private Farrier Patrick Malachy Kelly. They had me cured of clap in less than a month. By then, it was Christmas back home, singing the hymns. My hymn was the whine of the great wheels on the Union Pacific train, hauling me and the other recruits west.

I suppose it didn't matter if a feller wept for what was gone. Anyhow, there in the smoky coach, nobody seen me. I was huddled with the other cannon-fodder, some of 'em lads like me who had left homes in many lands. Some were toughs with the shaved heads of jailbirds. A few were Rebel soldiers who in the years since the War had never been able to catch onto anything better than fighting and killing. Our uniforms were rough-made blue sacks, saved over from the Rebellion. The train was moving at 22 miles an hour, they said, and it was a long way, cackling with one another or snoring or staring outside at the dark ghosts of the prairie, our fears riding on the backs of every one of them.

Few of us greenies knew what we were getting into, except maybe an old Reb veteran who had a silvery bullet scar on his cheek. "It don't matter whether you're fightin' for a slave owner or a Yankee nabob in his shoe factory. Us kind go get shot, them kind stay home. One war is the same as the next," he said, and spat his chaw out the window. "Rich man's war, poor man's fight."

I wondered right then if this wasn't the flag of my new land—a dollar sign instead of stars.

THE BIG LONELY

It was so peaceful in the white. Not to have a body, not to have a care. Like the Lord was saying: Have no fear, lad. I am with you.

Too soon the world roared back in. The St. Pat's day fight was long over. I'd been abandoned in the hostile camp. I was lying on my face, pain in my forehead, and my blood was streaking the snow. Hands were snatching at me, turning me over. The awful stink of it. Bear grease and sweat and tanned hides and smoke. Knives flashing. The sun full high and burning hot. Then, behind the knives, the faces. Gabbling hags. Hideous brown hooknoses and shaggy black shiny hair. They were poking me with the butts of knives, then tearing my tunic open and cutting the brass buttons from it. Mouthing gibberish, all the banshees of hell let loose. And then in it, an awful howl: "Mother of God...!"

Dirty fingers were grabbing my ears, twisting my head so I'd have to see.

In the smoking embers of a teepee, a few yards from me, reds in buckskins were dancing and shouting around a blue sack of bones. But a live man, still alive! His feet were kicking up puffs of snow, and his arms were trying to hide his face. Zwack! One half-naked buck slices with an axe and chops off the trooper's arm at the shoulder. I screamed too, till a dirty fist jammed in my mouth, and they were tearing at my hair, keeping me pinned there so I'd have to watch.

Whoever the trooper was, the banshees chopped off his arms and legs one by one, and then his head. A big Sioux wearing a soldier coat grabbed the bloody awful thing, the others fighting him for it like wolves. They began throwing it to one another, and the last I saw, those vermin kids were kicking it around like a ball, rolling a red streak in the snow.

I was next. I knew that. I whimpered, ah, sweet Jesus, take me back into the white.

I don't know how long I was out, waiting for death. But when I looked again, the sun was sinking over the far bluffs. I was so trembling cold I felt I was shaking the earth. But no, it was horses' hooves, thundering near me. Wild-eyed ponies, pintos, buckskins and runty little colts the color of mice. They were all painted and feathered, some of them rearing as a big flock of reds swirled in.

There was great commotion in what was left of the camp, the squaws who had been tormenting me, and the scurvy kids too, all

51

rushing out to greet these new Indians. A war party, mean, high-cheekboned faces smeared with reds and yellows. They were carrying lances, or bows slung over their deerhide shirts, and many had long rifles and a few carbines. Some of the buggers were leaping off their horses and snatching up the Springfields our dead troops must have flung down getting out of there. One giant of a man snatched a buffalo hat from a squaw, and I saw then that it was the lid Major Shaw must have lost.

These new reds coming in had saved me, I figured that out quick. Indians have brains about like coyotes. When a new rabbit runs in, they'd swarm after him, and forget the old one they'd been playing torture with.

They were dancing around like chattering magpies until one rider on a gray colt sweeps in from the upper end of the burned camp. I noticed him because when he came, they all flocked around him. Some squaws were wailing, chopping at their hair with knives, and flinging him bits of it. Mourning for the husbands or sons they'd lost.

But the Indian on the gray horse pushed through the squaws. He'd grip the shoulder of one, or touch another on the top of the head. To my eyes, there wasn't anything special about him, except that he was slight of frame, boyish, with lighter color skin and greeny eyes. Mean in the face. He didn't have the fancy decoration of the others, but only a few white dots like hailstones dabbed on his cheeks. And no headdress either, except for one eagle feather sticking up from his black hair.

His eyes spooked me because they had a burn in them, like he'd seen me, yet he was looking beyond me, too. Then, quiet-like, he starts jabbing his rifle in different directions, and the camp reds began whooping off to catch ponies or scurry in with slabs of venison and blackened strings of buffalo meat that hadn't all been lost when we burned the camp.

I kept thinking: recall. The retreat that I'd sounded. We'd put our tail between our legs and run, even leaving our wounded to be butchered by the divils. But was this why? I wonders. This new man. Captain Bloxham had said Crazy Horse was camped nearby, and if he got into it, we'd lose the whole command.

I was looking at him. I knew that.

But I was in luck, too. Those savages had forgotten me. While the camp lads were wrangling in new mounts from the pony herd, and the squaws were painting the mens' faces and draping cartridge belts on them, I began to drag myself across the snow like a crippled crab. There were some rocks not far from where I lay. I got behind them, and then into a little coulee. It led down into the big ravine that we'd had so much trouble crossing. But when I found myself

52

down there beside the frozen creek, I saw the air hole in the ice that Surgeon Munn's hospital stewards had cut to unfreeze the boys' feet. I shouldn't have risked it, maybe, but I was burning up with fever thirst. I plunged my head into that icy water, already starting to freeze again. When I came up, I was dizzy and seeing stars, sure I was going to faint away.

But I says, No Patrick. God took you into the white, just to bring you back and make you live. So I *will* live. I'll beat these reds.

By dark, I'd gone so far up that ravine, I couldn't hear anybody now, or smell the fires of war. But Jesus God, they'd robbed me of my buffalo coat, and even cut the buttons from my tunic, so I couldn't close it shut. No hat, no gloves. I'll die out here of freezing, I knew. I'd crack and shatter like the red mercury in Surgeon Munn's bulb.

Then the stars came out, icy cold, and I was so weak I was crawling over sticks and stones, my hands gone numb. I kept thinking: I've got to sleep. Dig myself a snow hole like the veterans taught me on the march from Fetterman.

But I was out of the snow now, in a rocky canyon. It felt hot, too, and as I crawled on, I began smelling smoke.

Then, ahead, I saw a red glow like a giant with one eye, glowering at me. Who the hell is out here, I thinks? But soon, one eye becomes two, and five, and a hundred. Little red winks in the earth. I crawled to one and touched it. Fiery hot! Jesus! I cry, and then I was laughing, cackling, plumb mad in the deliverance of it.

Like a peat bog at home that had caught fire, and burned with the stink of sulphur, this hot earth I was ripping out with my hands was coal. A hod carrier's hearth of a live coal seam, and I fallen smack into the middle of it.

I kicked around with my boots, which the squaws hadn't stolen, and made a nest of burning coals. I kept thinking: if they find me now, they'll have a warm body anyway, to send down to hell.

———

As best I could figure, for two days I traveled southwest by the sun, hoping to reach the command, and above all, to stay scarce from the red devils. Jesus and Mary, they had struck a fright into this lad.

But then soon, a greater terror chilled my heart. I was going to die out here. Miserable and alone, I would starve to death. Slogging in deep snow, clawing up those endless hills and down a valley to the next one, I was burning out the juice that drove a man. My vitals were gnawing at me, making me so weak I could hardly lift my boots, and sometimes dizzying and falling in a heap.

Once in a while I'd see snowshoe rabbits popping up out of a drift and peering at me. Or coyotes would stare down from a rocky ledge, bared of snow. Kill the curs, I screamed to myself. Give me just one, let me tear his hide loose with my teeth and gnaw his bloody flesh.

But they'd trot away and leave me lying on my face, melting the snow with my tears.

I had neither gun nor knife. No way to make a fire. Far ahead to the west, I could see black smears of timber, running up the slope of a mountain. I thinks: Get in the trees, I can be warm at least, and hidden. For the way it was on these empty, snow-glistened hills, a savage could see the black dot of me from miles away, and no doubt come charging in to finish the job.

All that second day, getting to the distant timber was what drove me on. I could scoop up snow and drink it, so I had no thirst. But to have something to eat, ah, sweet Jesus, I knew there must have been grass to put in my mouth like a horse, but the snow was so deep I couldn't burrow down to reach it.

About then, my poor dumb brain began dancing tricks before my eyes. I was seeing the great green fields of Mayo. I was munching berries from the moors, or sometimes sitting by the hearth in our cottage and gnawing a sweet grouse I had stolen from His Lordship.

By now, my head was aching something fierce, and my face burning with fever. Having no glass to look at myself, and better that I couldn't, I'd trace my frozen fingers up to my right temple and feel the deep gash that was there. Who knows, maybe it went into my brain, and was leaking my wits away. But the wound throbbed, and once when I picked at it, out falls a small piece of brass, from the damn Army trumpet that the ball had blasted into me.

Catch hold of yourself, Paddy, I moans, you didn't come this far to die!

I was so weak by then I was clawing myself across the snow, like I was pulling the whole blanket of it toward me and bringing in the trees. They rose up like a cliff, slender green lodgepole pines, towering into the lead sky of dusk. And even before I reached them, I slid over an icy crest and into a swale. A little canyon it was, filled with underbrush, and God Almighty, it too was green.

I began tearing at the leaves and chewing them. Bitter as hell they were, but at least something in my mouth. Then just ahead was a clump of dark bushes with orange berries on them. They were hard as buckshot but sweet, too, and I stuffed my cheeks with them.

I was thinking in my daftness that the berries tasted like smoke. I bolted up, my nostrils shouting: Smoke that is, lad!

I slogged toward the dark cliff of timber. The light of the sun was gone, and the forest still, but the smoke was sweeter now, the scent of pines. I came into a clearing and stopped short in fright.

Life! A human sign. Man had built this! Four poles had been

speared into the snow. Lashed to the tops of them was a platform heaped with green boughs and dead gray sticks. The fire that I'd smelled was just embers and winking coals, wisping up smoke through the platform.

I took a gulp of frozen cold breath, my heart pounding. First I thinks: It's a tree, squeaking in the night wind. But there was no wind and the trees stood still. The sound came again, and now it was a low howl, rising. I swung around, peering through the dark caverns of the timber. Wolf! I thinks. Are you a wolf out there? But I knew, from the veteran troopers, that a wolf never eats live meat. They just wait.

Finally I bellers: "What the divil are you?"

The echo boomed off through the trees. But the wail had stopped, and with it, my poor heart. The branches were rustling on the platform. I took a step or two toward it.

Mother of God! A gray shape rose up from the sticks and was staring at me.

I fumbled, I stammered. Finally I shouted: "Well, say! Are you dead or alive!"

A tongue answered me. Heathen was all I knew, a hoarse, cracked voice, beginning low and then half-howling in a jeer. The light was almost gone, nothing but the wink of the coals. But the ghost was moving, beckoning at me with something that looked like a stick. When I edged closer, I saw that it was a lance, with white feathers on it.

Next thing I knew, the ghost was leaning down to me and I was touching a dry bony hand. Then the next hand, both gripping mine. I was smelling a strange kind of grease, stinking sour, and when I gave a half-pull, the whole human contraption was onto my shoulders, a face and smoky hair next to my face, and I swung the cursed thing to the ground.

Ah, the damned goblin! Bulging cheekbones like a skeleton head, the dark skin drawn tight, wizened and cracked, eyes beading out, and a matted mane of gray-black hair. "*Waiscu*," it whispered, and then I knew.

A woman, by God. A crone so old she didn't belong in the world. Then it came back to me that I'd seen these same death houses in the hills around Fetterman. Set up a lodge of poles and lift the corpse to the sky. That was how the Sioux gave their souls to the Great Mystery that they figured to be their Creator. When firewood was low at the Fort, troopers would go out and chop the damn scaffolds apart, to warm their feet by in the squad room.

By then, the mummified bodies would have rotted away. Dust that we threw to the coyotes.

But this one now? Alive? She was still gripping my hands and staring at me. Her eyes began flashing, plenty alive. "Well," says I, "did they make a mistake with you, Grandma? The wrong corpse in the church?"

That loosed a chatter out of the old dame. Of course, she couldn't understand what I was jabbering about, nor me her, but she began smacking her shriveled fist into the other palm. Then she lifted her hands to her breasts and cupped them, jiggling up and down and grunting like: good, alive, plenty left here!

By then, over the shock of it, I got a better look at her. She was dressed fit to kill all right. Maybe that was part of the savage ceremony. They buried you with your best finery on, and hers was a squaw sack of soft elk hide. I could tell because I felt of it, and what's more, she had a necklace of bear claws, which must have put a lot of grizzlies down. Sewed all over the dress were gleaming elk teeth, too. All these trappings were money to the savages, so the old crone, I figured, had to be well off.

"Why did they leave you to die, and you didn't?" I blurted.

Ah, hell, she just cackled back. Then she whirled to one of the four poles of the scaffold and seized an eagle feather dangling from it. When that didn't mean anything to me, she stalked over to the dying embers and kicked them with her foot. Stamped her moccasin on them like a damn queen.

She gave me a throwing sign with her hands, and I caught on. "Ah, you're freezing, dame, and me too," I said. But when I started to rip some dry branches from the sacred platform, she struck me across the cheek with her lance.

At that, I burst out laughing and broke the lance in two. "We'll start out even here," I said, but I did move off and gathered some dry wood and pine cones at the base of the trees.

A few minutes later, we had a blaze going, and the warmth and the flame was God's mercy to me. I hadn't but sat by the fire before she creaked down beside me. Then, with her cruel, empress eyes tracking over my face, she took my cheeks in her dry fingers, and when she touched my wound, I winced. "*Lakota! Ethiti!*" she cackled.

I'd picked up few words of redman lingo from the loafers around the Fort. *Lakota* meant Sioux, and *Ethiti* good. Good for the Sioux to kill this *waiscu*, white man hair face!

"Like hell they killed me, you old hag!" I said, and laughed at her.

Well, that touched her off. She threw back her head and howled. Next thing, she fished into a pouch sewn into her elk dress and came out with a red clay pipe and a beaded sack of tobacco. "*Chashasha*," she grunted. And though I hadn't fallen prey to tobacco yet, never being able to afford the stuff, I sucked that pipe like it was food from the gods—after, of course, she had offered the heathen thing to the four directions and the sky.

The smoke was so strong it made my head reel. "Mother of God," I said to her, "I can't eat smoke. I'm starving." I began putting my fingers into my mouth in the best sign I knew, and she caught it.

From another pouch around her belly, out came a coil of skin. Some animal gut it was, intestine, and from it she squeezed out a handful of fine ground stuff, and when I put it in my chops, I realized that it was meat. Strong as hell, concentrated, buffalo probably. She said, "*Pemmican*," and I, mouth full and beaming, said, "Old gal, I'll eat your whole yard of it if you give me the chance."

Well, the good Lord himself must have been beaming down on us, for he give us all the chance we'd need, me and my heathen queen. Her name was Atsina, and I suspected she was some kind of Lakota royalty. Cranky bugger, she sure treated me like trash. Yet sometimes in the nights, she'd stroke my face and whisper gibberish as if maybe I was a son or a husband she'd lost in the wars. I seemed to give her company, and a reason to cling to her life. Maybe that was enough reason for her to spare me.

Her people had left her an old smoothbore musket to die with, and a skinning knife. With them, and her wisdom in the mountains, we managed to move steadily lower toward the plains until I could see the familiar Big Horn mountains, gleaming in the snow. From here I was hoping to pick my way back to Fetterman, and maybe get an Army doc to cure her lungs.

Never happened, though. On a bright spring morning when she finally coughed her last, I knelt beside her, took her dry old head in my hands, and kissed her dead lips. "God rest ye, old queenie," I whispered. "Bless you for what you done."

When I looked up, I saw the legs of a spotted pony above me, then more and more, stamping in the frost and snorting out the white breaths of hell. "Jesus God," I said. A war party of about 40 hostiles descended too quick to react. Little Big Man kicked me aside. What a mean-faced bugger he was, his forehead cliffed down and his cheeks wide and cut with scars. I later learned that he'd fought all the wars at Crazy Horse's side. They were closest friends. His plug-uglies picked up Atsina's frail body like sixty pounds of grain, and lashed it over one of their pack horses.

Then they whipped out a horsehair lariat and noosed it around my neck. With leather thongs they tied my wrists behind me and tightened a rotten, greasy rag around my eyes. The end was sure now. They heaved me up on a pony, and when we were ready to go, I felt my neck jerk like I'd been hung.

But all they were doing was leading me to the hanging, someplace far away, and in their own time. Mine, God help me, had pretty much run out.

THE LAST FREE DAYS OF THE LAKOTA

The great camp of the Sioux lay in a canyon far to the north of where I'd ever been. Hundreds of lodges stretched down along a stream in the bottom, and on the pinion sidehills grazed vast pony herds. When I first seen it, I gasped.

All the Injuns in creation must have been gathered here. Against them, I felt pitiful small, and doomed.

Out in the big lonely, I'd pretty much lost track of the days. I'd been hit at the St. Pat's day fight, March 17. Maybe I'd traveled a month with Atsina, and about the same with Little Big Man. So now it was probably late May, that dusk when I stumbled in. I looked like a shiftless old squaw man. I was still white in the brain, but traveling with the heathen had played savage with the rest of me. My Army blouse was in shreds, the lower half of me in buckskin and moccasin, sorely abused on the long trail. I had enough beard to pass for Rip van Winkle, and what didn't fit on my face was hanging down over my shoulders.

As I hobbled closer to the camp, Little Big Man gave a grunt and quit prodding me. He lifted his rifle like a stick in his hand and fired it at the sky. While the smoke was drifting away, he signed at me, Go!

He was pointing at the lodges. When I didn't savvy, Jack Red Cloud edged next to me. He was a fat-faced kid in a celluloid collar who'd been traveling with Little Big Man's bunch. When his father, Red Cloud, the great war chief, had signed the peace paper back in Washington, the Army give Jack some white schoolin'. I clung to the lad as my best hope of getting out of here alive.

Jack grunts: "Little Big Man has told the people you come in peace."

"Well, I hope like hell so!"

I started moving foot by foot toward the camp, my heart in my throat. Only later did I learn that among the plains tribes, if a visitor, unarmed, even the foulest mortal enemy, announces himself in peace, and asks for the hospitality of the camp, the savages are bound by custom to give it to him.

In the next few weeks, other than mongrel dogs sniffin' me and Sioux kids pokin' me like a circus animal in a cage, they pretty much ignored me. With Injuns behind every tree, I had no way to escape and nowhere to go if I did. So in that time, I got an education in what the old free life of the Lakota used to be. But when the world started rushing in on us, I had a pretty good hunch, too, that

58

I was seeing the end of it.

Early one dawn, hundreds of warriors swept into the camp, driving a herd of ponies, and packhorses loaded with plunder. Squaws were tearing calico dresses from the packs, or running around with other glinting white man's junk, frying pans, coffee pots, even an old music box that was tinkling a waltz from back home in the States.

The camp criers were running through the lanes, hollering the news of what must have been a great victory. Some of the scalps were Indian all right, but just as many were the bloody, tawny hair of whites, and it chilled me.

In a clearing, hundreds of ponies they'd captured were milling and kicking up dust. Indian boys, who were the horse herders, were flinging up their arms and trying to keep the beasts corralled. The warriors were divvying up the spoils of their raid, lassoing the ones they felt they were entitled to, and scrapping with any other buck who got in their way.

But there was a prize horse in the lot, and I spotted him quick. He was a big, roman-nosed roan, an American horse, with a fresh guvmint brand on his hip. No doubt some poor trooper had died giving him up. But the roan was fierce. He'd probably been a stud before the Army vet cut him. He was rearing and striking at the warriors, his nostrils flared like he couldn't stand the stink of them.

Ah, sure, that was it. An Indian pony wouldn't let an American near him, on account of the smell we had, and the same went for our horses with them. Besides, I noticed quick that the roan was gimped up bad in his left hind leg, which didn't improve his disposition the way the reds were chowsing him.

As I watched, he give one lad an awful kick in the gut that would have killed a white man. The kid ran off gripping his belly and screaming, but nobody paid any attention to him because they were too busy trying to tame the wild roan. Somebody struck him with an iron whip and he was bleeding on the flank.

I couldn't watch that. "Leave him be, you divils!" I cried, and elbowed through the warriors until I faced the horse alone.

His eyes were red and bulging. He was pawing dirt about to strike me. But I says, "Settle yourself, lad. Use your head now." Then I eased around so that the little breeze there was blew my scent to him. He snapped his head to me, and the red-mad began to clear in his eyes. He'd plopped steaming, scared manure in the dirt in front of me. I knelt and rubbed it onto my hands. I kept talking to him gentle, until slowly I lay my hand on his neck and stroked it. He wasn't sure yet. He pulled his head around and sniffed what was left of my Army blouse. By now, the warriors were crowding in. I seethed: "Stay clear, you buggers."

As they drew back, the roan settled more. Patting his belly first, I slid my hand down his foreleg, my ear against him. The thumping of his heart was slowing. "Have you been shod?" I says to him, slowly lifting his foot. The U.S. shoe was there, thank God for some decent farrier in the ranks who hadn't quicked him. "Why lad, you could be a brother to my Freckles roan," I whispered, and knowing the Army style of shoeing, I edged toward his rump. The left hind leg was the bad one, the hurt one. I patted it slow, eased my hand down and picked up the hind foot.

Jesus and Mary, he gave a wince and tried to kick me loose. "No, no," I whispers, by now half under him and holding his leg across my knees.

Pus and corruption in the hoof. The hind shoe had broken in half, and the part that was left had twisted itself into the sole. The nails that were left were quicking hell out of the poor beast.

I tried to pry it loose with my fingers, but it wouldn't give. I only had a few seconds, I knew that. Even a calm horse won't stand forever with his hind leg in your lap. So I swept my eyes over the warriors and signed that I needed something to pry with.

A moment later, something taps me on the left shoulder. Some Indian, I didn't have time to see his face, had slid me an old rusted piece of iron. But God was in his heaven, because it had a sharp point like a knife.

Working slow, with the roan trying to kick me loose, I edged the point under the broken shoe and pried it off to fall in the dust. Then I loosened the bad nails and got them out. When I finally cricked up, that roan stamped his cleaned hoof in the dust, and just from what his eyes said, he looked like he was going to kiss me with his mean red lips.

"You ain't done yet, lad," I said. "You had best be barefoot out with the heathen." One by one, I pried off his other shoes. When I was done, I didn't even have to put a rope on him. I just led him around by the mane.

The warriors stood there frozen in astonishment. Then one mean-faced devil gave a grunt and clapped me on the back. With that, they howled. *Ethiti, ethiti!* Good, good! They began running in to slap my shoulders. They were like kids let loose in the candy store. By then I was so tuckered from the work of it, I wanted to get back to the lodge and sleep.

But as I turned, something hard pressed against my belly and stopped me. I was staring down at a nickel-plated revolver, civilian kind, not Army. The Indian holding it flipped the revolver and handed it to me, butt first. At the same time, he reached out and took the iron bar from me that I'd pried the shoes with.

Right then, I realized that he was the Indian who'd given the bar to me. My breath caught in my throat.

Crazy Horse. The same gray-colored eyes I'd remembered from

that St. Patrick's dusk when he'd come swooping in with the warriors. The eyes that were close to me now, staring right through me. Something about the way he moved was like a cat, ready to kill. When he handed me that revolver, the other warriors rippled out their approval.

His thin, cruel lips were tight. He was looking me up and down from my moccasins to the top of my head. He fingered my blouse, studied the last Army button that was left on it. The power of his eyes on me told me just one thing. He was deciding whether I would live or die. Then, behind him, a giant Lakota, Touch the Clouds moved in. So did the plug-ugly Little Big Man. He began grunting at Crazy Horse, jerking hard signs with his hands, mostly toward me. Crazy Horse listened to him in silence, and his eyes swept across the people. Nobody dared say peep.

Then Touch the Clouds moved forward, towering over all of us. In his hand he had a leather pouch with U.S. on the flap. It was a dispatch case they must have picked up in the raid. Papers were stuffed back into it, by warriors who couldn't read them.

Touch the Clouds jerked a fistful of them out and showed them to Crazy Horse. Though I was a few feet away, I could see that Crazy Horse was looking at the papers upside down.

Touch the Clouds grunted something, and Little Big Man thrust in, arguing. Crazy Horse snapped his eyes at both of them. That was the end of the talk.

He stepped before me, took the cheap white-man revolver from my hands, and slid it into my belt. The people let out a roar, and parted as Crazy Horse walked through them. Little Big Man twisted away from me with a last murderous look in his eyes. Then I felt a shove on my shoulder. With his ham hand, Touch the Clouds pushed me after Crazy Horse. Follow the warrior, the holy man. For reasons known only to him, he had spared my life.

———⟫●⟪———

After that, they started puttin' me through bravery tests, like they had to be sure whether I was worth keepin'. In their pony herd were captured American horses from settlers, miners and troops. Some of these monsters had been sorely abused. Trust Crazy Horse to select for me three of the worst fierce buggers, and make me ride them into the ground.

Two I tamed, taking my share of falls, I will say, and the heathen howled at my discomfort. But the last horse, a giant bay stallion with feet as big as my head, was so spoiled and insane that, unable to mount him, I tied a sack of rocks on him and he bucked all day and night, never quitting until there wasn't a rock left. The next morning after he had struck me, kicked me and bit me on the shoulder, I reared back at

Crazy Horse and shouted in my pain, "You want him, you ride him! I will not waste my life on a wild beast that should be dead!"

Though I didn't know much Lakota, I was learning, and hoped by then to get my point across. Maybe no one had ever talked back to the great man, but when I did, I thought I saw a faint flicker of a grin cross his lips. He had the stallion's throat cut, and gave the meat to the poor.

Ah, the tests were childish in a way. Could a weakling *waiscu* soldier fight by hand, in the Indian style? With the whole camp watching, they gave me a knife and a club and matched me against a bruiser who had the same. I glowered at Crazy Horse and flung the knife and club at his feet. Then I squared off with the big Sioux, knowing full well that back in Laughrasheen, I had tangled more than once with bully toughs. I was lucky with this man. The knife slashed my blouse, the club swished past my head by an eyelash. But I caught him full square with a fist to the jaw, and he dropped like a sack of flour. Not done yet, though. He was clawing, ripping at my throat and eyes, and trying to bite off my nose. But when you're fighting for your life, you have strength that even my past fevers hadn't burned away. I got the savage's throat in my hands and almost had him choked before I banged his head in the dirt and staggered up.

The crowd growled angry, but they quit when Crazy Horse lifted his hand and turned away. I must have passed my test, but God in heaven, I lay in the lodge all that afternoon, getting over it.

Every day now, more hostiles were coming into the camp, streaming up from the agencies. As well as being a horse people, the Indians are gun crazy, too. The new weapons the hostiles were bringing had U.S. marks all over them. A gang of reds were trying them out, blamming at a white-man's shirt they'd draped on a beaver house.

Crazy Horse had brought me up here to watch. Jack Red Cloud was with him, and though the great warrior was his uncle, he had little use for the lad.

After the warriors had blasted the target a few times, Crazy Horse snatched one of the guns and handed it to me. I was angry to be holding a piece like I'd once used. It was the standard Springfield 1873 model carbine, .45 caliber, 50 grains of powder. Single shot, it would kill up to 500 yards, if you could keep the damn thing from kicking your head off. When I told Jack Red Cloud what the gun would do, he passed it along to Crazy Horse, who stood there squinting at me. Then he flicks two fingers, signing for me to shoot it twice. I aimed, fired at the target shirt, and ejected the shell which flipped out with the trapdoor mechanism in the breech. Loaded a second shell and fired, but this time, the cartridge case didn't pop out.

Crazy Horse gripped my hand. His eyes were gleaming. "My uncle wants to know why the bullet case doesn't fly away," says Jack

Red Cloud.

I lay my finger in the breech. "The damn piece is dirty, that's why." Jack frowned. "So how do sojers get the case out and shoot again?"

It wasn't the first time any of us had asked that. It was no secret among the troops that the rotten design of the breech made half of the empties stick. I told Jack that some of us carried a little iron tool or used a knife to pick out the spent hulls.

By now, Crazy Horse was coming as close to laughter as I'd ever seen him. Not joy, just harsh and cruel. Touch the Clouds, Little Big Man and the other leaders were clustering around. In quick hand motions, Crazy Horse got right to the heart of it. The soldiers fire two or three times, Jack Red Cloud explained, then their rifles jam. They can't get the shells out. At this, the savages howled. While the poor *waiscus* were picking at their breeches, they were defenseless. Wait for them to fire twice, then sweep in, strike them down!

The other chiefs were praising Crazy Horse for his wisdom, and jeering at the worthless Army guns. The Sioux had managed to steal lever-action Winchesters, which never jammed, and could spray out a whole volley while the soldier wretch was still trying to put in his third shell.

But Crazy Horse shrugged their praises aside. His eyes were burning intently. He was signing how they'd fight the troops. Jack Red Cloud told me some of it, and because Crazy Horse never said many words, it was pretty easy to follow. In the old days, the Sioux had fought singly, one man here, one man there, sweeping down with all their brave glory to count coup on some pitiful *waiscu*.

But no more! Watch the way the white troops fight, Crazy Horse was telling them. They fight in bunches. He was scraping his fingers in the dust, making a crowd mark. So will the Lakota warriors fight. Not alone, not one man anymore, but in groups, like wasp's nests. His quick fingers showed an exploding nest, swarms of wasps striking the *waiscu* soldier groups from the sides, the back, the rear. Stinging the bear and then running away from the swipes of his angry paws.

Little Big Man grunted in puzzlement, like he was angry for not thinking of such tactics himself. But how would the wasps know when and where to strike?

Watch the sun, Crazy Horse signed. He draped a thong over his neck, and tied to it was a small mirror. Aiming it at the sun, he burned the reflection across the eyes of Little Big Man.

It was chilling, watching them plot how to put us down.

Later, Crazy Horse flung a U.S. dispatch case at my feet. He spoke quietly to Jack Red Cloud, for a longer time than I had ever heard him speak, but without a flicker of hope or pity in his eyes.

"Open your ears," Jack whispered to me when the harangue was done. "My uncle has given you the safety of the camp. He thinks you are a brave man, even though a dog of a *waiscu* killer. It is good to have *waiscus* with us. You are not the first. They know things we do not. They have the tongue to speak for us. But when they cannot help us, when they are so"—he groped—"foul in the tongue to spit at the people, we kill them like whining wolf pups and scatter their bones for the rats. You choose this death, sojer."

"Maybe so," I blurted, "but it's a helluva sight better than trying to put on your red skin and dying with you. You're doomed, the lot of you!"

At that, Crazy Horse sprang at me like a cat and his hand gripped my throat. I could smell the wild onions on his breath, and the ugly scar on his cheek, which I hadn't noticed before, was pulsing pale and livid. But even staring at him that close, my eyes never left his. His fingers dropped away from my throat and he turned his back on me.

Touch the Clouds patted my knee and grunted something I couldn't get. "He admires your bravery, and now asks," Jack said, "in the bigness of his heart, if you would have a woman with us? Make your lodge here. You do not even have to fight your people if you choose to stay with the women in camp."

I looked at Touch the Clouds and saw a gentleness in his face that I didn't believe could be there. "Tell him I thank him," I passed on to Jack, "but if he was away from his country and his own kind, his heart would grieve, too. Not even a fine, strong Indian girl would change that for me. My duty is not with you."

When the gist of that circulated back to Crazy Horse, his thin lips tightened. He wasn't getting his way with me, but what he wanted I didn't know. He ripped open the dispatch case and thrust me a fistful of papers. "Read," Jack snapped. "Tell what they mean."

Looking at the typewriter printing, I felt the same old tug of sadness, longing to be with my own. The papers were military all right, dispatches from Camp Sheridan to Fort Fetterman. I couldn't make much sense of them, and said so. They were dull requisitions for supplies, mules, horses. One was a dispatch signed by George Crook, General, asking for new cavalry troops from Kansas.

When I read his name aloud, Crazy Horse snapped to me. "Cluke?" he said, groping to get it. "Cloak?"

"Crook."

Crazy Horse was nodding. They were passing the name around, doing their best to mutter it, or sneer it. Jack Red Cloud began pressing me. Did I know Crook? I says I did, had served under him at the Crazy Woman Fork. What kind of man is he?

I had to puzzle for a minute, because it seemed a lifetime ago when I'd last seen him. Finally I said, "He is a hard man. He sleeps side by side with the soldiers. He starves if they starve. But he is a fair man. He has honor, I have heard it said, and I have seen it. I trust him. If you had any sense, you would, too. It's not from hate he kills you. He wants peace as much as you do."

My words circulated among them like butter running across a hot pan. The sizzle was in their eyes, and yet they seemed to be thinking patiently and seriously, too.

With no warning, Crazy Horse leapt to his feet and stalked out of the camp circle. All eyes followed him as he picked his way like a mountain lion up the rocky side of the canyon. There were tall pines and scrubby pinions on the top, and he disappeared among them.

In anger, I grabbed Jack Red Cloud. "What in hell does that mean? What is the answer for me, lad?"

"He has gone to pray."

The hell with praying, I wanted to groan. Set me free! But then Touch the Clouds muttered to Jack, and the lad turned to me. "He is waiting for a sign. So will you wait."

That very same afternoon, having nothing else to do, I decided to take a bath and wash the rags I was wearing, for I stunk worse than a pigpen. The weather had turned hot now, and as I followed the stream that flowed through the camp, grasshoppers were clicking and bees were humming. Beyond the last lodges, the stream rose into greening willows. Beavers were at work, gnawing down aspen and making their dams. When one caught sight of me, he sniffed, then slapped his tail like a gunshot and dove into the protection of his house.

It was a pretty little glade I'd come to, all the lovelier because I was away from the noisy camp for a change. But just as I was standing on the path, admiring Mother Nature's handiwork, brushing through the grass came a strange sight. It had four legs with a blanket over them, and was making giggles.

I'd seen such pranks before in the camp. Jack Red Cloud had told me that when Indian girls wanted to tease the lads, they went two by two under the blanket, hoping to find some buck with the balls to whisk it off them.

"All right, dearies," I chuckled, and ripped the blanket away. Did they howl! One was a fat little thing with a face like a moon. She poked me in the belly and stuck out her tongue. But the other girl, who was tall and swelling out of her elk hide dress, took hold of my Army blouse and jerked it sharply. She scowled at me, hissing something in Lakota.

My heart caught in my throat! I knew those Chink eyes, that go-to-hell look! Her, here? "God help us," I blurted, "that day at Fetterman, the snow! Ain't you the one?"

"The 'one'!" she sniffed scornfully. "What you think, sojer? Every dumb Injun look alike?"

"It ain't that, just the surprise, finding you here. I figured you for a loafer Indian, not in a war camp."

"Where else would I be, if not with my people!"

I chuckled. "So it's Walks Outside again, is it? God in heaven, gal, am I glad to see you! I've been talking Injun so long I've forgotten my own lingo. What the divil are you doin' here?"

She whirled and her eyes had a sudden laughter. "Cause I leave Fetterman! Remember fine madam, gold hair, monies on her wrist? I don' want to be Lakota slave."

"Well, dearie," I chuckles, "you ain't heard the end of it. That day after you'd run off in the snow, damn if the Captain didn't hang your job on me. I'd be the one washing the lady's pots and pans and maybe even her panties."

Walks Outside scowled. "Pretty woman. Talk so sweet. She is yours?"

"Mine? Hell, I'm a common soldier. She belongs to my chief, my captain. You been around Army. Enlisted man is a slave to officers' women. Can't do nothin' else."

She frowned. "But that day, snow blowing on her, I have eyes. You watch her plenty."

"Sure I did. Them folks give me my orders. If you want the truth, Injun gal, I spent more time looking at you."

Her eyes lifted, and the savage smokiness in them seemed to be gone. As shy and honest as a child, she said, "I am happy you live. Many sojers dying now, I hope not you."

With a wriggle of her fingers, she ran off her pouty little girl friend, like sayin' find your own man! Then she put her hand in mine and led me up a sidehill into an aspen grove. With the bright green leaves whispering and shivering above us, she bedded down gentle as a deer, not lying, though, just seating herself cross-legged Injun style, and silently running a blade of long grass in and out of her wide lips.

"Damn, ain't it peaceful here," I says, shaking my head. "A whole world away from that miserable Fetterman."

"It is where the people always come in spring."

"Is that why you left Fetterman? Be with your own again?"

She didn't answer, just tilted back her head and stared up through the leaves. Finally she murmured, "At first I don' want to come. On the Platte River, white man road, we were safe, war can't do nothing to us. Some days I think, the old way is over. We have nothing anymore, so be white Injun, dumb little Lakota girl again. Maybe go back to Fort Robinson. School, working."

"Was you there long?"

"Three years. Camp Sheridan they call it then. You know officer, Major Weldon?"

"Naw, ain't been around that post."

She turned from me and stroked her fingers through the long

grass, snatched up a bunch and let it fall. "My family, we were never Bad Faces, agency loafers. We lived free, along the Loup river. My father say, 'Show *waiscu* we are tame Injuns, peace people.' He tie American flag to our lodge poles. By'm'by come sojers. Nobody ask, Who are you? Why you here? No! Just come screaming, running through camp, shooting. My father, he has his hands to the sky in peace, cry 'No! No shoot!' Bang-bang-bang-bang. Four times they kill him. Kill others, too. Soldiers grab me and carry us all off in wagons, small children, old women. When we come to Camp Sheridan, they pull off my clothes, look at my body, say, You are strong, not sick, you are the only one who can work. They shake dust on my body to kill Injun bugs. Then cut off my braids. Same for boy or girl, look like white person. Must not talk one word of Lakota, whip us if we do. Then take us into church house, teach us praying to God. The Christ man on Cross, weeping. I weep. Oh, tears were on my face so much! Missing my home, my people. But soon the Major Weldon comes. His wife, she wasn't like the fine pretty madam at Fetterman, no, no. She was Quaker woman, not lovely. Heavy, face like old squirrel. But very religious, sitting for long time in the dark room, saying no words. Their custom for praying, she says. Major does not pray, but a good man. Both very kind. Long ago, in the big war before—the Rebellion, you say?—Major had caught a black woman and all these years she take care of his house. Then she died out here. Now they have nobody so they make me her. Give me her name, Dinah."

"So you were their house servant?"

She smiled. "Sure, yes! But it is the same if I was still here. Lakota girls are raised to work before we have babies, and many years after them, too. But Weldons say I am like their daughter. Long time before, they had a daughter and she died of coughing sickness in some fort, Nebraska, Kansas? I don' remember. So they put her dress on me, send to Army school. Missus teaches me at night. She says, Dinah, you are very intelligent. See, see!"

With a suddenness that made me jump, Walks Outside clapped her hands together and howled. "Like fine madam Fetterman, captain madam! All white women are the same. Need slave. Oh, my! I talk too much. Does it hurt your ears?"

I chuckles. "It's like music, lass. I mean that."

"I would have come before," she said softly, "but Lakota girls not supposed to push in where not asked. Our mothers train us to be shy, be good. It is what Lakota men want from us." Her eyes flickered. "Are *waiscu* men the same?"

I shrugged. "Hell, dearie, I ain't been *waiscu* for so long now, I don't know what they are or want anymore."

"Yes. I watch your face. So sad, so lonely."

"A fish out of water I am. And maybe you, too, I'm thinking.

Why would you give up the white-man life, when them Weldons were caring for you and treating you so fine?"

"It was not always so," she said quietly. Uncrossing her buckskin leggins, she turned from me and lay like a cat, face down in the grass. I thought for a moment she was weeping and didn't want me to see, but when her cheek lifted and she lay it flat on the back of her hand, her dark face was hard and her eyes open but distant. "I am Walks Outside," she murmured. "I can only be what I am. My people are here. Mother, brothers, sisters. When the Lakota were attacked on the Crazy Woman Fork in the snow, the soldiers ran from them. Did you know that?"

"Ah, I did indeed! A Sioux ball hit me in the face. I was one of the runners, Walks Outside."

She squinted at the scar on my temple. "Yes, I can still see the place. Besides, the warriors talk much about your fights. They wonder why Lakota can't kill this man. Anyway, so you didn't die at the Crazy Woman camp, but many of our people escape. Come quick back to Fetterman. Everybody excited, everybody saying how weak you whites are. Then our men in the camp on the Platte, they tell us, 'Don't let them keep us here like starving dogs. We can be free and they can't stop us.' When my mother came to me in the night, she said we must go to our cousin, the great Touch the Clouds. He would save us from sojers. My heart broke that night. It was like saying goodbye to the Majors again. I couldn't do it for fear of weeping. Over there, leaving Robinson, I had made a pillow case for Madam, so I picked some flowers and sage and wrapped them in it. Then I went off with my mother and the men. I am Lakota woman. This is my place." She lowered her forehead to the grass and lay still.

"Ah, you poor thing," I whispers. Before I knew it, I'd gripped her shoulders, turned her to me. Gently, I took her face in my hands and wiped her tears away. She didn't protest or push me back, just held her face next to mine and murmured something in Lakota that I didn't understand.

Jesus God, the sweet earthy smell of her was arousing me, her hard breasts pushing against my chest.

"D'ye have a Lakota man?" I whispered.

She drew away and sniffled. "One has been chosen. I am waiting to go to his lodge. He is a good man. But so are you. I don't want them to kill you."

"Walks Outside—have you ever lain with a man?"

She closed her eyes and shook her head. Then she began to giggle, and pulling away, ran her fingers through my beard. "I would think of this, yes. This strange skin with fur on it, oh, how it frightens me. And I could weep, too, that I do not have it. Sometimes, bathing in Madam's lavatory, I would scrub my skin so hard to get the color out of it, make it white. But still just 'Injun'. That's what sojers say. They were so bad at Fetterman, fighting sojers all gone, nothing but dirty mouths left, tramp people. Make me dance with them, put hands under my dress. They buy many Lakota girls with sweets and pretty clothes. Then, you know…" She slapped her palms together like bouncing up and down. "But always I ran from them. I don't live there, and they don't live here. I cannot change my skin."

"Well, lass, I'm here sure enough." No sooner had I spoken it than I was ashamed.

She was nodding. Her hands dropped to her breasts where, God almighty, I wished mine were. "My cousin, Touch the Clouds, says I should give myself to you. My Lakota man who will be my husband one day, he will take me to his lodge, no matter what with you. He is a generous man. He would forgive me. Perhaps he would be proud if I bore him a white child, at least one who could live with both peoples. Is that what Fights Without Club wants?"

I frowned. "Who wants?"

"You," she laughed, gripping my hands. "The man you fought without your club—he will be my husband."

"Ah, God help me!" I breathe. "Of all the Injuns I had to pick!"

She smiled, and kneeling next to me, put her hands on my shoulders. "If it will save your life, Patrick Mister Kelly, if it will make you one of us, I will give myself to you."

I took her in my arms and held her tight. She neither struggled nor encouraged me. She would give herself to help me, if I needed her so bad. It was like I was holding life here, holding the earth, the common clay of truth that our Maker had put into both of us. If the heathen had a soul, I was gripping it, and I wanted to weep at its simple beauty.

Slowly, I pushed away. "You're a grand lady, Walks Outside, and I thank ye for that."

"You will always be my friend," she whispered, and slowly stood up. "Even in death."

"Dammit to hell!" I cried, "there ain't no reason for our people to kill each other! You seen how it is in the forts. We're too many for you, too many guns. Can't you tell your people they ain't got a chance against us?"

"We have life!" she shot back. "Who are you, the Jesus God, taking ours away? I am sick of *waiscu*. Your monies, your killing, your fine gold hair madams making Sioux girl slave!"

I reached out for her. "Now cool down, damn ye! Don't be stupid about it, don't play the stubborn Injun on me because I know you know better. I'm telling you what I've told Jack Red Cloud until he's sick of hearing it. Some way, between us, we've got to stop the killing while we can!"

"It is not for us to say!"

"Who then? Watch these squaws and kids get shot down like we did at Crazy Woman? I killed one myself and ain't proud of it. But you just want to let it happen! Suffer some more because it's in your damn holy signs I suppose! I'm sick of you Injuns leaving everything to your Person Above, never trying to understand or lift one finger to make peace."

Her face went dark. "What are you?" she spat. "Nothing to us! A camp rat is worth more than you." Her strong lips curled down. "I have heard you. These lies you tell us are the same as all the sojers! What have they ever brought us but more death! The signs are given to Crazy Horse. He is the only one who knows. He will tell us what we must do."

Then, her mood shifting as quick as the moon ducking behind a cloud, she thrust up from me, brushed her hand over my forehead almost in a slap, and moved away, stopping once to scowl back at me. Savage style, she honked her nose out onto the leaves of the willows, and was gone.

I set there in the grass a long time, clutching my knees to my chest. Aching for a woman, I was, and admit it, yes, this proud, surly one, never knowing if she'd be holding me tender or ripping my throat out. Loneliness, was it, wanting her so much? Or maybe just plain fear that the reds would kill me before I ever had a last woman to go out on. Yet, as I cooled down, I began to see that it was probably lucky, her leaving me when she did. In the surging of my hot blood, I could have raced after her, caught her and flung her in the grass. Maybe she even wanted me to, like that was how Injuns done it, proving their bravery. But still, having felt the other side of her, I knew there was gentleness and the trust of a child in her, too. Even after having her life snatched from her and her Injun lice powdered away, she clung to a ray of hope that we'd spare her. God knows, I wanted to now, for I seen how senseless this fighting was. Humans were on the other end of our bullets, and that alone pretty much drained the war out of me. I was grateful for the touch of her I'd had, and my heart ached for the both of us.

What would we gain by a few fierce moments in the grass? No peace in it, nor future either. It wouldn't change our spots. Too different, too far apart. We still had the fires of hell to burn out of each other. I wished I knew a better way!

That very dusk, a heavy rainshower struck the camp, fierce lightning and thunder, and after it, the air grew cold and a fog covered the great camp.

In it, Jack Red Cloud found me and led me up the trail to the top of the canyon. Here, in a grove of pinion, sat Crazy Horse. The mist was rising above him. When Jack led me closer, I could see the wetness of his naked body. He was sitting cross-legged, again in one of his trances of prayer. His teeth were gripped on a hard stick, and wedged between his toes were large stones. He was giving his body pain so that he wouldn't drift off to sleep, and thus keep his wits clear to listen for the Person Above.

We stood there with the fog racing past us. Crazy Horse didn't even seem to see me. Presently, he took the stick from his mouth, and when he spoke, it was in a brief whisper. Jack nodded and quickly drew me away and back down the trail.

"Well hell, lad, what now?" I says, bursting in curiosity for my life.

"He has seen messengers coming to us. They will tell us what the people must do."

"And me?" I blurts.

"By'n'bye," Jack grunted.

It came at dawn the next day. Four mounted warriors clattered into camp, and the criers were running the lanes, the people spilling out, barefoot on the wet grass. Touch the Clouds and the other chiefs gathered around. The newcomers had ridden a long way, their war paint crusted with dust. The squaws were giving them pemmican and buffalo pouches of water. All the time, the warriors were talking and signing in great excitement.

The *waiscu*s were coming toward the camp. On the trail, ready to fight.

God Almighty, I thinks, Crazy Horse, up there in the mists, had seen exactly this. But how? It was a good twelve hours before that he'd had the vision of messages coming. No wonder the people were so awed by his powers. So now my eyes were searching the crowd, wondering if he'd be there to watch his prophecy come true.

But there was not a sign of him. As the warriors milled around, running their ponies in and getting their guns and trappings ready, Jack Red Cloud hurried me over to Touch the Clouds, who was standing tall as a pine tree in front of his lodge.

The chief gripped my arms and made a long speech, much of which I couldn't savvy, except for the look in his eyes. It was stern, but also hopeful in a strange way, like he trusted me and would miss me as he would his own son.

I wasn't far wrong. Jack passed it back to me that Crazy Horse was setting me free. But there was a price. I was to help him save the people. His, and mine.

The Army that was moving north toward the Tongue River was led by Crook. The couriers had found this out. I was to hurry to Crook and warn him that if he crossed the Tongue and tried to attack the people in their camps, he and all the white soldiers would be slaughtered.

"I wouldn't count on that," I says to Jack. "Don't let them hotheads bluff ye!"

The lad whipped to me angrily. "Open your ears! You do not know! There are more Lakota and Cheyenne gathered here than have ever been together! We are too many for you. Go to your homes, leave us at peace to dance and hunt, or all white sojers die."

The force of his words, and Touch the Clouds' towering visage, sure caught my attention. Not that I could believe what they were threatening, but even less could I believe that I was finally getting loose.

They'd already led in a big strapping pinto, slapped a U.S. McClellan saddle on him, and slid into the scabbard the Winchester carbine Crazy Horse had given me. I started to say, But where are the troops, which direction from here? And worse than that, turned loose alone, I'd be easy picking for any hostiles still streaming up from the agencies.

Touch the Clouds smiled. He'd already thought of that. I wouldn't be going alone. Turning, he beckoned at one of the warriors. God help us, who steps forward but the bruiser I'd bested in the knife and club fight.

The husband-to-be of Walks Outside. My eyes swept the crowd, searching for the precious thing, but all I could see were hags, old squaws and urchins fairly dancing in glee at the prospect of a fight.

The bruiser was in full warpaint and wore an eagle feather headdress as long as he was. Jack Red Cloud says, "He is Cut Meat," and well he could have, I thinks. "He will take you to within sight of the *waiscu* dog killers. Then you are no longer one of us. If you hope to live, tell them Crazy Horse's words."

That was all. No goodbyes. No final glimpse of that gentle heathen lady I was leaving behind to her fate.

Cut Meat grunted and jerked my pinto's buffalo-hair bridle. I followed him through the long camp and out into the lonely of the big open. Green as the mother sod it was, and ah, Jesus, how free I felt! I don't know if Walks Outside had ever told her man about me, but he was as surly as if he'd caught me under her blanket.

It only got worse as the days went on. But I was armed and I didn't fear the bugger, having bested him once. And he did slip me past some hostiles who well could have lifted my scalp.

About noon on the third day, we were close enough to the Big Horns to see the last snow glinting and melting on their awesome slopes. Cut Meat pulled up short and pointed his rifle to the south.

A wasteland of hills rolled away here, beautiful I do say, dotted with red and yellow and purple wildflowers. Red-tailed hawks were soaring above us, and smaller hawks darting in the tall grass searching for field mice. Far off, I saw the white butts of antelope, racing away from us. I thought Cut Meat was pointing at them. But he

72

jabbed his rifle further toward the mountains.

There were distant bobs of white there, too. When I squinted at them closer in the blinding sun, they were canvas. The tops of Army wagons in a great column, heading my way at last.

Cut Meat looked at me, then spat in the dust and wheeled his pony. With a whoop, I put my heels to the pinto and started racing across the hills. An hour later, eyes burning with dust and my throat crying out for water, I pulled up over a sagebrush hill and saw a red and white guidon streaming in the breeze.

Three troopers were riding hard toward me, my Indian pinto already winding their fierce smell and rearing in terror. The buggers were tearing their carbines out of their scabbards. "Jesus God," I cries, "hold your pieces, byes! I'm one of ye!"

In a great clatter and swirl of dust, they were reining in, milling around me, hard-faced men I'd never seen before. "I'm Kelly!" I cries. "Trumpeter, Captain Bloxham's troop!"

"Christ Almighty, will ya look at that?" one bellows at the sight of me.

"Goddamn deserter," growls a big corporal, leaning out to grab hold of my pony's bridle.

"In a pig's ass! I'm a prisoner coming back. The reds have had me for two months now!"

By now, more troops were streaming over the hill, all of them spoiling for a fight, the wild way they rode and flung their weapons up. The corporal, not believing me a whit, jerked my Springfield away and the others pulled me down from the pony. "Get an officer up here!" the corporal shouted.

"You sonsofbitches! Take your hands off me. I'm as Yank as you!"

Then a dusty officer cut through them. A lieutenant from his straps, a fine-looking man, taller than me, and when he stepped off his horse, the rabble troopers pulled back. He looked me up and down, with the rest of them muttering I was hostile or deserter or God knows what.

"Lying bastards!" I cried. "I've been in Crazy Horse's camp!"

The officer nodded and said quietly to the troopers, "That'll be enough here. Get back to your columns." As they pulled away, he turned to me. "You said Captain Bloxham's troop, 3rd Cavalry?"

"Yes, sir. They left me for dead at the St. Pat's day fight. My Captain can tell you the truth of it."

"He's not with us. But General Crook is. He'll want to see you."

"He better sure as hell. I'm carrying word to him from the reds."

"I imagine you are, or you wouldn't be here to talk about it." The lieutenant's dusty face cracked into a grin. As he stepped back onto his horse, he thrust out his hand. "I'm Crawford, G company 3rd, commanding. Good work, soldier. Welcome home."

73

BLEEDIN' IN THE ROSEBUDS

Officers' country was in a grove of cottonwoods alongside the Tongue River. I heard an enlisted striker mutter that this was the last night we could have a fire, so he was making one. Get warm. The sun died over the bluff across the river. Lieutenant Emmet Crawford led me through the orange shadows, where the officers were sitting against trees, writing letters, or others cross-legged on their blanket rolls, finishing up their last bit of supper. They were lean and fit, and not bad educated either. Here was one, reading aloud from Shakespeare, and another, in his long red undershirt, had a harmonica and was tooting a tune that some of them sang.

When Crawford led me in, one or two officers got up. A darkhaired wiry Captain introduced himself as Bourke, and with a grin added, "We're both Other Siders, Kelly. I'm happy one of us had a shamrock in his pocket."

I remembered Bourke from the cursed winter march to Crazy Woman Fork. With his Congressional Medal from the Rebellion, he was a bonafide hero all right, yet now in an old pajama top and Indian leggins, he looked as common as an ordinary trooper.

When Crawford brought me to Crook, he was sitting at the base of a cottonwood, a fly rod beside him, and his hands bloody with the guts of fish. He'd caught a string of gleaming little trout, and one by one, he was slitting them from the bum up to the throat, and flinging the innards into the silver stream.

Now that it was summer, his bushy beard had thawed the ice I remembered in it, and was light brown in color, with the two points of it swirled together in braids. He wore an old canvas hunting coat and gray woolen pants that even a squawman would have flung away. Atop his head was a slouch hat that shaded his eyes. His hat moved, his sunburned cheeks above the beard caught the last light, and I took from his signal that I was to sit down.

"Emmet," he says to Crawford, "you'd best stay. Colonel Royall and Bourke, too. And get Mills." In a moment, out of the shadows, I saw another Captain I'd remembered from St. Pat's day. Anson Mills, who was a hell-for-leather Texan, commanded the black horse troop that swept into the camp. Scipio Shaw had the troop of grays, but I didn't see Shaw here. Mills had an Indian blanket wrapped around him and was clean-shaven. When he shook my hand, he said, "I knew there were two men we left in that camp. I didn't realize it was three. Old Bedlam Bloxham didn't even record it in his action report, which is nothing less than criminal."

"Ask Kelly about that," Bourke says.

74

Crook frowned at me, and now I saw that cold look in his eyes. "How did they treat you, soldier?"

"About like a mule, sir. But maybe I have the hide for it. At least I'm here."

Then Lieutenant Crawford, who was the biggest man of all of them, and a handsome one too, kicked some sticks together with his enormous boot, squatted down and started making a small fire. "Retrace your steps for us, private, from the Crazy Woman Fork to now."

As best I could, I did exactly that. Escaping, finding Atsina, then into the frying pan with Jack Red Cloud, Little Big Man and the whole murderous lot of them. Finally to Crazy Horse. Crook kept nodding, skinning his trout. He was a man who didn't speak much, I could tell. Once, in fact, I says that Crazy Horse was pretty much like the General himself. He didn't use many words. "But what there were," I adds, "he made pretty plain, sir. He don't want the troops coming after him. He says he'll kill you all."

Crook glanced at me with a hard grin. "Did he say where this killing was going to happen?"

"Someplace above the Tongue, sir. If you set foot in the Tongue."

Crook tossed another handful of guts into the stream.

Bourke asked me how were the hostiles armed? I described what I'd seen. Lever-action Winchesters, fresh in grease from the agencies. "And worse, sir, they've been practicing with our Springfields. The devils have figured out what we already know, that the damn breeches jam after two shots."

"They've had Winchesters for years," Crook said quietly. "Not enough to do real damage. Nor do they have the stomach to go against infantry long rifles, which do not jam."

"But sir, they're going to go against you different, fight different, from what I saw."

"How is that?"

As quick as I could, because he acted impatient with me for bringing this all up, I told how they were planning to fight us in bunches, wasps stinging the bear from all sides. Even using mirror signals."

"I'd look forward to that," Crook answered. "Every Indian I've ever fought runs away." Then he looked at me intently. "Did you get any sign from Crazy Horse that, if we guaranteed him land of his own, he would come in, lead his people in, at peace?"

"Nothing like that come up, sir. It wasn't like we were chatting over ale in a tavern." Some of the officers smiled, but Crook didn't.

"He gave you no sign that he was willing to talk peace, short of war?"

I shook my head. "I'd say they're spoiling to fight. General, I ain't been Army long, and I don't know much Army thinking neither. But I have been living among these heathen, and I seen what I never thought was there. They aren't serving time like us, or winning stripes or stars. They ain't hired to fight. They're fighting to stay alive, which means down to the last of them to save their squaws and tykes and their land which they hold damn dear, and only sell with blood. We're talking about killing their camps. They know that. We call 'em bucks and sell their scalps in saloons. These are people, General. They ain't elk or buffalo. They got a banshee, Crazy Horse, telling them it's a great day to die. I'm saying they're ready, and we'll pay with our blood."

The way the other officers looked at me, I knew I was out of line. Enlisted didn't dare speak to officers unless asked, and I hadn't been. Just mouthed off what I felt was the truth of it.

Some officer behind me muttered, "Give that man a stretch on the picket line, he'll get over it."

But Crook was watching me quietly. "Soldier, I went to war against Indians before you were born. I have heard all their threats and their boasts. It's part of their war bag. They want to terrify you, and then they can work more concessions out of you..."

"Sir," I blurted, "I had nothing to give them. I'm telling what I saw."

"Then see this," Crook snapped. "Not one treaty we've made with them have we ever kept. Not once have we put them on a reservation except to rob them and starve them. The miracle is not that we've had so many wars, but so few. I don't hate these people, nor do I blame them for fighting against the swindling they've been given. I regard war against them as a distasteful task, and my duty is to get it over the sooner the better. They are victims of an expansion that isn't going to stop, and neither you nor I nor any man here can do anything about that. The Indians know full well that peace, and as much justice as I can give, will come only when they want it, not before. I intend to bring them to that happy day in whatever way I have to. The dreams of any other solution or the inflated fears of soldiers who shouldn't be in the field have no place in my command." He turned to Crawford. "Feed him and put him back in uniform." Then he humped away, his dead trout in a sack over his shoulder.

As I was walking back toward the enlisted camp, I saw Mills, Royall and Crawford sitting down beside a fire. Their faces were hard and ghostly in the flames. Mills was thumping a map that he'd spread out on his blanket. "Napoleon's Fourth Axiom of War," he muttered. "Never try to join three columns in face of an enemy on his own ground. He will beat each one separately. So we have three columns, Terry-Custer, Gibbon and ourselves."

"Sheridan's plan," Crawford said. "The hero of Winchester."

"But what's he trying to do to Crook?" Mills snapped. "Ruin him? This thing won't work. We're split up across a wilderness, can't even communicate with each other."

Then they fell into muttering among themselves. I heard only a little of it, not wanting them to catch me eavesdropping. From what I could understand, the pouter-pigeon Sheridan, whom I'd shod for in Chicago, had been the roommate of General Crook at West Point. Closest of friends, they were. Then the Rebellion came. At the battle of Winchester in Virginia, the Union troops were having the hell beat out of them until Crook leads in his cavalry and turns the tide. But who sweeps up then to claim the glory for it? Little Phil, bedecked with his medals from that night on.

"I don't blame Crook if he never forgives him," Lieutenant Crawford said.

"There'll be blame enough for all of us right here and now," Colonel Royall said. He was a dignified old Virginia man with a full gray beard. "Sheridan has Grant's ear and Sherman's too. That's why Custer is commanding the 7th again, and they'll not keep that hotspur on their leash."

"Are you saying Crook is a scapegoat in this?" Mills asked.

Royall shook his head. "Sam Grant has never tolerated backbiting among his generals. He holds Crook in high regard as an Indian fighter. But I have never trusted Phil Sheridan. Perhaps it's guilt over snatching past glory from Crook. Or it's just practical generalship. Sheridan, in my view, would like to see his pet, Custer, or Miles or MacKenzie, some of the younger men, take full command out here. Our expedition, gentlemen, may well be the holocaust in which this will be settled."

At that point, I caught Crawford's wary eye glancing at me in the shadows, and I moved on. The last thing I heard was Mills saying: "Crook has no idea of the force against us. He doesn't want to know. If I were you, Colonel Royall—you're second in command— talk some sense to him before we have to fight."

But nobody was talking any sense to anybody. Maybe the only one who was right was old Napoleon. He saw it coming.

Three hours before daybreak of June 17, Crook broke camp and marched us along a stream that the scouts called the Rosebud. Good reason, the banks of the flowing rivulet were choked with wild rose bushes, and when the dew burned off, the bees came swarming around the flowers. I says to a trooper riding at my side. "God help us, if this ain't a pretty place to die."

The man had been asleep, slouched there in his saddle like a sack of grain. Angry that I'd waked him, he grunted, "Nobody's dying, you thick-headed greenie. What d'ya think them is?" and he flung his arm at the long dusty file of horsemen on both sides of the creek. I'd heard it said in camp that there were twelve or thirteen hundred of us now. Nobody had a real clear count, what with Shoshone and Crow scouts whooping in and out of the ranks, and then, too, a grizzled gang of Montana miners had joined us the night before. One of the officers said that this was the finest Army ever put together, and no Indian with a grain of sense would dare take us on.

About eight in the morning, when the sun was beginning to cook us, and the horses playing out, a command trickled down from Crook to dismount, unsaddle, and help ourselves to hardtack and cold coffee.

While the lads were untacking their beasts, a corporal comes slogging through the tall grass, green as Ireland it was, and hollers: where was Kelly, the trooper the reds had caught? I steps forward and he says: "Gineral wants you, up the creek." Some other wag cracks, "Officer's pet now, ain't he?"

Well, maybe yes, but probably no. Anyhow, I was glad to leave these rag-tags, for they were all strangers, none of my old bunkies among them. I led my mount, a sway-backed chestnut, along through the company camps that were forming on the banks of the stream. The infantry were mounted on mules, which had been another of Crook's ideas, to give us better mobility for fighting. But the mules were green-broke buggers, kick you as soon as look at you. They were braying and getting loose, bucking, and filling their bellies with the sweet new grass. Just to make it even noisier, the Indian scouts were racing their ponies up and down the banks of the stream. The devils had painted themselves like holy hell, and their boasting and horse-racing were all childish bluffing to build up their courage, I suppose.

But I must say, just the commotion everybody was making and the cocky gorging of the soldiers on their vittles sent a chill through me. You're raising hell out here like it's a grand lark in the sun, I thinks, but lads, you don't have a notion of what you're up against, or what could be lying in wait for you behind those hills.

When I led my horse into the officer's camp, which was by a pretty little spring, Crook and Bourke were sitting on a log, playing a hand of cards. It was a Yankee game they called Twenty One. They were flipping cards down just as carefree as school lads, and using revolver bullets for chips. Crook's gray eyes twinkled when he turned over the cards. "Five and under, Bourke," he said. "You may learn this game if the campaign lasts long enough."

Then he takes note of me, standing there, and beckons at a couple of civilians, sitting nearby in the grass. One I recognized, a wizened-faced fellow in a derby. It was Mr. Strahorn, the newspaper writer who'd been with us for the St. Pat's day fight. The other, who was scribbling notes, glanced up with the map of Ireland on his face. "John Finerty," he says, grinning, "Chicago Inter-Ocean."

"I know the paper," I says. "I worked in the Yards."

78

"You look it, lad. But tell me, now that you've been a guest of the lesser race, and come home with your scalp, how does this particular situation look to you?"

"The what, sir?"

"Are we going to have a fight?"

I glanced around at the officers lounging on the grass, one lighting his pipe and another whittling a stick. As far as I could see up the stream, the whole command was knocking back and resting. Ah, sure, we'd earned it maybe, after a three-hour ride before breakfast. But when I looked above the stream, I could see that we were in a big basin, with hills all around us. "Are we going to have a fight?" I repeats to Finerty. "I hope to hell not, sir. Not in this place."

Finerty frowned. "You've been here before?"

"No. But the furthest one of them hills is still close enough to have a swarm of reds behind it. And close enough that they can fire from there, down into us. They have fine weapons, mister, and they ain't the lesser race neither, as you say. Far from it."

"Trooper," Mr. Strahorn cut in, "your feelings are understandable, having been among these people."

"They're spoilin' to fight you," I cried.

"I doubt that. Because they know what you probably don't. These men here, this command, are the finest troops in the world. Look around you, Kelly. Ex-Confederate cavalry officers, now in the ranks. Union officers who have been in steady combat for twenty years. There are probably more bullet wounds and saber scars in this bunch than any army in the world, which is why the foreign professionals have joined us. Italians, French, a Prussian colonel." He pointed at one big fellow in suspenders and long underwear who was shaving beside the stream. "It's not an even match-up, for a savage to go against these, and they know it."

"They're fightin' to stay alive, sir. That's the difference."

Then somebody laughed, and one of the young officers said to Finerty, "John, maybe you could write a dime novel about Kelly? *My Sioux Captivity*. Something like that. They tell me they're eating up this pulp, back in the States."

Just about the time he said the word Sioux, far off in the hills, there was the thump of a gun, then a quick rattling of others. Bourke was dealing another hand to Crook right then, and neither acted as if they'd heard a thing. One officer said that it was probably the Indian scouts, shooting at buffalo, like they'd been doing every day. But then Lieutenant Emmet Crawford pulled on his big boots and stood up. He beckoned at his striker to bring him his horse. "No, that's not buffalo," Crawford said. "Too many shots in too many different directions."

It was one of those moments that more or less froze in my brain, like I'd seen it all before, knew what was coming, and everyone else was just sleep-walking through it. Far off on the northern rim of hills, a plume of dust was rising, sweeping toward us. Down along the stream, the horse races of the Shoshones and Crows had stopped dead. They were staring toward the hills, then breaking out into howls and racing toward the dust. By now, the plume was horsemen, riding fast down toward us. Here and there I could see that they were wearing pieces of blue uniforms, and closer I could make out the red patches that Crook had hung on the Indian scouts so that we could tell them apart from the hostiles. Now their howls echoed across the hills: "Lakota! Otoe Lakota!" Sioux, many Sioux!

Then, like a nightmare come to life, there they were. On the skyline, first on the left, then on the right, rose up masses of mounted Sioux. God almighty, their screeches alone filled the whole valley, the blood-curdling death songs of banshees, not hidden from us anymore, not ghosts, but glittering lines of horsemen, feathered-headdresses trailing down to the ground, and their raised lances and guns spearing up at the sun. I knew enough Lakota by then to savvy what their shrieking was about. They were daring us to die.

Everywhere around me, officers and strikers were scattering. Bugles were sounding, horses being galloped in, troopers trying to snatch up their saddles and mount. Finerty's face, and Strahorn's too, were pale in the sun, as they stared at that awful horde of Sioux sweeping toward us.

I glanced over at Crook. Bourke had already sprung up, but Crook was methodically patting the cards together, slipping them in his jacket pocket, and then picking up the revolver shells they'd used for chips. "Present my compliments to Captain Mills," Crook said to Bourke, "and have him drive those hostiles off the bluffs."

God help us, I thinks, the man is as cool as if he were swatting a fly. By then, Crook's striker had hurried in with the General's big black horse. I was surprised to see that he wasn't riding a mule anymore. Maybe now he was needing a mount that could carry him fast into the middle of this mess—or away from it. As he wheeled past me to start fording the Rosebud, his eyes smiled. "Ride courier for me, soldier. You might get to see some of your old friends."

I followed him, naturally, it being an order. But I didn't follow long before the battle of the Rosebud had swallowed us up, and the odds looked bad because we'd been caught by surprise.

There is no way to tell time in a fight like this, nor did I have the faintest notion where we were, chasing the heels of Crook's black horse up and down gulleys and hilltops. A common soldier, getting shot at, is the last man to make any sense out of the wild death dance we were trapped in that day. Crook fairly ate up the hills, and now that we'd climbed out of the stream bed, I could see that we were in a basin so vast that the columns of us were like ants

80

in the palm of a giant's hand. I could count five different fingers of hills sloping down toward the Rosebud, and troops and hostiles were blasting at each other on every one of them. As far as I could see in all directions, knots of bluebellies were dismounting, wriggling up the hills, firing as they went, with the savages coming hell for leather right down into them. Even the heavy booming volleys of the infantry Long Toms didn't seem to stop the red divils. They were charging in and out on horseback, wasps stinging the bear just as Crazy Horse had taught them, and our cavalry was soon afoot, one trooper holding the horses of four shooters who were spread-eagled on the firing line.

"They're cutting us into separate fights," I heard Crook shout to a dusty officer who'd ridden up. By now the rising dust was so fierce we could hardly make out friend or foe. Streaming past us were Captain Mills' companies, lashing their horses up the slopes and rocky ledges, trying to beat the hostiles to the high ground. Then Bourke swept in from behind us and nearly spooked me off my horse. He was pointing: "Those bluffs, General. To the west. Royall is trapped."

There was heavy firing in that direction, first volleys from the troops and then the lighter, faster chatter of the reds with their repeating Winchesters. I wondered if our poor lads were crouching on that bluff top, picking out their damn second shells that were stuck in the breeches.

Crook whirled his horse. Though there was anger in his eyes, I never heard him cuss or give any sign of fear. "Royall has to close up with us, or they'll split off half of our command. Nickerson should have given him that message by now. Why doesn't he comply? Good God, man, move your troops off that bluff!"

Bourke was standing on a big yellow rock, watching to the west with his field glasses. "Hostiles are on both sides of Royall, sir. Hundreds at least, maybe more."

A bullet sung into the rock at Bourke's feet. The wiry Lieutenant scurried for cover, and the sky fell in. A pack of heathen came thundering down the ridge right at us. They were close enough so that I could see the gleaming buffalo horn headdresses of the Cheyennes, and hear the shrilling of their bone whistles. Far above, on the furthest ridge, I saw flashes that weren't from guns. They were from a mirror, and when it would burn across the painted faces of one horde of savages, they'd veer their ponies off in another direction, our troops so busy shooting at them that they didn't see the next lot of murderers striking us from behind.

All I could think of was the cruel sneer on Crazy Horse's face when he showed his war chiefs how to beat us. They were doing it, bullets and showers of arrows whizzing around us. Crook slashed his arm toward the top of the bluff where there were big boulders sticking up, and a reddish ledge of shale. His black charger was leaping up the ledge, Bourke and I following him. We'd been joined by maybe twenty dusty infantrymen, fighting cut off from their outfit, but they were giving good measure with their Long Toms. Now, when the two columns of Indians that were stinging us from both sides rushed us, I heard the thock of .45-70 caliber bullets smashing into ponies or savages. No way to tell. Indian ponies were falling in bouncing heaps. Here and there, a red would come howling at us, firing under the neck of his horse so we couldn't get a good shot. Then, before we could get aimed again, he'd whirl his pony and snatch up one of his wounded comrades from the dust. Our own were already wailing down in the basin. I don't know how many had been hit, but I was sure hoping the next one wasn't me.

We tried to take shelter in some scrubby pinions on the ridge. Infantry troops, hospital stewards and the surgeons were already running into the rocks where Crook was setting up his headquarters. From here we could see the whole swirling fight. But then, just as Crook spurred off, signaling to another troop of cavalry, his big black horse gave a lurch and a shudder, With a bloody snort, he went end over end, hurtling Crook hard into the rocks.

I was the closest one to him, trying to follow as he'd told me, but the way he shook himself and shivered, I thought he'd caught the bullet. "Are you shot, sir?" I grabbed hold of his shoulders and helped him up. There was fire in his eyes.

"No damage, soldier, except to my pride. I have never seen Indians fight like this." Then he shouted at Bourke and the others who were running up. "Get word to Mills on the north slope. Fall back, take five troops of cavalry. March up that canyon and hit Crazy Horse's camp. Kill the camp. If we don't, we'll starve."

Bourke's face tightened. "Sir, the scouts say that the canyon is a trap. Rocky ledges, downed timber."

"We'll take that chance, Bourke. It's our only one."

"General Crook," cried Surgeon Munn, "we've got dozens of wounded, more coming all the time. Your headquarters soldiers are down to ten rounds apiece. We can't hold this place if you send all the fresh cavalry with Mills."

"We *will* hold it," Crook said. "We'll swing Royall's troops back to us. If Nickerson hasn't already shaken him loose, send more couriers, Bourke. He must follow my order!"

Bourke began running through the milling horsemen, slapping two non-coms and then a young lieutenant. "Tell Royall to withdraw at once, wheel eastward to this position. He's got at least a thousand hostiles pinning him down, so you'll have to fight your way to him, and fight your way back."

Bourke was whirling toward Crook when his eyes caught mine.

"Sir," I says, "I ain't attached to no troop here, but I've been up against these reds. I don't mind hittin' 'em a lick just to get this mess over."

"The more the merrier," Bourke said, and he wasn't laughing. "Follow the others."

I went galloping northwest toward Royall's bluff, plunging down into one coulee and scrambling up the other side. At every turn, reds were shooting at us from back, front, side. I was so busy staying on my crazy, leaping mount, I hardly had time to fire back. A flash of a painted face or a headdress trailing in the wind, I'd blam off a round, never knowing if it hit. Then I raced into one coulee just in time to see a trooper go down. He'd been cut off here, with swarms of the vultures swooping in on him cackling, smashing his head with clubs. I reined in and fired at the devils. Hit one, he spun away, moaning. But the rest of the bloodthirsties were howling, and in the time it took my horse to race fifty yards, they had hacked off that trooper's arms and legs, and the blood was spraying into the sun.

Racing past, there was nothing I could do, I ran into two groups of Indians, fighting each other on the rise just above. The red-patched Shoshone scouts had trapped a small bunch of Sioux up here, swarming around them, hurling lances and clubbing them into the dust. In the noise of it, I heard an awful scream. One young Sioux, down on his knees, was sobbing, begging the Shoshone to spare him. It took me an instant to recognize him in his nakedness and paint.

Jack Red Cloud, blubbering pure coward, with the Shoshones whipping him with coup sticks. I shouts: "Leave that lad alone!" But the Shoshones were sneering at poor Jack, gripping their crotches like they were peeing on him. They'd already ripped off the gleaming eagle feather headdress his father had given him. One big Shoshone was waving a trophy he'd snatched from Jack. It was a gold-inlaid lever-action Winchester that President Grant had given to Red Cloud as a peace present. But then the Shoshones were gone, sweeping past me, and in the shame of it, Jack had scurried out of there, too. A Sioux was lugging him fast up the hills on the back of his horse. Covering him with fire was a gang of painted Indians, their bullets ripping through the tall grass where I rode. I caught a glimpse of one man. He was wearing no warpaint, only a single eagle feather and a breechclout. What's more, he fought on foot, unlike the rest of them. He'd snap off a few shots from his Winchester, then wave it in the air, rallying the other Indians to stand their ground and not run away. Clear in the sun, the glint of a mirror struck my eyes. It was hanging around his neck. The strange one, the messiah, Crazy Horse.

Well, my friend, I thinks, you weren't bluffing, were you? You sent me home to warn against just this kind of slaughter. But nobody listened, not my people, not yours. Maybe they never will, until enough of us are writhing in the dust with our guts leaking away.

I hurled my horse off the bluff and into the last coulee between ourselves and Royall. No need for the message. His dusty troopers were already flaming across the big broad bottom, heading east to Crook, but between them and me was a swirling horde of reds, fighting hand to hand with the troopers. I had no choice but to plunge into them, spraying lead wherever I could, but damn, it wasn't enough to keep the dervishes from ripping two troopers out of their saddles and spearing them like squealing pigs in the killing lane.

A big Sioux was hurtling toward me, half of his face painted white, the other half black. I'm thinking: What a ferocious, ugly bastard, even his dun pony was coming at me, teeth bared and biting. Losing my wits for just that instant, I barely ducked a lance that he whistled past my head. "Not yet, you devil!" I howls, swinging my carbine over the pommel and blasting him square in the gut. The .45-70 slug should have blown an ordinary man off his horse, but this banshee only swayed. With a scream of pain, his big muscled arms drew his bow so fast, so close, I never saw the arrow coming.

My left leg, closest to him, felt like it was on fire. I was starting to puke in the pain of it, gripping my horse's neck so that I wouldn't fall down into that swirling lot. I kept thinking: This little bee sting can't stop you, lad. It's just a savage's arrow. Flesh wound. But somewhere during my time with the reds, I'd heard them boasting about a few men in the tribe who were so strong, they could shoot an arrow clean thru a buffalo's ribs and guts, and watch it fall loose out the other side.

I tried to move my leg so I could get free and dismount. It wouldn't budge. I clutched at it and felt the big bone snapped and flopping, the arrow driven right thru it and spearing me to the side of my horse.

All I remember was rough hands reaching under my saddle pad and cutting the shaft loose from the horse. I heard somebody say, "Can he ride?" And another answers. "Hell no, look at the blood he's leaking. He won't live to get back to the stream."

The stream? I thinks. The Rosebud? Then I began seeing ghosts of the past, dancing in my eyes. Where was Crook? Where was Crazy Horse or Walks Outside? What were we doing in this godforsaken slaughter?

It didn't matter anymore. We'd let our blood mingle with the sweet Rosebud's, and none of us would ever be the same again.

MY CAPTAIN'S WIFE

For much of the time that followed, I was daft, drifting in and out of life like I didn't much care whether I lived or died, only to end the pain, God help me.

Along Rosebud creek that night, surgeons with bloody white coats, Munn and two others, were working on all of us crippled lads. Ah, I was better off than those who were gut-shot and had no way to live, not with the primitive Army doctoring that we knew then. When another poor soul would wail and give up the ghost, weary, grumbling troopers would drag him by the legs into a big pit they'd dug nearby where maybe thirty or forty stiffs were heaped like cordwood. Beyond them, up and down the creek, worn out officers and troopers were huddled around campfires, the licking flames dancing goblins in the dark. I saw one man stand up and spear a Sioux lance into the fresh-dug dirt. "They beat us, damn them!" he cried.

Ah, the shame of it! We'd put our tail between our legs and run, lucky to get out with our skins. The Shoshone and Crow scouts were blubbering and wailing their death songs. Crook, with a blanket over his shoulders, was hunched up like an old man as he stared at the mass grave. "March a troop over that," he muttered. There'd be no bugle playing Taps, no rifle salute for the dead, least of all a Bible for the forgotten. Our horses would tromp the earth until there'd be nary a sign that humans were buried here, lest the damn reds rip up our bones and piss on them.

By the time Surgeon Munn worked his way down the line to me, I was well on the way to dreamland. A hospital steward named Rawley, a quick, ratty faced little bugger, had jabbed me with morphine, and it was starting to take hold. An old Sergeant, who'd been plugged long before on the Washita, gave me a flask of whiskey. "Arrow hurts more than sin, youngster," he said, "and when they get to cutting the point out, use this." He stuffed a fresh-cut stick between my teeth, but not before I let the whiskey burn down me. Then I started to swim away good until I could hardly see Munn's tired face floating over me like a moon.

He was telling the other surgeon and Rawley that the arrow had not only smashed the big bone in the leg, but was corrupting the wound. Either the point had carried in with it part of my uniform pants, or more likely, had been dipped in heathen poison. "I want to save your leg, soldier," Munn said, "but that arrow has broken in two. Part of the shaft pinned you to your horse. The steel point, however, is still in your leg bone. If the infection spreads as I think it will, you don't stand a chance."

85

I was sweating from the pain of him probing the bloody hole. "Jesus God, man," I cries, "I ain't givin' up my leg!"

"It's a metal point, I can feel that now. They're using them more and more, and they're wicked." He started telling me how the point clamped over, no way to get it loose. The bone would never heal, I'd have a leg full of jelly. The other surgeon, a younger man, had already brought him a kettle of boiling water, and from it Munn drew out a foot-long saw with big ripping teeth.

I struck the cursed thing away. "No cuttin'! If I'm croakin', it'll be with my leg on!" They'd pulled my pants off, I was lying there naked, Munn's finger striping a circle below my crotch, where he was going to start hacking and leave me with a stump. I lashed out again, flinging the saw into the darkness.

"You'll regret that, soldier," Munn grunted, and moved off to work on somebody else. Faintly, through the morphine swimming my brain, Rawley turns to the young surgeon still beside me and says, "I've been working on a technique to use a hook that might fish that bent iron head out and save the leg."

"Show me, and I might believe you," the surgeon answered.

"Don't have it with me," Rawley muttered. It was back at the cantonment where he was stationed. I heard him say, "Camp Connor." It might as well have been St. Peter's throne, for all I knew. But Munn never started sawing on me that night, and by dawn I figured he'd written me off as a guinea pig, more or less, for a lowly hospital steward to practice on. If one more trooper died out there in the disgrace of the Rosebud, nobody was going to miss him. There'd be new recruits to walk in on two legs, and replace this old broken wheel. The war was all that counted. The war had to go on.

Ah, God, what a trip it was, getting all of the wounded out of the mountains and back to civilization. They lashed me, like the others, onto travois, a canvas stretched over two poles. The cavalry horse that was dragging me managed to slam into every damn rock on the long trail. When we had to cross and re-cross the Rosebud—about fifty times, it seemed—four troopers would lift me onto their shoulders and slog the stream. My leg, swollen twice its size, was yellow blue and leaking corruption. I drank all the whiskey in the old sergeant's flask, and I bit a dozen sticks apart in the pain of my leg being jostled. In three days, after we'd hit Crook's base camp at the foot of the Big Horns, Rawley loaded me into an ambulance wagon. They'd made a bed of straw in it, but that cursed wagon was so hard-wheeled and hard-springed that it jolted me more than the travois ever had. By now, it was just Rawley and one trooper escort rider, guiding us south. I was so drugged and feverish, I lost all track of time.

Late one afternoon, I felt the ambulance creak finally to a stop. Chains rattled as somebody unhitched the horses. Outside, a man was talking. I thought, I'm dreaming this, but damn, don't I know that voice? Then, big hands with a gold ring on one finger pulled open the canvas dust flaps. "Kelly? By Jove! You indeed! Bully luck, young man. I'd given you up for dead."

"Ain't quite," I croaked, squinting at him until I knew for sure. It was Captain Bloxham all right, the same old jowly face and piggie eyes. He pulled his specs down, then turned and shouted: "Orderly! Bring Mrs. Bloxham, on the double!"

He was holding the canvas flap open. I saw a row of frame barracks that must have been newly flung up Army style, the lumber fresh cut. Cantonment Connor it was, a sorry, God-forsaken place with a flag drooping over a huddle of old log cabins that had probably been a ranch or stage station years back. By then, I was so dizzy that the dying sun flamed into my eyes and like to blind me. I started to sag back into the straw when another face peered in. Daft as I was, it looked like a cameo I'd seen dangling on Lady Cavan's bosom. Seeming carved out of ivory, there stood Mrs. Bloxham, her blonde hair piled atop her head and more trailing down her neck. Ah, God help me, I thinks, did she look so lovely when I seen her at Fetterman, or am I just paining so bad that I'm playing make believe?

Captain Bloxham was blustering in the sun: "Leah! This soldier is Kelly, don't you remember? My trumpeter at the Crazy Woman fight. With him, we have our witness! We can turn the court!"

"Oh, Clete, hush up that nonsense! The poor man is half dead. Steward Rawley." Her blue eyes flashed, "Bring him to the sutler's store. Since you've been gone, I've readied the back room for these wounded they keep sending. What are you going to need?"

"Boiling water," Rawley answered. "Whiskey, morphine."

"Hurry," she said, letting the flap drop and leaving me in darkness.

I remember murmuring to Rawley, was the Cap's wife a nurse? He said, hell no, just worked in Reb hospitals during the War. Out here, you took whatever help you could get.

The last I saw, she was squinting at me and patting a chloroform rag over my nose and mouth. "Don't fight" she whispered. "Breathe hard...you won't feel anything..."

When I awakened at daybreak, I was lying on a bench in a bare pine room, and she dozing in a camp chair beside me. She had a hospital steward's rubber coat wrapped around her. It was way too big, and the blood stains on it were mine. Her hands were folded in her lap. But when I gave a move to feel down toward my leg, she stirred.

"I imagine you're looking for this, aren't you?" From the folds of rubber in her lap, she handed me a steel arrow point, crimped at the base so that it would never come out.

"God in heaven," I breathed. "Rawley done it! I got my limb!"

"You came through it beautifully. You were as brave as Rawley was skilled."

"I surely thank you, ma'am. Never expected nothin' like this."

She stood over me and drew the sheet away. Carefully, though, because I was naked as a jaybird beneath it. "See for yourself," she said, and I could look at my leg for the first time without shuddering. Though they had a bandage over the wound, and a splint tight up into my crotch, healing the bone, I suppose, the ghastly color had left my limb and the swelling was down, too.

"You're not out of the woods yet, soldier." She whisked the sheet up over me and smiled. "These things take time to heal, so I'll be coming to change your dressings quite regularly."

"And won't I be looking forward to that, ma'am!" I was laughing in the joy of being in one piece, never realizing how it must have sounded, enlisted talking so bold to a lady. But Rawley caught it. He was glowering. "The Captain is waiting for you at your quarters, Missus Bloxham."

Then they were both gone, leaving me in that bare, medicine-smelling room, with the point of a Sioux arrow clenched in my fist.

Little did I dream that before very long, I'd be wishing the damn thing had struck me in the heart and put me out of the misery that lay ahead.

Missus Bloxham was the only woman on the post, and the only white one I'd seen for months. So I suppose it was natural that when she'd come by the hospital, I couldn't take my eyes off her. Like Her Ladyship Cavan she was, all thoroughbred with her graceful neck and fine bones, and me a common drayhorse plug not fit to sniff her harness.

She was business-like enough peeling off my bandages, and it wasn't hardly private with other sickies in the hospital peering at us, or Rawley playing doctor while she was changing my dressings. Yet still, I found myself counting the hours until she'd come. Her hands were gentle and skilled, and her southern accent so soothing that it might have nodded me off to sleep, except for wanting to watch her as long as I could. Sometimes when I couldn't savvy her way of talking, she'd laugh. "Grow up with black nannies and you never can get their gullah out of you. But I learned a great deal from them, too, the way they'd heal sick people down in the slave cabins. All sorts of herbs, rabbits' feet, chicken bones. I saw it work." Then she went on to tell me that when the Rebellion swept over Mississippi, there were so many wounded, somebody had to treat them. Even though she'd barely lifted a finger in her girlhood, she did her best to learn Confederate nursing and making do with very little medicine. Another time, she told me that she'd helped a surgeon amputate her younger brother's arm. "I wept so much for him I was hardly any use. But at least he's still alive." That's when I noticed the sad, faded beauty of her smile. It died on her lips and left them twisted and hard.

While she'd be working on my dressings, I'd notice the way the other wounded men watched her. She'd sit down in a camp chair and they'd be staring at how she crossed her thin, pretty legs. Sometimes she'd have to lean over, and though she wore a rubber hospital coat, it parted enough at her breast to make you think she was trying to let us see a little of her body.

Often, I thought about that day in the snow at Fetterman, Walks Outside, dark as sin, fondling this fair lady's bracelet. I wondered if the Sioux gal would be sneering at me, watching me being pampered by one of my own race? But hell, who knew where Walks Outside was now? If the troops had hit the hostile camps after the Rosebud, she could well be laying dead someplace, or moldering in a burial tree. My time with the Injuns seemed so long ago I couldn't hold onto the feel of it anymore. I was alive and back with the troops, and I sure could have had it worse than my officer's wife caring for me.

Not everybody saw it that way, though. Once, after Mrs. Bloxham had treated a lunger with T.B. and left him no better than before, he sat up angrily. "Perfume on her, powder on her ass. D'ye catch the way she queens it around here, treating us like we're her nagurs. I was with Sherman in Georgia. I seen her kind. Secesh, south in her mouth! Goddamn all of 'em, they dangle it in front of you, boys, and tease you with what you don't dare touch."

The next morning, that soldier was dead, and I was glad he was gone. I didn't believe for a minute that she was coquetting herself in front of the men. There was too much fine lady in her for that, I thinks. Yet Steward Rawley was always sour about her, and that puzzled me.

Presently, she stopped coming to the hospital room, and anyhow, my leg had healed up enough that I could hobble around on crutches. Not having any real duties, I took to wandering around that miserable, lonely Cantonment Connor.

Captain Bloxham had built it with two troops, about ninety men, and not a dozen of us were sound of mind and limb. All the losers the field commanders didn't want had ended up here. Most were sickies, lungers and the like, or crazy in the head from getting shot at by an Indian. Some were oldtimers waiting for final discharge, and more than a few were caught deserters, sent here instead of Leavenworth.

"This fort is yer perfect example of money chasing fear," an old sergeant told me. All that spring and summer, the sagebrush and mournful hills had been running with blood, thousands of Lakota, Cheyenne and Arapaho swooping down on wagon trains, far flung cow ranches and dog holes where men were trying to mine gold. From Colorado up into Dakota and west to Montana, country newspapers were wailing that nits make lice. Burn out their damn nests, exterminate the reds to make room for decent, civilized white people. After the settlers had hollered loud enough, Congress began showering money their way. Army headquarters got the wild notion of building a string of tiny outposts, to replace the old forts like Kearny on the Bozeman Trail that Red Cloud had destroyed after beating us in the 1868 war.

So Cantonment Connor and others like it came crusting up out of the sagebrush, with new lumber and old men, so understrength and isolated that a determined band of Lakota could have ground us into the dust in a couple of hours.

"A losing proposition," the sergeant grunted, "which is why they give us Old Bedlam Bloxham as our commander. He's as washed up as we are. A damn relic."

One afternoon, I was out on the sagebrush parade ground when couriers rode in with news of the massacre of Custer and the Seventh at the Little Big Horn. I pegged over to them while they were unsaddling their sweaty horses, and asked, "When did it happen, byes?"

"Happen?" one of them snaps. "Why, six-seven weeks back. Didn't nobody tell you?"

"We got no telegraft," a trooper answers. "Our old man don't let us patrol noplace 'cause they ain't soldiers enough to guard this post."

My heart sank, hearing the truth of what the lad said. We were so far out of it we didn't count. Our war was over, and nobody cared.

That very hour, the men began grumbling worse than I'd ever heard. Some were boldly making plans to desert and run for the gold fields. By mess call that evening, Captain Bloxham assembled the ragtag ranks of us in front of the barracks and began huffing out a speech.

Ah, it was proud Army talk, and I felt sorry for the poor old man, trying to whip these bindlestiffs into being soldiers again. The noble sacrifice of Custer and his Seventh made it imperative, the Captain said, for us to perform our duties with diligence and bravery. We must become avengers of a great tragedy. Regular patrols would now be sent out. Warpath Indians were known to be streaming down from the northern battlefields. Even as he stood up on a cartridge box and talked, I could see hazy trails of smoke in the sky, and smell it too. The hostiles were setting the whole country afire, burning away the forage our horses would need to live on. The Captain warned that we'd be sternly punished for dereliction of duty, but by then, the shiftless troopers were slouching against their dirty Springfields and grumbling close to mutinous.

"Duty!" grunts a shave-headed ex-deserter beside me. "Ain't that old fart the one to talk. If he hadn't run off at Crazy Woman Fork, we wouldn't be stuck out in this hole."

"You wasn't there, mister," I grunts. "If you was, you'da probably skedaddled first, from the miserable look of you."

He tries to whirl me and cock a punch, but I lifted my crutch and jabbed him away. By then, the old sergeant was shouting: "Order in the ranks! Captain is speaking!"

Well, nothing come of it. The troops grumbled off to kill more useless time. We were all rotting out. That night, for lack of anything better, I drifted over to the hospital room and peered in the window. Steward Rawley was mopping the board floor with some kind of disinfectant, and Mrs. Bloxham, in a long riding coat, was standing, hands on her hips, giving him orders.

After she'd gone, I eased inside and asked Rawley if I could help him. Didn't have anything else to do. He gave a little snort. "Don't con me, soldier. You're hanging around to get a sniff of her."

"Not true," I says, lying in my teeth. He handed me the mop and told me to wring it, which I did. Then he slapped it back in the pail.

"I'm going to tell you something for your own good, You're done, you're healed. We've got other men to treat. Stack your crutches in the corner. I signed your ticket this afternoon, putting you back on light duty."

"Well ain't that a shame," I says, and grins. "I was getting to like it here."

His face hardened. "Don't."

"Meanin'?"

"You ain't the first, Kelly, and you won't be the last. I got eyes. I see how you look at her. Yes, you've been hurt and you've been through hell, living with savages. But you're back in the Army now, and if you're too ignorant to notice, I'll do it for you. An enlisted man does not so much as look at an officer's wife. You do not touch her leg when you help her into a sidesaddle. Your eyes are on the ground, on the dirt, because that's what you are." He turned on his heel and walked away.

I followed him outside into the darkness. It was a hot dry night in September, rumblings of thunder on the horizon, and occasional lightning flashing over the log huts and mud hovels of the camp. "If you're warning me about something, Rawley, you'd best spit it out."

He'd walked over to the camp well, pumped the arm once or twice and water spilled into the tin cup. He swilled it and splashed the rest onto the rocks. Then he took a bent, half-smoked cigar from the pocket of his white steward's coat, lit it and blew smoke at the stars.

"I'm not blaming Mrs. Bloxham," he said quietly, "or judging her either. She's a kind you've never known, greenhorn. A lady, born to it. Leah Leatherton of Leatherton, Mississippi. They owned it all. I rode into what was left of the parlor of that big house the night after our division burned it to the ground. It'd make you cry. We robbed them, looted everything they had. Made them walk north, and whipped them even more in the damn Reconstruction, letting nagurs order 'em around. Maybe they had it coming, I don't know, but here was this fine lady, raised by a dozen slaves, ended up washing clothes in Memphis. Give her credit. Some of her kind were getting by in whorehouses. Captain Bloxham, he was lieutenant then in military garrison. She found him and hooked onto him as a ticket out. Eventually they had a child, a boy, Andrew Jackson Bloxham. I used to play with that kid when we were all serving under Crook at Camp Grant, Arizona. The boy was maybe five years old, when one afternoon, summer thunderstorm, lightning struck him dead. Up until then, Mrs. Bloxham was popular enough with the other officers' wives, though her beauty was against her. They resented that. She played the Army game and did her best to advance her husband's career, the way they all do. But when that kid was struck down, she broke apart, went wild with grief, and her true colors began to show. She turned whore."

"I don't believe that," I says, flaring.

"Ask any man who's been around her, soldier. Look at Bloxham, what's he but a dull plodder? D'you think he could fill her breeches? Ah, no. I'm not saying he's a coward, but he had a pretty ordinary record in the Rebellion, and in the regulars, the heroes with the medals get the promotions. Mrs. Bloxham knew that well enough, so they say she whored with somebody to get him captain's bars. No, it wasn't Crook, he don't play that way. But she started using her looks to go after the power. Live on these dry, forlorn posts all these years, ah no, that hussy wants dinner parties and drawing rooms with fine laces. She wants Washington. Her Cupid could get her there. Cupe, they call him, for good reason."

"Cupe?"

Rawley whirled. "You served with him, didn't you? Major Scipio Shaw. That's the hot sword she went after, stinking bastard. I've personally seen him cause one divorce and one suicide, playing with other officers' wives. You think it's all peaches and cream in there, soldier?" He jerked the tin water cup toward the yellow smear of lamplight in the Bloxham hut. "Put men and women together out here on these lonely plains and you've got big trouble. If I was running this Army, I'd keep every damn pair of bloomers back east of the border."

"She and Major Shaw?" I echoes, and couldn't believe it.

"Just get back to your duties and forget that tart, soldier. She'll grind you under her heel, I guarantee you, if you get in her way." He walked off in the darkness, and I stood there, face flushed and half-sick in my belly. I hated him for telling me all that, staining her, robbing me of my gentle dream. Even more did I hate the damn Army game, where jealousy and clawing for promotion was more important than winning a war.

I wished none of it had ever touched me. And yet still, I couldn't get her out of my mind.

I drifted across the dark cantonment, past the horses stomping on their picket lines. A few sentries were out, shuffling their posts, and I took care that they didn't see me. I edged against the log wall of the captain's hut, and peered inside. The devil was in me, snooping like this.

Captain Bloxham, in his underwear top and big belly, was slumped in a rocker, his eyeglasses hooked over one ear, and a map spread across his knees. He was asleep, twitching once or twice and shifting his weight.

Beyond him in the shadows, a white shape moved across the lamplight. Leah, in a bluish cotton nightgown, the light flowing into the shadow between her legs. She was looking down at him, then gently unhooked his gold-rimmed glasses from one ear and lay them on a table beside him. She moved to the bed, a double-issue cot, with the covers rumpled, and when she sat down on it and stooped to the floor, I could see into the swelling front of her nightgown. She began to crank a small music box, and the song that came out I'd heard at Fetterman. A war song, "After the Ball Is Over." One night, I'd seen the officers and their wives waltzing to it. But now, the way she played it, the tinks came slow and sorrowful.

When I looked at her again, she'd gotten up from the bed and gone to the far window of the hut. That was the dark side, facing the prairie. She stood with her arms clamped across her breasts like she had a chill. Then she tilted her head against the cold pane and stared out into the night.

Ah, God help me, I wanted to run around that cabin and look into her eyes. But I heard a footstep and whirled.

"Troop quarters are on the other side of the parade," grunts a sentry. "Are you lost, soldier?"

"No," I whispers, "I ain't lost."

But still, I was puzzled at the way I was watching her like a common Peeping Tom. Why? Was it pure loneliness that made me hound dog around, trying to find excuses to look at her? Hell, the woman was years older than me, and when the sun hit her powdery face wrong, she sure showed her years on the dry, harsh plains. At least with Walks Outside, the Injun gal was young and had all of life ahead of her. Forget Walks Outside, I says to myself, and this Leah, too. Females of any stripe and Army don't mix. Someday, if I ever got out of this hole, if my manhood got screaming at me too bad, I'd do what the other troopers done. Plug it into some blowsy harridan at a hog ranch. There was whorehouses crusted up beside every major fort, and before long, I was bound to get back to one of 'em.

The very next afternoon, assigned to light duty, I was shoeing a horse down at the adobe stables when a shadow crossed between me and the sun. It was Captain Bloxham, wearing a white pith helmet, his uniform blouse unbuttoned. I stood up and tried to salute, but he patted me on the shoulder.

"At ease, young man. I'd heard you were back to duty, and that's a good sign. Do you have any limp from the cursed thing?"

"Ah, it ouches me once in a while, sir, but a long way from the heart, it is."

"That's the spirit, Kelly. We need it. Now that you're on your feet, you and I have business to do. Come by my quarters when you're done here. Mrs. Bloxham serves dinner at six. I imagine you could use a change from meat and beans."

"That I can, sir."

"She's a fine cook, I can vouch for her."

Then shy, almost embarrassed, he turned and hulked back across the parade ground. In the long, dusty sunset, I stared after him, puzzled at what might be coming now. Enlisted never dined with officers, and never expected it either, unless it was something far out of the ordinary.

I got shined up as much as I could, and when I knocked on the door of the hut, it wasn't the captain but Mrs. Bloxham who let me in. There was a fire going in the hearth and the hut smelled of fresh baked bread. Her blonde hair was wet in little ringlets from standing over the stove. "Oh, do come in, Private. Forgive me, I'm never on time for anything, and the captain is still out back in the bathtub." She took my cap from me and hung it on a wall peg. Our hands happened to touch doing it, and I stood there kind of awkward like I'd never been in a decent house before. "That wretched stove is out again." she said. "Would you mind putting some more wood in?"

I grabbed hold of the stove door, looking at her instead of it, and burned hell out of my finger. "Oh, I'm so sorry," she said, and handed me a rag. When she did that, she brushed the stove by mistake and got a smear of soot on her face.

"You...you dirtied yourself, ma'am." I pointed at her cheek.

"So I did." She laughed and dabbed it with her handkerchief. After I'd got the stove loaded, she swished ahead of me and showed me to a folding camp chair. "I wish there was more, but it's so hard to make these dreary cabins homelike."

"You sure done nice with it, though." I glanced at the log table, set with tin issue cups and plates. She had a bottle of wine out, and had picked some prairie flowers that she'd put in a canteen in the

94

center. She wore a long dress that had lace flowers on the breast, and puffy sleeves. Under it were elegant ladies riding boots, scuffed with prairie dust.

"Do you ride horses, ma'am?"

She smiled. "Oh, wouldn't I love to. I grew up riding. My father ran blooded horses. But it's dangerous now. The Captain doesn't permit anyone to stray far from the post."

"Well," I says, "this morning after stable call, I went out on the bluffs to the east, exercising ponies off the picket line. It's a piney little ridge up there, and safe enough, I believe. You can see a long way. Nobody could sneak up on you."

I just blurted it out innocent enough, because it was what I was thinking at the time: a good place for me to get away from the humdrum of the Army.

Her face lit up, but her voice was quiet. "Some day, if you'd want some company..."

Holy God, her hand had just brushed mine, and fireballs went off in my eyes. I couldn't help but wonder: Was this all by accident? People didn't rub up against each other and pretend they hadn't. Ah, I supposed, maybe it was just her Southern habits. Them kind of folks touched and kissed much more than the stiff-backed Yankees. I couldn't believe that a lady so far above me could think of me as anything but dirt. Unless she had some reason for treating me otherwise, and I sure didn't know what it might be.

By then, though, Captain Bloxham had plodded in, buttoning his tweed coat. It was an old riding coat, like a gentleman would wear, except it had leather patches sewed on the elbows. The only Army he showed was his dusty gold-striped pants. "Oh Clete, this is good news," she said. "Private Kelly has offered to take me riding someday, in a safe place."

"I doubt if there is one, my dear. We had a picket fired on this afternoon, about a mile south. However, if you insist, this young man might be responsible enough. I daresay he's seen the elephant, what with living with these savages." Then he pats me on the shoulder and says, "Sit down, Kelly. We have a lot of talking to do."

Night comes fast out on the prairie, and soon it was just the two candles spluttering on the table and the glow of the stove embers. Mrs. Bloxham had cooked venison somebody had shot, canned spinach with fresh mushrooms in it, and she'd baked biscuits, served with wild honey. I helped myself again and again, and mopped up the venison gravy with biscuits. Her eyes were soft in the candlelight, and more than once, I saw her smiling at me, the way a mother might while her son was contenting himself at her hearth.

Between mouthfuls, the Bloxhams had me telling them tales about my wandering out with the Sioux. I mentioned a few things that had happened, and Mrs. Bloxham said, "How fascinating it must have been. You're blessed, you know, to be alive and here."

"I do know, ma'am, and thank my lucky stars for it."

She looked at me intently. "Is it true that you actually befriended Crazy Horse?"

"Well, ma'am," I chuckles, "with his kind you never make friends. They don't let you inside their heads. On the other hand, there was a few who spoke American. Jack Red Cloud, the chief's lad, and a girl, too. 'Fact, one you'd remember."

"Oh?"

When I tells her about running onto Walks Outside, she cried, "Why, that one, that rude thing. I'm surprised she didn't cut your throat, after the way she behaved when I tried to hire her."

"No, ma'am. She made life pretty good for me."

She frowned. "But the girl had been with whites. Why in the world would she run off to the hills and risk getting shot? Or is she just as stubborn and impossible as the rest of them?"

"Savage is all." I shook my head and glanced at Captain Bloxham. "When they got word, sir, that we'd been licked there on St. Pat's day, whole bands of 'em rode north and threw in with the hostiles. Maybe that's why we got our backsides kicked so bad at Rosebud. Too many numbers against us."

"Well, you've come through," Captain Bloxham muttered, "and not the first time, don't forget. All of us could have been wiped out at Crazy Woman Fork, and precious little thanks we got for it."

She glanced at him sharply. "Oh, Clete, do we have to get into this?"

"We are and we will." Captain Bloxham's big hand trembled. He poured wine into his tin cup, and splashed me a draught. "Face the facts, young man, which Mrs. Bloxham seems unable to. The Powder river fight was a disaster, not only for the command, but for me personally. Surely you've heard it, they must be talking about it out in the troops, Kelly."

"Well, I've heard there's going to be a courts martial, but it's way above my head, sir."

"I am accused of gross cowardice in face of the enemy for sounding recall," the Captain said heavily. "Colonel Reynolds is so harried and confused he says something different in every testimony. He does not clearly remember giving the recall order."

"Well, sir, I heard him…"

Captain Bloxham's eyes gleamed, and his fat cheeks thickened when he smiled. "Bully for you, young man! You heard him give me the order!"

"I did indeed."

"But," Bloxham crows and grips my forearm, "did you also hear

Major Shaw countermand the order and give his own order to charge the bluffs?"

"Well, sir, just about then, so much was happening and I got hit…"

"Think, man! Remember!"

Mrs. Bloxham gave a little cry and pushed back from the table. "You're not in court, husband! Leave him be. Please, we don't need this now."

"I'm speaking, my dear."

"No! I'm asking you a favor! Drop it!"

Her hands lay like wounded little birds on the table. Slowly, he reached out his thick hand and his fingers crushed hers. "Long ago, my dear," he said quietly, "you would have insisted that I carry this affair to its just conclusion. It is a matter of honor, which you fail to see, and I will not permit you to sweep it under the rug." He swung to me. "Answer me, Private Kelly. Did or did not Major Shaw countermand the recall order?"

By then, looking from his face to hers, and trapped between them, slowly it did begin to come back. I rubbed at my eyes and could still feel the dished-in scar in my temple. "Major Shaw asked me," I said, taking a deep breath, "was I supposed to sound recall? Yes, I says, and he says, by whose order? I says, My captain. Then Shaw, the major, stands in his stirrups. Carry it out, he tells me, or something like that. And the next minute, he turns to the other troopers who were fighting mad, and tells them to charge the bluffs. We'd hold the bluffs all day, if need be, until Crook joined us."

"There you are!" Captain Bloxham banged the table. I jumped, and Mrs. Bloxham just covered her face and whispered, "Don't."

"Yes, damn you!" Bloxham cried. "Cupe Shaw made sure that I'd be tagged the coward, blowing the retreat. And him the hero for taking back the bluffs. For winning the day, God curse his soul!"

Leah got up unsteadily, her blue eyes fierce. "You have what you want," she whispered. Then she nodded toward me. "I apologize for our rudeness, Private. If you'll excuse me, I prefer the night air to the smell of dead coals." Her shoulders stiffened, and she crossed out of the candlelight. I heard the door creak open, and she was gone.

Captain Bloxham was sitting with his face in his hands. "Ah, how hard it gets, this constant backbiting of our brother officers. One doesn't know where he stands anymore. Yet we took the oath of duty. Mrs. Bloxham has no idea what that means, particularly since war has hurt her so much. But mark this, we are not permitted the luxury of the easy way, of quitting with dishonor. I'd rather fall on my sword than surrender in such shame." I didn't know what he was mumbling about, maybe the scars of old wars, or from her. But there was nothing I could say. He rubbed his eyes clean of whatever it was, took a last swig of wine, and cleared his throat. "Very well, young man. You will testify in my behalf, just what you recounted. Is that too much of a favor to ask?"

"Well, sir, you done me favors, too. What I said was true, as I remember. But I've got to admit I ain't liking being mixed up in the middle here, all this damn Armying..."

"Armying." Bloxham chuckled. "That's a good word for it. Arms and legs windmilling. Don Quixote. The point, young man—for reasons you don't know and I refuse to reveal—Major Shaw intends to step on my face to get his star. Why else am I here, exiled to this dog-hole post, for the stain of cowardice that he is squarely putting on me? If he were to have his way, with his connections, Sheridan and the rest, they'll junk me off to retirement after the court martial is done. And him, meanwhile, the hero of the Crazy Woman Fork who tried to stand and fight. Why, do you realize, Shaw should be limboed like me under investigation, but I've just heard that Crook has given him his battalion back. After the Rosebud defeat and then poor Custer, Crook is now making a major campaign down through Dakota, with Shaw prancing at the head of his own troops. Imagine! Another fight on his record, another glory. While my men eat ground squirrels and dig trenches, waiting for an attack that will never come. Exile, Kelly. Your words, the truth in your heart, can spare me from it. Will you do that much for an old man?"

"Of course." Then I felt a draft across my legs. I hadn't heard the hut door open, but when I looked, Mrs. Bloxham was standing in it, framed against the stars. "Well," I stammered, feeling uneasy caught between them, "I'd best be going now. I thank you for your kindness."

"The thanks are mine," Captain Bloxham said, gripping my hand. "You're an honest man, Kelly. I won't forget that."

As I lifted my cap off the peg, Mrs. Bloxham opened the door for me. Maybe I just imagined it, but I think her hand trailed from the latch back to mine. "We'll still take our ride, Private," she whispered.

I said, "Glad to oblige, ma'am. Anything I can do." That green I was, not realizing that I'd already been done. My goose was all but cooked.

———

A few days later, the mail wagon come rattling in from someplace. The troopers were crowding around the tailgate where a corporal was flicking letters at 'em or tossing packages, many of which were beat up from the long, hard trip. I wasn't expecting nothing, nobody knowing my whereabouts, indeed I didn't have nobody except on the Other Side. But, for lack of something better, I hung around the tailgate, watching the soldiers' mooning over the words of their loved ones.

Then the corporal stands up. "That's all they is, boyos, hope for more on the next trip. While you're at it," he glances into the mail sack, "got two here for a Missus Bloxham. Anybody know her?"

"Captain's wife," I says. "That hut yonder, over by the flagpole."

"You connected to the Cap?"

"His striker. But he ain't around. He's out with troops."

He hands me a package and a letter. "Sign here in the book, laddie. I'm running late and got to hit the Emigrant road before dark."

As I started across the dusty parade ground toward the Bloxham cabin, I glanced at the mail he'd handed me. The package was flimsy pasteboard, maybe a foot square, with a smudgy postmark on it from Camp Grant, Arizona Territory. The letter, though, had only a bold scrawl "By courier: Mrs. Cletus Bloxham, Cantonment Connor, W.T." The envelope was crinkled and stained with mud like the Pony Express had run it through.

When I come up to the Captain's hut, I knocks and hollers for Mrs. Bloxham. No answer until, from out back, I hear the tapping of a hammer and a woman's voice cries, "Damnation!" Going around the cabin, I sees Mrs. Bloxham, her hair mussy and a faded Army bathrobe on her. She sucked her forefinger, then jerked it from her lips and shook it in pain. Her eyes snapped to me. "Didn't the Captain ask you to do this, put up our wash line?"

She kicked at a rope that was dangling from the cabin. Clothes pins were scattered in the sagebrush. She'd been trying to pound a nail into the hard logs. I picks up the hammer from where she'd flung it, and sets it into a basket of laundry she was going to hang. "I'll get you strung up, ma'am. Sorry you had to hurt yourself."

"So am I, soldier! I don't do carpentry for a living." She squinted at me. "What is that you have?"

"Mail just come in. Maybe lift your spirits, I'm thinkin'." When I hands her the letter and the package, she snatches them, reads where they're from and cries, "Oh, I can't believe this! You don't realize…"

Her fingers tore open the letter. As dusty and bedraggled as she looked, she might have been a cranky washerwoman, but a moment later, her blue eyes were sparkling, her teeth flashing. It was almost as if she didn't know I was there. "Such good news," she cried. "Forgive me, private, but this is from the expedition. Written only four days ago. A miracle it even came through to me. They're still in Dakota."

"Ma'am?"

"General Crook's expedition," she flared. "I thought everyone knew. They've hit a Sioux trail, Major Shaw says, possibly even Crazy Horse, and they should catch up to him any day. But, oh my God," she glanced at the letter, "torrential rains, mud so bad the horses have no footing. Awful suffering of the men. Well, anyway, it's so good to hear word." She studied the letter again as if not wanting to

99

let it go, and then, with a faint smile, slid it into the basket beneath the dirty laundry.

"Now this one," she said, and laughed, tearing her fingernails at the wrapping of the package, "who in the world in Arizona? Here, can you read that name?" She showed me the corner of the package, ink on it all right, but it had been rained on and smudged out.

"Can't tell, ma'am."

"Well then, maybe it says who inside. If you'd open it for me, they've made it so tight."

I pulls out my clasp knife and slit the top of the box where it had been squashed down. When I hands it back to her, she pulls out a small object wrapped in old newspapers and tissue beneath. A card was pinned to it. She stared at it, ripped away the tissue. Her hand flashed to her lips and she groaned. "Oh, my God. Andy's."

She sank down in the dust, clutching the thing to her breast. It was a furry little monkey dangling between two sticks, his paws on a wire. Back in Chicago, I'd seen kids running that exact same toy. If you pushed the sticks together, monkey'd jerk up in a somersault and flip down on the other side.

She kept clicking the sticks together but he didn't budge. Her eyes lifted to me and she sobbed. "They broke it! Damn them, they broke Andy's—it was his favorite, he had it that last day!" She covered her face with her hands, and her thin shoulders shook.

Watching her so broken, one part of me longed to reach out and comfort her, but the other part hissed, Git back in your place, common soldier. Skedaddle, let her burn off her own sorrows.

At that moment, up comes a clopping of hooves, a slide of dust, Captain Bloxham reining in his horse. "Leah!" he cries, glowering from her to me, "what the devil is wrong? What's happened here?"

Sniffling, she glances at him and holds up the monkey, her hands clicking his sticks, but the little thing wasn't jumping.

Bloxham's face reddened, his jaw gritted tight. Swinging off his horse, he knelt beside her and held her in his arms. "Oh, my dear, dear Leah. Why this, why?"

"I want it, Clete! It's mine!" She dabbed at her face with a handkerchief. "The quartermaster down there at Grant, our friend, Major Valentine? He was having the barracks cleaned, they came across some of our old things. Thoughtful to send it."

"Thoughtful!" Bloxham echoed. "Man ought to be shot, opening this grave again." He swung to me. "You're not needed here, trooper. Personal matter."

"He came with our mail, Clete," Mrs. Bloxham said, and pushed up, "though I surely could have used him earlier to fix this damn wash line."

Bloxham glowered. "Kelly, I tried to find you after reveille. I want it done. Hop to!"

"Yessir."

He put his arm around her to lead her back inside, but she stopped. "Please, soldier, if you're good at fixing, could you do this for me?" She started to hand me the monkey.

"Don't, Leah! Forget the damn thing!" Bloxham fumbled to take it from her, but she jerked it away.

"I'm not going to leave it broken, Clete. It's mine, damn you!"

Wearily, Bloxham turned to me. "It belonged to our son who was killed at Grant. Why it ever came back...?"

Trembling, she handed the monkey to me. "If you can make it work just like it used to when Andy had it, I'll hang it over the hearth."

"I'll give her a try, ma'am. Maybe a new wire."

"And the one on the clothes line first," Bloxham snapped. "Now please, dear, get hold of yourself. I'll fix you a spot of tea, wouldn't that help?" With his big arm around her shoulders, he patted her and took her away.

I hammered up the line in short order, but when I come to the basket of clothes, I just let it lie, with the letter from Scipio Shaw still winking out at me.

⟶≫◆≪⟵

After the roaming hostiles started sniping our pickets, the captain sent us out riding patrol for the next few days. I barely had time to fix the damn little toy. When I finally put on new sticks and got him jumping, after reveille one morning I drops it by her cabin. There were no sounds within. Maybe she'd gone off someplace, or was still sleeping, so I just slid it inside the door.

Late that same afternoon, the troop corporal thought he'd seen some stray government horses running loose up on the piney ridge. We sure didn't want some red thieving 'em, so the corporal sends me to run 'em home.

The piney ridge was the kind of hangout Injuns love. Well-protected with its crags high above the prairies, they could see enemies coming from any direction. For centuries now, they must have been camping in this jumble of yellow slabs, some of them as big as boxcars with curlycue Injun signs of snakes and lizards pecked into the sandstone. The wind had howled the bluffs long enough to carve out holes where lions nested, the old bones they'd fed on scattered about like white leaves. From the bluff, I could look down on Camp Connor, about a mile west, the sun glinting on the hut windows, and dust rising from comings and goings of troops. To the north and east, the prairies rolled out to the end of the world, tawny as sand, and striped with little dark coulees, shadows promising water, but there never was any. It was a dry old piece of hell to me, having walked so many miles across this forlorn country.

As it turned out, there were no Army horses running loose on the ridge. Could be some wily red had already run 'em off, or more likely they were just ghosts in the corporal's mind. Like all of us, he was a mite crazy, looking for ways to eat up our deadly time.

But the bluff was so pretty in the sunset, and quiet, too, I decided to kick back here until mess call. The best way to get out of Army work is not being there in the first place. I got off my horse and tied him in the blowdown timber among the rocks. I began picking up dry pine cones, for they lighted fires quick in our camp stoves, and it was getting cold, these September nights. The sky went streaky orange, and the sun died behind a black mountain of clouds. Wind was coming up now, whipping the prairie, stinging dust into my eyes. Then far off, lightning crackled and dark rain began pelting down in great rumbles of thunder. My guvmint horse, number 306, a thin bay, begins shaking himself and rattling the saddle. I says, "A few more minutes, lad, you're going to get yourself a bath."

Then he gives a little tug on his halter and tries to whirl, his eyes showing white and fear. A voice says, "You didn't wait for me. You made a lady ride alone."

Mrs. Bloxham! I was fumbling up, dropping my pine cones. "God help us, ma'am, you give me a fright."

"My, how spectacular this is. You have good taste, Private." Her voice was laughing, soft and Southern now. She picked up her long gray skirt, dainty-like, and stepped over the blowdowns, coming to me.

"How did you know where I was, ma'am?"

She smiled. "In a camp this small, doesn't everybody know everything?"

"I suppose. Sometimes that ain't too good either." I was thinking of Rawley when I said that, and as if she'd read my thoughts, she shrugged.

"Oh, come now, in the Army you can never believe all you hear. I swear, you soldiers gossip worse than our darkies used to in the kitchen."

Watching me, with her soft eyes steady, she untied her blue silk throat scarf, let it drift to the ground, and slowly undid the buttons of her gray jacket. "That's better," she said, and sat down on an old dead log. "What a lovely place this would be for a picnic. I swear, I should have brought sandwiches. But then again, the Captain would worry." She sighed and looked at me. Pulling off her gloves, finger by finger, she said, "Anyhow, I came mainly to thank you in person for fixing Andy's little toy. I'm sure you're puzzled, why it would mean so much to me. After all, the child is dead. Long dead."

"Well, ma'am," I says, my eyes on the ground, "the heart don't die so quick, I suppose."

"Yes. Yes, that's a good way of putting it. Have you ever lost a child?"

"No, ma'am. Ain't never had one, least that I know about. Not figuring on it neither, I guess you might say."

Her eyes smouldered. "Well if you do, and if you lose him, you never really recover from it. You carry that little face day and night. Why did I ever let him go out? Why was there lightning so close to our quarters? And yet," she sighed, "there was always lightning in the rainy time in Arizona. We were going to a ball that night, so I was fixing my dress. My Indian girl couldn't sew worth a damn. I wasn't watching the child, didn't even realize it was raining. He just strolled away, over there by the cottonwoods and the irrigation ditch." Her hand lifted out beyond the rocks as if she was seeing it all right here.

"Ma'am," I says, "maybe it ain't my place to say this, but what I seen of life, and the Maker snatching one away and letting the other run free, I don't understand who makes the choice, and I don't have the wits neither, ever to hope to."

In the fading light, her face seemed to harden, and she looked older for just that moment. "You can't always stay out of things, though, just let them slide and hope for the best. You do have to make choices, soldier. You can't just let life rush over you like a giant wave, hurl you along like a stick. I've been there." Her voice caught and she turned her face away from me. Her riding boots slid back and forth, making little cuts in the sand. The wind made a shivery sound and pelted the first drops of rain.

"I ain't quite followin' you, ma'am."

She whirled. "Of course you wouldn't. Silly that I'd expect you to. You're an immigrant, aren't you?"

"Indeed," I chuckles. "Ain't the brogue enough!"

"Well, I am not an immigrant." She sat erect and smoothed the gray skirt over her knees. "When I was a little girl, my great-grandmother still lived on the plantation, and I clearly remember her telling how General Washington rode her on his knee. We had silver from Lafayette! Oh, I'm talking gibberish. What does it mean to you! Choices, I said. We lost everything down to the last serving spoon! Robbed by coarse men, those goddamn foul-mouthed Union troops. Do you know something, when they burned us to the ground and ran us away without even a mule to pack us, I never looked back. Just saw the flames in the sky and ran into the woods. We had 20,000 acres of woodlands alone, not counting cotton land. But all of it dead. Theirs! I said, by God, I would find my future in some new land, on my own." Her eyes flashed. "And I did!"

"Yes, ma'am," I murmurs. "Steward Rawley has told me a little of it..."

Her eyes tightened. "Soldiers' lies!"

She had me flustering now. "I ain't saying that, ma'am. Just that you is something special, particularly out here."

"Oh yes, here." She laughed bitterly. "Do you have any idea of how many posts we've served on? How much packing and unpacking I've done, never having a roof I can call my own, never holding onto anything because it won't fit in their damn ambulance-regulated loads. And you wonder why I could weep, trying to hold onto my son's last toy?"

"I said I understood, ma'am."

"Yes, I appreciate that." Her voice changed and she looked at me with a slow smile. "Here I'm trying to thank you and all you get back is an old lady's dreams."

"I wouldn't say old, hardly."

She laughed. "Like the old darky used to say about the whiskey my mother let him steal, 'If it was any worse, ole Miss, I couldn't have drunk it, and any better you wouldn't have give it to me.' What I mean is, yes, I do dream about a settled life, after all these years. Major Shaw, for example, having served General Sherman so loyally, is just on the verge of getting a post in Washington. I know that, feel it in my bones. But what's it to you?"

"I don't know, ma'am," I says, still standing above her, and not having the least notion what she was wanting out of me. Just an ear, I suppose, lonely as all of us. But then, sharply, she stood up and gripped my hands.

"So this is Private Kelly," she said lightly. "Do you Irish have first names?"

"Patrick, ma'am."

"Oh, how nice. My father had a horse named that. How old are you, Patrick?"

Her eyes were watching me so intent and hot that I flustered, lapsing into Other Side brogue. "Just now twenty I be."

She threw back her head and laughed. "Not be, soldier! Am! Oh, you precious Irish. They ought to put you all in troopers' school until you learn the King's English."

It stung, having her mock me. "Not for one of them bastard sons, I will not. I got no allegiance to a King."

"What about to me, though?"

I frowned. "You what, ma'am?"

"Don't be dense, damn you! I'm your commanding officer's wife."

"That I know, and I'm having trouble with it, too. You oughtn't to be here."

"But I am here. You invited me, remember?"

"I—I wasn't thinking, not like this anyhow..."

"Well, I'm thinking and have done little else. I'm tired of inventing

104

jobs for you so my husband will bring you by the cabin. Do you have any idea how alone I am there!"

"We're all alone, ma'am."

"Not like me. And stop calling me ma'am!" I couldn't believe it was happening, God forgive me I didn't want it to, but couldn't help myself. She had too much lust in her, too much control over me. "Oh you dumb stud, you magnificent rock!" Her hands were on my shoulders, her fingers digging in, gripping me hard. I towered above her, and her perfume was in my nose and eyes, with the scent of roses. "Ah, God, don't wait!" Her voice went hoarse. She was burying herself against me, my face in her hair and her breasts pressing my heart. "Now, Patrick, now!"

"But, ma'am...?" I was exploding in my jeans, burning all over. But then she had my hands, pulling off the lacy flowers of her blouse, her nipples red in the thunder sky, and the rain lashing down heavy. She kept gripping my hands, guiding them over her thin hips, slicking off her skirt. I was crying, "We're gonna get soaked," and she screamed, "Let it come, you bastard, let it!"

With dry crackling leaves going wet under us, we rolled and clawed our way into a cave of sandstone, just a ledge, covering us from the storm. She was riding me, like a mare whimpering in heat, and then I her, and all that there was to life was pumping away in lightning.

When it was done, we huddled together, naked under the ledge, the rain pissing down and making brown pools in the dead Indian ground. I couldn't believe it was me, smelling her sweetness, stroking her forbidden flesh. "Suppose," I says, grinning, "somebody had come up and caught us?" And she says, "They would have seen beauty, Patrick." She was running her fingers over my face, twirling little knots in my chest hairs, and my blacksmith arms, that's what she called them, digging her fingers into them. Playing games, laughing at me, until she got me started again, and we never could get enough.

When the storm let up, just about dark, I helped her dry off and dress. "Now you'll go back," she whispers, "and I'll go back, and every time your eyes see mine, you'll know I'm blessing you for this. Do you forgive me?"

"Forgive, ma'am? God in heaven!"

"Leah," she says, and touches my lips.

"Leah."

I boosted her up on my horse, and led her out of the blowdown. She sat a horse erect and proud, the wind whipping her blonde hair, and the light rain blown away. "It ain't a good idea to go into camp together," I says, "but I'll get you to the creek anyhow. A lady hadn't ought to be riding out here alone."

"Some lady, my boy." She smiled down at me, and kept running her fingers through my hair.

When I got her to the creek and took her off the horse, she clung to me again, and I stroked her wet hair and kissed her. God Almighty, I had never been with a woman like her, never been in love, and if this was it, I wasn't worrying about rules, just doing what was bursting from my heart.

"Oh my dear Patrick," she whispers. "There's so much to tell you, and so little time. Please God, there will be time one day. But for now, all these rumors and fights, this vile Yankee army. Trust me, dearest boy. Don't listen to my husband. Stay out of this dreadful mess..."

"Well," I says, and plucks the gold button on my blouse, "with this suit on, I'm pretty far into it, seems like."

"Not about Major Shaw! He's not your concern. Please, Patrick. He's a good man, perhaps too rash and too bold. But if you do what my husband wants you to do, you'll wreck Major Shaw's career. Don't put that on your conscience, I beg you."

"I'm wishing I wasn't mixed up in any of this. But if they ask me to set it down in front of God and that Army court, I have to tell them the truth. What I saw."

"Too much truth can be cruel."

"Then you're asking me to lie for you?"

She cried harshly. "Come on, soldier. You're already lying. An enlisted man with an officer's wife. Think about what that's worth, what it might mean to you." She smiled in the dark, her teeth glowing faintly. Then she put her hand on my private parts and held them. With a giggle, she turned, snatched up her skirt, and went up the bank toward camp.

I sighed there like a stuck pig, and finally plodded my horse toward home. Somewhere in the dark plain, I heard the hammer click on a sentry's gun. "Password," he barked.

"At ease, soldier," I heard her answer. "I am Captain Bloxham's wife."

"Yes, ma'am. Sorry, ma'am."

"No offense. You're only doing your duty." Then her voice trailed off, and the truth of it twisted at my heart.

Captain Bloxham's wife. Major Shaw's whore. And me, the next piece of dirt to be ground under her heel, on her way back to the man she really wanted.

Ah, God, she robbed my soul. I hated her and craved her so much, I was bewitched as a leprechaun, moping around the post, longing for a look at her, or to hear the sound of her voice.

Then, at stable call the first day of October, an Army ambulance came rattling in, followed by a file of troopers. Horses were lathered, everybody hot and shouting orders. An officer in a drooping black hat got out of the ambulance. He was a major, an adjutant.

A few minutes later, our sergeants mustered the scraggly troops in front of Captain Bloxham's hut. Holding his pith helmet under his arm, he moved down the line of us, talking in a disjointed sort of way. I was in the rear holding some horses, so I got only the gist of it. General Crook had fought a big action in Dakota Territory, against a hostile chief named American Horse. Not only killed him, but sent Crazy Horse and the rest of his devils packing. "This post," Captain Bloxham bellowed, "is now deemed superfluous to the protection of this region. Troops will begin closing it, emptying all barracks. Military stores will be carried by wagon back to Fetterman. Corporals, assemble your work details."

While he spoke, I saw Leah, standing in the door of his hut, a white shadow, finally turning and going back inside. I thought: She's looking for me, out in these dirty ranks of baggy bluecoats. Maybe indeed she was, for even as the camp was starting to be ripped apart, and team horses wrangled for the wagons, Steward Rawley found me and snapped, "Captain Bloxham's orders. Grease the wheels on the ambulance that just came in. Replace the team with fresh horses."

"Is somebody going someplace, Rawley?"

"You. If there's a lucky way out, Kelly, you always seem to find it. But don't count on a cakewalk this time. Major Adjutant is taking Captain Bloxham to Fetterman for court martial. You're served as a witness. That's why you'll get to drive the ambulance, for your little Rebel dove."

I whirled him. "I don't like the way you talk about her, or me either. Mind your tongue."

"Well, she is a wounded dove, soldier, because I've just given her barbiturates."

"She ain't sick, is she?"

"Man-sick, you bet. I warned you, Kelly. Stay clear of that one. The fight in Dakota where they killed American Horse? The adjutant just told her that her lover boy Cupid caught a ball through the jaw. Should have been his own balls blown off. Major Scipio Shaw, your lady's dandy, has left half his face lying in Dakota."

A couple of hours later, when I helped Leah into the ambulance, she was like a sleep walker, eyes red wet and a brown shawl wrapped tight around her cheeks. I heard the adjutant say to Captain Bloxham, "They're sending Major Shaw and the other casualties out by travois. Mean as Cupe is, he'll probably be the only one who makes it."

"If there's justice in this Army," Captain Bloxham answered, "Major Shaw will live to stand trial." Then he grunted at me to start the team. We had a long way to go.

The second morning out from Camp Connor, we were angling toward the Emigrant Road, and felt safe enough. The Road was the main north-south route along the Big Horns, and in the distance we'd seen wheel dust, probably miners, pilgrim wagons or Army troops moving somewhere. When we came to a little coulee with water in it and a few red-yellow willows, Captain Bloxham had me brake the team, and we all spilled out for coffee and bacon.

I was building a campfire of dead sticks, and Rawley opening the paniers to get at our vittles. Two recruits, Swede farm boys from Minnesota, were riding flank for us. Captain Bloxham signaled them to go over the far ridge, where they ought to be able to spot the Emigrant Road. Report back when they'd located it.

The adjutant major had his blouse off and was kneeling by the alkalai creek, washing his face. Leah, I imagined, was still asleep in the ambulance. Then I noticed a red-tailed hawk soaring in the sunlight above us. He was making a strange cry, I thought.

Hiss. Thuck! Rawley screams, "Hostiles!" Captain Bloxham was up on the back step of the ambulance, trying to get something out of the inside, and he toppled off.

The adjutant was down on both knees, groaning and tearing at a Sioux arrow in his belly. Rifles crashed, one slug pranging into the coffee pot, the other ball thudding off someplace. I was scrambling to get under the ambulance. I had a carbine, but it all happened so fast, I didn't know where to shoot.

Then I heard an awful howl and the rattling of hooves. Our two flankers were streaking back from the ridge, a cloud of dust pursuing them. Spotted ponies, five Indians, slicing into the Swede boys. An Army Springfield boomed, then a second, and a campaign hat flew into the air. Two riderless horses were milling, and a Sioux, his nakedness painted with green lightning streaks, was cutting the horses away from us, snatching at their bridles and finally catching them.

"Leah!" Captain Bloxham cried. "Stay down, don't let them see you!" A flash of her hair, and she was ducking back into the ambulance. Then Bloxham's revolver exploded close to my ear. Two screaming Sioux were racing by us, firing bows, the arrows ripping through the cloth sides of the ambulance. Captain Bloxham was prone and trying to shoot again, but his glasses had fallen off and lay glinting in the dust. He couldn't find a target.

I saw mine clear enough, though, a pattering of moccasins, a brown body leaping. I aimed at the flash of his long knife, pulled my carbine trigger, and when the foaming devil crashed into me, I'd blown a hole through his neck.

"Good man, Kelly!" Bloxham cried. "Keep firing!"

By now, maybe a dozen were coming at us from across the creek. When they saw the adjutant clawing at the arrow in his belly, a pair of them leaped off their horses, clubbed him down and started dancing around him with coup sticks.

Steward Rawley was walking slowly toward them. "Don't!" I shouted. "Take cover!" But on he went, his face dead set, long hospital coat dragging like a shroud. He had revolvers in both hands, their muzzles flashing as he fired methodically at the hostiles. One Sioux screamed, hit, and a pony buckled with blood spouting from his flank.

We were hollering at Rawley to come back, but he never wavered, just kept walking right into the midst of them. I was firing now to cover him, but it was too late.

The Sioux could have reached out and grabbed him, but they stood dumbstruck at his bravery. Finally, a rangy buck lifted a lance with feathers on it, shouted an oath and hurled it through Rawley's chest.

By then, I'd scrambled up onto the ambulance box, dragging the captain behind me and dumping him over the sill into the bed. "We'll fight from here," he cried. "Stand your ground!"

"Captain! You got her to think about! They've seen her now."

"Then keep firing, Kelly!" he screamed. "They can't take us!"

"They will, sir. Sitting ducks!" I knew by then that somebody had to run this thing, and it had better be me.

I lashed a crack at the team, thank God I hadn't unhooked them, the poor beasts neighing and pawing amidst the shooting. When my whip lick hit them, they leapt out like Irish hunters, rattling the ambulance away.

I wasn't seeing any Sioux, but from their blood-curdling howls, they were surely behind us, the ambulance knocking rocks, lurching so bad I thought she'd tip. But the creek bottom was level for maybe a hundred yards, and gave us the start we needed. When we banged up the bluff and went soaring out into the sagebrush, I heard a few booms of rifles and a spent ball cracked the side of the wagon.

"I'm going for the Emigrant Road, Captain," I shouted. "We're bound to run onto somebody, and the Sioux know that. They'll scare off."

He gripped my shoulder. "Bully for you, young man! We'll beat them yet!" Leah, crouching behind him, looked white as death, hanging onto the rocking sides of the bed with both hands. Then she let loose and picked up a Winchester lever action that was clattering back and forth on the floor. "I can shoot," she cried.

Bloxham thrust her back. "Stay down, my dear. If they haven't seen you yet, we might still make it!"

"Give me that, ma'am," I said, and took the Winchester from her.

As fast as we were going, the sun was in her eyes one moment, and shadows the next. She was swaying and seemed lost. "Ma'am?"

she whispered at me.

"Leah, then," I whispered back, as if it mattered any more. Dropping the reins, I stood up on the box and looked behind us at the streaks of dust. Four of them, still coming on strong. I picked out one, fired, and spilled his pony. Then the team swerved left, and the wheels smoothed. We'd hit the Emigrant Road. God Almighty, when we came up over a ridge, I could see trail north and trail south, it seemed like a thousand miles of it through those mournful hills. We flashed by an old cavalry guidon flag that some trooper had speared into a pile of rocks.

But on the road itself, nothing. Godawful lonely empty. Not a fresh track or dust cloud as far as the eye could see.

Captain Bloxham kept smacking his fist into his palm. "As many times as I've been on this road, all the patrols. Where are they, damn them?"

Leah cried from behind us: "Can't we go faster?"

I whirled for another peek and it wasn't pretty. Four Sioux in full gallop were eating up our dust line, as bold as jockeys in the home stretch at Epsom Downs. Captain Bloxham kept muttering that their ponies were too fast for us, out here on the flat. Couldn't I get more speed from our team?

Poor damn beasts—yes, I was driving four, but the two leaders, a roan and a bay, were about at bottom. "The wheelers are sound," I shouted to the Captain, "but that roan is starting to lame. We ain't got much time left."

I heard Captain Bloxham shoot twice, the Winchester cracking out of the back of the ambulance. Then he crawled up to me, face flushed red and breathing hard. We were sweeping down into a canyon with willows and some cottonwoods in the bottom. He grabbed me by the shoulder. "There! This coulee. I remember...!"

I didn't know what he meant, we were rattling so fast downhill, but he fumbled past me and grabbed hold of the right hand reins. "In here, Kelly! Go right, little road. Ranch, on the high ground. Camped there once!"

I wheeled the team right and we swerved, almost tipping over, heading into a rutted track that ran along the bottom and then up onto a big bronze hill. Ahead, against a sandstone cliff with a canyon cutting through, I could see a sagging frame house and a mud hut beside it. Maybe it had been a ranch once, the captain was right about that. But when I looked closer at the corral beside it, most of the poles were torn down. I even shouted toward the for-lorn place. The echo wailed away on the wind. Nothing came out. The slab door of the shack was torn off its hinges and creaking in the wind. The rest of the place was just burned-out frames, three chimneys, and one scraggly coyote, running off to hide.

"Damn them, they were here! Where are they?" the captain moaned.

In that instant, hoping like him for something that wasn't there, I'd taken my eyes off the team. I felt the lines jerk. The roan leader had grabbed the bit in some kind of panic, shying off from a bloated sheep carcass lying in the trail. Next thing I knew, the roan gave a squeal, his knees bucking the dirt. He thudded down on the trail, cartwheeling, and the bay next to him tripped and fell. Lines snapped like gunshots, the ambulance tongue spearing into the earth. I was flying off the box, Leah screaming, and the whole top of the ambulance rolling, wood cracking into splinters and ending backside up, wheels spinning in the sun.

I crawled over and gripped Leah. Her body was warm and soft, her eyes wild. She didn't know where she was, but the force of the spill had flung her clear. No wood had speared her. Captain Bloxham's face was cut and bleeding, his hat and specs gone. On all fours, he crawled back to us like a dog, then stopped, breathing hard and shaking his head down at the dirt. "Oh, God, my dear, my dear, what have I done to you? What is happening to us?"

"Clete, I'm all right. I'm not hurt, but you are." He kept moaning, and she took his head against her breast and hugged him.

"Please now, don't worry about me. I'm not afraid to die," she whispered. "It may even be better, you know."

"Better, hell," I growled. "Nobody's plannin' on dyin'. Come on, both of you. Catch hold. Sir, get up now." Hoping to move him, I scrambled to my feet and glanced at the wheel horses. They were still in their traces, but pawing and rearing something pitiful, the leaders down, the roan with a broken leg. I took a Missouri clasp knife from my blouse pocket, slashed the wheelers' lines and knotted them quick into riding reins. I dragged the horses over to the Captain and Leah. Bloxham was peering at me foggily. "Kelly, what are you doing, it's too late, man..."

"Not if we slick out of here, Captain. Horseback, three on two. Look there." I pointed toward the sandstone cliff behind the ranch. In it was the dark red slash of a canyon, leading up into the mountains. Far off, I could see smears of pine timber. "We got to get into that cover, and quick."

Captain Bloxham was standing, swaying, shading his eyes with his hand and trying to focus on the mountains. "Up there?"

"The only place, sir."

"No! Madness. We never could last. There is no one here..."

"Captain! Listen to me! If we get to the high ground, we've got a chance of holding, and after dark they'll leave us be, for they don't like to fight at night. I know how them heathens' minds work. They want a quick easy kill. Even if we have to fire our last rounds at 'em, somebody down on the Road might hear the echo of our guns."

"You don't understand," he said hoarsely, and began shaking his head. "I've heard all the guns, used up all the chances. I've been to the edge, I don't fear it. There's a time to die, young man. I have no shame for the way I've lived."

"For the love of Christ, sir! Listen to what I'm telling you. We can get out of here!"

He turned from me, and touched Leah's face. Her cheeks were wet from weeping, and his big fingers tracked over them and left streaks of dust. She grasped his hand and kissed it. Beyond her on the slope of sagebrush, I caught sight of a dark speck, like a slow moving elk that didn't belong. It was edging toward us from the Emigrant Road. Not much time now. Maybe the Sioux were puzzling what had happened to us, but it wouldn't be long before those sharp-eyed devils sorted it out.

I grabbed the Captain's arm. "Get horseback, sir. Put her up. It's got to be now!"

"Yes," he said, "I know. You're a good man. A loyal man." He looked at me, foggy-like, and then at her. He was standing, his thick legs wide apart, and she was on her knees, gripping one of them. "God help me, my child, my Leah," he murmured. "I did love you. I loved you more than duty itself. I wasn't enough…"

"Clete, Clete," she sobbed. "Stop it! We're still together…"

"Strength, my dear. Godspeed. I will always forgive you." Slowly, he turned from us and walked to the wagon, tipped over on its back. "Kelly," he said. "The rifle. The brass, too."

He was pointing at the Winchester, lying in the dirt. I picked it up and gave it to him, also a fistful of cartridges. "Captain, you ain't figuring…?"

He bellowed: "Of course I am, young man! Strong defensive position, a stout wagon. Do you think I've never been under fire before? Go! You'll have a lead on them!"

She clutched at him. "Clete! No!"

He flung her toward the horse, and then he knelt down beside the wagon and began laying the cartridges neatly in the dirt, as cool as if he was on a rifle range. She was screaming in the wailing wind, until finally I had to grab her by the shoulders and boost her onto the horse. "Captain, I'll hide her a ways up the canyon, then come back for you."

He either didn't hear me, or didn't want to. He was crouching against the ambulance, his eyes sweeping the bronze hill for the hostiles that would soon be rising from the rocks. "You heard my order, Kelly. Go, damn you!"

I looked at Leah and wanted to say, That's a brave man. But what was the use? She knew. She was nodding, tears spilling down her cheeks. I hit my horse a lick and jerked hers along with me. We went clattering up through the slash in the rocks, and I kept her going, without looking back, until we struck a dark hiding place high in the pine timber.

I got her situated by a little creek, where she had good visibility on all sides. Then I left her my carbine and the five cartridges I hadn't shot. I tilted her head up to me so that she had to look me in the eyes. "If I ain't back, and if they come for you, Leah, put yourself out of it. Promise me. Don't get taken."

Then I held her against me and she was shaking in a chill. I whipped off my U.S. blouse and wrapped it around her. When I reached in the pocket to get out my clasp knife, my hand touched her breast. She gave a little moan and wouldn't let me go. I didn't blame her. I didn't want to go either.

All the way back down the trail, I kept thinking: What the hell are you going to do with a four-inch knife? By now I'd dismounted and was leading my horse, stopping every few yards to listen.

But not a sound came up from the big open below. And when darkness fell, it was quick and pitch black, not even stars to guide me. I stumbled around for a while more, finally seeing there was no sense to it. I turned and slogged my way back up the canyon.

When I found her, she was lying face down in the wet grass like a doll somebody had flung away. I broke off some dry pine boughs and gently rolled her onto them. Then, for the warmth of it, and the senseless rage, too, I held her to me tight, but there was no man-woman in it, no teasing flesh. Just two lost souls, clinging to whatever was left.

In the first light, I got her up. She was like a sleepwalker. She had cramps in her belly, her face was flaming with fever. Still trying to cling to being a lady, she kept whispering that she didn't want to be such a burden on me. I got her some water from the creek that she drank from my hands. Then she had to stumble off into the brush and sicken it all out.

When we finally mounted, I got up on the one horse behind her, so I could keep her from toppling off. The other horse followed us, not wanting to be left alone.

To cheer her up, I said, "The only help we'll get will be back down on the Emigrant Road. I'm even thinking that the Captain took care of those reds. We'll just pick him up now."

"Please God," she whispered.

Moving slow and cautious, I eased us to the edge of the rock cliff. Below me, the old ranch was glinting in the first sun. I let out a whoop. "Jesus and Mary, look at that!"

A dozen or more government horses were tied up in the wreckage of the buildings. Troopers with carbines were poking around the ambulance, still on its back where we left it.

We came thundering down off the cliff, with all eyes whipping to us. The bluebellies had their rifles up and I was hollering: "Hold your fire! We're with the Captain. Captain Bloxham!"

Leah cried out: "Where is he?"

By the time we'd pulled up to the burned out buildings, she was sobbing, "I'm his wife."

A dusty young lieutenant, wearing a red bandana over his head, rose up from behind the wagon and came to us. He touched his forehead in a salute, and smiled. "We've met, ma'am. You probably don't remember, but my first post was with your husband's troop at Camp Grant, Arizona. Tom Prendegast."

She was fumbling, trying to brighten. "Yes, of course. Mr. Prendegast." Then, desperate. "Lieutenant, my husband! Where is he?"

"Let me help you, ma'am," the Lieutenant was saying, and gently slid her down from the horse. "You've had a bad scare, Mrs. Bloxham, but it's going to be all right."

"What have you done with him?" she cried.

"Please, ma'am," he stammered, stalling it. He turned from us and began picking up some empty cartridge cases lying beside the ambulance. "Captain Bloxham was firing. Fortunately, we were down on the Emigrant Road, we heard it and came as quick as we could. There were five or six hostiles, we think from the tracks. He must have held them off for a time, but they were too many. They took him."

She screamed and clutched his shoulder. "In the name of God, Lieutenant..."

Mr. Prendegast glanced at me helplessly, and then at the other troopers who had gathered around and were staring at the dirt. "You must believe me, Mrs. Bloxham. He never knew. They didn't harm him."

"Never knew...?"

The Lieutenant turned stiffly and pointed at distant dust going down the bronze hill. An Army wagon was creaking slowly away. "They didn't harm him, ma'am, because by the time they found him—you know how they are, superstitious savages. He had gone mad, Mrs. Bloxham. They never touch the insane. They run from them."

Leah looked at the Lieutenant, then at me. He tried to take her hand, thinking she was about to faint, but instead, she just sunk to her knees, kind of melted there, her face in her hands. "Then he's alive," she sobbed. "Tell me he's alive!"

"Of course he is. He'll probably be at Fetterman before we will. I've told the drivers to hurry."

She thrust up, groping for her horse which a trooper was holding. "I must go to him. Please, let me!"

"We'll take you there, ma'am." The Lieutenant ordered the troops to mount up. Leah was so wild to chase the wagon carrying the captain, the Lieutenant had to gallop to keep up with her.

I followed at some distance behind. A trooper riding beside me shook his head grimly. "That lady, she better be a hard one."

"She's been through a lot, and come up on her feet," I answered.

"Not this, soldier. Them reds, when they caught the old man, they blinded him first. Cut out his eyes. Must have figured they didn't want him seeing no more goblins. Crazy as a tick, he is. I've watched it happen before, men out here, face to face with the reds. They never come back."

"He will!" I cried, and wanted to sob.

The trooper shook his head. "You ain't seeing your captain no more. It's better that way." Then he whipped his horse ahead of me, and we went following the dust, taking a brave man home.

He never did come back. Three months later, in the Army asylum in Washington, Captain Bloxham died. Merciful, it was. Though Leah was with him all that time, he never recognized her or spoke to her again. It was said out in the troops that they buried him with full honors, with a new medal on his breast that he couldn't see. General Crook himself had written his eulogy. Final salute to a noble old war horse, who went out like a man, and left a trail of pity for us who were left behind.

By then, I was on station at Fort Robinson, over in Nebraska. Waiting out the winter, waiting for the Sioux war to be done with. In the deep snows, the hostiles couldn't hide anymore. Fresh troops, blasting howitzers at the cliffs, were shelling the winter camps. The snows ran bloody all those dark months, God knows how many squaws and kids were killed too.

Once, in February, when a handful of starving reds straggled in, I recognized a young buck who'd been hanging around Touch the Clouds' lodge during my time with the heathen. He could speak a little American. I edged up to him when he was drawing food and blankets from the ration issue. Curious, I says, "Wasn't we together in the big camp last June?"

His dark eyes flickered, and he turned away from me.

"Hold it now," I says. "I had friends there. One girl, Walks Outside?"

His head jerked up, his eyes burning. "When sojer kill Dull Knife, she in Cheyenne camp. Husband, too."

"Cut Meat," I whispered.

"Gone! Dead, sojers shoot him. She run to north."

I grabbed his shirt. "Where north?"

"Maybe Oglalas. Maybe dead. Many die now."

"Ah, God," I cried. "Man, how do you know?"

"She my sister!" He flung his new issue blanket up over his face so that only his eyes showed. The sullen, flaming look in them stayed with me for longer than I wanted to remember. I kept trying to see Walks Outside's face again, but it was gone, too, just like Leah's.

So the frontier was dying, everybody said, and my war dying with it. Good riddance. What started out as a cure for clap was now a broken heart.

I'd had a bellyfull of frontiers. But there was still one left that I'd have to cross. God Almighty, I never asked for it, and didn't know how to run from it, either.

But I should have, while I still had time.

In May 1877, Crazy Horse surrendered at Fort Robinson. I watched him come in with hundreds of his warriors. Proud, well mounted and armed with more Winchesters than we could believe. But his women and little ones were starving. He had no other choice.

When he surrendered, face to face with Crook, he thrust his left hand to the General. The one, he said, that comes from the heart.

There would be peace, now. For all time.

Less than three weeks later, with Crazy Horse a prisoner, and me assigned to the troops that were guarding him, an Army ambulance with escort rolled up to the parade ground.

I was quite far from it, walking my dreary post. But when I happened to look at the ambulance unloading, the first person to get off was dressed in a fancy tan riding habit, and a broad lady's sun hat. The kind gentle women wore in the South, to keep the sun from darkening their lily white skins.

God help us, I breathed. Leah! Here again with me!

But not quite.

The second person off the ambulance wore cavalry blue. Erect, stiff as a ramrod. My eyes swept to his face. Even at the distance, I could see the horribleness of it. Twisted eyes, a jaw too small and hanging in the wrong place. A gargoyle, staring out from a tomb.

Major Scipio Shaw.

What was left of the bastard. He was taking her hand, walking her slowly up the gravel path to Officer's Country, where I knew that I didn't belong, and never would again.

RATS IN A TRAP

That summer of 1877 was a dangerous time for the USA. And for common soldiers like me, in the steaming hills of Nebraska, the thunder clouds that rose up every afternoon were flashed by lightning that came from far off.

Back east of the border, the nabobs who owned the railroads had cut the pay of their workers by ten percent. And the gandy dancers out on the tracks and the car barns weren't about to swallow it. They began rioting in Chicago and other big towns, burning and looting the rolling stock of the roads. Rutherford Hayes was President. He'd served under General Crook in the Rebellion. From Sherman, Sheridan and the high-brass muckety-mucks came orders for Crook and the other commanders to rush troops east. Gun down the rioters in the dingy streets I used to know, like Back of the Yards. I was glad they didn't order me off for such scab work. But many of our foot and horse regiments went clanking east on the cars, leaving us with far less men than we needed to patrol that grim frontier.

At Fort Robinson alone, and at the nearby Red Cloud and Spotted Tail agencies, we bluebellies were sitting on 4500 Lakota. To be sure, some were tame, bickering rascals who'd been loafing around the forts for years. But when Crazy Horse and his hotbloods were dumped in their midst, you had a pot of sullenness and jealousy that began bubbling foul.

Then, in August, another prairie fire swirled up in the west. The Nez Perce chief, Joseph, had broken out of his agency. He and his well-armed warriors were cutting a swath of death through the mountains of Idaho and Montana. And just to the north, in what the Sioux called Grandmother land, Canada, Sitting Bull and his unsurrendered cutthroats were smouldering. The way we heard it out among the troops, if the northern Sioux decided to make a run for their old hunting grounds on the Big Horn, Crazy Horse would escape from us and hurl several thousand of his own warriors into another slaughter, even worse than what we'd gone through in the summer of '76.

Fort Robinson began to rattle with wagons and pack trains. More troops that we couldn't spare were sucked away from us, the rumor being that General Crook himself would lead the attack against Chief Joseph.

And, as if this wasn't enough, the court-martial over the retreat at Crazy Woman Fork was now ready to begin. The charge was that Major Shaw had disobeyed orders in combat, and I was the only man alive who could prove it.

About that time, I happened to run into Captain Bourke who'd

117

just come from General Crook's headquarters in Omaha. He clapped my mitt genial-like and seemed pleased that my leg had healed so well. Because he was Crook's aide, I had a notion to blurt out, Why not stop the damn court-martial? It didn't make any sense now, and what's more, a private testifying against a major put me square in the middle of a fight that was going to hurt somebody bad—chances are, me.

But tell him what? I thought. Blubber out that a piece of dirt from the ranks had loved an officer's wife, and was mooning for her still? Ah, hell, I just swallowed it, and wanted to be shet of the whole lousy business.

"You know, Kelly," Bourke was saying, and his eyes twinkled, "I'm glad I stumbled onto you. This has just come to me, but it's worth a try. Remember that day at the Rosebud when you were regaling the correspondents about your captivity among the lesser race?"

"Well, sir, they proved they wasn't no lesser, if I remember right."

He laughed. "Exactly my point. During that time, you knew Crazy Horse. Had some contact with him?"

I nodded.

"I want you to start over again."

"Sir?"

He was already scribbling a note in the dispatch pad he carried. "Give this to your company officer. The general's order, by me. It assigns you to the detail guarding Crazy Horse's camp. But you're different from the others. You can speak some Lakota, can't you? At least understand?" I nodded and he said, "I'm sending you there as our eyes, Kelly. Crazy Horse is going to take watching, particularly now, with all this turmoil about Chief Joseph. We want to find out what he's thinking. We might be on the short end of a fuse here."

I went back to the barracks, got my bedroll, Springfield and guvmint horse, and rode to Crazy Horse's camp, a few miles up on the bluffs behind Fort Robinson. It was a far cry from the old free-roaming camp that I'd left so long before. Beaten now, the Sioux seemed to have turned into a seedy bunch of bums, their feathers and finery pretty much gone. Most of the bucks were lounging around in cast off charity clothes or Army hand-me downs from the Civil War. Tin ration cans littered the camp, and women, kids and dogs were wrangling over scraps of a beef carcass.

As I edged through the camp lanes, trying to locate Crazy Horse's lodge, and present myself to him face to face, which is Indian custom, all I got were hard, heathen looks. Maybe it was my *waiscu* skin, but more likely, it was the uniform I wore. Idle bucks, lying in the dirt along the creek, would turn away from me as I passed. When I asked one of them where I could find Crazy Horse, he shrugged and went back to work restringing a bow that a kid had handed him, along with two pitiful arrows.

As the sun died, I was shaking out my blankets to bed down when I heard a dog growl behind me. Then, thump, a foot kicked him away. I whirled.

I thought it was a trooper, for he wore a blue cavalry blouse and black campaign hat. But then I saw bare, bandy-legs and a bulging, half-naked chest under the blouse. "What you do here?" he grunted in English. "You bring trouble maybe. Long time, I no forget you."

Nor me either, I thinks, for I was staring into the mean, slitty eyes of none other than my old captor, Little Big Man.

He was glowering like he was going to cut my heart out. Sharply, he struck me across the arm with his rifle, and began chuckling. "Hey, how you like? Got sojer suit. Little Big Man big scout. Sergeant stripe. Go sojer school. Talk like *waiscu*, what you think?"

"Pretty good, I suppose."

"Very good! Smart Injun. Sojer see this, you salute!" He slapped the stripes on his blouse, like he was ordering me to.

"The hell I will. Last time I saw you at the Rosebud, you were shooting at us."

"Yah, you run off too. But change now, all change."

"I hope."

"You gonna be friend Little Big Man now? What you think?"

I said nothing.

He jabbed me with the rifle. "Yah! Tell!"

"I'm thinking," I said slowly, "that I ought to put a rope on your blackguard neck and drag you around like you did me!"

He made a thrust at my throat, then stopped in midair, and began guffawing. He gripped my arms and bounced me up and down. "No more kill. Lakota good Indian. Open your ears!" He whirled me.

In the shadows a few feet away stood Crazy Horse.

His thin, cruel lips were tight, and his eyes gave not one flicker that he'd ever seen me before. Even though it was cold that night, he was wearing only a breechclout, and he looked more gaunt and sullen than I remembered.

He brushed his hand at Little Big Man, who stepped aside. Five or six tall, mean bruisers moved in beside Crazy Horse, northern warriors without a doubt, who had surrendered with him. Slowly, he came forward and studied me from tip to toe. Then, without any change of expression, he snatched off my cavalry cap and jammed it on his own head.

The other Indians grunted and chuckled as Crazy Horse ripped off the cap, spat in it, and slapped it into my belly.

"Cluke!"

I stared at him, not savvying until Little Big Man butted in. "Back then, Rosebud, he send you to Crook. Three Stars. Stop fight.

But you don' go. You lie!"

"Did like hell! I went to Crook straight off…"

"How come fight?"

"Because they don't listen. Nor you. Crook wanted peace, you wanted war."

They were staring me down, not hearing a word I said. "You think I'm lying," I cried, "put this in your pipe!" I jerked my belt buckle open, dropped my jeans and showed them the slick and purple scar on my leg. "One of your damn Lakota arrows did that. I paid for the Rosebud just like you!"

Crazy Horse thrust next to me and his fingers touched the scar. He was nodding, and when he drew away, his eyes smiled hard. "Hola!" Then the others began grunting and enjoying the hell out of it. They'd drawn *waiscu* blood on me, so maybe now we were settling old scores.

Crazy Horse turned sharply to Little Big Man, motioned at my blanket roll and horse. Little Big Man started bundling it up, and grabbed hold of the horse.

"He will take you into the camp," said a voice next to me. "You have the hospitality of the camp."

I was looking at a young man about my own age who was dressed in a white-man hunting coat and buckskin leggins. His face was high-cheekboned Indian, but his black hair had been roached short, Army style, over his ears.

"You belong with these people?" I says.

He nodded. "Interpret sometimes for the General. Billy Garnett. My father was an Army officer, my Mother Lakota. I've spent all my life around 'em."

"Well, mister," I breathed, "ain't I glad to see you."

By then, Little Big Man and the others were already lugging my outfit up toward the lodges. As we began to follow, Crazy Horse shoved Garnett between us, so that he could speak through him to me.

"He will show you the camp," Garnett said, "and what is happening to his people. He says, You have talked to Crook once, you can do it again. Is that true?"

"Ah, hell, Garnett, sure I've talked to him, but you know Army. Them brass don't listen much to a common trooper."

When Crazy Horse got the gist of that, he grabbed my forearm and shook it. "He thinks you talk straight, he has watched you before in his camp," Garnett translated. "So now you tell Three Stars, Crazy Horse wants to talk to him. Man to man. No other officers, no other Indians. He will show you why."

When we reached the main part of the camp, it didn't take much translation for me to understand the fire in Crazy Horse's belly. He flung his arm across the Army tents and sorry lodges. His people were rotting out, no question. Idleness, bickering, lies. In the dark shadows, knots of bucks were lounging around gambling. Some were dead drunk and sprawled on their faces, sleeping it off. Traders weren't supposed to be in the camp, but they'd snuck booze in all right. And goods too, white-man trinkets and calico dresses that the squaws were wrangling over. As Crazy Horse walked through them, naked urchins would follow him like a Pied Piper, clutching at him for some sign of hope that wasn't there.

"Crook," Garnett said, "promised to give these northern Indians, Crazy Horse people, a reservation of their own, someplace far off from the jealousy and lying of the loafers here. This Crook said. I heard him say it, and Crazy Horse believes him. But it has not happened."

By then we'd reached the top lodge on the bluff, and I took it to be Crazy Horse's. It was a big teepee in the old style, with a small brush shelter beside it. A fire was glowing inside. I heard soft voices and the hacking sound of somebody coughing.

Little Big Man and the others had already tied my horse up to the brush shelter. Crazy Horse signed that it was where I should stay. He repeated, "Cluke!" and speared his finger at the earth. Here! Then, he turned abruptly and went into his lodge.

"You can stay all right," Garnett said, "but don't bother him unless he sends for you. He has a lot of worries now." The coughing began again and Garnett shook his head. "She gets worse every day. Black Shawl, his wife. When the soldiers ran 'em around all winter, below zero, deep snow, she got lung sickness. Tuberculosis, the doctor says."

"Army doctor?"

He nodded. "Surgeon McGillycuddy from the troops. That's one thing Crook has done, sending him up here with his pills. But Crazy Horse believes you can do even more. Bring Crook here."

"I'll try, Garnett, but I ain't a bit sure he'll listen."

When I went back to the post the next morning, the sergeant major was waiting for me "I see on your record that you're a farrier. The major needs one. He's waiting for you at stables."

"The major?"

"Shaw, soldier. He was in here looking at the court-martial schedule, and he knows you all right. Get down there, on the double."

The stable was a big booming barn, echoing with the stomping of dozens of horses, troopers pitching hay here and there, and the veterinary and his helpers doing mend-ups on animals that were being readied for the Chief Joseph war. I felt sorry for the poor things, and in a minute, sorrier for myself.

Damn if that barn didn't remind me of Francis His Lordship Cavan. Death in the place. When I slid open the door of one stall, a leggy chestnut thoroughbred wheeled to me, nasty, daring me to ride him, like I'd done with that wild lad on the Other Side so long ago. I could almost hear my soiled sister Nora, whimpering just beyond, plunging me into that awful night of murder. But this time, I was hearing a woman's voice, leaping out from the past. "I told you," she was saying, "I don't want a horse. I have no interest in it anymore…"

"Of course you do," a man answered. "We'll have a canter in those hills, that's what you need."

I spun around. Major Scipio Shaw had slid open the door and was leading Leah right smack up to me.

My breath caught in my throat. Shaw's curly black hair had gone gray as a ghost, and the face on him, ah God, it sent shivers through me. From the Sioux ball blasting into him, his left eye and cheekbone had been twisted up, bulging, and his other eye too small and glinting at me. His jaw on one side was scarred and drooping slack, so he talked with a mushy mouth I could hardly understand.

"High time you got here, soldier," he slurred. "Kept us waiting. You recall him, Leah? Kelly, serving the captain?"

She was staring at the stall floor, the wet manure and straw. "Yes, we know each other. Good day, Private."

"Ma'am," I said, and touched my cap. Ah, how I longed to reach out and hold her, whispering to her, What are you doing with this broken wretch?

But Shaw had his arm around her waist, where mine ought to have been. She was wearing a straw yellow sun hat, and had another tailored riding outfit on, gray this time, too, like our first time. "They tell me that Kelly is pretty good shoeing a rank horse," Shaw was saying. "This one has some fight in him, but after you get his plates on, he's a lamb. Do you realize, he was one of Custer's. Should be dead now. I wouldn't put you up him, Leah, unless I was damn sure you could handle him."

"You drag me down here, I told you, Cupe, I'm not in the mood to ride, so I don't care what you do with him. Have your own canter, you like that better anyhow." She turned on her heel, but the stall was tight, with the horse's butt there, and she brushed my arm as she went past me and out into the aisle.

"Get at it, soldier," Shaw said, and followed her away.

I set three shoes on, with some fight, and was sweating when Shaw came back. He stood, hands on his hips, watching me work. Finally he said, "You and Mrs. Bloxham went through a lot together, didn't you?"

I glanced up. "Sir?"

"The day the Captain was taken. She told me everything."

How damn much? I thought, my face burning. But I only grunted like a coolie. "Yessir, we seen enough."

I stopped tacking nails then, and straightened up to get the cricks out of my back.

Shaw was leaning against the stall, licking a thin cheroot in his twisted lips, "I'm waiting for the horse, soldier."

"I can see that," I retorted, and shoved my shoeing toolbox over to the other flank of the animal.

Shaw had lit the cheroot, blew out smoke and then, quick for a big man, thrust in at me. "You're pretty good at seeing, Kelly, so take a look at this." He held the cigar under my nose. "What is it?"

The foul thing smarted my eyes. "Seegar."

"Wrong. It's a gift, the kind you'll never get in your life because it costs one dollar each. Last week, at the White House, General Sherman gave me a box of these out of his own personal supply. Now, does that mean anything to you? What does that tell you?"

"Major, are you wanting me to shoe this horse or talk all day?"

He kicked over my toolbox. "Mind your tongue, or you'll be in leg irons! Now listen to this straight. General Sherman is a friend of mine, so is Sheridan. I go all the way up with them, from the Shenandoah to burning Atlanta to now. They know what I am, and it didn't just happen. I bled my guts for my major's leaves—five wounds, six medals— and I'll bleed more for the star that's going to replace them." Slowly, he reached out and held the cigar under my nose again. "Smell that good, trooper, because any common ranker who tries to stand in my way will burn in hell first. If you say one word against me at that court- martial, I'll see to it that you're branded as a lying illiterate, trying to smear an officer's good name, an officer known for courage through- out this Army. You want me to prove it, you hardheaded sonofabitch, then go against me, and you'll be wishing you'd deserted while you had the chance, or better yet wish you were dead!"

Before I could answer, he turned, slammed open the door of the stall with such a clang that the chestnut jumped. But then Shaw stopped, his back to me, and his voice was low. "I've had a thousand men like you under me, Kelly. Hod carriers, farm boys, ex-felons. But do you know something? They all have one thing in common. When they follow me, carry out my orders, we win. Every time we've won. That's my lucky star. Custer and I used to talk about it. He had a flaw, too impatient, but that's not mine. I've helped a hundred up through the ranks, and I'll do the same for you. Provided one thing: that you know you're in the ranks."

"If I wasn't, Major," I grunted, "I wouldn't be standing for a tongue-whipping like this."

"Learn your place, Kelly. I'm only going to warn you once. You and Mrs. Bloxham have had an acquaintance, because of your duty station and the events that happened. Well, that's over. She's had a great deal of suffering and she doesn't need you as a memory of it. We're making a new life, she and I. There is no room in it for a common soldier, despite his loyalty to her former husband." He sucked his cigar and stared at me. "Finish the last shoe and turn the horse out," he said, slamming shut the door and striding off down the barn aisle.

Two mornings later, they convened the court-martial. I was in the soup now for sure. If I lied and saved Shaw's bacon, the miserable bugger might make it easy for me, give me cushy jobs or even stripes. He'd about promised as much. And yet what I'd have to stomach was watching him mincing around with Leah, and me trotting at their heels like a pet mongrel to be tossed a bone or kicked in the teeth as it pleased them. Worse, I'd have to live with myself, knowing that I'd backed down from the bastard.

Yet if I told the truth, that he'd broken orders, I'd surely clear old Captain Bloxham's name, and very likely wreck Shaw's chances at any further promotion. It was a rough game the brass played. These were men accustomed to killing or being killed. Let an officer get mad at some pitiful soldier, he'd slap a malingering charge on him, slam him into the Hole, a dark, dirty box below ground where the accused would stay weeks at a time, lying in his own filth, never hearing a human voice or seeing the sun. We were little better than animals, and the officers knew that they could get away with treating us accordingly. I'd heard of one trooper ragged so badly by a young lieutenant that he finally hung himself in the barracks. If he'd had any gumption, the poor devil should have deserted first. And thinking that, I wondered if Shaw hadn't made the very same suggestion to me?

If I cut and ran before the court-martial, then there'd be no testimony, and maybe just as important to him, he'd be shet of me, looking in on him and Leah. Ah, the damn conundrum of it galled me. Sitting in that hot, smoky courtroom, I must have dozed off, for the next thing I felt was a hand gripping my shoulder roughly, and I was staring into the grizzled face of the sergeant major. "You got no need to be gold-bricking in here, Kelly. They won't use you yet, maybe a day or two more. But I'll damn well make use of you."

He jerks me out of the courtroom, and from the steps of the post headquarters, points at a loaded wagon out on the horse path. "They're shorthanded down at the sutler's store. Haul 'em those Indian-issue supplies. Requisition to the agent, or if he's not there, to one of the preachers."

The sun was going down by the time I'd rattled the wagon over to the post gate. Just beyond the military fence, in a grove of cottonwoods, was the sutler's log store, agency beef corrals and slaughterhouse. Half the Sioux on the reservation seemed to be clamoring around the place. I could hear the braying of cattle, milling in the corrals, waiting for slaughter. At the sutler's store I couldn't find any agent or sutler either, just sullen Sioux pretending not to speak

English. So I hupped the team ahead toward some dark buildings along the creek. A few were old cabins and huts of a frontier settlement crusted along the reservation fence. Mixed among them were new Army frame houses, flung up by soldiers or drummers and shills hoping to feed on the carcasses of the surrendered Sioux. I'd seen such a place down at Fetterman. The Hog Ranch, we called it, home of post laundresses, squaw men and just plain whores, working the troops for whatever they could get.

But I soon saw that there was something different here. On a dark plain, stretching back from the creek, were several big Army mess tents with lanterns burning inside. When I stopped the team, God almighty, what was I hearing but footpedal organs and the throaty voices of Indian women and kids, trying to sing hymns. From one tent they were bleating "Mine eyes have seen the glory of the coming of the Lord." When I drew my rig up to the next tent beyond, it was echoing with "Amazing Grace:" "I once was lost but now I'm found, and Grace has set me free."

Free, hell, I thinks, and got slowly down out of the wagon. The Sioux that weren't in the church tents were crowding around long tables in front of each tent. There were hundreds of Indians here, squaws, kids, all gabbling and wrangling over food, blankets and geegaws of white charity. At the end of each table sat a pair of religious dames, pinched white faces half-hidden under their big bonnets. In front of them was a big ledger book. I couldn't get the gist of it right off, but when I did, I wanted to groan for the pitiful buggers.

A squaw could draw rations for her family all right, but the catch was, when the religious biddy wrote her name down in the book, from that moment on, the squaw—Red Bonnet or Bright Eyes or Rises with Sun—was hooked as a full-fledged member of the church that was feeding her.

What a clever deal it was, like recruiting sailors out of the Dublin slums. The Episcopals were in one tent, Presbyterians in the next, and a black-robed priest from the Pope himself roaming the fringes to see what starvies he could sign on for life everlasting in the Holy Mother Church.

A slovenly soldier was lounging by one of the tables. I says, "Man, am I seeing this right? They're convertin' the heathen?"

"You said it, mate. They either sign the ticket for one Bible-thumper or the other or they don't get grub."

"Aw, that ain't fair," I grunted. "These people got Indian religion, and what I seen of it, livin' with 'em, it's a helluva sight truer than this crap they're being fed."

"You lived among them bums, hah?"

"Yas. When they were free, and not beggin' like this." As I started away in disgust, I stopped, thinking of the wagon I had to unload. "Soldier, how's about bearin' a hand and helpin' me with this stuff. Set her on the tables, I suppose."

"I'm on sick leave," he whined.

I jerked him to his feet. "You just got better. Come on now."

As we started pulling the goods out of the wagon and setting them on the table, a tall white man dressed in black edged in beside me. "This is fine, soldiers. Government generosity. Our cup runneth over."

One look at him was all I needed. What a sanctimonious bastard, a long face about as sincere as an undertaker, and his slick white hands fingering the goods as we laid them down. Next thing I knew he was separating out coffee cans, sacks of sugar and flour. "Hey, mister," I says, "that's for the Indians, and you gotta sign my requisition for it." I reached into my pants to pull out the paper the sergeant major had given me, but Black Suit smiled me aside.

"Allow me to introduce myself, soldier. I'm Deacon Lowery. This is my mission. Well, partly my mission, divided with the other faiths of course. So all the paperwork has long ago been taken care of. Now, the second of those two houses over there, the far one…" He pointed through the darkness and I could see a pair of frame houses, fresh-built they looked like from the raw lumber, eastern style with high-pitched roofs. "My congregation owns them both, use of myself and staff. When you've unloaded here, would you be a good fellow and take the kitchen accoutrements over to the far house…"

"Accoutra what…?" I stared at the oily bugger and wanted to slap the smirk off his face.

"The necessaries. Here, I'll box them for you." Damn if he didn't, took an empty crate from the wagon and stuffed into it the coffee, sugar and flour. "God blesses you for your help to our children."

Then he minced away to get more squaws signing his book. "Mary and Joseph," I grunted to the other soldier, "if that sonofabitch has got the key to heaven, I'll take hellfire and damnation any time."

The lounger soldier smirked. "Hey, sonny, you don't know the half. That house down there where he's running you with this stuff, guess who was living there but his wife's sister. A Bible teacher for the poor Indians. Well, one day she must have had the Good Book open to the saucy part, because in walks the wife and what does she find but the Deacon humping Sis like a billygoat." The soldier chuckled and blew his nose into the grass. "Hallelujah, Praise de Lawd! The wife whacks him over the head with a fry pan, and before he can even pull his pants up, she's screaming bloody murder to Chicago, where they got the congregation. She's on the next train out, but not before she kicks little Bibely sister's ass west—Frisco, I heard—but the Lord's vengeance may not stop there."

"So what in hell's the necessaries for?" I says, staring at the crate

I was supposed to lug.

"Way I heard, the horny fart is trying to rent the place out, bait the nest for his next angel. Give one of these squaws a soft sack and grub, you can get in her pretty quick, the way I hear."

Just then, a big scraggly-haired squaw had edged beside me and was fingering the goods in the crate. "Gimme, sojer."

"I'd like to," I says wearily, "but white folks got there first."

Lugging the crate off through the darkness, I was glad to get shet of the mumbling and mouthing of conversion. Making 'em into good little Indians, imitation white men. What a sham, every crook and pious parson plucking for a piece of them. Seeing the Sioux groveling like beggars was a hard knock for me. Ah, yes, punish the fierce bastards that had hurt us so bad. My leg was still aching and would ache for the rest of my life. But to remember how free and proud they'd been in their big summer camp of '76, and the gentle dignity of Walks Outside—something big had been lost here, and I missed it too.

When I reached the second house, it was dark as a tomb, the shutters drawn, and not even an Indian mongrel to sniff at me as I stood on the stoop. Yet there was smoke wisping up from the chimney, and that struck me strange. "Halloo!" I said, and rapped on the front door. Nothing. Then I tried the knob, and damn if it wasn't open. I slid inside, figuring to set down the crate of necessaries and be gone, but the parlor was dark except for a red glowing light in one corner. It was the wood stove, ticking and flaming away, and atop it a kettle was boiling and beginning to whistle.

"Anybody home?" I says. Hell, there had to be somebody. Then, fumbling around the bare wood furniture, I edged into the hall. There was a slit of light here, coming out from under a door. By then, I was tired of hollering at ghosts. I banged open the door and saw a soapy head rising up from a bathtub. God help us, that wasn't all I saw, the smooth white shoulders, the pink nipples bubbling with soap suds.

"Leah!"

"Oh, my God," she cried. "You! How did you find me?"

I grinned. "God himself, I reckon. That parson had me run some grub over here, stealing it for his tenant. I never dreamed it was you, Leah."

"Patrick, Patrick!" She was out of the tub by then, wet and sweet and clinging to me. She was soaking my blouse and pants. I said, "Let me dry you," and she was just moaning. "No, like this. Please, now!"

My eyes closed and we were swaying there, loving as hard as we could go, all the fury of the months apart screaming out like a cry in the night, and it didn't matter who heard anymore.

I was gripping her wet blonde hair, kissing the frail beauty of her face, and she was laughing, sinking us to the bare pine floor where we lay in the puddles and the feet of the cast iron tub seemed like they were galloping over us. "I can't get enough of you," I whispered, and she was sobbing, her tears salty in my mouth.

When it was finally done, I helped dry her body, and she put on a long blue bathrobe, Army blue, with USA on the breast. Whose? Captain Bloxham's, or Shaw's?

Then we went out into the parlor and she had me light one lamp. The blinds were tight shut, except on one side window, and she patted over to latch it. "Reverend Lowery, or whatever he claims to be, I don't trust him for a minute. And Patrick," she said and smiled, "you shouldn't be here, you know, and that just makes it all the more delicious."

"Well, Leah, if I die now, I've already gone to heaven, from what you give me." I hugged her and stroked her again, and it was maybe an hour before she could even get coffee on the stove. That and some hot biscuits. We sat on the hard wooden chairs in the parlor, and it was like making love in the sanctuary of a church. On the bare pine walls were pictures of Jesus leading little lambs, or rising up into the clouds.

"Well, you better tell me," I said, not wanting to end it. "What about the Major? Where do I run if he busts down the door?"

"He won't, not tonight anyhow." She was drying her hair with a towel, and her blue eyes darkened with sadness. "He's gone with General Crook over to Fort Washakie in Wyoming. They're starting the Chief Joseph war. I pray to God it keeps him busy and away from me."

"It ain't good, is it?"

She shook her head. "I wanted it to be, Patrick. Really I did. Oh, there's so much to tell you. Those months, back in Washington watching poor Cletus die. I really loved him then, please understand that. I treasured him. But I'm not a woman who can be alone. I can't play widow. When he was gone, all that was left was Cupe. Everything I wanted, I thought. The Army, promotions, just the comfort of being safe and secure. And yet," she stared at the Bible pictures on the walls, "look at me now. Whoring, my mother would have called it. God has a way, I suppose, of taking away what you love most. First my son in Arizona. Then Clete, out here on these awful plains. And finally Cupe Shaw. The wreckage of him, the bitterness. A purely rotten man. Oh, Patrick, I fear him now. Desperately. You don't know how utterly mean that bastard can be."

"I'm getting a notion," I said, and went on to tell her how Shaw had threatened me. "I'll be on that witness stand any day now, Leah, and I've got no way to duck it."

"Finish him," she whispered. "Tell the truth. Clete was so right, and I was so vile to have cuckolded him."

"I don't believe that, Leah. I sure ain't making no confessions for what you and I done neither. Things happen, that's all. My momma used to say, Dear God ain't no punisher. But I will say this, when I go against Shaw, I believe that bastard will kill me."

Her eyes flared. "He can't do that. The Army has laws protecting enlisted men."

"Sweep 'em under the rug, they do. It happens all the time. I seen it. But what I don't know now, where does that leave you and me?"

She sighed, got up and took the coffee pot back over to the stove. "Cupe wants to marry me. That was the understanding when he brought me west with him."

"You agreed to it?"

"I did. What else could I do? I was alone back in Washington. I had only the clothes on my back. My widow's pension, when they finally get it straightened out, is the grand sum of eighty-three dollars a month." She smiled bitterly. "I was better off back doing laundry in Memphis after the war. So yes, I went with him, lying to myself that someday I'd learn to stand the sight of him. Oh, it's so cruel, so shallow. If I loved him as he once was, shouldn't I love him just as much now, in the bitter, shattered vileness of him? In sickness and in death. Oh, Patrick," she sobbed and came to me. "I don't want to marry anyone anymore. I just want to be free."

"Seems like we're a long way from it, Leah," I whispered.

In the upstairs room, we didn't sleep much that night, nor did we make love again. She lay beside me, staring at the narrow peaked ceiling. "How do I start over?" she murmured. Then, disjointed-like, she got talking about her past in the South. Her brother, who had survived the War, was trying to put together what was left of the burned out plantation at Leatherton. "He's asked me to come back there and help him, Patrick. We have nothing, even between us. The nigras, with this awful reconstruction, won't work the fields anymore. Too uppity. They stay in town and wait for the Yankee politicians to feed them. But you and I could work, couldn't we? Maybe, together, we could make something there."

I was staring out the one narrow window, looking at the stars. "Well hell, Leah, it ain't a question of wantin' to go with you. I've been with you all these months, longin' for you. But the Army's got a chain on me."

"Break it, fling it off!"

"Desert, you're saying? That's what Shaw would like all right."

"Forget him, damn you. It's us, Patrick. Don't you understand, I'm 32 years old. I've burned away the flower of my life out on these forlorn plains. I want to settle now. Want more children while I still can. Want something of my own."

Gently, I turned to her and held her. "When you desert, Leah, you quit and run. I seen dozens of worthless bastards doing it. And I ain't sayin' either that I'm in this Army for life, because it ain't worth a fart, compared to you. I know that. But when you desert, they track you, they hunt you. I run from the Other Side over here because I killed a man."

"You did?"

I nodded. "He needed it, I'll say. But now that I've run, and seen so much, I'm beginnin' to know that I ain't just the settlin' kind, Leah."

"Roamer, drifter, tramp. No, no, you can't want that!"

"I ain't sure, dammit. But I don't want to be hidin' out in barns and gutters neither."

"They don't catch all the deserters, Patrick. Not a fraction of them!"

I just shook my head and held her close. "We ain't going to settle it tonight, Leah."

"Could it be every night? Please, Patrick, until he comes home..."

Well, it was every night. Two nights, that is. Not easy to do, but God almighty, worth it. When I heard the reveille bugle from the distant camp, just before dawn broke, I'd slide up the window, drop down to the woodshed, and gallop through the main gate to camp before any of the slugabeds were awake or could notice. Same thing in the nights. Wait for dark and slip in again.

Ah, God, I had a chuckle out of it, those two times. Beating the system, I thinks. With the courts-martial on, the sergeant major wasn't checking very sharp in the barracks. And, as I say, many of the troops had gone off on the Chief Joseph war, or banging strikers heads back in Chicago. Now that they'd pulled me out of the Crazy Horse camp, my only duties were drill or stable call, shoeing horses.

But on the morning of the third day, Leah and I still wrangling out our future, if any, I must have slept through the reveille bugle. When I waked up and scurried away, just as I leapt off the woodshed, I hear a low, nasty laugh. "Still delivering groceries, or haulin' ashes, is it?"

I whirled to see the slovenly soldier I'd met on the first night. "What in hell are you doing here?" I asked. "Ain't you got troop duties?"

"I kind of guard the church property, mate. Deacon Lowery makes it worth my while. Can't have no monkeyshines going on down here."

He stood in the first sun, smirking at me. I knew right then I couldn't trust the bastard, and that very same night, he proved it.

BLOOD IN THE MOCCASIN

Along toward sundown, I was riding on the gravel path beside the parade ground when I heard the rattling of wheels. A big Army ambulance swerved up in front of headquarters. Captain Bourke was first out, followed by General Crook. I dismounted in a leap and went after Crook, who was still wearing his hunting jacket and slouch hat, and looked trail-weary.

Bourke started explaining who I was, and that he'd sent me up to Crazy Horse, but Crook cut him short. "What's on your mind, soldier?"

"Just that, sir. Crazy Horse. He wants to see you alone, no other officers or interpreters because he says they tell lies."

"Wait for me in the courtroom," Crook told the major and other brass, then whipped back to me, not a bit pleased at the delay. "Sure he wants to see me. So does every Indian at this agency. Now what's new here? Don't waste my time with hearsay."

"I've been in that camp, General. Crazy Horse is surly, on the fight. The way he tells it, everybody has lied to him, the old chiefs, the Army. Promised him a reservation of his own, but it hasn't come. Those northern Indians of his are rotting out, and they're still warriors at heart, you can bet. It ain't going to take much of a spark to touch 'em off."

Crook blew out a long breath and glanced at Bourke. "What would a meeting with Crazy Horse accomplish?"

"Buying time, maybe," Bourke answered.

"If we had it." Wearily, Crook stared at me. "You don't know this, soldier, nor does Crazy Horse. But over these past few months since he's been here, I've been pleading with everybody I can think of to deliver that Powder River reservation to him. I've talked to senators, ministers, the Eastern Peace Policy groups. The answer's always the same. Only the President and Congress can legislate that land. And sitting squarely on the lid of it is Sheridan, who wants no deals with any Indian. There's too much hue and cry about Sioux atrocities, and pressure from the border state communities. The country isn't forgetting Custer overnight."

"Those same Indians that put him down are three miles from here, sir, and thirsting to try it again, if I'm any judge."

"A risk we have to run," Crook snapped. "Kelly, get this straight. I have never lied to an Indian yet, nor will I lie to Crazy Horse. Much as I want to treat him fairly, it's up to Washington to decide what happens to him. I'm waiting just as much as he is, but I don't think it's going to be for very long." He turned from me, his boots grinding the gravel as he walked up the path toward headquarters.

It was how he looked after the Rosebud, shaking his head and his shoulders hunched up like an old man.

Though I sure didn't want to do it, I felt I owed the truth to Crazy Horse, so I grabbed my horse and rode out to his camp.

The place seemed heavy and dead, like the air gets before a lightning storm. When I came up to his lodge, I tied my horse and hesitated, a few feet from the teepee flap. You don't just barge in on a man like him. I doubted if anyone was there, until I heard a low, faint coughing from inside. That would be the wife, and from the sound of her, anything but cured. Then I heard whispering inside, and the teepee flap lifted.

Crazy Horse came out, naked except for a breechclout and moccasins. His eyes burned me with that same look, as if he'd never seen me before. Not knowing what else to do, I put out my hands, to show that they were empty, harmless.

In his quick, catlike way, he sprung forward. "Cluke? Cluke!"

It had begun to rain, a storm cloud whipping over us, drops pelting my Army blouse, and running down Crazy Horse's cheeks.

Fumbling in Lakota and sign, I told him, Yes, I'd seen Crook, and Three Stars wasn't lying to him. He was doing his best to help him, but it was going to take time. I ran my finger across the weak, dying sun, which was how they counted days.

Crazy Horse nodded, sat down crosslegged in the wet dust and signed me to do the same. We stared at each other, one on one. Finally he murmured, "*Ethiti*," good friend. His eyes lifted to the clouds which were furling black and spilling rainshowers onto the distant yellow hills. He was watching something. I glanced up and saw a red-tailed hawk screaming above us, riding the wind of the storm. Crazy Horse's fingers lifted to his headband and touched the hawk feather that was there. The Sioux all had an animal, and the hawk was his. Then, face hardening, he took off one of his moccasins and turned it upside down, as if to drain it.

Hell, it was empty, yet I knew that he was trying to tell me something. Slowly, he touched the moccasin against my left thigh, right on the spot where I'd showed him my arrow wound from Rosebud.

He flicked his hands in the all-gone sign, then jabbed his forefingers down at the dirt.

End of conversation. After he'd stalked back into his lodge, I felt a shiver. Down, I remembered, was how they showed death, and I had no way of knowing whether he meant his, or mine.

Just after midnight, I waked up with a start. Sergeants with lanterns were stomping through the barracks, hollering stable call for three troops, ready to ride. As the boys pulled on uniforms and rattled chains off the carbine racks, everybody was cussing and growling rumors. They were shipping out for the Chief Joseph war, groused an old vet, but another man said, No, it would be Sheridan back in Chicago, calling for more troops to bust the railroad strikers' heads. Then a corporal ran out from the squadroom and said he had it straight. Lieutenant Clark and his Sioux scouts were going for Crazy Horse's camp, and needed backup in case it got hot.

Well, my night's sleep was wrecked for sure, and hoping to find out what was going on, I went clattering downstairs with the troopers. On the porch, sergeants were counting the squads out, and giving tally sheets to officers who were commanding this wild ride.

I froze in my tracks. Major Shaw was staring at me in the darkness, his eyes gleaming. Beside him stood a soldier. God almighty, it was the slovenly bastard who'd caught me coming out of Leah's house. Damn if he wasn't from Shaw's troop, and putting the finger on me like Judas.

"Arrest this man!" Shaw snapped to one of the sergeants. "Keep him in the guardhouse in irons until I get back!"

He whirled and clattered down the steps, the sergeant calling after him. "Major, what charge?"

"Insubordination!"

The sergeant grabbed my elbow. "You heard it, boyo. Off with ya."

In the milling of the soldiers running past, I could see that the sergeant was losing his troop tally, so I cut in quick. "Sir, you got men to count, so at least let me fetch my boots and pants."

Well, he bit on it all right, giving me just enough time to grab my duds, slick out of that barracks and down the back fire ladder. With the confusion of three troops mounting up, soldiers were running every place and nobody was asking questions. In the darkness, I cut across the parade and along the blind side of the darkened buildings until I'd reached the post gate. A sentry was there, half-asleep but not so much that he didn't throw up his carbine. "Post on alert," he says. "Nobody out."

"Just why I'm going," I lied in my teeth. "Sergeant Major says warn the civilians at the sutler's store."

"Shoot the lot of 'em, as far as I care." The soldier shrugged and I ran past him, not stopping until I'd reached the creek winding through the cottonwoods. I moved more cautious now, not wanting to set the camp dogs howling, edged along the creekbed until I took cover against the woodshed behind Leah's house.

The place was dark as death, but the narrow window of her bedroom was open, catching the hot night air, I suppose. Just as I started to climb up on the shed, I heard the rattle of troops, going through the post gate. After they'd galloped away, I grabbed hold of the sill and let myself into the room.

The bed was white and rumpled, slept in, but a ghost now. "Leah?" I whispered. I creaked open the door just beyond it, and waited, listening, at the top of the narrow stair.

From below in the parlor, there was a faint sound. A sizzle it was, like something had been spilled on a hot stove. A moment later, a white shape came around the bottom of the stair. It was Leah, in her nightdress, starting up the steps with a teapot.

"Waiting for you," I whispered.

She let out a cry and almost dropped the pot. She took a step or two toward me, and then sank down on the stairs. I leapt toward her and took her in my arms. "What's wrong, Leah?"

"Him." Even in the dark, I could see a ripening bruise on her cheek, and one of her eyes was puffed, half shut. "He found out about us. Half-killed me for it."

"That goddamn sonofabitch!" I was already lifting her, carrying her up to the bed. She still clung to the teapot, for she had a towel on the floor and had been putting hot dressings on her wounds. "His ring made the cuts," she said, and tried to smile. "West Point ring. Officer and gentleman." Then she began sobbing, her shoulders trembling and her fingers pressing my head against hers.

I put her under the covers and lit a candle so I could look. I wish I hadn't. He must have punched her out something awful, and there was a welt on her shoulder and more on her buttocks where he'd lashed her with his officer's quirt.

As gently as I could, I began dabbing the side of her face. She'd put Epsom salts in the hot tea water, to draw the pain away.

"When was it, darlin'?"

"After supper. He came down here and seemed pleasant enough. He didn't mind my renting this place, said it was better to be away from those jealous Army wives. He even wanted to go to bed with me, but just as we were starting up...."

"You were going to let him!"

"Patrick!" she cried, "You let him or he ravages you! Oh God, I despise him. I lied, said it was my female time. But even then he was tearing at my clothes, trying to see proof and..." she shook her head. "I didn't have to, thank God. Just then, a courier came rushing down from camp and was banging on the door."

"Courier? You mean with orders?"

"Yes. This is the night, Patrick. They're going to arrest Crazy Horse."

"Not without a fight, they ain't. I just ran here from the barracks. They've got three troops covering the Indian scouts. Trouble for sure. But Leah, that courier? What did he look like?"

She frowned. "Oh, a soldier, common sort. But I have seen him before, hanging around here with Deacon Lowery."

"That's the sonofabitch that saw me and fingered me, Leah. And got you hurt so bad. I'm sure sorry for doing this to you."

Her eyes flared. "Well, I'm not, Patrick. Oh God, I bless you for our times, and our future too. I'm free because of you, don't you understand?"

"Not hardly," I grunted. "First it was the courts-martial, and now we've got this fierce bastard stompin' the both of us. He's jugging me, in irons, and that's only the beginning."

She shook her head, and gently her fingers trailed down my cheeks. "It's our beginning, dear boy. It has to be now. We've got to go. Clear out of all of this."

"Go? Leah, where in hell to? And how? He's got us trapped just like Crazy Horse."

"That's exactly why it's our chance! If those Sioux start a fight, this post will turn upside down. Cupe, damn his hide, will have to stay with his men. But you won't. We'll be out and far away before they even miss us. Oh, Patrick, it's our freedom, it's everything we've longed for. Like the darkies used to sing, it's de hands of de Lawd, carrying his sinners home!" For the first time, she tried to laugh, wincing in the pain of her swollen face.

But where, though, and how, I said heavily. Sure, I wanted to go. I'd been aching for her. She was the only future I had, my chance to get out of the mess we'd made. But the idea of running hit something deep in my heart. Maybe it was what my Momma said: curse of the Irish, restless roamers, pissing in the fire and moving on.

But for all the doubts I had, Leah wouldn't hear them. She'd been Army long enough to know how the deserting trick was pulled off. First we'd need a good team and wagon. She had the money to buy it, with enough left over to get me some civilian duds at the sutler's store. When the Indian fight broke out, which could be any time in the next few hours, we'd light out for the railroad at Chadron, Nebraska. There was an eastbound train every day. She didn't know the exact hour, and they never ran on time anyway. We'd just wait in the dark station at Chadron until the cars pulled in, and we'd be gone.

East? I said. She smiled. Or south. Out of Chicago to Mississippi. She'd heard again from her brother. He even had a little cottage fixed up for us, and two new mules, to help with putting the cotton crop in. I says, "Do you think you'd be happy back there, Leah?"

She smiled. "With you, Patrick. All our lives. Please now."

I nodded and pushed up from the bed. When I kissed her and held her bruised face, she was giggling like a little girl putting one over on her father. When morning came, she'd fix up her face, go over to the sutler's store and get the wagon and duds. We arranged to meet the next dusk, where the creek crossed the road below the church tents. There was a heavy grove of trees there. I could hide out until she came for me.

By the time we'd planned all the details, it was dangerous to stay with her any longer. I slid out the window and down from the shed just as the first streaks of light touched the sky.

I dassent go back to the post, I knew that. The Army had a long memory. Shaw's order to put me in irons would still be on somebody's mind.

About nine in the morning, I was hungry as hell, so I drifted along the creek until I came to a few teepees and brush huts of Sioux loafers. These were Bad Faces who made a business of hanging around the post, scarfing up bones or crumbs. But an old squaw had a cookfire going, and a big pot on it smelled awful good. After I'd said a few words in Lakota and signed her, she thrust me a ladle and I swilled the soup. She was gumming me a grin in her toothless mouth. "Dig deep. Puppy in bottom."

Presently, some young Sioux horsemen came hurrying into the camp. They pretty much ignored me, but the excited way they were jabbering sure caught my attention. I edged close enough to pick up some of what they were saying. Apparently, the troops and scouts had hit Crazy Horse's camp at daybreak. There was almost a fight, but what pulled the fuse out of it was that Crazy Horse had either been warned or had a vision. Before the captors could nail him, he and his sick wife fled off on their ponies. According to the young Sioux riders, they'd made for the safety of Chief Spotted Tail's camp. Like old Red Cloud, he was also an uncle of Crazy Horse's, and Crazy Horse figured he'd be safe there. Sioux custom said, You can't turn out a fugitive if he comes in peace, and God knows, they had let me come in to them that way.

After I'd heard enough from the riders, I began worrying. Suppose there wasn't a fight. If Shaw just trotted home and surprised Leah in midst of her preparations, the rotten bugger would really tromp her this time. I almost wanted to duck back to her house and warn her, but by then, the loafers camp and the church tents beyond were crowded with Indians. In wagons, on horseback and pulling travois, Sioux seemed to be streaming to the post from many parts of the reservation. I asked the old squaw what was happening. Her eyes darkened, and she reached out and grabbed my Army blouse. "Go back to sojer! This Lakota people here!"

She hadn't but said it when I heard a sound behind me. I whirled at the sight of a corporal cocking his carbine. Behind him were three mounted troopers. "Don't I know you, Jacky?"

"Never seen you before," I grunted, "and it ain't Jacky."

"Is now," he said. "Sarge left word at the squad room. We been hunting you all morning."

Off swung the other troopers. Hell, they were on all sides of me, carbines cocked. The corporal grabbed one of my wrists, clicked a cuff on it, then twisted my arm behind me and got the other wrist.

"What in hell for?" I cried.

"Ask Major Shaw!"

"He ain't here. He's out with the troops."

"You'll be waiting for him, Jacky, when he gets home."

The end of the dream, I thinks, Crazy Horse and me, both running, but nowhere near fast enough.

The guardhouse was a bare pine shack at the edge of the parade ground. Beside it stood the Officer of the Day's shack, which I could see through the barred window. "Hell, man," I said to the corporal as he started to chain up the iron door, "I got no way out of this coop. At least take the damn cuffs off, will ya?"

He grunted something about having his orders, but I grabbed his arm. "The regs give me rights, too, mister. Officer of the Day has to approve my arrest."

"Ain't you the guardhouse lawyer, though! Allright, Jacky," he muttered, and snatched off my cuffs, "hang on the bars like an ape." I did just that, watching him stride off, and with him, my freedom.

There were two other soldiers in the narrow little hutch. One was a mean-eyed deserter, head shaved and a ball and chain on his leg. The other was a blond-headed, pimply-faced punk, didn't look sixteen, his eyes red with weeping. He was lying there moaning like a baby, knees up and cradling his iron cannonball against his belly.

When I asked the poor devils what they were in for, the shave-head deserter sneered: "You're in it with us, boyo. I was at Julesburg when they wiped out the post. Before this night is done, them reds are gonna torch this place and fry your balls!"

I figured he was just a malingering grouser, but as the long afternoon died away, I began hearing bugles up at the stables. Troops were mounting. A plume of dust raced across the parade ground, a team of artillerymen rattling past, dragging a light field gun.

I whipped to the other side of the guardhouse. Two troopers had just galloped up, hollering for the Officer of the Day. A young lieutenant banged out of the shack to meet them, and they began pointing to the east. From what I could make of it, the troops and Sioux scouts had hauled Crazy Horse out of Spotted Tail's camp. They were bringing him here on the double, and had promised that he could see General Crook.

"Impossible! He's gone to Wyoming," the lieutenant shouted. "Report to General Bradley, post commander. Tell him to send reinforcements, or I'll have to pull back to the barracks line!"

As the troopers swept off toward headquarters, I could feel the tension, hell, hear it. I ran to the other window of the guardhouse. Across the darkening parade ground, a black line was moving slowly toward us. Sioux, and not tame loafers either. Tall northern warriors, some with paint on their faces. They gripped their blankets tight around them, and it was my guess that they had enough rifles underneath to blow us to kingdom come.

On the fringes of the line, squaws were moving like dark ghosts, blankets pulled across their noses so all that showed was their glinting eyes. Even the Sioux kids, scurrying after them, weren't horsing or playing games. They were chanting low, the same Lakota words over and over again. "Tasunke Witko." The chant was Crazy Horse's name.

Down from the barracks clattered another column of troopers, but too few to hold back the tide moving toward us. An officer's whistle shrilled in the darkness. Somebody shouted, "No shooting, no weapons. Keep them back. Stand your ground here!"

Abruptly, several hundred yards from us, the Sioux line stopped, the ends of it curling in to surround us. No one moved or spoke. The only sound was the neighing of horses and the clink of weapons on Army saddles.

Then from behind the line came a God-awful cry, the wail of a single voice. "Tasunke Witko!" Like a black wave in the sea, the Sioux parted in a deafening roar. Moccasined feet began rubbing the dirt, then stamping it. They were moving toward us again, pressing close against a file of blue-coated Sioux scouts and a handful of grim-faced troopers, caught in the middle.

The scouts were screaming Lakota curses and jabbing their Springfields at the northern warriors who were crowding in on them. Then I saw why.

In the center of the file of scouts walked Crazy Horse. I didn't recognize him at first because he was dressed differently than at his camp. Now he was wearing a buckskin shirt and blue cloth leggins. But the way he walked hadn't changed, the pride of it, his head high and his motions quick and coiled as a panther set to spring.

In the roaring of the Sioux, I barely heard the hoofbeats of a horse flashing past the guardhouse door. When he careened to a stop in front of the Officer of the Day shack, I recognized the damn animal from his white back feet. Scipio Shaw's chestnut, and the bastard himself wheeling off him. "Officer of the Day!" he shouted, and the young lieutenant came flying out of the shack.

"Fix bayonets!" Shaw slashed his revolver at several troopers, and they came pell-melling toward the guardhouse, tearing their bayonets out of scabbards.

"One gun goes off here and we're all dead," Shaw shouted to

the lieutenant. "Hold the prisoner in your office!"

"Major, I can't! General Bradley has ordered him into the guardhouse!"

"Countermanded! He won't take that. He was guaranteed safety and a chance to talk!" Shaw whirled his chestnut. "Hold him where he is, then, keep the troops back. I'll drag Bradley down here myself!"

As Shaw spurred away, nobody knew what to do. A sergeant had run in from headquarters with orders to open the guardhouse for the prisoner. He ripped off the lock and banged back the iron door. I made a leap to get through, but a soldier slapped his bayonet against my chest.

His scared, ratty face was trembling, and luck was with me, for I remembered him. Gentles, a recruit who'd turned tail at the St. Pat's day fight. "Hey, lad," I cried, "if we could beat 'em at Crazy Woman fork, we can do it here!"

That calmed him enough to swing his bayonet aside and let me pass. "Guard this door," I said. "I'll try to talk sense to Crazy Horse."

The scouts had formed a tight knot around him, against the northern warriors shoving and wrestling to get through. Touch the Clouds, towering over all of us, hurled himself in like a battering ram, knocking down scouts and ripping rifles away. Little Big Man was holding Crazy Horse from behind, shoving him the last few yards to the guardhouse door. "You damn Judas, let him go!" I cried. Crazy Horse heard, his eyes snapping to me. With a lurch, I busted through to him, just as Touch the Clouds ripped Little Big Man off his back.

Crazy Horse seized my hands. "Kola!" he whispered. Friend.

"Three Stars!" I signed him. Wait. Talk to Three Stars! But the others were tearing at me, trying to get me loose, and I grabbed Crazy Horse by the wrists.

God almighty! I touched something hard in his buckskin sleeves. Knife, had to be! A knife hidden in each sleeve. Little Big Man flung me back. "Kill sojer! No belong here! Vamoose!" he spat, he and other scouts dragging Crazy Horse toward the guardhouse door. I ran around them, trying to get out front and stop them.

But Crazy Horse had already stopped. He was staring inside at the two soldiers in ball and chain. With the cry of fury, he whirled, ripping the knives from his sleeves, slashing Little Big Man across his wrist, blood spraying up.

The Officer of the Day was shoving in behind me. "Stop him! He'll get away!"

Scouts and northern Indians were flailing, hammering each other, Crazy Horse crouching ready and flashing the knives. Little Big Man leapt on him from behind, grabbed one of his arms and tried to snatch the knife. The Officer of the Day was shrieking. "Kill him! Kill the sonofabitch!"

Gentles lunged past me, Crazy Horse jumping aside, the bayonet crunching into the wooden door of the guardhouse. Little Big
Man had torn the first knife away and was going for the other one,
spinning Crazy Horse, holding him so that he couldn't move. "No!"
I cried, just as Gentles hurled a second thrust, and the bayonet
buried itself to the hilt in Crazy Horse's back.

There was no cry of pain. Just sudden, deathly silence. Crazy
Horse's face went gray. Stunned, he was looking at Little Big Man.
His lips moved. Kola? Had a friend done this? Slowly, he sagged to
the ground. I thrust in after him, but Touch the Clouds held me
back. He was staring at Crazy Horse's moccasins. Blood was running
into them, filling them.

Jesus God, exactly the vision he'd showed me, two days before!

The Officer of the Day was shouting: "Somebody. Pick him up!
Help this man!"

Crazy Horse's head was tilted back and he stared at the sky. He
whispered something to Billy Garnett, the young interpreter, who'd
rushed in and was kneeling beside him. "What is it, Billy?" I gripped
his shoulder.

He glanced up at me, his dark eyes smouldering. "He is saying,
'I think you have hurt me enough, my friends. Tell the people it's
no use to depend on me anymore.'"

"Ah, God," I whispered, and stumbled away.

A great cry rose from the hundreds of warriors, outrage roared
at the heavens. Squaws began hacking their hair and buckskins in
mournful death wails. Soldiers were running across the parade
ground, trying to get out of there before the powder keg blew.
More mounted troops were racing in. I thought I saw Shaw, leading
them, but I sure wasn't waiting to find out.

I ducked behind the Officer of the Day's shack and raced for
the post gate. Shots were booming across the parade ground, flat,
tinny cracks that sounded like makeshift Indian guns. Officers were
shouting to the soldiers: "Hold your fire!" One blast into that angry
mob, and those warriors would wipe out the whole garrison.

God Almighty, the futility of it! All the months of freezing and
clawing our way through fight after fight. To win what? Not peace,
only the bleached bones in butchered camps, ghosts wailing in the
graveyard we'd made of these forsaken plains. Captain Bloxham,
fumbling his brave cartridges out in the dirt, to go mad, blind and
alone, so that a pair of betrayers could live. It was all gone now,
ripped away like the knife that had stabbed into Crazy Horse's
back. The bugle calls to glory had murdered what they told us was
an enemy, yet he'd spared me and been my friend. What was it
for? I was sick of war and bloodshed. All I had left was Leah, run

140

free and start again, far from this world that was flaming away in the fires of hell.

The miracle was, in all the confusion, I not only found Leah, but the sweet brave thing was rarin' to go. Bought the new team and wagon and was whipping it up to her house just as I caught her. "Oh, Patrick! Thank God," she cried, and jumped off the wagon box into my arms.

For a few moments we just held each other and blessed the luck that had put us there. Even the sadness of the night was burning away, our high hopes healing the old wounds. Finally she laughed and said: "I declare, you're so worked up you haven't even noticed my traveling dress!"

"Hell I ain't! Best one you could have picked, darlin'!" It was the same gray riding suit she'd worn on our first night together, way back at Camp Connor. But now she had a straw hat on too, and was tying the scarf of it under her chin, so the wind wouldn't snatch it away.

When I dumped her two flowered valises in the back of the wagon, we were so footloose and carefree that we didn't even go back to shut the front door. "Let the wind blow through it!" I boosted her onto the wagon, hugged her narrow waist and up into her breasts, holding her bruised face and kissing her pain away.

We'd had a close shave all right. When she'd heard firing from the post, she knew the Indian fight was on, and it had to be now. She was praying me thoughts to run to her, so she wouldn't have to go alone to the bridge where we'd planned to meet.

"Well, I ain't here by much!" I told her about being jugged at the guardhouse. Only the coming of Crazy Horse and his shameful murder had set me free.

"Patrick," she said sharply. "You look so worried. Don't be. We're out!"

"I'm just watching them buggers." I pointed to Indians and white loafers streaming past us, heading toward the post gate. In the big church tents on the dark plain, there were lanterns going, and agitated Sioux swarming the ration tables, snatching what they could get. Some damn preacher was even playing an organ in the tent. More hymns, to settle the savage's souls. "Leah, too many folks here. We've got to get scarce. I ain't even changed into my civvy duds."

"They're in the back." She laughed, and waved her hand. "Your whole new life. Oh, go fast, Patrick!"

I whipped the team ahead, and barely heard a shout behind us. "Stop, I beg you! We need that wagon to move mission supplies to safety!"

I knew that voice and wished I didn't. When I whirled, Deacon Lowery was loping after us like a tall, flapping scarecrow, waving his arms.

"Wagon's under orders!" I shouted. "Army business!" And when the wheels rattled it away, I said, "Go to hell, you miserable bugger! Save somebody else's soul!"

We swept along the creek and finally away from the noise and consternation. The big dark cottonwoods that lined the road were flicking above us, their branches making a canopy with bright stars glinting through. "You picked a good team, Leah," I said, for I had the horses in a fast trot now and they never wavered.

"I picked the right driver. Just think of what a different ride this is than that last awful one with poor Clete."

"At least now, all the heathen are behind us, I hope." I was grinning, looking ahead, because we were rattling into the big thicket where the bridge was. You could hide an army in the darkness here, and never know that a soul was around.

Feeling so safe, I pulled the team up and we slowed, just before the bridge. "Oh, don't stop, Patrick. We've got a train to catch!" She was laughing, leaning back on the wagon box.

"Well darlin', you'll be happier without a stinkin' bluebelly beside you. I'll duck these duds and stash 'em in the stream. Then, if anybody stops us and asks questions, we're just ordinary, peaceable citizens, going out for a night on the town."

"I like honeymoon better, though I do despise that word."

I lifted her hand. "No ring, though."

"In God's eyes it is." She clung to me, and when I kissed her, I tasted her tears. Joy, it was.

I started to unbutton my Army blouse, fumbling with it, my fingers trembling and she saying, "Hurry, I can't wait to see you in civvies..."

Something splashed in the creek just below us. I'd barely whirled when I saw a streak of white. Blaze-face of a horse, big strapping chestnut. He'd come out of the brush on the other side of the creek, and now thundered up the bank beside us.

Scipio Shaw, breathing hard, leaned forward in the saddle and aimed a revolver at my chest. "Going someplace, soldier?"

"Cupe!" Leah cried, her hand clapping over her mouth.

"Surprised, are you? Well, what were you expecting? Maybe the next stud, something even more rotten than this immigrant tramp? When you wear him out, throw him into the ashcan." His twisted face sneered. "No, I'm the last lover back, Leah. Remember? The old one you sneaked with all those years to feather your own nest..."

"Cupe, stop this!" Leah cried.

He laughed harshly. "So you really thought you could pull it off?

I'm astounded. What did you think you were leaving behind? Some burned out staff officer or helpless cripple? I was running down Rebel bushwhackers in your foul swamps before you'd even soiled your pants with a man. So you and your clod from the barracks, do you think you could keep your trail from me? Deacon Lowery saw you, and if it hadn't been him, an army could have tracked your scent! Bitch in heat! Whore, with her newest son to raise, sucking the fire from her loins!"

"Cupe!" she screamed.

"Get out of that wagon! Both of you!"

I glanced at Leah, her face white, too frozen to move.

"Out!" A flash of flame, his revolver crashing a bullet over our heads, so close I could hear it hiss and the powder smoke stung my eyes.

Shaw was crazy wild, his lips trembling in rage. Gripping Leah's icy hands, I drew her across the wagon box and we got down, to stand in the dirt. Shaw's lathered chestnut was as twitchy as him, jangling his bit and throwing his head almost into my face.

Leah stared up at him. "All right, Cupe," she said hoarsely. "You have us. You've won. But just know this, I'm not going back with you. Not ever. When you struck me, you ended anything we might have had, and it wasn't much anyway. Over! Go your way, we'll go ours!"

He lashed out to seize her hand, pull it up against the livid pulp of his face. "Is it this?" he cried. "Feel it, whore! Kiss it!"

That I wouldn't take. I thrust against his horse to push him back. Shaw whirled and struck me on the side of the head with his revolver.

"You're under arrest! One more move and I'll shoot you like a dog. Desertion in face of the enemy, in time of war!"

Reeling back, seeing stars, I had a mind to rip the gun out of his hand, but Leah had already cut between us and was gripping Shaw's leg.

"Cupe, listen to me! Please, I beg you! Yes, we're running and yes, he's deserting, but don't you see, it's your way out, Cupe! You can save your career!"

"Don't you tell me what I can save, you tramp!"

She clutched his hand. "The court-martial! If Patrick's gone, there'll be no testimony against you. We'll both be gone and you'll be rid of us!"

His eyes squeezed shut and he rubbed the revolver barrel across them. "I'm not losing you," he said hoarsely. "Isn't this goddamn face enough suffering? Maybe I'm done for anyhow. The snobs on the staff, do they want to look at me? They're sickened by me. Career? What's that? They trash you tomorrow and let you die alone in an old soldier's home."

"Cupe," she pleaded, "I know how you feel, really I do. But you belong with troops. It's your life. You have to go on. They need you…"

Shaking his head, he dismounted slowly, reached out and took her face in his hands. "You're not getting away, Leah, not with your lying talk or your honeyed tongue. A deceitful bitch you are, but you're all I've got. I'll never let you go!" He whirled to me. "Walk, scum!"

His eyes were gleaming in pure madness. "Walk?" I echoed.

"Better yet, run!"

Ah, God, I saw it then. Running away from deserter's arrest, no court in the land would convict him for shooting me down. No way to stop him either, just the three of us out on that lonely bridge of death.

"I ain't runnin' for you or no man, Shaw!"

He fired the revolver at my feet, pebbles blasting, stinging my legs. Leah was screaming, "Cupe! No!"

"You've had your last warning, soldier!" He was lifting the gun to my face, and I knew he'd use it, just as I'd known His Lordship Cavan would. I leapt toward him, grabbing his arm, twisting at the gun as Leah sprung in to help me. The revolver blinded me, flash, roar and a sickening wet spray. Blood was in my mouth, on my face, Leah sinking away in the smoke. Half of her head was gone.

"Ah, Jesus God!" I screamed, falling on my knees to clutch at her, but the revolver clicked again behind my ear, the cylinder turning. "She had it coming!"

I roared up to strike the barrel just as it fired, slammed my fist into Shaw's face and reeled him. But the gun was still his. I flung myself under it, butted my head into his belly, and when he staggered, I snatched the revolver and fired the last three rounds into his face.

Then, choking for breath, I flung myself down in the dirt beside Leah, held her still warm flesh, and wept.

I don't know how long it was. Long enough to feel her go cold in the night chill. I couldn't think straight. I didn't even want to live, with her gone. So maybe it was lucky then, or God's mercy, that I heard distant hoofbeats pounding the road. If it was a patrol, and chances are that it was, I wouldn't last a minute out there in the middle of this bloody mess. An officer shot, a woman killed. Who would believe the word of a private, with blood and powder burns all over him?

I gripped Leah's hand, kissed her fingers and tasted her blood on my lips. Then I flung myself back down toward the creek, the way Shaw had come. But I stopped short, my better sense screaming warnings. Afoot, unarmed, I was a goner for sure. I whirled back, ripped off Shaw's gunbelt, and leapt onto his chestnut. The hoofbeats were racing toward me, but there was a bend in the road. What they were sure to see first was the empty wagon and the tragedy of the dead lovers. It would take time for them to sort it out, and I prayed that it would be enough time to let me go free.

Leave it to them! There was no more I could do for my Leah. Just remember. Hold her to me, for the rest of my life.

Tears running down my cheeks, I went crashing off through the underbrush, whipping past the giant cottonwoods, vines and briars snatching at me. God knows how long I fled, but when I finally stopped, the brave, strong chestnut stood trembling, heaving his flanks in exhaustion. He hadn't quit me. He never would. A thoroughbred, like her.

I was on a big hill of white rocks and scattered bones. Who died here? I wondered. And then I knew. It was me. A wild colonial boy, sobbing his dreams away with all the anguish of Job, until finally he'd have to stand erect and find the courage to face the lonely horizon. Go on, that was all. Alone, but at last, a man.

WANTED

For Desertion and Murder
of Major Scipio Shaw, 3rd U.S. Cavalry

PATRICK MALACHY KELLY

Private, deserted 3rd U.S. Cavalry,
Fort Robinson, Nebraska Territory,
September 7, 1877

Description: 6'4", eyes blue, hair black,
age 22 years. Has Ireland accent but can read
and write. May be armed, dangerous. Last seen
heading for Arizona Territory or Old Mexico.

Report his presence to nearest
U.S. Provost or Peace Officer.

REWARD: $10,000 U.S. Dead or alive.
If dead, must show proof of corpse.

WITH THE RENEGADES

For the next nine years, I was on the lam in old Mexico.
By September of 1885, I was thirty years old, and a far different man than the lad who had fled from Mayo so long before. In truth, not a lad ever again. My years of running and slaving to survive in Mexico had baked my skin as hard as an armadillo, dusted my black beard with the first streaks of gray, and burned a lifelong squint in my eyes from the desert sun.

In the fierce flaming deserts and mountains where I prowled to eke out a living, you'd either habla in Spanish or starve, and when I worked the silver mines in Sonora, there were enough renegade Apaches and Yaquis on my crews that I had to savvy a smatter of their tongues, or the brigands would have slit my throat in the dark.

Staying alive was all that counted in those years. And, more important, staying scarce where no lawman or bounty hunter could ever track me down. Hell, I even shoved coal on ships out of Guaymas.

Near the pueblo of Bavispe in eastern Sonora, I'd hooked onto an Apache band and was sellin' the furs they trapped. They give me one of their girls, Nah-thle-tla, a sulky, wild little thing. I took to calling her Nati, like "nothing," but she kept me good company. On account of her, my negocio for the furs turned into a right smart business. Month after month, she'd snake me up secret trails in the Sierra. I had a horse for myself, a mule for her and three more pack mules trailing behind. Bringing in presents and tradin 'em for hides in the strongholds of the various bands.

The Apaches then in the Sierra were runners from the reservations. San Carlos, White Mountain, Fort Apache in Arizona Territory, and Warm Springs and Mescalero in New Mexico Territory. When we'd come on a band of them, in rocky, fortified hideouts, I blessed my luck for having Nati at my side.

The bucks were as wary as pumas, and as quick to strike as a rattlesnake. Hell, they'd been running from troops and Mexican rurales for years now. They knew every rock and spring in that scorching wasteland of jagged peaks. They even knew where the other scattered bands were, though they had precious little contact with them. So when we'd barge in on them and start our parleying for trade, more than once I had my heart in my throat.

The wiry devils went around naked except for a breechclout and leggins. Most had headbands around their long black hair. Sometimes they tied sticks and leaves into the headband, so you could walk by them and think it was just a bush. And arms, God almighty, they had the finest shiny new Winchesters and Colt revolvers that any frontiersman could hope for. They'd killed for these guns, lashing up into Arizona or New Mexico, burning ranches, plundering freight outfits.

Many times, Nati and I had run onto Geronimo. Once when we came to his stronghold, the rocky knob high in the Sierra looked like it had been hit by a cannon shell. Apaches were sprawled everywhere, and Geronimo so drunk, he was writhing and clinking around in a litter of smashed mescal bottles. Nati got him to explain that they'd just looted the town of Huachinera, below Bavispe, and emptied the cantina of everything the poor dead Mexicans had.

I told Nati to brew up some strong coffee, and she doused it with some kind of herb. We trickled it into Geronimo's mouth until he finally retched it all out and purified.

Then, the horny goat plopped his dear relative, Nati, in his lap, squeezed and fondled her, and started talking. God Almighty, what a talker! Many of the Apaches had no use for him, saying he was a thief and murderer, robbing them of living a soft, cushy life on the reservations. But others were cowed by the slippery brigand, and you could understand why when you sat face to face with him, the campfire flickering hate and treachery in his scowling eyes.

He had 25 fighters in his band, a few being old, trail-wise coyotes, but the majority were young hotbloods who had no fear of U.S. troops. As for Mexicans, Geronimo spat: "Even alone, I can kill all the cabrones in this valley. You think I lie?"

I just shrugged and let him orate on. He'd stomp around the campfire, telling how wronged he'd been all these years. When he was a boy, the treacherous Mexicans had lured his people into Janos, Chihuahua and slaughtered them, including his mother and father. Then came the Americans, robbing the Apache of their ancestral homes. "Now your soldiers say, this Crook, Nantan Lupan says, be farmer, Geronimo. Here, a wagon, a mule, make little corn patch! Ayyy! What does Apache know about woman's work on a farm? We have never planted a seed since the beginning of time!" He leapt toward me with a scream, and for sure I thought he'd cut my throat.

Well, nothing come of it. His bucks didn't trade much, robbing and killing being more to their liking. After they lit out for a raid in Sonora, Nati and I spent more months prying hides out of the closer bands.

Finally I says, "The hell with this running around like a ground squirrel. I'm settling in one place."

I'd wheedled out a gold claim about ten miles northwest of Bavispe. It lay on a tawny mountainside, a pretty little place with an old adobe beside the shaft where the last miner had got his throat cut by Apaches.

When I moved Nati inside, you'd think she'd treasure having a roof over her head, but oh no, not that wild one. First thing she does is build a wickiup out back and sit there sulking.

She was weeping for her people. Always they had lived together and traveled together. Life was meant to be roaming, never staying put.

"Well, we are now, dearie," I tells her. "I'm sick of beating my way up these trails to the clans. They can jolly well lug their hides down here to me. Nobody'll see 'em out here, no rurales or gringos."

"It is not good to be alone," she pouted.

"Ah, your stinkin' damn relatives, I'm sick of 'em. Give 'em up, will you?" The trouble with Apaches, they were so damn inbred and suspicious of each other, they'd walk 50 miles just to peer in on one of their relatives. Spy out what he was doing, in case he was getting something they weren't. "We stay here alone, you help me fix this place up, and you'll be seeing more than enough of your people, believe me. They'll beat a track to us."

Two days later, they did.

————

They struck us in the middle of the night, slit the throat of my camp watchdog so I had no warning. Strong hands jerked me up from my sleeping mat. I could smell Apache, hear them cursing me, Nati screaming in fright. Then somebody struck a match, flamed up my kerosene lamp and I saw a ring of Winchester muzzles pointing at me. The men gripping them were the finest killers the U.S. Army could recruit from the Apaches.

Ah, what proud, saucy bastards they were, knowing they were protected by their blue troopers coats. A surly brute named Kaytennae even had sergeant stripes on his sleeves.

All these years, all this way, only to end up trapped by these devils. I ripped their hands off me and shouted in Apache, "Cabrones! You've got no right breaking in on a man! I'm no Mexican you can kick around like a dog. Look at my woman! You'll kill her in fright. Now clear out of here, the lot of you!"

Kaytennae's lips twisted in a sneer and he said in bad American, "You talk Apache just like Mexican prisoner. But you not one of us. Just for trade, robbing. We know what you do, man. Mexican tell us. So we got plenty business you." He swung on Nati and cursed her in Apache, calling her a cut-nose white man whore, selling out her own people. "You know so much, you gonna show us where Geronimo is hiding like coyote!"

Nati spat in his face, and then they really started slapping her around. She fell, knocking over the pots on the stove. Tussling with them, my head whacked an earthen olla hanging from the eaves, shattered it and water showered down on all of us.

"Bastante!" A voice cracked like a whip. The Apache scouts

whirled. A tall man stooped to enter the adobe. "Well, what do we have here?" he said quietly.

"Gringo. American man," Kaytennae grunted.

"Yes, I can see that."

What I could see, and it chilled me, was a pair of dusty cavalry boots that must have been size 14. The tall legs were in torn canvas hunting pants, above them an Apache buckskin jacket with a rusty silver captain bar pinned crooked on one shoulder. Stunned, I looked at his face, the stubborn jaw, wide forehead and unflinching gray eyes. Cool courage that I'd never forget, and, God help me, maybe he hadn't, either.

He was so tall he couldn't stand straight inside the low adobe, so he squatted down and stared at me. Finally he said, with a trace of a smile, "A prisoner coming home, wasn't it? Only you were running from the Sioux then, if I remember. Am I mistaken, soldier?"

"Ten damn years," I whispered.

"Private Kelly, wasn't it?"

No point lying, he had me dead to rights. "Yessir, 'fraid so." I tried to grin. "I see it's Captain Crawford now."

He nodded. "Eventually. And what are you, Kelly?"

"Gettin' by."

"But you're not, though. Come outside." He cricked up and I followed him into the darkness. We stood looking at the dark skeleton timbers of my mine stope and the yellow mountains lit by the stars. "Some of my scouts understand English, and they don't have to hear this. You were a good soldier, you served well. Why did you do it?"

"Sir?"

His face hardened. "I campaigned many years with Cupe Shaw. He had his faults, plenty of them, but in this Army, an enlisted man doesn't kill an officer and live."

"The bastard give me no choice, sir!"

"That's what they all say, Kelly."

"Mine was different. Major come after me because I was loving his lady. Captain Bloxham's wife."

"Leah?"

"Yessir. And a good woman, gone bad."

He sighed and turned from me. "I'm not judging her, soldier. I knew her for many years. I'm not saying it couldn't happen, but I find it hard to believe."

"Sir," I said and seized his arm. "I have killed two men in my life, one on the Other Side, and him, Shaw, that set me fleeing. But I ain't no muderer. With the both it was them or me. If you don't believe that I got a side to it," I blurted, hoarse by now, "I even wrote it down. I got it all in a diary book."

"Where?"

I jerked my head at the adobe.

"Get it," he said, "and anything else you're going to need. You won't be coming back here. The scouts will bring your woman along. They say she's connected to Geronimo."

"Him and most of 'em. It helps me buyin' hides."

When I returned to him with the diary book, my rifle and a few duds, the Apache scouts already had poor Nati roped and tied like a hog. They were going to drag her after them, and I shouted: "Turn her loose, you beggars! She'll stay with me. She's not going anyplace."

The scouts sneered me aside until Captain Crawford thrust in. "Put her on a horse," he said, "tie her to the pommel." Then he took the diary from me and thrust it in his own saddlebag.

"Where are you taking me, sir?"

He swung onto his horse in one tall step like he'd done that afternoon I came in from the Sioux. "We're camped upstream from Bavispe. First time I saw you, Kelly, you demanded to see General Crook. Well, you'll get your chance now and wish you hadn't."

"He's down here?"

"He's been here on and off since 1883. It's a mystery to me why we haven't turned you up before now." He pointed at a guvmint horse and told me to mount.

"And Captain Bourke? It wouldn't be that he's around?"

"You're riding his horse."

"Don't tell me," I sighed, "the same old Rosebud bunch."

"You make it a full house, trooper. You better hope that you can show us a good hand."

He jerked the reins on my horse, and we started down the hill. Mother Mary, all my years of running, only to end up right back where I'd begun.

Captain Crawford led me some miles through rocks and cactus until we finally reached Crook's temporary camp above the Bavispe river. Sorry place. The Apache scouts had flung up a few wickiups, and the white officers were living under canvas shelter halves, and mostly getting soaked from the miserable rains that were beginning.

It was still dark when Crawford brought me there and set me down beside a big split rock which was going to be my jailhouse. Though he didn't say as much, I knew damn well I was under the keeping of the sergeant, Kaytennae, and a big-headed Apache corporal they called Dutchy, supposedly because he looked German. To me, he was just another cutthroat from the stripe of Little Big Man.

After Crawford had gone off to an Army mess tent that at least had the glow of a fire in it, I hunkered in the mud by the rock and tried to keep the rainwater out of my neck. Before I knew it, Dutchy had twisted a hair lariat around my feet. I cussed him in Apache, saying what in hell was the matter with him? I wasn't going noplace. Then I peered around in the gloom and there was no sign of Nati. "What have you done with my woman?"

They told me to shut up, not white-man business.

I hunched there most of the night, building a red-mad anger until I could have ripped out the throats of the lot of them. But why try? They were treating me like another caught deserter. Besides, there must have been 60 well-armed Apache scouts in that camp. I didn't have a chance of getting loose, and they knew it. The only white men around seemed to be Crawford and maybe a couple of other junior officers. But as dawn started to break, I saw a bearded, shiftless-looking gringo, slogging his way into the rope remuda where the mules were corraled. I could spot that man anyplace, for he was a true frontier type. Tom Moore, chief packer for General Crook.

"Mister Moore!" I hollers. After he was done sorting his mules, he came over to me, stared at my tied legs and shook his head. Then he cut his chaw of tobacco and give me a quarter. "Well, ain't this a sorry squaw man. You'd a done better with a Sioux woman, I'm thinking."

"You ain't far wrong, Mr. Moore. I'd have done better than to be anyplace but where I am now."

"Reckon. Army swings a wide loop, soldier. But looking at it one way, you'll be getting outa this forsaken desert and into more habit-able regions."

"How is that now?"

"Way I hear, Captain's having me ship you across the line on the next mule train I send to Fort Bowie."

My heart sank. "Look, Mr. Moore," I said earnestly, "I done what I done, ain't denying it. I was just hoping, though, to talk to the General, or if not him, Cap'n Bourke."

"Matter of findin' 'em." Moore arched a spit of tobacco toward the rocky mountains, amber in the first gleam of sun. "Up there is the General, Captain too, hunting turkeys or whatever. Do they fig-ure to be in today, Tom?"

A sharp-faced man in a gray civvy suit had come up beside him. He wore a felt hat which he took off, wrung the water out of it, and put back on his balding head. When he turned to me, he smirked in a way I didn't like and sure didn't trust. "So you claim to know the General?"

I nodded. "Served with him, Rosebud. Mr. Moore too."

"How long have you been bedding Apache women?"

"Long enough, if it's any of your business."

"Don't smart me, soldier. I'm Tom Horn, chief of scouts here under Captain Crawford. I speak more Apache than you'll ever

152

learn, and that little bitch of yours isn't telling me the truth."

"Well, you ain't gonna scare it out of her, mister, if that's your idea. Where have you got her?"

Without answering, he turned and strode off, grunting orders in Apache to the few scouts stirring out of their wickiups.

Presently, Kaytennae flung me some old stale bacon, hardtack and a tin cup of coffee. It galled me, having to sit there among the Apaches like a camp mongrel, while the white officers were up and messing at the big tent. Then my hopes lifted, for there were two new men among them. First off, I recognized Captain Bourke. He was wearing an old pith helmet and had a blanket wrapped around him. The other man was handing Mr. Moore the reins of his mule, then his guns and a brace of turkey. He was dressed in khaki hunting pants and shooting coat, and just from the slow, almost tired way he went into the tent, I knew that General Crook was back.

The rainstorm got worse as the morning progressed. Hours later when my belly was aching for food again, Tom Horn slogged up through the mud, jerked his head at Kaytennae, who undid the lariat around my ankles. "On your feet," Horn said, "or have you been playing skylark so long, you don't take orders?"

"From them with the power to give 'em," I snapped. Horn shoved me through the flap into the mess tent.

The rain was drumming the canvas in earnest now, the tent so dark it had to be lit by a Mexican kerosene lamp hanging from a pole. Beneath the flicker of light, General Crook, in a long underwear top and his hunting pants, was sitting crosslegged on an Apache blanket. He was spreading the wings of a black and orange bird and pinning them to a slab of wood. I'd heard tell, years back, that he hobbied by taxiderming the fowl he shot. As I watched, he was dusting the bird with preserving powders.

He was so busy at it that he gave no notice of me standing there, stiff as a ramrod. A voice behind him said, "Well, soldier, since the last time we met, it looks like you've lost your lucky shamrock." I glanced over and saw Captain Bourke, lying on canvas with an Indian blanket keeping him warm. On it, I saw my open diary book. He put it down, peeled back the blanket and got to his feet. "But I will say, as a struggling diarist myself, you didn't leave all your blarney on the Other Side."

I felt my face burning red. "What I wrote, sir, was how I seen things, crude no doubt, but I stand behind it."

"Bourke," Crook exclaimed, his eyes flashing as he glanced up from his bird. "This was a damn lucky shot. A single cock, off by himself in the sacaton, and what does he turn out to be but a Sonoran Masked Bobwhite. Look at the mask on him. Perfect! Black as a hangman's hood, and the orange breast of the male.

Exactly fits the pamphlet from the Natural History people in New York. Coronado's quail, creature of the Sonoran desert grassland. Just what the hell was he doing 8000 feet up in the mountains, east of the Chihuahua line?"

Bourke smiled. "Quite a traveler, I daresay."

"Not anymore," Crook grunted, and admired the bird, pinned now to the wood slab like Jesus on the Cross. "That's what we're going to do to you, Kelly. Clip your wings."

My shoulders slumped, realizing he'd finally spoken to me, and not liking the sound of it one bit. "Normally, when I meet a veteran of one of my campaigns, I put my arm around him or at the least shake his hand. I thank the men who have been under fire with me. The little I saw of you back in the Sioux days, you served well. But this nonsense you've put down in there..." he nodded toward my diary, "what's it going to gain you? What purpose?"

"Well, sir," I fumbled, "I wasn't figuring on nothing. Just keeping myself company, you might say."

"With lies? More frontier pulp?"

"I told what I saw. I was hoping the General would remember."

"Every man, soldier, has a different sieve through which he screens the truth. You put in there that you warned me about Crazy Horse, and I didn't listen. I was like—I think you said—a stone." I gulped and by now my face was boiling. "Did it ever occur to you that I wanted to end that fight before it began? And after it was finished, and Crazy Horse was tricked into surrendering by my superiors, that I tried my damndest to get fair treatment for him?"

He pushed up wearily. "So a good man is dead, and more are going to die down here. A rotten job, Kelly, but mine to do. I regret losing good soldiers like you. Men who don't quit." He turned to Bourke. "Send him to Bowie, court-martial for the murder of Major Shaw. Dismiss."

"But sir...?" I pleaded.

"Out. You chose your way. I don't shake hands with killers."

"But you bloody all are!" I shouted, and both of them whirled to me for the insubordination of it.

"Mind your tongue, soldier," Bourke warned.

"Kill or be killed is what the Army means, and there ain't no justice to it. General, you seen what I wrote. Shaw had to get rid of me. If I told the truth about Captain Bloxham at the court-martial, I could finish the Major's career and he knew it. And sure, I did wrong with Mrs. Bloxham, God knows, maybe I shouldn't have done it, but I loved her."

"An officer's wife?" Crook said coldly.

"She come to me, sir, and I'll not blame her neither. Shaw was whacking her around. In truth, man to woman, I had as much right to her as he did. Don't that give me a side to it?"

"Take your word against a dead officer's?" Crook echoed and shook his head. "I wouldn't have a command left, Kelly, if I operated that way."

"Seems to me, sir, you ain't got much of a command here, or you would have caught Geronimo before now." Crook's face hardened but I blundered right on. "General, when I warned you about Crazy Horse before the Rosebud, you wouldn't listen, so I'm begging you to hear me this time. I've been with these Apaches, Geronimo too, know how they think, and they're laughing at you. You can spend the rest of your days killing off bluebellies in these miserable rocks and you won't bring the wily devils to heel. Call me deserter, killer or whatever you want, but with me, you might have a chance to put an end to this. My Apache girl, Nati, is a favorite relative of Geronimo's. She can lead you to his hideout anytime she chooses. And if not her, I can."

"You picked yourself the wrong squaw, soldier," Bourke answered. "Horn's questioned her, so has one of her uncles, the scout Tsoe. She spits in their faces. No cooperation whatsoever."

"Then leave her out of it. I know the trails, General, better than your damn scouts, because I've been traveling 'em all these months."

Crook glanced at Bourke with a faint flicker in his eyes. "Am I hearing this correctly, Captain? A soldier asking for amnesty from the prior charges of desertion and murder?"

"Highly unusual, sir," Bourke answered. "But then again, this is an unusual war. A long way from anyone, mostly from regulations."

Crook nodded. "So who would know?"

"And whoever might," Bourke added quickly, "would have long forgotten if the General brings Geronimo and company across the line."

Crook sighed. "No, too much of a gamble. Kelly, yes, in your case, there are a few extenuating circumstances. You have provided me certain intelligence in the past, as regards Crazy Horse's intentions before the Rosebud, and prior to his assassination. That sets you a little apart from the ordinary court-martial criminal. But in no way can I as a general officer waive charges against you." He looked at me keenly. "Do you understand that?"

"I'm wishing I didn't, sir, but I suppose I have to."

"You have to. Let me make this crystal clear. Even knowing these terms, are you are willing to join this command, and risk your neck, for nothing except court-martial at the end?"

His words fell heavy upon me, but for some reason, I found myself half-smiling. "Well, sir," I whispered, "when an Irishman comes over from the Other Side, he ain't got a pot to piss in to begin with, and if he don't have nothing at the end, he's no worse off, is he? So, it's gambling, General. If I get myself killed up in this Sierra, trying to help you, it ain't much different than dying from a firing squad. The only thing that comes between is like you said, Captain Bourke. It's holding onto a shamrock, no matter how the race ends."

"The luck of the Irish," Bourke said. "We're all gambling on it, for we have damn little else."

By that time, I hadn't noticed, but Captain Crawford had stooped to come into the tent. Crook turned to him. "I'm giving you another pair of eyes and an Apache tongue, Emmet. You know the man."

"Well, I've brought him home twice already," Crawford said with a faint smile. "I suppose we can risk a third shot at it." He jerked his head at me. "Get a mule from Tom Moore, soldier. Two hundred rounds of ammunition. We leave at dark."

When I went out of the tent, I was practically flying, soaring there in the freedom of it, and yet lying to myself. Free, hell, the noose was still around my neck. God alone knew how I could ever shuck it off.

Only a few days later did Captain Crawford hint to me that wise old Crook had been planning to use me all the time. He and Bourke had scared me into volunteering to go, counting I suppose that I'd be too feisty proud ever to quit while there was a ray of hope left.

It was up to me now to track Geronimo to his end, trade his life for mine. It was a bad hand going in, but the only one I had left to play.

CURSE OF THE SIERRA MADRE

Of all the soldiering I ever did, I prayed this would be my last campaign. One thing for sure. It was the worst.

From the eleventh of December, 1885, to the tenth of January, 1886, a pitiful handful of us slogged our way up into the worst hellhole in Creation: Espinosa del Diablo, the Devil's Spine, a rocky blood-red wilderness of fortress after fortress, dark canyons slashing down several thousand feet, and scorched peaks above them over 11,000 feet tall. From their hideouts up here, and watching us every minute of the way, were fifteen Apache bucks, 33 squaws and 29 children. Seventy-seven all told.

Against them, Crook's command was hurling God knows how many thousand troops and Apache scouts, if you counted such small columns as ours moving like ants up the Sierra from Chihuahua and Sonora, and down from Arizona and New Mexico Territories. More troops were guarding the lonely passes on the border, and still more playing watchdog on the Apache reservations of San Carlos, Fort Apache and Mescalero.

But numbers alone couldn't describe what this war truly was: a blood hunt against proven killers. The little band that was our target included not only Geronimo but the last of the great Apache war leaders: Chihuahua, Natchez, old Nana and Magnas. When they busted out from the agencies and started this mess, by Crook's own words in his report to General Sheridan, they had "traveled not less than 1200 miles, killed 38 people, captured and wore out 250 horses—with the loss of one fighting man."

Against these, our little gang under Captain Crawford had about 50 Apache scouts, and for white men, Lieutenant Marion Maus and William Shipp, both West Pointers, Tom Horn and yours truly. To say we were outnumbered didn't tell the half of it. We were tracking the canniest, most vicious savages left on the continent. Hell, they had to be, just to have survived all the troops chasing them for all these years.

Ah, hell, I knew some of their trails all right, but by the second night out, when the lashing rains hadn't let up, all the trails turned to mud, and the dead campfires they'd used were ashes bleeding into the arroyos. Crawford and Horn too wanted to keep us on mule back to cover this hellish country quicker, and also to keep our extra ammunition and grub with us. But many a time when I'd kneel and stare up some devilish slope, I knew full well we couldn't ever get to where our quarry was, crouching on the top.

I says, "Mr. Crawford, I've been up that thing, maybe a month back. No way to do it except hoofin' it. Better to leave the mules camped here below."

He didn't believe me. In the dark we started up that awful cliff face, our mules clicking on a trail about two inches wide. We couldn't use torches or fire, lest the hostiles see, and we couldn't see a yard in front of our eyes, with the rain slashing down. I hear a cry and then a pitiful bray, crashing and screaming down the rocks. We lost two mules that night, and three the next, trying to do the same thing.

Finally, sitting hunched on the crest with water running down his handsome face, Crawford muttered, "We're afoot, Kelly."

I nodded. "About the only way, sir."

When we located the camp that I knew was on the top, it appeared that the hostiles had run out of there while we were still going up. You would think, Well, we have a fresh trail, so we'll just follow them higher. But it didn't work like that. An Apache could run 50 miles a night through those mountains, while we'd still be panting, trying to catch our breath.

In the steady rain, discouragement soon set in. Alone in this savage land, we were wet, scared animals, fighting for life. Some of our scarce ammunition was already lying among broken mule carcasses on the bottom of arroyos we couldn't even get down to. Climbing steadily on rocks day and night, our apache leggins were torn apart. Much as our scouts tried to patch them, the rain made the rawhide swell and tear. Finally, most of us were going barefoot and with empty bellies because we couldn't cook for fear the hostiles would see our fires. So it was hardtack, raw bacon, rainwater swilled out of holes in the rocks.

Day and night like this. Crawford never quit, and wouldn't let me, much as I cursed the senselessness of it. Worried about the condition of his men, Crawford ordered me to cut a crippled mule's throat, and we tore into the beast while his blood was still warm. Dutchy, the scout, grunted bitterly, "No damn good, mule carry white-man all day, now eat him. Bad sign."

Maybe so, but we were wearing out fast. Then, in the first light of daybreak next morning, I happened to turn my head and gaze down into a canyon far below us. Wet fog was running here, but through a patch of it, I saw something moving. Buckskin color. Maybe a deer? But deer was darker than that. This could only be a tanned hide worn by an Apache.

I scurried over to Crawford and told him what I'd seen. By then, the fog was coming in heavier and I couldn't show him anything. "If I've got the right canyon, Captain, and I ain't sure," I said, "there's a trail down below that they use. I was on it with my woman a while back."

"Every one you say you've been on before has led noplace,"

Horn grunted.

"Didn't ask you, Horn. I'm asking the captain. If I could slip down there, sir, maybe I can pick up fresh sign, even if I don't run onto anybody."

"If you do," Crawford answered quietly, "we're not going back to pull you out, Kelly."

"Yessir, I understand. But ain't it worth a try?"

"Help yourself, soldier," he said, and slapped me on the shoulder as I left.

I went over the cliff, and hunching and slicking through the protection of the fog, started scaling down that fierce canyon, taking care not to loosen any rocks that might give me away.

By the time I reached the bottom, I was so badly used up that when I saw a little stream in the arroyo, I lay beside it and let the water run over my face. Fast water it was, clunking stones in the streambed as it ran. I'm thinking, Now ain't that a pretty sound, like frogs croaking.

I'd pulled off my hat, which was a tattered Mexican straw, and set it on a rock. Thuck!

I sprung up to see my hat kiting away with an arrow through it. Not twenty feet from me was an Apache, grinning mean, his tiny bow raising with another arrow ready to fly. "Cabron!" I cried, swinging my Winchester, and then he was laughing, and me, too. Apache joke, winging my hat when it could easy have been me. Hell, he was a kid, maybe eight, ten years old. One of Nati's damn relatives, and who was sitting in a patch of maguey cactus just behind him but my little bronze lady herself.

"Well, ain't you the one!" I breathed. I strode over to her, gripped her hard little hands and jerked her to her feet.

"I came to you, husband," she said in Apache. "Now I suppose you will beat me." The Apaches were a physical lot.

"I ought to, curse your hide." But damn, it felt good to feel her body again. I stood there hugging her and patting her tight butt under the buckskin. Hers was the dress I must have seen from way above. "How did you know where I was?"

"I follow you."

"But they had you prisoner?"

She giggled, nodding at the tyke. "Kazshe, my little cousin, has big knife."

The kid pulled a ten-inch pig sticker from his breechclout belt and showed it to me gleefully. "Apache don't stay prisoner for white man."

"You're going to now, you mean little bugger." I tousled his black shiny hair. Next thing I knew, Nati had pulled me down and was sitting on my lap. Family reunion, you might say, and after a month of sweating up rockslides with the bluebellies, I loved the feel of her.

Then, sure enough, she went back to her old tricks, and began pouting and scolding me for leading the soldiers up here, against the People.

"I have to," I said. "If I don't, they'll kill me."

Her lip trembled. "My man would be dead?"

"As a stone. No more furs, no more house for you. Nothing."

"No. We stay with Geronimo. All of us. He takes care of the people."

"Where is he?"

Her eyes narrowed and she shrugged.

I slapped her, not hard, across the cheek. "Your husband asks you where!"

Her head lowered, and finally I wormed it out of her that Geronimo, Natchez, Chihuahua, the whole lot of them, were camped on a big rocky plateau several miles from where we were sitting.

"You're a good wife," I said, and kissed her. "Someday, when this is over, maybe we'll live in the canyons, have plenty of fine dresses. Kazshe will be with us, too, The People living as one."

"Oh, yes, that is how it is meant." She was giggling again, saucy, hiking her buckskin dress up her thighs like she wanted me to bed her down right there in front of Kazshe, God and everybody.

"Not now, Nati. First we're going up the mountain to talk to the big soldier. He's a good man. You take him to Geronimo and we'll have peace."

"Soldiers kill us," Kazshe whimpered, and Nati began to waver.

"Look, woman, the both of you. If the soldiers wanted to kill us, they would have done it back at camp when they had us prisoners."

Her eyes lowered. "I want my husband, that is all."

"You got him, dearie." I gave her another hug and a bite of tobacco that she popped into her mouth. Then I led them back up the steep canyonside. Hours it took, clawing our way on the narrow trail. It was almost dusk when we neared the top, and I saw the glint of fieldglasses watching us from the rocks. Captain Crawford. Maybe he wouldn't have come down to rescue me, but sure as hell he wasn't going to abandon me either. I thanked that man.

What a sorry sight the command was, scattered there in a jumble of boulders, cholla cactus and big-eared green nopales. You couldn't turn around without pricking yourself on something. After a month of what we'd been through, even the hard-bitten Apache scouts were showing wear. Some were rubbing cactus oils on their bleeding feet, and others were sprawled out sleeping wherever they fell. Lieutenant Maus, a powerfully built officer, had had the sleeves ripped out of his Army blouse, and his craggy face and handlebar moustache was so caked with dust he looked like a rock with whiskers. Tom Horn's gray civvy suit was hanging in tatters, and the sun had fried his fair skin. Only Captain Crawford had come through it with any military bearing left. He had a cartridge belt with a U.S. buckle cinched around his buckskin jacket, and one silver double bar still hanging loose on the shoulder. He handed me a piece of hardtack from his belt, and I suspect it was his last.

Horn had pushed to his feet, squinting at Nati and the boy. "Well, Kelly," he said grudgingly, "I've got to hand it to you, you weren't seeing ghosts. Will the little bitch talk now?"

"Not to the likes of you," I snapped, seeing that he was already trying to lord it over her. He snatched the bow from the terrified kid and broke it over his knee.

I whirled to Crawford. "Captain, if you want to get anything out of my woman, keep this bugger offa her! Them, too." I nodded at the scouts who were crowding in, threatening Nati about how she got loose from the rear guard camp, and did she kill any of the People?

Crawford shooed them away like a bunch of cackling chickens. Then he, Lieutenant Maus, Nati and I went off by ourselves and squatted in the gloom of dusk. She smoothed the earth clean and with her finger traced a trail that led around the end of the arroyo and up to the rock fortress where Geronimo was supposedly camped.

Crawford sliced Nati a big cut of tobacco, and let her swill his canteen. "Well, Kelly," he said with a faint smile, "if God's in his heaven, we might just have them this time."

"I sure hope so, sir. It's been a hell of a trip if we don't."

He pushed wearily to his feet. "I thank you for going into that canyon. So will the General." He turned to Maus. "Issue extra ammunition. If the terrain favors us, I want to surround the camp, so nobody gets out. If not, it'll have to be a straight frontal attack."

Maus swung his hard face to me. "Squaws and children in there? How many? Ask her." I did, and Nati signed a bunch. "Maybe 80, 90."

"Nuisance," Maus grunted. "Hard to avoid killing them in the dark."

"Do your best, Marion," Crawford said. "I want prisoners, not bodies."

By then, night had fallen. The scouts were already streaking their faces in hideous paints, and wiping their knives and Winchesters clean of dust so that they were gleaming in the starlight. I says to the Captain, "Nati's our ticket in, sir, and I don't want them cutthroats to hurt her in the excitement of it."

Crawford glanced at me, with a strange smouldering look in his deepset eyes. "It's not every soldier who would say that, Kelly. Care about a squaw."

"Well sir, she's the only one I got."

He nodded. "I know. I feel the same. What remarkable people

161

they are. These scouts, good God, their loyalty to us, the suffering they've gone through, getting us here. Finest troops I've ever had. Take Kaytennae, the scout sergeant. When I was down here with the general in '83, that man fought us like a tiger. A real killer. For his crimes, the general sent him to Alcatraz. And brought him back a year later, to be the best soldier we have. So one minute, you do your best to exterminate them, and the next, love them." He sighed. "It's a strange, mixed-up world, son. Find yourself an extra bandolier. Take us there, and maybe we can end this."

The trail Nati drew was about five or six miles, going the long way around the canyon, but God in heaven, we were all night on the cursed thing, wriggling through rocks and cactus on our bellies, and nary even the light of a match. But Nati knew the trail like the palm of her hand. Once, when Crawford busted through a rock ledge from the sheer size of him, she clung to him like a bulldog to keep him from falling off a precipice. As the three of us lay panting in the near miss of it, Crawford grinned and cupped the back of Nati's neck in thanks. She chomped her teeth and signed tobacco. He cut her off a half a plug. Good man.

Crawling like lizards, smelling the wisping smoke of dying camp-fires, we finally wriggled into position overlooking the camp. Hell, you couldn't see anything. Horn had dropped back to bring up our one mule that carried our extra ammunition. Wouldn't you know, the damn mule lets out a spine-chilling bray, and who answers him but a burro or some pony in Geronimo's camp.

God in heaven, that touched 'em off. The whole mountain came alive. I could hear shouts from down where the Apache fires were. Then the boom and flash of rifles. Crawford groaned at the scouts: "Hold fire! Pick out targets!"

But they didn't. Howling death cries, they were blamming away, rushing the camp, bullets whizzing every place, and me biting my teeth in the dirt, hugging Nati and the boy to me. Hell, after getting the troops there, I was done, I'd had my war.

When the powder smoke finally lifted, we could hear the cack-ling of Geronimo and the other warriors, high in the rocks above us. They were rejoicing, taunting. The mule had warned them, and they'd slicked clean out of there without the loss of a single warrior, squaw or kid either.

All we'd gotten for our trouble was their moldy old blankets, dead fires, pots, pans and a few razor-thin ponies. The scouts kept wanting to run up the next peak after the hostiles, but Crawford sat down wearily and shook his head. Though it was still mostly dark, we could see the rock ledges where the warriors were holed up. Crawford muttered, "A company of infantrymen couldn't break them out of there."

Even the hard-bitten Lieutenant Maus agreed. It was like hunting quail. When they started going high on you, they'd run you to death. "On the other hand," Maus added, "we've got all their food and we've wrecked their camp. That's bound to mean something to them, isn't it?"

When I said it probably would, Crawford turned to me. "Tell your woman to go up to Geronimo. Take the boy, too. We have their camp, ponies, meat, mescal. We have everything they need to live on. Have her tell him, Come down here, talk to me, and I'll give him safe conduct across the border." Then, dead serious, he took Nati's chin in his big hand and spoke a few words in Apache. Geronimo knew that the big captain with the big boots didn't lie to him, never had, and for that reason, trusted him. "Go tell him what I say. Come in now, or we'll starve him to death up there."

Crawford had the respect of all the scouts, and their faces showed it as they crouched beside us. Nati must have caught it. Her eyes lowered and she gripped my hand.

"If my husband sends me, I will go."

I nodded, and kissed her on the forehead. She pushed up, snatched Kazshe, and they scampered off toward the distant rock ledges. We watched them for a long time, until they were out of sight. I didn't know if I'd ever see the tough little nut again. Geronimo was such a vicious bugger, he could well cut her throat just for leading us to him.

Slowly, dawn came graying in, and with it a ghostly fog. The camp that we were occupying now must have been a choice Apache hideout. Shiny black malapais, vomited up by some forgotten volcano. Great slabs of burned and twisted stone made rifle pits for God knows how many Apaches, and what's more, from this knoll, we could see all the way down to the distant slash of the Rio Aros, and even the plains of Chihuahua yellowing far off to the east. Crawford had Maus and Horn scatter the scouts in the old Apache positions, in case the hostiles tried to come storming down on us. Then the sergeant, Kaytennae and Corporal Dutchy began passing out the spoils of war. All of us gorged on dried meat, not caring if it was deer, horse or stolen Mexican cow.

Plumb tuckered out, and down at the mouth too, I lay beside Crawford in an old lava pit, and we chomped away in silence on roasted mescal. "Well, Kelly," Crawford mused, "the soldier's life is mostly wretched and hard, but there's a reward, you know."

"Sir?"

"Like you, trooper, I was an enlisted man once. Joined a Pennsylvania regiment at seventeen. Thought the Rebellion would end before I could get myself blooded. Sixty-one, that was, right after Manassas. By '64, they'd commissioned me. I've been fighting

163

ever since." He shrugged and sat up, his deep eyes shielded from me. "At times like this, you wonder what it's all been for. One failure after another. But you know something, Kelly. It isn't. For you know by then, in your heart, that it's not the bars you're fighting for. Not even for the U.S. It's for your men you fight. Comrades of your unit, your troop. Knowing you'd give your life for them, and they for you. That's all it's for, Kelly. That's the reward."

I was moved. For him, a man of such few words, there seemed to be pain in getting this out. And yet a kind of peace, too. That's what his face showed. He was smiling, watching the fog lift, his eyes sweeping over the scouts lying in the rocks. Comrades, ready for his command. All one we were, in that moment, because of him.

Maybe I dozed, because when I stirred again, it was light enough to see that he'd left me. Worse, the scouts were jumping around in agitation, pointing to a grassy basin that lay below us. In Apache and Spanish both, they were crying "Troops! Mexicans!"

Grabbing my Winchester, I ran up from the pit to a black ledge of rocks where the captain, Maus, Horn and Kaytennae were standing. Maus whirled to the higher ground in our rear. "Up there, too! On the Chihuahua trail, behind us!"

By then I could clearly see two files of Mexican soldiers. One was snaking in and out of fog on the high trail behind us, and the other scattering into battle lines in the grassy basin below.

"For God's sake," Crawford breathed. "Can't they see we're American troops! Horn! Call to them. Identify us!"

Hand it to Horn, that icy bastard never flinched from danger. Out he runs from the protection of the ledge and begins waving his battered civvy hat. "*Estamos soldados Americanos. Tenemos permiso para estar aqui. No tires! Somos Americanos regulares!*"

In answer, a volley ripped through the camp from the Mexicans above us. I heard a scream, one Apache scout writhing on the ground. He hadn't even been awake when a ball ripped through both his legs.

"No!" Crawford shouted. "*No tires! Soldados Americanos!*" He was already pulling his captain's blouse over his buckskin and Maus digging in his pack for his long blue Army greatcoat.

Horn cried to the scouts in Apache: "Put on your soldier blouses. Show yourselves as Americans. Do not fire back!"

One band of scouts had already run up to a high knob that commanded the whole field, and they were pinging away gleefully at the Mexicans until Crawford bellowed and shut them down.

I knew what was happening, and every white man among us was stunned at the senselessness of it. Apaches had been slaughtering Mexicans in these mountains for hundreds of years, so now the troops that surrounded us figured they'd settle the old score in bitter vengeance. Sitting ducks, we were. Canny Maus had already eye-balled the numbers of Mexicans, and told Crawford it looked like 150 at least. Twice our number.

But we had the rocks and the good ground, except for the bastards still above us on the high trail, and digging in for a fight.

By now, though, about ten Mexicans had split off from the riflemen in the basin below. They were coming toward us, waving their sombreros, telling us in Spanish to come down, they wanted to talk.

Horn was squinting at the Mexicans, moving guns ready, up toward us. A sorry bunch they were. Soldiers, hell, they were peons, wearing white baggy cottons and fieldhand straw hats. Double bandoliers of ammunition and machetes gleaming in their belts. In my nine years in Mexico, I'd run onto many of these miserable buggers. Most were convicts or ex-convicts, working off their chain-gang sentences out chasing Indians. Horn grunted: "I don't trust 'em, Captain. They're here to rob and plunder us. Open fire while you've got that first bunch anyway. The scouts will take care of the rest."

"No," Crawford said quietly. "That won't do. It proves nothing. They want a talk, they'll get it." Without a glance at either Horn or me, he moved slowly out of the rocks, unbuckled his cartridge belt with the revolver on it, and started toward the muzzles of the Mexicans.

"Captain, no!" I cried, and broke after him, Horn, I'm glad to say, running right beside me, and Lieutenant Maus, his long great-coat flapping, coming in from another direction.

The Mexican leader was one cut above a peasant, at least from the dusty cavalry boots he wore and a Mex Army cap. His American Winchester was halfway raised, covering all of us, and his dark shifty eyes were trying to see behind us how many men we had.

Maus bulled right straight up to him before Crawford and the rest of us could get there. In Spanish, Maus said: "Don't you see we are American soldiers? Look at my uniform and the captain's."

The leader and others began pupping their lips nervously, muttering, "*Si, si! No tieres, no tieres!*"

The Captain assured them that nobody was going to shoot. We were friends. Allies. We had official Mexican papers showing we had the right to be here in pursuit of hostile Indians.

By now, more of the Mexicans had crowded around, and I heard one cutthroat whisper in Spanish, "These are the *jefes*. Kill them while we can."

Before I could warn the captain, he turned to Maus and whispered coolly, "For God's sake, go back there to the scouts and see that not a shot is fired. I'll talk this out with him." He glanced at Horn and me. "Go on, go back."

Every bone in me screamed, Don't! But we were all unarmed.

We had just barely got back to the protection of the rocks when the talk must have ended. Out of the corner of my eye, I saw Captain Crawford, walking back maybe thirty feet from the Mexicans, shaking his head. "Senseless, killing each other," he muttered. "It must stop." I had a white silk bandana, which I used to keep the dust out of my mouth. It was trailing from my belt. Crawford nodded to me, took the bandana and crawled up on a big rock. He started waving the bandana, shouting in Spanish. "Cease firing on all sides. We are American troops. Friends!"

Horn was scrambing up beside him, shouting the same thing. The bastards, the murdering sonsofbitches we'd just been talking to, crashed out a single shot. The leader did it. Then a flaming volley, hissing balls our way. I flung myself down in the rocks. Horn let out a curse and came stumbling, bleeding into me, shot through the upper flesh of his arm.

"Aw, Christ!" Maus groaned. "Emmet!" He flung himself on Crawford's body, gripping him. When I wriggled up, the great captain was lying there with his head back and his eyes open. On the black tall stone where he'd been trying to plead for friendship lay a piece of his brain as big as my finger. The Mexican leader's bullet had hit him squarely in the forehead.

Kaytennae and all the scouts let out a fierce howl and their rifles flashed in volleys. Of the nine or ten Mexicans who had done this dastardly murder, four of them, including the leader, were ripped apart, the scouts' bullets tearing into them, and winging the rest of the bunch as they limped and crawled back to their lines.

After that, the scouts, in fury over the big captain falling, were hell bent to wipe out the whole lot of the treacherous bastards. Kaytennae kept shouting to Lieutenant Maus that we had them so scared now, the fight would be over in the time it took to light a match.

But Maus was just as sturdy and cool as Crawford would have been. He knew the odds. We were surrounded and at least two hundred hard miles from the U.S. line. We didn't know how many more Mexican troops might be coming up behind these. And worst, saddest, Captain Crawford hadn't died. He was still alive. No hope for him, but he was still ours. We had to get him out.

On top of all of it, someplace in the rock ledges above us was Geronimo and maybe several score warriors, the roughest killers in Apacheria. No doubt they were watching what was happening to us. I thought of Nati, up there, trying to talk them into coming with us. Well, that dream was gone, too. The Apache knew the hate and treachery of the Mexicans far better than we. As far as Geronimo was concerned, he'd just be licking his chops, watching all the soldiers, Mex and U.S., kill each other off.

By then, the Mexicans were howling at us again from their fortified positions in the basin below. "Come over and talk." They wanted to explain.

"They'll explain all right," Maus grunted. Horn wanted to go do it, but because the scouts were still cleaning out his arm wound, I said I'd do it, being as how I savvied Mex, American and Apache tongues.

With his handlebar moustache and cold blue eyes, Maus was as hard a rock as Crawford. "It's your choice, soldier. Whichever one of us doesn't get out of there, the other one must. No weapons. We go in empty."

God in heaven, I wanted to curse him for risking that, but being on borrowed time in this man's Army, one way out was as good as the next. I followed him down into the Mex camp.

They had a strong position, surly, crouching curs, growling at us from behind every rock. A big, fat-bellied sergeant named Santana Perez was now in command. He moaned that we'd killed his captain, Mauricio Corredor, and his lieutenant too. I snapped hotly in Spanish, "*Cabrones!* You killed our best man, trying to talk peace to you!"

Perez began moaning, *Ah, si, lastima.* Tragedy. All a terrible mistake. They thought they were fighting Apaches.

"*Mentiras!*" Maus roared. All lies. They could plainly see our uniforms. We had permission from Mexico City to be here.

Well, then, they wanted to see that permission, and Maus had me skedaddle back. I dug an official paper out of the poor captain's pack and returned. Perez and the others studied the paper. Hell, I doubt if any of the brigands even knew how to read. Anyway, they pouted that it wasn't much. It didn't make up for their men we had killed. And what about the Apache horses and mules we had stolen? Those were Mexican animals. "Give them to us. Now! Bring them here!" Perez spat on the ground.

Patiently, God help me, more patience than I could feel with all those guns on me, Maus explained that the animals the scouts had captured were booty and belonged to them under their enlistment law.

The thieving buggers would hear none of it. "Ours!" they cried. Then Perez told me, his dark lips curling, "Neither of you will leave this camp alive."

I glanced at Maus, both of us knowing full well that they had us trapped. Slowly, one of his cold blue eyes gave me a wink, and he whispered: "Call to the scouts in Apache. Have them show themselves. Every man stand up, weapons in hand."

I pushed Perez aside, cupped my hands to my mouth, and hollered a long angry message up the hill. Within an instant, the Apache scouts set up their own howling. They came bristling out of the rocks, the sun catching their Winchester barrels until it looked like there was 700 of them, instead of a mere 70.

Perez and his barefoot killers got the idea quick. If the gringo officer would give them all the food stolen from the Apache, and half the animals, they would march beside us and protect us until we got out of Mexico.

"Absolutely not!" Maus growled. "I will give you six mules. As far as protecting us back to the border, if one of you tries to enter our camp, my scouts will kill you all. Take what I give you, turn around and get out of here. That's the end of it!"

The way he said it, planted there like a rock, set them to whining even more. I heard the same old man whispering to kill us quick. But Maus never wavered, stared Perez down until finally the bandit shrugged and said, "You lie, we think, so we keep you here till the mules come."

Maus nodded, and told me to go get them. "Sir," I whispered, "they got you prisoner and I hear them saying they mean to kill you. Let me stay. You go back."

He shook his head. "This is my command now."

It took me an hour to get the mules together. The scouts didn't like losing them. They were hell fire to rush in on the Mexicans, but I warned, "If you do that, the lieutenant is a dead man."

Talk about discipline. We call the Apache a wild savage, but that line of bandy-legged, wiry scouts stood there gripping their rifles as proud as if they were on a parade ground. "If they harm either of you," Kaytennae said to me in Apache, "not one of them will ever leave this sierra, even if we have to die with them."

When I led the mules down, the miserable wretches kept whining that the animals weren't in good shape. We had given them our bad ones. More arguing, Perez wavering. I nodded at Maus and he must have been thinking the same thing. Without a word, because that's the best way to bluff Mexicans, we turned on our heels, and as casual as if we were strolling on a boulevard, we hiked back up to our own line of Apache guns.

Maus barked orders: "Make travois for the captain and the wounded scout. One squad of scouts take the high ground, cover our withdrawal." As the men scurried around, picking up our gear and getting ready to go, Maus turned to me and gripped my arm. "Glad you were with me, soldier." Then he stalked off and attended to getting Captain Crawford as comfortable as we could make him.

Seven days he lived, shot through the brain, joggling all the way down that awful trail. When we straggled into the old pueblo of Nacori, he finally gave up the ghost. The scouts wept, and so did I. All we could find in the miserable dump were four boards to make a casket. The scouts who loved him fired one ragged volley over him, we had so little ammunition left. Then we lay him to rest in the dry sand of Mexico, Lieutenant Maus kneeling beside the grave and muttering, "We'll be back for you, old friend. We'll never forget."

ARMY JUSTICE

Three days after we'd buried poor Captain Crawford, Lieutenant Maus started our ragtag column north from Nacori. With our wounded men and not enough ammunition to swat a fly, we were still in danger from the Mex who were prowling everyplace now. So we lit out for the U.S. line as fast as we could go, never realizing that far beyond us a bigger storm was already flashing the sky, and when its black clouds finally busted open, they'd lash us with a torrent of treachery and shame. Like an arroyo in flood crest, the dirty water would sweep away all the sticks and bones of them that I'd loved.

Because we'd chased him so hard, Geronimo decided to surrender to General Crook. They met in northern Sonora in the rocky *Canon de los Embudos,* meaning the place of tricksters, and it damn sure turned out to be. The old coyote agreed to Crook's terms, and promised to walk his people across the Arizona line and turn himself in.

Well, they hadn't but hit U.S. soil before one of the thieves from the Tucson Indian Ring slips into Geronimo's camp, fills him with mescal and scare stories. Even though Geronimo was so drunk he'd keep falling off his mule, he managed to flee back to the Sierra that night, and take a lot of his cutthroats with him.

It was a known fact that the Indian Ring bunch didn't want the Apache war to end. They were making too much money out of it. You'd think that Sheridan in Washington could have seen the scam, and maybe he did because he grabbed it as his excuse to dump General Crook and replace him with President Cleveland's pet and fellow Democrat, that strutting peacock, Nelson Miles.

So, Crook, after his hard years on the trail, was booted out in failure, and I, in another way, got the same treatment. Though I can't prove it, I'm sure it was that miserable bugger, Tom Horn, who was jealous of me or hoping to feather his own nest. Anyhow, he turned me in as a deserter. Next thing I knew, I was in the guardhouse at Fort Bowie.

The rotten Army game! I cursed it, little knowing that the purest treachery of all was still to come. But I couldn't see it. The iron window of the guardhouse didn't face the parade ground, so I could only hear the rattling of troops and wagons, and sometimes in the nights, the drums and mournful wailing of Apaches. Lt. Maus had managed to gather up the majority of Geronimo's band and brought them to the post, but they might as well have been in Siam for all I knew.

Then, one night a guard, bringing me hardtack and water, lips off that General Crook had got shot in the face. God help me, I was grieved. But next morning at grub, a guard says, "Ah, hell, the Old Man ain't hurt. Just loading paper shotgun shells he was, and one blowed and singed his beard."

On the eleventh day of April, '86, about dusk, two new troopers came to my cell. They were grizzled vets that I could have known from the Sioux times, but if so, they didn't let on. One says, "Git them prisoner rags off ya, wash your damn face. You're going to the Big House."

I didn't know what they meant until they led me across the parade to an adobe two-story with an Eastern kind of shingled roof, and big dark garrets staring out. A couple of Army ambulances were parked in front, a soldier walking guard post on the board porch. The troopers knocked on the door, then opened it and pushed me inside. Got out of there they did, and left me standing in a parlor where there was a party going on.

Maybe not exactly a party, just some officers taking drinks from a couple of Army wives in crinkly, fancy dresses. Over by the fireplace, which was roaring, I spotted a little golden-haired girl. Five or six, I suppose she was. Some officers were laughing and lifting her up onto a man's lap. He was sitting on a cane rocker, grinning, and a couple of plaster bandages were on his face.

The little tyke starts fussing with his beard. "Oh, Crookie," she pipes up, "I don't like you this way. You're just an old bump on a log."

Didn't he howl at that, hugs her to him and starts trotting her on his knee. One officer looks at me like I was tumbleweed that got blowed in there, and says, "A man from the guardhouse, sir."

Crook's gray eyes flickered, and I was close enough to him to see that his rusty beard had a black stripe down one cheek, and his bushy eyebrows singed from the shell exploding.

He didn't give any notice to me, for the tyke was jiggling on his lap, goading him. "Horsie, Crookie. Go fast."

"Tomorrow, little lady, I'll take you on a big horse, all the way to the train."

"Promise?"

"Promise." Chuckling, he grizzled her with his beard and got up. Then he motioned me to follow him. Smelling the perfume of the officer's wives, and catching their looks like who let this piece of dirt in, I went right on after Crook into an office with a mesquite wood desk and a picture of President Cleveland hanging above it. Captain Bourke was sitting on the edge of the desk, and another officer was staring out the window. When he turned to me and nodded, I barely recognized him. It was Lieutenant Maus, shaved clean except for his handlebars, and spiffed up in dress blues.

"At ease, soldier," Crook said, creaking into the chair behind the desk. "Do you have the proceedings, Bourke?"

The captain nodded and placed some typed papers on the desk. Crook fingered them, then tossed them aside. "Court-martial of Private Patrick M. Kelly. Do we have quorum?"

"Aye," said Captain Bourke, and Lieutenant Maus nodded.

Crook leaned forward on his elbows and his intent eyes tracked my face. God almighty, I thinks, with his burned beard and plaster patches, he looks like a used-up scarecrow, his face thin and lined, and his hunting jacket so frayed it was about gone. "Well, Kelly, desertion and murder. Are you guilty as charged?"

It come so direct, I stood there caught off guard and gulping. Finally I mustered, "I had to desert, sir, and yes, I killed the major, but only to keep my own head from being blowed off. Believe I told the general that."

Crook swung his chair away from me, slouched back and put his boots up on a low table. "I have Crawford's field reports on you, Kelly. You did us good service. It all doesn't come down to much, the way things have turned out, but for your part of it, like so many others, there damn well should be rewards. Lieutenant Maus, who has also spoken for you, has been recommended by me for the Congressional Medal of Honor."

"Well, now," I blurts, swinging to Maus, "high time somebody seen what you did, sir."

Maus shrugged, and Crook said, "Remains to be seen if the President will grant it. Coming from 'old bump on the log Crookie' here." The others grinned, but Crook didn't. "Kelly, I'm leaving this command tomorrow, and I've written so many declarations and apologies, I hope I never see another piece of paper again. So we'll do this just verbal and quick. Bourke will make it official. This is a field court-martial, in time of war, and the findings are…"

He glanced up at me. I was frozen there like a pillar of salt.

"Guilty as charged."

Captain Bourke nodded. "Aye." Maus: "Seconded."

The bottom fell out of my feet and I stared at the floor.

"Pending," Crook added, "probation. The appeal now made by the present officers who, having campaigned with this soldier, warrant that, in light of his loyal service beyond the call of duty, his sentence is hereby suspended."

"Sir?" I croaked.

"Under the condition," Crook snapped, "that Private Kelly, who has proven his worth as a soldier, will now exercise his probation by giving his government continued service. Re-enlistment in the 3rd U.S. Cavalry for four years."

I was struck dumb, blood rushing to my face. "Another hitch?

Ah, God help me, sir, I'm out, I been out all these years. I was making a life for myself below the line!"

"When you agreed to scout for us, I gave you no guarantees, Kelly. But this one means you're clean. No pursuit, no sentence. You're still a young man. You've got many years ahead that I wish I had." He slid a piece of paper across the desk. "You'll sign for four, soldier, and I'll tell you why. This Army, this whole western push is not done yet, not by far. Without good officers, good men in the ranks, fair people, seasoned people, God help both the settlers and the Indians. Somebody is going to have to keep them from each other's throats, or the bloodshed will never end."

Desperate, I looked from Bourke to Maus and their faces said nothing. "General," I stammered, "I'm grateful to you, truly so. But down there below the line, with my Apache woman, I was getting by. I even got a grubstake stashed away. Now if I sign, I'm gone off again, ain't I?"

"But you're not running either, Kelly," Bourke said, and smiled. Then he went over to the corner of the office where there was a heap of old canvas packs from some campaign. As he pulled up a big bundle with its leather straps black and twisted from rain, I recognized it as Captain's Crawford's. I had dug into it that morning at the lava rocks to fetch the Mex permission paper for Lieutenant Maus.

"Emmet Crawford," Bourke said, "must have thought well of your diary. Interesting document. Time for you to have it back, soldier, and finish it in the next wars." With a grin, he handed me my old dusty, crinkled copy book.

I stood there gripping it. "Sir," I finally says to Crook, "if I don't go back...?"

He shook his head. "I won't walk away from military justice, Kelly. I've bent it as far as I can. It's this or a sure sentence. Even life. It's out of my jurisdiction, as of tomorrow. I'll get you to a good troop, a good officer, son. That's all I can do."

When Crook spoke, there wasn't an iota of bluff in the man, and I should have known it by now. Part of me wanted to weep, and the other part to rejoice. Finally, I just blubbers, "Sir, my little Apache gal, Nati. She says we're husband and wife, Indian style. But I reckon I'll be leaving here. Could I see her again?"

He got up slowly and sighed. "All of them, son. They'll be at Bowie Station tomorrow. I'm on one train, they're on the other. And the only damn thing I can do, like you, is to watch." He turned to Captain Bourke. "Issue Kelly a good mount, full uniform, assign him to Emmet's burial detail."

"I'll take him along with me, sir." Bourke turned to me. "We're re-interring Captain Crawford in Kearney, Nebraska. He asked to be

172

there. It's as much of a home as he ever had, considering that he's been campaigning steadily for 25 years."

"And the Apaches, sir?"

Bourke stared at the floor. By now, General Crook had already pushed up from his desk, ripped the court-martial papers in two and dropped them in the ashcan. "The Apaches, at least the Chirichauas," Bourke murmured, "will become the most disgraceful page in our history of dealing with Indians. Those people, the scouts you served with, all of them who remained so faithful to us, have now been found guilty of acts of war against us by the President and General Sheridan, and will be punished accordingly."

"Ah, God help us," I cried. "Why? Ain't there a way to stop it?"

"Maybe someday," Crook said wearily. "Not now. Put what's left of the Indian in a zoo, and let our grandchildren look at what he was." He gripped my hand and murmured, "Good work, soldier. I thank you for it. Report to your troop."

Then he was gone, shuffling away, a beaten old man. Hell, we all were, busting our guts out to end all this, but it wasn't good enough for the nabobs above, and least of all for the poor savages that nobody cared about, except men like us who were supposed to kill them off.

Right after reveille next morning, six troops of us came to attention on the parade ground, our red and white guidons rippling, and the post band playing Old Lang Syne. Ah, I suppose it looked like glory, pretty as a picture, officers' wives fluttering their dainty handkerchiefs, saying goodbye. Out across the sunbaked desert we rode, to the Bowie Station on the Southern Pacific track. Lonely, glinting strand of iron that I'd seen so long before.

Two short trains were waiting there, engines hissing steam and soldiers inside the dingy yellow cars were already jerking the windows open, for the heat was fierce.

When my troop rode up, I could see Apaches clustering around, the bucks dressed in their best white cottons and straw hats, and the squaws a merry-go-round of bright-colored dresses. Even the naked little urchins had been spiffed for the occasion. They were cackling, rejoining old friends and families. Some of the wild bronco Apaches from the Sierra were gaping in wonder at the snorting engine, and wriggling in to peer beneath the big wheels. Likely, many of the poor innocent buggers didn't even know why they were here, except for having some kind of a hoe-down with Nantan Lupan.

When Crook rode through them, on his lap was jiggling the little blonde girl he'd promised the horsie ride. But after he'd dismounted, other officers snatched her out of harm's way. Apaches were swarming around Crook, catching on finally that he was leaving them. The squaws began mourning and wailing. Some of the scouts in their blue jackets were saluting him. Then they broke ranks and began hugging him like everybody wanted a last piece of their beloved father.

My troop was at attention maybe a hundred yards away, so I couldn't pick Nati out of the crowd. Hell, I didn't even know if she was there. Could be, when Geronimo gave us the slip, she'd fled back to Mexico with him. Or there was always the chance that the Army had freighted some of the Mexican bunch back to their homes on the San Carlos reservation.

But one thing puzzled me. There were a helluva lot more Apaches gathered here than what must have come up from Mexico. While I was pondering that, our lieutenant ordered us to close in. The Apaches were agitating so much that they might get out of hand.

But Crook raised his arms and the roaring stopped. He was standing by the steps of one of the dusty coaches, officers and conductors around him.

Then I hear a bugle. The death song. "Taps." Crook, staring down the track, took off his battered hunting hat and clapped it to his heart. Soldiers were lifting the flag-draped coffin of Captain Crawford into a boxcar at the end of the coaches. Captain Bourke was with them. When the remains of that brave man disappeared into the darkness, Bourke ordered a soldier to slide shut and lock the boxcar door. Then he walked up the track to where Crook was.

The general looked out across the brown sea of Apache faces. I think he started to say something to them, but finally he just shook his head. He nodded to the conductor, all aboard, then turned and hulked up into the coach.

I couldn't see his face, but I think he was weeping. A soldier beside me whines, "How long they gonna keep us standing out here, fryin' our brains?"

"You ain't got one, mister, it all went out your mouth!"

The engineer screeched the whistle, and the iron wheels began grinding.

A ripple of fear swept across the Apaches. They stared at the second train like they'd finally figured out that it wasn't just for show. It was meant to snatch them far off to some terrible place. The troopers were crowding in, prodding the Apaches up the steps with their Springfields, loading them like dumb beasts going to market.

I kept searching for Nati in the swirl of them, hoping against hope she wasn't here. Couldn't be, Jesus God, after all she'd done for us, certainly somebody in the Army would be protecting her. Then I caught a glimpse of an old grayheaded squaw, Geronimo's aunt. "Stay in rank!" an officer shouted at me, but I leapt off my horse and ran through the Apaches until I caught the old one. "Nati!" I cried. "My girl! Where is she?"

The squaw was weeping so much I could barely understand her. "Is she here!"

The old one lifted her arm toward the last coach. "Someplace, maybe there. She has come with us. They say they're taking us home. Isn't it so?"

I thrust past her and began tearing through the other Apaches, frightened kids and pleading squaws being crowded up the loading steps by the soldiers. Black hair, flashes of colors, tears glistening on many of the bronze cheeks. "Nati!" I cries.

Did I see her?

I never knew. Soldiers shoved me aside and wouldn't let me search the train. Guards were on the coach platforms, the engine whistle shrilling, and the big wheels started grinding again. All I could see were a few Apaches, poking their heads out like animals in a cage. Stunned, wailing, their pitiful black eyes sweeping across the desert, clinging to it before it was gone. The bluebellies inside were jerking them back, slamming the windows shut, to keep them from jumping out and running free.

This was their last chance, and they knew it.

I watched the train all the way up the long track, until its smoke was a black wisp smearing the copper sky. Beside me, a young lieutenant barked, "Troop mount!"

Jangling their brasses and gun scabbards, the troopers swung to saddle, and a few of them began crowing about what a great thing we'd done here, every murdering Chirichaua snatched out of the territory in one fell swoop.

"Meaning just what?" I says.

"Why, we even got them peacefuls," pipes a pink-cheeked recruit who couldn't have been sixteen. "We was pulling duty at San Carlos this week, see? Officer up there says, How we gonna round up all them Chirichauas here? Got no excuse to arrest 'em. They ain't done nothing wrong, they been staying home with their families, never did join Geronimo or nothing. But our major snorts back: They started doing wrong when they were born! Chirichauas, aren't they? All the same stripe. We're going to round 'em up like we always do. We ring the dinner bell: Get your rations. They'll suspect nothing, just come streaming into the issue corral. Only this time, boys," the recruit grins, "there wasn't no beef, no cookies. We slammed the gate on every damn one, and put 'em on that train what just left! How's that for beatin' injuns!"

"Stinks!" I says, and spits.

The young shavetail butts his horse against mine. "Did I hear you correct, soldier?"

"Damn right you did. Lousy stinkin' treachery."

"You call me 'sir' when you address me! Nor will I tolerate your

175

malingering lies undermining the morale of my command. For the killing they've done, these wanton murderers deserve every whit of punishment we can give them, and they'll jolly well get it where they're going. Across the continent from here. Fort Pickens, Florida. They'll rot in the dungeons before the youngest child among them ever comes back to terrorize the southwest again! Where the hell have you been stationed, anyhow?"

"Sierra Madre! 'Sir'!" I spit it out. "Maybe they're just look-alike Injuns to you, but not to me. I served with them scouts, and they ain't done nothing but save our butts." The shavetail was blinking like he couldn't believe I was lipping him. "You want all of it? Yas, I married one of your murdering savages, too. Good woman, brave woman. She ain't done nothing but riskin' her life to bring Geronimo to us."

"Only he isn't! He's still at war!"

"She tried, dammit! And she ain't even Chirichaua. She's White Mountain Apache, at peace since before you was born. I wonder what she thinks now about US of A justice!"

Months later, I wrote Nati at Fort Pickens. Presently a soiled envelope come back with one sheet of paper. In the wiggly letters they must have taught her, she wrote: "My husban him name Nahthletla wife. One year hab tree hundre sixti fibe day." She never even got that year, just eight months before the stinking hellhole finally broke her heart and set her free.

With a curse at the rottenness of it, I turned my horse and started eating the dust of the column. A common trooper again, choking down a four-year sentence, but by damn, it was better than life in prison or the firing squad. I'd make the best of it, God help me.

BLACKMAILED!

When I left Arizona Territory on the second day of January, 1886, I figured that I'd paid for my sins and buried my enemies. Little did I know that the ghosts of my past would be rising from the grave, waiting to bushwhack me on my trail to freedom.

With no wars to fight on the frontier, the Army found us a new one close to home. In the smoky cities, they turned us loose against the working stiffs, bustin' their heads if they dared cry out for better wages, or their piece of the American Dream.

To protect the city of Chicago from the mobs in the streets, my regiment of the Third Cavalry begun building Fort Sheridan, a monument to little Phil. There on the lakefront 25 miles north of town, we camped in a tent city and did the coolie labor that would soon loft up barracks and towers of granite. On the bluffs there'd be polo fields for the officers and rifle ranges for us bluebellies. I says to a sergeant, "Hell, there ain't an Injun within a thousand miles of here. Why do we need a fort?"

"It's war enough downtown," he snaps. "All these immigrants crowding in here, strikers, anarchists, waiting to rip the gold out of the Gold Coast. Burning trains, bombing factories and public parks. The city fathers aren't about to let that rabble destroy what they've built."

"Flyin' with the eagles and featherin' their golden nests ain't the kind of soldierin' I signed on for."

He jabs me in the chest. "The Army is the servant of commerce, Private, and you will do what it tells you!"

I found that out all right when Ora Zachary come into my life. I'd been at Fort Sheridan about a month, layin' tent floors and diggin' latrines, when I noticed the bugger idling up to the work crew. He never said nothing, or give orders. Just stood there with a cavalry quirt clenched behind his back, his icy blue eyes following every move I made. He was a tall, big-shouldered lieutenant, his lantern jaw shaved so clean it was blue in the sun. The Army had a Trojan in this one, I figured, and the thought chilled me. Another Scipio Shaw.

Late one afternoon, Zachary thumbs me out of the mess line, tells me to pack my gear, we was going into Chicago, no questions asked. About nine o'clock that night we hits town, me lugging my barracks bag, and slushing after him in the snow. At the corner of Dearborn and Lake he unlocks a side door and leads me up a narrow stair, three flights, to his private apartment.

I couldn't see much of the place, but it sure looked like fancy digs on a lieutenant's pay. Zachary turned up a gas lamp, and there

177

were newspapers, photos and books littered around. He beckoned me at the fireplace which set between two big windows that looked north toward the river. "We don't need much light, but the heat will help. Touch up that fire, Kelly, I'll be right back."

We sure didn't need much light. While I was stoking the fire, here come a roaring, rattling that scared hell out of me. The black iron skeleton of the new elevated railway was right outside the window. One of the damn Loop trolley trains burned its headlight through the parlor, and its iron wheels like to shake the building down.

When Zachary came back, he'd shucked off his uniform and was wearing a tweed jacket, old riding pants and carpet slippers. "You're here, Kelly, because I'm on detached duty to the Inspector General's office, reporting direct to General Sheridan. Special agent kind of work. Undercover. You won't see me in uniform nor will you address me by rank. Most people call me Zack. But when we're in front of superiors, it's Mister Zachary." He squinted at me with a hard smile. "So now you're wondering how you got into this?"

"It's a long way from sleepin' in a tent, I'd say."

"Maybe not as far as you think, soldier." He thrust away from the fire, went over and rummaged in his desk. When he came back, he said, "Put out your hand."

I did, and he dropped a cold, hard ball into my palm. "Ever seen one of those?"

I held it up to the light. It was pitted iron about as big as my thumb. "Looks like something out of an old smoothbore. Big caliber."

"It's older than that. You weren't in the Rebellion?"

"No, sir."

"That's a minie ball. Mostly the Rebels used them. Lethal. Blow your arm off at 200 yards. But this one has a different history. Would you have any idea where I got it?"

I shook my head, and his sleek jaw tightened. He took the ball from me and closed it in his fist. "Out of the face of Major Scipio Shaw."

My cheeks went hot, my heart give a thump. "God help us," I whispered. "You—with him?"

Zachary squatted down beside me, his eyes burning into mine. His voice was hoarse as he tossed the ball up and down. "I picked this thing out of his face at Slim Buttes and carried him back to safety. I probably should have let him die then and there instead of by your hand."

"Self-defense! I was tried for that and acquitted!"

"I know about your so-called trial." Slipping the ball into his jacket pocket, he pushed to his feet. "Crook rewarded you for service, that's what it came down to. But he isn't the whole Army, and there are some of us left who won't swallow what he did."

"Meanin' you?" I mutters, my hands tightening into fists. The man loomed above me so big and threatening, I started to push up out of my chair. He shoved me back down and turned away.

Staring into the fire, he said, "I served under the Major in Virginia, eighteen-year-old Kentucky squirrel hunter, and I would have gotten my head blown off if he hadn't taken a liking to me and made me his orderly. I went to the frontier with him, still enlisted, a sergeant by then."

"Crazy Woman Fork," I whispered, my face hot. "Wasn't it there?"

Zachary laughed harshly, but another train was rattling past, grinding the sound away. "In front of the cliffs at the Sioux camp, I saw you sounding retreat for Bloxham, and struck the bugle from your hands."

I kept nodding, unable to believe it. "A sergeant with a beard done that. I ain't never forgot, just couldn't place him as you."

"Shaved it off. Styles change. You were going to ruin Shaw, Kelly." He shook his head. "What a greenhorn, siding with Bloxham over him."

"I was tellin' the truth!"

"Don't give me that! What Crook did for you, saving your ass, Major Shaw did for me. When I packed him out of that canyon at Slim Buttes, held my fingers on his neck to keep him from bleeding to death, he put me up for a Congressional and a battlefield commission. I got both. That's what Shaw meant to me. He gave me a career in this goddamn brutal Army. Who knows how far I would have gone if you hadn't shot him to death!"

"I told you the reason," I flared, "and I ain't gonna keep repeatin' it." I pushed up out of my chair. "If you brung me here to get even, you best start right now, face to face!"

Zachary smiled and kicked at the fire, the sparks showering up. "I am even. You're here, and assigned to me by the General."

"I ain't seen that order."

"You won't. My kind of work doesn't write 'em. I've got you in my hand just like that minie ball. I saw a man like you go to Leavenworth for killing an officer. The slacker bastard, he figured that behind bars he was safe for life. Two months later they found him with a knife in his back. Friends remember. So you're the ball in my hand, my friend. You throw it up into the air and it falls right back down. Throw it further and it can roll into a lot of places. It can roll further than an illiterate Irishman like you can ever dream. Depends on how you want to play with it."

"From what you said, I ain't got much damn choice." In fury, I stalked to him and grabbed his arm. "I been on the rough side, mister, and if you're working me up to put me out of your way, start now!"

He flung off my arm. "Don't you touch me again, and don't be stupid either. If I wanted you dead, Kelly, I could have done it anytime when you were in Arizona. I had friends in that command. I want you alive, on your feet. I want a brave man covering my back, and you're it. You pull off what I want, and you can go far in this Army." He grabbed some newspapers and photographs from his desk. "Do you know anything about civil disturbance? What's going on now in these cities, the radical, foreign element?"

"Not much," I grunts, "but they did send us to Noo Yawk, bustin' trolley workers' heads."

"And how did you feel about that?"

"Lousy. Job for a peeler, ain't it? A copper. I don't call it solderin'."

"Well, you can damn well bet it is, laddie, because if this country comes apart, if it's torn apart by the rabble now in the streets, you're going to think that the War of the Rebellion was a picnic. There'll be that much bloodshed. My job is to head it off, and that's the work you'll be doing. Saving lives. Saving the prosperity that's only going to get bigger in the years ahead. You've seen the factories around here, the network of rail lines. We're in a boom, Kelly, we're the envy of the world, and no mob in the streets is going to rip it away."

Pacing slowly around the darkened room, he said, "I went over your service record with General Sheridan. This team we're setting up will establish Army tactics for the future. The best fights are the ones you can avoid. Get inside the heads of the enemies, turn them before they hurt a lot of people. You're going to be our man who gets inside those heads."

"You're talking spying?"

"Saving lives, soldier. We want information on these radicals, what they're thinking, how we can put out their fires before they light them. To do that, somebody has to enter their ranks, be one of them."

Wearily, trying to sort it out, I shook my head. "Turn-coating, ain't it? Lowest form of life, trying to be what you ain't. Suppose they don't let me in with 'em?"

"From your records, Crazy Horse must have let you in, Geronimo, too. You did it by standing up to them, I hear. Jumping through their hoops until they trusted you. What's the matter? Are your guts leaking out now?"

"They ain't, mister, when you stand there and threaten to put a knife in my back."

"Kelly," he growled. "You can either fight the system, or turn it around and make it work for you. I'm giving you that chance. You goldbrick, bull against my plans, you'll end up dead in circumstances never to be explained. On the other hand, you make this work for me, you bring me what I want, you're going to fall into the shithouse and come out with a new suit. The leaders of this city demand an end to this radicalism, and they're willing to pay for it. The Chicago police are working with us, and so are Pinkerton agents. The problem with both of them is that they're hated by the radicals who can spot them at a thousand yards. They can't get inside, but you can."

"Just how is that now?"

He smiled, walked over to me and jerked up my hand. Running his big fingers over it, he said, "You can take the Irishman out of the brickyard, but he'll still be carrying hod. Working man. Your record said you did common labor, and you'll do it again for your government. For me, Kelly."

Turning, he walked over to his desk and pulled on a greatcoat and felt hat. "I've wasted enough time with you. These newspapers, backgrounds on the radicals, photos. Stay here tonight, read 'em, get to know every face. One of my agents will come by for you in the morning, and put you behind the lines, with instructions. After that, it's up to you. Let's hope you're smart enough to take advantage of—" his heavy jaw tightened and his pale eyes smiled—"my good will."

Tightening the belt of his greatcoat, he started to leave, but then stopped. Reaching into his pocket, he took out the minie ball and dropped it into my lap. "Don't stretch it."

The door slammed shut behind him just as another elevated train came roaring down the track. Its headlight beam flared through the room, passed on and left me alone in the darkness of a dying fire.

Courtesy of the grand American guvmint and the city fathers of Chicago, a lowly Irish working man took up residence on West Randolph Street in a smoky brick building that had survived the Fire. Once it had been a pickle factory, and I could still smell the stink of the things. Next door was a tannery, and down the block the dingy printing plant of a German newspaper, the *Arbiter Zeitung*.

This sheet, written partly in Kraut and the rest American, was the hotbed of the radicals. To sneak me into their midst, Zachary and his agents had me playing the same raw greenhorn I'd once been, just off the boat and looking for a fair shake and a full dinner pail. I wore a cloth cap, tattery clothes and worn-out boots. Zachary was holding my Army blues like a hostage over at his flat, with orders that I should never go there except in emergency. We'd meet on street corners in the Loop, or at saloons when I had something to tell him. Most of my days were spent pounding the grubby pavements like I'd done back in '75, a strapping Irish mule looking for any kind of labor for whatever pittance the boss would give me, to slop it away in some beer joint like the other immigrants.

The only difference was, I didn't have to earn a penny. The Pinkerton assigned to me was a flatfoot named Rolph. He'd put me into my digs in the basement of the pickle factory and came by once a week to slip $25 in greenbacks under my mattress. When I needed more to buy somebody's mouth, the price could rise into the hundreds, and nobody was the wiser. I shuffled around the hiring halls and job sites, one step above a bum, watching and listening to the radical whispers that were sweeping the city.

If these hard-faced foreigners ever found out I was a stool pigeon, they'd shiv me quick in some dark alley. I was their enemy in ways they never understood, and what's more, I was getting to be my own enemy, too, doing this rotten job that I couldn't see no way to escape.

At heart, I had to root for the workingman. Hell, the poor devils were no different than me, coming from the Auld Sod where the likes of His Lordship Cavan had been making dray horses of my people all these centuries. An Irishman wasn't alive if he wasn't a rebel. And yet, as I'd ponder in my basement room at nights, maybe Zachary had a point. Whether you was a working stiff or a common soldier, the system ground you down until you were a spavined old mule, pastured off to die without ever knowing what you might have amounted to. With Leah, we would have started out poor but at least we'd have been making lives of our own on what was left of her land in the South. We'd be pulling ourselves up out of the mass of nobodies, and yes, for a poor man, despite my sympathy for the workers, I was more than ready to take the risk and make something of myself. Nobody else would do it for me. With the shadow of Zachary hanging over me, I had no choice but to let the ball roll and see where it would lead. Instead of pissing outside the tent, I'd get inside where the power was, and use it to beat the bastard and his system at his own game.

I hadn't spent but a few weeks undercover before I seen that Zachary was living high on the hog. Saloons where I'd meet him, he always had a different flossy dame with him. He wore a derby hat and a checkered vest with a big gold watch and chain. "Gift of the Board of Trade," he tells me. Sometimes he'd treat me to a big beefsteak dinner or try to push whiskey on me. He had money to burn, and more than once on the streets, some dignitary from the Chicago Association, the nabobs who ran the town, would greet him like they was long-lost brothers.

I won't say that Zachary was a braggart, but he sure didn't hide the fact that he was an authentic hero, on his way to still more glory. He had ambition leaking out all over him, and it made him dangerous to be around. Moody. Sometimes he'd be all grinny and the charmer. Next day I'd strike him like flint. He'd spark off, demanding more information, names and dates written down in reports, which wasn't my strong suit.

The *Arbiter Zeitung* was the radical mouthpiece. "Revolution! A fair wage, an eight hour day!" If the bigwigs didn't start listening, the anarchists vowed to blow their ears open with dynamite.

"Totally irresponsible," Zachary muttered to me. "No American has ever used dynamite to resolve disputes, wouldn't think of it. But this element we're letting in now, the Statue of Liberty ought to be torn down if this is the scum it brings." We were walking together under the elevated scaffold, and when the train above passed, he pointed his finger at me like a gun. "Dig into those *Zeitung* people! Bring me backgrounds on Schwab, Spies, Fielden, Fischer, Engel, Lingg. Particularly on Albert Parsons. Slippery bastard was a Rebel cavalryman in the war, and now we think he's ring-leading the whole anarchist movement. Check deliveries to the printing plant for anything suspicious, black powder, cast iron. If they're making bombs, I want to know!"

With him hounding me, I had to keep plodding the streets, taking day work so I'd be shoulder to shoulder with the radicals. After I'd paraded with 'em in picket lines, and even done some of their slugging, they pretty much seen I was on their side. But damn if I could pick up even a whisper about bombs, until one I never expected struck me right in the kisser.

I'd been following a lead on a Mexican laborer named Alejandro who supposedly had some connection with this Parsons. He must have been a boozer for I had to track him through a string of saloons and finally to a charity shelter over on DesPlaines Street.

What a stinking dump it was, one step up from a soup kitchen. The building had been a factory way back, and the dark, clammy rooms were now being used as a make-shift hospital ward. A few orderlies in white coats were tending the pitiful souls lined up on rows of cots. Some of them were moaning and others staring blankly at the walls. Harridans, whores, bindlestiffs or just plain crazies, they were the kind of riff-raff the coppers found lying in doorways or giving up their ghosts on crowded streets where the peddlers' wagons never even stopped, just splattered 'em with mud. The drinkers among 'em were screaming off their D.T.s, and the pale lungers coughing out their lights. I never did find the Alejandro feller. Probably he'd conked and gone to potter's field.

I couldn't wait to get out of that miserable place, stinking of alcohol and human waste. It was one thing to watch wounded troops suffering after a battle. At least they thought they were dying for something. But here, what kind of hope did these dregs have? If they got back out on the street again, there wasn't no work for 'em. They'd starve and die in some other shelter with nobody knowing their names.

There was a side door into the alley, and just as I starts tugging it open to get out of there fast, I brushes against a cot beside the wall. I probably wouldn't have noticed it except that the feet of the body lying there were out from under the blanket. What struck me wasn't that they were naked, but that the color of 'em was strange, brown skin pale and faded like an old sunburn. Then, from under the blanket, a thin brown arm topples out and weakly scratches toward me. The whisper was in Lakota. *"Fights Without Club."*

I lets out a cry and drops to my knees, clutching at the blanket and the pitiful sack of long, hot bones until I had her face buried against mine. "Walks Outside," I whispers, feeling the fever in her cheeks, and when I could draw back enough to bear to look at her, ah God, she was a ghost of the girl I'd remembered in the Sioux camp so long ago. Her slant eyes were sunken and burning dull, the skin drawn tight over her cheekbones and fever blisters on her lips. Her black hair, once so thick, was now cut short and frazzled wild as a witch. "Ten damn years," I blurted. "I never did know what become of you. I figured you'd probably been killed off in the wars."

"Oh, Mister Patrick," she sobbed, shivering against me. "I was dead till now. You hear? I speak. Better…?" Then her body began to wrack with coughing, and just in the effort of it, she sagged away from me, her face buried in the dingy blanket.

I bolted up from the cot and finally found the head orderly. "That girl over by the doorway, she belongs to me."

"Hell, take her," he grunts. "I got too many anyway."

"What's the matter with her?"

"How do I know? Injun, ain't she? Probably drunk, patrol brought her in couple of nights back."

I grabbed the front of his white rubber coat. "Ain't you got a medical doctor in this place?"

He laughed. "You think they worry about people like these? Get her out of here if you gotta have an Injun. I need the bed."

A half hour later, I had the poor thing bundled up in my great-coat and carried her in her high button shoes and ragged dress out to a hansom cab. I tells the hackie to get me to the best sawbones in that part of town, and slipped him a greenback to do it fast.

There was a clinic a few blocks away over on Halsted, and with a fiver this time, I get a young Chinaman doctor to interrupt his charity work on Hunkies and take her into an examining room. He stripped her and I was stunned by the look of her body. Strong as an elk she'd been, and just as proud, but now her skin was stretched tight over her ribs, her belly hollow and her female place a dying mound of wispy black hairs. "Save her, Doc," I pleaded. He shrugs and sticks a needle into her arm, after cursing the thinness of it where he had trouble finding a vein. "At least she'll sleep now," he says. "Take her someplace warm, feed her well. It's fever in her lungs. If she's strong enough she'll throw it off. Some do, but not many."

"She's strong enough," I breathed, and by then she was asleep.

For the next days, I dropped out of the Army and the snooping game. I hadn't felt so charged up for years, because now with her, what was left of her, I at least had somebody to care for and care about. "You're our hope, Injun gal," I'd whisper to her, stroking her. "Don't quit us."

To get her out of my cold basement flat, I rented us the top floor of a dingy frame house over on DesPlaines. It had a big brass bed and a flush toilet, too. Many's the afternoon we'd lie together on the four poster and watch the first weak sun of spring glistening on the trees. "All them years we've been apart," I'd murmur, "what in the world ever brung you to me again?"

She sighed. "We have no hope on the reservations. An old nun, Mother Grace, let me help her in the hospital at Pine Ridge, but we could do so little. We had few medicines. Our people were dying faster than anyone knew how to cure. Even the medicine men, forbidden, too, were not having good luck anymore. So I talk to Mother Grace: 'How can I help my people? Perhaps I become a doctor, or a law person to fight against these treaties that always rob us?' With sadness in her eyes, she says, 'Yes, you are an intelligent woman, Walks Outside, but it is hard for any kind of woman to enter the professions, least of all a Plains Indian.' At last she says, 'Nursing, though, you could do that. My order has a nursing hospital far away, in the great city of Chicago.' That was just six months ago, and how happy I was! The hospital is out there on the west side with a church beside it. Maybe I should pray more but there was not time. Every day I work with the nurse sisters in the wards. Doctors too, they try to teach me. At nights we have training, reading so many books, learning the body, the *waiscu* ways of curing. One day I'll be ready and bring these gifts back to the Lakotas."

"Sure and you will, dearie. But I ain't clear on it neither. If you was there with nuns in their hospital, what was you doin' in that charity shelter?"

She drew herself erect and with her hands made the Lakota slapping sign, meaning gone, done with. "In the last moon, some weeks ago, the hospital closed. The big church above moved the order to Milwaukee city, or near there. I don't know why. Maybe no money left. But when the Chicago city people came in, the hospital belonged to them. White nurses. No room for Injun gal. With the Sisters gone, I have nobody, just the streets."

"But God in heaven, Walks Outside, there's other Injuns in this town, I seen plenty. Couldn't you hook on with friends or find somebody to help you?"

"I try, Patrick. Very hard. One place I wash dishes. They give me food, nothing else. In the paper I read a notice, a family looking for servant to care for infants. But when they see me, the babies start screaming, Injun scare them. I have no money anymore. Sleep beside buildings where it is warm. Have a blanket from home, one old dress and high button boots. One night a man stops me on the street and says, 'I'll buy you a nice nightie, dolly, and get you in a good clean crib.' At first I don't understand what he says, but when he takes me to the place, ahh, whores! Get rich laying with *waiscus*. I ran so fast! Then, you have seen the rest. It was very cold by then, no food. Sometimes I steal apples or took scraps from the ash cans. When the fever came, I thought, Well, the Person Above has sent me this. In a vision he was saying, I will take you out of this terrible land. You are better dead with the ghosts of your own people. Come back to us now." She clung to me, nodding hard and tears running down her dark cheeks. "Do you know, my dear Patrick I was ready to go. When you came by my bed, and I saw you, I couldn't believe that the vision was happening! My heart almost burst in joy! I was dead and you were there with me, Injun and squaw man floating like clouds in the Beyond."

"Beyond is just beginnin'," I whispered, and held her until the sun was down and she slept.

In the weeks ahead, we were so happy it didn't seem like there was anybody else in the world. She recovered fast, and with spring coming, I'd get her out in the sun as much as I could. But my undercover work did puzzle her. "What is this war, Patrick? Why are soldiers in the streets?"

I'd grin. "Because there ain't no Injuns left to fight."

"This one is left! What kind of soldier are you? Don't carry a rifle, don't even wear the blue suit? Who are the enemies that take you away from me so much?"

Hell, how to explain it to her? I'd give her some vague notions that a soldier's duty in the city was to save lives. The streets were crowded with foreign people who were trying to rip the country apart.

"Why would they do that?"

"Ah, they come here for a better life. Want to get rich like everybody else."

She'd frown. "What is rich, Patrick?"

"Well, dearie, it's everything out there on the street. The factories, trains, trolley cars. The stores with the big windows where you see all them dresses."

"All I see," she murmured, "is *waiscus* hurrying every which way, with faces so sad."

The next day, to cheer her up, I took her over to the Loop where I'd deliver my latest report to Zachary. When he wasn't around, I slipped the papers under his door and we strolled down LaSalle Street to the grand new Board of Trade building. I figured Walks Outside would enjoy a lift in the elevator, never having been in one. We hadn't but got out on the second floor when who do I run into but Zachary himself! He was striding down the hall with some of his big-wig pals, spots us, his jaw drops. Twisting away from the others, he grabs us, kicks open the door of a toilet room that said "Ladies" and shoves us inside. A dame comes screaming out of the can, still hiking up her bloomers, Zachary grunting at her, "This room is in use." After she'd hurried out, he planted himself with his back against the door and glowered.

"I told you, soldier, when you want me, you come to my apartment!"

"I was just there and left you a report."

"You better had!" He whirled on Walks Outside and looked her up and down. "A pretty goddamn fancy Indian, I'd say, and what the devil business is she of yours?"

I took a step toward him. "Now simmer down, mister. Read the report and you'll see."

He whirled to Walks Outside. "Savvy English?"

Her face tightened. She was clearly scared of the way he was storming. "I speak," she muttered.

"Lay off her, Zack! Her name is Walks Outside. Lakota. I knew her in Crazy Horse's camp, and run onto her here in the city. That good enough for you?"

"Not quite!" he snapped. He grabbed Walks Outside by the wrist, slowly turned her, looked at her beadwork, her high button boots and Sunday-go-to-meeting lace blouse. "You're a hell of a long way from your blanket, woman. What are you doing in the city, dolled up *waiscu* style?"

Her lips tightened. "Is it against the law for an Indian to be here? Are we not Americans?"

"Don't sass off to me!" he cried. "I asked you a question."

"My husband takes care of me," she said quietly. "You talk to him."

"Husband!" Zachary's jaw dropped open, and he whirled to me. "Since when do you have an Indian slut, Kelly! Why didn't I know this!"

"Because you ain't never asked. Now back off her, Zachary. She's no part of this and a good woman too. You got business, you do it with me!"

Walks Outside's eyes flashed with scorn and hurt. She thrust past Zachary, jerked open the door behind him and went out into the hall. For a moment, I thought he was going after her, but he pulled the door back shut and blocked it with his bulk.

"You're playing with fire, soldier," he said quietly. "Rolph told me you moved your lodging. He pays you every week, and I see why. Bought yourself a whore. Jesus Christ, couldn't you even find a white one!"

My fists tightened. "Like your women, Zach? I wonder who's paying for them. Ain't it your swell pals at the Chicago Association?"

He lashed out to whack me but I was too quick for him, twisting his arm around and flinging him into the door with a thud. "This street goes two ways, mister!" I cries. 'What's an Army officer doing, selling himself to a gang of bankers and factory owners? You think I ain't got eyes, or a lot of voices whispering to me on the street. You're in a rotten racket, and you got me by the balls all right, you and your minie ball. But there's a limit what I'm going to take from you. Get yourself another spy, damn ye! Start some other clod fresh and see if he can come up with what I've brung you all these months!"

He wrested loose. "Don't crowd me, Kelly, or you're dead! This city is about to explode, and I don't have the time to waste on you. What's in your damn report?"

I tells him that Parsons, Spies and the *Zeitung* crew were fixing to make trouble on the Black Road, McCormick works.

"When?"

"As soon as they can. They're rounding up street enforcers. Sluggers."

"All right, that's good, that's something. But I can tell you, Kelly, the Chicago Association, to a man, the leaders of this city are fed up. Do you have any idea how dangerous these anarchists are?"

"Probably better than you, because I'm out on the street with 'em."

"Ahh," he sneered, "you don't know the half of it. My position lets me see the overall strategy and I mean to implement it and end this rebellion. I've ordered 1500 militia brought to the armory, battle ready. I'm also calling in the First Infantry from Fort Sheridan, and General Sheridan has been so informed. This is on an if-needed basis. But right now, what you don't know, the entire nation is paralyzed by labor strikes. Why, here in the city, one-eighth of all working men have left the plants and taken to the streets. Railroad workers, gas company, iron men, meat packers, plumbers. One spark, this thing blows, and by God, I welcome that chance!"

"Meanin' what?"

His pale eyes flickered. "When these radical bastards assemble, do you know what they do? Pretty damn smart. They flock into these meeting places and bring along their wives and kids. The cops are Irish-Catholic mostly, and they hate the very smell of the longhairs, and most of all hate 'em because the bastards are athiests, Jesus-killers. But even a Chicago policeman hasn't the balls to fire into a crowd of women and children. So here's what I want from you, Kelly!" He pushed his finger into my chest and held it hard. "I don't care what they do out on the Black Road. No, find me a meeting, or better still, cause one to happen right here in the middle of town where there's going to be say, two or three thousand of the anarchists, men only. Then, when they start hurling their brickbats at the troops—and I'll have troops—you're a soldier, you know what will happen. We return fire, and in one volley right into the face, we'll blow away this goddamn labor war. That will be the end of it. Finished. The country will go back to work and never again will these foreign sonsofbitches threaten us. Shiftless bums, what did they ever earn? They have nothing but greed and envy. Cowards, the lot of 'em! They won't stand up to U.S. troops."

"I ain't so sure of that, Zachary. Them people have been chowsed around by coppers for too long now to take more from anybody, flag or not."

"You're dead wrong, Kelly! Mayor Harrison agrees with me, and has had a bellyful of these socialists. All we're waiting for is the right moment. You'd better be there for it. If you're not, nobody's going to know where you went, not even your squaw!"

After he'd stalked off, I went out in the hall and looked for Walks Outside. She'd vanished. Hurrying down to the lobby, I raced through the crowds and finally come on her leaning tall against a street lamp, out in the fresh air.

"You give me a fright," I says. "I thought I'd lost you." When her eyes smouldered and she didn't answer, I added: "I'm sorry about running into that mean bugger, but he's my officer."

"You are his dog?"

"Come on, gal." I starts to walk her through the crowds, but she acted like I wasn't with her at all, striding on in front of me, her head high. Only when I grabbed her arm did she whirl her dark face to me. "Oh, yes, he is your officer. But what am I, Patrick?"

"Well, you know. I told him. My gal."

"Wife, is that?"

"Why, sure."

She stopped short. "But you were ashamed to say it to 'your officer.' You don't even present me like you would a white woman. No, just a squaw. Injun slut with lace on her neck."

"I said nothing of the kind, damn ye!"

"You said nothing!" she whispered. "You just let that man look at me in his foul way! Was that enough for you, Patrick? Were you so afraid of him you couldn't stand up for us?"

"Goddammit!" I flared, "Zachary is holding Major Shaw's murder over me. I can't do nothin' but take orders from him, but that don't mean I like it!" She stopped and gripped my hands, people shoving past us until she drew me into an alley. "That man," she seethed, "oh, Patrick, he is death for you. I don't care what happens to me. It is just for you! Run! We must run now, it has been shown to me!"

I put my arms around her and we stood there, swaying together. "I love you, darlin', and maybe what you say is true. I ain't never trusted that bastard and even less the nasty job he give me. But out of it, I got you. We're together, ain't we? That's why we can't run. We've got no place to go and less to hide. Best we can hope for is that the end of this damn thing will come soon."

It wasn't long in coming. Out on the street I picked up word that Spies, Lingg and maybe Parsons himself would be over on the Black Road speaking to a meeting of the lumber shovers union. Figuring that it was heading for a showdown, I hops a car toward the McCormick Works. Before I could even get there, copper wagons came clanging past, and people were shouting out of the dingy worker houses that there'd been killings over at McCormick. When the lumber shovers noticed Pinkertons and scabs lighting into the picketing workers, they come clattering down the Black Road to help their brother working stiffs. I never did get a clear story of what happened. Somebody started shooting, and when the smoke cleared, several union men lay face down and dozens of others slinkin' off with revolver bullets in 'em. By nightfall, the poorer classes of the city were howling for vengeance.

The thought chilled me, thinking of Zachary's pale cold eyes, and knowing he was waiting to pounce on the next incident that would give him his bloody chance. But just what was it, where would it be? And more important, could I head it off some way?

The next morning, after I'd soused one of my informants with a tank of ale, he leaked out that a *Zeitung* German named Lingg was making bombs.

A half hour later, I'd tracked Lingg to a basement room over on West Washington. Crummy place, a hole under an empty iron works. No sign of him, and the door was locked. Going around the alley in the back, I found an airshaft window covered by an iron grate. Using a rock and an old piece of scrap, I twisted back the rusty grate, squirmed down the shaft and smashed open the small window.

I'd no sooner got into the dark, clammy room than I smelled something familiar. God in heaven, no wonder. It was black powder. The place looked like it had been an old shop for the iron company, and under the long, metal-topped workbenches were six wooden canisters of blasting powder, and beside them a small box with yellow cubes in it. The label read: "Dynamite." I fumbled around further. Cast-iron pipes lay scattered on the floor, and when I pulled up a canvas at the far end, here was a neat row of pipe bombs, about three feet long, with knuckle nuts screwed on to block the ends, and wispy white fuses trailing out, ready to light.

"Jesus and Mary," I whispers. The buggers, or Lingg alone, had it all here, ready to use. Just then, I heard a scraping sound up toward the street. I made a quick lunge at the shop door, cracked it open a peep, and could see into the anteroom, where Lingg must have lived. A cot with a rumple of blankets, an old stove, and daylight hitting them from the street above. The front door was opening and I heard men talking.

Whirling, I fled back into the shop room, no time now to get out of there or worm my way up the airshaft. The only thing I had going for me was the semi-darkness. On the far wall, I spotted one of the workbenches with a metal sink in it, and a cabinet below. I made a lunge toward it and crawled in. The dark space had plumbing pipe in it from the sink, but I scrunched around until I fit inside, just barely, and pulled the cabinet doors almost shut. The men from the street were in the room, not ten feet from me. I couldn't see much through my crack but they had a torch, spearing around through the darkness. I was afraid to move lest they'd hear me. Then one of 'em lets out a shout, "Just like we thought, boys!" I hear iron scraping and craned around to look. They'd flung back the canvas and were pulling out the pipe bombs. One of the men says, "How many we going to need?" "Every damn one," a voice answers. "He wants us to have enough to take care of the other targets. Use that canvas when you go out to the wagon. Cover 'em."

By then, even at the risk, I had to crack open the cabinet door further. There were three big men in the room, but they wasn't Germans. A couple wore slouch hats, another a derby, and just the footpad way they moved, lugging out the pipe, told me only one thing. They were Pinkerton flatfeet. When they switched off their torch, I heard another voice coming from the door to the anteroom. "That satchel over there," the voice said. "Bring it. Right size to do the job."

"Right size?" I'm thinking. Then, God help me, I knew that voice! Ora Zachary! Had to be, but before I could get the door cracked open enough to see, one of the Pinks had picked up a worn-out old leather valise, carried it away, and he and the new man were gone. I heard the front door crunch shut, the place was dark again. Pushing out from the cabinet, I rushed across the shop and into Lingg's bedroom. Damn my luck! By the time I looked up the short flight of steps to the street, all I could see was a black, police-type wagon and the back doors closing. Only there was no City of Chicago lettering on the wagon sides. This was private stuff. Secret. Pinks, sure, but was Zachary with 'em?

I'd never know, and even less what so-called law enforcers were doing with the bombs. I milled around on the street until about five that afternoon when I see a horseman come clattering down DesPlaines. He had flyers under his arm and was kiting 'em out to workingmen. "The Haymarket!" he was shouting. "Bring your men!"

I picks one of the flyers out of the muddy street. The same big type was smeared across it: *"Arbiter Zeitung!* In palaces they fill goblets with costly wine and pledge the health of the bloody banditti of the Order. Dry your tears, ye poor and suffering. Take heart, ye braves. Rise in your might and level the robber rule in the dust!"

Hurrying back to my lodging, I says to Walks Outside, "They mean to do it tonight, I think. You stay here, lock yourself in. I'm going over to the Haymarket."

"You have found something?"

"Enough, and I don't want you around it."

She gripped my hands and smiled. "Ah, the fire is in your eyes, Patrick. I am so happy to see it again. Of course I will not stay in this cage, waiting. A wife is meant for war too!"

I couldn't talk her out of it. Finally, I just grunts, "All right, damn ye, but wear your old dress and a blanket around it. Looks like rain out there." She smiled, and when she pulled on the dress, she slid a small clasp knife into the skirt pocket.

The Haymarket, a big oblong square on Randolph between DesPlaines and Halsted, was only a few blocks from our house. On the way over, I seen another flyer plastered on a telephone pole: "The Haymarket! Tonight, 7 o'clock. WORKINGMEN ARM YOUR-SELVES AND APPEAR IN FULL FORCE!" As we hurried down the street, we passed the DesPlaines police station and there was enough paddy wagons pulled up here to make it look like a livery barn. Coppers in blue uniforms and caps were going through drills on the sidewalk, making the workingmen heading for the meeting stream around them out onto the streets.

By the time we hit the square, the sun was gone and gray rain clouds were whipping in from the west. I tightened my arm around Walks Outside, for there must have been two or three thousand workers already in the square. Factory buildings rose up like cliffs on all sides of us, the biggest one being the Crane Plumbing works at the north end. The mob was growling or shouting at the speakers, the noise of it booming off the factory walls like we was in a canyon. "I don't care for the looks of this," I says to Walks Outside. "There ain't no women and children. Just the way Zachary wanted it."

"Will the soldiers come?"

"I don't know. There's already a helluva lot of coppers."

The rough-dressed workingmen were crowding around a wagon parked at the far end of the square. I wanted to get close to it, but it was hard to lead Walks Outside through the noisy, haranguing crowd of these brawny buggers. In the humid air, I could smell the sweat on their grimy clothes. Finally, I pulls her around the end of the crowd where a bunch of coppers were forming up. It was dark here, all the street lights off, but I see the flaring of a match and a man in a brown derby lighting a seegar. It was Carter Harrison, the mayor. Somebody says to him, "Sir, it's dangerous to draw attention to yourself this way."

"Rubbish!" snaps Harrison, sucking on his seegar to keep it going. "The best thing in the world is to let the people know their Mayor is here with them."

A police captain pushes in beside him. "I've been through the crowd, sir. They're angry enough but I'd say we have it controlled. Those long-winded speakers are going to put this mob to sleep."

Harrison nodded. "I intend to watch it for a few minutes more, then let it fade away." He turned and the police led him off someplace else. In the dark, it was hard to pick out anybody's face. I'm sure there was Pinks mingling with the workers, but I couldn't spot a familiar one. Least of all was there any sign of Zachary, and not a single bluebelly soldier.

I pulls Walks Outside around the back of the crowd and leads her in as close as we could get to the wagon. The little *Zeitunger,* Spies, was waving his arms, shouting over the noisy workers, "Attention! Listen, I ask you. There are, in the city today, between forty and fifty thousand men locked out because they refuse to obey the supreme will of a small number of men. The families of twenty-five or thirty thousand men are starving because their husbands and fathers are not men enough to resist the dictation of a few thieves."

The crowd roared back, "Hang 'em! Hang McCormick!"

Then Albert Parsons got to his feet, and I figured it had to be serious if the head radical showed up. "Is this Germany or Russia or Spain?" he cried.

Voices shouted: "It looks like it!"

"If you love your wives and children, if you don't want to see them perish with hunger, killed or cut down like dogs in the street, Americans, in the interest of your liberty and your independence, arm! Arm yourselves!"

The crowd began growling: "We're ready. We'll do it!"

There was more roaring, and finally he turned to a white-haired Limey windbag, Samuel Fielden, who started his own harangue. I pulls Walks Outside away where I could see over the slouch hats and derbies of the workers. "What is it, Patrick?"

"Don't know yet." I points toward the distant police station. "The Mayor must have left. He ain't over there where he was, and them coppers are forming into ranks." I pulls her across to a doorway of the Crane Plumbing building which had an alley beside it. "Stay here, gal. Don't you move."

Turning, I starts back into the crowd which was beginning to thin. The rain was pelting harder now, some of the workers holding newspapers over their heads, and the others drifting away. In that instant, I hears a clatter of feet and it wasn't the tired workers going home. It was a line of police, coming in on the trot, whacking the mob aside with their billy sticks. The police were in four ranks and there must have been fifty men in each. When they neared the tailgate of the wagon where Fielden was mouthing off, the head copper, a captain with a gleaming badge, hollers: "In the name of the people of the State of Illinois, I command the meeting immediately and peaceably to disperse!"

Fielden cries: "But we *are* peaceable!"

The crowd was muttering angrily, milling around in confusion as the police ranks pushed on in, several coppers reaching up to jerk Fielden and Spies out of the wagon. The fear and anger in the air give me an awful hunch that this was the flashpoint. Whirling, I started to run back to the Crane doorway to get Walks Outside. But the workers were shoving and pushing to beat it out of there. In the dark, two bruisers thrust past me, and, unlike the others, they were heading toward the wagon and the coppers. I might not have noticed 'em if I hadn't stumbled and glanced down to catch myself. One of the men shoving past me was carrying a leather satchel. Even in the dark, it could have been the twin of the satchel I'd seen the Pinks carry out of Lingg's basement! In just that flash look, I seen that the handle of the satchel was loose. Only one end of it was attached to the leather. The other was gripped in a man's big hand, and his arm, which was all I saw, was in a black, shiny raincoat. But too quick, he was lost in the crowd.

I stumbles up onto the sidewalk, heading for the Crane doorway when I hears a scream from the wagon. A strange orange light crackles and fizzles. Then a shattering roar, blasting off the walls of the buildings, the sky flashing clear as day, the whole square bouncing up and down in the force of the explosion. It was like a hand had struck me from behind and knocked me flat on my face. Fragments of iron hissed past, shattering windows of the buildings, glass tinkling onto the pavement. Down on all fours, I turns toward the screams. Under a white cloud of powder smoke lay the whole front rank of coppers, writhing, dying, blue bodies ripped and broken, the ones still alive kicking in their pain. From behind them, the next ranks of coppers were rushing in, Irish voices screaming curses, their revolvers crashing fire and steel into the workingmen. Hats were flying off, close-range bullets ripping into the chests and faces of the working stiffs. The square was roaring with anger and terror, everybody trying to run at once and not knowing where to escape. A few workingmen were firing back, gunflashes spitting out of the darkness as they pulled away, cursing in their Hunky tongues and covering their bloody faces with their hands.

Thank God, Walks Outside was just where I left her, the flames of the burning wagon flaring over her face. Just as I runs up, she drops to her knees. One of the wounded coppers had come whirling in like a broken top and fell beside her. "Mary Mother!" he cries in a thick brogue, "help me—the arm—bleedin' to death!"

Walks Outside already had hold of him and eased his shoulders down to the street. With her knife she cut open his ragged blue sleeve, and when I see the look of his arm, it was all but chopped off at the elbow, the bottom of the grisly thing held on only by a dangle of broken bones and tendons. His blood was spraying up on her face.

"Handkerchief." she cried to me, and when I jerked it out of my pocket, she tied it in a hard knot just above the shattered elbow. The copper's eyes were rolling, his bearded face drained pale in shock. He tried to say something but he was gargling, choking. Walks Outside reached in and seized his tongue, pulling it out to give him air. "You'll live," she kept whispering. "The blood is stopped now."

Just as I tried to help her, or find somebody to care for the poor bugger, I hear above all the shouts one loud voice barking: "Over there! That's him! The bomber, canvas coat!"

I hears footstep slamming toward us. In all the confusion, it never crossed my mind, but the coat I was looking at with the copper's blood on it was my coat! Light canvas to keep off the rain. Whirling, I see two shapes racing toward us out of the crowd, flames of the wagon flashing on their revolvers. I grabs Walks Outside, jerks her up and we run toward the alley, she screaming in the terror of it and not knowing why it happened. Just as I fling her in front of me, rounding the alley corner, two bullets ping into the side of the building, stinging my cheek with bits of stone. "Run, gal! There, down to the end!"

The alley was maybe a hundred yards long and we flew past the garbage cans and parked wagons. In the running, my throat was burning, sucking in air, but Walks Outside was even swifter than me. When she got to the end of the alley, she cried, "A trap! No place to go!"

I hear the feet slamming behind us, one more shot, the bullet hitting something and singing away. Stand and fight? But I had nothing on me, no gun, only her knife. "No chance," I cries. In that moment, I spots an iron ladder bolted to the factory wall. I shoved her at it and she scrambled up the rungs ahead of me. When we reached the top, it was the flat second story of one of the factory buildings. "Gimme your knife," I says, crouching down behind the little wall on the roof. "If them buggers come up the ladder, I'll take 'em one by one."

She was clinging to me, both of us peeping over to look down. But the alley was noisy now, torches of coppers stabbing the doorways and flashing over other workers trying to escape. I never could see who'd fired the shots, and sure didn't plan to hang around and find out. Keeping low, I leads Walks Outside across the roof of that plant, and when we hits the end of it, facing the street, I see the rungs of another iron ladder leading down. I rips off the canvas coat, and then, hands trembling, gets her down onto street level.

Thank God, there were so many people here, running every which way, we just melted in and high-tailed it through back alleys until we got home. Behind us, the sky was lit with the flames of Haymarket, and the roar of the city was dying off except for the clanging of paddy wagons and ambulances, rushing in to pick up the dead.

For me, though, there was no regaining what I'd lost here. The violence of Haymarket was like a knife plunged into Walks Outside's heart. The next morning, I went out to get the newspapers, and when I come back, our room was empty. All she'd left me was her headband, beaded in the colors of the American flag.

Though I'd seen it coming, I was overwhelmed by grief. I had no idea where she'd gone, and no way to reach her. Letters I wrote to the Sioux reservations were either trashed by the slovenly agents, or came back scrawled, "Not known."

If the loss of her wasn't sad enough, the fraud of Haymarket sickened me. The whole world was stunned by it. Sixty-seven coppers wounded, seven dead, and God knows how many radicals. Nobody was counting the anarchist stiffs, the poor shot ones crawling back to their hovels and the dead dumped forgotten into potter's field. The city fathers were howling for justice. I seen then why the Pinks and coppers had taken the bombs out of Lingg's basement. After planting them in radicals' houses all over town, they swooped in and arrested the poor stiffs on the "evidence." Every man connected to this tragedy would be hung. Hell, they were convicted before they'd even been caught.

The trials dragged on into the fall of 1877, going all the way to the U.S. Supreme court. Claims were made that the original twelve jurors had been paid $100,000 each by the Chicago association. For the hanging, troops were rushed to Chicago from as far away as Salt Lake, and the association donated hundreds of rifles and a Gatling gun to "preserve order." Hundreds of Chicago police surrounded the courthouse, and they were armed with Springfields and bayonets in case the radicals tried to charge and set their heroes free. In the last hours before the hanging, Lingg, the bombmaker, had a small dynamite cartridge smuggled into his cell. He bit it in his teeth and blew his head off. That left, on the gallows, Parsons, Spies, Fischer and Engel, the last three from the *Zeitung* bunch. As the hood was pulled over Parsons' head, the gutsy ex-Rebel cavalryman cried, "Let the voice of the people be heard!"

Somebody heard, all right. On a snowy December 11, 1887, a quarter of a million people, workingmen mostly, turned out to carry the radicals' bodies to Waldheim cemetery. It was the largest public gathering in Chicago's history. The anarchist movement was blown apart by Haymarket, shot in the face as Zachary had predicted and helped come true. Nobody had won the eight-hour day or a fairer shake, and it would be a long hard fight before the nabobs ever let it happen.

And yet, sickened as I was by my part in Haymarket, something big had changed here. The rumbling in the streets wasn't going to die out. The next time the thunder flashed into fire, I prayed I'd be on the side of the underdogs and let the eagles burn in hell.

I never dreamed how quick it would happen. And not in the cities this time. We still had the last ghosts of the frontier to kill.

FIGHTS CLOUDS

In the spring of 1889, my luck changed. I'd read in the paper about a new law Congress had passed. The Dawes Act, they called it, and under it, the Sioux would give up eleven million more acres of their ancestral hunting grounds. But as a sop, any Sioux who signed would get his own 160 acres, free and clear.

Just as I was thinking what a raw deal it was, I see at the bottom of the story that General Crook would be the man going to Dakota to administer the land grab.

I wrote him a letter that very night. About ten days later, a sergeant wakes me in the Fort Sheridan barracks and dumps some papers in my lap. By order of General Crook, I was assigned to him in South Dakota. "You'll be my interpreter, Kelly," he scribbled on it. "Last of the old Rosebud bunch."

For a month or two, we traveled all the Sioux reservations, me parleying with the old chiefs, trying to explain the deal Crook was offering. I grieved for the buggers. They couldn't read the damn maps I was showin' 'em. Their brains didn't work on paper, they just flowed with the land as they'd done for hundreds of years. They had no way to imagine that the old times were truly gone. Up on Standing Rock Reservation, Sitting Bull raised hell about the land grab, but Crook cut him short, telling him that he'd lost his power and respect among the people. The guvmint needed three-quarters of the adult males to sign, and little by little, they trooped in and scrawled their marks.

By the time we reached Pine Ridge, Crook had brightened momentarily over the success of his treaty-making. To entertain the dignitary commissioners and mainly himself, he put on his seedy hunting duds and led us into the piney hills of Nebraska to shoot wild turkey. For a day or two it was like old times, all of us settin' around the campfire swapping yarns about how this country used to be. Though Crook was still a crack shot, I noticed him hanging back more and more. There'd be toms gobbling in a patch of timber, but he'd just sit on a rock and let the others do the killin'.

The trip come to an unhappy end. Lewishon, one of the soldier wranglers, was a surly bugger, and one morning, over how to pack a mule, he gets into a fight with Clanahan, a big Mick corporal who clubs him with a trenching spade. We thought Lewishon was on the way out, so Crook folds up the hunt and we clatter back to the nearest doctor who was at the Drexel Catholic Mission, five miles from Pine Ridge.

The mission itself was a giant three-story brick building, gables in the roof and spires with crosses on 'em. Standing way out in the middle of lonely prairie, it looked like a castle somebody had dropped in here from the Old World. After I'd got Lewishon into the sawbones and saw that he'd live, I started back down the hallway to go care for our pack animals. Like churches anyplace, this one had the musty smell of holy candles and whispery nuns in black habits gliding through the shadows. They'd frown at my uniform like what in hell was a soldier doin' in God's house?

Hurrying to get out of there, I come to the second floor which the priests used as an Injun boarding school. In a classroom at the end of the hall, I hear squeals and glanced inside. It was a nursery for Lakota babies, a few tykes playing with bright toys on the floor. Other brown-skinned babes were in cribs and a nun and a nurse were fussing over 'em, gettin' bottles into their squallin' mouths.

The nurse in white stood up from the crib. She'd half-turned to say something to the nun, but in that turn, God help me, I saw how tall she was, her face dark against the starchy uniform. Her black hair was still in a rope down her back, but instead of her headband, she wore a white nurse's cap. The button on it gleamed gold.

In Lakota I cried out, *"Wife! Walks Outside!"*

She whirled, the proud nose, the Chink eyes squinting. Her hand flashed to her mouth!

"Jesus God," I whispered. "It's you! Ah, gal, where have you been!" I swept her into my arms, but savagely, she pulled away. Running to the door of the adjoining room, she cried, "Father! Father Craft!"

A thin-faced young man in a black robe came quickly to her side. "What is it, girl? What?"

She whirled and pointed her finger at me. "I have seen a ghost, Father. Tell me if it's a ghost!"

He was smoking a cigarette, and when it wisped up into his eyes, he tapped the ash from it. "No," he said and smiled. "I would say, my dear girl, that your ghost is a soldier."

She looked at him, then at me, and plunged her face into her hands. When I took her back into my arms, her shoulders were racking in sobs. Sniffling, laughing, she kissed me all over my face and ran her fingers down through the tears on my cheeks. "Oh, Patrick, dear Mister Patrick! God has sent you, he must have!"

"Did you think I'd ever forget you, gal?"

"No, no! Not that. But so long now, no word, I try for word. I wrote you all over the place, but you didn't hear!"

"That's Army, darlin'. And the same out here, all my writin' to you. How'd I ever know where you were?"

Father Craft had lit another cigarette and was sizing me up. "Well, you're not exactly a stranger, Mister Kelly."

"You knew about me?"

Walks Outside was clutching his hand and mine. "What do you think I've talked about all these years, Patrick! Look, look here, sisters!" More nuns and nurses had hurried in, their spectacled eyes mooning at us in curiosity and joy. "He is my husband. My child will have a name!"

"Your...your what?"

"Ours! The baby, dear Patrick. I have given you a son!"

"Aw, for Christ's sweet sake," I moaned, and it didn't matter if the nuns were gasping in shock, I just stood there blubbering and holding her to me like I'd never let her go again.

The nuns were giggling and Father Craft put his arms around both of us. "Show him, girl," he said. "Meet the prettiest blue-eyed Lakota you've ever seen."

By God if he wasn't. When she lifted up the child who was plucking at her skirt, his shiny little face was dark-skinned all right and his hair wisping black. He had her nose, too, proud and sharp. But when he sniffed the smell of this big *waiscu* stranger hugging him, the little eyes flickering at me were as blue as the sea crashing the rocks of County Mayo. "God in heaven," I whispers, "next thing we know he'll be popping freckles! What the devil are we going to call him?"

Walks Outside had it all figured out. For the Christian he'd be Matthew—"Not by bread alone does man live." And for the heathen, Fights Clouds.

She gripped my hands. "We give him you, Patrick! Fights Without Club. But more. In my father's family we have the great Touch the Clouds. So this little one must fight the clouds, in the courage of your people and ours!"

"Matthew Fights Clouds Kelly!" The nuns were blessing the poor tyke, who began squalling in fright until Father Craft says, "Too much excitement all at once and it doesn't need on-lookers. Girl, take your family to your quarters and rejoice at what the Lord has brought. I'll do his baptism at six this evening following Mass."

In her cubicle down on the first floor, we put Matthew Fights Clouds to sleep at the foot of her hard cot, and then, in all the tenderness and passion of the loneliness apart, we made wild and grateful love. I just couldn't get enough of her hard, proud body, or she of me. She wrapped the earth around me in her strong legs and arms, and our joy was shaking the little crucifix cockeyed on the wall. For hours, praying the babe not to wake up and end it, we sobbed and laughed, trying to put our lives back together.

The morning after Haymarket, she told me, she'd been so furious at Zachary that she rushed down to his flat on Lake Street. "I had a knife," she whispered. "I was going to kill him for trying to kill

200

you, but when I got there, he was gone. He must have just left. The fireplace was still roaring, things were burning in it. I did something bad, Patrick."

"What was that?"

"I hated that man so much for taking you from me, I said I will take something back from this foul one. In the fireplace, he had clothes burning. Mostly gone they were, except for a black raincoat. It was rubber, maybe that's why the fire wouldn't eat it." She peered at me. "Why do you look so strange?"

"A black rubber raincoat!" I muttered. "Gal, don't you remember! Somebody in that kind of raincoat was at the Haymarket!"

"Shooting at us! He must have been the one!"

"I don't know, Walks Outside. Whoever chased us into that alley I didn't see. But out on the square, before the bomb, it could have been him. Ah, hell," I shrugged, "no way to prove nothing. It's over now, thank God." I grinned and stroked her cheek. "So my little Injun counted coup on her enemy? Good for you, darlin'. An old burned coat. Was it worth anything?"

"Of course it is, to people who have no clothes! I brought it home with me. My old aunt wears it around her camp when the nights are cold. The foul one was good for something, anyhow."

The rest of her tale made sense, though I sure couldn't have figured it out at the time. She'd simply fled back to her people and finally hooked on with the sisters, doing nursing at the Drexel Catholic Mission. Without the proper address, my letters never got through.

Later that afternoon I reported to General Crook. When I told him that Father Craft was waiting in the church to shake the waters on my babe, he glanced at his watch and smiled. "If you don't mind a pagan, soldier, let's go."

"Sir?"

"Can't hurt, I suppose. We're all getting closer to that time when we could use a little churching. Besides, I've heard good things about Craft. He's been with the Sioux for many years. Valuable connection. They trust him."

In the shadows of that frontier chapel, with candles flickering and the echoing of the holy words, a feeling of peace swept over me, and it was strange after all these years of war. Here was old Crookie laying his conqueror's hand on my lad's little head, and then turning, still the gruff General, not showing his heart, he drew Walks Outside to him and kissed her on the forehead.

When it was done, Father Craft led us up to a small dining room and the sisters fixed us beefsteak and potatoes. There was red wine on the table, probably from the altar, and Father Craft was puffing his cigarettes even as he ate. Crook, though, didn't touch either of the vices, never had the taste, he said, and that was rare for an Army man in those lonely years on the frontier.

Walks Outside, with little Matthew in her lap, sat across the table from Crook. She was wearing a pretty yellow squaw dress and beadwork around her neck. When it come time to nurse the babe, shamelessly she pulled the dress down from her shoulder and gave him the blood-red nipple of her breast. Ah, I was so proud of her, the erect way she sat, her stately beauty. Crook squinted at us, his leathery face crinkling. "Well, soldier, I can see why you wanted to come back here. I commend you both for finding each other. Burying the hatchet, we might say."

As I looked at him, I thought: yes, he'd won, we'd won. The scattered few bands still able to resist had been ground down in the thundering glory of our cavalry charges, blasted by howitzers in their winter caves until the starving wretches had no choice but to come weeping in to surrender.

Father Craft murmured, "The Indian was in our way, General, that's what it amounts to. No room for him in our plan. He had to go. Well, we've done it for 300 years now. Are we finally at the end? And perhaps more important, how does the Lord judge us for the enormity of our genocide?"

Crook took a deep breath and stared at his hands. For a moment, I thought he was going to push up from the table and leave. But then he did a strange thing. He reached out and took Walks Outside's hand. "I can make no apologies to your people. I did what my duty called of me, and your warriors, the bravest I've known, were forced by our collision on this continent to do the same. In our war of the Rebellion, I fought against my own wife's brothers and uncles. It's never easy sorting out which of us is right. You talk about God. I'm not a religious man, but I doubt if he's on anybody's side. Look at the survival of species that nature demands. It's harsh. The old must die so that new life can be born. There have been wrongs on both sides in all this bloody history. You see your burned camps with innocent children slain, ponies with their throats cut, your lodges looted by ruthless invaders with hair on their faces. And for every one of those, miss, I have walked through the wreckage of frontier shacks, soddies, broken wagon trains where, because we were the strange ones to you, your people wreaked unspeakable horror and depravity on our defenseless settlers. Who makes it right on either side! Who is wise enough?" Sadly, he shook his head. "I'm not the man to know. All I can hope for, now that the tides of 'progress' have swept your old lives away, I hope to bring justice to your people, and some measure of recompense for the wrongs you've suffered. Do you understand me?"

Walks Outside's eyes glistened with tears. "I see that you have a good heart, sir. Even remembering what you have done to us, I love you for that."

"Well, General," Father Craft said, "I second it. But I do wish that people of good heart like yourself had more control of the outcome."

Crook squinted at him. "You realize, I'm sure, the political constraints any General officer must work under."

"Don't I though!" Father Craft smiled. "How often I've testified to Congress, telling those august gentlemen that I, too, am under severe constraints in the Society of Jesus. Think what it's like to have distant, medieval Spaniards telling me how to operate in the New World! Why, it's their creeds and their minions who have littered our continent with the bones of millions of aborigines. But that said, dear General, this Dawes act of delivering land in severalty to the Indians will only be a death-knell to what's left of the people. Oh, we look out the window at these vast sweeps of emptiness and we think that there's too much land, that it doesn't mean anything. Why should 30,000 shiftless Lakota be occupying 'American' land that's the size of New Hampshire and Vermont? That's what you're demanding they give up. And what's left, why, they won't hold onto it, can't possibly. Settlers are already flocking in to rob them of their tracts. As Crazy Horse said, 'You cannot sell the land on which the people walk.' Land is not property to them. Nothing is privately held. It's communal, for the common weal. But I heard today, perhaps it's just an agency rumor, now that your land treaties have been validated, already Congress is cutting the beef ration to these people. What do they have left, I ask you!"

Wearily, Crook tapped his fists on the tabletop. "I've begged the Army, the President, the Congress, to listen to observers like you, Father. To cease and desist from their crass, politically-motivated clutching of their purse strings. But they don't see. Their budgets, their appropriations are year to year. All they care about is being re-elected and sharing the spoils of office with these political hacks they send us as Indian agents. The long-term effects of plundering the tribes means not a whit to them. But God help me, I'm sick of it, and have fought against it every day in our months of discussion. If the beef ration is cut, these Indians to whom I've pledged my faith will only blame their signing that treaty for bringing them this disaster."

"But sir," I butts in, "can't you change the way it works? Hell, I been watching you these months. I know damn well you ain't happy with this damn piece of paper."

"It was the best I could get, Kelly! Sure, maybe I dread the implications, but in war and politics, and there's no difference between them, you move a step at a time, advance a foot, retreat a foot. In whatever time I have left, I mean to keep fighting. That's all I can say to you, or to you, Father," he glanced at Walks Outside, "and to you and your people. Wait, be patient."

She smiled sadly. "By'em'by, the Lakota say."

"By'em'by," Crook murmured and got to his feet. "I thank you all." He walked around the table, patted little Matthew's head, and was gone.

As I watched that grizzled old warhorse shuffle away, I had the sorrowful feeling that we were coming to the end of our trail. For a moment, I saw him slogging the snow with us before Crazy Woman Fork, and again at the Rosebud, his black horse cart-wheeling down, gut-shot. Even the fierce rocks of the Sierra Madre were melting into a sad memory. He was a brave man, doing a nasty job that no one would thank him for. There was so much bad blood on both sides that only time and maybe new generations could ever heal it.

That was May of 1889. On a morning eight months later, in his hotel room at the Grand Pacific in Chicago, Crook called to his wife, Mary, and said, "I feel tired." Before she could take him in her arms, he'd gasped his last breath. Dead at 61, all his years of hard campaigning finally catching up with him, and, I truly believe, his heart breaking in his failure to bring a just peace to his enemies.

When I told Walks Outside the news, she whispered, "For all the death he brought, he was a good man. Strong for the people. Who is going to carry on for us now, Patrick?"

"You, darlin'," I says and smiles. "Me, too, if I can."

"We must, husband." She picked up Matthew and held him to her breast. "His world can be better than ours if we make it that way."

We tried, but the times were against us.

A Messiah craze called the Ghost Dance was sweeping the West. On the reservations, 40,000 Injuns were said to be dancing. The settlers were screaming in fear to Washington, and the greatest number of soldiers ever put in the field since the Civil War began rumbling our way.

A warrior chief named Kicking Bear sat with Walks Outside and me in our cabin and with eyes gleaming, told about the dance. The Lakota would form into a great circle around a sacred tree, a rock or sometimes even around a Christian cross. The dancers could wear no metal objects, no knives or even traditional jewelry. Hour after hour they'd chant their many prayers. Kicking Bear sang one: "A'te he' u-we, ya'nipi-kta, e'ya u'-we lo." Meaning, "There is the father coming. 'You shall live,' he says as he comes." Soon, the dancers would spin around dizzy in their belief, many falling to the ground and foaming at the mouth. As I listened to Kicking Bear's powerful new medicine, my heart tightened in fear, but mostly pity that he could have swallowed such guff, and passed it on as gospel.

According to him, the Ghost Dance was not for war, it was for peace. He slapped his hands together in the off-sign, this man who had helped kill Custer at the Little Big Horn and almost us at Rosebud. *"The Person Above takes hold of the land like a great blanket that is the height of a white man standing up. When he pulls it back, all the white-eyes fall off the top, all the houses. The earth that is left below is just as pure as it was for all of the People's time. Buffalo herds are darkening the sky with their dust again. The soldier forts are gone, too. The scars of the wagon wheels have disappeared from our soil. The world is ours again!"*

Fat chance, I thought, and the sadness of it struck me hard, coming just at this time when I was happier than I'd been in years. Walks Outside, young Matty and I had run onto a real streak of luck. My cavalry cantonment, #6, was up at Deadwood, South Dakota. We had a few patrol duties but not much else. To kill my spare time, I got a job with a feisty, hell-and-brimstone newspaper-man, Freeman McTighe. His *Sentinel* was no more than a one-room print shop on the main canyon street of Deadwood, but all the labor in town was so gold-crazy McTighe couldn't find a gopher to clean up the shop at nights. So I started out lugging paper bales and melting down old type-trays, and it led to a real friendship.

Freeman McTighe was more than a boss to me. For all his ranting about politics and injustice, he was a clever little scamp with a big heart. He went around in shirtsleeves with garters on 'em, his red beard smudged with ink and a dead seegar clamped in his teeth. "What I can pay you, Kelly," he said, "won't buy you a cup of coffee. But what I can teach you will tell you the tale of the under-dog in these great, glorious United States, and maybe give you the guts to fight back. Do I have the right man?"

I grins and says, "Try me, Freeman."

"I'll do more than that," he snaps.

Damned if he didn't. First off, he sells us for 10 bucks an abandoned miner's shack that lay in a coulee off of main street. "If the wife and you can fix it up," he says, "move in. You'll be close to your work at the paper, and ride your horse up the road to your military duties."

The rough-hewn old shell wasn't much, but it had a little spring and two acres of hillside land with pine trees. "This is ours, gal!" I cries to Walks Outside, "the first piece of ground I've ever owned in the US of A."

What a thrill it was to ride home from the cavalry camp after colors and see Walks Outside tackin' up white lace curtains, and our tawny babe giggling in the grass with a tree-frog in his mitt. Walks Outside would grin and scold me for thinking the land was ours. "It's his," she'd cry, sweeping the scampering tyke into her arms. Then she'd tell him in Lakota that his grandfathers were watching him play here. Matthew, nearing three years old, was already starting to chatter, but it was mostly in Lakota, mixed with American. "Matt," I'd say, riding him horsie on my knee, "how are they going to understand you when you get to school?"

"I speak soldier then," he says. "Gimme button, Papa," and he tries to bite one off my cavalry blouse.

Next thing McTighe did was to let Walks Outside write in Lakota for the Sioux and put it in the paper. "We need Indian voices," he said, and was hoping that her words would tell the restless bucks the truth of what was going on. But again, we run out of time.

In November, I had to take a patrol down into the Pine Ridge reservation, and what I saw was pitiful. Just as Father Craft had predicted, the crooked agents, backed up by their cronies in Congress, had slashed the beef ration until the people were starving. On top of it, the weather had turned hot and dry. Their pitiful crops withered away, and like Job's boils, the last straw was sickness. Measles swept the reservations, then the influenza. With the kids weakened by hunger, they began to die faster than Craft or the Holy Rosary nurses could treat 'em. I'd parley with the old proud chiefs, and their angry wailing pierced my heart.

On the heels of that come even worse news. Up north on the Standing Rock reservation, Sitting Bull threw in with the Ghost Dancers, and for the first time, I could smell war in the air.

With Walks Outside begging me, I finally got leave from my officer and took her and Matty horseback northeast over the frozen prairie. The hope was that she and I could talk sense to the cranky old charlatan before he bulled himself into a fight.

We were too late. It had already begun.

THE 7TH CAVALRY'S REVENGE

In the dusk of December 18th, Walks Outside pricked up her ears even before I did. She held her head high and sniffed the air. "The People are close."

We come out of a coulee and onto a plain, streaked with the silver coils of the Cheyenne River. In the distance, I could see a few log huts that must have been there a long time, and around them, the wagons and teepees of a big camp. Hurrying in, we found hundreds of Injun families, all in a state of great excitement. Three days before, Injun police and troops had stormed Sitting Bull's camp. In the ruckus, his followers lit into the police and killed some of them. But as they were falling dead, they had managed to blast down old Sitting Bull himself. Maybe the circumstances were different than the killing of Crazy Horse, but the reason was the same. The holy men were a threat to peace. The last real fighters were gone.

That night in the camp, the People were still mourning, squaws hacking their hair and slashing their arms. Walks Outside got right back into it with 'em, and Injun tykes took Matthew off to play in the dirt and chase ground squirrels. I noted some surliness on the part of the warriors, eyeing my uniform, but mostly they just lay beside their lodges, their eyes smouldering like the dying fires.

These Lakota were in the band of a chief named Big Foot, and they were confused and scared. Walks Outside and I kept telling them that the soldiers didn't mean them harm, and wouldn't do nothing if they just trooped peacefully back to their reservations. Yet that same night, dozens of more mounted warriors came clattering in, and by daybreak the camp was humming with wild tales of soldiers shooting at them and claiming that the whole Sioux nation was going to be packed up and sent to the hated Indian territory of Oklahoma.

Walks Outside, Matthew and I slept in the lodge of Mary Sweet Grass, her aunt on her father's side. Mary was a wispy little thing, her skin as crinkly as old paper. She looked about 90 and wore spectacles from some Army post with the lens missing on one side. I'd twit her and say in Lakota, *"My beautiful aunt is only seeing half the world in her waiscu glasses."*

With a snort, she snatched up Matthew. *"What half of the world is his, mister soldier? Tell me that! His world is gone. You took it away and my niece as well."*

About mid-morning the camp broke up, and the whole kaboodle of us, maybe two or three hundred people, started creaking the wagons and travois southwest toward the Badlands.

Big Foot was known to be a pretty fair and pacified chief, been to Washington many times. I'd hoped to visit with him on the march, but he was all bundled up in his travois and his wives led Walks Outside to believe that he was suffering in his lungs. I could hear him coughing as the day wore on, and figured I'd best wait for a time when his ears might be open.

But it never come. On toward dusk, I told Walks Outside that I'd scout ahead of the bunch, hoping to find some grass for the wagon teams, horses so skinny their backs was like knives. She frowned, "Husband, along this river there are squatters now. Whites who have taken our land and shoot at any red skin as they would a wolf coming too close to their shacks." She made me take two young buck warriors with me, for they knew this country better than me, and where we might run into trouble.

About dark, the three of us come down into a valley partly hidden by tall cliffs of that miserable Badland soil, clay streaked in reds and whites and the wind for all the centuries carving it into spires and whistle holes. I thought I seen a flash of light just ahead. It wasn't a campfire. It went out like maybe a match in the wind. I didn't know if I was just imagining it, or had I heard a click of steel, too? Whatever, I told the Sioux lads to hang back. I'd go down off the hill and snoop.

Next thing I knows, there's more clicks, a smear of buffalo hats and black faces that I could hardly see against the night. "Halt, you!"

Then other shouts: "More, boys, up yonder ridge!" A Winchester spurts flame and crashes. I hear the clatter of the Sioux lads' ponies above in the rocks, and by the time of the next volleys, they was long gone.

"Goddammit!" I cries. "Friendlies! Hold your fire!"

"Who is saying dat?"

Rough hands had seized me, whirled me. I was lookin' into the face of a black man. Nagur, he was—buffalo soldiers, and they had me dead to rights.

"For Christ's sake," I cries, "look at the uniform I got on! I'm from Cantonment 6, over at Deadwood. Trooper Kelly, 3rd Cavalry."

"Ain't no 3rd here," grunts one of the black men. "We're 6th Cavalry, up from Texas."

"Well, ain't that somethin'," I grunts, and then, just bein' common soldiers together, they unhands me and takes me over to their officer.

He was sitting in a cave the wind had howled out of the Badlands and with a stick was drying his socks over a fire. He had a bristly moustache and a hard, lean face that had been pointed into a lot of prairie winds. He wore a broad-brimmed hat, not reg, and when he pushed up wearily and looked me over, I could see that he was a steely-eyed bugger without an ounce of pity in him. Just get the Army job done.

And profane! He cussed like a teamster. "You stupid black son-sofbitches!" he roared at his nagur troopers, "pissing your breeches when any shadow moves out there! I told you there was to be no firing, and I want the ass of the first whore's son who started it!"

Finally he cooled down and got to me. I told him what I was doin' out there, the wife and child traveling with Big Foot's band and trying to keep the peace. He scowled. "Squaw man soldier? Where'd you learn that?"

I grunts something about Rosebud and Walks Outside, even back to Nati, down with Crook in the Sierra. "Jesus Christ," he grunts, "am I by some stroke of luck to find a bonafide soldier still left out here! Speak Lakota? You got to, don't you?"

"Yessir."

"Detached are you? What is this bullshit?"

I tries to explain how it come up, Crook and all, and he cuts through it. "You're attached, trooper. I've got black recruits here, and if somebody don't start stopping 'em from wetting their pants, they'll blow their feet off. I also want a Sioux talker and you're it."

"Sir," I says, "only thing is, I left my woman and child back with the People. Your lads blasting at them Injuns ain't gonna make 'em very settled. I'd best go back to that camp and explain things."

He smiled coldly. "I attached a soldier, not a barracks lawyer. Mess with my troops, bed down. We pull out before dawn."

When I joined the darkies around their fire and shared their beans, I says, "Who in hell is that rough-talking lieutenant you got?"

They chuckled. "Why, man, ain't you heard? You can hear him cussin' all the way from the Staked Plains to the North Pole. Not a man to cross. That's Black Jack, and if he ain't got a bodacious temper, his name ain't John J. Pershing!"

Hell, he was just one more Army man to me, back in harness again and I couldn't do a damn thing to get shet of it. I was worried as hell about leaving Walks Outside with the People, tempers so edgy now on both sides, troops ringing Big Foot's band and crowdin' the Injuns more every day. But there wasn't no arguin' with Pershing. I was on Army time now, and he couldn't care a damn if my woman was left grievin' for me. He had a lot of old Crookie in him, honest and hard with the troops, looking after their welfare before his own, but tolerating no slackers and ducking no danger that he'd ask another man to risk.

So off we went plodding, west through the Badlands, the December winds spittin' snow into our faces. But now, unlike in '76 at the Crazy Woman Fork, the Army had figured how to protect soldiers fighting in this fierce cold. The darky troopers all had big buffalo coats and caps, and gloves so thick you couldn't lift a pail of water with 'em, let alone try to pull a trigger. When Pershing seen me in my civvy Hudson Bay jacket over my summer cavalry blues, he began sonsofbitching the bastards in the quartermaster and finally barked to the troop sergeant, "Get my scout here the buffalo coat of that worthless trooper who died on the trail!"

"Hell, sir," I says, "I'm warm enough, and if I ain't, maybe I'm gonna be." He squinted at me and I pointed toward a ridge line above us where I'd seen a shadow that didn't belong. "That ain't no Christmas tree up there." Until I said it, I didn't realize that Christmas was already past. This was the dusk of Christmas day. So much for the dreams of Walks Outside, little Matt and me.

Pershing was scanning the ridge line with field glasses. "The hell you say," he murmured. "But no, wait. Something did move." He whirled to his men. "Stamp out those fires. Get into the rocks! On the double!"

Just as the troopers started to scurry for cover, slugs from the ridge begin hissing and pinging into our camp. "Hold fire until you have targets!" Pershing shouted. But the black troopers were blasting anyway, their bullet puffs kicking up on the ridge.

Whoever them Injuns was, they knew how to fight way better than our lads. They'd shoot from one part of the ridge line, then scurry down to another. Pretty soon I seen the dust of horses, maybe more joining the hostiles. By then, they had the range on us good. We didn't have no place to hide, we were hugging the only rocky cover there was. But Pershing wasn't down. He was striding back and forth just behind our firing line, kicking butt and sonsofbitching others when they were quitting their shooting and trying to wriggle to some safer place. Finally I growls at him, "Mister! Get down, willya. They wouldn't know where we was in here if you wasn't standin' up drawin' fire!"

He roars at me like I was the yellow-belly of all time and that flamed me. I jumped to my feet and placed myself square in front of him, facing the flashes of the Sioux guns. "If you ain't gonna get your thick head down, mister, then I'm gonna stand here until I stop one for you."

I hadn't but got the words out when a trooper besides us screams, a slug ripping his arm, blood spraying me and the Lieutenant. With a faint nod, as close as he could ever come to thanks, he says, "Move those Indians out of range, Sergeant."

I blinks. "It's private, sir."

"Not now. I believe you're just mean enough to wear three stripes."

I slaps a few troopers on the backs, rallies 'em a little, and gets 'em to follow me runnin' down the slope, not taking the ridge head on, but going around the base of it. By the time we were over there, it was dark, the reds hadn't seen us coming, but were still plinking away at Pershing's bunch. So my lads and I crawl up the hill. At our first volley, catching them from behind, the hostiles scattered, and the only noise left was two hit ones moaning, and the sound of ponies thundering away.

When we came back to camp, I told Pershing that one of the warriors who'd escaped was Kicking Bear, the other Short Bull. "Kicking Bear," I said, "come by my place in Deadwood a while back, all puffed up with ghost dancin' and the magic power of the damn shirts. I ain't personally acquainted with Short Bull, but they're the old breed. Hit us at Rosebud and put Custer down."

Pershing nodded. "That is remembered."

"Sir?"

"I had a dispatch this morning. The 7th Cavalry is now out here and has taken position on our west flank. They haven't forgotten, Kelly. If these old warrior fools give them the slightest provocation, those soldiers mean to avenge the Big Horn, you can bet on it."

Just as Pershing had said, for the two days after Christmas, we began seeing the dust of other cavalry patrols, moving like black ants on the frozen prairie. Then snow showers would whip in and we'd lose sight of them. But one thing was pretty clear. The Army had spread a big net around the north and west. As they tightened it, any Injuns caught within were being slowly pushed southeast toward Pine Ridge reservation.

In the dark, squally skies, there was a feeling of doom. I began fidgeting and chafing, longing to get back to Walks Outside, at least be beside her if things got rough. Late on the afternoon of December 27, after units of the fresh 9th Cavalry had joined up with us, a dispatch rider comes streaking in from the north. Pershing beckoned me over and shows me the dispatch. "What do you make of this, Kelly?"

The sum of it was a white squatter and squawman named Dunn. I'd heard of him from the Injuns. He had a Lakota half-breed woman all right, and like many of the *waiscu*, thought that give him claim on a hunk of Injun land. However it happened, a Colonel Sumner and the 5th Cavalry had caught up with Big Foot's band and started making parley with him. Colonel Sumner promised Big Foot that he'd take him peacefully down to Pine Ridge. Nothing was said about stopping dancing or any kind of punishment. But, Injuns bein' Injuns, they had to yammer it out among themselves, and when they were too slow to decide, the Colonel sends 'em Dunn, who could speak Lakota, to goose 'em along. The next thing Sumner knows, the Injuns had fled in the night, and he lost 'em.

"Sir," I says to Pershing, "I don't necessarily trust this Dunn. My hunch is that he told them people some kind of wild lies, just to get

211

'em off his turf up here. Maybe he was even straight with 'em that they wouldn't be harmed, but I've seen it happen too many times before. When you parley with Lakota, just the faintest lift of an eyebrow or the way you say one word louder than the other is apt to touch a trigger in them."

"You're thinking that they got scared and fled?"

"Something like that."

"So what do you recommend?"

"Well, sir, first thing is, somebody's got to find 'em. I've got a hunch that they'll keep moving south. Pine Ridge has always meant safety to 'em. The old chiefs are down there, Red Cloud and others. And besides, there's enough guvmint people and missionaries around to give 'em some sense of comfort."

He was squatting and stood up slowly. He took off his wide hat and wiped his finger around the dusty headband. "Do you think you could find Big Foot's people, Kelly?"

"As well as anybody, maybe."

"No, I think better than anybody," he said. "You've got a wife and child with those people. Your fat is in the fire. Get down there, see what you can do. Talk some sense to them."

"Thank you, sir," I says. "I been waitin' since Christmas to do just that!"

"Get out of here. Bring me word when you have some." Then he turned and began growling at his black men, preparing the column to move.

I waited until dark and then lit out on a gallop for the south. I'd only been down to Pine Ridge on my one cavalry patrol, but having traveled with Injuns enough from my old captivity days, I had a pretty good notion of how the warrior leaders read the land. They was like game animals who always took the low side of ridges and the trails that would be the least work for their tired animals. They looked for basins, too, where there might be a springhole or nibble of grass. But now the land was frozen tight, snow clouds rolling over me and not even any stars to steer by.

I did have a good mount, though, and when I took him down to an easy walk, with just enough touch on his mouth to keep him awake, his perkin' ears told me that he knew he was leading me someplace that he could scent, and I didn't. Being a herd animal, a horse was always looking for his own. "So am I, lad," I whispers. "Find 'em."

It must have been close to midnight when the Badlands had fallen away and the country was rolling south in great dark waves like the sea. My mount began quickening his steps, his head switching from side to side. With a jangle of the bit, he stops short, getting wind of something. As I started to wheel off him, he gives a little pull-away and almost dumped me. There was fear in his eyes, the wrong scent striking his nostrils. He'd whiffed Injun ponies, no doubt about it. Moving carefully on foot, I come around the bend of a coulee and could see faint smudges of red. Closer, they were Injun fires, some of 'em inside the ghostly shapes of Lakota lodges. A few wagons were scattered about, bony black skeletons on the silvery plain. There was more snow here in the lower country and as I crunched through it, I was surprised that the Injun wagon horses didn't get to neighing at my beast. Maybe his scent wasn't strange to 'em, and even the camp dogs weren't barking. Could it be that other whites had beat me here?

Too late I got my answer. In a basin just below the lodges, a bonfire blazed up, its flames dancing over the blanketed shapes of Injuns. They were milling, being crowded together and chowsed by a dismounted line of troopers, carbines at the ready.

Behind me, like a volley of shots, hoofbeats rattled the frozen ground. A cavalry patrol swept in, its red and white guidon streaming. 7th U.S. Cavalry.

God in heaven, it chilled me. I bolted toward the fire because I could already hear the angry bucks growling in Lakota. They didn't want soldiers in their camp and weren't about to give up their guns to them. An officer was barking to a half-breed interpreter, "Tell 'em we're only asking for 25 rifles. Nobody's going to harm them. They'll be kept here under our protection until morning, and then moved to Pine Ridge."

As I shoved through the growling Injuns and the swirl of soldiers trying to push 'em back, a low whisper cut my heart: *"Husband! Get out! Run!"*

Walks Outside came rushing to me, Matthew bulging under her blanket and old aunt Mary Sweet Grass clutching her for dear life. "Now quit this," I laughs, hugging 'em. "I'm here, you got no reason to be scared..."

"Too late!" Walks Outside hissed, pulling me through the crowd to the edge of the fire. Big Foot lay on an Army litter. He was covered in blankets, a wool cap on his head and his wives sobbing beside him. When he tried to answer the Army interpreter, he'd start racking with coughs, finally falling back pale and gasping for breath. Ringing him were the warriors of the band, clinging to their rifles or tryin' to hide 'em under their blankets and cast-off charity greatcoats. The troopers were so impatient and nasty that I started to bust into it and warn 'em not to disarm these people so fast.

"No!" Walks Outside pulled me back, her hand ice cold in mine, terror in her eyes. Cavalry officers were moving around the fire toward Big Foot. One was a captain, flinging back his blue cape so that he could get his hand on his revolver. Behind him come a colonel with a white goatee and broad white hat. A whistle shrilled and a tall officer muscles out in front of the others. He was beckoning the soldiers to back off from their disarming. In his buffalo coat and cap, and his bare hand holding the whistle in his lips, I couldn't get a good look at him until he came up to Big Foot and stopped. With his hands on his hips and his face smirking power, he looked down on the poor old man with all the scorn of a conqueror.

God help us, didn't I know! Ora Zachary!

I froze. Him with the 7th? How, why? Hell, I'd never find out, and there wasn't time neither, Walks Outside tearing at me, turning me, but it was too late. Zachary's quick eyes had spotted yellow cavalry stripes standing where they didn't belong in the midst of the Injuns. "You, soldier!" he barked. "Out of there! Stand in your rank, we..."

He never finished. His big jaw had dropped, his cold eyes gleaming like a cat that had just found a mouse under his paw. "Lieutenant," the colonel barked, "I can't deal calmly with these Indians if your soldiers are in the middle of them."

"This man is not from the 7th, sir. He's in where he shouldn't be. Front and center, you."

As I stepped forward, the colonel glowered at me. "What the devil do you think you're doing? Deserted from some other unit, that your story?"

"Nossir. I'm under orders to be here."

"Leave him to me, Colonel," Zachary said. "I know him from way back. I'll settle his hash."

As the colonel grunted and moved off with the others to work out the disarming, Zachary took hold of Walks Outside, Matthew and me and led us into the shadows beyond the fire. Eyeing us up and down, he said, "So, what do we have here! The two bad pennies, isn't it? I'll say this for you, Kelly, you've got an instinct for putting yourself in harm's way. Don't you ever learn?"

"Not from a sonofabitch like you," I muttered, fists tight.

"Now, now, that's no way to address your superior. How did your head get so big, soldier? Is it this?" His teeth bared in a smile and he drew the blanket away from Matthew's head. "Family man, are you now? An Indian-lover makes himself a little half-breed to go on the ration rolls, suck more charity out of the great White Father. Oh, yes, Kelly, you know how to work the system all right. Don't even mind who you lie with to get what you want." He flicked the blanket back and smiled at Walks Outside. "Does he share his pay with you like he did buying you fancy clothes back in Chicago? Oh, you're some Hiawatha, you are! How does it feel to be back here where you belong, starving and freezing your pretty black ass!"

"She don't have to take that, mister, and I ain't!" I shoves him

214

back with my Winchester.

"Sure, Kelly, talk big, make your bluff and you can't do a damn thing about it." He brushed the rifle aside. "My command has this camp, and you're under me. Don't get yourself dead any quicker than you have to, because I'd be delighted to oblige!"

"I'll bet you would, you miserable bastard." My face was flushed, my hands trembling. "I'm going to tell you something, Zachary. I don't know if you can count nothing except them goldpieces the Chicago association bought you with, but if you can, count just a few more days. January first, the new year, and my hitch is up. I done my time. I can walk out of your racket and you or no bluebelly can lay a hand on me!"

He laughed harshly. "So you really believe that, do you? Keep dreaming, you thick-headed Mick. The Army don't write discharges in time of war, and this is war. Even if it calms down in a while, I can keep your papers buried so long you'll have gray hair before they reach the War Department. In the meantime," he leveled a finger again, "you get restless, try to desert and run off with your latest whore, I'll see to it that you get what you gave Shaw, in full payment." His face was trembling in fury, the veins bulging in his neck.

"You mean," I said, lookin' him in the eye, "after you and your Pinks didn't get me in Chicago, now you'll do it right?"

He scowled. "What in hell are you talking about?"

"You knew I was on to your game, mister. After you'd rigged your damn Haymarket, you figured you was finished with me, so you'd gun me down in that alley and I'd never spill the beans!"

His lips tightened. "I wasn't even at the Haymarket! I was on a train going to Washington. My work was over, and by God you'll start doing yours now, or I'll put you in irons. Why are you in this camp? You know these people?"

"Yas, I know 'em!"

"I said why! What did you do, desert your command so you could be with your lady love?"

"I come here on Lieutenant Pershing's orders. 6th cavalry, attached to him."

"Oh? So now you're a black man, too, Kelly? You change your skin color more times than a chameleon. You like passing, I suppose. Jesus Christ, a blue-eyed Irishman! What in hell is your trouble?"

It was all I could do to hold onto my temper. "Pershing's orders!" I flared. "He told me to stay with these people, persuade 'em to surrender peacefully, and mostly to protect 'em from rotten sonsofbitches like you!"

He grinned. "Well now, isn't that just fine! Fits like a glove. Forget Pershing's orders and your gold-bricking, too. You're under this command and finally you're going to do something right for your government."

"What's going on here?" said the goateed colonel, striding up.

Zachary whirled. "Sir, I've served with this soldier in the past. He's gone squaw man, but I think we can use him to get these hotheads simmered down and complete the disarming."

"I have fifteen rifles already turned in," the colonel said. "I know they're hiding more, but it isn't going to amount to a fart, and I haven't time to argue about it. We have the camp surrounded. We'll move south in the morning. I've dispatched an order to the troops at Wounded Knee. It's a big open site, close enough to the agency that we can protect it. Get your men back into ranks, Lieutenant."

"Yessir. But I'd suggest keeping this soldier in the camp and calm down the hostiles during the move-out."

The colonel frowned and scratched at his goatee. "Make him a hostage from us, you're saying?'

Zachary nodded. "Indians think that way. They like to have a piece of the enemy's hide in their war bag."

"All right," the colonel grunted. "Don't suppose it can hurt." He glanced at me. "You're to stay in uniform, soldier, so there's no confusion. But you're not to carry weapons, too much risk of accidental discharge and blow the whole thing. Take his rifle, Zachary."

"Yes, sir!" After the colonel had stumped away, Zachary's face went cold. He snapped his fingers at me and held out his hand. Slowly, my jaw tight, I slid the Winchester at him, barrel first, pointed at his gut. He pulled back my buffalo coat. "Get it off." With a jerk, I unhitched my U.S. belt and handed him my Colt and cartridges. He nodded, his big teeth flashing in a grin. "I like having you back with me, Kelly. This isn't Chicago where you can melt away. Here, I know where you are—and got the minie ball right here in my pocket. Sweet dreams, Hiawatha." He winked at Walks Outside, turned on his bootheel and strode off to rejoin the officers.

LAKOTA DEATH SONG

For what was left of that night, I lay with Walks Outside, staring at the winking fires of the 7th Cavalry and the shadows of sentries. "Oh, husband," she sobbed, "can't we run away?"

"Not a chance, darlin'. He's put me here and those pickets mean to keep me here. If everything works out right, they'll take us down to Wounded Knee and surrender the band. It will be over, and better still, I'll be outa this bloody Army."

I glanced up because the tent flap lifted and in come three Lakota. They were strangers to me, a pair of young hot-bloods who, even in the cold, were stripped down to breechclouts, their hard bodies and faces painted in war colors. The third man was Dancing Eagle, a mean-faced fighter from the old days. He scowled at Walks Outside. *"You, the daughter of a great warrior, you lie with a hair-faced killer. You take him to your loins! Why?"*

Walks Outside's eyes flickered. *"He is my husband. He means no harm to us. He will help us with these troops that have come."*

"Help! What do you call that?" Dancing Eagle cried, flinging his arm out toward the ridges above us. *"Do you not hear the sound? They have rolled in cannons to blast our camp. They are already loading them! Why do they do that,"* he swung to me, *"unless they mean to shoot us down like coyotes?"*

By then, more of the northern Lakota had pushed into the lodge. They were frightened, surly and well-armed, mostly with Winchesters they'd hidden from the 7th. One young buck had an Army-style roached haircut and wore a soldier blouse. He'd been off to Injun school at Carlisle barracks, educated and uppity. "What do you tell us that we don't already know!" he cried in perfect American. "The troops had those same Hotchkiss guns ready at Sitting Bull's camp in case he didn't surrender. Why do they bring so much power here now? This is like trying to kill an ant with a war-club. They have the power because they mean to use it!"

I shook my head. "I doubt that, my friend. The way the Army thinks, they always back themselves up with more than they think they need. There wouldn't be no point in blastin' down innocent Injuns when they're already surrenderin'. There'd be no excuse for it."

"So what is this?" he flared and thrust a wrinkled newspaper into my hands. "You think we don't read what you people are saying all over your country. They are screaming for our scalps. Punish the Custer killers!"

The paper was the *New York World*, and when I skimmed the front page columns, I could see what was terrifying the lad. Correspondents from all over had flocked into Pine Ridge like they was waiting for the works to blow on the 4th of July. "Historic moment!" one reporter blared. "We are here to witness the last surrender of hostile Indians in the United States. From gore to glory, three centuries of warfare with savage peoples will end on these frozen plains."

The other bucks were growling, one of 'em plucking at the newspaper as if he could read the secrets in it. As he did so, a middle sheet fell out, and a column on the left caught my eye. The headline read: "Local Reporter Considers Sioux Dancing Peaceful. No Threat." Below, the story began, "Freeman McTighe, special correspondent to the *World,* and a Dakota newspaperman of long experience with the Sioux, reports that the entire Indian trouble on the Plains has been inflated far beyond its reality. Though thousands of Indians are dancing all over the West, McTighe regards it as a civilization's last cry for justice. As the *World's* correspondent, McTighe is riding with the famed 7th Cavalry and filing his...."

I never finished. "God in heaven," I whispers and thrusts the paper to Walks Outside.

"Oh, Patrick," she cried. "This is hope, don't you see! Do you suppose he is with these troops around us?"

"I don't know. But one thing about that feisty bugger, with him lookin' in, and knowin' all these other reporters as he does, the Army sure won't pull any shenanigans in front of him."

"But if we could reach him, Patrick, have him know the terror our people feel this very night—please, you must try!"

Then she translated it out to the Lakota, telling them that we had a friend nearby who put down the words on the paper, and that these were more powerful than guns. Her husband would bring this man to us.

Ah, the childishness of them Lakota. They began grunting *how's* and *hola's,* slapping me on the back. They didn't understand Army, and that I was under orders to stay put. Least of all could they understand a murderous bastard like Zachary. I drew Walks Outside away from the others and we left the lodge. There were no stars and the cold was biting fierce. She had her arms wrapped around her breast. "Gal," I says, "it would be one thing if I stumble onto McTighe when they break camp in the morning. That would be the best of luck. But hell, we don't know how old that story is or when he was out with the troops. He could be long gone by now, and you've got these people all fired up with false hope..."

She squinted hard at me. "I don't like your words. Say the truth! You're afraid of that foul Zachary!"

"You're goddamn right I am! If I cross that man's orders, if I give him one chance to rack me, he'll do it. You know what that means? When I come up for discharge, he could hang another violation on me, hold up my damn papers and I'd never get loose."

She drew away. "I want the People to live. I thought I had a man with the courage to face his enemies." Turning, she stalked back into the lodge.

Mary Sweet Grass had flamed up the fire and I could see that there'd be no sleep for the rest of this night. The bucks threw scraps of meat into the stew pot, the pipes come out and the wrangling begun. The ghost-shirt wearers were ready to fight at dawn. I didn't know what in hell to do. Any course of action seemed a longshot. Stay put and wait for things to happen, or plunge in and make 'em happen, even at the cost of my freedom, and possibly my life.

At length, I just lay back, rubbed by the legs of Injuns and smellin' 'em crammed in there, and says to myself, it's out of this lad's hands. Maybe it's in yours.

Funny thing, I had just started to doze when little Matt, wide awake by now, comes snugglin' up to me and ticklin' my face. I loved to play with the little blue-eyed tyke, but I was tired and too worried to want to bother with it now. "Go to sleep, son," I whispers.

He wasn't listening. He kept rubbing my cheek with something, scratching me hard, and when it hurt, I finally pushed up. What he had in his little mitt was a leather neckband. I'd noticed it before when Mary Sweet Grass was braiding the thongs and beading them. But not until now did I see how she'd finished it off. Threaded into the center of the band was a leather handle, torn at the ends like it had been ripped from a satchel.

"Matty!" I cried, gripping it. "Where did you get this!"

His hand flashed toward Walks Outside. "Momma have. Make present, pretty boy. Here, Papa, you put on."

I hugged him and crawled over to her. She was sitting with the Carlisle Injun, proudly showing him what she'd taken out of her canvas sack. It was a clipping of a Lakota story she'd written for McTighe.

I dropped the handle in her skirt. "What is this, gal? You keepin' souvenirs?"

She laughed. "Oh, husband, Auntie found it when I gave her the coat. It was in the pocket."

"What coat?"

"I told you, Patrick. That last day in Chicago, I went to Zachary's place. The coat was burning in the fire. Now anyway it keeps Auntie warm." She smiled at old Mary, the shiny black raincoat flapping on her like a raven's wings as she stirred the stew pot.

"God Almighty," I breathed. "Walks Outside, don't you know what this means! I can't prove it, but by damn, if this was the handle on the suitcase at Haymarket, and if it was in the pocket of the black coat, then Zachary *was* there, and maybe even flung the satchel with the bomb!"

She stood up sharply. "Oh, Patrick, I never thought that. I would have said! Do you really think this could be him?"

"It's all I've got, darlin'. Let's pray it's enough."

Her eyes tightened. "You mean, if you could prove?"

"Hell, yes. All this time, gal, you've been after me to start fightin' another way. I see it now, and maybe this is where we start. Gimme that sheet, your story." She took it from the Carlisle Injun and handed it to me. "Now we need a pen, pencil, somethin' to write with."

She fumbled in her pack. "I brought nothing, Patrick."

"Well, I did." The Carlisle lad pushed up. "In my lodge I have been putting down the story of what is happening to us."

When he came back with an old pencil that he sharpened with his knife, the other bucks crowded around Walks Outside and me. I lay the clipping on the hard top of an old cracker tin, and writing more painstaking than I'd ever done in my diary, I printed: "This is the last will and testament of Sergeant Patrick Kelly, 3rd U.S. Cavalry and his wife, Walks Outside of the Lakota nation, set down by us in the 7th Cavalry camp, north of Wounded Knee, 28th of December, year of 1890. Upon the death of either of us, to be opened and attached statement and evidence placed in hands of proper authorities."

Following that, as short as I could make it, I set down the facts of my service under Lieutenant Ora Zachary for the sole purpose of destroying the labor movement in Chicago. I put in all the accusations I had against the man, told of the Haymarket, the satchel and the black coat. Then Walks Outside, in the graceful, flowery hand she'd learned from the nuns, described finding the black coat and handle in his apartment. When it was done, I signed it and so did she. The Carlisle lad signed as witness, "John Roving Bear," and aunt Mary Sweet Grass, who'd once known some American, painfully scrawled her name.

"Oh, Patrick!" Walks Outside cried. "You will go?"

"With this, darlin', I've got a weapon anyhow. God knows where it will come down, but we'll sure find out."

Stuffing the papers and the raincoat into Aunt Mary Sweet Grass's buckskin pouch, I give Walks Outside a last hug, and little Matt, too, and slipped outside into the dawn.

Mist was rising, gleaming on the brass barrels of the Hotchkiss guns pointed down at us from the ridge. "You miserable sonsofbitches," I whispered. "This might just be the one time you ain't gonna get your way with the People."

A few minutes later, when the troops had chow on their mind, and using the Indian wagons as cover, I managed to get away. My first hope was to find Freeman McTighe, but that meant tangling with the 7th, in some unit someplace that didn't know me. I was sure that the whole regiment had been split up into patrols, and God knows which one Freeman would be riding with, that is, if he was still even around. Toward noon, I run onto some Army wagons the 7th was escorting. Lazing in, pretending I wanted a borrow of oats for my mount, I asked a corporal was there any correspondents ridin' with the 7th? He said there had been, he'd run onto one or two, but they was down around Pine Ridge. After I'd got the oats from him, I realized I was chasing a needle into a haystack. It could be that as long as the 7th was herding the Injuns south to Wounded Knee, Pine Ridge was the place I ought to be going.

But then I pondered. If I didn't happen to find McTighe, just who in hell could I leave my evidence with? There wasn't all that many people I could trust with something that had my life written all over it. On the other hand, if I could get as far down as the Holy Rosary mission, Father Craft would be out there. Or would he? Hell, it had been months since I'd seen him, and I knew very well from what he'd said once, his Jesuit honchos were always running him hither and yon, raising money for the mission. It would be just my luck to find him far away someplace, and nobody at the convent but some doddery nuns, so far out of the world that they wouldn't know how to get my words into the right hands.

By dusk, I realized the folly of this ride. Yes, Walks Outside and I had set down on paper our own ghost shirt against the bullets of Ora Zachary, but it didn't mean a fart in the Dakota wind if it just lay in a ditch, blowing away. With McTighe and Craft probably longshots, the only man I knew and figured I could trust was Lieutenant Pershing. If all the troops were moving south, following the one band of hostiles, didn't that mean that his lads would have to be with them?

About dark, I did stumble on a lonely camp of black buffalo soldiers. They were huddled in a coulee making their dinner fires. They offered me some of their meat and beans, which I wolfed gladly for my belly was growling. But when I says I had a dispatch for Lieutenant Pershing, they knew him all right, and my mount better have wings. "Mister man," chuckles one darky corporal, "dat cussin' Black Jack flew off on us yestiddy mornin', headin' north to that stronghole the Injuns got in the Badlands. More shootin' up there. Be couple of days at least before his troop joins up with us pore folks."

As I rode back south, my heart was heavy. I was so dog-tired I had to slap my face to stay awake and keep from toppling off into the snow. Even failing on my long ride, all I was dreaming now was to get back to Walks Outside, put us both in the Lord's hands, for I damn well couldn't solve it on my own.

Wool-gathering as I was, I didn't realize that it had been hours since I'd passed the old basin where I'd left Big Foot's band. The country was just waves of bleak, rolling hills, slashed by the dark veins of coulees where cottonwoods and willows stood frozen. Staring at it so long now for signs of life must have numbed my brain. I come up on a ridge, walking my mount who was all but played out. I didn't even realize that the strange smell was fires, and that shapes on the plain below were Army tents and lodges.

A shuffling in the snow, jangle of harness. Rifles click behind me. Out of the darkness ride two buffalo-coated troopers, Winchesters across their pommels. "That's him!" one barks. The other shouts, "Dismount, mister. Under arrest!"

Before I could even swing out of the saddle, another horse swirls in, rearing back in a shower of snow. "Take his mount," the rider says, and after the trooper had pulled my animal away, I was staring at a Colt revolver, lying across the arm of Ora Zachary.

After the troopers had ridden off, dragging my mount with them, Zachary and I stood alone on that dark, lonely ridge, and in the faint starlight, I could see the glow in his eyes. He squatted down, the revolver ready on his big thigh. "Didn't you think I'd check the camp for you, Kelly? My troopers knew you were under arrest. One saw you slip out just before daybreak. Why did you leave camp when you were under my orders to stay there!"

"This, you sonofabitch!" I jerked the buckskin pouch from my shoulder. I was unprepared for him catching me again, and I knew that after failing on my ride, I didn't have a leg to stand on or anybody to protect me. One shot in the dark night could be a deserter trying to escape in time of war. My only hope was to bluff him to the showdown. "You and your 7th are crowding these Injuns. Maybe you ain't got a plan to put 'em under, Zachary, you ain't that cocky. In fact, you're a damn coward, but you got your finger on the trigger. If you chowse these people too hard, you damn well know what you'll get back! Just like Haymarket! You'll get your excuse to blow 'em all away. That's why I rode out. I wanted to find Pershing or some newspaper man who would at least be honest eyes lookin' over your murderous shoulder."

Zachary stood up slowly, "You're making a lot of accusations, soldier, and nobody's around to hear them but the coyotes. I've come to the end of the string with you."

"You ain't but started, mister!" I ripped open the pouch, shook from it our letter, the satchel handle and the black raincoat sleeve. "Pick 'em up, you bastard! Read what it says!"

Warily, he jerked the Colt barrel at me and motioned me back. Then he dropped in the snow, fingered the handle, the raincoat and the piece of paper. "What is this garbage, Kelly?"

"Read it, and remember!"

He had the letter crinkled in his big fist, squinted at it, and finally jerked a match out of his blouse. The flame sputtered in the cold wind, and his eyes narrowed as he read. Then he flung the match away, rose up and howled. "'The Last Will and Testament,' is it! You goddamn thick-headed immigrant, are you a barracks lawyer now? Have you never heard about libel, about hearsay? You should have stuck with killing Indians, Kelly, instead of screwing them. Your whore came to my apartment and found an old coat with a handle in it? What the hell does that prove!"

"That you was at the Haymarket, mister, and probably flung the bomb. I seen the satchel when you raided Lingg's place—I was there—and I seen you in that black coat in the crowd. Maybe you saw me, too, and had your Pinks try to kill us in the alley."

His big jaw had tightened and there was a tremble in his lips. "Who have you showed this to?"

"You figure it out."

He leapt at me and pressed the Colt into my cheek. "Who!"

In that one second, my whole world seemed to flash across my eyes. The old instinct was to fist him in the belly, grab the Colt, blow him down and run. But he was a big, strong killer at heart, and his chances just as good as mine. The other way was to lie. That I'd found Pershing and found McTighe and the whole world knew. But somehow, that bugger breathing into my face was the devil I'd sold my soul to, and the only way to kill the lie I'd been living was the truth.

I shoved him back. "Nobody seen it, Zachary. The men I wanted to find, the honest ones, ain't around, and maybe that's good. Now it's just you and me."

His big teeth bared. "You're even stupider than I thought, Kelly. Nobody saw it," he howled, "nobody but a couple of Sioux and an already convicted murdering soldier. Well, your time is up." He dropped to his knees and stuffed the sheet, handle and coat sleeve into the pouch. "Right here, I've got all the evidence I need against you, and what's your word and the lies of Indians against mine?"

"It won't come to that, Zachary. There ain't gonna be no court-martial, at least not yet."

"What do you mean, not yet?"

"Why," I said quietly, "you find a deserter out here in time of war, you shoot him down. No problem with that. I ain't the first. And hell, Zach, you talk about evidence. You ain't gonna be showin' anybody that paper or them objects, now are you? What good would it do but maybe make some general officer tie you back to the Chicago association pay-offs, and the Haymarket murders you done for 'em? Hell, mister, you're movin' right up the ladder. The nabobs who own this country owe you a real debt for blowin' the working-men off their backs. You got big ambitions in this Army. It don't pay to rock the boat. You said it yourself. Get inside the system and you can win big. Best leave it at that."

He drew away from me, looked down at the revolver and checked the cylinder. When he snapped it shut, he said, "On your way, soldier. Run, if you want."

"Nossir." I smiles. "With the Lieutenant's permission, I'd like to take it walking."

"Goddamn you!" he shouted.

"That way," I said quietly, "I'll have time to think how this is gonna come down. My woman will hear that I've been shot. So will another Lakota, John Roving Bear. Smart Injun, studyin' at Carlisle to be a lawyer for the tribe. And there on the back of that evidence paper, you'll see what my wife wrote for the publisher of the paper up in Deadwood. His name is Freeman McTighe. He covered the Haymarket, and wrote about the men you sent to the gallows. He knows all the wrinkles, Mister Zack, and how to get to the big ears. Why, right now, he's even out here, riding with the 7th Cavalry, and reporting for the *New York World* exactly how you're crowding these Injuns into a war."

"Are you threatening me?"

"How can a dead man threaten anybody? The only hope I've got is seeing you in hell with me, knowing that decent men finally caught up with you, ripped off your bars and pitched your career into the ashcan. Good night, Lieutenant, sir! Shoot well. You'd best not miss."

I turned from him. I heard the revolver click. My shoulders tightened, waiting for the slug to crash into my back. If there wasn't another way to beat the bastard, at least now I'd show him a brave man going free. My mind hurtled me all the way back to the Sierra Madre of Mexico. *Ley del fuego*, they called it down there, law of the fugitive. If a prisoner ran like a rabbit, they'd blast him and howl at his groveling death. But if he had the guts just to walk, then who was the coward, them or him? Run! he'd said. That was fear. Show no fear! Walk slow, count the steps. My face was on fire, I was breathing hard. Quick, damn ye, make it quick!

I stared at my feet, sliding through the snow. I was moving downhill, getting further yard by yard. Do it! my heart screamed. Get it over! But there was no shot. Once, I thought I heard him thumping close to me, making sure he wouldn't miss, but then it was only the distant hoofbeats of a courier.

A shot blasted behind me, the bullet hissing past my head. I whirled. Zachary was standing wide-legged, the revolver steadied across his arm. It was my last bluff, and it had to be good. "Why, you sonofabitch," I whispered. "You're coward enough to shoot a man in the back. I never thought that. So I'll just make it easier for you. I'll give you the heart! Close in, where you can't miss." All the time I was saying that, I was edging toward him. But when I saw his hand tighten to pull the trigger, I pulled the oldest trick in the world on him, raised my hand and shouted at the darkness, "Soldiers! Troopers, over here!"

There wasn't nobody, the echo booming away, but in the split second it took him to turn and look, I flung myself into him. He was off balance, trying to look behind him. The force of my blow against his belly knocked the revolver flying. The strong, mean bugger wrestled me off him, lashed a kick at my balls, but I'd already turned on my side, grabbing his legs and dumping him again. He scrambled free, tore his fingers across my face, trying to gouge my eyes. I felt the skin tearing, and knocked him back. Before he could throw a punch, I got a clear shot at his jaw and heard it click with my blow. He shook his head, dizzy, down on all fours, scrambling toward the revolver, but I stepped on his hand with one boot and with the other kicked him in the face. He groaned and went down. Breathing hard, I staggers over and picks the black Colt out of the white snow.

When I turned to him, he was kneeling, his teeth bared. "I'll kill you for this!"

"Naw, but you won't, Zachary. You had your chance, and you know what I got on you. I don't need a bullet to put you in the ashcan." Stooping down, covering him with the revolver, I picked up the dispatch case and stuffed the evidence into it. Then I looked at the Colt in my hand. "When you get another one of these, 'Lieutenant', just remember, I got one, too, and you ain't never fought in Irish pubs. I'm ready when you are."

I turned and walked slowly down the hill, glancing over my shoulder lest he was gathering up to make a run at me. But maybe the shock of being beaten had put him down for the time being. I didn't know how long my luck would last, but I was out of this one, anyhow. When I got down to the bottom of the hill, my whole body was shaking. Slowly, I turned back. He was a lone black shadow on the silver land, his empty hands dangling beside his legs. His voice floated down to me, a low laugh like a sneer. "Major Shaw and I started out with the 7th, soldier. You don't beat us."

"You cowardly bastard, I just did, and you ain't ever gonna try me again."

By the time I'd reached the camp, even in the cold, I was shivering with sweat. When I come into the warm lodge of Mary Sweet Grass, Walks Outside sprang up and ran to me. She stroked my cheeks and stared at me, her lips tight. "There is no help for us? Oh, Patrick, your eyes are saying that! Is no one listening?"

"Zachary listened," I whispers, holding her to me.

"But he hurt you! You're bleeding!"

"Not as much as he is, darlin'. Forget him, he's over."

BURY THE FRONTIER

December 29, 1890.

Big Foot's camp lay on the bleak plain where Wounded Knee creek snaked down through through the low hills. There was a log postoffice at Wounded Knee hamlet, and a church setting up on a hill. Below it were the lodges of maybe 400 Injuns, squaws, kids, old ones and at best 150 bucks and veterans who could be called warriors.

Surrounding the camp, and blocking any escape route were the 7th Cavalry, First Infantry, maybe some of the 6th and 9th Cavalry, too, I couldn't make out the guidon flags, there was so many, and a battery of Hotchkiss guns on a rocky knob overlooking the people's lodges.

The guns, which the reporters called our latest technical miracle, could crash out thirty half-pound shells a minute. But of course they wouldn't do that. They were just there to strike fear into the savage hearts. Last hostile Injuns in the US of A, beaten down, half-frozen, all finally corralled here, sulking and mourning in their tiny, terrible trap. There'd never be a surrender as sweet as this, that's what the newspapers were crying. Bust open the doors of the saloons, raise your glasses high! We'd won! Hurrah, lads, wave your flags for the glory!

As the dawn broke, gray and cold, the Injuns raised a white surrender flag beside Big Foot's lodge. I'd heard in camp that the old chief was close to death, and that doctors from the 7th had put an Army stove in his lodge. Keep him warm and alive at least until he gave up.

But as I came out of our lodge that morning, even the sham and pomp of this military rigamarole no longer wounded my heart. It was all going to be over any moment now. No more campaigns of chasing and killing and hating. Peace at last. The end of my long ride, fourteen years of my life coming to a close. As I stretched in the sun, Walks Outside took me in her arms and lay her forehead against mine. "Oh, husband, can we believe this?"

"I hope so, darlin'. At least the people have got here safely, and they know they don't have to go any further. That's a good sign. So is he." I smiled, nodding toward Matthew. Dressed in buckskins and carrying a tiny bow and arrow, he'd scampered out of our lodge only to run into a group of older Lakota lads. They were visitors in the camp, Walks Outside said, and had come from a boarding school, their hair cut white-man style and wearing neat blue uniforms. At the sight of our little savage with his tiny bow, they began chuckling and ragging him. They were maybe ten or twelve years old, not meaning to harm the tyke, but Matthew's face flashed toward me, fear in his eyes. "Show 'em how to shoot your arrows, Matty," I cries.

"Momma?" he pleaded, wanting her to rescue him.

"*Stay there, son. Be brave. You're a better Lakota than any of them!*"

"Claims he don't speak English," said one of the school lads.

"Sure he does," I answered. "He just wants to see if you speak Lakota, or did they whip it out of you?"

"We got a good school," the lad cried. "Play baseball."

"Then show him how. He's got to learn."

After Matty had gone grudgingly into the gang, Walks Outside murmured, "How strange, to have this little creature of both worlds. But it will be easier for him, I think, than it has been for us. At least, the killing time is over."

"Please, God," said a voice, and then I saw Father Craft, a cigarette wisping in his thin lips. He was wearing a charity overcoat and an Army cap. "Are you back with troops again, Patrick?"

"Yessir, and damn if I ain't out in two more days. Just an ordinary civilian husband then."

"It must agree with you, though. You look well, both of you." His pale eyes smiled. "What a blessing this has ended with only a little bloodshed. But I must say," he frowned toward the distant white flag above Big Foot's lodge, "the troops have asked me to be present and calm the people, yet Army impatience is no way to go at these things."

By then, I realized that the troops were already coming down into the camp. Some of the bucks, blankets tight around them, were running toward a council that was forming in front of Big Foot's tent. "I warned the 7th commander against an immediate disarming," Father Craft said. "Yes, they have a few old hunting weapons, but they're emphemeral against this assembled might. My God, up there on the hill, it's a wagonyard of buggies, all these correspondents, some of them with their dolled-up ladies. Photographers, and, if you would believe, the *New York World* has set up a bunting-draped reviewing stand for the dignitaries." His face darkened. "I doubt if they'd come so close if they knew that some of the young men are muttering Ghost Dance songs."

"But Father," Walks Outside said, "nobody could think of making trouble with all these guns around."

"Probably not. Still, dear girl, I'd advise you to remain here in your lodge, away from the center of things."

By then, I could hear voices rising over at the council circle. "They need me," Father Craft said. "Come by the mission tonight if you can. We'll sup together."

As he moved away, I caught him and said, "Father, if you're going to be milling in the midst of these Injuns and troops, hadn't you ought to be wearing your black robe and Cross?"

He smiled. "The Indians all know me, Patrick. Besides, your

Army blues are warmer than the cloth."

After he'd gone, I told Walks Outside to collect Matty and the two of them stay in the lodge. "Do you worry?" she said.

"Naw, gal, but these parleys always take time. You know how the Army is. Just stay clear of it."

I give her a kiss and started running toward the hill where the wagons were parked. Hell, it looked like a carnival, every stripe of civilians from agency loafers to dignitaries. Some of the ladies had brought picnic baskets and were serving coffee. A few had American flags, and some of the reporters carried banners advertising what papers they were with, Chadron, Nebraska, Omaha, Chicago, San Francisco. Photographers were setting up their cameras, sighting them on the milling camp below. I kept inquiring about McTighe and finally somebody points at a buggy where a man in a derby was hunched over, scribbling notes. I caught sight of a red-bearded head, so big the derby was perched on it like cork. "McTighe!" I howls, "I could smell your damn seegar 50 miles away!"

He scrambled out of the buggy and poked his stogey at me. "Note that it's unlit, my boy. I'm down to sucking dry and hoping. Given up the habit, and by God, I've been worried about you. Where in hell have you been?"

Before I could tell him, a new troop of cavalry clatters in, the men dismounting, jerking their carbines out of scabbards, and starting in ranks down toward the camp. A voice shouts: "You people! All correspondents, all civilians here, leave this area! We're moving you back to the next ridge. It's only a hundred yards further from the site."

"We can't photograph from there!" shouts a lad, popping out from under his camera hood. "Leave us stay. We're all set up."

"No! General's orders. Move back now. After the surrender, we'll give you full run of the camp. Photos, souvenirs, whatever you want."

"Jesus God Almighty," McTighe muttered. "You'd think it was Gettysburg."

"Or the Little Big Horn." By then, I'd looked up and seen that the officer on the horse was Ora Zachary. As McTighe started to climb into the buggy, I said, "No, stay put, Freeman."

Zachary's dusty face was set in fury. He had a Winchester across his pommel. "You-heard-the-order-soldier! Clear out!"

I grins. "Yessir, Lieutenant, we're just leaving. But first, though," I jerked a thumb at McTighe, "like you to meet Mr. Freeman McTighe of the *New York World*. This is Lieutenant Ora Zachary, Freeman. Old hand with the 7th. Won a Congressional."

"You were with the 7th at the Big Horn, Lieutenant?" Freeman asked.

"Naw," I cut in, "just a pissant fight that everybody's forgotten. But Freeman, you was covering the Haymarket in Chicago. Being as

228

the Lieutenant was there, you might want to do a story on him."

Before the stunned Zachary could answer, a captain from the 7th swept by. "Goddammit, Zachary, move out these civilians! Join your unit in the camp!"

Zachary took a last look at me, his eyes flaming. Then he jerked his horse around and thundered down the hill.

"I better get into that camp myself, Freeman. This thing is heating up."

"I wouldn't, Kelly. Just watch from here."

"I can't. Walks Outside's down there."

He seized me, spun me. "Aren't you seeing, man? I was in the Rebellion. I fired artillery. They're loading that Hotchkiss battery and aiming it square at the council. Something go wrong, how can a gunner tell soldier from Indian?"

"Ah, Freeman, nobody's gonna shoot. No reason to, not at sitting ducks!" But even as I said it, dust was rising in the camp and people already scuffling. I tore away from him and ran down the hill. The last thing I saw was Zachary and his men charging right up to the edge of the council circle. They swung off their mounts and joined other troopers who were already running through the camp. It was hard to tell at the distance, but I could see bluecoats dragging paniers out of the lodges and ripping apart squaws' belongings, searching for guns. Closer, one soldier was wrestling a tiny knife and stitching awl from a squaw. Then he began trying to search under her dress. Two bucks jumped him and flung him down.

In front of Big Foot's tent rises the low howl and prayer of the Ghost Dance. "Don't!" I cries. Somebody flings sacred yellow dust into the air and the sky split with a roar, a crash louder than any lightning, a point-blank volley ripping through the circle of bucks in front of Big Foot's tent. Injuns were falling, writhing, bluebellies all over 'em, clubbing them hand to hand, and then more bucks, a black tide crashing over the soldiers. Rifles were stabbing orange into screaming women and kids running like rabbits. Soldiers were dropping to their knees, aiming better, levering in cartridge after cartridge until I couldn't see, just smelled the burned powder of a giant cloud of smoke, pressing down on the camp, hiding even the teepees, many of which were flaming, and black figures stumbling out, wailing like banshees in the whiteness.

On the rocky knob above, the Hotchkiss guns kicked back on their trails, the shells screaming into the camp, hissing, roaring, flinging bits of bodies into the sky. All that time I was racing toward Walks Outside's lodge at the far right side of the camp. No shells bursting here, not yet, but already, with Injuns trying to scurry under their wagons for protection, shells were blowing them apart, wheels hissing through the air.

In one last glimpse, I seen a line of troopers leaping over the bodies of the dead Injuns and firing at some who were running and crawling to get away. A tall officer was waving his buffalo hat at his men, roaring them on, but I couldn't see him close enough, didn't know who. As the big smoke swirled around him, gunners from the hill couldn't see nothing but Injuns escaping, and with two flashes, their rounds blasted friend and foe alike. I never had a chance to look again.

Walks Outside, shrieking, had already seized me. She swept Matty into her arms, and I grabbed Aunt Mary's hand. "Over there!" I cried, "the coulee! We got to get out of range!"

Just as we began to run, I hear a whimper, didn't even see the shell or the bullets that had done it, but laying torn and shattered on the frozen earth were the blue-uniformed Injun school lads, the whole gang of 'em, if not dead, then dying fast.

"I can't help 'em!" I cried to Walks Outside. "Go! Go!" I snatched Matty from her and we flew out the far end of camp, following a stream of Injuns who were limping and crawling toward a coulee. There were willows and cottonwoods in there, at least some cover. After I'd got Walks Outside, Matty and Mary safe under the lip of it, I raced back onto the plain to pull in some wailing squaws. One was a young woman, her breasts bare, with an infant squalling at 'em. She was sitting upright, dazed, whispering, *"They have killed me fifteen times."*

The poor thing was a bleeding pin cushion. She thrust her babe to me and fell back dead. A leather cap was scrunched down over the infant's little head. The mother had beaded it with the American flag!

Exposed as I was, slugs began kicking up around me. I ran, holding the child. When I got into the coulee, about 30 injuns were huddling there. An old squaw, her arm half blown off, took the babe from me and gave it to one of her daughters. By now, though, the Hotchkiss gunners had spotted us. A shell crashed down a towering cottonwood and it exploded in dust and splinters. I shouted in Lakota, *"Run up the coulee, spread out. Go far!"*

Some of them were too dazed or hurt even to follow, just lay sobbing against the frozen bank, waiting for death. But I got Walks Outside, Matt and Mary again and we ran up that coulee until our lungs were on fire. "How far do we have to go?" Walks Outside cried.

"I don't know, gal. Forever if it keeps up like this!"

We weren't far enough yet! The sonsofbitches had spotted us again. Maybe we'd run a mile, us and a handful of Injuns, and even though the gun-roar from the camp seemed to be dying out, the Hotchkiss battery was walking shells up and down the coulee. One flash hit close to us. I see a raven fly into the sky. When it came down, it was Aunt Mary Sweet Grass, her black raincoat half torn off her, and her wispy gray hair red with blood. Walks Outside was clutching her, screaming, and I finally had to jerk her away. "Save our boy, save yourself!"

I was still carrying Matty, his little fingers clutched in my hair like he couldn't let go. After we'd run another mile or two, the coulee was playing out, coming up level with the surface of the plain. When we finally fell heaving into a last clump of willows, there were a few other Lakota around us. One buck, wounded many times, was trembling an old smoothbore shotgun up over the lip. I growled at him in Lakota, *"Don't shoot! You just make it worse!"*

"You, sojer!" he cried in American. "Tell 'em what they do! We are miles from those dogs now, yet still they kill us!"

Walks Outside lay beside me, her hard breasts pressing me and her shoulders racking in sobs. "Why, Patrick, why?"

All I could do was shake my head. Finally I says, stroking her, "I love you, darlin' gal. We got our boy, I got you, we're still here, we'll make it."

She was peering past me, her dark face wet with tears. I raised up over the lip of the coulee, and to my surprise, saw another parallel coulee about a hundred yards away. Shapes were moving along it, bluebellies. Once and a while, one would stop and his rifle would crash into the coulee. There'd be an Injun scream and wails. But then a loud voice cried out. "You! You Indians over there east of us! We see you, we know where you're hiding! The fight is over! Come in to us! Throw down your weapons, walk over here! No one will be harmed!"

There must have been an interpreter with that officer, for a half-breed voice sang out with the same message. *"We make peace now. Soldiers not your enemies."*

"Do they lie, Patrick?" whispered Walks Outside.

"I don't know, darlin'. But the shooting's sure falling off. Maybe they finally got the blood out of their eyes. I've got to chance it."

"You'll go there? Oh, husband, no!" she sobbed.

"It's the only way, gal! I'm wearing a uniform. Once they see it, they'll let up on us. They're down to picking single targets now, and they won't shoot their own, except by accident."

"Patrick!" she screamed. "I see death! All of us! Don't you ever believe what I see?"

"With all my heart, God bless you. I have to go, Walks Outside. I can bring us help."

She sat erect, her eyes closed, and she wailed her death song. Then, with a deep breath, she seized my hands and nodded. "Take our child, husband."

"No! Hell, no! I got to get close enough to 'em so they can see my blues."

"Take our child. You can protect him better than I, alone here with other Indians."

"Yes, maybe you're right. Come on, boy," I whispered wearily, and covered him with my arms. "But you, darlin'," I said to Walks Outside, "promise me you'll stay in this ditch and not show yourself. In battle, bullets fly too many places that nobody expects, and nobody's name is on 'em either. Them troopers probably got sharpshooters with 'em. Don't give 'em a chance."

She smiled and gripped my hand. "I've been in war before, Patrick. Care for yourself. I love you."

One of the wounded Lakota had an old bloody flour sack wrapped around his neck like a scarf. I said, *Brother, let me borrow that for a flag of peace.* He nodded and with trembling fingers tied it onto a willow branch. Then, with a last glance at Walks Outside, a touch of her black hair, wet with snow, I eased up out of the ditch, shielding Matty behind me.

"Troopers!" I shouted, "hold your fire! I'm Sergeant Kelly, 3rd Cavalry, coming in!"

I could see blue shapes moving in the ditch across the plain. There was silence, and I began walking faster, straight toward them.

A volley crashed and slugs whined past me. I ducked and almost fell. "Goddamn you buggers!" I screamed. "I'm coming toward you with a white flag! Look at it!" I waved it back and forth. "Hold your bloody fire!" I whirled to glance back at the ditch where I'd left Walks Outside and the others, but there was nothing moving. They must have been huggin' the dirt like I told 'em, and I was grateful. That volley of long range .45-70 slugs had to have gone right over their heads.

I had Matt tucked under my arm like a sack of flour, my other hand holding the willow stick high. "They gonna boom us, Poppa, boom us down?" he whimpered. "I scare."

"Sure you are, son, but I ain't gonna let nobody hurt you. Quit your squirming now, you're heavy to pack." Then I began walking faster, because hurry was the best chance we had. Get in close enough so that they could be sure of my uniform.

Two more slugs slammed into the dirt beside me and sung off in ricochet. A shout from the ditch. "Halt, you! Hold it right there!"

"I ain't armed!" I cried. "I've got a little boy and a white flag. I'm 3rd Cavalry, damn ye!"

By then, I could see the buffalo coats rising out of the ditch, and behind them, a bare-headed bald man in a greatcoat. He took several steps toward me, then studied me with field glasses. "You got hostiles over there?" he barked.

"Who's askin'?"

"Lieutenant Cressy, 7th! Are you a soldier?"

"Christ, sir, I been hollering it at you. Kelly, Sergeant, 3rd!"

"Lyin' bastard," cries one of the buffalo coats. "The 3rd ain't here, no 3rd troops in this fight! He's a breed, sir. Don't trust him."

"I'm from Cantonment 6 up at Deadwood! Detached for service with the 7th!"

"Who? Whose command?" Cressy shouted.

"Zachary. Lieutenant Zachary!" I couldn't believe I was using his name for protection, but it was the only one they might know.

A roar of anger came back. "Zachary's dead in the camp! Kilt by you buggers!" Then I could hear Cressy shouting, "Hold your fire, men!" but one shot singed off anyway and whistled close to my head. The buffalo coats began to run toward me, white-faced recruits, terrified and blood-thirsty in their first fight, and they scared hell out of me, for their officer had obviously lost control of 'em.

I glanced back at the coulee I'd left. Too far to get back there. If I turned and fled, they'd shoot for sure. Nothing to do but stand firm. "This is Sergeant Kelly, lads, you hear my order! Put down your arms!"

That slowed 'em a bit. One of them stopped, no more than ten yards from me. "What you carryin' there? Kid, ain't it? Injun kid!"

"He's my son."

"Then you ain't no soldier!"

"Fourteen years, sonny, from Rosebud on up! I was assigned to the camp to protect the People. My wife and child were in there. Now get those goddamn rifles down!"

By then, Cressy, the bald-headed shavetail, had dared to move in. He was squinting at me. "All right, men, back off. What did you do, run out on Lieutenant Zachary when he was under fire?"

"I never seen him, sir. He had me in a different part of the camp. All I seen of that fight with the Injuns was the flash of Hotchkiss shells. Was that what killed him?"

With a wary glance at his men, the lieutenant nodded. "Friendly fire. A mix-up. The gunners had no way to tell."

One of the recruits cried, "He wouldn't have been there if it wasn't for your goddamn people! You killed him, squaw man! Turn us loose, officer. This ain't done yet!"

He started to break past me toward our coulee, but I tripped him and he sprawled. When he came fumbling up, I kicked him in the face. "Your sergeant is talkin' to you, boy. Stand easy, I told you. I'll shoot the next man that breaks!" They pulled back, cursing, scared, and I turned to the lieutenant. "What in the name of hell are you people doing, running Injuns down three miles from the fight? Jesus Christ, mister, these are women and kids! Don't you have no shame!"

"It gets out of control," the lieutenant said weakly, "but if you have prisoners, sergeant, we can take them in."

"Prisoners? Ah, you greenhorns, there ain't no prisoners here, nothing but butchered cripples! Yes, we're gonna take 'em in, but first," I snaps my fingers, "hand the rifles down, soldiers. Just the officer and me go in armed."

The recruits growled back, one of them twitching his trigger finger. I grabs the rifle from him and he pulls it, blows a booming hole in the sky. Poor little Matty let out a shriek. I swung the rifle on the other recruit. "Now, sonny, you want to play, too?"

Slowly, he stock-ends his Winchester to me, and I bundles both of 'em under my arm, and set Matty down on the ground. "Carry this flag," I tosses it to one of the recruits, "and now you walk in first and make peace with those people."

As they moved out ahead of us, the lieutenant whispers to me, "Good work, Sergeant. These men are not qualified even to hold a rifle. I don't know who put 'em into the regiment."

"Well, it's over now," I breathed. "For Christ's sake, the bloody awful murder of it!"

The lieutenant stopped short and stared at the dark willow clump at the edge of our coulee. "What's that?" he said in terror.

I hadn't heard it till then. It was a low moaning, at first sounding like another of the poor wretches dying. But then I could hear the words. It was the Lakota death song, a man's voice wailing, "*She stood up to watch him and keep him safe with her eyes. She feared no waiscu bullets, she had seen them before. But the Father says so. She saw her death and it has come. The Father says so.*"

Flinging the lieutenant aside, I bolted into the coulee. The singer of the death song was the young wounded buck with the smoothbore shotgun. When he saw me, he raised the gun with both hands above his head. "*They shoot at you, and they kill what you have left behind.*"

He nodded at the bottom of the coulee. Walks Outside was lying on her back, her long legs spread and her arms flung wide like Jesus on the Cross. Her beautiful breast had been ripped open. Why! my heart screamed. I warned you, you promised! It didn't have to happen! Accident? No! The whore of war, the devil's dice in a random shot, striking down the innocent! When she'd seen that I was in danger, she dared the soldiers, exposed herself for one split second, just enough for the angry volley meant for me to blow her life away.

The world spun in my eyes. I lost my balance, fell, and moaning, raging like a madman, I crawled to her and cradled her in my arms. Rolled with her, rolled in her blood, kissed her dark lips, tried to open her China eyes. "Walks Outside," I sobbed, "ah, my darlin', darlin', it was over! Why did you have to go! Why did I ever leave you?"

But her face was at peace, her thin lips parted, her head held high. Proud, accepting, her suffering over.

I was still holding her in my arms when hours later, almost dark, two Army hospital stewards in white rubber coats drifted in and knelt beside me like ghosts. My mind was so gone I almost thought one of them was Steward Rawley, and now he'd be reaching in with his hook to pluck the pain from my heart. One of the stewards was saying, "Your son is in the wagon, soldier. All the wounded are there. It's over. We'll take you home."

"Home?" I flung their arms from me and fell again when they tried to pull me up. In the madness, I was lifting up with her through the black fingers of the willows. The world was clutching at us no more. We were in the sky, drifting together, outside all the fury, Walks Outside, Fights Clouds, the only peace was here. "Leave me alone," I whispers, "I ain't one of you."

A steward whispers to the other, "Git some morphine into him."

"The hell you will," I roars, staggering up. And when they tried to put her on a litter, I kicked them back and lifted her myself, so light, so frail, a bird soaring away free.

In the Army wagon, trembling in the icy grinding of the wheels, I lay beside her and held her all the way back to the end of our dead, cold world.

I blocked out much of what happened after that. Voices would come to me out of the swirling snow, a new blizzard laying peace on the land, but the people who spoke were all strangers, fumbling into my sorrow, trying to take away my loneliness. I'd stare through the drifting flakes and see only her, striding proud across the parade ground that first day at Fetterman. Sometimes I'd be dreaming that we were together in the sweet green grass of the Crazy Horse camp. I'd see her hands on her breasts, and then mine, and we were twirling like tops in the blessed joy of our bodies.

"Dust thou art, and to dust returneth."

I didn't know the old hunch-backed German priest who was saying the burial. Father Craft had wanted to do it, but the last I seen of him, he was lying on a litter on cold straw. The frame church that loomed up above the slaughter-ground at Wounded Knee had been turned into a hospital, the pews ripped out, and nun-nurses and a few Army medics walking down the rows of the dying people. All were Injuns except Father Craft. When I knelt beside him in my daze, still sobbing about Walks Outside, he put his hand on my shoulder. "The Lord has her, Patrick. But just know, you gave that girl hope, and happiness, more than most of these people ever get." Then, weakly, he smiled. "And see what I get for wearing Army clothes?"

He'd gone to the camp to calm the Lakota during the surrender, begged the colonel in charge to go slow and not barge into the lodges and rip them apart. But who listened? The awful first volley crashed out, red and white whaling into each other. In the confusion, some blood-crazed buck had stabbed him in the chest, figuring he was a hated bluecoat. Any other man, the doctor said, would have gone under, but not Craft. That spindly bugger with his pale blue eyes had kept ministering Injuns and wounded soldiers, too, until the blood drained out of him and he keeled over.

There was no point saying that I'd tried to warn him. He shouldn't have gone in there without his Cross. But maybe even that wouldn't have spared him. I thought of the Injun babe with the American flag on his cap, and Walks Outside with the beaded crucifix around her lovely neck. Too much hate, too much vengeance. All the warnings we'd tried to give had spared no one. I gripped Father's cold hand in mine, and then, trying to smile, I moved to snatch the wisping cigarette out of his lips. "I know," he whispered, "bad for the lungs, but it keeps me alive, Patrick."

Yes, he lived all right, the Good Lord had him in his plan, I suppose, to keep helping these people. But what could he do, when so few others cared? The Lakota kept dying, some of wounds, but most, I'm sure, of broken hearts. Nobody from our guvmint was there to mourn these bloody, twisted sacks of flesh and bones, crammed into pine boxes by the Army medics so that the great US of A could get 'em out of the way as quick as possible, hoping that humanity would never know the foul outrage of what we'd done here.

I stood swaying in the snow, the flakes so thick I couldn't even see the iron fence around the cemetery. Lucy Bird Eyes was a cousin of Walks Outside. Though she'd been wounded in the fight, she insisted on coming to the burial, one eye bandaged and maybe gone. She held Matty to her breast during the long-winded priestly orations, and the confused little tyke could only try to peek under her bandage to amuse himself. How could he know what was going into the ground here? Or maybe he did, better than us.

I was the only soldier present, all the rest grieving Injuns, the squaws who hadn't been wounded hacking their hair and ripping their sleeves. The bucks were being held in an Army barbed-wire stockade. The men here were kids and a few crippled warriors, too old and useless to fight anymore. Their eyes were clouded with memories of the life they'd lost. Other Lakota, some of them wearing scout uniforms, began sighing into their shovels and heaping yellow, snow-wet dirt onto the pine boxes. I didn't count the dead, maybe nobody did. Only later, I seen a newspaper that said 84 Lakota men and boys, 44 women and 16 infants were buried here. My beloved Walks Outside was a number now. So was Aunt Mary Sweet Grass and the blue-uniformed Lakota lads from the boarding school. The coffins were stacked layer on layer, and when the mass grave was finally closed, all we could do was look at each other. Far off, from the white tents of the 7th Cavalry camp, a bugle squealed some call that I couldn't tell anymore, or care about. In the distance, cavalry were moving like black ants across the snow. Guidon flags were flying in the glory of it all. General Miles himself was here, taking charge, making the peace. I could see the swaggering officers on their chargers, and behind them, to pick over the dead ground like scavengers, come the photographers and reporters and blood-mongers who'd be shilling the remains of the Sioux, the bead-work, the frozen, cut-off trigger fingers, the bloody punctured Ghost Shirts. Cheer for the memories of the last frontier, put 'em under glass in museums, hang 'em on the walls of saloons, and mostly, when they'd lost their value and were forgotten, let 'em rot in hock shops far across the land.

What a twist it was in my heart when I heard the distant fifes and horns of the 7th Cavalry band. They'd turned out for the conquering general and the picture takers from Washington, and the song they played was Custer's. "Garryowen."

Before the grave was even closed, I left Matty in the care of Lucy Bird Eyes. Seizing my government mount, I raced down through Pine Ridge agency, knotted with civilians and soldiers, the whole world flocking here to pick the bones of the dead, and more than that, wagging their tongues about the great bravery of this last Injun fight. That very afternoon, Miles had awarded thirteen Congressional Medals for the heroic killing his soldiers had done!

Custer had been avenged. So had Rosebud, the Fetterman massacre, all the generations of bloody race war. We'd buried the frontier. Now we could forget what we'd done. But not I! my heart cried. You, Zachary, choked on your minie ball! Ah, the sweet justice of it, friendly fire, was it, burning you up in hell? And Shaw before you, and Leah. Well, we'd won something, we'd learned something, and we'd paid for it dearly in all the awful sorrow of those years.

At the shack town of Rushville, Nebraska, troop trains were steaming in. The 6th Cavalry, the only unit I had left, was departing this night. I raced up and down the tracks through the grinding smoke of the trains, and finally, from an end Pullman, I see a tall, elegant lady alighting, buffalo soldiers scurrying up to fetch her luggage.

But she didn't have eyes for anyone except big, leathery Lieutenant Pershing. He sweeps off his broad hat and spins her in his arms. They stood there smooching like they didn't care who watched. A buffalo soldier beside me cracks, "Hey, don't the lieutenant have himself a swell! I don't know how he finds these dames way out in the sticks."

It didn't mean nothing to me, but with Pershing as happy as he was, I figured this was a good time to hit him up. "Pardon me, sir," I says, "Sergeant Kelly, reporting back."

He turned to his lady, "Excuse me, darling, be just a moment." Then he scowled at me like he was going to start sonofabitching again. But when I blurts what had happened, being caught in the massacre and losing my wife, his face softened. "It was a rotten thing. I'm sorry, soldier. What can I do for you?"

I told him about Crook, my court-martial and my hitch of punishment which had ended two days after Wounded Knee. He frowned. "You want out, Kelly?"

"Yessir. Just as quick as I can shuck these blues. Had a bellyful."

"What are your plans?"

"I wish to hell I knew, sir. Ain't caught up to myself yet, losing her."

With a glance at his lady, he jerked his head at me and we walked a few steps away, along the grimy side of the Pullman. "You've got an Indian child to raise, Kelly. Are you going to do that alone?"

"I hope to. Seems like I owe it to the both of us, and mostly her."

"Over the years, soldier," Pershing said quietly, "I've watched hundreds of good men like you sign the ticket and finally walk out the gate of some miserable, forlorn western post. It's been that for all of us. But do you know what happens, Kelly? These brave men, set free in civvies, they try it for a few months or even years, and only then do they realize that when they left the Army, they left home, and maybe the only family they ever had."

"Are you askin' me to ship over, sir?"

"Just to use your head. It's no bed of roses out beyond the troops. Jobs are hard to come by, and the adventure you've lived, it's not there, clerking behind a store counter someplace. Besides, the Army can help you raise that boy. Jesus Christ, we ought to do something for these people."

I nodded. "I thank you for sayin' that, Lieutenant. But them Injun boarding schools whip the tykes for speakin' their tongue. If the truth be known, sir, I'm more on their side than I am on ours anymore. Sick to death of what we done."

"Yes, you've earned that right. You'll get no argument from me." Reaching inside his blouse, he took out a dispatch pad, scrawled on it, tore the sheet off and handed it to me. "Take it to the paymaster, Sergeant, muster out. Maybe Washington wouldn't do it like this, but I run my troops my own way."

"You've shown me that, all right. I wish you well, sir, wish all them officers were your breed," I says, and salutes.

He paused a moment, and his hard eyes twinkled. "I'll tell you this, Kelly, we're going to need good men. You may think you're over and done, but our wars have just begun. Mark my words. I've got a hunch you'll be with us again. On your road, mister." He snapped me a salute, turned and strode back to his lady.

From the moment I left him, an emptiness closed over my heart. He was right. This was more than a discharge. I was leaving home, leaving the memories of good men like him, Crook, Crawford, Bourke, Maus, old Cap Bloxham. I'd miss 'em all, mostly dead now, but as I stared at the icy railroad tracks with the troop train hissing

238

away, I wondered if young Pershing and I would ever cross paths again. Were there more fights ahead? Was that the best our people could hope for? Ah, God, I whispered, leave us at peace until we can remember how rotten war is. There ain't no winners, never will be. Our enemies have the same blood as ours, the same hopes and dreams. It not you or me, it's us. We're all us. That's what my beloved had taught me, and died for, trying to make it come true.

Three days later, Freeman McTighe was standing beside my wagon at the Holy Rosary Mission. Some of the nuns were there, too, shivering in their black robes as the harsh wind from the west swept across us. Each of them kissed little Matt and gave him enough blessings to send him to the Vatican. Then I put him beside me on the wagon box and he set up straight, a little American in a cast-off sailor jacket and a wool cap pulled down over his ears. I was in charity civvies myself, gray Confederate Civil War trousers, a battered felt hat, and a discarded Union Army blouse. All my mustering out pay had gone to buy the team of horses and wagon, a Winchester and enough grub for a few days down the trail.

"Why did we ever let it happen?" I says to McTighe. "They didn't deserve this!"

"No, no, of course not. But you don't understand, my boy."

"Don't understand what?"

"It will always be this way, and always has been!" Angrily, he punched his unlit cigar into his lips and bit off the end, like he was dying to smoke it, despite his swearing off. "There are three levels in humanity, my young Irish friend. At the bottom are the dregs, the immigrants like you, Indians, Mexicans, blacks, Bohemian wage slaves in all the Chicagos of the land. In their suffering, their strikes, their screams, they're grasping for the pot of gold that America promises. Give us our daily bread, our share of the rich pork pie. But the system says, No. Who is the system? Why, ex-soldier Kelly, it's our second level of humanity, its your officers, your elected politicians, your police, your Pinkertons, your petty employers like me. It's even the rich factory owners who had the dregs shot down at Haymarket. This second level is the precious few who have risen from serfs to become artisans, tools of the system, Praetorian guards. But you say, why does a Wounded Knee happen, why a Haymarket? Aren't these second-level functionaries the ones who perpetrated these horrors? And you saw it, Kelly, physically they did just that. They killed to preserve what they'd won, this frontier, the future markets for their goods. But ah, my boy, they are as deluded as thou and me. They just think they run things."

"Freeman, that don't explain nothin'. I seen what these bastards done here!"

He nodded bitterly. "That's the shell game of it, Kelly. You will never see the top level of humanity, that tiny handful of faceless barons who control the world. England, France, Germany, U.S., who cares? They care not for flags or borders or glory wars. They care not for Presidents or kings. They create them, they own them. For this top level, this handful, owns the ships and the seas, they own the transfers of money around the globe, the banks, the insurance, literally the treasuries of nations are in debt to them. When a functionary fails, they replace him with one who will enrich them more. When a serf fails, serfs by the hundreds of thousands, they simply move them aside as you would a hill of ants, sometimes by disemployment, often by death. For they know that if you have the money, you can buy them all, buy the world."

I stared at him, that red bull-dog face with the seegar clamped in his teeth. "You're sayin' it's set in stone, Freeman? There ain't no hope for the little man, or the second one neither, not even you!"

"I'm not religious," he said quietly, "but that girl you left here, when I think of her, I think of the wise old Lakota medicine man who told me once, 'The person who has searched for the Person Above has found him.' She did that, by her life with us, and her death by us."

"But if you're dead," I cried, "where's the hope! There ain't none!"

"If enough people seek the truth, live it and die for it, Patrick, they're going to make a difference in the world. Why else would I scribble my guts out, flinging bits of paper to the wind, a nobody, and nobody listening? I may be a weak, cranky-headed old bastard, but I'm one of a kind for all that, I mean something and was put here for a reason just like she was. Just like you were. The reason is the trying. And damn," he scowled, "the whiff of a good cigar! Now get out of here, you've got a long way to go."

"But where?" I grinned and gripped his mitt.

"You're asking the wrong man. But wherever you go, it'll be a hell of a trip. Have you got a light?" He held up his cigar.

I pulled a match out of my blouse pocket and lit his stogey. In the flame, he beamed. "Bless you always."

"Ah, burn yourself up in hell," I whispers, "but I'll never forget what you done for this sinner." The sisters were pecking Signs of the Crosses on their black chests, and I gave 'em my own.

Then it was just Matty and me, creaking up the long empty trail west. His blue eyes lifted to me. "Where we goin', Poppa?"

"Far. Far off."

"Is it a good place?"

"The best," I said, lifting him into my lap. I put the reins into his little brown hands. "Take us there, Matt."

"Drive horsies like a man?"

"Like a man. That's what you are now."

I closed my eyes, hugging his tiny warmth, and he drove us away to the sundown.

240

PATRICK

SECOND FRONTIER: THE OCEANS 1896-1918

A DAISY AT LAST

Well, ain't this Alice in Wonderland! I thinks when I seen her. On that September afternoon of 1896, here sits a princessy female, perched like a canary atop her steamer trunk. The grimy Chicago and Northwestern station at Lander, Wyoming didn't have but one dumb shuffling porter who was trying to sort her baggage. Pointing with her parasol, she was telling him, "No, no this one here, that one there."

"And while you're at it," I cuts in, "stuff that damn trunk in the storage room, 'cause I ain't about to pack it up no mountain."

She whirled, like who was I, and right then, I felt like saying, "I wish to hell I knew, dearie!"

The years had treated me hard since Wounded Knee. Just like Pershing had predicted, I hadn't found no bed of roses outside the Army. I'd hoboed from job to job all over the West, at the same time trying to raise young Matty all by myself, and give the lad some sort of future. But it wasn't in the cards. Depressions come and went. Jobs was scarce. Finally, I packed up Matty and sent him back to his mother's people at the Rosebud Reservation in Dakota. Then, drifting to Wyoming, I hooked on in the lowest of trades, and a new one at that.

I was wrangling what they called dudes up into the mountains, helping them blast down game animals. Seemed like the whole world was flocking out here now, rediscovering the grand, free life of the used-to-be. The owner of the outfit was a worthless souse named Ringgold. He says, "There's money in these here eastern personages, Kelly. You stick with me, some will rub off."

I stuck, all right, and the rub was, there wasn't nothin' else.

"I'm your ride to Ringgold's camp," I says to Miss Princess.

She plumps her dainty hands on her hips. "I never intended taking the trunk. It's for San Francisco. My cousin told me that he had servants engaged here, but I must say, my good man, I don't enjoy sitting three hours in the broiling sun waiting for somebody to come help me."

She got down from her perch, flicking orders with her gloved hand. This went, that stayed. "Also, kindly tell me, where are the ladies facilities?"

"The what?"

"Can," the old porter grunted. "I tole her we ain't got one."

The C&NW station set close beside the creek and a bunch of willows, growing up under the cottonwoods. "Over there," I points. "It's them bushes, or you pretty much got to hold her and squirm."

The color flared in her pale cheeks. "I'll thank you not to

242

address me in that manner! Do I make myself clear!" Her voice caught and she turned her face from me. "Oh, God," she whispered, "why did I ever come!"

By then, I'm thinking the same, and half sorry for her, too. Talk about not belonging out here among the leering station loungers and tobacco spitters, why, she was hardly even a woman. Young girl, slim as a lad, a fancy hat tied with lace under her chin. If there was a bosom on her, she had it swaddled in so many scarves and corsetries that a piece of dirt couldn't possibly have got in and soiled her lily skin.

"Ah, lady," I says gently, "come over here, there's nobody can see you." I guides her down through the fallen leaves to the willow bushes. Turned my back and waited.

When she came out, holding up her skirts, she was sniffling and I noticed her eyes. Dark brown, the color of her hair. In the pale of her skin, they were so big and sparkly that her eyelashes flickered like leaves of a flower. "Thank you," she said. "Do forgive me. I'm on edge. It's a dreadful trip out here, but I'm sure you don't know that."

Only from riding it on the rods, dearie, I thinks. But hell, I was a common servant to her, why should she give a damn? Turning, I signed Stinky Face, my young Shoshone buck, to begin packing the mules. She watched intently as the nimble bronze lad humped up her valises and balanced their loads in the paniers.

Cupping her gloved hand to her mouth, she whispered, "It's beastly to call one of them 'Stinky Face'."

"Not if you had smallpox all over it. Probably the Army Doc seen it delivering him, and hung on that moniker."

"Well," she sighed, "this will be an experience. I pray I'm strong enough."

"If you ain't yet, you're gonna be." I nodded at the horse and told her, "Git up." She started fumbling around, clawing at the saddle and kicking her foot to get high enough for the stirrup. Finally I grabbed her by her thin little waist. She gave a flinch, not liking it one bit as I boosted her onto the big tall horse. The stirrups were set too long. I had to thread them up shorter, which meant pushing her thighs back so I could see to work. God help me, the softness I was feeling in her crinolines or whatever they was. When I grabbed her calf and stuck her foot in the stirrup, she flared. "I don't think this is quite necessary, do you? After all, I have ridden horses before."

"Maybe, but out here, you grab hair when you mount. Take hold of that mane or you'll pull the saddle off like you was trying to do."

It went on like that all the way up the mountain. If she had ridden a horse before, she sure set uneasy on this big buckaroo. Not that he was mean or nothing, gentle as a puppy, but he loved to eat them rocks. Every time we come to a steep place, he'd leap up it and she'd let out this little moan.

But as the trail hours dragged on, I could see that she was gaining confidence, probably figuring that she'd got this far and hadn't died.

She had a pretty sounding voice, and sometimes she'd get nattering about something or other. But since I was some yards ahead, I didn't want to have to pull up and keep saying, "What?" all the time. Anyway, hell, her kind of people didn't expect no servant to talk back, so I just humped on, lost in my own silence. Jabbering up a trail like magpies don't make it no shorter, and only drives away the game animals, which was our bacon for her and her personages.

By the time we come to a big high basin with wildflowers all over it, I could see that she was out of sorts about me not waiting on her hand and foot. So she starts the snippy, spoiledy princess act again. "Oh, my," she cries, flinging her little hand out at the meadow of flowers, "how beautiful, the sun tinting them with every color of the rainbow! Wouldn't Mummy love these!"

"Ma'am?" I reins in my horse, having trouble hearing her natterin'.

"My mother. She has a big cutting garden of flowers. We live by the Lake near Chicago and they do well there. Do you suppose if we snipped a few of these, they'd keep long enough to have Mum's gardeners identify them? I'm not a flower person. That's her. Well?"

"Well, what?"

"Could we stop and pick some of these?"

"We could if you want to drag into camp way after dark. I ain't in love with that idea. You'll have days to pick your damn flowers. The mountains are full of 'em."

She frowned. "Well, could you at least tell me their names? I could write her. Those yellow ones there, what are they called?"

"Yaller flowers." I give 'em a squirt of my chaw.

Her dark eyes flamed. "Do you know the name or not?"

"Daisy!"

"A daisy?"

"Yas!"

Pouty, she wheels her horse ahead of me and clatters on to the next bunch of flowers. They were red as blood and growing out of the side of a rock. Her teeth flashing in the sun, she reins in: "And these?"

"Daisy!"

"But they can't be! They're not the same as the others."

"Are. Just more of 'em!" Hoping to get loose of this foolishness, I whacks my mule past her, but damn if she hadn't stopped at a scarlet flower, standing all by itself. She smiled like a kitten. "All right, then what is this one, pray tell?"

I jerks the mule up short. "Mountain daisy!"

She began laughing. "Obviously, my good man, you don't know

244

one thing about it, and that's fine, just say so. But please, stop playing me for a total dunce. I am not a child."

"Well, you damn sure act like it, pullin' us up short all the time, what's this, what's that? I don't know where you come from, missy, or what kind of lackeys you run, but out here on this mountain, I ain't your good man or nobody's. You want your goddamn daisy, then git off your fancy tailfeathers and pluck it yourself! Find your own way to camp."

By God, if she didn't scramble off her horse with her eyes flashing fire. She breaks off that flower and jabs it down between her breasts like a red tongue raspberrying me. All the way up the trail she packed it just like that, and we never spoke again.

When we got there, high in the black timber above Bull Lake, we had a surprise waiting. Suckling Calf, my Shoshone cook woman, told me that Ringgold had taken the hunters far off above Trail Lake, and him so drunk he could hardly stay on his horse. I glanced up toward the cliffs of the Winds, black and flashing with lightning. Storming like hell, and the way the air felt, it would be snow before dark.

I told Suckling Calf to get the *waiscu* girl into a tent, attend to her trappings and feed her. The squaw waddled over, sniffed her perfume, scowled at her little pointy boots and grunted, "Chicken with No Feathers."

The lady frowned. "Is she trying to speak to me?"

"Ah, that's the tribal way. Suckling Calf is one of these old bats that's got to shake her medicine on anything strange. It's like a dog liftin' his leg, pissin' territory. She's just puzzling out a name for you is all."

She winced when I said "pissin'," but then managed a weak little smile. "Well, it's Diana. Diana Archibald. Some people call me Liberty, my middle name."

I frowned. "I ain't never heard that handle on nobody."

"As well you wouldn't. I have very formal parents and they were determined to mark me like launching a ship. Mummy's aunt, Diana, is a great huntress to the hounds in Virginia, so first I was supposed to be her, but when I happened to pop out of the womb on the second day of January, 1876, Father said, Aha, Centennial Year, we'll hang the flag on her. Hence, Liberty. So silly, I'm sick of it." But then her petaly eyes darkened. She stared at the gloomy camp with the pines closing in like sentries. Suckling Calf had squatted down and was scowling at us. "Don't tell me you're intending to leave me here?"

"No place else."

"With her?"

"Why, hell yes, her. Something wrong with that?"

"It's, it's just...." her eyes swept the dark, sagging tents, and bloody deer carcasses hanging in the pines. "Oh, I suppose it has to be filthy on these camping trips. I've never done it. But if I can't speak to this Indian person, and if I'd want to clean up, or even lie down…?"

"Well, dearie," I chuckled, "in that case, you better holler for your French maid."

"I don't find that one bit amusing."

"Ain't supposed to be. This ole bat, what you call Indian person, probably knows more about raising spoiled brats than you'll learn in your life. Meaning getting you off this mountain if anything happens to me, and feeding you like Queen Victoria in the meantime. She ain't gonna bite you. The last paleface lady's heart she ate was years ago. Now git down and cool out." I grabbed her and took her off the big tall horse, getting a whiff of the sweet mountain daisy as I brushed against her. "If I don't haul your people in before it storms, who knows when you're gonna see 'em next."

Her eyes widened. "It's like that out here?"

"It's like that."

"Well, what could happen?"

"Plenty, but don't have to, so stop fretting your pretty head, missy. The most glorious place in the world is these mountains, if you treat 'em right."

She frowned. "What does that mean?"

"Knowing you ain't alone up here."

"You…you mean the Indians or…somebody to help?"

"I mean whoever put all this together. Injuns call him the Person Above, and you're closer to it out here than you ever been, I believe. That's what you're trusting. Grab hold of the big horse's tail and he'll lead you home. Been my experience anyhow."

She was nodding. "Quite poetic, really. I…I just wasn't expecting…" Her eyes lowered and she whispered. "Thank you, my…." she stopped and laughed. "I was going to say 'my good man', but dear me, it's not that anymore, is it?"

"It sure ain't."

"But what do I call you?"

"Mountain daisy," I says, and grins.

"No, no. That's me now! Can you believe it, I truly love the name Daisy."

"Pleased to meetcha. I'm Patrick, or Kelly, whichever. One thing for sure, there ain't no Liberty in my moniker or I damn well wouldn't be up here wet-nursin' dudes."

"Oh, I hope there's liberty for you someday, don't you?"

She was smiling, and me thinking, how in hell do I fluster out an answer, not even knowing what she means, talks so strange. All I could do was turn away and climb up onto my mule. I had the feeling, though, that she was still watching me, and she must have been, for she called softly, "Please hurry back, Patrick..."

My name rippling across her lips shivered me like a flash of lightning. I hadn't been socked this way for years now, if ever. Why? Had I gone daft? Proud little princess, she was half my age and as far above my head as Finnegan's rainbow. But there I was, snatching and dreaming. Hurry back, she'd whispered. Jesus and Mary, I'd fly all the way home to that one, just to pinch her and see if she was real.

But I couldn't carry her in my heart for very long that night. We did have a raging storm, in more ways than one. In the biting cold and drifting snow, I finally tracked Ringgold and his personages up to a hellish side hill, above timberline on the slopes of Spire Peak. In fall storms in Wyoming, you often get lightning cracking and splitting apart the snow clouds, like God Almighty hadn't decided which season was supposed to be dying and which to be born.

The lightning flashed across dark figures huddling in the slide-rock. There was not a stick or boulder to protect them, and when the bolts sizzled down, the thin air was so charged with electricity that my scalp was tingling and my rifle barrel humming. "Name of God, Ringgold!" I bellowed. "Git 'em down from here! Take cover!"

"We're lying flat," he whines. "Best we can do. Little lightning ain't gonna hurt nobody."

"Not you anyhow, damn souse, pickled as you are." I got a good whiff when I crawled past him. Just beyond, I see the black shape of a downed horse, poor beast pawing his forelegs and trying to get up on the wet-slick rock. Couldn't, though, for his left front leg was flopping cockeyed. Busted.

Not far from him, a man was lying on a little white ledge, and two others in hunting greatcoats, snow streaming down their faces, were trying to roll him into a tarp. One of the hunters was wearing specs that were running wet too, and when I crawled up, he swung to me. "Damn stupidity. No excuse for this. It's my fault, Fish," he gripped the fallen man by the shoulders, "but try not to move until we can get a look at that leg."

"I'm perfectly fine, Teddy, nasty bump, but it's going numb now. I'll be able to hobble, I'm sure."

This Fish personage was a big, strapping bugger, and brave enough, too. When I sliced open his canvas pant leg, and felt of the wound, he didn't even wince. The horse had fallen atop of him and ground him around in the rock, gashes here and there and everything swelling. "It's a long way from the heart, lad," I says, and put my arm under his shoulders. "Now ease yourself up and start walking on it. Git circulation going." With me helping him, he tried gingerly to take a step or two. "And the next thing that's going is us getting to cover."

Right then, another boomer of a bolt crashes the sliderock about fifty yards from us, the electricity crackling and the handlebar moustache of the man with glasses stood out straight. "Who are you?" he gasps.

"Supposedly the partner of that dumb sonofabitch who got you up here. But I ain't no more. Move, all of you. Git off this slope."

"No!" Ringgold staggers up and starts waving his arms. "Left their packs up on the rim, sheep-hunting. Got to get 'em."

I grabbed him by the collar. "You go hunt a hole, Ringgold. If you wasn't so pickled you never would have took 'em up here. Git your own damn packs and clear out. This ain't your hunt anymore!"

I flings him back and he starts whimpering. "The horse, Kelly! My best horse!"

"Was," I says. "Never should have put people up here in a storm, animals neither." I strides over to the poor flopping beast, covered his eyes with my hand and slit his throat.

"How am I going to get back?" Ringgold howls.

"You got here, didn't you? Figure it out." Then I turned to the personages and says, "You, Specs, and the other lad, grab holt of the big feller and ease him down. I'll pick trail just ahead of you."

It wasn't easy. Ringgold had got 'em in a place so steep and slidey that it wasn't meant for nothing but sheep or goats. In the driving snow, I couldn't see much trail, and every time we'd make a misstep, we'd send more slides of rock grinding and crashing off the mountain.

Finally we reached the first timber below, and by then the storm was easing up too, rumbling away and splitting the peaks to the west.

"That's bully work, chap," says Specs. "The right man at the right time. Kelly, is it?" He pulls off his big, western gauntlet glove and gives me a shake. "Call me Specs if you like, but the name is Roosevelt. Teddy Roosevelt. Our walking wounded here," he grinned at the big hobbling feller who was now leaning against a lodgepole pine, "my dear friend, Hamilton Fish. And the eyes of both of us, one of the finest hunters ever to trod the Adirondacks, Freddy van Wyck."

"Pleasure," said van Wyck, over his shoulder. He was taking a leak on a tree. When he finished up, he wiped his hands on a soggy red bandana and gave me a shake. "I wasn't sure we'd get off that place. We're in your debt, sir. You seem to have done this before."

I nodded. Few times.

"More than I can say for your associate, whatever his name is. He's quite a bottlehound. Will he get down all right?"

"After he sleeps it off, he will. If not, I'll catch up to him presently. We'd best be heading out, if the Fish there is ready to move."

"The Fish!" Roosevelt chuckled. "Well, Ham, I doubt if you'll ever trust me on another sheep hunt, will you?"

"Why, we'll go after him again tomorrow," Fish said, and pushed away from the tree. "By Jove, that was a superb ram!"

"Almost a full curl, Kelly," Roosevelt exclaimed. "Now mind you, I'm not new at this. I've taken some outstanding sheep on the Missouri bluffs. My ranch up in Dakota. But I do believe your animals here are bigger in the chest, more gross volume. Has that been your experience?"

I looks from one gleaming face to the other and thinks, So them is personages, are they? Imagine, standing there with wet snow leaking down our necks and a good five miles from camp, and here these spoiledy snots are measuring up game animals, like they're already telling tales over fine cigars and whiskey at their private club.

"My experience," I snaps back, "is that only a dumb sonofabitch tries to go up sheephunting in the teeth of a storm. Aside from taking a spill like you did, the game don't work well neither. They huddle up and wait it out, just like you ought to have been doing. Now let's git on our way..."

We hadn't gone a quarter mile through heavy timber and black jungles of blowdown before I hear a shuffling coming up from below. A clink or two. I pulls up short and Roosevelt frowns. "Why are you stopping?"

"Just listen."

We didn't have to wait for long. What I'd heard was Stinky Face, slogging to us through the timber. When he'd got to camp, following the Daisy princess and me, Suckling Calf had put him on our trail with the camp horses.

I gave him a slap on the arm, then signed him to help the big one, Fish, and gentle him into the saddle. Roosevelt and the handsome dandy, van Wyck, swung on their horses like they'd done it all their lives, and may have at that. Jumping and blooded horses, wouldn't you know, fancy riding.

Roosevelt, wiping at his specs, pulls his mount up beside me. "I notice you speak sign, Kelly."

"Some."

"The spoken language as well?"

"Few words. What I don't know, I habla Lakota at 'em, and even sometimes Tex-Mex and Apache. They git the idea well enough."

"I should think so! Why, this is quite fascinating. Do I take it that you've been on these various frontiers, among the different tribes?"

"Some," I grunts, hoping that was the end of it, but he keeps blustering at me, enthusiastic as a tyke in a toy store. How did I happen to be in these places, and when I says soldiering, he exclaims, "The devil you have! How I envy you. All my life, Kelly, I've longed to be out with troops, even to lead them. But it was not in the stars for me. Born too late for the Rebellion, in fact, I was still in velvet knee-britches when I watched Abraham Lincoln's funeral parade in New York. By the time of the frontier and those glorious fights you were in, why, they'd stuck my nose in a book at Harvard, or we were traveling abroad. Pity. There's so much a man proves about himself in the smell of powder."

"Well, Mister Specs," I says and grins, "about all I proved was the difference between the quick and the dead."

"You were never hit?"

"Ah, a Sioux arrow at Rosebud, and a glancing ball at Crazy Woman Fork. Maybe a nick from the Apaches. Tell you the truth, I stopped counting. There ain't a whit of glory in none of it, mister. That's what you didn't miss." Far off, through the timber, I could see the flicker of our hunting camp fire. I turns to Stinky Face and says in Shoshone, "Flame up that fire, get the woman to boil water for the big man's leg."

I didn't have to say, Get the vittles on, knowing that Suckling Calf would have them waiting. When we cricked down from our horses and warmed our butts in the roar of that fire, van Wyck already had a leather flask of brandy out and was passing swigs of it around in a little silver cup. "When Johnny comes marching home again," he cried. "To the light of our life, warming our hearth." He lifted the silver cup, took the first swig of it, then held it out to my Daisy princess.

I hadn't noticed her coming up to the fire, but there she stood, a Shoshone blanket wrapped around her, and her eyes dancing in relief. "I can't believe it! I've been weeping in that dreary tent all these hours, certain you were doomed, but he did get you home!"

Roosevelt laughed. "Flying colors, Diana, albeit with one badly bruised Fish."

"Hunter's luck," van Wyck cried. "Drink to it, darling."

My eyes snapped from her to van Wyck. I had to hand it to him, the lad was a charmer, cool and cocky enough to sing the birds off the trees.

When she took the silver cup, her frail fingers closed gently around van Wycks', and her petal eyes smiled at him. Roosevelt was huffing about what a grand experience it was, and how provident that the packer had found them when he did. The packer, is it now? First it was 'he' and she was 'darling.' Ah, I knew where I stood. Outside. The personages were huddling by the fire, laughing, telling tales about people and places I'd never heard of. Suckling Calf was ladling them out tin cups full of stew, the firelight glinting her gold teeth and the gaps of the missing ones.

The personages began tearing into the beef ribs, hearty as wolves with greasy mouths. Quietly, I slid my tin plate into the fire and burned the garbage off it. Then I went off by myself, crawled into my blankets and lay there listening to the rustling of the pines.

That crazy Roosevelt was hell to hunt, and to be honest, I was just as pleased to be hauling them dudes around the game trails than to set mooning in camp, sneaking glances at Daisy. I managed to get Roosevelt a three-quarter-curl ram, and van Wyck shot through the eye of a bull moose at further range than I would have ever tried. Hell, he had some kind of glossied up English rifle, the finest money could buy. Even the Fish kept limping and trudging along after us, until I helped him kill off a cinnamon bear, a scrawny boar, but he was as tickled with it as if it had been Captain Ahab's white whale.

In the talking they'd do among themselves, maybe thinking I wasn't listening or wouldn't catch on, it come out that Prince Charming van Wyck was Daisy Archibald's intended. He was a young lawyer in New York, going to go into politics, following Specs Roosevelt, no doubt, who was already running for something or other. But to hear van Wyck tell it, his family and the Archibalds had been connected to one another ever since the Dutchmen bought NooYawk island, or come on the Mayflower. Hell, when you're a greenhorn, the history of the USA don't mean a damn to you, because you ain't in it, and never would be. One time, I hear the Fish ask, "All right, Freddy, the truth. When's the wedding planned? I'm sure you two have worked it out these last few days."

"Delightfully," van Wyck answered, cocky as ever, but a frown darkened his sunburned face. "Oh, a few technicalities. Diana wants to finish Vassar, which I find totally unnecessary. We'd have been far better off, boys, if they'd never invented colleges for females. And of course, the Commodore and Grace Archibald are determined to keep their baby girl firmly in Chicago. Guaranteed future, he assures me, meaning that I drop a practice in the best firm in New York to go stumping around the cornfields of Illinois!" He laughed, "Oh, bother. I'll tame that old lion."

"Love conquers," said the Fish.

And Teddy whispered, "Quiet, chaps. I hear elk bugling."

I was counting the days until the hunt was over. Git 'em outa here and me back down to earth. When we came to the last night, Roosevelt was smacking his fist and saying a fitting celebration was in order to end this delightful experience. So that afternoon, I sent the bloodthirsty buggers off to hunt by themselves. Hell, we didn't need no more game, couldn't hardly pack out the carcasses we had. I set Stinky Face to chopping up the meat. Some I'd give to the Shoshones, for I couldn't believe the personages would want to haul it all back on the cars and risk spoiling it. "Anyhow," I says to Daisy, "you're going on to San Francisco, didn't you say?"

"I was. Yes. But plans change. That happens, you know." She glanced at me kind of shy, and I noticed that her hand trembled when she took a drink of water out of the camp scupper.

It had turned out warm that afternoon, almost hot for fall. Indian summer. I set in the shade of a lodgepole and watched while she fussed with draping an oil cloth over a rough pine table we had, and then putting tin cups with wildflowers in them at each place. Such a pale girl. She was wearing a man's hunting shirt, probably Prince Charming's, and she'd rolled up the sleeves. Her hands were dark from the mountain sun, but her forearms were white as lillies. Perspiring she was, pretty little dots of it on her brow. Her kind didn't sweat like us working people. When she'd wipe her sleeve across her forehead, wisps of her oak brown hair would get loose and start flirting with her eyes. Finally she just laughed. "Oh dear, go native, who cares!" She pulled out the bun at the top of her head until her hair was spilling loose over her shoulders. "I've decided, in fact, just this minute I've decided, not to go to San Francisco. And somebody I know will be very upset."

"Your feller?"

She sighed. "Oh, it gets so involved. We were going out there for the wedding of his closest friend at Porcellian." When I looked puzzled, she said, "Their club at Harvard. It doesn't matter. Freddy is such a romantic dear. He's dying to learn surfboarding. They do that in Hawaii, you know, and I can just see him, once we're in San Francisco, sneaking me off on a boat to Honolulu. It's all so dreamy and wonderful, but it's all...." she shook her head. "Too pat, too set, too ordained."

"I ain't following you, missy."

"No, you wouldn't, I'm sure." She dropped to her knees beside me, for I was still setting against the pine. "Please, Patrick, don't call me missy."

"Well, what then? Princess, d'ye want?"

"Oh bosh. You thought I was joking the first night, but I'm dead serious. I've decided to keep on being Daisy. After our little excursion, I find it a lovely nickname for Diana, which I despise, and we all have nicknames in our set. So now I'm a whole new girl and that's that. Agreed?"

I grinned. "Daisy it is. As long as you pick the damn things yourself."

"But I can't, Patrick," she said quietly. "I'm not supposed to."

"Like who says?"

"The way I've been raised. My parents are very strict. Their whole value structure is based on stiff upper lip. Our code is straight from Calvin." When she seen me puzzlin', she added: "Calvinist principles. I take it you don't study religion?"

"God help us, I hope not."

"Well, it comes down to wearing the Protestant hair shirt. If something doesn't hurt, it's not good for us. Nothing should give

252

pleasure. Only pain counts and redeems us. Nothing is up to me. Not the name I'd want, or who I marry or how I live. Everything's planned. Forgive me for saying this, but I'm sure it's obvious to you. I'm just different from anything you've ever known. My life has been laid out in little squares, building blocks, since the day I was born. Proper schools, proper college, make the right friends, make my debut, marry, bear children, grow old and die. Oh yes, there are a lot of boards and good works and functions in there, too, that I'm expected to grace with my name. But in the end, I'm being sentenced to be exactly like my mother, and her like her mother, all the way back as long as anyone can remember. Marching in the lockstep of our class, our values, our specialness as the leaders of society."

I blew out a long breath. "Some years back, the day I left my Sioux wife dead at Wounded Knee, a friend of mine and hers, a newspaperman named Freeman McTighe, told me about how it is with the bigwigs. How just a handful of 'em, bankers and such, run the world. Well, this world you're talkin' about, this lockstep life at the top, it's part of that, ain't it?"

"Of course it is, Patrick! All interlocked, interrelated. Look at Teedie and me. That's T.R.'s nursery name, you know."

"I didn't, but it kind of fits. Like a little Teddy bear."

"Oh, quite! Cuddly, funny, sometimes truly noble. Though he was years older than me, I used to have a crush on him when we little cousins were scampering around on one of the various family estates. Only when I grew up did I see how pathetic he really is. Not only is he trapped in our awful caste system, a victim just like me, but he thrives on it. He's become the part our rules demand that he play. What outsiders like you can't understand, our families go so far, far back we're a closed corporation. Teedie's mother was a Bulloch from Georgia, important leaders in the Rebellion, and my father is connected to him on the Livingston-Jay side. Those bloodlines, it's like racehorses, they go back to the Revolution and long before. These are the people who are bred to own the country, and, as I think Alexander Hamilton put it: because they own it, they're entitled to run it. Here's Teedie who was sickly as a child, but by God the family plan was to make him into a strong boy. He grew sideburns and went off to Harvard, flailing away as a pugilist. Bully, get in and whack, seek the strenuous life, so off he charges to his dreadful ranch in Dakota. Our old-line leaders are expected to be men of war in their games, their colleges and then out into the money-grubbing world. Run the world. But for the females—and this has always struck me as so dreadfully unjust—under our caste system, a woman doesn't own her own body or her labors or her right to govern herself through equal suffrage. Why, even we ladies-in-waiting to our great princes aren't allowed to decide anything in our privileged society...." Her eyes lowered and her finger trailed a circle in the pine needles beside me. "So what do we have left? Cool, quiet mansions, maids to bring us tea, and migraines in the afternoon. Don't complain, they tell us, just curl up in our womb. Pull up the covers and go to sleep in the warmest, most comfortable womb in the world. But, oh my God, Patrick, it is not the world! You know that. Every bone in you says that you live in the real, and I in make-believe. Even in these few days out here, the sunsets, the flaming dawns—just the freedom! Beside this grandeur, all that old stuff that I've been raised by, the rules and the codes and the cliques, oh, it's so small, so hollow. So meaningless."

Her eyes flashed up at me, as wide and wounded as a trapped doe. "Do you think I can get out, Patrick? Is there any way?"

"Ah hell, Daisy," I muttered. "Ask one of your own kind. I'd be the last one to know."

"Don't use that word 'kind'! I despise it. That's what I'm running from. But you ran, too, Patrick. That's why I'm asking you."

"If I ran, it was to save my skin."

"No, no, not at all. Teedie's been telling me. He's fascinated with how you've lived, the battles, the adventures. All these places you've been, the strange tongues, the dark cultures. I've just read about such things in books. I want to live it, don't you see?"

"Daisy," I said, and slowly pushed up, for I didn't know how to end this, or answer it either, so stunned was I. "What I done, or what you got to do, all rests on the hand you've been dealt, the way the coin has flipped."

"So I can't change?" she cried. "Is that what you're saying? That I'm too soft for it?"

"Not at all, girl. You wouldn't be talking like this if you didn't have the heart for it. But you can't expect that changing your spots or your calling in life or the roof over your head is going to put out the fire in your belly."

"And what is that?" she whispered.

"I ain't sure, Daisy. My dear Momma would tell me that it's God himself, trying to a bring a soul home. With me, though, all the roaming I've done, I've never got there, I'll say."

"But you keep going?" she said hopefully. "Trying?"

"Ah, yes, looking under the next rock, I suppose. Perhaps someday I'll find the green grass beneath."

She seized my hands in her small, soft ones, and sent a chill through me. I thought I saw her lips whisper, "Thank you, Patrick." But whatever, it was lost in the hilarity of the hunters, storming back into camp. God help me, they'd shot two more muley bucks and some worthless sage hens, tough as boots. When van Wyck runs up to her, his face had a tight look, like he'd seen her letting go of my hands. Well, now, lad, I thinks, I don't know what's happening either, but whatever it is, we both better get used to it.

That night, with the fire crackling, and the brandy and whiskey passing around, we had our farewell feast. God almighty, these personages had a strange way of entertaining themselves. With Stinky Face hunkered down in the leaves, and Suckling Calf in her greasy squaw dress sagging her old breasts against the table, here was the Fish, standing up and crying, "Let the toasting begin!" The big feller had a sense of humor. In his hunting pack, he'd lugged up a top hat and celluloid collar, so there he prances around, big as a horse, and starts reciting "Horatio at the Bridge." They told me the name, for sure as hell, I couldn't savvy it. He was saying the damn poem by memory, in Greek.

Not to be outdone, van Wyck leaps to his feet and starts doing a speech about Julius Caesar, and by God, not in English either. Latin.

Mind you, they was spouting all this in front of common Injuns, Stinky Face slumped down, letting it lash over him like a hailstorm. Once in a while, his dark brow would knot and he'd stare at me, like who is crazy around here, white man? Poor old Suckling Calf had a brandy bottle in her mitt by then and was puddling away until finally she was face down on the board table. I grabbed the bottle and said to the Fish, "I told you buggers not to let 'em get into this."

Nobody was listening. Mister head honcho, the bully-huffing Roosevelt now stands up and starts his own oration. He had a fistful of papers he'd taken from his pack, and with his eyes mooning through his specs, he'd bang his fist on the table whenever he thought we wasn't listening. His gibberish meant nothing to me, for he was running on about some U.S. sea Admiral named Mahan. "That man," he cried, "is a visionary. Admirable book, his *Influence of Sea Power on History*. Here's what I said when I reviewed it for the *Atlantic Monthly:* 'Sea power is the key to the ultimate triumph or failure of the mighty races to which the fleets belong.' Wake up to what that means!" He was fist-smacking like a hell-and-brimstone preacher, at which Suckling Calf gives a twitch and hiccup, moaning in her cups. "The frontier is ended. Face it! America's ability to produce manufactured goods will soon outstrip her capacity to consume them. The only thing we can depend on is sea power! If we have it, we have the world!"

"Come now, Teddy," rumbles the Fish, "it's one thing for you to deliver this litany to your friends in your neat, Harvard Quad accent, but it's something very different if you try to choke it down the throats of Congress. Those are crude men up there. If McKinley is elected next month, he's so timid he'll run from you imperialist jingoes."

"Beveridge won't! That young firebrand from Indiana. Here," Roosevelt rattled another paper, "his exact words on the floor of the

Senate just before we left the East. I quote: 'God has not been preparing the English-speaking and Teutonic peoples for a thousand years for nothing but vain and idle self-contemplation and self-admiration. No! He has made us the master organizers of the world. We are the adepts who must administer government among savage and senile peoples. God has marked the American people his chosen nation to finally lead in the regeneration of the world."

As he spoke, Suckling Calf sogged over onto my lap, and the dead weight of the poor old bat was more than I needed to pack. I grabbed hold of her, rolled her into a blanket, and let her sleep it off beside the fire.

When I come back, Teddy was firing even more barrages. "Why here," he roared, "if you don't take my word, listen to this young newspaper man, White. A comer. William Allen White, he signs it, *Emporia Gazette* out in Kansas. 'It is the Anglo-Saxon's manifest destiny to go forth as the world's conqueror. He will take possession of the islands of the sea. Hawaii, the Phillippines, all of the sea. And of course, closer to home, Cuba must at once be filled with Yankees!'"

"Cuba Libre!" Fish bellowed, and started waving his top hat. Then they were drinking to the fuss that must have been going on in Cuba, revolution, oppression, outrages. Hell, how would I know, or care?

Finally the Fish cuts through it, "Gentlemen, if I still have the floor, Enough of politics, cigars and smoke-filled rooms! I say, a word from the fairer sex. The fairest!" He swung to Daisy and lifted his glass.

"Here, here!" van Wyck put his arm around her. "You've been so quiet tonight, my dear, I'm afraid your cousin Teedie has bullied the wind right out of you."

"Oh, not at all," she said, laughing. "I was just waiting to be asked."

God almighty, how pretty she looked, with the flames dancing in her dark eyes. She was wearing a blouse of silky blue, puffy sleeves, and the front of it cut low over the pale bosom that she didn't have much of. But her hair was made up different now, fallen long, with red mountain daisies threaded into it. From her flowing skirt, she took out a small paper book. "There's a new poet that my literature professor at Vassar is just crazy about, and now I see why. I picked up his latest work on the way out here. He's an Englishman, I believe, but has spent years now in places just like where we're sitting. Canada, Alaska, the north country. Robert Service is his name." Turning away from van Wyck, she began softly to read:

"'The Wanderlust.

The wanderlust has got me by the belly-aching fire,

by the fever and the freezing and the pain,

by the darkness that just drowns you, by the wail of home desire,

I've tried to break the spell of it—in vain.

256

Life might have been a feast for me, now there are only crumbs;
in rags and tatters, beggar-wise I sit;
yet there's no rest or peace for me, imperious it drums,
the Wanderlust, and I must follow it.'"

She glanced up from the book and her eyes crossed mine. Then shyly, she smiled, closed the book, and sat down.

"Bravo, bully!" Teedie cried. "You have such a beautiful voice, my dear, I would enjoy listening if you were just reading the telephone directory."

Van Wyck took her hand and lifted it. "Three cheers for Vassar. But I must say, that's depressing stuff they pump into you back there."

She looked at him sharply. "To you, perhaps. I find it terribly apt. And now, gentlemen, I love you all, but I'm not a good traveler, you know. I must pack." As she passed among them, they gave her little hugs and pats. When she came to me, our eyes met, and she handed me the book. "I'm done with this, so why don't you have it. You might enjoy Mr. Service. 'Belly-aching fire, the wail of home desire.'"

I stared at the book, and then she was gone, a pale shadow drifting away to her tent.

"I fear that our lady is right," Roosevelt said. "It's exhilarating to feel those mountains in your legs. Nothing beats the strenuous life, but all good things must end." He walked over to me and gripped my hand. "You're an interesting chap, Kelly, and a fine woodsman. I hope we'll hunt together again."

"Seconded," said van Wyck, with a strange look in his eyes. "Provided he's not too busy reading Diana's poetry. Well, my good man, what's the bill of fare? Do we settle with you here, or when?"

I shrugged. "Tomorrow down at the railroad is good enough. Closer to the bank."

When we come to the railhead next day, the cars were already there, and also another private Palace Pullman that had been hooked on. This glittery coach was filled with other fancies, including dames with little snapping poodle dogs that they claimed could hunt birds. These new personages been shooting everything that walked or flew over in the Jackson Hole country. They'd come out from Philadelphia, Boston, NooYawk and God knows what other burgs I'd never see. What struck me strange, all of my personages seemed to know all these new ones, like they was just one big happy family. Now how, I thinks? But then I remembered what Daisy had said. Interlocking they were, as joined together as a tribe of Siamese twins. It didn't matter which part of the nation they lived in. They were all the same kind, so rich that there were only a few of them, in a land still stricken by the Panic back in '93. I suppose it was natural that them that had the silver spoon would be clinging together like spiders woven in one glossy web far above the heads of the rest of us. They were dancing and hugging and swapping tales, to be told many times, I'm sure, in their fancy parlors and private clubs.

I got the baggage loaded and the game cared for by black porters who stuffed it into a special boxcar full of ice. By then, they'd all swirled up into the Palace Car. I kept looking for Daisy, longing for one more touch of her, but when she came running back to the rear platform Roosevelt was huffing to the conductor to get started. Various people had important stops and connections, no delays possible. So all I got from Daisy Archibald was a wave. In the confusion of everyone laughing and taking off, I thought I saw her gloved hand rise to her lips, like she was blowing me a kiss.

The cars clanked up the dead yellow hills out of Lander, and snaked off into the mournful gray sagebrush. The whistle was howling like a coyote baying at the moon. Wearily, I turned to Suckling Calf, who was sitting in a heap on the bricks of the platform. "You're paying for falling into that bottle last night," I says, and helps her up. "Now get the boy and start putting the camp gear away."

She was chuckling and the breath on her you could bottle. She grinned her gold and gappy teeth. "Chicken with No Feathers, hah? I theenk she take home white man heart."

"You theenk! Why, you ole bat, what would you know about it?"

She leered and gave me a slobbery kiss on my cheek. "Chicken in pot now. You wait."

I waited all right, until the snows had come, and the sagebrush lay frozen and dead, along with my wild dreams. All she'd been was a shadow, the eyes of a doe deer flickering at me in the timber, maybe trapped once, but run away now for sure. Ah, hell, I thinks, give it up. I didn't know where she'd gone, least of all where she lived. I'd never find that lass again.

As it turned out, I didn't have to. She found me.

———

Just before Christmas it was. I'd come to town, trying to find work for winter. Ringgold and I had split. I was field-mouse poor and would have to resort to trapping in the mountains. In fact, I was over at the Mercantile pricing traps when a lad runs in from the depot. He had snow all over his coat and on his little cloth cap. He was dancing there, fluttering a telegram envelope, pretending it was so valuable he wasn't going to give it to me. "You little scamp," I says and snatches it, him all the while peering over my shoulder to read it.

From Chicago, Illinois
Patrick Kelly, huntsman
Lander, Wyoming

My daughter informs you have access to game animals. Sender desires to purchase breeding pair American Bison for gift to friend. Urgent. Christmas deadline. Two thousand five hundred dollar bearer funds held your name Wyoming State Bank. Use as necessary for purchase and transportation of yourself and animals to J. Ogden Armour, Armour and Company, Union Stockyards, Chicago. Wire confirmation at once.

Commodore E. H. Archibald
Archibald Hoe and Disk
Archer Avenue Plant, Chicago

I stared at the white piece of paper until the stripes of words pasted on it danced in my eyes. Holy smoke, the Union Stockyards, even the Armour company. What a lifetime ago, it seemed, that I was driving their meat wagon and killing steers in the stink of their corrals. Yet now, just like I'd told Daisy, the coin had flipped and spun me full circle right back where I'd begun. America the beautiful, I thinks. By God, it could only happen here.

Yet something struck me fishy, too. The Commodore was her papa all right, but how had the old devil known that this "huntsman"…get that name, will you…knew anything about buffalo? It wasn't like they were common as ground squirrels anymore. Bones on the prairie, except for a precious few the Sharps rifles hadn't crashed down. And who knew that?

I grinned. My little Daisy. Had to be, bless her pretty head. While we were riding up onto the mountain that first day, buffalo was one of the beasts she was nattering about. I told her they were hard to come by, but some of my Shoshone friends had a few scraggly survivors grazing in the dirt behind their teepees.

I fairly flew to the bank, pinching myself all the way. But it was true. The President of the bank himself sniffed at me in my rags and counted out 2500 greenbacks, which was probably more money than he'd ever seen. At least, he sure whined while he was parting with it.

That very afternoon, I rode out to Crowheart Butte and made parley with Suckling Calf's-wizened old grandma. I let her moan it out and wail for the old life, all the while sitting with bills in my mitt. But finally her old eyes gleamed and she counted out five hundred U.S. By dark, the Shoshone boys and I had roped a good, wet young cow, and though the old nasty bull that was running with her had seen better days, he was all they had around to go along with her.

As luck would have it, there were steers going out of Lander bound for the Yards in Chicago. So I hooked on, and my bisons rode in a special coop in the cattle car. I put down dry straw and mounds of hay for 'em, saying to the railroad boys that these here beasts were going to the nabob Armour himself, so treat 'em good. And me, too, while they were at it.

The road done a lot of business with Armour, so they sure listened. I bunked in the caboose, right behind my beasts, me and a couple of brakehands, and a cowman I knew from the Sweetwater, riding all the way to the Yards to see that he got fair price for his beef.

We come rumbling into Chicago the morning of Christmas Eve. It was snowing so hard I could barely make out the dingy city, stinking with smoke from the trains and river boats, and far off, the rows upon rows of dark squatty houses where the working people lived. Praise the Lord, I thinks, that ain't me no more, at least for this moment of being Cinderella.

At the Yards, the flunkies hopped to, and right quick you can bet. They knew about the buffalo, but they didn't stay here. The Mister wanted them shipped direct up to Melody Farms.

When I says, "Melody?" the Yard foreman chuckled in a brogue you could cut with a butter knife. "Well now, lad, I'll tell you how it is with Mister J.O. When he wants something, he gets it. North of the city, east of the lake in a settlement they call Lake Forest, where the swells live, Mr. J.O. finds an Irish farmer by the name of Patrick Melody, who owns a big swatch of land, beautiful trees and ponds and the like. I says, it's a bloody swamp, sir, but the Mister says, Oh, no, my man, it will be superb. An Italianate villa will rise here. Get that, Italianate, which don't mean Dago, lad. So he ups and buys old Melody out, for a fortune I hear, and puts his name on the farm to ice the cake. Your beasties are going to their new home this very day."

It was getting on toward dark when we rattled up the long track, north out of the smoke of the city, beyond the hovels of the working people, until we were cruising through beautiful oaken woods, dotted with lakes and fields. When we finally pulls up, we're just one cattle car now, a special engine and my caboose, the brakeman hollers, "Armour station, mister."

"He's got his own?"

"Why shouldn't he? This is his track."

There it was, a lovely red brick depot with a blue slate roof. Maybe this was the Italianate fooferaw, how would I know, but alongside it was a shiny purple brougham with a big yellow A painted on its doors. Two liveried coachmen sat on the box as stiff as their whips like they was expecting a general instead of a pair of moldy, manure-caked shaggies.

More flunkies scurried up, wearing the white rubber coats of yard workers that you could get the blood off easy. They prodded the buffalo down the loading ramp, and when the beasts hit the slick snow, they stood snorting and pawing for about one second, and then, lickety-split, went thundering away, splashing into the marshes and booming through the giant oaks.

"God help us, byes!" I cries. "Your boss has paid a fortune for them buggers! Ain't you even going to pen 'em up?"

"It's all a pen," snaps one of the yard flunkies, "all under the Mister's fence. Nothing gets in here, and nothing gets out."

Just then, I hear the rattling of another brougham. I'm standing in the slush, mud and crap on my rubber boots, and in the wet cold dying to take a piss after being so long on the cars. In fact, I was reaching for my buttons when I hear a cry. "Patrick! Oh, Patrick, it is you! We've done it!"

The carriage door flies open and Daisy comes running toward me, her doe eyes wild and rejoicing. Her hands were in her fur muff, but she ripped them out, snow running down her face and onto her fur collar. When I held her against me, we just stood there, rocking back and forth. I lifted her chin. "You darlin', you rigged this, didn't you now?"

"There had to be some way," she cried. "Aren't you glad?"

We were throbbing against each other, and out of the corner of my eyes, I see the Armour flunkies with their mouths gaping open, at the sight of a lady losing herself in the arms of a common drover. "We've done it," she kept saying. Ah, God help me, how we both wished it'd always be so easy, never dreaming of the heartaching years that lay ahead. Like the wild bisons that snorted off into Armour's giant pen, we found our own pen, we did, and for me at least, what came out would never again be the same as what went in.

BECOMIN' A GENT

That very night, at the Archibald great house, standing like a castle on the bluffs of Lake Michigan, I got my first look at how the other half lived.

As a fitting welcome for the bisons, I suppose, the Archibalds spiffed me up and dressed me like a doll. Daisy's three brothers had gathered for the holidays, Eben, Enoch and Ethan. The "E" boys, Daisy called them, and it was surely for excellence, expected now or sometime later. Perfect puffers they was, slick-cheeked, pomaded hair, true gents, knowing the best wines, cigars and costly haberdashers, from which they swaddled me into a fine Irish tweed suit, vest and all, monogrammed shirt, cravat and cordovan brogans.

Yet when Daisy's mother, Alice Archibald, pats me down beside her at the long, lacy table, the queenly thing says, pleasant enough, "Why, I'm delighted to have you with us, Mr. Kelly. I understand that you're both Irish and Catholic?"

"I suppose, ma'am. Born that way anyhow."

"How nice! The only Irish Catholics I've ever known before are my servants."

Daisy, sitting next to me, grabs my hand, her voice like a shot. "Mother!"

"New blood is always stimulating, my dear. One gets isolated. One can learn. Must, the way things are now."

My eyes flicked back and forth between them, and God help me, they were shooting sparks. Queen Alice must have been a beauty at one time. She had Daisy's lovely pale skin, but her eyes were glinty gray and her jaw set strong. That old gal knew just where she sat all right. Top of the heap. Her hair was a mound of spun silver, with eyeglasses dangling on her expansive bosom, which Daisy didn't have. In her presence, Daisy seemed to melt down small and frail, a quivering doe, her eyes looking for a way out. She wore a mouse-colored tailored suit, velvet lapels and all, with a choker of pearls glistening in the lace of her blouse. But when her hand gripped mine, I felt the wet in it, and the trembling.

Small wonder. Even the Irish maids, as they bowed to serve our fancy plates, were casting glints at me like, Didja lose your way to the pigsty, mister?

It appeared that special celebrations such as this Christmas Eve were made to order for Himself, the Commodore. He presided from a grand carved throne, his hands spread flat on the oaken table, and when his own wife had the gall to speak to him, it was Mr. Archibald. The whelps called him Father, but she didn't have that

262

privilege. I kept wondering, what in hell does he let her call him when he's trying to get her between the sheets? I stared at him with his florid face and bristling white moustache. His hooded eyes and sagging jowls give him the look of a lordly walrus, perched on top of his iceberg. When he smiled, which wasn't often, he gleamed big fang teeth, and God, how he could shovel in the groceries. It showed in the girth of him, a rich liver, three fine wines at dinner, then brandy, seegars, and a whiskey and soda to put him to bed. Even Alice Archibald, with her puffing pigeon breast, tended to the portly, and the oldest E boy, Eben, was sure heading the same way. Big drinking was their habit all right, but when the lackeys kept passing us whiskies, wines and seegars, I'd just shake my head.

"What is this?" bellows the Commodore.

"I don't indulge."

"And why not?"

"If the truth be known, sir, I couldn't afford it on soldier's pay."

"Well, there's a new excuse for you, Father," Eben chuckled, and Daisy steeled him with a glance.

"I just never got the taste is all, and seen too many lads put down by it."

"Temperance, bah!" the Commodore grunted.

"It's to his credit, Mr. Archibald," Alice sniffed. "It's something we can be thankful for. And besides," she looked at me warningly, "alcohol is the curse of the Irish people. How well I know, the last coachman we had."

Then somebody started a story about the poor coachman, so sotted that he drove the team into a ravine. Listening to their silly tales, the brothers putting their oars in, trying to please their papa, I glances at Daisy and thinks, How in hell, girl, did you ever spring from these loins? They'd cowed her. She was too sensitive for the pomp of it. She'd just smile sadly or sigh.

When the grand feast was over, they must have had a pre-arranged signal. Alice Archibald rose in her long flowery gown, and the ladies swished away with her up the grand, curving staircase. There were two other young women at the party, one a princess in the making, they said, Lolita Armour, J. Ogden's daughter, and Daisy's schoolgirl chum. It was the two of them, I learned, who had rigged up the bison racket to get me there. Whether Lolita was the intended of one of the E boys, I couldn't tell. The middle one, Enoch, had eyes for her all right, and young Ethan looked fairly smitten by the other young one. A Pullman daughter, she must have been, for during the dinner, she told a wild tale about the wretched strikers burning down her father's model city.

The signal for the men was to troop after the Commodore into his library. The oak-paneled walls were hung with portraits and photographs. Over the great hearth were gold loving cups, trophies that the walrus or the boys must have won by their exploits in pasture games. Golf-stick trophies, horse-hockey sticks, polo it was, and young Eben standing against a fence, bulging out with a white Y on his chest for his heroic football playing at Yale.

"When you came in on the train, Kelly, you passed this." The Commodore pointed to a colored lithograph showing a whole town full of identical brick factory buildings. "Our original plant. Archibald Hoe and Disk. From here, my grandfather used to say, 'Let the prairie yield to the plow.' Well, sir, he made it do just that. When Diana went off to Vassar, I told her, 'Instead of filling yourself with this psychological garbage, far better, my dear, to dig into your own roots.' History was made here, Kelly, this breadbasket of the nation, and by God, our iron and steel played a big part in it."

Bridey, the upstairs maid, had pattered in and was trying to palm me a snifter of brandy. I shook my head.

"Gad," said Young Ethan, looking out the window, "what a superb night for a skate! Bridey, have the coachman sweep the pond. I'm going even if nobody else is."

They all thought that was a great idea, but the old walrus harrumphed. "I have reading to do, and then to bed. Christmas Day. Breakfast at eight, we will light the tree at nine, carriages in for church at ten. Goodnight, my boys. Enjoy yourselves." When he came to me, his jowls were pursing and I could see the blue veins in them. He studied me from my borrowed brogans to the top of my head. "I find you quite as my daughter described you. Larger frame, possibly, but Eben's tweeds fit nicely and take off some of the rough edges, one might say. I'm sure Armour will be pleased with the animals you've brought him. We're awfully close. He's done many things for me. And for this city. Well, when will you be leaving?"

The hoods lifted from his eyes and I could see the brown pupils. Same exact color as Daisy's, only his were cold and hard.

"I ain't sure, sir. Hardly been time for Daisy and me to talk about it."

"Daisy! Who is Daisy!"

"Your daughter. At least, that's how she wanted it in the mountains."

"She often wants what she can't have. Goes through these damn phases. When she was sixteen, it was a fishing guide from our club in Wisconsin. Indian, mind you." He blew a long breath through his saggy lips. "Don't worry. You'll be taken care of for your trouble. It is Christmas, after all. I gave my plant people the largest bonus we've ever issued. The economy is improving. One has to do these things. They expect it nowadays."

Then he turned and clumped out. Ethan was grinning and

plucking my arm. "Come on now, fellow. I'm sure I can fit your size skate. Have you ever done it?"

"Not in this lifetime."

"Well, watch Diana," Eben said. "Fine little athlete and great on the figures. She can teach anybody."

"That'd be me," I says, and followed them outside into the cold.

Hell, I'd be the tail of their donkey all right, amusing them in my flounderings. But I don't think the brothers planned it that way. They wasn't bad lads. And I know damn well Daisy hadn't. "Patrick," she kept saying, "you don't have to do this. Do you really want to?"

"I'll damn well try," I says.

While we was lacing up the skates, one of the coachmen went scurrying around, sweeping the snow off the ice. What happened then was pitiful. I see how Daisy stroked away so easy and the boys too. So I lurches out, sliding, and my feet go straight out from under me, skates flashing up to the stars, and me cracking down on my spine.

Daisy swooshed beside me. "Oh, Patrick, are you hurt!"

"Me pride!" I grunts. "But I'll learn this damn racket!"

While she was pulling me up, her lips brushed my cheek. "You're such a good sport. They can't beat us. We won't let them."

I got the hang of it before long, her strong little hands gripping mine, and I stiff-legged around there like a spavined horse. The pond where we skated was right at the edge of the bluff. When we set on a snowbank to rest, we could well topple off and go crashing down through the great trees and underbrush that ran to the lakeshore. There was white ice at the edge of the lake, and beyond it, a black sea, hardly a wave in it, and burning with the light of the stars.

I stared back at the great house, a castle of granite it was, with warm yellow lights in the downstairs windows, the servants, no doubt, cleaning up after us. I glanced at Daisy beside me, her fur collar tight against her lovely neck. "You've got some kind of outfit here, I'll say."

"It is lovely, yes. We're so privileged, aren't we? Too much."

I shrugged. "Well, that depends who's looking at it, I suppose."

Ethan thrummed up on his skates with his lady friend. "Don't capture the poor man, Diana. Come on, we'll play crack the whip."

"I'm not capturing anybody, Ethan," Daisy retorted. "Just go on, you do it." As he skated off, she sighed. "We're a very competitive bunch, as you may have noticed. It's hard to be oneself here."

"I can see that."

She snuggled against me on the snow and her eyes laughed. "Tell me the truth. Are you overwhelmed by them? Are they truly insufferable?"

I shrugged. "Take a little getting used to, I'd say. Never being

265

around the likes. It does strike me strange, though," I said, and stared at her leather gloves which were gripping my bare mitts. "How did you get so different from 'em, Daisy?"

"Am I? Do you think I am?"

"What I seen in Wyoming was. Ah, not all the way. You've got the talk they have, the finery. That would be natural, of course, growing up in palaces like this. But there's more to you, girl, at least as how I sees it. Where did it come from?"

She took a scoop of snow and tossed it over the bluff. "Down there, I think."

"Under the bluff? In that damn thicket?"

"Oh, but Patrick, that was the wild side of me, my escape from all the silly rites of growing up. It wasn't that I couldn't do the little games we were supposed to play. I'd even beat my brothers sometimes. I was good in athletics. But somehow, I always felt I was losing my real self in all the noisy competition, jockeying and fighting. Do you understand that?"

"Mebbe, yes. Soldierin' is much the same. Feller ain't never alone."

She stared down into the darkness. "I'd slip away from all the organized things. I had trails to secret glades and arbors where the creeks ran down the bluff. So peaceful, so wonderfully quiet. There were springs and frogs. Once I found an ancient tortoise, took him to my room until Mother made me give him up. Said he'd shit on the rug." She giggled. "Do you mind me saying that dreadful word?"

I grinned. "Hell, dearie, it's life, ain't it? Join the human race, eh?"

"Oh, Patrick," she whispered, "how I'm trying! In those years I spent, dancing to my own drummer in the glades of this bluff, I began to see that so much of the way we lived, what we believed, it *was* shit. It was wrong. There are other humans on this planet beside us. Why," she pointed south along the bluff, through the big oaks, "we're so screened in here, we don't even see that crowded, tortured city seething just a few miles below us. Oh, the men go in there, of course. They go in, strike steel on steel, draw blood." Her voice rose. "But I don't want to be so protected out here! I don't want to hate what you called 'my kind.' There shouldn't be any kinds, Patrick. We are all human animals on one level, and saints and souls on the other. Can you understand at all what I'm saying?"

Beyond us, on the black ice, the brothers were cracking the whip now, skating like fury and flinging the squealing girls off on the end. The Pullman lady came toppling into me, showering me with ice from her skates. "Oh Diana," she cried. "It's fun. Don't be a poop!"

"We're freezing. We've had enough," Daisy said, glancing at me. "Let's go warm up."

"Fine by me." But the Pullman lady flickers her eyes, snotty-like. "Di—an—a! Are you up to your old tricks?"

When we trooped back to the house and out into the kitchen, I says to Daisy, "Now what's this about your old tricks?"

She laughed. She'd stripped off her fur coat and was wearing a white woolen sweater with a high collar up to her chin. So bulky it was, she looked like a lad in it. You couldn't see no woman there. She lit the big gas stove and put on a pan of milk. "I hope you like cocoa," she said, and I nods. Then she came over and plopped down on my lap. "My old tricks, Patrick, mean that I do crazy things sometimes. I'm not formal like my family or my school chums. When I see something, some place or person or whatever that interests me, I don't pedigree it, don't plan any attack or any tricks. I just go to it. Help myself."

I smiled and trailed my fingers down her lovely oaken hair. "Like the daisies on the mountain, hey?"

"Yes, Patrick."

"And the Commodore?"

"Oh, they're horrified. Mother, too. One time, when I was sixteen, such a crushy age, I was guided by a fascinating young Indian, a Menominee, up at this fishing club Father has in Wisconsin. The poor boy had never been out of a wigwam in his life, so I just said, Come down and visit us. Well, down he trots. Mother and Father were absolutely mortified. Sent him packing the second day, terrified that he was going to, well, you know..."

"That ain't my business, Daisy."

"But it is, dammit! I never even held the boy's hand. It wasn't that kind of thing. Never is for me. I just want to open up new lives, reach out and touch something human for a change." She looked at me intently, her arms draped around my neck. "Patrick. I never have."

I frowned. "Never what?"

"You know. Been with a man. Does that make me so...so awfully unappealing?"

I held her to me. "It makes you, Daisy, like nobody this lad ever knowed."

The milk began to boil over, and me with it. We had our cocoa and talked on, like there wasn't enough we could tell each other, nor the time to do it.

Shortly after the brothers come huffing in from the ice and packed their girlfriends off in the house carriages, a quiet voice trailed down from the top of the stairs. "Diana, dear, really, it is past midnight."

"I know, Mother." She rolled her eyes at me. "Well, maybe she's right. You've had an awfully long day, the buffalo and all."

"Them was the easy part," I says, and she led me up to bed.

On the second story, the grand palace looked like a hotel. Separate rooms for the brothers and Daisy, where they'd grown up. In one wing was a suite for the sire, and adjoining it, another for her ladyship. Frosty as they were, it didn't surprise me that they slept apart. Right next to hers jutted out another suite that Daisy told me was for guests.

She'd just opened the tall doors, and I could see a fireplace, two lace-topped beds, fluffy covers and a scent like pines coming from little pillows.

"Dear," Alice Archibald called from her doorway. "May I see you?"

Daisy stalked toward her, leaving me at the doorway of the guest lodgings. All I caught was a glimpse of Lady Alice, puffing out of her pink kimono, her hair spilling long and angry. Daisy stormed in to her mother's room, but they went at it so hot, they didn't even shut the door.

"He *is* sleeping in the guest room, Mother, he *is* my guest!"

"Absolutely not. Your father and I forbid it. He will sleep in the coachhouse with the other servants. That's his class, and if you don't know it, I beg you to learn it, and quick!"

Then there was muffled shrieks and finally sobbings, until Daisy's voice shot out clear. "If you won't let him—damn you, Mother, I am grown and in college—then I will go into that guest room and sleep in the bed beside him!"

"You are to stay in your own room with the door locked!" The Commodore had banged out of his suite, and I ducked into my room to take cover from the glowering old walrus.

"If I stay, he stays!" Daisy cried.

Her mother had grabbed the Commodore and was pushing him back. "Oh, Mr. Archibald, you dear man, look at your face, it's not worth your blood pressure!" When she got him cooled and out of there, she whirled on Daisy. "All right, you proud little snippet. Your little playmate, your trophy stays. But by creation, young lady, you shall hear from me about this when the holiday is over!"

"Merry Christmas!" Daisy cried, turned on her heel and stalked back to me. She pulled me into the room and I held her, sobbing against me. "I'm so sorry," she whispered. "Inexcusable that you had to hear it. Oh, they're so horrible! Beastly!"

"Now, now, darlin', they ain't. They're just protecting their flesh and blood."

She looked up, sniffling. "You're so big, to say that."

I smiled. "Hell, I wasn't expecting to be no crown prince. You want the real world? Well, you're in it, dearie. Now go on, rest your pretty head. It always looks better in the morning."

She kissed me square on the lips, hers hot and trembling, and then, still sobbing, ran down the long hall and slammed into her room.

268

The next morning when they gathered at the tree to give out their lavish presents, Daisy pleaded with me to stay there with them, but I begged off. Family time, I says, and went out for a long walk, slogging slush trails in the snow that was melting under the giant oaks.

The next day, Daisy's pale cheeks seemed to take fire. She was yawning a lot, and didn't seem like herself. Well, the poor little thing wasn't, indeed. About two o'clock in the morning, I hear voices in the hallway and people running. The town doctor was beside Daisy, and she was sitting up in bed with her nightgown lowered. He was listening with a stethoscope, placing it below her firm little breasts and all around her back. God in heaven, I had just blundered in there because of the commotion, thinking the house was on fire or something. I never dreamed to be gazing at her in nakedness. Yet the Commodore, in his flapping nightshirt, whirled to me and bellowed: "Out, damn you! Don't you know your place!?"

"I was thinking maybe to help you," I says quietly, and started out the door.

The Commodore's bare walrus feet came clopping after me. "You'll help by getting out of here tonight! Pack your bags, go. It's pneumonia, raging fever, we're rushing her to Presbyterian in Chicago!"

"Patrick!" Daisy cried. "Please, momma, don't send him away!"

"Impossible, my dear. You're delirious. Tell her it's impossible, Doctor." The sawbones was muttering, "Oh yes, impossible, of course. Keep her warm, plenty of fluids, and hurry the carriage."

"I'll phone Armour!" cried the Commodore.

"Emory," Alice pleaded. "You can't wake him in the middle of the night!"

"Bosh! He'd insist on it. He has a special railway car waiting at his siding. Told me just today." As he thundered past me toward the telephone, he roared, "You heard what I said! Out! You are not needed or wanted here!"

They carried Daisy past me on a stretcher the sawbones had brought, him and the brothers lugging it. Her thin arm trailed to me. I gripped her flaming hand and kissed it. Then she was gone. Strangely, Alice, bulging in her kimono, turned to me with tears in her eyes. "You only really love them," she whispered, "when they're being taken from you."

I nodded. "I know how it feels, ma'am."

She gripped my hands. "Forgive my husband. He's just so terribly upset. Please go back to sleep. You can leave in the morning. The servants will arrange it. That will be perfectly satisfactory."

"I love your girl," I says quietly, "and I ain't gonna quit her in a time like this." Letting that soak in, I turned and went back to the guest lodging. Down below in the courtyard, a carriage rattled away on the icy gravel, speeding the stricken thing to Mr. Armour's Palace Car.

I leaned my head against the cold pane. God help us, I breathed, spare that little one. Don't take another from me.

For a couple of days, she must have fought it out bad. Father, Mother and brothers were at her bedside in the Presbyterian's hospital. By then, the upstairs maid, Bridey, from Cork, was taking pity on me, moping around alone in the big house. But the wispy, birdy little spinster, praying her beads, just made my heart ache worse. She'd come to the family years ago, and when Daisy was born, the baby of the bunch, she took her over. They had a prim English governess, of course, but Bridey was the soul of the little girl, it seemed. Pattering around the house, Bridey kept up a steady chatter with her Maker, like He had nothing better to do than listen to that pious woman all day. "Ah, you believe like my own Momma does," I'd say, and she'd sniff at me, "What else is there, lad?" She delighted in showing me snaps and portraits of Daisy, the toys she'd played with, and all the heart-throbs of her short life. "Let up on me, woman," I finally says, "this ain't helping me none."

Bridey turns to me, crinkling her wise old eyes. "Back in Cork, we had a little sister who fell in the hearth. She burned and burned, and when we finally saved her, she'd become a leprechaun."

"Dead? A ghost, you're saying?"

"Not at all! She lived, lad! No bigger than the man in the horse's eye, but she graced our house for all them years. The fire made her. That's what I'm tellin' you. Go to the little Daisy, you call her. Ah, Jesus and Mary, she is that. Go to her. Go! She needs you!"

Bridey got the carriage arranged with the head coachman to take me to the Chicago Northwestern cars. Just as I was going out the door of the great house, here's Eben, the oldest brother, stalking in. He was wearing his business clothes, a fine Chesterfield and derby hat. I says, "Lad, how is she?" and he says, "Fighting the good fight."

He pulls an envelope out of his coat. "My father, for Mr. Armour, wants you to sign this bill of sale for the buffalo. So that there'll never be any misunderstandings."

I frowned and scribbled my name as drover. "Well, there ain't, are they? The beasts has been delivered."

"There's money left over, Kelly. Quite a considerable sum, from the original 2500 wired to you. I don't have to know how much, I don't want to know how much, but it's my father's wish that you keep the remaining funds. They'll help you get back where you came from."

"For my trouble, is it? A tip?"

His brown eyes went cold. "Call it what you like."

270

"What I'd like, lad, is to see your sister back on her feet. I love her."

He pursed his lips just like his father. "That is not for you to say, Kelly." He turned to the coachman. "You have your instructions."

The coachman nodded, and I went out of their world just as quick as I'd come in.

When I hit Chicago on the cars, I had almost 1400 U.S. in my jeans—and a determination, too. I was going to stay around for awhile, until I learned poor Daisy's fate. When I picked up a hack at the booming, sooty station, I got to talking with the driver, who only had one arm. I asks, How? and he says, "A Comanche ball." He'd served on the southern plains when Custer was there. We got to jawing about soldiering, and he says, "Well, if a greenhorn don't have a coop in this town, there's a safe lodging for us old rankers. It ain't the best part of town, out on North Avenue. Guidon Hotel, an ex-sergeant from the Sixth Cavalry, McNamara, runs the place."

I told him, "Take me there and wait." A dump it was all right, but they had a room overlooking the streetcar line. I paid my first night's tab, dropped my bag and had the hackie run me through the slush and driving rain over to the Presby's hospital near the Lake.

What a damn morgue, rising up with gray stone turrets and black windows weeping for the dead souls who were daily flitting away to purgatory. Them starchy nurses wouldn't hear of letting some common drover into the private rooms, and besides, the Archibald family had given firm orders: no visitors.

I nods polite enough, then finds the back stairs and walks myself up. God in heaven, I have hated hospitals ever since the sawbones had tried to cut me at the Rosebud.

It didn't take no city detective to find which was Daisy's room. Why, it was like a flower shop out front, big pots of every kind of plant, waiting to go in and cheer her. I glances around at the blooms, finally picking out a big spray of them that I knew would tickle her.

"Mountain daisies," I says, after slipping in and staring down at the thin body underneath the blankets.

God almighty, she was pale as a corpse, her brown hair flung lifeless over the pillow. There was a tube sticking into her arm, draining something into her. Life, I hoped. When she didn't answer, I set the pot down and took out one of the flowers. Gently, I opened her dry little fingers and placed it in them.

She stirred. Her eyes flickered open, and she gave a moan. She tried to sit up but I held her down and kissed her cheeks. "You're coolin' off, darlin'," I whispers. "You're beating it, you're gonna live."

She kept nodding, tears now glistening, running like tiny streams of hope. "You're staying, Patrick. You stayed?"

"Till the last shot is fired," I grins, and tells her about lodging at the Guidon dump over on North Avenue.

She was so weak she could hardly lift my hand, but she took it and kissed it. "Come every day, can't you? I'm better, really stronger. The cough is going…"

"It is not!" rumbled the Commodore. He'd barged in, big as an ox in his overcoat. I felt the draft from the door, and Daisy's fingers tightening on mine. "You are not to be here, Kelly. Leave her!"

"Father!" Daisy sobbed, her voice cracking. Then a doctor came rushing in, and with him a big hospital orderly and a bruiser in civvies who looked like a copper of some sort.

I cries, "I ain't leaving you, Daisy, don't you worry." And to the others, "Back off, can't you see, you're upsetting her worse with all this!"

I waited, breathing hard, out in the hallway, with the stretcher carts creaking past, and the look of death on the nursely faces. Daisy must have calmed down, or they give her morphine to do it. When the Commodore came out, he'd stripped off his greatcoat and tall hat, threw them in a chair. He seized my arm in a steel grip and walked me down to a little porch at the end of the hall. He stood staring at the misting lights of the city, and the files of ants on the pavements below. Working people, going home.

"All right," he growled. "How much?"

I whirled. "What in hell does that mean?"

"A daughter. My only girl." His voice cracked and he strode over to the window. His big forefinger traced a slow line across the pane. "I deal in lines, Kelly. Numbers are lines. Some drop through and are lost to everyone. Some rise above, and profit everyone. There is no way I can put a number on the life of my little girl in there. But I know this, if I don't, you shall destroy her. We shall all lose, and her the worst." He turned to me, lips trembling. "What is it going to cost me to get you out of her life?"

Ah, the cold hardness of him struck me in the heart. "I don't take bribes, mister, and I'll thank you not to offer one again. What do you think I am? Some stiff in one of your factories!"

"I asked for a number!"

"You'll not get one! I'm asking you to give me your girl, for I love her and she loves me."

"Bah! She couldn't! You've known each other a few days, a charade, an infatuation, pure and simple!"

"God help me, I hope it's pure and simple, Mr. Archibald, and I'll do my best to keep it that way for the rest of our lives. I ain't for sale!" My fists were shaking so hard I didn't know whether to bust him in the jowls or smash the window. But what use, it wouldn't help her. Finally I says, "You can't stand the sight of me. That's your business. I'll leave you now, but you're going to see me again. You'd best get used to it." I whirled and started down the hall, but his voice cried after me, a plea. "Kelly!"

When I turned and came back, he'd heaped into one of the chairs and had his face in his hands. His big shoulders were heaving. I finally grabbed one of them and said, "Come now, sir, I didn't mean to shake you so bad. We both love her, ain't that all?"

He was nodding. "I do, I do, Kelly, That's the tragedy." The hoods lifted in his eyes and he stared at me like he'd never seen me before in his life. "I have never breathed this to anyone," he whispered, "and I don't know why I'm doing it now, least of all to a total stranger, even a threat to us. But damnation, man, watching her suffer, I feel so powerless. She makes these beds and lies in them. She's always done it. Hurls herself at life and breaks apart. Diana is so odd, so beyond reason, totally different from anything her mother and I have known, sometimes I wonder if she's even my child."

"Well, she is, ain't she?" I blurted, thinking, though, how strange it was that she didn't even look like them.

"A figure of speech." He shrugged. "Mrs. Archibald had wanted a fourth child. It was planned, of course. I was traveling to Washington a great deal in that winter of '75. Corrupt Grant administration, terrible farm problem. We were helping. Bah," he scowled, "I'm wool-gathering. Of course she's ours. Just so, so impossible."

"But sir, that's families, even litters of pups. It ain't a sin to be different from one another. The world would be a sorry place if we wasn't."

"No, no, you don't understand. I can't expect you to. Even when she was born, right in this hospital, and for years thereafter, she was so sickly, so ill-equipped to progress in the normal stages, we took her to specialist after specialist. She was too excitable, wild, living in total fancy. Her brothers were never like that. It was even thought that in her birth, there could have been an oxygen shortage, and she damaged her brain."

I smiled and patted his shoulder. "What I seen of her, sir, she's got a better head on her than you and me both. Why, she's rebelling, that's all, and God help her do it, I say. New ideas are coming into the world, Mr. Archibald, and she's riding on them, I think."

"Think all you want, but you don't have the say about her future, Kelly." He blew his nose loudly and his eyes hardened. "I'm all for Diana kiting off to the East to educate herself, if she thinks she needs it. But her oddness, her rebellious instability is unacceptable to Mrs. Archibald and me. This mucker-posing."

I frowned. "What is that now?"

"Abandoning her station in life. Putting on clothes that are not hers. Lying down with dogs and getting up with fleas. Her family, her community, has a certain standard of values, tried, proven and handed as a legacy to us down through the generations. No willful snip of a girl is going to fling those away, not in my house and certainly not on my funds. When Diana finishes Vassar, I'm planning to give her a grand tour, her mother and I together. All the European capitols. Broaden her culturally, after which I expect her to return to Chicago and fulfill her obligations in a social and charitable sense. She has a name that means something, Kelly, and one does not lower one's self to escape from it. When the proper man comes along, I pray that her oddness, her childish immaturity will have been hardened out of her, as we harden steel for our plows, and that she will make him a strong and sane wife."

I shook my head. "Your girl could be in there dying, yet still you're not letting her go, are you?"

"Not until she's well enough. Children are an investment, Kelly, requiring constant maintenance."

"Well now, what about her intended back in New York, van Wyck who was hunting with us?"

"Commendable chap, no doubt. Promising career. But she's not ready. Doesn't know what she wants. Crippled some way in her nervous system, and still must heal."

I sighed and shook my head. "Well, sir, you ain't me and I ain't you, thank God. But I'll tell you what I think, and you can put it in your pipe and smoke it. If that girl is a cripple, which she ain't, you're making her one. Control her, shape her like some goddamn tool in your plant, until she's perfect enough to go out and be sold. Let her go, Archibald, for if you won't, she will anyway. Maybe to me, maybe to God, but whatever, you can't do a damn thing about it."

I turned on my heel and stalked off down the hall, wanting to bust in for a last look at Daisy, but the bruiser was planted in front of her door with his arms folded over his chest.

It all come to an end in a way that Daisy and I didn't dream. For I knew by then that I had met my match with her. Our stars had crossed, melted together in the wild sky. Madness it was indeed, and there wasn't a man or woman who could rip us apart. Not even God himself, it seemed then, and we took that chance. We dared Him.

A week after I'd left Daisy at the hospital, I was lying in my dingy bed at the Guidon hotel. I'd finished the evening paper and had dropped it to the floor, the room dark save for the flashing lights of the saloons. It was storming, sleet running down the panes, and below, on North Avenue, vendors were buttoning up their carts, trooping off after the horse drawn street cars, creaking the working people home.

When the door opened softly, and the papers rustled beside the bed, I thought I'd dozed into a dream. But Daisy was there, standing above me in a long fur coat. When she opened it, her slim body was still in her hospital gown.

She'd escaped from them. Though wan and weak, she'd escaped to me, and there, in that slum room, she made the two of us one.

She stayed with me a night and a day in that Guidon room, the happiest we'd ever have. But it wasn't to last.

The following morning, while we were having coffee like royalty in our bed, two Pinkerton dicks busted down the door, with oldest brother, Eben, shoving in behind them. Pinkertons protected the Archibald plant, and he paid them a fortune this time, to get his daughter back.

In the end, after all the scrapping and threatening, it was Daisy who left, weeping and dragged away. The Commodore wanted to press charges against me, but I heard his own lawyer tell him that there wasn't a court in the land could convict me. The girl was free, white and 21.

What they done was to ship her back to Vassar college to complete her studies. They wasn't even trying to buy me off anymore. Them and the Pinkertons were making sure I'd never touch her again.

The only hope I had, Daisy knew where I was, so I stayed put at the Guidon, hoping for a letter or some word. Nothing come, but I figured it was still better than rushing back to the Wyoming winter and freezing my butt out on a trap line. As my Archibald money began to trickle thin, old sergeant McNamara let me tend bar for my board and room. I enjoyed the smoky noise of his saloon. I'd meet some old vets of the plains, we'd swap yarns, and the world pretty much stood still until the April Fool's day, no less.

I'd gone out in front of the Guidon's frosted glass doors and was stretching in the sun for a bit, putting off going inside and sweeping the foul sawdust from the saloon floor.

A shiny black motor car pulls up to the gutter, popping and rattling. There were so few motor cars around, I could scarcely believe that this one was close enough to touch. The street folk were just as curious as me, shaggy vendors running over from their carts, and the usual beggar boys with their shoe-shine boxes squatting down to look under the bowels of the thing.

The man driving it had a spiffy gray suit on, with goggles and a floppy cap. Getting out from behind the high wheel, he was grinning, flicking his thin seegar at the rabble so that they wouldn't dirty his machine. "Is it a German Benz?" pipes one of the street snots. And the driver says, "No, we beat the Benz in the Washington Park race. Also the de la Vergne and the R.H. Macy. This is the Duryea Motor Wagon Company's machine, the only American-made entry."

Shoving through them, he spots me, and cries, "You there, Kelly. Aren't we in luck! Remember me?"

He pulls down the scarf from his mouth and lifts up his goggles. "God Almighty," I says, "Ethan!"

He claps my mitt, and then puts his arm around my waist like I was a long, lost relative. "How about a drive, fellow?" he says.

"Well, sure. I ain't never been in one, though."

"You'll never forget this ride," he says, and sweeps me away.

Four lurching, backfiring hours later, Ethan wheels me up to the great Archibald house, rising above the Lake in all the budding glory of pink and white spring flowers.

And then came the best of all.

My Daisy. She'd come home to me, for the good and godly reason that she was carrying our child.

We hugged and danced in the sunbeams of the parlor. She took my hands and pressed them on her belly, but I could feel nothing but the slim wonder of her soft flesh. "Oh, Patrick, my darling," she whispered. "We've won, they've given in." Her brown eyes lifted to mine, as wide and bright as the petals of a flower. "Could you ever believe such a dream?"

"You're the dream, darlin'," I says, and kisses her hard and long.

That's when murderer's row trooped in. Ethan, Eben and Enoch came over and shook hands. Then the waters parted and made way for the Commodore and lady Alice, their faces as grave as if they were at a wake. Though the Commodore wore a stiff collar and morning coat, the starch had drained from his face. Alice's eyes were weepy and she kept dabbing them with a lace handkerchief she'd stuck up her sleeve.

"One doesn't want these things to happen, oh please God," she sniffled to me, "but now that it has, we stand shoulder to shoulder and put it behind us."

I nodded. "I thank you for that, ma'am. All of you. The boys, too, and you, sir."

"There are conditions," barked the Commodore.

Daisy gripped his hand. "Father, please, not now. Poor Patrick, can't we even offer him a drink or something? Make a toast! This is a celebration!"

"The fellow doesn't imbibe," the Commodore answered gruffly, "but sit down, sit down." He motioned at the soft green sofa with big flowers stitched to it. I settled into it, Daisy beside me, wanting to pull it over our heads. "You and I, Kelly, at the hospital, discussed my daughter's upbringing and the values to which this family hews. We will not plow that ground again, except for these conditions, which highlight the differences between us. Beginning with the matter of her child..."

276

"It's his, Father," Daisy cried. "Ours!"

"My first grandchild," barked the Commodore, "shall be received exactly as if it were one of ours. Just so that you understand, neither the grandchild, nor Diana, nor my sons, have one cent to their name."

I frowned. It come so hard and quick, I didn't know what to make of it.

"Hah? Surprised, are you?" He glowered at me.

"Father!" Daisy cried. "Do you have to turn everything into money?"

"Let your Father explain, dear," Alice said, and reached for Daisy's hand, which she jerked away.

"I support my children, of course," the Commodore said, "with education, travel and, in the case of my sons, I give them employment in the company. I will do the same for Diana. Have done. When Mrs. Archibald and I are gone, our securities holdings will pass down to our heirs." He looked at me intently. "But since you are not one of my heirs, Kelly, I will require you, as a condition of marrying my daughter, to sign a legal paper by which you make no claim on one cent of her assets."

"This is so cruel," Daisy whispered, "just so beastly, I can't believe I'm hearing it. Patrick, please, forgive him. Can you?"

I took a deep breath and glanced across their faces, tight lips, hawky eyes. I gripped Daisy's hand. "You people come at life in a way I've never knowed. For sure, I never had nothing to protect, the way you do. But Daisy is carrying a new life for us, and I'm not loving her or the little one neither for the money that's in it." I looked hard at the old man. "When the Injuns deal for a squaw, the parents put a price on her, so many ponies or trappings the young buck has to pay. Well, mister, you already paid mine for me. I've got her, and there ain't a red cent in the world that could ever buy her back."

"Well spoken," Ethan said, and his father gave him a glower.

"You will sign the document?"

"I will, that. Now what else is in your craw?" By then I was heating up.

"The matter of the birth," the Commodore said. "It will be an embarrassment."

I glanced at Daisy. She was staring at her hands, weeping. "For God's sake," I grunted, "what is this now? She's just having a child...."

"But soon they'll see," Alice said stiffly. "Everyone will know. Of course, we'll rush a wedding...."

"I don't give a damn about a wedding," Daisy flared. "God's already married us, and because it's out of your control, you can't stand that!"

"If-you-will-not-interrupt!" Alice lashed back, "it will be an intimate family wedding, not one whit more, after which you and Mr. Kelly will move away. Out of the Chicago area."

"Move?" Daisy echoed, and glanced at me. "But where, dammit, why?"

"We don't know where. Father is working on that. When you start to show, my dear, and of course when the child is born, people always count the months, count back to the wedding date. We want you out of sight and out of mind for that period. Then finally," Alice smiled coldly, "when you, Mr. Kelly and your family return, it won't matter anymore. People will have forgotten."

Daisy stared at me. "Can you believe you're hearing this? I can't."

I smiled. "I can't believe you come from 'em, darlin', but it's their house and their way. Let it pass. We'll be gone soon enough." I turned to her parents. "I'm going to call you Emory, sir, and you, ma'am, Alice. If you're done with your rules and regulations, your little girl and me are going out for a walk in the flowers." As I started to stand, Alice reached out and seized my hand.

"You've taken this much better than I would have expected. I thank you for that. But there is one last, important matter. I know that it will be difficult for you, and I don't mean it to be hurtful...."

"Shoot," I says and grins. "If the money didn't hurt, what else can?"

"You will have to change, Mr. Kelly. We expect a certain standard."

I frowned. "Standard? I ain't following you...?"

"Oh, Mother, for God's sake!" Daisy cried and tugged at me. "Come on, Patrick, we're not listening to one more word of this!"

"G'wan and spit it out, Alice," I says quietly.

"It's talking like that," she answered. "Crude speech. It's common, Mr. Kelly, and frankly the same goes for your manners, or lack thereof. And the way you dress. I realize that you come from a different background, but here in the set where you and Daisy must move, we find such behavior not only unattractive but quite offensive at times."

"Take off the rough edges, fellow," Ethan cut in. "Hell, read a book or two, get a tailor."

The Commodore was sitting in a heap, his lips trembling. "Don't mock this, Ethan. I want to be proud of the man, take him to my clubs, meet my friends. Kelly," his hand started out toward me, then held back, closed into a fist. "You will be my son-in-law. My first, my only. So much to do, so much load to take from me. How I've dreamed of the time. If you could help make us," he shrugged, "a little more comfortable with it."

"Ah, God help ye, man," I says, went to him and gripped his shoulder. By then, he was covering his face in his hands, the E boys

278

saying, "Please, Father, he'll be all right. We'll help him to be."

When I finally got Daisy outside and away from the nonsense of it, she led me across the lawn, green as the Old Sod now, and the skating pond chirping with birds and croaking frogs. Slowly she led me down the bluff into her secret glades. We sat in the quiet of the wet leaves and she wept. Stroking her lovely face, I says, "Darlin', let 'em all go, they don't matter to us."

"But those rules, those insults!" she cried. "How can we ever get free?"

"But we already are, Daisy." I gripped her slim tummy. "This little one, and more, more, eh?"

"Oh yes, more, Patrick. Forever!"

"And me," I says, "in a boiled shirt and derby hat!"

Then we got to giggling about how comic it was to take an old dray plug like me and turn him into a prancing blooded stallion. "Ah, hell," I laughs, "give it a try. I've been far worse!"

"Just so that you never change inside, Patrick."

"How could I, darlin'? You're there."

And she was, God bless her. We didn't have an idea of where we'd go or what life would bring us, but I had her and her love and all the rest didn't matter.

HONEYMOON IN PARADISE

They got rid of us all right, out of sight, out of mind so that the fancies back in Lake Forest wouldn't be counting how close to our wedding our love baby arrived. Though the Commodore and Alice had rigged the first part of our hiding out, Daisy's cousin, Teedie, finished burying us. Mr. Specs Roosevelt had become not only assistant Secretary of the Navy under President McKinley, but was storming around Washington, trying to find a war.

"He should have been in Rome, wearing a purple toga," Daisy said sadly. "Great Caesar Teedie, now that he's smashed his childhood toys, he'll find himself a whole new playroom, an empire this time."

"Ah," I says, "he's just bully-huffin' like a braggy kid."

"Read it and weep, darling." She hands me a letter from him, supposedly sending us congrats on our wedding, but even in the first line, in his bold, strong hand, he'd scrawled: "The expansion fever is everywhere. Leap the barriers of the seas. Claim our destiny. This nation must be willing to pour out its blood, treasures and tears, rather than submit to the loss of honor and renown. Bully for it, my dear Diana. You have a brave soldier for a husband. How well he knows the times when men and nations must fight. With this in mind, with the need as never before for good, strong patriotic men, why in the world is the Commodore shipping you off to a dreary coal mine for your wedding trip?"

Before Daisy could answer him, the Commodore and Alice had exiled us to the slag dumps of Festus, Ioway. Archibald Hoe and Disk, AHD, had a coal mine here, to supply their furnaces for melting iron into plows. Problem was, they had a surly bunch of Hunky and Dago miners on their hands. The mine was struck, and my job, said the Commodore, was to get it unstruck.

So right from the first, I went on his payroll. Daisy didn't like it one bit. "I won't have them buying you off, Patrick. We mustn't start that."

"Hell, darlin', it's only till the baby comes, and besides, it puts grub on the table, don't it?"

"But Patrick," she said quietly, "it's a matter of what you want to do, what we want to do with our lives."

Right then, I was so much in love with her the future didn't seem to matter. And, as things turned out, we couldn't do a damn thing about it anyway.

One morning, a Studebaker motor car rattles up to the farmhouse where we were living. The driver was a Federal marshal. He had a tellygram in hand, ordering me to meet the Assistant Secretary of the Navy when the personage's train passed through Des Moines that evening. Daisy was excited about seeing Teedie, but the Marshal says, "No, ma'am. Mr. Roosevelt specifically forbids you to take that long motor trip on bad roads, due to your delicate condition."

"Oh bother," she laughed. "This will be a tough baby. Frontier child."

I finally got her talked out of it, and glad I did. Helluva trip up to Des Moines, and maybe fifteen minutes with Specs on the smoky station platform. He had the usual flunkies following him around, but he shooed them off and said, "We'll stretch our legs, Kelly. A vigorous walk is in order."

He was swinging his arms, taking deep breaths as we went crunching off down the track and out into the freight yards. "Let me say first, I'm delighted by you and Diana. Gad, we need strong people these days. But when I think of her, stuck down here, with so much going on, out there…." He punches his fist into the darkness, and I says, "Where is that, now?"

"The world, man!" He sucked in a deep breath and grinned, his teeth flashing under his bristly moustache. "Kelly, what I see in my job is incredible opportunity for this nation. Here," he pulled a pad out of his coat pocket, "even as I travel, I'm drafting this to Mahan." When I puzzled, he said, "Why, Admiral Mahan, the visionary, now my closest adviser. I write him: 'I am fully alive to the danger from Japan, and I know that it is idle to rely on any sentimental goodwill toward us. We should build a dozen new battleships. If I had my way, we should annex Hawaii tomorrow, blocking the Japanese. Once we have those islands, we shall neutralize in one stroke the Spanish in the Philippines, and with our strong Atlantic fleet, send them packing out of Cuba.'" He stuffed the pad in his pocket. "Important stuff, Sergeant Kelly. Do you want to play a part?"

"Sir?"

"I've liked the cut of your jib ever since our time in the mountains. You're one of a special breed, Kelly, rough riding men, taming what we thought was the last frontier. But it's not. Far more awaits us." His eyes gleamed and he gripped my arm. "The advanced nations are poised to divide up the spoils of the dark, primitive wildernesses beyond the sea. America must be there first."

By then, we'd strode up to an iron switch that parted the rails in the yards. It had a glowing red lantern atop, and a lever arm sticking out below. I itched my back on the lever and then squatted, looking up at him with his face bathed in red. "Do you follow me, Kelly?"

"Well now, Specs," I says and grins, "I ain't sure. These last months with Daisy and your kind of folks, I've been hearing all kind of notions I never dreamed of…"

"Of course you have," he grunted. "Perfectly understandable."

"...and what you're saying is just more of it. Great nations, powers, Army games. When you're a trooper in the ranks, all you're worrying about is where your next beans come from or how to duck a bullet. That gleam in your eye ain't just the lantern, mister Specs. It's wars I'm seeing."

"If forced to it, an honorable nation has no other choice."

"But who's doing the forcing? It ain't enemies, from what I can see. I'm thinking that it's the nabob bunch, up there in your White House or NooYawk or wherever the money gathers. For sure, it ain't common working stiffs or troopers hunting a hole that want more shooting."

"We all belong to the same nation, Kelly," Roosevelt said sternly. "I see things that the man on the street cannot. Those qualified to lead must lead. You're one of them. I'll be specific, just to check my own judgement about you, I had the Secretary of War locate your service file. It's shocking what a poor department they run. Your papers are quite incomplete. However, young Jack Pershing, and he's a comer, gave you fine reports. There's also mention from a Captain..." he frowned.... "Boyle, is it, or Breen, some Irish name...?"

"Bourke, would it be?"

"That's the one. I'd hoped to chat with him, but he died last year...."

"I'm sad to hear that. A good man he was, about the last of our old Rosebud bunch."

Roosevelt frowned. "Your what?"

"An Injun fight we had in Montana. Seemed big at the time, but ah, who remembers them things?"

"Whatever, this Captain Bourke, as General Crook's aide, reported favorably on intelligence work you'd done for him with the Sioux chiefs...?"

"Crazy Horse," I murmured.

"And thereafter, with the Apaches. A mission dealing with Geronimo, I believe."

"Him too. Yes."

"In light of this, Kelly, an idea struck me. You are a man who knows how to work behind the lines. Infiltrate the enemy. At the Navy Department, we have rudimentary intelligence, officers assigned to supposedly diplomatic or commercial missions in many parts of the world. The fellows give me reports in formal terms. I do get information. But not near enough. I want my own man, Kelly. Looking through my specs as you call them. Multiply my vision a hundred times." He took off his specs and began rubbing them with his handkerchief. "Gad, it's sooty in this yard." Then the train whistle blew and he swung toward it angrily. "This damn schedule they assign me! McKinley is a dreadful politician, why, he won't even leave the White House porch, so I have to stump for his programs. Well now, fellow," he said, and began leading me back toward the dark, steaming Pullmans, "I'm assigning you and my dear cousin to one of the most lovely places in the world, and, at this moment, highly strategic. Honolulu, Hawaii."

I stopped short. "Maybe I'm missing a turn here, Specs, but you're wanting us to go way out there?"

"Not a matter of wanting, Kelly. I'm sending you, under my personal orders. Private citizen, sub rosa, no connection with government, but I will make it worth your while."

I frowned, getting warier every moment. "And just what the divil would I be doing way off in the seas?"

Roosevelt smiled coldly. "Peeking under the covers of our dear friends, Germany, Japan and Spain. Of all of them, the Germans are the greatest threat at this point, Japan second. The Spaniards are," he sniffed, "ephemeral. The Federal marshal who brought you here has been given a confidential envelope. In it are your specific instructions. He'll sign it over to you when he takes you back to Diana. Do give her my love." He chuckled. "She'll have a Hawaiian baby, Kelly, and please God, by then, that soil shall be ours."

We'd come to the steps of his Pullman, official flunkies waiting there for him, and the conductor asking, "May we pull out, Mr. Roosevelt?"

T.R. waves up the track, then claps my mitt. "I knew you'd do it, and you'll do it well. Good luck, Sergeant. One more thing. When you have read your instructions in the pouch, destroy them."

Then he bounded up the Pullman steps, and the wheels clanked the lot of them away.

When I come home that night and told Daisy that her Terrible Teedie had hired me, I expected a fight for sure. To my surprise, she jumped up out of bed and almost started packing our bags. "I thought you'd be sore," I says, but she plopped onto my lap and hugged me. "Oh, silly, don't you see. This is your shamrock that's popped up. It's our jailbreak from Father, Mummy, too. This so-called job at the mines is going noplace. We both know that. Certainly Teedie is family, but he's different, and in a whole other orbit. He's got adventure in him, and for all his bully-bluffing that I dread, he can open doors for you, darling."

"You're right there," I murmurs. "Too long now I been pissin' outside the tent, ain't I? Time to come in."

"Yes, it is that time, and could very well start you on your own road, Patrick. Us, I mean, why, it's so exciting, spur of the moment, sailing off on the high seas. Yet," she said, and frowned, "you dare not pay Teedie's price. We've got to watch that."

"Watch what?"

"Ambition. His overwhelming ambition. He does want to be Caesar, Patrick. He's got his little imperium, his royal court of Harvard Yard intellectuals feeding his ego. The Adams brothers, Cabot Lodge. They're so much smarter than Teedie that he doesn't realize they're steering him toward their own dreams. Don't let them steer you, too."

"Hell," I grins, "them buggers is so far above me they don't know I exist, and could care less."

"Exactly, darling. That's how it is now. But someday—I truly believe this—with your courage, your military skills, the unique background you've had, you could become an instrument of real value to these men. They're greedy. They use anybody who'll help them on their way up. Please don't let them use us, mostly you, my love."

"Jesus and Mary," I whispers, patting her belly with our babe in it, "stop your damn worryin'. We're off to the high seas, darlin'. Why, look here," I rips open T.R.'s secret envelope, "he's got us a stateroom on the top deck. The bridal suite! Now ain't that a helluva trip for a lad whose last sea crossing was steerage!"

We laughed then and made love, on the surging hopes of the waves themselves, sweeping us west to paradise.

On the ship out, I didn't know that Daisy had written her mother. A lot you don't know when you're first in love. Years later, old Alice give me the letter, thinking we'd want to remember them good times.

S.S. Mariposa
en route to Hawaii
June 21, 1897

Dearest Mummy,

Oh, this God-given ocean, the enormity of the cobalts and the greens, rising and falling in the swells. The sunsets, which I can see right from my berth, slowly turn the Pacific into a plate of molten copper. When the last twilight has flashed, the world goes from scarlet to black and the only sound is the whisper of our wake, a bubbling string of pearls on the dark water. Forgive my gushing, Mum, but I've never been so happy in my life. I literally feel I'm an angel on gossamer wings. Yes, maybe I'll fall someday, or wake up with a crash, but do you know something? I don't dread it. My Patrick, strong and noble, will be waiting there for me with open arms.

I do miss you so much, and am writing to tell you of our decision. We have taken Patrick's son into our family. Matthew Fights Clouds Kelly, nine difficult years old, is at this moment draped over the stern of the Mariposa, dangling down a long line that some sailor gave him, and trying to catch a fish.

Who in Lake Forest would ever have dreamed that your dainty Diana would not only have gotten herself pregnant to a common soldier, but end up mothering an Indian child! Now, in your shock, don't leap to conclusions. Patrick didn't "put" this on me, Mummy, but I've seen for months now that his heart is truly with his boy. On some level, I know he feels guilty that he's never been able to provide a home for Matthew, and really doesn't know how to cope with him. So when Teedie gave us this blessed assignment, I was the one who saw more in it than just our honeymoon in paradise. Rather, couldn't it be a time of healing for my husband? That's why I suggested to Patrick that we bring the little fellow with us. His first response was puzzling. Despite his affection for his boy, he's also, I'm delighted to say, awfully possessive of me. We have such an encompassing love that he resents even a fly who buzzes in to interrupt us, let alone a hellion kid. On my side, Patrick knows, and you must know, that I've always been stupidly jealous that he had a wife before me, and a red Indian at that. He never talks about her. He lets the past go. But I just can't. Finally, after enough silent tears on my pillow at night, I resolved to meet the challenge head on. I can't change the past, or what Patrick did, or the presence of his child. The only thing I can change is myself. Don't you think that's right? Isn't that mature?

My hope is that our home, our values will eventually overcome the savage in young Matthew's veins. Patrick agreed to try, and when we headed west from Iowa—I purposely didn't tell you—he changed our tickets. After much dust and interminable carriage rides, we ended up in the most desolate wilderness I ever hope to see, the Rosebud Sioux reservation in South Dakota. Wilderness connotes trees, lovely tall pines. Why, there isn't a single one! Nothing but the bleakest sort of prairie, and when you get near the Indian towns, the foul stench of them is overpowering! I was appalled by the garbage, old broken wagons, bones of dead animals, and every variety of tin can and rusty stoves. I had the impression that Indians treasured God's beautiful nature, but Patrick shook his head. "Ah, Daisy, the nature they did know, the free life they used to have, has been taken from them. They junk the rest. They think it's no different from them, thrown into the trash heap by the *waiscu*."

These people are bitter beyond belief, and I don't blame them. The shacks where they live, and the few ugly frame houses, built for them by the government, exude an excruciating sadness. I had this glamourous image of Indians, the Catlin paintings, the Wild West shows, but they're anything but those noble savages now.

In that dark, awful shack, we were surrounded by leering squaws and tall somber warriors, some of whom had helped kill Custer, Patrick said. Then young Matthew was standing before us, a total Indian, naked except for a breechclout and moccasins. Patrick hugged him and presented him to me, "Your new momma, lad."

What a dreadful moment! I can hardly describe the look on the boy's face. He has the tawny skin of the half-breed, high cheekbones and a sharp nose, but his eyes are so haunting. Sometimes they laugh like Patrick's, other times, they're so penetrating that you can feel hate burning through you.

Matt tried to speak in Sioux but Patrick wouldn't let him. "Her name is Daisy, son, and she's a flower I picked in the mountains. We're going across the seas and you're going with us."

Matt's alert eyes focused on my stomach, bulging out of my dress. Quietly he said, "You're already making a child for your new house. You don't need me, Papa. Leave me alone where I belong."

I said gently as I could, taking his hands which were cold as ice, "I want to be your mother, Matthew. We'll have a house full of children, in a beautiful place, and you'll never be alone again."

He stared at me. "I already have a mother. She is in the earth near here. She doesn't want me to leave her."

"Dammit," Patrick blurted, "she ain't comin' back, lad! This is your father talking, and her husband. I know what she'd want for you, she said it many times, a better life, our two worlds joined now, in you."

"People can't live in two worlds, Papa. I tried yours. I tried always moving everywhere, and had nothing."

"It ain't like that now, son!" Then Patrick went on to tell of the great house where I'd come from, and the people of my blood who ran the great cities and even talked directly to the great white father in Washington. Though the boy didn't seem to get it, the English-speaking Sioux did. I couldn't tell if they were offended by our apparent connection to the power that had destroyed them, or if, rather, they could see future benefits for Matt that they could never know. His adopted mother had been admiring my shoes (those little brown pumps from Marshall Field's). Rather impudently, she snatched one from my foot, removed Matt's moccasin and fitted the pump on him. He gave a little cry and kicked it away as if it were a snake. But clearly, the squaws were as practical and covetous as any mother for her child. My footsteps could lead him on a path he could trod no other way.

Clearly, young Matthew wanted nothing to do with me, but after the elders had spoken interminably, he tightened his long lips and squared his shoulders. "My mother, Walks Outside, was outside of my father's people who killed her. So I will go inside them, for her, without looking back."

The chiefs nodded assent. Then Matty smiled in his cold, cunning way. "I am my books. I go only with my books."

One of the squaws turned to me. "He reads all the time, new mother. Let him take his books and he will go."

"Why, Matt, darling," I cried, "of course! In fact, when we get to San Francisco on the train, I'll buy you all the books you could ever read."

"*Ethiti*," he said, which Patrick told me meant "good." It was done. We had him, for better or for worse.

Once we got on the train in Nebraska, Patrick feared that Matt would be overcome by homesickness and try to escape us. But my instinct was correct here. "This little creature," I said to Patrick the first night, "has such a proud, stubborn streak in him that once he's given his word, he'll never go back on it. That would be shaming himself, don't you see?"

Patrick sighed. "I hope you're right, darlin.'"

Well, so far I have been. In a strange sort of way, Matt has almost switched from Patrick to me, as if I fill the mother-void in him that Patrick never could. I do want to do just that, not to take him away from his father, but just to reinforce him with a kind of gentleness a father really can't show to a son.

Tap wood, we've only had two incidents up to this writing. The first was curiously embarrassing, but poignant. Our last night on the train, I had to get up in the wee dawn hours and do what pregnant ladies must, use the facilities. We were in a compartment, Patrick in the upper berth, me in the lower, and Matt in the third bed opposite me. When I visited the little toilet room, he was sleeping soundly, I thought. Well, lo and behold, as I tiptoed back to my own lower berth, this muscular, strange little man stopped me, oh, gently enough. He simply took one of my hands in his. With the other—I have trouble saying this, Mum—if he doesn't slowly lift up my night dress and stare for a moment at my most intimate lower body, including my baby-swollen abdomen. I was horrified, of course, and yet, there was something so wonderfully open and natural about his curiosity that I didn't even try to stop him. He had his look up and down me, then gently let my dress slide down. Smiling, he took my hand, kissed it, and went back to bed.

The incident on shipboard, first night out, had a more jarring effect. As I say, perhaps it's the Indian alertness, but he notices everything. When the ship's purser was showing the passengers the boat drill and the fire-alarm system in the main lounge, Matt had to try out the latter. While we were peacefully having dinner in the salon, the little imp balled up a paper napkin and tossed it into one of the tall, fluted lamps attached to the side of the salon. As he expected, when smoke arose from it, the fire alarm went off. Patrick was furious. He collared Matt and so did the purser and the Captain himself. As punishment for endangering the ship, it was deemed that Patrick would take Matt on a tour of the fiercely hot engine room, make him work for a few minutes shoveling coal to a boiler. To my amazement, it turned out to be sort of a blessing. "Why," Patrick exclaimed when he returned to the cabin, "the little bugger is a whiz with engines. Machinery and the like. I never seen a kid so curious to learn."

"Then that's a good sign, Patrick. Wonderful. It's hope. By filling him up with all he wants to learn, we can straighten him out, don't you see?" I did not mention to Patrick the boy's earlier curiosity about my femininity, but it all comes down to the same thing. He's an empty vessel waiting to be filled.

Oh, Mum, isn't that my job? Please tell me if I'm on the right track here! I do love you. This has gotten way too long, and they're sounding the first dinner chime. Hawaii tomorrow, the palmy isles! I'll send this back by the Mariposa, butterfly in Spanish, Patrick says, and winging to you again my thanks for being my Mum. I wish I could wrap it with a sweet Hawaiian lei, instead of just,

Your flower,

Daisy

When I first saw the green mountains of Hawaii rising from the sea, I thought of the poem Daisy had read me up in the mountains. "The belly-aching fire, the wail of home desire." Indeed, it was my heart wailing now, aching for that other green island, the Old Sod, that I'd fled so many years before. And always wondering if the running I was doing, one wild leap after the next, would ever take me truly home? Would this new green grass finally be the place? Who the hell knew? Surely not me.

Yet, there was a comical side of it, too. I kept thinking of my saintly Momma. If she could see me, lazing my toes in the waves, she'd be crying, Ah God help us, a sinner lad has slipped through the pearly gates. She, poor dear, would still be thumbing her beads back in Laughrasheen, while I, the divil's own, was stringing mine with daisy petals on a lei.

How we laughed in those days, frolicking in the sand like Adam and Eve. An old Hawaiian woman we'd hired as Matty's nurse told Daisy about the healing powers of the sea. "Every day," she said, "go

288

to the water, sit in it, put it on your skin. Be like Hawaiian people. And this little boy," she grabbed Matty's chin, "he look like us, too. You like play in the water?"

"Sure," Matty said. "You come down, too. Bring your net. Show me how to catch the little fish." So, right from that morning on, it became a ritual. Lilia, the big, waddling Hawaiian, Daisy, Matty and me would all traipse down to the beach at Ewa plantation. Matty not only learned how to toss a net into the shallows, but some Hawaiian lads got him started riding a surfboard through the crashing waves. He never wanted to leave with us and go home and eat, but by then, Daisy had a pretty short leash on him. The way she'd been raised, kids didn't just play their days away. Had to be some pain in it, she'd smile, and afternoons, she'd give Matt another stack of books to eat up. I will say for the little bugger, he could flick his eyes across a handful of pages in the time it would take me to read a single one. Anyhow, the time passed as pleasant as if we were in heaven. If there was war someplace in the world, we sure couldn't hear the sound of the shot and shell. Only the whispering surf, sweeping our footsteps away, and bathing us in the Ocean of Peace.

We lived in an old shacky plantation house, where we could look east toward the few buildings of Honolulu, and Diamond Head rising beyond. Closer to us, around Pearl Harbor, lay the undrained swamps of Ala Moana and Ala Wai. The rest of the island went jungling off into mountains, where the misty rain made for soft days, like those in County Mayo. The native Hawaiians were a pleasant lot, never killing themselves with work. They'd pluck their food from the trees or the ocean, and spend the time left over lying in the shade of banyans, plinking ukeleles. The only coolies seemed to be a few Japs and Filippines, wearing peaked straw hats and slogging after oxen in the paddies and cane fields.

At first, my secret instructions from T.R. mostly came down to working with a pair of field glasses. I'd sit out on the shack porch and make a log of what ships snaked through the swamp and into Pearl Harbor. The clever muckety-mucks back at Naval headquarters in Washington had worked me up a code. As far as the sleepy port of Honolulu knew, I was just a purchaser of sea stores for the Grand Pacific Company. This outfit was a made-up scarecrow too, but they did have a cable address in San Francisco, and several times a week, I'd trot to the cable office and send them my "purchases."

The code was, if a German man of war steamed into Honolulu, I'd buy "black tar," for the ship ropes, I suppose. If a Japan ship come in, I'd order myself "red deck paint," and if it was a Spaniard, I'd order "white canvas hatch covers." The amount I bought was the number of ships from each nation that hove in each week.

"Now, ain't this plumb silly," I'd laugh to Daisy, as she'd bring me tea out on the porch. For a time it seemed about as harmless as playing cribbage in the barracks. But all the while, too, I could sense that there was a bigger game being played far beyond me, not only on the sea, but in the mud streets of Honolulu city. The native Hawaiians might have been loveable enough, but behind their sunny smiles, their dark eyes would more and more be flashing with surly anger. Sometimes, loafing on the docks or at Vierra's rickety Beehive saloon on Nuuana Street, I'd hear native Hawaiians talking revolution. Good reason. The white haoles, missionary families, planters and nabob merchants were robbing their ancient kingdom away. The last Hawaiian queen, Liliuokalani, had been dumped from her throne by the white gang, and when the natives rebelled, it was Uncle Sam, standing off with gunboats, that put them in their place.

Hawaii was a big bubbling kettle of sugar cane, ready to boil over. There was so much intrigue going on that it was hard for an outsider like me to get to the bottom of it. But then, a break did come. About a month before our little one was due to be born, Daisy and I were invited to a fancy luau at the stately Iolani Palace. I suspected that T.R. had a hand in this, though, as always, he never peeped to me what he was up to. Because the guests at the party were the head honchos in the islands, Daisy made me buy a white linen suit like they all wore, a straw lid and cravat too. She spiffed herself up in a flowery mumu that hid her tummy, and with leis on her and gardenias in her hair, she was as soft and sparkly as a Hawaiian sunrise. We left Matty at home with his Hawaiian nursemaid, and when I took Daisy on my arm and we swished up the velvet carpet into the Palace garden, I noticed the spiffy guests casting glances at her, hoping to meet this new pale-skinned beauty. "You're knocking 'em dead, darlin'," I whispers, "and I'm sweatin' like a hog." She laughed and squeezed my hand. "I do love parties, Patrick. God knows, I've been raised on them." Then, while she was straightening my tie, up strides President Dole himself, a starchy, preacher-looking gent who'd kicked out the Hawaiian queen. "Why, my dear," he said, "what a pleasure! Aloha!" He give her a kiss on both cheeks, and began prattlin' how delighted he was to meet Mr. Roosevelt's lovely cousin. "I have so much respect for T.R., and at this point in time, his strongly stated opinions offer these islands a real ray of hope."

"And how is that, sir?" I asks, when he finally lets go of Daisy and shakes my hand.

"Why, common sense! We are Americans here, you are Americans across the water. We need each other now as never before."

While Daisy was being lorded away by the personages, and hospitable ones they were, I drifted off among the looser-lipped gents

290

hanging around a big crystal bowl filled with punch. From the talk I heard, President Dole, backed by Thurston, Castle and other haole nabobs, were hanging onto Hawaii by their fingernails. Bumping at the gate were the Germans, Japanese, even the damn English. They had many mercantile interests in the islands, and as any Irisher knows, when John Bull gets his mitts on the sod, you play hell getting it back. "We are virtually surrounded, young man," one bearded planter says to me. "Do you have any idea the number of foreign ships that are putting in here lately? This is not mercantile. This is munitions, men of war, sheer, naked colonialism."

Playing dumb, I just grins and says, I had no idea of all them ships, and why in the world would they be coming?

With a glance over his shoulder, he whispers. "The pearl, fellow! Pearl Harbor. Finest deep-water anchorage in the Pacific, possibly the world. Either the United States takes it, and I mean now, or we shall lose freedom's last bastion in the West."

Right there, I saw the handwriting on the wall. Uncle Sam was going to snatch these islands pretty damn soon, and me, a consignor of naval stores, was I? Hell, wily T.R. had plumped me down here as his private stool pigeon, hoping I'd blow my whistle when the fruit was ripe for plucking.

That night, Daisy and I lay out on the porch of our shack, mosquito netting draping down over our sleeping mats. The moon was full, melting yellow as butter on her limbs. The scent of ginger and pikaki was still in her hair and her neck, and I kissed her often, to be sure she was real, and to keep her from drifting away from me. Finally I whispers, "What is it, girl? What's got your pretty head?"

She sighed. "Those people today at the Palace. Oh, polite, charming, but so cold in the eyes. So much power, and the ruthlessness to use it. Look what they did to the Hawaiians. Why, I heard tonight, when they dethroned the poor queen, they even sentenced her to forced labor. Of course, the charge was lifted shortly, but the humiliation for that proud woman, to say nothing of the rape of these native people, their lands stolen, their old, gentle way of life ripped from them. It breaks my heart. Sometimes I feel like, well, this...." She trailed her fingers down through the silvery folds of the mosquito net. "We're all in their net, Patrick, these power people are suffocating us in it, and neither we nor the Hawaiians have any way to get out. Why, one geezer was even asking me about Father. They were classmates at New Haven."

I smiled. "Your birds all got the same feathers, darlin'."

"That's just what scares me. It's how they think, Patrick, our white race superior to any other, and the rest might as well not exist. Oh I love Teedie, of course I do. But my God, how many years I've listened to him and my eastern relatives, enraptured by their dreams of glory. They want the world and nothing less, and they feel that they're the only ones who should decide how we seize it and plunk it in our wallets. That's why Teedie is always sounding off in the *Atlantic Monthly*, or striding around the salons of Washington or Fifth Avenue. He's building a claque, and every day is getting more determined to cram his narrow view of the world down the public's throat. Foul cigars and fouler dreams."

"When you've got blood in your eyes, girl, you don't see much else."

"But think what it means, Patrick. If they jingo us into war, it's our lives, our baby, the futures of all of us. Yet we allow ourselves to be run around like toy soldiers by a precious handful of these people. They'll fling us over a cliff."

"Ah, darlin'," I whispered and stroked her hair, "I don't know history like you, ain't been educated for much but staring at the dirt. But my notion of it is, the bigwigs have always run the little people around. The proles, T.R. calls them, under the whip of the plutocrats."

"I know." She sighed. "That's the Adams gang. Teedie, Brooks Adams and Cabot Lodge were Porcellian at Harvard. It's so terribly inbred. Brooks Adams is Henry Adams' younger brother, all descendants of John Quincy, of course, and Brooks now fancies himself a historian. I've tried to read his latest book, *The Law of Civilization and Decay*. He says that in the luxuries of the Gilded Age, we've become soft and effete. Money is all that counts. Economic man rules us. Teedie, naturally, rebels at that. He wants to smash his fist in somebody's face to show that we're manly."

"Ah, Daisy, the English redcoats were the same. If you want to fight, you'll jolly well find an excuse."

"But it's so repulsive, Patrick! How many dinner parties have I attended where the talk is always taking, taking, greed, greed. If it's not the Eastern people steering this crashing dreadnought of Teedie's, it's my own flesh and blood. Father, his friends on LaSalle Street. The industrialists of the bread basket, with their strings of factories and interlocking trusts. He won't even discuss it with me. He says that my teachers at Vassar were anarchists."

"Well, I hope to hell, darlin', 'cause you married one."

"It's why I married one," she whispered, and held me tightly. "Oh, so much I want to fight this elitist thing, Patrick. But a woman is a third-class citizen, and you, dear, are second class at best. They don't listen to us and never will. They steamroller on. Look at the evidence. Why did they put McKinley in? He seems front porchy and harmless, just a dreary midwestern politician. But they got him elected because they can run him. A friend of Father's, Marcus Hanna, is a powerful industrialist in Ohio, and he literally bought the White House for McKinley. He extorted millions out of the Rockefellers and the old guard to make sure they'd elect a man who preserved the system. They did it. They created a landslide. The business of America is business, and oh, Patrick, how I shiver to think of these coarse, fat-fingered men, about to gorge themselves on the pie of the world. What happens to the human beings in it, poor defenseless people like these Hawaiians, who dare to stand in the way?"

"They go, darlin'," I said quietly. "Just like the Injun. It makes me sick, thinking back, that I had a part in all that murderin'. Ah sure, them bigwigs sugar-coat it with high sounding monikers like Manifest Destiny. But when you see them savages, frozen stiff on the dirt at Wounded Knee, you know what it was for. Get 'em out of the way is all. They don't count."

She turned from me and stared out at the stars. "Now, now, stop that," I whispers, for she was weeping.

She whirled back to me, her eyes wide. "I'm frightened, Patrick. I want to get out of this! It's like rolling down a hill in an avalanche. Can't we stop it?"

I shrugged. "Some day, maybe. But right now, darlin', it ain't worth fretting yourself about, or this little kicking thing either…" I stroked her belly. "Rest in peace, I'm saying, and leave it at that. More than good enough, for this lad anyhow."

"For us," she whispered. "Oh Patrick, teach me to have your faith." We clung to each other, loving hard and long until the mynah birds were crying in the dawn, and her fears had trailed away.

The next afternoon, two Japanese warships come into the harbor. It was surprise enough to set Honolulu buzzing, everybody wondering if Japan was now going to beat the other scavengers and grab the islands themselves. I hurried down to the cable office to send my report, then got caught in a heavy rain squall and took an hour getting home. I'd no sooner banged open the screen door than I heard Daisy's wails.

In our big, dark bedroom where we'd had so many nights of love, she was lying naked and writhing, with our new life trying to bust into the world. Our nurse, Lilia, and another Hawaiian woman were kneeling beside her, their strong hands kneading her tummy and their giggles and grins trying to calm her. God knows, they'd been through this kind of fight hundreds of times. In their simple, native way, there was no fear about it, only joy. "Ah, Daisy," I whispers, stroking her pale face, "you're doin' just grand. Be brave, I'm here for you, darlin'."

She was weeping, trying to grin and push at the same time. "You mustn't watch, Patrick. It's too awful. Oh God, make it end!"

Damn, all the violence I'd seen in my life was nothing compared to watching my beloved suffering. Finally Lilia cried, "Men no good now. Shoo, you!"

It wasn't five minutes before the Hawaiian women started hollering. I heard a tiny, squally cry. When I ran in to Daisy, she was hugging a little wizened thing to her breast. "Girl lady," Lilia cried. "So nice pretty woman for *haole* pop!"

I knelt by the bed, clinging to Daisy and our little one. "Ah, my God, darlin', you did it! Look what we've got! Ain't she grand!"

Daisy's lip trembled. "But Patrick, it's not a boy! Didn't you want a boy?"

"Hell, no! Boys are trouble! We already got that. But this one here's an angel."

"I know." Tears were running down Daisy's cheeks. "I want to love her so much."

When I touched the babe's wispy hair, it struck me that I hadn't even noticed the color. The wet little strands were flaming red! "God in heaven," I cried, "and where did we get this baby dear?"

In a flash, I knew! Of all of us Kellys, only Nora was our redhead, my little sister whose terrible night on the Other Side had sent me fleeing across the sea. So I says to Daisy, suckling our girl for the first time, "Darlin', for me she's got to be Nora."

Daisy smiled. "Yes. I love that name."

"And for you, Daisy, ain't the rest of it for you? Your own name, the Liberty you ran off to find, the Liberty that set us free."

"Oh, yes, Patrick! That *is* her! I never would have thought of it." Gently, she drew the child away from her breast. "Nora Liberty Kelly. Long may you wave."

Little did I dream that on that second day of October, 1897, our innocent babe had already been wrapped in the caul of war.

AN EXPLOSION ANY DAY IN CUBA

I never seen it coming, T.R.'s splendid little war, but young Matty sure figured things out early. Years later, scribbled longhand on New York Central paper, he wrote Daisy and me why he done what he done. Hell, he had it in his blood. All the tears in the world couldn't stop him.

August 25, 1906

Dear Papa and Daisy,

You said I owed you an explanation because I offended you by, as Papa put it, "taking the bit in my teeth" and going direct to cousin T.R. Yes, I did, and I'm not sorry either. I am sad, though, rattling down this long railroad track east, finally all on my own, and into a strange world. I know I'll do well, but I'll miss you.

Anyway, it's high time I left home. At 18, if I were still among mother's people, and if they were still living in the old way, I would have long ago taken my first hunts, been on the war trails and had my vision quests. It's only your *waiscu* world that refuses to let young braves grow up.

I was bred to be a warrior, and more than that I intend to become a decider of events. The one man I know who can help me is our cousin, T.R. He can take me into the council lodge.

When I first realized this, I was nine years old. It was that Christmas holiday of 1897 when we all came back to Chicago from Hawaii. I was shocked by that giant city, the noises, the smells, the overwhelming masses of people. That night, if you recall, there was a blizzard whipping across the Lake. I'd grown up on snow in Dakota, of course, but here to see those miles and miles of buildings blanketed in white, their chimneys spewing out smoke, and thousands of people with angry faces plodding down dark streets to houses that all looked the same—why, I said to myself, "They must be mad, living this way. It's a monster wrapping us in its arms and I don't know which direction to go to escape."

Yet, I saw immediately that we were the lucky ones. Commodore and Grandma Archibald had sent two steaming motor cars to the depot, one for us and the other for Daisy's baggage. To keep us warm, the chauffeurs wrapped us in curly gray lap robes, and when our motors honked the crowds out of our way, the poor, cold people stared at us in wonder and, no doubt, hate. When we pulled up to the Archibald's four story brick house on Astor street, I thought I

295

was entering a castle. The great hearth was glowing, and so were small chimneys in the bed chambers. The Irish maids were pattering around, the butler and footmen attending to our luggage. Exploring at once, I was stunned that there was a separate room for billiards, and even a ballroom and piano on the top floor. Totally empty. Such space! An entire clan of Lakota could have lived here. I must admit, Daisy, when I first met you in our shack on the Rosebud reservation, I couldn't dream that you'd come from something like this.

Envy, you say? Far from it. Your elegant parents, your handsome brothers with their fine cigars and gold watch chains made me feel wonderfully welcome. When I heard the house maids chattering in their Irish tongue, I could only think how far my papa had risen from their servant station. Good for you, Papa. I wanted that great house to be all yours. You had married the chief's daughter and paid him 40 ponies for letting her go.

But I quickly saw that Commodore grandfather Archibald, for all his big belly and booming voice, was not the chief, and you, Papa, were at best only a shirt wearer in the lodge, a respected position to be sure, but not a decider, not the power.

The real power struck my life on New Year's Eve. It was cousin T.R., striding in, beating the snow from his hat, and his fourteen-year-old daughter, cousin Alice, a blonde, curly-headed princess, ordering the servants to remove her wet boots. Here, I said to myself, are leaders of the *waiscu*. You were ashamed of me that night when I called T.R. "Laughing Horse," yet when he flashed those big teeth in a jaw that was like a horse's and kept snorting, "ha, ha!", any Indian would have named him so. While you and he and grandfather Archibald were in the smoking room, talking about our experiences in Hawaii, I eavesdropped enough to know that Laughing Horse was a man of the entire world. When he talked about Cuba, Puerto Rico, Guam and the Philippines, I had to scurry to my room and look them up in my Rand McNally atlas. The way Laughing Horse kept punching his fists into the air made me know that he was planning to make war on the whole world.

I kept thinking, How does he have the means to do this? He's not the President, not an admiral or general. He's merely a Navy official in Washington. Yet when I followed him around, and helped the butler carry his bags up to his room, I was struck by the confidence that swelled his big chest. "Lakota, are you!" he boomed to me. "Truly noble people! Dee-lighted to have one in the family!" Every other word seemed to be "dee-lighted," and when Alice, or Baby Lee as he calls her, told him to pipe down, he simply shooed her aside and kept up with his bombast. When Baby Lee and I had milk toast that night out in the kitchen with the servants, she sighed, "Oh, don't mind Papa. He's just a rambunctious boy who never grew up.

Mother and I pay absolutely no attention to his ravings."

But something struck me about T.R. and made me want to be around him. For all his thrashing like a bull moose trapped in deep snow, he had so much energy and hope that I knew he was going to go someplace in his life, smash down something. That night, if you remember—I have a clear picture of it still—you grownups went off to a costume ball. Daisy said it was *the* social event of the season, and was taking place at the Potter Palmer mansion, overlooking the Lake just a few blocks from our Astor street house. Papa certainly knows how Indians love painting up for dances and tribal festivals, but this *waiscu* shindig had more fuss to it than I'd ever seen. T.R., the boy who never grew up, had brought his own costume, tailored specially in New York. To the giggles of all, out he pranced in a white sailor suit, short pants and a silly cap that should have been worn by a six year old. Then came Daisy, blushing plenty, I'll say, wearing the flimsy satin pants and curly-toed shoes of a harem girl. You were laughing, "Meet Miss Little Egypt!" and the jewel in your bellybutton gleamed. "Shocking!" cried Mrs. Archibald. "Dear, you're positively naked, and it's not flattering when you still haven't slimmed down after your baby!" But T.R. hugged you. "Bravo! Hootchy-kootchy from the Columbian Exposition Midway, right in this city!"

Then out you came, Papa, and everyone gasped. You were wearing dirty canvas pants, brogans, a workingman's cap, and a blood-stained rubber apron. Grandfather Archibald, who was dressed as Napoleon, roared, "Doubly offensive! That's no costume, man!"

"Ain't supposed to be, Commodore," you answered, "just a mick immigrant showing them Armours and Swifts how we used to kill steers in their Yards."

"Art imitates life," T.R. cried. "The most honest man at the party!" Then you bundled into the motor car and swept off in the snow, your laughter trailing behind you. How I longed to be a fly on the wall in that Palmer ballroom, watching you twirl about dancing and when the lamps dimmed and the band played Auld Lang Syne, lifting your champagne glasses to welcome in 1898.

But it wasn't all a happy new year. Sometime after midnight, I heard the motor car bringing you home. While you'd been gone, little Nora got one of her squalling spells and began throwing up. Her Irish nursemaid, that dumb Bridget person, didn't know what to do, so I thought I'd better tell you. When I tiptoed down to the door of your room, you were arguing about something I couldn't understand, and I was sad because I'd never heard harsh words between you. "Patrick," Daisy cried, "you mustn't believe those awful things he tells you about the Spaniards. They're just his excuse. What makes it ludicrous, the business interests—they were all there, bankers, industrialists—the last thing in the world they want is a war, just when our country is finally coming out of the doldrums. You saw how they treated Teedie, a spoiled little bully. Mr. Palmer called him 'That insane Harvard cowboy.' Patrick, if he wants a war, let him have it, but include us out. Why should we have any part of it? What's it to us?"

"It might be bigger than us, Daisy," I heard papa growl. "There is times...." I was embarrassed to be eavesdropping, so finally I just tiptoed away down the dark hall. When I passed T.R.'s room, his door was open and I glanced in. He lay on his back, sprawled on the bed, and because he was still in his sailor suit, he looked like he'd fallen overboard and washed up on a beach. The funny thing was, he held a book over his face, about two inches from his nose. I marveled that anybody could read so close to the print. While I was watching, though, his hands sagged and the book dropped to his face. Then he sighed off into sleep, snoring, grunting. It sure didn't look comfortable, so I tiptoed over and lifted the book.

He waked up with a start. "Hah!" he barked and grabbed my arm. There was laughter in his pale blue eyes. "What do we have here, a warrior about to cut my throat!"

"You were sleeping with the book on your nose."

"Why, it has to be there. I'm blind in one eye. Closer the better."

"Aren't you reading awful late?"

"Have to, have to, boy. Curiosity never sleeps." He plumped up a pillow behind him and stared at me.

"Will you make a war, Mr. Roosevelt?"

"*I* make it?" he whooped. "Of course not. I dread it. Say good-bye to my wife and children for the last time, go into the eternal darkness, no, son—what is your name, Michael, is it?"

"Matthew."

"No, Matthew, it's not given to me to make anything. But should this great nation be threatened, should any infidel ever pluck at the hem of our flag, you can bet that I'll be in the front rank and yield up my life in pride and eternal gratitude for our United States." His eyebrows beetled. "And you? Is this not your country as well, red-man?"

I shrugged. I didn't know how to answer. Finally I blurted out about Wounded Knee, and so many cruelties of the blue coats that had puzzled me all these years.

"Bully!" He smacked his palm. "Get it out, get it on the table! What do you want to do with your life, Matthew?"

"What you have done."

"How's that?"

"I will be a warrior first. That's my blood. But I will also be a decider. A leader of warriors."

He seized my hand in both of his, which were warm. "And just how will you do it?"

"I don't know yet, sir. But I will."

He laughed and hugged me to him. "Strong medicine, strong brave. When your day comes, Matthew, call on me. I respect a man who intends to fight."

Yes, Papa and Daisy, I did call on him. An Indian never does anything until an elder asks him to do it. He asked, "Are you ready for West Point? Can you stand up in battle like your father?"

"More than my father," I answered. "His time was then. Mine is now."

The train has taken me into Ohio in the darkness, and tomorrow in the dawn, I shall see the Hudson River and the United States Military Academy. He gave me my first step. Don't blame him. Don't blame me. As the Ghost Dance song cried, *"Aiee, says the Father!"*

I love you both. Good night and God speed.

Your son,
Matthew

New Year's night on 1898, on the Pennsylvania cars, I left Chicago myself, heading for Noo Yawk and God knows where. But down deep, I did know where, even though I'd tried to hide the truth of it from Daisy. Coming home from the masquerade party, T.R. took me for a short trudge in the quiet, snowy street, him in his sailor shorts and a fur coat wrapped around him. He thanked me for what he said was a bully job in Hawaii, valuable information, but that affair had cooled temporarily. "At this point, Kelly, Japan is really no threat. The Germans bear far more watching in the Pacific and elsewhere. They thirst for colonies. But nothing at all can be settled while McKinley insists on waiting for a resolution to the Spanish question. We need to move the man toward reality. You're fluent in Spanish, aren't you?"

I says, Well, I used to speak pretty good Tex-Mex, but what the divil was this now?

"Haven't you read the papers, man? Spain has been ravaging Cuba, throwing the peasantry into concentration camps. Weyler, that butcher the Spaniards call a General, is stooping to torture, starvation and worse. Why, just yesterday, the correspondent, Richard Harding Davis reported that male Spanish officers actually stripped and searched high class Cuban women, and tomorrow it will be American ones. Imagine such treatment of women! No red-blooded American will stand for that! The Spanish, Kelly, are trying this nation's patience to the breaking point! I don't know when we'll draw the line, but draw it we will, and very soon. I want you in Cuba to see what we're up against."

New Year's morning, he began sending telegrams from the Archibald house, and before I'd kissed Daisy goodbye, he'd given me instructions about who to meet and where. The rest was up to me.

So many times, it seemed, all the way back to 1876 and the Sioux war, I'd rattled out of Chicago to go fight somebody. But this time, a blizzard was raging, and wet snow was weeping on the Pullman windows. Daisy's tears, I thought.

Ah, God, the poor sweet thing. We hadn't never argued up until then. She loved me so much I could have ripped the moon out of the sky and she would have laughed and put it in her pocket. But a woman grows in marriage, they say. She has to give up the old adoration and become herself again. Daisy was doing that over this Teddy Roosevelt business. She had a stubborn streak when anybody tried to push her around. Though she loved Teedie as a bumbling kid cousin, she bridled when he'd pull his charm boy act on us, all bravo and enthusiasm. "He's so thick-skinned, Patrick, he doesn't have the slightest sensitivity about the feelings of others. He's a bully in the playroom. You simply must not let him make you into one of his newest toys. I watched him do it while we were children. He'd get, say, a new little auto model. He'd do everything but sniff it and lick it, he was so fascinated by it. Then quickly he'd tire of it, run the machine all over the floor, smash it into walls until finally the wheels would come off and it was a wreck. Please, darling, I don't want you coming back that way, just for him."

I tried to point out that I was a soldier first, and having worked behind the lines for the military—sure, maybe it was a nasty, dangerous job, but didn't I still owe something when my experience could help our country in time of need?

"But, dammit, Patrick, they make up that need! Teddy and his jingos invent wars! They're new toys to smash. Can't you see the fraud of it? They have not the slightest remorse if people happen to get killed. Teedie said it himself, something to the effect that you can't make an omelet without breaking a few eggs."

"I got a tough shell, darlin'," I laughed, trying to jolly her out of her fears. But when I left her, in the snow on Astor street, she turned on her heel and buried her face in her hands.

Alone on the rocking, clanging Pullman, I couldn't sleep. Finally I went back to the parlor car, close to midnight, it was, nobody there in the red plush chairs except a black bartender and a lumpy, pudgy gent sitting at the far end by the observation platform. He had his feet up on another chair and was puffing a rich seegar. A drummer, I took him to be, traveling the road to sell somebody something.

Though it wasn't my custom to imbibe, I calls to the nagur, "I'll have a tap of ale, me boy." While he was fizzing it out, up strolls the drummer. "By jove, that's music to my ears. Irish, are you?"

I looks at him, a jowly face and twinkly eyes. His accent was English, high class, like Lord Cavan on the other side. "If it's your business," I grunts, "I'm Yank."

He laughed. "But the brogue lives on. I don't mean to be rude, sir, just curious. What part of Ireland?"

"Mayo, God help us. Long ago."

"Beautiful place! I've fox-hunted there. May we sit down? Please. A cigar? Finest Cuban." He starts reaching into the pocket of his tweed jacket. Tailored clothes, wouldn't you know? Not a drummer, this one.

"Don't smoke."

"Well, I picked up the delicious habit. Three years ago. Hard not to, when one is in Cuba."

At that, my ears perked. I set down beside him and he thrust out his plump, soft mitt. "I'm Churchill," he says. "Leftenant Winston Churchill, Her Majesty's Fourth Hussars."

"Well, God in heaven," I says and grins, "I took you for a peddler, lad. What are you doing over here in the colonies? Stamping out another rebellion?"

He was a genial sort. "Oh, I'm not that bad, mister Irishman. My mother is American. Actually I visit this superb country often, if I can get away. Not an easy thing, though. My regiment is stationed in India." He said it "Inja." "We'll soon be going off to fight the Boer, it appears. Have you read it in the press, the Jameson raid and all that?"

"I've heard of it, yes. The sun never sets on the British Empire, so it keeps you Johnnies traveling around looking for scraps, I suppose."

He chuckled. "Whenever possible. It's the road to promotion and a challenge I find quite stimulating. Cuba was much the same. A crude, fetid place, but on every front, one learns something. And you, sir, Mr....?"

"Kelly. Cavalry trooper, retired."

"You don't say!!" He bubbled up, wanting to know where I'd been and who I'd fought. The wheels rattled us down the track and through another glass of ale. He told me he'd been attached to the Spanish general staff in Cuba, military observer, and then shipped over to observe the rebel side, General Gomez. This was one of the names on T.R.'s list, so I listened close.

"What do you think, Churchill? Do them rebels have a chance?"

"I daresay not much, and I hope not."

"Why is that?"

He wrinkled his nose. "A rabble! Inferior arms. They neither fight bravely nor use their weapons effectively. To a large extent, their army is colored men, an undisciplined gang."

I nodded. "I served with black soldiers, Churchill. Maybe it's a different breed down in Cuba, but ours is among the best troopers we had."

"But, man," he cried, "it's the potential outcome, don't you see? On the remote chance that they should win, these people are going to demand a share of the Cuban government. That's going to bring a bloodbath of a racial war, and after years of fighting, inevitably, another black republic!"

I frowned. "But if the island is theirs?"

"A black republic," he repeated, and sadly shook his head.

After we'd parted, I went back to my sleeper, lay in my berth and pondered what he meant. Ah, indeed he was the English gentleman, descendant of the red coats who had ravaged my people, despite the fact that they was white. But to the proud English, the poor Irish or Scots were no more than animals. I remembered Francis His Lordship Cavan talking about the East Indians in the same way. Turbaned rabble, vile black bodies no decent person would want to touch. So here was Churchill, a leader in the making for the English side, like T.R. was for our side. If these ruthless divils ever got to the top of the heap, there'd be more slaughters like Wounded Knee. Their kind would always win. They had the power and the money, and divil take the blood and shattered bones of stiffs like me who would be rallied to die for them, and never know why.

When I hit Noo Yawk, a young, moustached Cuban met me and took me to a dingy brick building at 120 Front Street, overlooking the masts and funnels of ships in the harbor. On the 4th floor of this dump was the office of the Cuban Revolutionary Party. Mind you, it was illegal for them to be raising money and getting their arms in the U.S., but these fiery Cuban men and women were hard at it anyhow. The office was a printing plant, presses churning out propaganda sheets, trying to get America to plunge into war on the rebel side. I could see right off that the Cubans were canny. They'd made important reporter friends on the Noo Yawk papers. They told me that the nabobs, Hearst and Pulitzer, were outdoing each other to get the dumb American public to support the rebels and shed our blood down among the palm trees. The truth of what Daisy said struck me. Everybody back here was trying to invent a war.

I hadn't been in town but a few hours before the Cubans took me to a saloon down by the waterfront. Being mid-afternoon, there wasn't anybody at the tables except a few Cuban cigar-makers just let off from work. In a back room, though, a *gringo* was waiting for me. "Meet the hero of the *insurrectos*," says my Cuban guide, and then

302

leaves me alone with a feller who claimed to be a lieutenant colonel of the rebels. He was an American soldier of fortune named Frederick Funston. When he stood up to greet me, I got a shock. Hell, he was a little stump of a kid. I stood at least a foot taller than him, and he couldn't have weighed a hundred pounds. His face was gray and he looked like he hadn't shaved for days. Beside him on the table was a bottle of whiskey and he was doing his best to wipe it out. "Kelly, are you?" he said. "Professional soldier?"

"Something like that."

"Well, friend Kelly, I'm a mercenary and this is my medal." He thrust his left hand out to me, his arm bandaged in a sling. But when his fingers gripped mine, they were hard as steel and I could see the muscles bulging out of his chest. "I've been shot full of holes, Kelly. Welcome to the most vicious war on the face of the earth. Sit down, have a drink."

For the next hour or so, the cocky little bugger fell into the bottle hard, tellin' me horror stories about all sides in the Cuban war.

He looked at me groggily. "A vile war! We have to end it down there!" Weakly, he pounded on the table. "The public is so slow to understand. McKinley is spineless, a shoddy manipulator who only cares about keeping his political skirts clean. He won't risk a confrontation with Spain!"

"Funston," I finally says, and lays my hand on his slumped shoulder. "Catch hold of yourself, lad. What can you tell me that will help all of us?"

His head raised, his eyes trying to focus. "Maybe it's already done, Kelly."

"Done?"

"A friend of mine saw a letter written just yesterday by Cabot Lodge. D'you know him?" I shook my head. "Very powerful senator, Lodge," he slurred. "My friend sees diplomatic correspondence. This letter went to our embassy in London. Lodge wrote: 'There may be an explosion any day in Cuba which would settle a great many things.' Figure that out if you can."

I shook my head. "Beyond me, lad."

He slapped the table. "Somebody knows something! Maybe we've already decided on war. They just haven't told the public. It needs the explosion, whatever that is, some incident to touch it off." He lifted himself up from the table. "Maybe you and Rowan can find out something."

"Rowan?"

"Andrew Summers Rowan. West Pointer," he laughed bitterly, "a shavetail infantry officer, but I will say this for him. He's spent some years studying Cuba, a 'military hobby' he calls it. Whatever, he had a meeting yesterday at the War Department, and now he's up here, waiting for me to get him passage to Cuba."

"What's he up to, Funston?"

"I wish I knew. Secret orders, verbal only, and he won't tell me a damn thing. I'd go with him if I could to cover his back, but I'm anathema to our Army and the rebels. If I go down there again, the Cubans will have me commanding a brigade of their damn rabble, and I'm not well disposed to that now, or healthy enough, either. I've been to that rotten war. Help yourself, Kelly." His eyes blurred over my face. "What's your rank?"

"Sergeant."

He laughed bitterly. "A sergeant and a shavetail, trying to get a message to Garcia. *Buen viaje, compadre!*"

Four days later, Andy Rowan and I had been smuggled ashore in Cuba. Rowan had a big nose and sad eyes, a little too West Pointy for me, but I sure liked his guts. He kept plodding on behind our guides who were Cuban rebels in white pajamas and carrying machetes. They led us through the worst kind of jungle and swamp. I had no idea of which way we were going, or if General Garcia even existed. Mostly, the country was empty. We'd stumble onto occasional *casitas* of Cuban cane-choppers, the whitewashed adobe walls pocked with bullets and the red-tile roofs blasted by shells. Entire little *pueblos* would have been burned and the nearby fields scorched black. The *gente,* said one of the rebels, were long gone. Them that weren't dead had been swept up and placed behind barbed wire in the reconcentrados of the *peninsulares* General Weyler. The rebels called the Spanish "*peninsulares.*" "The Boche pig!" spat one. "The butcher of Cuba. He has imprisoned thousands of our people in these dreaded concentration camps where they kill each other over a crumb of bread. Starving, dying like dogs! Why have these wretched Iberians come among us? Cuba libre!" he cried, and the other two rebels slashed their machetes into the side of a palm tree, leaving yellow, oozing wounds.

That same afternoon, we saw another sign of what this war had done to Cuba. *La trocha,* they called it, a giant clearing two hundred yards wide that had been hacked out of the jungle, and great felled trees piled up on each side like barricades. This particular *trocha* ran for 50 miles, and there were many others in different parts of the island. The idea was to bottle up the rebels in their mountain strongholds so they couldn't attack cities like Santiago and Havana. To make sure nobody would cross *la trocha,* the Spanish had strung it with barbed wire on both sides and planted electrically-triggered mines along its full length. To make it even more leak-proof, every few hundred yards were blockhouses and machine gun pits. Ugly shellholes in the red earth showed a trail of death when distant Spanish artillery had zeroed in, catching a pitiful handful of rag-tags making a run for it. Hell, one place I looked at with glasses was stacked with bloated white bodies, swollen and stinking in the sun, with ravens and rats feasting on 'em. "Look now," I whispers to Rowan, "if you bluebellies got to fight through stuff like this, you'll bury a lot of lads."

"Our commanders aren't madmen. You don't attack these fixed defenses. You go around them and leave them to rot. Relics of the European trench-warfare mentality."

"What about these concentration camps?"

"A crime against humanity. Do you see now why we'll have to join this wretched war and wipe out such bestiality?"

"Ah, lad," I sighed, "they always make the enemy into a divil. If they didn't whip us into hatin' him, we couldn't bring ourselves to shoot him down. That's the risk of it."

He frowned. "I don't follow."

"In order to beat our enemy, we'll probably have to turn ourselves into the very same divil as him. War rots a man, Rowan."

He glanced at me and his eyes seemed even more sad, but he said nothing.

That same night, we managed to slip across *la trocha* and put some distance between us and the awful clearing. About dusk every day, the way our rebel guides had it figured, they'd squat down in some jungle clearing and begin digging with their machetes. Sure enough, every time they'd finally uncover a canvas sack that some other rebel had stashed there, and it would be filled with yams. Some of them were old, stale and even green with mold, but by damn they tasted awful good because they was the only grub we had.

About then, there was a rustling in the jungle. The rebels sprang up and chased after it. When they came back, they'd caught two prisoners wearing the straw hats and blue pajama uniforms of the Spanish army. One was a young blond boy, the other, a grizzled, swarthy cob with a beak like an eagle. But they wasn't armed. Deserters they were, and starving, too. After much yammering with the rebels, they claimed that they wanted to join our side. When the war was over, they hoped to settle down in Cuba. The older one even showed us a photo of his Cuban wife, a squatty little peasant gal with two tykes clinging to her white skirt.

I wasn't pleased that the rebels let these *peninsulares* throw in with us, but Rowan shrugged it off. "They'll be under guard, Kelly. These rebels know what they're doing." He squinted at me. "What bothers you?"

"They surrendered too easy."

About then, we shared our yams with the buggers and soon had

305

all bedded down on palm leaves to pass the night. Jungle birds were cawing, and in the dampness, land crabs come clicking around us, beading their big, ugly eyes and snapping their pincers. I tossed, trying to sleep, and when I happened to glance at the older Spaniard, he was face down on a palm frond, but one eye slowly opened. His hand snaked out and he touched the younger soldier who quietly pushed up on all fours. Damn, he had a machete in his hand that he must have stolen from the rebels. He raised it over Rowan's head!

"*Alto!*" I cried, flinging myself toward him. Caught in the act, he whirled, flung the machete at me. It struck me in the chest with the pain of a rock, but, thank God, it wasn't the blade going in, only the handle whacking me. The older one tried to wrestle me down. "*Corre!*" he screamed, the blond boy leaping toward the underbrush. I ripped my Colt out of my canvas jeans and fired, a roar, a flash. He sprawled, but not from my bullet. Wiry little Rowan had tackled him, the lad blubbering that he wasn't going to tell the Spanish troops, he and his compadre were just running to save their lives.

By now the rebels had swarmed in. "No!" Rowan shouted, but they shoved him back. One seized the lad by his blond hair, a slash of a machete in the darkness, a sickening spray of blood, the body fell, headless. Behind me, the older Spanish soldier lay writhing and screaming. A machete through his chest had pinned him to the ground. The rebels began rifling his pockets to get out the photo of his family and anything else worth stealing.

"*Cabrones!*" I kicked them aside. "At least let him die!" Just as I knelt with my revolver to put him out of his misery, a rebel reached in and slit his throat. Then they began dancing around the bodies and howling victory songs.

I smashed into them. "*Caiete!* You'll bring the whole damn Spanish army!" I glances at Rowan who was staring dumbly at the corpses. "Forget 'em, mister. We got to get scarce. Run!"

When we hit the trail again, I was too sickened ever to touch another yam again, or black-hearted rebel either.

As luck would have it, the next morning we heard the sound of artillery, and by afternoon came straggling into a gang of rebels, lying in underbrush and pot-shotting at a distant red-roofed pueblo named Bayamo. Straight off, they took us to General Garcia who, compared to their blood-thirstiness, looked as gentle as a country preacher, an old man in simple gray pajamas and a white walrus moustache. The middle of his forehead was cleft with an unhealed scar. For years, Rowan told me, the old man had been fighting this vicious revolution. The Spanish had often jailed him, and once, in the hopelessness of it, he'd tried to kill himself with his own rifle. Though he was a walking scar of a rotten war, he give Rowan and me *abrazos* like a kindly father, and told us how *encanto* he was, enchanted that we'd made it through to help him. Then he pulls out a crumpled letter and says in good American, "Yes, my brave compatriots, I have been informed you were coming. Cuba has so many friends. It is touching how many want to help. And here," he squinted at the letter, "you have already been introduced, Lieutenant Rowan. They have written that you are a confidence man."

"I'm a what?" Rowan gasps, with a glance at me.

"What it says. A confidence man. Am I reading it correctly, sir?"

Rowan was trying not to grin, but I couldn't hold mine back. Finally I says, in flowery Spanish, *"Mi General, the Lieutenant is a man to be trusted, that's what it means. You can put your greatest confidence in anything he tells you."*

"And anything we have is yours. I'm so flattered that you even speak our language." Garcia smiled, and his aide scurried in with hot Cuban beer. We all sat down under the shade of an acacia tree. There was a pretty stream flowing past it. I cooled my tootsies and my head, figuring I'd helped get Rowan here, and that was pretty much the end of our message to Garcia.

With the field guns booming lazily at the Bayamo pueblo, Rowan told the old man that the War Department was fully on the side of the Cuban heroes. Now, the question was, how could the United States best help in their valiant struggle?

Canny Garcia had a shopping list right in his mitt. Swatting at mosquitoes and puffing a thin stogey, he began rattling off the numbers of good rifles they'd need, cases of ammunition, grenades. Many of his troops were armed with nothing but machetes, while others were using smoothbore shotguns, stolen from plantations where the rich owners had hunted birds in the past. Artillery was almost non-existent. They need the latest heavy guns to smash the *peninsulares* well-built defenses. The meeting went on most of the afternoon, and when Rowan had memorized all the requests— couldn't risk putting anything on paper—Garcia stood up, gave us more *abrazos,* and assured us of safe passage out of Cuba. A small boat had been arranged to get us as far as the island Nassau. "Now, regrettably," the old man said, "the British will probably intern you. They want no part of our war or Yanquis meddling down here, but—" he smiled graciously, "even with three more days travel to get you to the boat, you still have accomplished a valiant mission. I am sure, Lieutenant Rowan, that a man of such confidence can talk his way out of the clutches of his British kinsmen."

After we'd left Garcia and got ready to set out on another trail of yams, I pulls Rowan aside. "This one you'll handle by yourself, partner. I'm staying."

His dark eyes widened. "Are you mad, Sergeant? Our work is done."

"Mine ain't, Rowan." I hadn't said nothing about T.R. up to then, but now I told him what Specs was interested in. Yes, we'd seen a little of the rebel side, and found it pretty shoddy. "But what about the enemy, the Spanish? If our lads are going to have to fight 'em, I want to know what we're up against."

"You can't go into the Spanish lines, Kelly. You'll be executed."

"I ain't intendin' to go in, lad, just around." Then I told him, which was the truth, my orders was to report to the American consul in Havana, General Fitzhugh Lee.

Rowan shrugged. "You'll never make it, but, do what you must. I doubt if I'll ever see you, but if I do, I hope it will be my privilege to campaign with you again."

"You're a pretty good confidence man yourself," I says and grins. Then, Spanish style, we give each other *abrazos,* and when I watched him trudge off into the jungle with new rebel guides, I prayed they'd cover his back and get him home.

As for me, it was lonely breaking off, but then again, I welcomed being on my own in a hostile land. I'd grown up on that kind of war, and always made it through. Luck was what you made by yourself, and I'd gamble on that. I turned my back on the setting sun, and struck east toward Havana. A few days later, beachcombing, I'd fallen in with a boatload of Cuban fishermen. We joked about our mother-in-laws and told dirty tales in Spanish. Because I had the lingo and was tattered and sun-burned enough to be a native, they made me one of 'em. When we rounded the rock jetties of Havana harbor, they let out a cheer. *"Compadre!"* they cried, *"see it before you. Our friends have come! Cuba Libre!"*

Dead ahead rose up a gleaming white dreadnought. Fluttering from the stern was the Stars and Stripes. The great battleship *Maine,* it was, thundering down here to save us from a war.

———⦿———

Maybe it was in the stars, who knew? With the 20th century ready to be born, the American people seemed determined to light the sky with a helluva fireworks display, celebrating, I suppose, that we'd lasted through a hundred years of Revolution, Civil War and Injun killing, but still we'd come out top dog. In the saloons, working stiffs were singing, "There'll be a hot time in the old town tonight." Nothing could stop the USA!

That afternoon I come churning across the green waters of Havana harbor. I was a long way from the tank towns and peaceful farms back home. It was February 15, 1898. When the Cuban fishermen pulled me up to the *Maine*'s gangplank, the neat white sailors were scowling at me like who in hell is this pitiful wretch trying to soil our ship? I was wearing white cotton pajamas, my beard grown out raggedy and my straw lid with a hole punched in the top. When they finally let me come up the plank, I was dumbfounded by the size of the *Maine*, a gleaming white castle, spiring up in steel towers taller than many buildings in Chicago. The deck was hundreds of feet long, bristling with armor-plated gun turrets fore and aft. Steam wisped out of the two giant stacks, and though we were dead in the water, I could feel the throbbing of powerful engines down in the hold. Remembering the dingy freight buckets I'd shipped on out of Guaymas years ago, I knew that the days of creaking wood and flopping sails were gone. Uncle Sam was building himself a navy of cold steel. Down in her belly, the *Maine* had nine thousand horsepower, a sailor told me. She could cut the waves at seventeen knots and not a vessel in the world could catch her.

After the sailor had led me to a starchy naval ensign, white choke collar and all, I presented myself as a special agent for Assistant Secretary Roosevelt and told my business. The ensign wrinkles his nose at the sweat of me and the slime from Cuban swamps. "This is a flagship, sir, and you are out of uniform."

"Well hell yes, I am. What did you expect?"

"Get him below," he says to the sailor. "Crew quarters, a wash, a shave, and issue whites. The people you want to see, 'Sergeant Kelly,'" he sniffed over the name, "that is, the Captain of this vessel, Sigsbee and Consul Lee, General Lee, will be dining at thirteen hundred hours, on the poop deck. Report there."

Poop, was it? Ah, the damn navies had a lingo all their own, prissy snots who'd never heard a gun go off. After they'd spiffed me up and done everything but powder my butt, they must have figured I was acceptable to T.R.'s great white fleet. Why, it was all pomp, a fancy party they were throwing. Under canvas awnings was a long table set with blue and white china, silverware and wines sparkling in crystal goblets. There was ladies present, swishing around in droopy sun hats and long fluttery dresses. If there was blood being spilled in Cuba, and I'd tasted my share, it wasn't about to bother these pretty heads. Above us, Old Glory was rippling on the flagstaff, pointing right toward the mean brown fortress of Morro Castle. No doubt about it, we were thumbing our nose at the Spaniards. Even at this distance, I could see black gun casements with their muzzles trained on us. Then, a Navy band, lined up against a gun turret, begins piping out "Yankee Doodle", and after it, "Marching Through Georgia."

"I never thought I'd be drinking to that song," laughs a portly gent, lifting his wine glass to some navies and ladies standing beside him. Though he had a flowing white moustache and the bearing of a soldier, I puzzled why he was dressed in a gray uniform. Only when he turned did I see his deck of ribbons and in gold on his collar, CSA. General Fitzhugh Lee, no less, the nephew of Robert E. T.R. told me that he'd led Reb cavalry in the Civil War, and after it fought Injuns on the plains. But now there was shrewd politics in taking these old warhorses back on the Yankee side. Bury the last bitterness of the Rebellion. As U.S. consul in Havana, General Lee was sitting on the powder keg, trying to find out whether it would be the Cubans, the Spaniards or us who would touch it off.

He didn't shake hands with me, but drew me over to the rail of the ship. "So, one of Roosevelt's field men, are you?" When I says, Yessir, he looks at me hard. "I have little use for people sent down here by Washington. They complicate my job. These damn writers in particular. That young troublemaker, Stephen Crane. *Red Badge of Courage*, is it? Why, that wet-behind-the-ears pup wasn't even born when we fought! As for that swaggerer, Richard Harding Davis, Hearst's lackey, you'd think any hostilities are going to be put on for his benefit alone. Hearst even has the gall to propose bringing his private yacht down here so that he and his coterie can watch the fun. What the devil do they think war is, a fancy dress cotillion? Were they meddling out where you were?"

"Ah, I heard of 'em, sir. The rebels like to get all the publicity they can, but Rowan and me was pretty much back in the swamps."

He frowned. "Who's this Rowan?"

When I explained that he'd been ordered to carry a message to Garcia, Lee sniffed. "Whose order! Never heard of such nonsense! Oh, it's typical War Department, no doubt, the worst bureau in the government, always horning in on everybody else's business. I suppose they'll send Remington down here next."

I frowned. "Who is that, sir?"

"Why, just another glamorizer for the military. Haven't met him myself, but they tell me he's a gross fellow who eats like a hog. Made his reputation sketching football matches at Yale, until someone in the War Department got the brainstorm of sending him beyond the border. Depict the romantic Indian wars! Why, the man never got close enough to smell a redskin. All he ever saw was peacetime maneuvers, with one exception, I suppose, the battle of Wounded Knee. I suspect he got there after they'd buried the dead."

"I wouldn't call it a battle," I grunted. "Massacre is what it was."

"You were there?"

"Yessir. I lost a Sioux wife in that rotten mess, and quit the Army because of it."

"But they still rank you as Sergeant? What regiment?"

"Third Cavalry mostly."

"Where?"

When I told him about Rosebud, Crook and the Geronimo chase, he rumbled a laugh. "By God, young man, we might just have

310

a soldier here, and some memories too! Old Crook," he said fondly. "George graduated from West Point the day I got there. I worshipped him. Then, in '63, the Shenandoah, wouldn't you know it would be my cavalry who caught him napping and captured him. My, there was one sizzling hot Yankee, you can bet! We laughed about it and I exchanged him. I've always admired Crook. Best Indian fighter we had. It was Sheridan who did him in."

"Yessir. I know."

He squinted at me. "I believe you do, Kelly. Well, your experience allows me to put trust in your report. I appreciate that. First off, how are the rebels armed? Have they received any of our new Krags, any Hotchkiss pieces?"

"Not that I seen, sir. I did talk to this Fred Funston, who'd run some of their artillery and said it was poor."

"Yes, Funston. I got him out of Cuba. Damn adventurer, soldier of fortune. But I'll credit him with being a fighter."

"The rebels are a ragtag bunch, General. Smoothbore rifles, old fowling pieces, shootin' tubes cobbled together with wire."

Lee sighed. "They're no match for the Spanish army. Miracle they've kept going this long. Do either General Gomez or Garcia have any idea of the number of Spanish troops now on this island?"

"I ain't sure, sir. I heard them mentioning about 100,000 regular soldiers."

He shook his head. "We think the number, including new reinforcements from Madrid, is well over 160,000."

"Well, I'll tell you this, sir, them *trochas* they dug are death traps to steer clear of. I passed through their territory pretty quick, but outside of Santiago, I seen good fortifications on top of the hills like this Kettle, they call it, and San Juan. It don't pay to hit these Spaniards head on. They've got smokeless powder. You can't see nothing to fire at. That's why the Rebs bushwhack 'em on the jungle trails, shoot 'em from behind."

Lee nodded. "I want all of this in a formal, written report, Sergeant. Meanwhile," he unbuttoned his gray blouse and took out a rumpled sheet of paper. "Did you ever see this?"

I glanced at the cheap-printed page, black letters smeared across it. "Nossir, I ain't."

"Spanish propaganda." He read from it, skimming, "'Long Live Spain with Honor…Yankee pigs meddle in our affairs…A greater taunt, sending a man of war from their rotten squadron, after insulting us in their newspapers…Death to the Americans!' I've showed it to Captain Sigsbee. He doesn't think it's authentic."

"Well," I says, "who ever got it up ain't very happy with us."

Lee's heavy hands gripped the rail and he stared at the slimy green water, lapping the plates of the Maine. "Nobody is happy with any thought of war, Kelly. We don't want it, the Spaniards certainly don't. I'm hoping that the presence of the *Maine* here will have a calming effect. Let cooler heads prevail."

"I couldn't help overhearing you, General Lee," said an elderly, sad-faced woman who edged up beside us. "But I would urge you to visit the concentration camps with me before you hope for an easy solution. You'd be appalled at the human wreckage. Children with swollen bellies, flies on their eyes. Living skeletons. We're filling fifty coffins a day."

"I know, Miss Clara," Lee snapped, "and I can't do a damn thing about it."

"We need more foodstuffs and medicines at once, sir, and I'll thank you to provide them."

"Sigsbee is trying, so am I. A ship next week, I believe."

"I can't feed my people on excuses," she said. Straight as a queen, bobbing the gray-brown bun of hair atop her head, she strode off toward the dining table. Lee sighed. "Clara Barton is one of the finest yet stubbornly impossible women I have ever known. She literally brands her damn Red Cross on all of us."

"Red Cross?"

"Oh, one of these new missionary works that keep springing up. Crusading females. Smash saloons or get the vote for women. Clara intends to minister to the walking wounded of the world. God help us, she's going to have her hands full with that dream."

When the luncheon was over, I was sweating like a damn pig, wishing I could plunge into the harbor and take a swim. But Lee hauls me aside with Captain Sigsbee, who was another bearded veteran of the Rebellion. A gentle sort, though, looking more like a scientist than a warrior seadog. If he was worried about being a sitting duck under the Spanish guns, he sure didn't show it. "Thank you for your news," he says, after I'd repeated what I told to Lee. "I'm going to use the rest of the evening for a long letter to Mrs. Sigsbee. I'm overdue, Lee." Then he turns to a deck officer and tells him to take me below, give me a typewriter to do my report. I grins, "Well, sir, it better have a brain in it, 'cause I ain't never run one of the contraptions."

The deck officer sighed at how thick I was, but he did take me down to a steamy place far below decks. With a tablet and common pencil, I started jotting words, knowing full well that nobody would pay any attention to them. Why should they? We couldn't do anything. With the war raging on the island, and the great powers arching their backs like dogs getting ready to tear out each others' throats, the *Maine* was only a cork bobbing on the dark waters of the harbor.

Listening to the waves slopping the steel of the hull, I started writing the stuff, but soon dozed off. The cubbyhole where they had me was a watertight compartment buckled in by steel doors. Ugly steam pipes ran across the ceiling, oozing so much heat that I burned my finger touching them. The hell with this, I says, cranked open the door and went out into a long, plated hatchway. The place stunk with coal smoke, for the boiler room was just beyond. As I walked toward it, I saw another hatch open, and peered in. From the floor to the roof, this cubbyhole was stuffed with white canvas sacks. A sailor was squatting in the dim light, fingering them. "What's up here, mate?" I says.

"Six-inch reserve magazine." He strips a string of sweat from his brow. "In case we got to blast them Spicks, Captain wants to know how many rounds we got. I'm tallying," and he goes back to jotting on a tablet.

"The heat in here is something fierce," I says. "Don't that worry you, counting powder?"

He shrugs. "Cap'n wants boilers up-fired at all times in case we got to pull the hook in a hurry. Yas, mebbe it's a mite hotter right now, but it's probably the spiggoty kid a-doin' it."

"The who?"

"Chamorro. Name of Carlos, from the island of Guam."

I frowns. "Where'n hell is that?"

"Far Pacific toward Japan. One of our cruisers put in there last fall, and this native kid swims out and gets aboard. Ah, the skipper took pity on him, made him a messman first. But he's bucking for rates now, that boy. He's all Navy blue, you can believe."

"Oh? Why is that?"

"Hell, mister, the Spicks have owned his island for 300 years. He hates 'em even more than we do, and he thinks he's helping us get that piece of rock away from 'em."

"Are we going to do that?"

The sailor grins. "Give us a war, you can bet on it."

Pushing up, I says, "I wish to hell he'd get the temperature down first."

"Tell him to do it," the sailor says. "He ain't a bad little nigger."

I went out on the hatchway again and down a greasy steel ladder to the boilers. Ah, they were monstrous things, the eyes in their steel doors pupping red with flames from the coals. In my sailing days, I'd been around boiler rooms, and they was always the divil's own pasture to me. No man on earth could pay me enough to work down in this furnace of Satan. "Carlos!" I hollers, over the ticking, boiling sounds. It was slippery going on the steel catwalks, everything I touched sizzling hot. Then, in the gloom behind the turbines, I hear a faint cry. A naked brown leg was stuck out, kicking, and when I stooped down and grabbed it, I knew I had the

Chamorro kid. He was wearing only a breechclout like an Injun and didn't weigh a hundred pounds. I got him upright, his eyes rolling and head lolling back and forth on his sweaty brown shoulders. "Carlos, is it? Are you hurt, boy?" I couldn't see no marks or blood. He tried to answer me as I gripped him, but all he could do was gasp and suck for air.

Then I knew! Gas had got him, like black damp I'd always feared when I worked in mines. I threw him over my shoulder like a flour sack, and went teetering along the catwalk and up the ladder, getting him the hell out of there. "Sailors!" I hollered. "Somebody! Bear a hand here!"

But my words just kept echoing back in the iron cavern. All the passageways were empty, the lights flickering weak. Something was screaming at me, Get outa this hellhole! I was like a rat in a maze. The poor Guam boy was so limp that he could already be dead, but I couldn't stop and look. Finally I hit a big ladder, leading toward deck, hauled him the last few yards, and pushed up a hatch cover above us.

Then the hot, sweety air of Havana Harbor was in my nose, and I knew we'd made it, this far anyhow. I lay the boy on the deck plates, and was just getting up to run and find somebody.

Hell blew! A great, flashing, splitting roar. The deck burst under my feet in a searing torch of flame. I was flung upward like a busted doll, arms and legs windmilling in the black sky, stars whistling past my eyes, the screaming and ripping of metal, lifeboats squealing down from their davits. Splash of the sea, and I was in it, writhing.

Wet and cold, dark, dying, the waves boiling away from the great hunk of steel that was sizzling, sinking, blasting with more and more thunders of ammunition blowing, and now the screams of people someplace above me. I was tearing at the water, choking, trying to get my feet and arms going, to keep me afloat, get clear of the shattering steel plates that were ripping and hissing through the sky.

Then my hands struck something. Wet, slimy, maybe driftwood or a wooden crate or a hatch ripped off a lifeboat. I couldn't tell, just kept clawing it like a slippery snake, pushing my head above the water, but the thing was trying to sink out from under me. Hang on, Patrick, I prayed. Don't go down. This ain't your time! Daisy, Daisy, flowers, shooting stars in the sky, and me, joining 'em, am I?

Is this how the end comes?

Maybe so. Far off, explosions rumbled in the deep, blasting out walls of water, hard as black steel, slamming me, crushing me until I felt no more. But that was good. I was glad.

Floating, drifting, my trip was done. I was at peace. Ah, lad, I thinks, it's like Crazy Woman Fork, when I let you drift off into the white. For now, it's all stripped away, all the noisy hurry and the

314

bugles and the wails of glory. The silliness of being a human being, when it's so easy and soft just to rest in the white. This is where you lived before you were, and where you're going back again.

Jesus God, the light, blinding, the brilliance of it. The soft hands, soaring you up the tunnel through the clouds where the sun was rainbows. Rest here, come home, Patrick lad.

But the divils were dancing still, screaming banshees. We will not let you go! The big voice, the light voice whispering, You're mine, lad, and the banshees wailing. Not yet, not done. There is more!

What more? God help me!

Dancing in the clouds, the divils had faces of Injuns, dancing under palm trees, black strange faces, muttering foul tongues, hooknose harridans and painted heathen from distant lands. We were dancing far off across the sea, swarming like wasps from island to island. Where is this now? Why here? I screams. What am I doing among you?

And they're wailing: suffer for your sins. The night we bury the *Maine* is the night when hell flames across the world. It has just begun. From this night on, you will dance with divils for the rest of your life. Your ears will be filled with the screams of the dying, the thucking of bullets into red, brown, black, yellow flesh. We will not let you stop. You will pay for your sins against us.

T.R. and Sheridan, the Archibalds, Crazy Horse, Crook, Geronimo, they're all dancing around the bonfire now, roasting heathen. But, lad, you're the one dangling in the fire. We'll make you pay, for them.

Ah Jesus, Daisy! She was in it now. She was trailing her lace handkerchief at me, saying goodbye. Saying her name was Liberty. But girl, I screams, you've never used that name. It's for Nora, ours together. But she was drifting off, and the name, ah no, it wasn't Liberty. She was whispering to me a name beginning with an "L", and I couldn't catch it.

I reached out for her hand, felt the smooth softness of it, and then it was gone. It wasn't her hand anymore. Jesus God, I prays, keep me here. Keep me home, resting in the white and the great beautiful light.

Then I was weeping, burning with fever, too. When my eyes opened, I was weary trying to get the lids up. A face was swimming there above me. Woman, old woman. She was holding my hand and whispering, "You'll live, young man. We'll keep you alive."

How many weeks it was, I don't know, but when I finally got my head straightened around and my strength coming back, they had me on a white ocean liner, steaming toward New York. I says, "How in hell did I get here?"

"When they pulled you out of the harbor," answers a Yankee doctor, listening to my lungs with a stethescope, "they took you to the San Ambrosia Hospital. Clara Barton pulled you through. Pity she couldn't have saved more of the crew."

"How many was gone?" I whispered.

"Two hundred and eighty six, I believe they said. Present count anyway. If it hadn't been for the Spanish doctors in Havana, the figure would have been higher. They may be enemies, but by God, they were humanitarians first."

"Enemies?" I whispers. "Are we at war again?"

He sighed and turned away. "You've had all the war you need, Sergeant. Just get well."

Three days later, they wheeled me off the liner at New York. T.R. had told Daisy what had happened. She was at the bottom of the gangplank, waiting for me. I was so tired I couldn't do much but weep, holding the sweet softness of her against me. "Don't worry, darlin'," I whispers. "The worst is over. It can only get better now."

It did. But not fast enough for us, and certainly not the way either of us wanted. The dream I'd had of dying kept coming back to haunt me, and it was like a curse, driving a wedge between my beloved Daisy and me. We had each other again. We had little Nora of our own, and young Matty of my old life. We had the world, you might say. But there was no way we could stop it, and run back to where we'd come from. The madness was too far gone by then.

In the months that followed, Daisy and I talked many a night about that wild dream I'd had, floating in Havana harbor. What did it mean, the howling dance of the heathen, making us pay for our sins? And why were all the strange, distant islands in it? At first, Daisy tried to laugh it off, saying I was just dreaming about our lovely days in Hawaii, or my horrid times with the rebels in Cuba. But secretly she was worrying that I was touched in the head.

She'd gotten T.R. to admit me to the Military Hospital in Bethesda. I'll hand it to Teddy, even busy as he was, he could pull the strings. He helped Daisy rent a house in Georgetown, plenty of room for her, Matt, baby Nora and a black nurse she'd hired. For a week or so, the Army and Navy sawbones worked me over with every kind of sticking and probing. What had happened, they said, the blasts of the *Maine*'s magazines exploding had damaged some of my internal organs. They couldn't tell which or just how, but as I strengthened every day, it come pretty clear that I wasn't looney. My brain hadn't been squashed. "We are learning all the time, Mrs. Kelly," the head sawbones told her, "that at the threshhold of death, these hallucinations are quite common. No one knows why, or what they mean, but I'm sure that in the upward march of science, rational answers will be found."

When we drove away from that hospital for the last time, I says to Daisy, "An Irishman is about like a mule, darlin'. It takes an awful big shellelaeigh to kill one, so I'm for putting this thing behind us and kicking up our heels again. That suit you?"

"Oh, so much, Patrick. Why, you hardly even know little Nora. She's growing like a weed."

"And why not! She's getting the finest milk in the world. Overflowing, you are," and I stroked Daisy's beautiful breasts.

"Oh, stop," she giggled, but didn't stop me either. We snuggled there in the back of the naval motor car, and the world seemed to lift from our shoulders. Spring was coming to Washington, and on the few warm afternoons, Daisy and I would take Nora out on the grass behind the house. The little tyke's hair was getting flame red, just like my sister Nora. "God help me," I was stroking her tiny cheeks, "I wonder if it'll be freckles too."

"Oh, I hope not," Daisy said.

"Well why, though? They're lovely on a lass. Irish love spots, we call 'em. Don't tell me that it's the Irish part of her that's got you?"

Daisy laughed. "I hope it starts bursting out of me a few more times, Patrick."

"Now, don't tell me you're makin' plans!"

Daisy picked Nora up, held her to her breast and patted her, for the little thing had started to squall. "The doctor thinks that my milk may disagree with her. That's why she cries so much."

"Ah, she's just a feisty one like her namesake."

"No. He's made tests. He thinks I should start weaning her. Which means..." Daisy smiled, "in just a few more weeks, I'll be ready for you. Oh Patrick, won't we want another? More, more, we said."

"God help me, yes, darlin'. A house full."

"Even if we don't know where the house is," Daisy murmured, her eyes flickering dark.

"Well, we've got a proper roof over our heads, don't we?"

"Yes, now. Temporary, I'm sure."

"Ah, why would you say something like that?"

She sighed. "Because it's what I love in you the most, Patrick. With you, things are never predictable. Everything is an adventure, and yes, I can accept not knowing where it leads. But the nesting part of me, and this little girl, and the others to follow, that has to get into it, too, Patrick. We're not born to be kites, soaring from sea to sea. What was it your mother used to say about you? Your hat on two hairs?"

I laughed and drew her hand into my black mop. "It won't be

317

long before they're gray, darlin', and then you can haul down the kites and sit rocking by the hearth."

She pinched one of my hairs, plucked it out and I squealed. Damnation! There in the pale sun of Georgetown, I was looking at a wisp of silver hair. "You had a terrible night with the *Maine*, darling," she said gently. "The shock of it would turn anybody gray."

Ah, how it struck me. I'd lived forty two years, most of them on the hard side, and pretty soon, some of the wear and tear was bound to show up. That night in Havana harbor gave me a look at death all right, dangling me there at the pearly gates. But something brought me back. And for what kind of road now? With a family coming on, with my life half done, was it always going to be more drifting, never knowing which way led home? I lay beside Daisy that night, and long after she'd gone to sleep, I still didn't have an answer.

But in truth, it was out of my hands by then. I waked up hearing marching bands in the street and newsboys hollering.

Cuba Libre! Remember the *Maine!* Hot time in the old town tonight!

The war nobody wanted had come, and it swept Daisy, little Nora and me into the howling bonfire. The banshees were screaming for vengeance, birthing the new century in blood.

My beloved ones and I would never know peace again.

ROUGH, ROUGH, WE CAN'T GET ENOUGH!

On our last night together, Daisy clung to me and sobbed. "Oh Patrick, this evil scheme of Teedie's, this whole wretched adventure is nothing but a fraud! You've said it yourself, why, you lived it that awful night on the *Maine*. You've done your duty, if that's what you think it is. Why be part of this madness again? Why must you go?"

"Because, darlin'," I whispered, "I don't know how not to. They need me."

"Of course they'd say that! But it's all lies, Patrick. They have millions of stupid men wanting to rush down to Cuba."

"Maybe so, only not that many who've been shot at, Daisy."

"But you hate the Army!"

"Indeed I do, girl. And don't you think that every bone in me isn't crying not to leave you. Yet if I lay back and do nothing, folks are going to die who maybe wouldn't have to, if they had a strong hand pushing their heads down so they don't catch a slug."

She shuddered. "Oh, it's so vile. Stop it, Patrick! I won't listen to that talk!" Her brown eyes were wet and wide. She was staring at me like she'd never seen me before in her life. "You love it, don't you?"

"What the divil are you saying?"

"I can see it in you, I've watched it building. They've infected you, Patrick. Blow their damn bugles and you dance for the glory. Jingo fever. War! You enjoy it. Stop hiding it, say it! You want the chase, the kill. Is life with me so boring that's all you have left?"

"Ah, God help me, darlin'." I drew her to me and stroked her little face. "In an hour or so I'll be gone. Don't let us part this way."

She turned from me and covered her face with the pillow. "You made your choice," she whispered.

It was the first time we'd ever had such harsh words, or failed to heal ourselves with love. So I went off to the damn Spanish war with a broken heart. Cursed the war, because Daisy was right. I knew better than being in it. What I didn't know was how to get myself loose from it. Like being in the black water of Havana Harbor, all of us seemed to be swept up into the curl of a monster wave that would hurl us, screaming and dying, onto the beaches of distant lands.

And for what? A sham, wasn't it?

I'd seen the crooked thing building. The *Maine* blew on the 15th of February. Two days later, Hearst spread a headline on his Noo Yawk *Journal*: "Destruction of the Warship *Maine* Was the Work of

319

An Enemy. Assistant Secretary Roosevelt Convinced the Explosion Was Not An Accident."

A million people bought the paper that day, and on the next, Hearst's headline read: "The Whole Country Thrills with The War Fever, Yet the President Says 'It Was An Accident.'"

Hurrah for McKinley! He wasn't going to let them stampede him into war. I wanted to shake the man's hand but the Navy sawbones still had me bedded down. If I'd been able to testify at the Naval Court of Inquiry, I sure would have told the muckety-mucks about the heat I'd felt below decks on the *Maine,* and the powder magazine cooking with coal gas. Before I could even tell T.R., if he would have listened, the Naval Court comes out and announces that the *Maine* was destroyed by a Spanish mine.

Lying buggers. They claimed that some diver, working in the mucky wreck of the ship, had found hull plates blown inward. Evidence of an outside explosion. Nobody listened to the few Navies at the hearing who said, Wrong. Coal gas had ignited on several other ships of the line. Couldn't the same thing have happened on the *Maine,* only worse this time?

By then, the pressure on McKinley was fierce, so he began teetering, begging God to help him choose between war or peace. But even the Almighty couldn't have stopped that runaway chariot of the jingoes. Roosevelt was saying right out in public, "McKinley has no more backbone than a chocolate eclair." And down on the island of Cuba, the artist feller, Remington, out with the rebels, was whining to Hearst that there wasn't any war, and could he come home? Some said that Hearst answered, "You furnish the pictures, I'll furnish the war."

Even across the pond in England, the old royal biddy, Queen Victoria, was pleading, "It is atrocious of America."

But who listened? By then, the working stiffs out in the streets were so whipped up by the yellow press that they were howling for blood. At the White House, poor befuddled McKinley kneels down one night and asks God Almighty to decide it. Out in a Chicago newspaper, the wag, Mister Dooley, was writing to his Irish pal, Packy: "By mornin', the Good Lord answers our noble President, straight from the pearly gates. War she'll be. Put up your dukes, Packy, and start swingin'!"

At the Navy Department in Washington, Roosevelt jots off a note to his fancy haberdasher, Brooks Brothers on Broadway, Noo Yawk. "Can you make me so I shall have it here by next Saturday a blue cravennat regular lieutenant colonel's uniform without yellow on the collar and with leggings. If so, make it. Theodore Roosevelt."

How I know about the note, T.R. asked me to deliver it in person. The haberdasher clerk was a pomaded gent, his eyes gleaming.

"How I envy you boys! It will be a splendid little war. I just hope that Colonel Roosevelt's regiment gets into it before the ball is over."

Tailored uniforms and a fancy dancing party, that's how it was to the jingo bunch, the patriots from cities and tank towns who were flocking to join up. By the time I'd delivered the spiffy uniform to T.R., he was down at a ranch in San Antone, Texas, galloping around with his own private army, the Rough Riders. "What grand fellows, Kelly," he cried. "Your kind of men. Rocks of the nation. You'll stay and help me drill them into a fighting force."

"Whoa, Specs," I says. "Playing soldier may be fine for you, but I ain't about to lose Daisy on account of it. We give her a bad scare that night on the *Maine*."

"Bosh! She's a courageous girl. She'll rise to the colors and cheer you louder than anyone. Besides, I'm not ranking you in the regiment. You'll land with us in Cuba, of course, but after that, due to your experience with the rebel forces, I intend using you as a military observer. Your actual job will be to nursemaid the newspaper people."

"Ah, what is this now?"

"The American public hungers for all the words and pictures we can give them to describe our glorious fight. These correspondents are ultimately valuable to us. We mustn't risk a one of them getting shot."

That night, I telegraphed Daisy from a hotel in San Antone, telling her that I wasn't in the Army, and she didn't need to start rolling bandages.

She fired back. "Hallelujah! Please come home!"

I answered, "Love you darling. Not yet. Soon."

After that, it was all dust and drilling Teddy's toy soldiers. "Rough, rough," they'd sing, "we want to fight and we can't get enough. Whoopee!"

What a cocky, bloodthirsty outfit they were, and pure greenhorns to boot. Though they didn't know squat about Army or war, God almighty, they made up for it in eagerness. When we thundered off, practicing cavalry charges, I had to whip hell out of my old Army mount to keep ahead of them.

Some of the Rough Riders were whang leather cowboys Teddy had known up in Dakota or on his hunting trips in the Rockies. Captain Bucky O'Neill of the Arizona Rangers was leader of this gang, and every day more starry-eyed lads kept showing up from ranches all over the West. My job was to pick out the fighters. One snip of a cowhand had rode the rods all the way from Idaho. I feels of his mitts and they was soft, so I asks him how long he'd ranched. "Not very," he says. What he really wanted to be was a book writer, and he begins telling me some nonsense tale about a white boy, name of Tarzan, being raised by an ape in the jungle. I looks at the enlistment paper he'd filled out, and says, "Well, Mister Burroughs, with them lily hands of yours, I'm thinking that you'd do better fighting with a pencil. Don't take it hard, lad. You just ain't had the experience to last with us."

Right behind him in the enlistment line was a hard-jawed youngster who said he'd pushed mules around back on the family farm. I give him a try at loading a mule for me, and then says, "You'll do." Feller's name was Tom Mix, and I made him a packer.

Another gang of the Riders were blanket Indians, mostly tall, hard-eyed loners from the Plains tribes. I grabbed every one of them boys I could, and sometimes in our tents at night, I'd talk sign with them, spinning windies about the great old days when we were fighting each other.

But the biggest bunch of the Rough Riders were just the kind you'd expect to rally around T.R. Fancies, they were, Eastern snots from swanky universities and private clubs. Polo players, larkers, out for sheer hell-raising. With all the millions they had between them, I says, "You fellers would be better off going home and starting a bank." Why, one of them, a jeweler named Tiffany, didn't figure Uncle Sam had provided us enough arms, so he buys us out of his own pocket a half dozen shiny new Colt machine guns. Him and his pals were blasting them off at anything that moved in the desert. Money to burn. And the one who was towering over the bunch, rallying them to the fight, was none other than my big old sheep hunter, Hamilton Fish. When I seen him getting issued his giant-size blue private's blouse and khaki pants, he lets out a howl, drops his duds to the floor. Standing there in his undies, he claps his arms around me and cries to the other fancies, "Here, gentlemen, is a man who's seen the elephant. An authentic. Saved my life, he did, and he'll save yours. Gad, Kelly, I'm delighted you're with us! It's going to be a ball!"

Quick enough, that dream ended. We had less than a month to train. By now, T.R. had seen what he was up against, playing soldier, so instead of him trying to command, on bully and bluster alone, he brings in a man who'd been shot at, Colonel Leonard Wood. He was a trim, good-looking gent, trained as a doctor at Harvard, but when sawboning proved too tame for him, he went cavalryman. The first time I met him in T.R.'s tent, we got to reminiscing about the Geronimo chase. Wood had served down there under Crook and Crawford, too, and, like Maus, he'd won a Congressional Medal for it. "Compared to the Sierra Madre, Kelly," he grins, "Cuba will seem like a skirmish. Do you realize, among others who cut their teeth in that cursed desert, we now have Adna Chaffee and Henry Lawton commanding the regular troops. Even Miles is at the top of the heap. You probably served with all of them."

"Ah, I heard of 'em, sir, but we was running up different rock-piles. Miles, though, I seen enough of him, the rotten way he dumped General Crook."

"Well, he has his hands full now, sergeant. The entire regular Army has been activated for the first time since the Civil War."

"And it's a blundering mess! Scandal!" T.R. snorted, banging his field desk. "Look at the uniforms we've been issued. Heavy winter khaki, when we'll be fighting in fierce jungle heat. Why, the word I get from embarkation ports in Florida is that there are no supplies, even less transport. The secretary of war is an incompetent boob, ranking right up there with Miles himself. We'll be damn lucky even to reach Cuba before Spain collapses."

It was beginning to look that way, all right. By the time we'd shipped into Tampa, Florida, Admiral Dewey had sunk the Spanish fleet, far off in the Philippine Islands. The papers were screaming his famous order, "You may fire when ready, Gridley." But he wasn't out of the woods yet. Steaming down from Hong Kong, German men of war were surrounding Dewey's fleet, and in the Atlantic, from Florida to Maine, East Coasters were pleading for Uncle Sam to protect them from the Spanish battleships that were supposed to be heading our way. Right about then, T.R. comes storming into my tent, waving a tellygram. "So, Kelly, you thought your service for me in the Pacific was meaningless, did you? Well, thank your stars that you were there. Congress has just voted to annex Hawaii. Those islands shall be ours! We'll turn Pearl Harbor into a major base, and after it, dig a canal through the Isthmus of Panama!"

The boys cheered, and were prattling about how Dewey's squadrons had already taken the far-away island of Guam. By God, Puerto Rico would be next! We'd own the seas!

It was all happening so fast, I couldn't keep track of it, or care much either. Tampa was a rainy mess. We were camped on mud flats near the docks, thousands of us, milling like ants. We didn't have any cook tents, and our shelter tents had been lost coming from someplace. Night after night, troop trains were clanking in from all across the land, spilling out more boys in khaki, dumb as sheep, falling into latrines in the darkness. T.R. was storming around, trying to find stabling for our horses, but they were already dying because some butt-polishing quartermaster had forgotten to send hay along with them.

Early one morning, I was running an errand when I sees a gang of Rough Rider troopers writhing in the mud in front of the hospital tent. "Dysentery!" Fish cries when he spots me. "Don't touch this stuff." He thrusts a tin can at me, bulging like it would blow up. It was leaking slime and the stink gagged me. "This is supposed to be

323

our ration," he cried. "Meat that the British government rejected last year because it was contaminated. Embalmed beef, no less! I'll see that the President hears of this!"

Before he flung the can into the sea, I caught the label on it. "Armour and Company, Chicago." Melody Farms, was it, with J. Ogden building his Italianate villa on the profits? Just like the old Reb veteran had told me back in '76, as we rattled west to kill the Sioux, "Rich man's war, poor man's fight."

Horses dying, men going down with gut fevers, what a hell of a sendoff. There were black troopers of the Tenth Cavalry with us now. Good men, frontier veterans, but when they hit the saloons or winked at the white girls of Tampa, the rednecks tore into them. Nagurs! Wrong color skin. Here was buffalo soldiers who had died bravely for our flag, and would keep on dying to free far off darky rebels, yet at home, all the freedom we give the poor buggers was a lynch rope and a flaming cross.

The night we loaded for Cuba, I caught a fat-faced kid trying to scurry up the gangplank. He wore a straw hat and spins me this windy that he's a full-fledged correspondent for a newspaper out in St. Louie.

"Sure now, and I'm a monkey's uncle! You're just a scamp trying to stow away." But damn if he doesn't jerk a paper out from under his arm, and smacks a story he's written. "All Troops in Fine Spirits. The Right Sort of Men to Defend Their Country."

The lad was sixteen years old, and son of the Eleventh Infantry bandmaster. He was trying to support himself writing until he could find a way to get into the war. When I kicked his butt off the ship, he left me the paper where his name was printed. Fiorello LaGuardia. Eager little Italian, that one.

"We are in a sewer!" T.R. roared, when we finally got loaded on a stinking iron bucket called the Yucatan. Hell, the ship shouldn't have carried 700 men, and we had twice that number. No place to lie down on the dark, steamy deck. We were swarming atop each other like blind rats looking for a hole. Had to piss over the rail, for the ship's toilets were plugged vile and leaking. No place to cook neither, and not near enough rations or fresh water to last us to Cuba. Then come the lowest blow. At the last moment, somebody, maybe even that strutting cock, General Miles, decides that the Rough Riders just stopped riding. He wouldn't give us the horses we'd trained with, because there was no room aboard ship. Nobody had planned for it. So the poor beasts that hadn't died, we left running and whinnying in terror up and down the Florida sand. We'd go fight the Spaniards afoot.

Or maybe, better yet, we'd swim to 'em. Middle of the morning on June 22nd, we spilled out of our transports into a steamy bay. On shore was a settlement called Daiquiri, a few palm-thatched huts and zinc shacks that an American mining company had left there. Thousands of troops began landing, the choppy green waters bobbing with dinky boats from the transports. So many blue-shirted troopers with bandoliers and bed rolls were crowded into them that the boats began wallowing and sinking before they even hit the beach. I heard fellers screaming in the surf, khaki hats bobbing and rifles being flung away. Many of the poor devils had never swum in their lives.

Worse was the animals. Despite Miles' orders, T.R. and some of the staff had sneaked their own private mounts aboard, and another small ship was carrying our pack mules. But nobody had figured out how to get the animals off, so they were splashed into the bay, floundering there to sink or swim. T.R. was standing beside me, howling, watching his pet mount, Rain in the Face, going under. Pretty soon, horse and mule corpses were washing ashore for the swarming bluebelly flies to feed on.

At that, T.R. bulls our ship captain into ramming the Yucatan square onto the beach, so most of us got out fairly dry, still clinging to our rifles and packs. But as I was running across the hot sand to form the lads up, I sees more boatloads of troopers coming in. Black buffalo soldiers of the Tenth Cavalry. As I watched, one of their skiffs, too heavily loaded, plows into a wave and goes under. "Fish!" I hollers, for the big boy was running beside me. We plunged into the surf and swam bloody murder toward the screaming troopers. Both of us dragged out a few before their lungs had filled. But two were lost. A tall lieutenant ran past me, cursing like hell, for these were his men. I only got a half look at his face, but that was good enough. It was Black Jack Pershing again, still stuck with darky troops. "Sir!" I hollers, but he didn't see me.

By now, out in the bay, bands were playing and troopers waving their hats. Steam whistles were tooting. The first of us lambs had made it ashore safely. Though there was a white Spanish blockhouse on a jungly hill above Daiquiri, not a shot was fired at us. Hell, a few platoons of Spaniards could have blowed us off that beach, but when it didn't happen, several sleek, private yachts began cruising close to shore. These were newspaper craft, belonging to Hearst and other nabobs. On the decks, I could see glints of black cameras and even dolled-up ladies waving their dainty handkerchiefs at us. They acted like it was just one grand party, and they were probably disappointed that they didn't get to see blood being spilled.

As I stood there in the hot sun, the bad dream that started with the Maine swept over me again. Here were U.S. troops, storming onto a palmy isle. This was something new for the US of A. Up until then, all our fights had been on our own soil, pushing our frontier westward until we had slain all the dark skins who stood in our way, grabbed all their turf. The West was ours, dead and buried. We had noplace left to go. But the empire-builders were hurling us on. We are not done. We need more! Leap out across the seas, take what's there, too, island after island in the years to come. And the dream, spinning in my eyes, was the howling heathen, red, black, yellow, brown skins, dancing around their bonfire of death, crying, We will make you pay for your sins!

That very afternoon, the Rough Riders joined with other Army regiments and headed up a jungle trail toward the next coastal village, a scatter of huts called Siboney.

T.R.'s notion that I was a military observer melted damn quick. I was just a common ranker like the rest, slogging and cursing in the mud. All wars are the same when you're out there with a rifle. All any trooper can see is the misery of the scant few yards around him, never knowing why he's there, where he's going, and wishing he was someplace else.

We spent a miserable night, huddling wet in the jungle. Far behind us, the beach where we'd landed was spluttering with hundreds of campfires. New boys, spilling ashore all night long. Ten thousand of us, they said now, against ten times that many Spanish. Beyond, on the jungle ridges between us and the city of Santiago, we could spot the wisping fires of the enemy, waiting in their trenches to cut us down. I was wearing a poncho and a floppy brown campaign hat like the rest of the Rough Riders. By then, though, I'd stripped a light cotton shirt and pants from a dead Cuban rebel, hell of a lot cooler than heavy Army khaki. I'd also found a new lever-action Winchester and about a hundred rounds that somebody had discarded on the beach. The issue rifle nowdays was the Krag-Jorgensen, but to me, it was a jamming piece of Danish pipe, and I'd stick with what I knew. T.R. had also given me a brace of .44 Colt revolvers to protect the newspaper snoops, so now I set out to do just that.

In our night camp, up on a ledge of jungle, I grabs hold of Stephen Crane first. Some said that though he'd never been shot at, he'd written the greatest war tale of all, *The Red Badge of Courage*. But what I saw was a prissy, cocky dandy, little moustache on him, and mincing around like an actor in a stage play. Richard Harding Davis, though, was a tougher sort, rangy, wearing hunting clothes and palling around with the officers. Leonard Wood was his close friend, and T.R. too. As for Fred Remington, who'd finally come back from the rebels, he was a portly gent wearing a pith helmet and lugging a bulky pack, filled with his papers and sketching tools. If he wasn't puffing big stogeys or pounding down whiskey, he'd sit by the fire, gorging himself on bacon and hardtack, and spinning tales to the other correspondents. The way Remington told it, he'd done a sketch of Spanish officers stripping white women naked to search 'em. Damn if Hearst didn't splash it on the front page of his paper, and sells a million copies that day. When red-blooded Americans saw dark-skinned Spaniards treating white ladies that way, you had a war ready to start. "But Fred," pipes one correspondent, "your sketch has been proven a fake. The Cuban woman now claims that no men were present. She was searched by a Spanish army nurse, a female." Then everybody chuckled and said, What the hell difference did it make? We were in Cuba, weren't we?

I hadn't been with them five minutes before I seen that T.R. had hung an impossible job on me. The fellers were as independent and skittery as a bunch of butterflies. Even worse than the correspondents were two young fellers in tweed caps and a big black moving picture camera. They were from Vitagraph Studios in Noo Yawk and said that the colonel had ordered them to make the first film in history of an actual battle. When one of 'em tells me, "Please put us as close as possible to the shooting," I knew how much war had changed. No longer was it the screams of dying men or the bravery either. Now it was all just a show to flicker in the darkness of nickelodeons and get swept away with the spilled popcorn on the floor. "Well, my Colonel's orders," I says, "is to keep you alive. That means none of you go running off in front of the troops or drawing fire. Sure, he wants you writing your stories or gettin' 'em however you do, but use your heads, keep 'em down. If you make targets, you'll kill some boys, and most likely yourselves. Stick close to me, and I'll try to bushwhack you up trails that lead to the fighting, where you ain't in the way."

"Fighting!" scoffs Crane, "Why, man, with all the troops we have ashore, we'll be lucky to get a sham battle out of this. The Spanish aren't fighters. At our first volley, they'll cut and run."

I looks at him, wearing a big black poncho and puffing contentedly on his pipe. "You're going to see some heroes die, mister. Don't make you one of 'em."

Hell, they wouldn't listen. They had to watch it happen, and it did. Before daybreak, we plunged into jungle where we couldn't see five feet in either direction. Remington was huffing along beside me when we hear the Spanish Mausers cracking someplace in the gloom. Then there's a zzzz, like a wasp, and a palm tree explodes beside Remington's head. He whirled to me, his face white. "That's a bullet!"

"Ain't it, though. What of it?"

"But what do we do?"

"Keep going, mister. Start crawling. Follow them other fellers who know how to do it." I started leading him on, but when I glanced back, he was on all fours like a dog, panting in the heavy grass. He kept shaking his head, saying, "I never expected it to be like this."

An old Confederate cavalry general, Joe Wheeler, was running our part of the attack. He had a white beard, and looked like a little cricket, but he was a brave man and kept stumping through us, waving his sword. "On, men, on!"

When we come out into a clearing of tall Cuban grass, the fire grew heavier. Davis had crouched down, looking through field glasses at a distant ridge. "T.R.!" he cries. "White up there, Spanish straw hats!"

Just as T.R. was hiking up his own glasses to look, a tree splinters beside him, and the force of the blast knocks him down. I ran to him, helped him up. He was wearing a polka dot scarf, and with it, I wiped the palm tree splinters out of his face and eyes. He looked at me blankly. "Pinned down. What to do now?"

"We ain't pinned, Specs. Keep moving, and say, get rid of that goddamn pig sticker, will you." He had a big sword strapped on and every step he took, it like to trip him. Then Wood and Joe Wheeler rushed in and began spreading the soldiers for the attack on the Spanish ridge. "You, Sergeant!" Wood cried. "Get a squad of Rough Riders, flank that position!"

I ducked back into the heavy underbrush where the Rough Riders were milling around, some crouching, others cursing that they couldn't see anything to fire at. "Hold your water," I says, "you'll get a chance." I grabs a few boys and starts off on a trail that led up to the left of the Spanish ridge. We were sweating, hacking at heavy vines and cactus. A couple of troopers with me must have been cowboys, for they moved quick and skillful, slashing through with machetes. Then another lad ran ahead, breaking trail, and when I caught a glimpse of his bulging cheekbones, flicked by the sunlight through the leaves, I was glad to have him. A Plains Indian, likely Lakota. I chuckled and signed him to get his scalp knife out. We were closing in on the enemy.

At that moment, a heavy volley tore through the trees around us. Somebody screamed, another cursed, but nobody was hit that I could see. A few yards beyond where I crouched, the sun was streaming into a clearing and yellowing the tall Cuban grass. "Soldiers," I cries, "spread out in here while you still got cover." They began wriggling away. "When I give you a whoop, we all break out, shooting. I want to hear a thousand rounds, sprayed right into that ridge line."

I crouched there, wiping the sweat from my eyes, then checked the breech of my Winchester. I had a full magazine, so I stuffed another fistful of cartridges into the pocket of my white cottons where they'd be quicker to get at. "Gad," says a voice beside me, "this is the most thrilling hunt we'll ever be on, Kelly."

I grins. "Well, if it ain't the Fish! I figured you was back with

Teddy. Didn't nobody tell you, never volunteer for patrol!"

His eyes danced and he gripped my shoulder. "I wouldn't miss this chance, my friend, not for the world. It must look like the old days to you, Kelly."

"Yas," I grunts, "and they don't get no easier, lad." I squinted at him, because tied around his big neck was a pair of extra boots. "You figurin' on walkin' a long way, Fish?"

"No," he said, and a strange frown crossed his handsome face. "I want to give these away to someone who can use them. You, Kelly. You'll make it."

When he started to hand them to me, I struck them down. "Keep 'em yourself. When it rains, them rotten issue they give us come apart. Two pair will come in handy. Now, be sure you're loaded. Then follow me out. We're going now, Fish."

Just as I stood up, a volley struck, but the bullets were high, ripping leaves. I caught a glimpse of my boys, flinging themselves forward into the clearing, black shirts, khaki pants, their Krags booming. "Take the ridge," I cries. "Run, damn you!"

One single shot whined past me, splatting with the sound of a rock dropping into a pail. When I flung myself back into the tall grass, Fish was lying there with a bullet through his brain. His eyes were staring at the sun that he'd never see again.

He was the first of the Rough Riders to go down. When I dragged him back after the ridge had been taken, he still had the extra boots around his neck. I wondered what he knew that I didn't. While I was giving the boots to another man, T.R. come up and stood wide-legged, staring at his old pal. Slowly, he took a step toward him, and stumbled over his damn sword. Dazed, he brushed his hand across his eyes and whispered, "It had to be. Yes. We're still doing the right thing, Kelly. We have to go on. It's only on."

The death of poor Fish choked me with the folly of this war. A lark, was it, a thrilling big game hunt that the dandies would be telling about for years in their private clubs? Ah no, me byes, save the glory for your dreams. The rotten jungle of Cuba began echoing with the wail of dying heroes. Captain Bucky O'Neill, who'd chased down desperadoes on the frontier, was so cocky that he claimed they hadn't yet made the bullet that could kill him. As he paraded before the lines, smoking a cigarette, a sniper in a tree blew half his head off. Day after day, more of the brave dumb sheep ended up rolled into ponchos and dumped into wet, moldy graves. By the time we hit the San Juan ridge of hills on July 1, bulky Fred Remington was kneeling beside me, sobbing. Stretcher bearers were slogging past us, hauling still more boys to the boneyard. "Atrocious. Obscene. I can't stand watching this," he whispered. Later, I read someplace that it had taken him a year to get over the nightmare of it. Well hell, what could you expect from a feller used to sitting in the sun, painting pictures of gallant troopers? Past glories, the yarns of old veterans were all he'd known. War, he figured, shouldn't have been any different than the football matches he'd played at Yale college.

What a hornet's nest we run into that morning of July 1. Like the fight at Crazy Woman Fork, the grand plans of the Army got knocked into a cocked hat. I never saw such stupidity in any battle, or panic either. The generals were ordering us to charge up an ugly, tawny ridge of hills that stood between us and the port city of Santiago. But as I swept the target with my field glasses, I saw a death trap. The hills were scarred with black trenches and silvery ribbons of barbed wire. Every crest had a blockhouse with thick concrete walls. There were fortified ranch houses, too, with red tile roofs the color of blood. In gun pits behind them were batteries of artillery, trained on us by God knows how many thousand Spaniards. Even as we watched the ridge that dawn, we could see the enemy strolling around in their pale blue pajamas and straw hats, like they was waiting for a Sunday school picnic to begin. One proud feller stood out in the open, leaning on a cane and puffing a seegar.

We were trapped between the Spaniards in front and the jungle behind. Joe Wheeler or wheezing old General Shafter, who was too fat even to mount his horse, had pumped so many troops up those jungle trails that it was like trying to push ants into a bottle. Whole outfits were jamming into each other, the lead ones mired in mud. But there wasn't anyplace to go or spread out. The jungle was too thick to crawl into. Trapped on the few trails, the men were sitting ducks, and the Spanish knew it.

They had their field guns calibrated to blast every known trail and each clot of desperate men. With their long-range rifles, all they had to do was fire high and soak the jungle with lead. They couldn't help but hit somebody. Barrage after barrage came howling down from the ridge, white, hissing puffs shattering the palm trees, the trunks crashing down, and in the mud below, poor jammed-up soldiers screaming and dying and howling for mercy.

On one stretch of trail that wasn't any longer than a city block, four hundred troopers got shredded into corpses, and nobody could even fight their way through the milling panic to haul the bodies away. I thanked my stars that I wasn't on that trail right then. I'd scurried up a hill about a half mile behind the slaughter. Our artillery troopers and some Cuban rebels had captured a Spanish blockhouse, and were already wheeling our field guns into place. T.R. had sent me here to take care of Mister Hearst. The nabob himself had decided that since this was the grandest attack of his damn war, he wanted to watch it from a front-row seat.

When I runs up the hill, our field guns had already started roaring away, hurling iron at two other ridges, off to our right. The hard-bitten Apache veterans, Generals Chaffee and Lawton, were charging these positions, which flanked us. "Splendid plan," cried some officer, explaining it to Hearst. "It's going like clockwork." The idea was, Chaffee and Lawton's bluebellies would have an easy time taking those hills. No handful of Spanish could stop our regular troops. Then the boys would swoop down and join the volunteers and the black Tenth Cavalry for the storming of San Juan ridge.

Clockwork, hell. Even with all the powder smoke, the shells ripping and shattering the jungle, the Spaniards wouldn't give up those hills. New troopers were already streaming past us to join that fight. Then I hear 'em shouting, "Why, Willie's here! That's Willie!" They were pointing at a sad-faced gent in a felt hat and business suit. He was sitting uneasy on a big guvmint horse, and not answering the boys, like he was sore that they were mocking him. But they began shaking his hand and saying, No, no, they were glad he was here. "Thank you, boys," he said. "Good luck, now. God be with you," and waved them on.

I grabbed hold of Hearst's leg on the horse, and told him I was Kelly, T.R.'s man, to keep him out of trouble.

"Why, I wouldn't call this trouble, would you? The attack is proceeding beautifully. Beyond anyone's expectations. They can't stand up against that." He flicked his hand at our field guns, crashing one after another and kicking back on their skids in recoil.

"Git down off that horse, mister," I says.

"What?"

"Right now! Bad place for you."

A staff major rushes up. "You're talking to Mr. Hearst, soldier. He can be anyplace he wants!"

"Then get your own goddamn heads blowed off," I cried, and flung my arm toward the ridges where our shells were exploding. "You haven't taken out them hills like you said, and they still got artillery there, and over on San Juan. You pull your guns up here and start blasting, them Spaniards got eyes. They'll find out where the shells are coming from. Move, Hearst," I says, swatting his horse away from him, for he'd dismounted. Grabbing him by the arm, I starts hurrying him away from the gun batteries.

We hadn't but toppled off the backside of the hill when there's an ear-splitting crash, flaming roaring, the blockhouse exploding, chunks of wall whistling out, bodies of Cuban rebels and our boys blasted like black crows into the sky. Hearst was screaming, quivering there as I pulled him down under me and we crouched together with the whole hilltop blowing now, a second Spanish round ripping square into our guns. Pieces of steel and rock were pelting down, stinging us.

"Oh, my God," Hearst breathed. "You saw that coming."

"And more," I grunts. "You're in the wrong place, mister."

He blinks. "But I can't run. Nobody's running. I have to write about this."

"You'll do it from the hospital tents, sir. The Spanish ain't blasting the Red Cross yet, but if they come to it, you'll still be far enough back to duck most of it."

He was flustered, frowning. "But Kelly, my horse. I can't walk. This heat is unbearable."

I glanced toward the hilltop where stretcher bearers were already scurrying through the smoking wreckage, shattered guns, caissons and mangled flesh. "Your horse ain't gonna feel the heat, Mr. Hearst. Come on now, I'll get you to a cool place."

I led him about a mile off to the headquarters tent. General Shafter was lying here, fanning himself under a palm tree. The bugger was so fat he couldn't button his uniform, and his belly was bulging out his underwear. The heat had got him. He was too sick to lead the troops. Hearst grabs me by the arm and says, "This man saved my life, General."

"I'm glad of that," Shafter grunted. "I wish he could do the same for those poor soldiers up front." As I turned to go, he called after me. "If you see Leonard Wood or that damn cowboy, Roosevelt, ask them why in the name of heaven they're still stalling their attack. I've sent two separate orders to them by courier."

I nods, Yessir, and starts toward the jungle where the front lines were supposed to be. About a mile from headquarters, I come on some weary soldiers, skidding a young lieutenant's body through the mud. He was one of Shafter's couriers. What happened to the other nobody knew.

God help me, the jungle along the banks of the San Juan river was a blazing hell. The troopers were packed so tight at the fords that I could hardly wedge my way through them. Pack mules, hit and braying, were splashing down and kicking their legs in the air. Steady fire from the mausers was rattling the trees like handfuls of gravel. Then big Spanish shells would crack and hiss flame. More would go down. Wild-eyed men, some of them black troopers, were running past me toward the rear, and just as many shoving them back to fall in the mud and curse. Why wasn't there any order to get out of here and charge?

Then, to make matters bloody comical, lifting up above San Juan ridge, what do I see but a big yellow air balloon, with two men in a wicker basket dangling below it. Troopers around me were shouting, "Them Signal Corps bastards. They're drawing fire right onto us! Move the damn thing away from here!"

But the balloon was stuck, its thick tether rope fouled up in the tops of the palm trees, and nobody could get it loose. By now, every Spaniard in the country was shooting at the fat thing, and every piece of lead was raining down on us.

As I stumbled into the San Juan river, which was only knee-deep, a horseman comes galloping past me, drenching me with spray. He was a tall man, stiff as a ramrod. His campaign hat was gone and floating in the river, but his lungs were sure unharmed. He was sonofabitching every black trooper who wouldn't cross the river, shoving the lads until he had most of them clawing their way up the far bank. Then he stands in his stirrups and shouts, "Miserable cowards, pissing your pants. Black cur dogs, where's your pride! I've trained you to fight. Now fight!" When I slogged over to him, he whirled to me, with his Colt revolver aimed at my face. "If you're one of mine, get up there and join your men!"

I chuckled. "Well, Mister Pershing, when you made me Sergeant Kelly at Wounded Knee, I sure never expected to be back with you again, not in this shooting gallery!"

He leaned down and scowled at me. "The hell you say! Is it Kelly? Yes, by God, my sergeant!" He holstered his revolver and clapped my mitt. "Damn I'm glad to see you! Get in there with my people. Put some starch into them. Shoot any scum who tries to quit!"

As he spoke, a Spanish shell whistled and blasted into the river, so close it ripped us with spray, but no iron that I could feel. Pershing's horse bolted into me and would have knocked me down if I hadn't grabbed hold of his stirrup. "Get out of this place!" Pershing roared. "Inexcusable to hold us here, taking such fire! Where in hell is their goddamn order!"

"Sir," I shouts, "I just come from Shafter. He wants you to go. Sent two couriers but they ain't made it!"

Right then, a horse comes splashing up with the little Joe Wheeler bouncing in the saddle. When the next Spanish round hisses over us, he glances at it like it was no more than a gnat. "I haven't seen this much shell since the War," he snaps. "Invigorating."

Pershing bellowed, "General Wheeler, do I have an order to charge the Tenth?"

Wheeler grins at the young Pershing, and there in the sunlight, I couldn't help but think, Here's the Civil War and the Indian Wars all rolled into one. And how many more fights would there be? For Pershing, probably many, but for the old Rebel, this was his last. "Take your men, sir," he drawls, "and remove the Spanish from that ridge."

Pershing salutes and starts to wheel away. "Hold on," Wheeler cries. "Bring young Roosevelt into it when you pass his position. He's been champing."

"Sir," I says to the General, "I'm hunting the Rough Riders

anyway. I can bring the order."

"Do so. Be quick! We'll win this day." Then he smiled in the sun. Pershing and the black troopers were already thundering up the far bank. "Hoorah!" Wheeler pipes, and spurs his mount after them.

There are times in a battle when things look so damn hopeless you want to lay down and die. And yet other times, for no real reason, the terror of huddling and hurting seems to fall away. No time to think what could happen. Suddenly you're moving, looking at the blue sky and every fine wisp of a blade of grass, each step getting freer and freer, as you move closer to life, or death. At least now, you won't be waiting any more. You'll get it settled.

When I found T.R., he was striding back and forth in a grove of palm trees. His men were lying down behind the trunks and some were shooting listlessly at the Spanish ranch houses on a hill above us. "That there is Kettle Hill, Teddy," I says, having seen it when I was skulking through the lines after leaving the rebels.

He blinks. "But we're attacking San Juan. Aren't those still the orders?"

"Specs, I don't know, but somebody's got to start moving or we won't have nobody left. Pershing's already going toward Kettle," and I pointed to a few black troopers running at a crouch up through the long, tawny grass.

"Bully!" cried T. R. "Join them, boys!" He turns, grabs his horse and starts to mount.

"Don't, Specs."

"But I have to lead the charge, dammit!"

"You're better off afoot. Them sharpshooters pick out officers, and mounted, you got colonel's leaves painted all over you."

"Yes, I suppose you're right. But I have to be in the front. I want to be! Not fair to ask others to do it."

I grins. "You'll be doing it well enough, Teddy. You'll get your war. Let's go."

Up we went, and the thing that struck me, there were so damn few. Later, Richard Harding Davis, who was with us, wrote that it was just a handful of men, scattered out, lonely little battles, mostly one by one, walking and half running up that slope. The paintings in the saloons would show bugles tooting glory, and Teddy bravely charging his steed up across the bodies of the Spaniards. But it wasn't that way at all.

Not that he wasn't brave. He was just as dumb and scared as the rest of us. That's brave, walking toward the hill in the sun, bullets hissing every which way, men screaming and dying on every side. Pershing's black troopers were soon mixed up with us. Their blood was just as red as ours, and I got it splashed on me as I carried one gut-shot lad back to his rest.

In the trenches above, the Spanish fought us with everything they had—artillery, machine guns, rifles at close range. To me, it was just a blur of their blue pajama uniforms, straw hats kiting into the air as our Krag slugs ripped them. Pretty soon, our boys were roaring, leaping the first trenches, cutting the barbed wire and racing toward the bullet-pocked walls of the old Spanish ranchhouse. There was a big kettle atop the hill, probably used once for cooking sugar cane. Bullets pranged into it. Spaniards were running out of the backside of the buildings now. It looked like we finally had the place.

Just as I leaped the last trench, a bullet whizzes a hot stripe across my left leg. I felt my cotton pants rip and there was blood on them. As I looked up, two young Spaniards were crouching in the trench, their Mausers aimed at me, glinting in the sun. I fired my Winchester from the hip, once, twice, three times. One screamed, and when I ran to them, they were both lying in the trench, reddening circles of blood soaking their pajamas.

One of them was kicking his legs, twitching. I knelt down beside them, to be sure they were gone, and wouldn't shoot me in the back.

They were gone all right. With the roaring of the battle raging in the background, the shouts of our boys and the rippling of our flags, I looked at the faces of the Spaniards. Enemies, was they? Hell, mere lads. One of them was black-haired, handsome, too, with a curving moustache. The other was blond, with a big farmboy's face, and eyes as blue as the seas he'd crossed, to come all this way to die.

He had a crucifix around his neck. I reached out to touch it, but then, a fierce dizzyness come over me. "I didn't hate either of you," I whispers, so what am I doing here, making you die?

A few yards beyond me, T.R. was running, waving his revolver. "We have it!" he cried. "It's ours!"

It was, that. We'd won his war. Only, like the boys I'd just gunned down, it was going to fling us across more and more seas, more years of dying for all the black, red, yellow and brown skins we were supposed to be setting free.

Ah, God help me, I mutters, why? Why do we have to?'

I cut the cross from the Spanish soldier's neck and slid it into my pocket. If he couldn't pray any more, maybe I'd better start. I was getting to that age when I'd need something more guiding me than just the madness of kill or be killed.

Yet, the very men who stood with me on that hill, Roosevelt, Pershing, and later Hearst, when he come up to see our victory, ah, them buggers would be in the thick of slaughter from then on. Not their fault, maybe, not anybody's fault. Just the times we were in. We were powerless to stop it, the greed, the bloodlust that had gripped our world by the throat, and wouldn't let it go until we were choking and weeping in graveyards across all the far-flung seas.

335

CIVILIZE 'EM WITH A KRAG

After the short and sweet victory in Cuba, the jingo bunch had blood in their eyes and meant to grab whatever was loose for the taking. Over in England, Rudyard Kipling was crowing about "The White Man's Burden":

"Send forth the best ye breed,
go bind your sons to exile
to serve your captives' need.
To wait in heavy harness
On fluttered folk and wild—
your new caught, sullen peoples,
half devil and half child."

To me, what we was doing stunk, and I wasn't alone in smelling the rat. In Washington, when the nabobs were trying to decide how best to grab the Philippines, a Senator named Hoar rises up and says, "If this be the first step in the acquisition of dominion over barbarous archipelagos in distant seas, if we are to enter into competition with the great powers of Europe in the plundering of the Pacific, China, Africa, if our commerce is hereafter to be forced upon unwilling peoples at the cannon's mouth, if we are to govern subjects and vassal states, trampling as we do it on our own great Charter which recognizes alike the liberty and dignity of individual manhood, then let us resist this thing to the death!"

Amen! I wanted to shout when I sees his speech in the paper. But McKinley, riding high with the success in Cuba, was now saying it would be "cowardly and dishonorable" if we gave the Philippines back to Spain. Nor could we hand 'em to France and Germany, "our commercial rivals in the Orient." And of course we couldn't leave the little brown brothers to govern themselves because they were "unfit and would have anarchy." Solution: "take the Philippines, educate the Filipinos, uplift, civilize and Christianize them as our fellow men for whom Christ also died."

On the strength of that hogwash, off to war we went again. In 1900, the birthday of our new century, I uprooted my dear ones and bundled the lot of us across the seas to the splendid Spanish city of Manila, capitol of the Philippine Islands. At that time, it was filled with mud and carabaos, which are water buffaloes, and thatch houses called nipa huts, side by side with beautiful Spanish haciendas. We lived in one of these, an enormous, spooky place with thick walls and angels painted on the ceilings. Barefoot servants were always pattering in to fan us or bring us ice, and in the flaming sunsets out on the verandah, they'd be serving lemon punches to beautiful American ladies, who were wives of our officers or diplomats. In their starchy white uniforms, the military men were erect, handsome, and courtly as knights. They spoiled little Nora rotten. It reminded me of old Crookie in Arizona, these warhorse generals and admirals trotting my little daughter on their knees and nuzzling her with their beards.

The first word I ever heard Nora say was "dapdap." In Tagalog, the Filipino language, it means a flame tree. We had a grand old one in our garden in Manila. Cruz, the Filipina nanny Daisy had hired for the kids, would set Nora down naked under the tree, and the scamp took to eating the leaves. "Be careful now, darlin'," I'd say, "or your hair will be turning the same color as them fiery things."

Well, neither tree nor God could change the spots on that little one. A redhead she become, even redder than my sister, Nora, and with a flame in her eyes that was going to make trouble for men all her life. Even as a tyke, when I saw her proud, independent ways, I groans to Daisy, "Who in the world is ever going to tame that one? I sure can't."

Daisy laughed. "Well, you'd better start learning, Patrick. I sometimes think she's got the worst traits of both of us. Spoiled, manipulative. A little rebel if there ever was one. What we sow we reap, darling. The only answer I know is to love her to death."

"That's my trouble, Daisy. I do love her, too much. Men I know. I can handle the wars of men. But a daughter for an Irish father, ah, I ain't no expert in the wiles of woman. Maybe it's like Teddy Roosevelt trying to handle that beauty he spawned. One day in the White House he says to me, 'Kelly, I can either be President or raise Baby Lee Alice, but I cannot do both.'"

It might have been a gentle time at home all right, but there was a spot on the dress, and a bloody one at that. Our rotten war against the Filipinos had turned into a snakepit. Though my assignment was to the Secret Service where I wasn't supposed to get shot at, I ducked more than enough rounds before it was done.

On top of it, I started having family troubles. During those years, I never wrote much down, for of all the fighting I hate, squabbling with my dear ones is at the top of the list. Daisy was trying hard to be a loyal military wife, but the sadness in her pretty face was like a knife in my heart. She didn't want to be here, or me to have any part of it. Again, it went back to her cousin, T.R. "He's pulling you around like one of his wolfhounds on a chain, Patrick," Daisy would say. "How long is this going to go on?"

I sure didn't know. After McKinley was shot down by an anarchist, T.R. took over as President, and from that moment on, I knew we'd be leaping from one war into the next because that was the ferocious bugger's way. To give him his due, though, it wasn't all his fault. He'd inherited a bloody mess.

One night out on the verandah, Daisy lit into me good about it. Young Matty was the reason, she said. The servants had taken the dinner dishes away. It was dark and hot under the big flame tree, and no sound but the distant city and over our heads the clicking of insects and the glow of fire flies. Daisy was shadowy white in her Spanish lace gown with puffed sleeves. "Tell your father," she says to Matty, "what you told me."

"I want to hear, too," Nora exclaimed. The restless little thing never could sit at the table when dinner was finished. She was down on the flagstones playing with a green iguana I'd bought her at the Escolta market.

"Oh, Nora," Daisy sighed, "I don't know which you torment worse, that creature or us. Will you please put him in his cage."

"Ah, darlin'," I says, "let her play. He don't hurt nothin', can't bite, don't have teeth." Then I turned to Matty who was sitting there with the darkness on his Sioux cheekbones and his teeth a hard white line. "What did you want to know, son?"

"Are you a spy? My friends at school say that's what you are. You go around like a Filipino, sure, your pleated linen shirt there and baggy pants. But just where do you go, Papa? Why do you hang around the cantinas listening to people, and then talk on the telephone late at night?"

"There's different kinds of wars, Matty."

His eyes flared. "Our soldiers wear uniforms! Aren't you proud of our uniform?"

I sighed. Matty was 12 when he come to Manila. Now he was nearly 15, gone to the American school with the kids of the MacArthurs and the other high brass. He'd started to sprout up long-limbed and strong, played at football and baseball like he was on the warpath. But deeper down, he was like the ashes of a smouldering fire. Late every night, he'd be up reading one book after another. Just like his Injun mother, he had a shell inside him, his own way of looking at the world that I could never penetrate. One thing for sure, he was too smart and hard to be put off by some fairy tale. Quietly I says, "Yes, son, you can call me a spy if you like, but what it really is is military intelligence. We've got a lot on our hands out here, and any war I can head off by hearing a slip from some Filipino, that'll spare enemies and our lads, too."

"Then I'm sorry for you, Papa."

"Ah? Why is that, now?"

"I thought you were a horse soldier?"

"I was."

338

"That's all you know," he said sharply. "I've read about the campaigns, the wiping out of Mother's people at Rosebud and Wounded Knee. Back then, you sent messages by horse."

"Ah, the tellygraft line worked once in a while," I cut in.

"Primitive! You never had any telephones. You didn't even know where you were most of the time. Just wilderness, wasn't it, three columns groping around with no communication? Your General Crook didn't even know where General Custer was!"

"That's right, and we all paid for it, son."

"But now," he cried, "here you are, an old man in the middle of fleets of warships, even autos and trucks churning around. We're thousands of miles away from what you know. We've crossed all the oceans. Where does it end, Papa?"

"How in hell do I know, Matt. But when you're a soldier—and you got the military bug in you, I can see that—you go where they send you, you do what they say. I ain't smart enough to figure the why of it."

"Oh, it's all so obscene!" Daisy cried, and her hand trembled as she finished her wine. "He won't tell you the truth, Matty, and anyway, you already know it, that's why you're so upset! The Spanish war was a fraud. Now we know. Teddy's little toy soldier war that won him the White House."

"It had to be, Mother," Matt answered coldly. "The Lakota people never shrank from wars that were necessary."

"Oh, rot!"

"It won us Cuba, Puerto Rico, Guam and the Philippines. The Spanish had no right there. Empires are over, particularly European ones."

"And what about ours? The glorious American Empire. Don't you listen to the song, Matty? 'Oh, the monkeys have no tails in Zamboanga. Under our starry flag, civilize the kakiak ladrones with a Krag.' That's what we're doing, outright murder of brown people whom we consider lessers!"

"Darlin'," I said gently, "it ain't so, and let's not start this again."

"What's a Krag?" Nora said, cuddling her lizard against her breast.

"Our U.S. rifle now," Matt snapped, "and a poor excuse for a weapon. You'd think this great nation could do better!"

"Great nation?" Daisy echoed.

Gently I took her hand. "Come, darlin', we'll take a walk under the stars, all of us, the lizard, too, and forget this politickin'. Just guff, can't do nothin' about it nohow."

"Oh, Patrick," she sighed and withdrew her small, moist hand, "sometimes your simplicity is perfectly appalling. It's so common of you, just to plod along like a drayhorse, taking orders that you don't even understand. Your son is trying to find out why we're here and what this all means. Tell him! We're in a pointless war—yes, Teddy inherited it, but he loves it, too—a war that has dragged on for years now, hundreds of thousands of people being killed, including so many of our poor soldiers out in the heat and swamps of these islands. Your history books that you're always reading, Matt, well, they lie. Our apparent reason for going to war with Spain was to set free the poor people of Cuba and the Philippines. In Cuba, the Spanish had driven the native populace into concentration camps. We were going to put an end to that barbarity, right?"

"We threw the Spaniards out, Daisy," I cried. "We done somethin', and you better remember it. It pains me to see you so bitter all the time!"

"Oh, yes, Patrick, we put an end to it, but how! We're now doing exactly the same thing as the Spanish! Right here under our noses, our own brave lads, as you call them, have been ordered to herd thousands of Filipinos into concentration camps. They were our allies, Matthew. They fought beside us against the Spanish, nobly I might say, but when we realized that their sin was only their longing to be free of us, free of our domination, we turned against them with every weapon we had. Tell him the truth, Patrick. How your admired friend, that cocky little Freddy Funston, sneaked into the camp of the Filipino patriots and captured their leader, Aguinaldo. Cut the very heart out of their resistance. Are we proud of that?"

"Well, goddammit, I am, Daisy!" I cried. "Funston did a brave thing and won the Congressional for it, too!"

Nora had crawled up into my lap. "Momma, you've got Poppa all red and shaking. Please leave him alone!"

"Medals," Daisy whispered. "Tell that to the Filipinos in our concentration camps. Without Aguinaldo, they've lost all hope. Who would think that in our desire to scorch this land and win, we would have become just as beastly as the Spaniards we replaced?"

There wasn't no point trying to reason with her, which was maybe why I don't want to remember them years. I was gone so much anyhow that she and I just seemed to pass each other in the dark halls of the big house. I'd lay down tuckered out and smell her perfume in our bed, but when I'd reach for her, though she never protested, she was gone from me in her heart and I didn't know how to bring her back.

One night late, when she was already in bed, three men come by the house. One was Army General Adna Chaffee. With his powerful build and handlebar moustache, he was every inch a soldier. We had a warm reunion, chuckling about that mess at Kettle Hill in Cuba where Chaffee's regulars got pinned down by the Spanish blockhouses and left us to take the high ground all alone. We went further back, too. While I was serving with Captain Crawford in the Sierra Madre of Mexico, Chaffee was chasing Apaches down on the desert below us. Miserable wars like them bond men together in ways that Daisy or no woman would ever know. That night, Chaffee had brought with him a heavy-set Marine Colonel named Littleton Waller. Though I hadn't been much exposed to Marines, I was damn glad to have this mean bastard on my side. He had the leathery look of an old toad and if he ever smiled, I never saw it. The third feller was a puffy-faced civilian who wore a tall celluloid collar. He'd come from Peking, where he'd been doling out food to the poor starving Chinese. His name was Herbert Hoover, and though he was a quiet-spoken engineer type, he had a confident way about him that pretty well shrugged off the danger he was about to lead us into.

We left for China that very night. While I was packing my campaign khakis and two revolvers, damn if Daisy didn't come sweeping in, her eyes red with tears, and Matty and Nora trotting after her in their night shirts. "The least you could do," she said, "is to tell your children why this is necessary. I'll never be convinced, but maybe they will."

"I'm under orders, Daisy, and there ain't time to talk about it, neither."

Poor little Nora took it hard, wanting to know where China was and why these funny-looking people were always killing each other. Matty been following the China war in the papers, and told Nora it was a religious uprising of fanatics called Boxers.

Nora's eyes widened. "You mean they wear boxing gloves?"

"Couldn't shoot if they did," Matt snapped. "Of course not, Nora. They're just wild men, killing thousands of civilians. They drove out the Empress of China and are smashing down her palaces and stealing her gold."

"Oh, Papa," Nora cried, "it's like a terrible fairy story. I don't want to hear anymore."

"Now, darlin'," I says and hugs her, "there ain't nothin' to this, and I'll be back before you even miss me."

"But isn't it true," Matt said, "that they're attacking the foreign embassies? The paper says that the Germans, French, English, Russians and Japanese are all sending soldiers to protect the wives and children trapped in the embassies."

"Son," I says wearily, "I don't know. I'll find out when I see it." Then I held Daisy to me, so frail and soft in the silk of her nightgown. "Does it have to be now?" she whispered.

I closed my eyes and swayed there, clinging to her. "Papa and these officers," Matty said to Nora, "are going over there to save the white-skinned people from the wrath of the yellow race."

It was months before I come home again. What happened on

those dusty China plains and in their stinking walled cities was a smear of more war I didn't even have time to write down. Ah, sure, we finally did save the embassies and the wives and kiddies. It was all mixed up in the politics and confusion of the great powers, everybody looking out for their own, and nobody knowing who was in command. I had one bad night that I thought I'd never live through, and wouldn't have if it weren't for a scrappy little lad named Smedley Butler. He was a Marine lieutenant that I fell in with when a column of us was trying to rescue a garrison of English sailors and their Admiral, cut off in an armory along the Yangtse River. Hell, Butler, a spindly little Quaker from Philadelphia, didn't have 50 Marines with him. Why, I thinks, this punk ought to be back home in the meeting house, calling his momma "thee," and praying up a storm, rather than catching it out here. How wrong I was! We had to plod miles in the darkness through a nasty stretch of flat country that didn't have nothing on it but mud hovels. Not a tree to hide behind, and what ditches there was were filled with human slime. We had several mules with us, packing our Browning machine guns, and the rest was just two files of tall, tough Marines, swinging along as cocky as if they were on the parade ground. These were old China hands, and Central American hands, hell, they'd been in every war, riding the Great White Fleet out across the waves to bust through all our frontiers. When we began hearing the Chinks closing in on us in the darkness, there were thousands of them, whipped up by the screaming Boxers and ready to die and bring a foreign devil down with them. "Butler, lad," I whispers, "there ain't a way in hell we're ever going to get through these buggers."

He smiles and raises his wispy hand. "Men," he says to his hardfaced Marines, "they're not armed well, and what they have, they don't know how to use. You will only shoot when shot at, and when you shoot, you will kill. Follow me, we go."

By God if they didn't stream right along behind him. I heard an old sergeant grunt, "Hell, the only bullet that kid ever heard was in Cuba, and that scared the shit outta him because I was beside him and seen. He ain't but twenty years old!"

Another Marine cracks, "The Chinks don't know that. Let's give our little boy a graduation party!"

Damn if they didn't. When the Boxers started flaming their smoothbores and fowling pieces at us, not a Marine broke ranks. Once and a while, I'd hear a shot hit home, somebody'd fall, and other Marines would just shoulder the lad and march on. At first, the Chinese were awed by such bravery, and Butler must have known it. Finally, though, they just went plain mad, hundreds of the screaming banshees blocking our road. Butler must have seen the moment coming, for he had the Browning machine guns already down in the dirt. When they opened up, and the Marines with their rifles, a scythe of lead cut through those Chinese, and them that was left ran and scattered like quail. By dawn, we was in the Armory and saving the wounded English Admiral. "Tip-top, young man," the Admiral says to Butler, and the word must have got through to Washington. Before I left China, Butler had won his first Congressional Medal, and, if I had to bet on it, there'd be more coming to him down the road. It was a privilege to serve with a lad so brave, and, from the looks of him, so unsuited for war of any kind.

By the time I'd come home, I was plumb wore out and had a touch of Chinese bowel fever, too. In the dirtiness over there, you couldn't help catching something. I was just glad it wasn't lead. For many an hour out on the cool verandah, I'd doze in our big hemp swing, conscious of Daisy drifting around like a pale ghost, bringing me boiled milk, trying to plug up my runs. When Nora would come home from school in her blue and white convent dress, she'd cuddle beside me in the swing, wanting me to tell her some story or other, but I says, "I'm storied out, babe. You tell me what's in your pretty head." And she would, jabbering away until I fell asleep again.

One thing about the service life, though, the brass don't give a man much time to feel sorry for himself. One afternoon, General Chaffee come by, visited a bit and then said a single word: "Samar." The island of Samar. Things were bad down there with the Juramentados. These bloodthirsty natives were Moros with a real talent for avenging the supposed wrongs we'd done to 'em. What they'd do was bind their limbs with wire so tight that they couldn't feel any pain. Then they'd come screaming into some Army camp. Our lads would shoot at 'em, but the bullets seemed to have no effect. Whipping their razor-sharp *krisses* around their heads, they'd butcher any soldier who stood in their path. "A Springfield won't stop them, Kelly," Chaffee says to me that afternoon. "Nor will the .38 service revolver. I've told Washington repeatedly that I want a new weapon developed. They've finally done it." Grinning, with a tug at his moustache, he beckons at his aide who takes a blue, bulky automatic pistol out of his briefcase and hands it to me.

"Colt Arms did this for us," Chaffee says. "You're looking at a .45 caliber with tremendous muzzle velocity and stopping power. You hit a man even in the arm with that, Kelly, you knock him flat on his ass."

I hefted the weapon. "Well, General, it sure looks ugly enough. How does she shoot?"

"Helluva kick. Better to steady it over your forearm." Then he smiles and lays the Colt beside me on the hammock. "We've got a boat leaving for Samar tonight. New troops. I want you to take this weapon down and familiarize our officers with it out in the camps. They'll be getting their own issue models very shortly, but in the meantime, they need a show of force, to give them some hope of good things to come."

"General," I says, "weak as I am, I can't hardly heft this thing."

He grinned and slammed a clip into the Colt. "Salubrious climate down on Samar, Kelly. You'll get better fast. Nobody is asking you to fight. Just look around for me and size things up."

I went to Samar, all right, and like always in the wars I'd seen, they never turned out as expected. I run some shootin' lessons with the new Colt, the last of which brought me to a small, lonely outpost at a nipa town called Mabang. There wasn't no Moros around, just our tired soldiers plodding through daily drills and digging new latrines in the wet, putrid earth. Come Sunday morning, I heard the church bell ringing in the valley town below our camp. Having nothing better to do, I strolls down there and peeks inside the frame church, sweltering under its thatch roof. I might as well admit it, with my heart aching for Daisy and not knowing how to reach her anymore, I was hoping to get a glimpse of some of them pretty Filipina gals. Ah, I wouldn't bed one down. I was beyond that. Maybe just set her down under a banyan and josh her a little in Spanish like I used to do with senoritas in the Mexican campaign.

But I'd just peered into the church and signed myself with the Holy Water when I realized that something bad was wrong. The church was full, but there wasn't a gal or old crone or kiddie in it. Wherever there were Latin people, the women did the praying. These here were all men, half-naked, wiry Moros, and sneaking dirty looks at me, too.

I backed out of the church and slid into the jungle where I hoped they couldn't see me. Then I ran like hell up the hill to camp, shouting at the tents for the Officer of the Day. Hell, I could have fired a cannon and roused nobody. The officers had had a party the night before. They were all lying drunk or sleeping it off. A few enlisted men in undershirts were shuffling into the mess tent for breakfast. "Break out your goddamn rifles!" I shouted, but they were chain-locked in the First Sergeant's tent, and he'd gone off to bed down his Filipina girl. By the time I'd got one second lieutenant out of his cot and pulling on his boots, here come blood-curdling cries. The Moros from the church and others from the jungle were racing through the camp, their *krisses* spraying blood as they cut off the heads of three lads in the medical tent. Then it was awful pandemonium, soldiers and officers stumbling awake, tripping over tent ropes, only to be swarmed by the screaming devils and hacked to bits. I fired all the revolver ammunition I had, and in the confusion even lost the demonstrator Colt .45. It wasn't no use. I grabbed two wounded lads and we run for the river in the valley, outrun the damn *krisses* and finally swam to the far shore. One of the troopers died soon, and the other I got out, whimpering with me, until we struck the next garrison camp to the south, and told the awful news.

The Moros had butchered over a hundred of our lads, Kansas farm boys mostly, whose families and widows wished they'd never heard of Samar.

But General Chaffee sure did, and vowed that the Moros would remember this day. He come storming down with fresh troops, and wouldn't let me go, neither. Samar must burn, Samar must die. Colonel Waller brought a battalion of Marines, and another frontier General named Jakey Smith come in with artillery and cavalry. I never seen such angry troops. Them generals just slammed an iron lid down on Samar, and for the next six weeks, the world never heard a peep out of that cursed island. The combined force of soldiers and Marines had orders to hunt down and kill every Moro on Samar above ten years of age. Even tough Colonel Waller couldn't believe it. I heard him ask Jakey Smith, "You are saying women and children, General?"

"Any Moro," Smith roared, "above the age of ten!"

The ones who wouldn't talk or tell where their allies were hiding would get water poured down their throats until they drowned. We give 'em even worse tortures that I heard about, but thank God, didn't have to watch.

By the time I come back to Manila, the papers and Washington were raising hell about the outrage. The Moros never fought us again. Samar had been turned into a graveyard. General Smith and Colonel Waller were tried for barbarity, but T.R. pretty much winked at it. They'd ended his war, which was unpopular anymore and costing him votes. He let his killers off by retiring them early.

Me, though, I did my own quitting. Samar had been my last straw. By the time T.R. declared peace, lifting up the White Man's Burden had buried 4200 American soldiers, wounded another 2800. As for the Filipino rebels who wanted to be free, we killed 20,000 of them and left another 200,000 to die of disease and starvation. So much for Christianizing the brethren!

When I told Daisy we were going home and out, regardless of anybody's orders, the color rushed back into her face. We danced around in joy. She kept crying, "I don't want to believe it yet, darling!" But even at that, she was running the Filipina servants around, packing this and that and pressing dollars into their brown hands for their loyal service. Everybody was weeping, Nora and Matt already making plans for the new lives they'd begin at home, wherever home was.

A week later, we were on a troopship, carrying wounded back to the States. We hadn't but cleared the harbor at Cavite when I hugs Daisy. We stood together on the deck, watching that misty green and tortured island slipping away. "Say goodbye to it, darlin'," I whispers, "because we ain't never gonna see this stinkin' Orient again. Nothin' more to cross. Eastbound now."

She looked up at me, her soft brown eyes smiling. "But to what, Patrick?"

"To you, my Daisy. Ain't that enough?"

It should have been, by God, we both wanted it to be. But as I looked down at that bubbling, foaming wake of the transport, I had an awful fear that the sea wouldn't be barrier enough to keep us at home and at peace. The sea was like a curse that the western mountains had been for me, and the southern deserts after them. Whenever there was a horizon that still lay unexplored, we Americans would find a way to leap across it, wouldn't we? Curiosity, was it? Greed? Boldness? I didn't know, yet, being the brawling mix of people that we were, would we ever change?

I doubted it, and it was doubt that took us home, hoping to begin again.

A NIGHTMARE COME TRUE

So far on these pages I've told tales of war, and love, too. Though I was scared plenty, I never did think there was a bullet made that could stop me, or, for that matter, a woman who wouldn't love me as I loved her. So what I wrote down was the way things looked to me at the time. Out there, I was writing, not in here, in me.

I never did have the guts to talk about the deepest wound to my heart. I can't hardly bring myself to remember it. Yet, the truth is there and must be told. That's why I'm letting young Nora do it for me.

She went off her head at the end of them bad years. What they called a "nervous breakdown" struck her when she was in her first year at Vassar College. She give me some guff about a man in Vienna, Austria named Freud, and how he had a way of curing heads by letting the afflicted person spout out all the garbage from childhood on that was torturing the soul.

At Vassar College, they had a head doc who was practicing this voodoo, and he took poor Nora under his wing. Years later, when it didn't matter anymore, he give me a couple of her letters to him.

Vassar Infirmary
December 3, 1915

Dear Doctor Galt,

You want me to pick a moment when things started to go wrong—well, okay, I think it was that ocean voyage that was supposed to take us home from Manila. I was only six at the time, so I'm shaky on the details. My half-brother, Matt, being fifteen, remembers it far better than me. I wish he were writing this! He doesn't have trouble in the head. (All right, I'm not going to feel sorry for myself, promise!)

On our troop transport, bound for the Hawaiian islands and San Francisco, other officers and their wives were traveling with us, as were many common soldiers down in the holds below. One afternoon, near the island of Guam, which lay like a dirty sock floating on the turquoise Pacific, Mummy and I were lying in our stateroom taking a nap when the door burst open. A young woman was standing there screaming. She looked like a ghost! I'll never forget her! Mummy cried out her name which was Louise, Louise Barnard, wife of a second lieutenant who'd served with Papa on Samar. Mummy

347

was hugging her, stroking her face, whimpering, "Dear, dear girl, it's not your fault!"

I could hear whistles and people shouting up on deck. The ship was slowing as Papa stormed in and seized my hand, then collared Matt and told him to take me down to the officer's mess and keep me there. Louise Barnard and Mummy were still wailing as we trotted away. I said to Matt, "Is the ship sinking? What's happening?"

"No skin off you," he said. "Fortunes of war," or some remark that was so mean I wanted to punch his nasty mouth.

You can't keep things from a child. They shouldn't have tried. In a few minutes the news was all over the ship. Mrs. Barnard had two children, a five-year-old girl and an infant of about a year. The baby had colic or something and was always howling. I didn't blame her. Our staterooms were unbearably hot. We'd just lie there naked and sweat.

But Mrs. Barnard had opened the porthole to get some air in her room. When her baby kept screaming and screaming, the exasperated mother finally said, "If you don't behave, I'll have your sister throw you out the porthole."

When Mrs. Barnard's back was turned, oh, God, Doctor, the five year old did just that! She thought she was helping her mother! I can weep now, thinking of it. A poor infant splashing into the sea!

Oh, we slowed and the sailors looked with field glasses for the tiny body but everybody knew it was hopeless. Mummy stayed with Mrs. Barnard and they were giving her shots of morphine to calm her. The lieutenant almost went mad with grief. But that night, Papa was so sweet to Matt and me, trying to make us understand. He said it all had to do with the risks of serving the flag, frontier wives and their children suffering greatly out in the Indian fighting days. He mentioned a Captain's wife he'd known, a woman named Mrs. Bloxham. At a desert post, lightning had struck down her only child. "All of 'em ought to get medals," Papa said, "and the folks at home, the civilians, don't know a damn what them brave mothers go through."

Matt said, "When I'm a soldier, there won't be any wife or kids."

"Ah, g'wan with you," Papa chuckled. "You'll have a whole teepee full!"

Matt had short-cropped black hair that came low over his eyebrows. When he was angry, his forehead would wrinkle and get a red blot like a birthmark above his eyes. "That baby going out the porthole is a sign," he muttered. "You better listen to it, Papa."

"Too much listening gets your head ringy, son. The babe's with the Maker and you'd best leave it at that."

"I don't believe in a Maker that kills. But I suppose the Irish always hide behind superstition."

348

Papa flared, "No more than your mother's people done. Here you are talking about signs. Now quit pesterin' your sister with things she don't understand. Go down to the troop quarters and play dice with the soldiers."

That put Matt into one of his sour moods. He stalked off, which wasn't unusual. He and Papa were always scrapping. If Papa said something was black, Matt called it white. When I was involved it was even worse. I sensed early that Matt was jealous of me because he felt Papa gave me all the attention.

Right about then, our troop ship developed trouble with its boilers, so we had to get off and go ashore on Guam for a few days. Mummy was in such a rush to get home to her parents that she threw a tantrum, but Papa sure knew how to handle her. He was so romantic. "Why, it's a blessing, darlin'. We'll stretch our legs in the sea and live like Adam and Eve."

Apparently when they were first married, they'd had months of a glorious honeymoon in Hawaii, and now Papa was determined to do it all over again here on that wretched little island of Guam. One afternoon on the beach, I eavesdropped on them when they were lying in the sand, talking about what kind of work Papa would do when we came back to Mum's home in Lake Forest. Mum didn't want him to be a policeman in the Archibald factory, which Grandpa had offered when he heard Papa had quit military life. Papa just laughed and said, "Darlin', I may be broke, but there ain't money enough in the world to make me bust another workin' stiff's head."

Then Mum got prattling about a new club in Lake Forest, the Onwentsia. She'd heard they had riding horses there, and maybe Papa could teach little boys and girls how to jump hunters. They never did settle anything, though. Papa was so gentle with Mother, and kept covering up her tummy from the sun's rays. Right then, in her bathing suit, I noticed some swelling that she'd managed to hide in ordinary clothes. So I'd stumbled on their happy secret. After all their dangers and even arguments in Manila, they'd put their lives back together. Mum would have a baby quite soon.

Oh, Doctor, it was the curse of the child going out the porthole! I know you won't believe that, it's so unscientific! But we'd hardly gotten off the ship in San Francisco before Mum began feeling badly. Papa rushed her to Army medical treatment. The blow struck in such a cool and wonderful place. The Presidio, the old fort in San Francisco with its green lawns, whispering giant redwood trees, and the fragrance of the sea, rolling in with the fog.

At the military hospital there, with the best doctors, Mother's newborn infant was horribly premature and died at birth. The baby flung out to drown at sea? Papa wept heavily, and said, God's will, over and over, as if trying to make himself believe it. But all I could be was terribly scared.

Mother had an awful time. The birth damaged her somehow. Her female organs had to be taken along with the baby, for the doctors said that they would infect her if left intact.

It didn't dawn on me until months later that I was all the family we'd ever have. Yes, of course, Matt was my half-brother, but Mum's maternal days were done.

But by then, though, it was peaceful summer. We were back in the house where Mother had grown up, overlooking Lake Michigan. My uncles, Eben and Enoch, were both married and had several children about my age. We'd scamper around the big bluff where Mum played as a girl. Grandma Alice and Grandpa Commodore were so overjoyed to have us with them, we were just wrapped into a wonderful, strong family again, and I felt so happy and secure.

We settled in a little cottage, north up the bluff overlooking the lake, and not far from the Archibald estate. Papa got me my first real horse. We had dogs and cats, and I began my years at the Lake Forest town school, slowly forgetting my childhood Spanish and Tagalog. Matt went to Lake Forest Academy, preparing for West Point which by then obsessed him. As for Papa, he never did teach riding at the Onwentsia Club. He said he had better things to do than squashing some lady's powdered butt onto an English saddle. The truth was, he couldn't keep any civilian job even if he'd tried. He was just too ornery and proud to let anybody boss him around. Eventually, against Mum's wishes, he went back to doing his secret work that took him away a great deal. Other men in Lake Forest would ride the Northwestern train to the city each day, but if Papa went to an office, it was only some dark cubbyhole at Fort Sheridan, which was an Army post close to us, and meant to protect the city, though I'm not sure from what.

You ask, was I close to Mother? Yes. In some ways, very. But first and foremost, she was a soldier's wife, and oh, how bravely she lived that role. She and Papa were so much in love I felt there wasn't room in it for me. That was partly Papa's influence. He was a big believer in children making their own way in the world. Though he loved me and we giggled and played together well into my teens, he was the most permissive father anyone could have. If I'd do some dumb prank like trying to start our Reo motor car, once almost rolling it off the bluff, Papa would just shrug and pretend he didn't see it. "Sure and you've got to take risks, darlin'," he'd say, "and I'm not wanting to look in on you either. You'll be all right. You'll do fine."

So I learned how to grow up, you might say, with my cousins there, and school chums, and the eastern cousins, too, the Roosevelts. I particularly liked Quentin and Archie, the boys, and of course I worshipped glamorous Alice Roosevelt, who was already the image of a Gibson girl, and took great pains to preserve it.

As for the excitement of my girlhood, such grand and wonderful things were happening to the United States. According to my Archibald uncles, the country had never been more prosperous or, as Uncle Enoch put it, "cocky." We felt that as Americans, we could do anything, and we really had. Why, motor cars were humming around everyplace. Telephones had come. Men were even learning to fly, and I'd see the pictures of their soaring in the *Chicago Tribune*.

Oh, I'm sure that around the world there were some problems. Papa's work would send him to far-off places like Nicaragua or the island of Santo Domingo. But I don't think he was really fighting. When he'd come home, he'd scoff that they were strutting little banana peels, the leaders in these countries, tin horn nabobs who needed to be taken down a peg. He and Matt used to discuss each war with great interest, because by then Matt was at West Point. The first Christmas he came home, I was appalled at how lean and stuck-up he was in his tight cadet grays. You'd think in a few short months he'd learned everything there was to know about the Army and how to push the common soldiers around. Papa just shook his head and muttered, "Maybe in four years they'll hone you down, mister Shavetail, because if they don't, I'll tan you myself. I've seen them cocky Academy punks kill a lot of men, just to prove their braggado-cio. Don't you get that way, son."

"It's a different Army than you knew," Matt snapped. "I can take care of myself. They teach us years of tactics."

"Teach ain't learn!" Papa snorted. "You only get that lesson when you hear your first bullet."

Matt's lips tightened. "Who said I'm even going to get shot at? The Army offers many different careers, many smart ways to fight. Science, engineering, diplomacy. A soldier has to be a man of the world now, Papa, not just cannon fodder on a horse."

"We'll see about that, mister smarty," Papa grunted, but then, like always, Mum came in and pulled them apart. I know Papa was proud of Matt, but I also think he was jealous that his son had already risen in military terms far beyond anything an old cavalry-man immigrant could have known.

I was proud of Matt, too, particularly when he stopped treating me as a pest baby sister and took note that I was becoming a woman. The June he graduated in 1911, he actually took me on his arm to the Ferry Hall Spring Dance. Though I was only a freshman, I really lorded it over the other fat, pimply girls, not a one of whom had a mature, dashing lieutenant as their escort.

By now, American heroes had dug the Panama Canal, and Matt, being an engineering officer, won himself a good billet down at the

Culebra Cut. During my next Easter vacation, Papa took Mum and me down there to see the wonder of the great ships, steaming from the Atlantic to the Pacific. Uncle Teedie, whose idea the Canal was, put in an appearance, complete with booming cannon salutes. Matt knew just how to play on Teedie's vanity, and was all heel-snapping efficiency with the other high officers as well. We had a grand reunion, all right, but on the way home, Papa just shook his head, partly in admiration and partly sour grapes. "That little redskin cuss has got the system all figured out. He'll get his star one day, if he don't choke on his polish in the meantime."

Then, when Papa had work to do in Washington with the government, which he still called "guvmint," he'd leave us with the Roosevelt tribe at Sagamore Hill, Long Island. Really, none of my friends in Lake Forest or here at Vassar had the opportunity to see the world as I did.

But there was another side of that world, too, that I shall mention only briefly, because I think it's the one area in which my mother and father haven't totally agreed.

Perhaps it was the loss of a child, and not being able to have more, but as Grandma Alice Archibald would scoff, "Your mother is a restless radical who insists on wearing her heart pinned to her sleeve."

Grandmother opposed the fact that Mum felt a sympathy for the suffering and the poor, and indeed, for the cause of women. "Your father is a soldier," she said to me once. "That's all he's really ever known. But there's another war going on, Nora, in the city of Chicago and all cities like it, teeming with immigrants, riddled with injustice. Grandmother says that I can't even make a dent in it, so leave it alone. She's embarrassed that I try. But by God, girl, I will keep trying, and I hope you shall, in your time. The Gilded Age is not going to last forever, and we'd damn well better do something about that. Bring some justice to it, because if somebody doesn't, the whole scheme will crash down of its own foul weight."

Frankly, I'd shudder. It all sounded so grim, so far from anything I cared about. More and more by then, Mother was running off to settlement houses in the slums of Chicago. She was trying to force better conditions in the factories and sweatshops. Sometimes she'd even bring some of the raggedy immigrants home, and Papa wanted very little part of them. This struck me strange. He'd been an immigrant himself, and one night he grunted to Mum, "Well, nobody helped me and wiped my butt, Daisy, not by a longshot. The country wasn't founded on the idea of babying all the riffraff who come here. Let the buggers get off their soapboxes and go to work!"

"There is no work," she cried, "or at best, at fifty cents a day. They have to eat, Patrick!" He'd just sigh and go back to reading his paper.

352

Sometimes Mum would take me downtown to women's meetings, which I didn't much like. I've always been more attracted to men. These angry-faced dames with rimless glasses and stern buns of hair just made me uncomfortable. Papa could always see the light side, but he had as little use as I for these strident suffragettes. Mother would choke down me all kinds of statistics, wanted me to put them in a history paper when I got to college. How a quarter of the states denied a wife the right to own property, or a third of the states wouldn't let her keep the money she earned, even if she was supporting a shiftless husband. "A woman," Mother said, "has no claim on this nation, and least of all on her own body. She's a breeder slave, Nora, and we have to stop it!"

I resented her putting her guilts on me, saying I should do this or that about the affairs of grownups that I had absolutely no control over. Wasn't she ever a young girl, wanting to kick up her heels with boys and dancing and the like? She'd become so bitter by then that bad things happened in the family on account of her. Grandma Alice broke down and wept to me one night. She said that Mother's radicalizing, her turning so totally against her class, was the real cause of poor Grandpa, the Commodore, bursting his heart.

After he was gone, things only got worse. The great Archibald Hoe and Disk Company, all those miles of red brick buildings, were having the windows broken out of them by angry workers. The kind Mother was encouraging with all her damn social work. My uncles were nice, polite gentlemen, but no fiber in them to run a big company that was dying. Oh, how business bored me! So depressing, fighting dog eat dog every day, and coming home so worn out that my uncles would sit in their big chairs and swill down whiskey until they went to sleep.

Archibald Hoe and Disk got rich making plows, but who needed them anymore? Not since our friends, the McCormick family, had blanketed the farm belt with their harvesting and threshing machines. And downstate in Moline, the Deeres were clunking out their smelly green tractors. Mechanical now, everything.

AH&D went under. Then Grandma Alice died in 1913, and how I wept. To me, she was a rock of strength, so generous, all the parties she'd put on for me, and the nights skating on her pond, and cocoa afterwards. All the safety and the rich life was dribbling away now. It would never be the same again.

I suppose Mum had money. Somebody must have saved something out of the Archibald disaster. But the Commodore's big house was soon sold and torn down to make smaller houses, one of which my Uncle Ethan lived in, until one day he died in a motor car wreck. Driving too fast as usual, and a girlfriend with him, his wife said. But that was hushed up. She didn't die, and was probably paid off to keep her mouth shut.

By then, out in the world, there weren't any wars, and I hoped that Papa could stay home and spend more time with us. But in 1914, he went off with the Army again, called to the mountains of Colorado to put down a strike by coal miners. It was a Rockefeller mine, and we knew some of the Rockefellers, of course, through the Roosevelts. I went to school with one at Dobbs Ferry. But apparently old John D. wouldn't stand for paying miners the wages they wanted, so he got the government to break them. Soldiers machine-gunned miners' wives and children in their company shacks. When Papa came home, he had a furious argument with Mother. He said he'd had no part of the Ludlow massacre, and it sickened him. But by damn, he wasn't going to quit his work either.

The very day Ludlow ended, American troops went storming into Veracruz, Mexico. To me, it was terribly complicated, and as silly as two bully boys in a schoolyard, trying to make the other one back down. Apparently, Mexico was in the throes of one of its perpetual revolutions, and some lowly Mexican officer had insulted the Stars and Stripes. When Mexico wouldn't apologize, the Great White Fleet stormed into Veracruz harbor, and soldiers and Marines took over the city. Our excuse at the time, said Mother, was that the Germans had sent a shipload of guns to the Mexicans, and we weren't going to stand for it. Monroe Doctrine forever!

Papa just let her rant on. By then, he'd come back from Mexico, and told me one night that he'd had a pretty good time, too. I realized then that the military life was sort of like a club to Papa. Of course, he couldn't belong to the fancy clubs where my uncles did business or played golf, "wouldn't be caught dead in them morgues," he'd say. So instead, his own club was made up of a handful of rollicking men who'd fought all the wars together for so long. I suspect that Mother resented the camaraderie he felt with these men. It was a part of his life that she couldn't share.

When he came back from Veracruz, he was chuckling about an escapade he'd had with a Marine officer named Smedley Butler. He and Papa had crossed paths both in the Philippines and the Boxer Rebellion. Apparently, Colonel Butler was so brave and foolhardy he'd already been awarded two Congressional Medals of Honor. So he and Papa cooked up a scheme of breaking through the lines at Veracruz and riding a train up to Mexico City. The purpose was to find out how many troops the Mexicans really had. Papa didn't go into details, but there were some hairbreadth escapes, and he loved them all.

He'd barely gotten back from that one when another member of his "club" took him off on an even more dangerous spying foray, this time, penetrating the Mexican lines on foot. That officer was a

Colonel named Douglas MacArthur. Papa said in his typical way, "The lad is a little cocky for my tastes, but he's brave enough, just like his old man." That was General Arthur MacArthur, who'd commanded all of us when we were in the Philippines.

But, like always by then, Mother was quick to throw cold water on Papa's enthusiasm. These wars, she said, were nothing but dollars and cents. Men's greed started them. When we had truly insufferable conditions at home, somebody up in Washington always decided to start a war, to get our minds off how bad things were in our society.

Maybe she was right, how would I know? By then, a serious recession was gripping the United States. Riots, breadlines. And worse soon followed. Though it seemed far from us at the time, and everybody was confused as to why it happened, across the ocean, the Great Powers had started the World's War. English, French and Germans were already dying, and beastly Huns were raping Belgian women. President Wilson was saying that our prosperity at home depended on our foreign markets. Mother laughed harshly. "Get ready for it, Nora. What he's really saying is that we'll only survive by joining their dreadful war. Make the world safe for American goods."

Typically, cousin Teedie was back on his warhorse, rumbling around the country, smacking his fist that we prepare ourselves to fight. Though he wasn't President anymore, he still wanted to be again, Mother said, and maybe war would give him his chance. He'd already concocted the scheme of setting up a military training camp at Plattsburg, New York, and all of his four sons would be there. I received letters from both Archie and Quentin. They were champing to get into uniform. Quickly, too, Matt, now a first lieutenant, pulled strings and got himself re-assigned as a camp instructor. When that proved too tame for him, he wrote me that he'd wangled a military observer post in British Army headquarters. "The real action will soon be here," he predicted, "and this little Injun is going to put himself in the council lodge."

After he'd sailed off into the darkness of Europe, a wonderful thing happened. To my astonishment, Mother and Father came rumbling up to Dobbs Ferry in a government motor car. I was playing field hockey that afternoon, for it was one of the last matches of my senior year. But Mum and Papa swept me up, bloomers and all. They'd already talked to the headmistress, and told her they were taking me to England, sailing on Saturday.

It was like old times. They both had their laughter back, Mum, pretty as a doll, dressed in a flowery print and wide hat. Papa was "spiffed up", that's what he called it, in a Panama hat and white suit. The other girls were so envious that I had such glamorous parents, whisking me away from the dreariness of boarding school.

"But Papa, what's this all for?" I cried.

He squeezed me, putting me into the motor car. "To have a hell of a time, darlin', that's what, and about time, too, ain't it, Daisy?"

She laughed. "He's won me over all over again, Nora. Your father is great for honeymoons, you know. We may be broke, and the world may be falling apart, but there's enough left for one last fling, and I think we've all earned it!"

Never in my life would I have such glorious days again. Down in the fine shops of New York, Mum bought me some dresses for the ocean voyage, and England after it. Not only would we see Matt, but we had cousins there, and though the war was grim and raging on, their country places wouldn't be touched. "And the best part," Papa grinned, "you're going to see where you come from, baby dear."

I couldn't believe it, for he rarely talked about Ireland. Probably he was ashamed in some ways about being Irish, such humble beginnings. But he had a gleam in his eye, telling me about my grandparents, and my namesake, Nora, who had seven kiddies by now. "You'll see 'em all, darlin', and bring joy to the Kelly hearth."

We had a riot of fun in New York. Archie and Quentin Roosevelt took me to Delmonico's. We rode carriages around the park and went to one superb ball at the Vincent Astor mansion. I danced with Alfred Gwynne Vanderbilt, the famous sportsman. He laughed and said, "What luck we're in, my dear. We shall continue our dance in the ballroom of the Lady L."

When I frowned and said, "What, sir?" he chuckled. "Why, the Lusitania, my dear. We'll be traveling together."

The Lusitania was the fastest and largest liner in the great Cunard fleet. Though I'd been on ship many times before—Asia, Panama and all our worldwide peregrinations—I was just bowled over by the size and splendor of the Lusitania. When we came aboard, tug whistles were tooting, everybody showering confetti. I never saw such fancy and famous people. Mother pointed out Mr. Charles Frohman, who was a Broadway theatrical producer, and then the author, Elbert Hubbard, whose famous *Message to Garcia* Grandpa Archibald used to quote ad infinitum.

Cousin Teedie couldn't send us off in person, due to the press of political work, but he sent champagne and a telegram of bon voyage to our spacious stateroom. A party was already going on here. Papa was delighted to find one of his "club" traveling with us, a handsome, charming Army Colonel named Archie Butt. They'd served together in the Philippines. Despite his dreadful name, he'd been cousin Teedie's military aide at the White House, and I was captivated by him, though of course he was much older. Another very charming man was Teedie's cousin, and therefore my relative, too, Franklin Delano Roosevelt. I believe he was something in the Navy Department by then. I heard him talking to Papa about a warning the Germans had just printed in the *New York Times.* "Vessels flying the British Flag are liable to destruction."

"And maybe with good reason," Papa grunted.

Mr. Roosevelt frowned. "Why would you say something like that, sir?"

"Well now, lad," Papa said patiently, "if you was a German and you saw us shipping arms to your enemies on these fancy ocean liners, wouldn't you shoot back?"

Mr. Roosevelt seemed flustered. "Well, sir, I personally have no knowledge that the Cunard Line would allow itself to be used for arms shipment."

Papa said something crude about the English, wouldn't trust the warlike buggers as far as he could throw them, but then Mum came up with refills for our champagne.

Papa doesn't usually drink, but that night he did, and it seemed to make him unusually cranky. Our first dinner out from New York was a sumptuous affair, stringed instruments and six or seven courses. Mum, looking so happy and beautiful, again tried to teach Papa how to dance, but he did it awkwardly and shyly. Not so, however, Mum's other dinner partner, the silver-haired and stately Mr. Elbert Hubbard. When they came back and sat down, he regaled Mum with the great success of the book he'd written, *Message to Garcia.* "My dear," he boomed, "when I first heard of an obscure Army lieutenant going down to Cuba, I said, 'Aha, this will be good filler' for the struggling magazine I was then editing. Why, it didn't take me twenty minutes to jot it down. I saw this Army fellow's mission as being a perfect moral lesson for corporate employees. No slipshod work. Once you've started on a mission, finish it! To my absolute amazement, I must have struck a chord, worldwide! The ink was barely dry on that magazine before reprint orders poured in. The New York Central bought 100,000 copies alone, Wanamaker's stores 200,000. The Japanese gave millions of them to their troops in the Russian war. Persevere, get your job done!"

"Tell the lady the punchline, Elbert," cried a beefy businessman from Kansas City.

""Well, at the risk of being materialistic," Hubbard sighed, "I've garnered at least a quarter million in royalties from an obscure Army officer's exploit."

I hadn't paid any attention to Papa during this rather braggy recital, but at that moment, he pounded his fist on the table and the plates jumped. "Don't you call him obscure, you sissified bastard! You're talkin' about Andy Rowan and I was with him bringin' that message through swamps and the killin' of Cuban rebels who stood in our way!"

"But, but I said that!" flustered Mr. Hubbard. "I wasn't trying to take any credit from him."

"No, just a fortune, blood-suckin' it out of a brave man, and leavin' him on the Army trash heap where they don't even know his name anymore." He seized my hand and was trembling. "Come on, daughter, you and me need some fresh air."

Mum was blushing, trying to apologize, but he just jerked me out of there and took me up on the top deck. He spat down into the dark water, and it was some minutes before he could speak again. "The brave deeds of men," he muttered, "ah, girl, how I used to believe in it, but it's all in the trashcan now. The cowardly bastards, writers, them reporters, have taken glory and smeared it with black ink. The hell with 'em, I say, burn in hell!"

I finally got him calmed down, and as much as anything to change the subject, I asked what the German message had meant. Mr. Roosevelt didn't seem concerned.

"Naw, his kind don't get concerned. They just give the orders and keep their hands clean."

"I don't follow you, Papa."

He was leaning with his arms on the rail, staring at the starlit water rushing by. "A bad dream," he murmured.

"But what?" I gripped his arm.

He shook his head. "I don't know what, darlin'. A long time ago now. The night the *Maine* blew, I was in the waters of Havana harbor, about ready to give up the ghost. When you go over the edge, that's when the dreams come."

I peered at his face, his burning eyes. "So it has something to do with a ship?"

"Yes, ship! Goddamn yes! That night I seen your mama, drifting away on a ship whose name started with 'L.'"

"Oh Papa," I cried, "maybe it was me, Nora Liberty!"

He shook his head and tears glistened in his eyes. I really thought it was too much champagne and I wanted to cheer him up. "Oh, you and your Irish superstitions!" I laughed. "Mum says you get these black moods, but please, Papa, not now. We're all going to have such a glorious time over there. Will you really take me out in the green moors where you played as a boy? And best of all, please show me a leprechaun!"

"Ah," he blew his nose and then hugged me. "That and more I'll show you, darlin'. Forgive an old man, livin' with his ghosts. You have fun now. Dance your little feet off."

"I can teach you to dance," I cried, "even if Mum can't."

"G'wan with ye! Catch yourself a young feller." He scowled, "And don't let me catch you with that front of your gown hangin' loose!"

I pulled up my front. I suppose it was a little too daring for him. Then he chuckled and kissed me goodnight. I watched him go slowly down the long deck, his arms folded across his breast.

I've wiped it out!

Please, Doctor Galt, I can't write this!

Once in Manila, I fell from my pony and struck my head. I've never remembered how it happened, or what I was doing before or after.

It's like that now. For the days of the voyage, Papa and Mum were so happy, they laughed and kissed so much, I didn't even want to intrude on them. It was only on the last day that Papa took me alone out on the deck where I could see Ireland with him. "God help us," he was whispering, "I never thought I'd make it back!" We were so close to the green shore, just few miles off. There were hundreds of others on deck, everybody crowding, cheering and snapping Kodaks at the misty, beautiful land. Mother was below in our stateroom, packing. Papa said she had far too many trunks.

The ship exploded!

Oh, don't ask me how. I don't remember! Everybody was screaming, and Papa was running for Mother. "Stay by the boats!" he cried. "Put my girl in the first boat, Archie!"

That was Colonel Butt, and when the boats came crashing down from the davits, there were already too many people in them, they'd hit the ocean and sink.

I was wailing for Papa, but Colonel Butt fought me into a boat. A woman was crying, "Archie, you come, too!"

He stepped back with a smile and said, "Women and children first."

There weren't enough boats! Do you hear me! Not enough. The *Lusitania* was heaving, plunging its bow into the depths. The boilers or something were exploding. Somebody shouted that we had ammunition aboard, that's why they'd sunk us.

How do I know, how does anybody?

They were all dead. Gallant Colonel Butt going down with his damn flag! No more plays for Mr. Frohman, no more yacht races for Mr. Vanderbilt, and Elbert Hubbard's last *Message to Garcia* was a drowning groan. Straw hats and ladies' corsets and yapping little poodle dogs were floating all around us.

Black, awful waves, and we were soaring up and down, British tars tearing at their oars, trying to get us to the Irish beach.

Then people were in the water, clawing at boats that were already filled. I was screaming and screaming. I saw Papa's head, his blue eyes fierce and his black hair plastered down from the waves. The strength of him, the courage. He was dragging something white along through the waves. Oh, my God, it was Mother in her undergarments only. In fury, he shouted at our sailors until they stopped and helped drag Mother and him over the side. Thank God we had room, just barely room.

Mother was coughing terribly, choking with water, and then finally she was unconscious. I stripped off my jacket and lay it over her, and some sailors stripped off their shirts too. Papa had her cradled in his arms in the tossing sea. "You'll make it, darlin'," he kept whispering. "She will, Nora. We'll get her home."

It took three days for her to die in a dingy little hospital, pious nuns pattering about and trying to keep me from crying. Papa had found several doctors, but a dozen of them couldn't have helped her. What did these dumb peasants know about modern medicine? With a crucifix of Jesus cockeyed on the wall, Mum lay in a bare room under a rough blanket, Papa and me taking turns sobbing and gripping her flaming little hands.

When all the lifeboats were gone or sunk, Papa had made her leap with him into the sea. But before he could reach her, in the billowing waves caused by the explosions, her lungs had already badly filled with sea water. Mother was a good swimmer, so maybe it was the shock, I don't know why. Then pneumonia set in and took her. Papa knelt there with his head against her leg, whispering that it should have been him, from that night on the *Maine*, to now. "Let me die," he sobbed. "Take me with her."

What else do you have to know, dammit?

I took Papa, that's who took him. The poor man was so distraught I was sure he'd leap out of a railway carriage and destroy himself.

Even coming home to his own turf in County Mayo didn't help much. His own father had been dead some years now, and Papa hadn't even known that. His mother, Grandmother Bridget, was a doddery old crone who couldn't remember what happened five minutes ago. In the little white hutches of Laughrasheen, all Papa's relatives trooped through the wake, praying their beads. Papa's sister, Nora, was a big strapping woman with a twinkle in her eye. I liked her, for she had Papa's wit, and courage, too. "We'll put your lovely Daisy down in the family plot, Patrick." A little priest was dancing around saying, "Indeed so, we'll have a mass in the morning." He said, "marnin'."

But Papa bellowed, "I won't put her in ground that is still owned by the damn English, the Cavans."

The priest said, "Oh no, lad. Things have changed. The new young Lordship was killed this winter on the Western Front. The bereaved Lady is now letting us have our own consecrated turf. Things have changed. You'd be surprised."

"Well, then," Papa whispered, "put my darlin' in it, for she's the best part of me, and I'll be joining her one day awful soon."

"Why, Patrick," cried his sister Nora. "You'll bury the lot of us.

Look at you, strong as a horse!" "Harse," she called it.

"Once," Papa said, "but you can't step in the same river twice, girl." Then he straightened up and wiped his sleeve across his eyes. "The daughter and I will be leaving in the morning, after the praying is done."

"Ah, God help us, brother, you ain't but home!"

"Home?" Papa cried, his eyes raging. "In the name of Christ, where is such a place? Can you tell me that, Nora?" He looked at both of us, then turned and stooped to go out of the little cottage. I saw him cross the purple moor in the mist, walking slowly, staring at the sea.

Right then I knew that I was all he had left, just the two of us, and that I could never fill the emptiness of his heart.

Oh, why did I say all this? Does it make me better? I think not. I'm weeping right on this page. Back to Vassar, plod along. I've lost her. Papa said it. We've lost the best part of both of us.

Where do I go? Are you saying that it's it up to me, now? Oh God, I hope not!

Nora Liberty Kelly. Amen.

PANCHO VILLA'S FIST!

The doc at Vassar sent me one last letter from Nora. Maybe his damn voodoo worked. Something sure did.

Headquarters, U.S. Punitive Expedition, Colonia Dublan, Chihuahua, Mexico.

April 20, 1916

Dear Doctor Galt,

Can you believe where I am! I'll bet you're reading about us in the newspapers! There's so much to tell you since I received your letter, by some miracle, that I hardly know where to start!

Don't you envy me, down here in the warm sun, while you're slogging around in the mud of Poughkeepsie? Well, I hope so! I envy myself, really!

Of course, as you said, I'm sad at leaving Vassar. You want me to admit things and mourn them. I do. But I've never been really that hot at studies. Anyhow, I had no choice.

It's about Patrick. I call him that now, instead of Papa. With Mother gone, we have a more mature relationship, I think. He's not so fearsome anymore. In fact, he's quite needy of me.

We had some real fights when I came home to Lake Forest for the Christmas holidays. Some holiday! Patrick was still wearing black on his sleeve for poor Mum, and ripping through the house and burning things. I just wouldn't hear of it, him and his damn black Irish mourning. Yes, she was gone, but we had to start again.

"So what is that?" he cried. "Your fancy parties and dancing gowns, is it? Ah no, me little beauty. You can kiss them frills goodbye."

It really hurt me how bitter, lonely and possessive of me he'd become. I suppose it's the old-country Irish way. I'd seen enough of it when we visited with his damn clannish relatives over Mum's funeral. Why, those squinty-eyed, pipe-clamping fathers just wouldn't let their daughters go. A young man could hardly look at them. The whole nation was filled with dreadful, pinch-faced old maids. I wasn't about to join that bunch and told Papa so. Patrick.

Why, the night after Christmas, there was a gorgeous debut ball at the Blackstone Hotel in Chicago. When a perfectly nice boy came by in his Reo roadster, planning to drive me to the city, Patrick flew into a rage. I kept saying, "What's wrong with motoring in?", and he cries, "Because you're alone with that snot too damn long. It could take hours. You could break down on the road."

362

"And then what?" says I. "Would he rape me, Patrick!"

"Don't use words like that! They do, fellers do. It happens, you flaunting yourself like a goddamn hussy. I ain't having it!"

"And you can't stop me either!" I shot back.

God, it hurt me to see him so dependent on me now. So sure, we both had a good cry then, and I went off with my young man, weeping all the way down Sheridan Road.

The problem was, and I saw it when Patrick got sensible about it, we were in financial trouble. He wasn't good at numbers, and I frankly had never paid attention to money things. When Grandma Alice died, I'd thought we were taken care of, perhaps not as lavishly as before, but certainly comfortable. I was dead wrong. It's so hard to be in a rich family one day, and practically paupers the next. Oh I know, I'm exaggerating again, feeling sorry for myself, you'll say. But the bitter truth is, poor Mother was a few months over 39 when she died. b. January, 1876, d. May, 1915. The Archibald family and their rigid lawyers had written Mother a trust that she wouldn't come into until she was 40 years old. Don't trust even your flesh and blood, control every damn penny. That's the Protestant ethic for you!

Papa has no truck with lawyers, he wouldn't even contest Mum's will. But the prim legal bastards, including my surviving uncles, read the trust to us on Christmas Eve, try that for sticking it in. If Mother died or divorced prior, blah blah blah, the money she had coming to her from the Archibald estate would return to her other blood siblings, which didn't include Patrick, and only half me.

I screamed at my uncles. "Half then! I get something!"

Oh, these awful family money fights! Everybody was practically broke by then, but still living beyond their means. The Archibald trust had been mostly invested in AH&D, so that value had dribbled away in the company failure. It came down to my uncles grabbing Mum's money, but for my half, my blood connection, I'd get half the proceeds of selling Patrick and Mum's cottage on the lake.

I said to Patrick, "Well, you take it. I have some nice things, and I'm quitting college anyway. Maybe I'll just go to work and support us. I type, I could be a steno."

"You will like hell!" he bellowed.

After a few days of raging like a bull and tearing up the house, he spent time on the telephone to Washington and New York. Apparently cousin Teedie had helped him, too, and Patrick had known Mr. Hearst in the Spanish War.

The very afternoon I came home from the grand ball at the Blackstone, there were two trucks standing in front of our cottage, loaded to the gills with our furniture and stuffed with Mother's steamer trunks that hadn't gone down on the Lusitania.

"Papa!" I cried. "What are you doing?"

He stood there laughing, his face flecked with the light snow that was falling. "Pissing in the fire, Nora, and moving on!"

I ran at the trucks. "But Mother's stuff, her treasures!"

Patrick put his arm around me and said gently, "Where she'd want 'em to be, girl. You know them bearded buggers she was playing around with, them starvies from the tenements? I talked to one of the settlement houses, and they'll welcome these things. They're putting a plaque to your Momma up on the brick wall."

I wept, standing in the snow, my mascara running down my cheeks. "But no house, no nothing! Oh, Papa, where will we stay?"

"In the sun," he answered. "A castle for you, darlin', a hacienda." Then he told me that Mr. Hearst had put him on the payroll. He needed an honest man down in Mexico to look after his cattle ranches and gold mines.

"But Mexico, Patrick! Aren't they fighting down there?"

He chuckled. "You think I ain't seen it before, girl? Why, them Mex bandit gangs, they don't know what fight is. Damn pesky gnats you can swat away with your lace handkerchief."

We left for Mexico that same night on the Southern Pacific. Despite a dreadful, dusty trip, and of course Patrick had lied—there was a perfectly horrible Revolution going on—when we finally came to the Tres Hermanas hacienda, at Babicori, Chihuahua, I almost wept with joy.

The place was gorgeous beyond my dreams. A wonderful rambling adobe, the walls two feet thick, and a patio with a fountain. An oasis, filled with the pungence of bougainvillea and date palms rustling in the dry air, and seeming to rub the stars in the clearness of the desert night.

I was hurtled back to my girlhood in Manila. Mexican women servants with their ropes of black hair were gripping my hands and murmuring, "*A sus ordenes, Dona Duena.*"

Dona Duena. The boss lady, and oh, how I loved it. From being almost dirt poor, I was now the *patrona* of thousands of rippling yellow acres, a high grassland so rich with cattle that Mr. Hearst hadn't been able to count how many head he owned. Lush, sensual hills, and elegant Mexican vaqueros in their big hats and tight-legged breeches, their horses' bridles clanking with silver.

Certainly there was fighting and killing down on the Chihuahua plains, but it was the last thing I worried about. Why, I hadn't been there but a few days before my childhood Spanish began coming back. The Mexican cowboys were shy and gallant, but sometimes as they groomed their fancy horses in the long stable sheds, I'd catch them glancing at me and whispering, "*La Rubia.*" The redhead. My coloration is apparently desirable down here.

From the ranch remuda and a hundred cow ponies, Patrick rode a half dozen before he found me a Spanish thoroughbred named, of all things, Patricio. I just loved him, he was so sensitive to my touch, and so fast. How many days Patrick and I would go cantering across the ranch, tallying cattle, or looking in at the way the vaqueros did their work. Because Patrick was so fluent in Spanish, and such a veteran horseman, the vaqueros learned very quickly that they weren't about to test him or push him around.

One night, a drunken vaquero came swaggering in from another ranch and muttered something about Hearst stealing his cattle. Patrick listened patiently for several minutes. We were having a candlelit dinner on the patio. Then slowly he stood up, collared the vaquero, and hurled him into the gushing fountain with its beautiful tiles. Our vaqueros rushed in, roped the miscreant's hands together and put him into our jail. Yes, we had a jail, where they gave prisoners or poachers not bread and water, just water. When their sentences were over, they came out very thin and dragged themselves back across the desert like beaten dogs. Life was harsh and cheap down there.

But what a joy it was to be with Patrick those few months. He was his old self again, funny, wistfully Irish at times, pointing to blue mountains huddled on the horizon, and telling me tales about his Apache days. I hadn't known until then, and probably Mother never knew, that he'd had an Apache wife. I wrinkled my nose at that, having seen some other shiftless Indians lounging around—ugly, really dirty people.

"What's got you, girl?" Patrick said.

I laughed. "Well, if you really want to know, are they like other women?"

He scowled. "Like? Now what in hell is that?"

"Stop being prudish, Patrick. Their bodies and everything. Making love."

"Holy smoke! Is that all you think about, girl?"

"Well, what did you think about when you were nineteen!"

He laughed then, reaching across from his horse and gripping me by the back of my neck. "And tuck your damn shirt in your pants," he said in mock gruffness. "I'm seeing too much skin, and that ain't for the Mexicans."

"Oh, Papa. I'd never...do anything with a Mexican."

"It ain't what you'd do, it's what they'd do. Come on now, we got steers to check." And we'd gallop off again. Sometimes I even dreamed that I was married to him—isn't that dreadful?—and that this was our ranch.

I made up my mind to get a very rich man one day and have a life like this. By now, as you can probably tell, I'd quit mourning poor Mother!

The best was to come, but it didn't seem that way at first. One

365

night, March 10th or 11th, I believe, the telephone began jangling in the big hacienda parlor. Patrick and I were both asleep in our separate, enormous rooms in the far wings of the adobe. The servants weren't permitted to answer the one crackly telephone, besides which, they were terrified of it. So finally I heard Patrick cursing and clumping down the long tile hallway. When I pulled a blanket around my nakedness and came to him, he was standing by the great hacienda hearth. The dying coals were all that lit his face. "The hell you say," he kept murmuring into the phone.

When he hung up, he told me that Pancho Villa and his bandits had struck a blow against the United States. A *golpe,* he called it, swooping down and attacking the U.S. Cavalry camp at Columbus, New Mexico. First time since the War of 1812 that an enemy ever dared set foot on American soil.

"Patrick! What's it going to mean?"

He jerked open a drawer of his giant mesquite-wood desk and took out a gunbelt and a key. Then he unlocked a tall armoire, a lovely Spanish antique, but now it gleamed with the ranch Winchesters and boxes of ammunition. "In the morning you'll get a gunnery lesson, but these will do for tonight." He handed me the heavy revolver belt, took two rifles for himself and locked the armoire with its heavy clanking chain.

"Are we in danger, Papa?"

He was clicking shells into one rifle. "Ah," he grunted, "life is danger, ain't it? Them Mex are sneaks, every one of them. That was Nesbitt on the tellyphone, Hearst's mine manager at Cusihuiriachic. Cusi, to you. It's south of here, but by damn if them Villista bandits didn't hit the place. Just tonight it was. They're streaming south from their raid on the border, and Nesbitt says U.S. troops are pursuing them."

"Well, that will be good, won't it? We'll have some protection."

"It don't work that way down here." He shook his head, and we started back through the shadowy hallway. "Ah, hell, girl," he sighed, "I seen it coming. Everybody seen it but that damn schoolteacher, Woodrow Wilson."

It was confusing to me, like their wars always are. Patrick said that President Wilson had decided to butt into the Mexican Revolution, so he recognized President Carranza as being the lawful government. Not only that, he even ordered the Southern Pacific to haul Carranza Federal troops along the U.S. side of the border and dumped them into Douglas, Arizona. From there, they walked across the line to Agua Prieta, Sonora. Villa didn't expect them to be there, and so when he attacked Agua Prieta, the *Federales* slaughtered 10,000 Villistas. "And we wonder," Patrick grunted, "why Villa's sore at us, and would punch his fist into New Mexico. Getting even, he is.

Just yesterday morning, out riding, one of the vaqueros told me that when Villa heard Wilson had given him the double cross, it turned him into a bandit with a price on his head, Villa roared that he'd kill every American he could catch." We'd come to my room by then, and he handed me the revolver belt. "Put this under your pillow, Nora." He ripped a blanket from my bed. "I'll sleep by the door."

"Oh, Papa, I'm all right. You don't have to worry about me."

"I ain't," he said, banging and locking the wooden shutters on the tall windows. "Now sleep, child. I been here before."

God, I loved him for that. I was frankly terrified, as you can imagine. We were so alone, hundreds of miles in the middle of the desert, coyotes howling far off, and every cactus out there beginning to tremble like a man was in it. Surely we had Mexicans with us, maybe twenty counting vaqueros, cooks, maids and yard boys. But as Patrick said, you never knew which side they were really on. Deep in their blood ran a hatred of any foreigner, particularly Americans. Could you blame them? In 1845, we'd taken half of Mexico away from them. "It's *la tierra,* darlin'," Patrick muttered, "their land. And when you mix that up with *la raza,* their race, and their strutting, cocky machismo, you get blood in the dust for sure. I seen it with Crawford. Treacherous bastards killed the best man I ever served with. Shot him down under a white flag. So grand Mister Wilson thinks that the Carranzistas are our allies, eh? Mark my word. They'll turn on us just as quick as a Villista, to get us the hell and gone from here."

Nothing happened that night, or the next either. At least a week passed, until one morning, when Patrick tried to use the telephone, the line had gone dead. Also, three of our vaqueros, with their women and children, had slipped off and taken their ranch horses and rifles with them.

In the sun in front of the hacienda, Patrick gave the remaining vaqueros a harsh dressing-down. His Spanish was so fluent and profane that I caught little of it. Where was their responsibility to their patron? Where was their gratitude? Hadn't he plucked them out of the barrios and made them proud *mayor domos?* What excuse did they have now to be groveling like terrified whores with urine running down their legs?

It was quite awful, but he'd been around these kind of people for many years now, and I will say that his bullying worked. Within minutes, he had the vaqueros fortifying the ranch gates and building rifle positions along the thick adobe walls. The housemaids and cooks were scurrying around, too, heaping Mr. Hearst's fine antiques into barricades so that nobody could rush the thick mesquite doors and break into the patio.

We had one motor car at the ranch, a fine new Dodge roadster with a canvas bonnet top. Patrick squinted at it. "Can you drive that damn thing, Nora?"

I laughed. "Why, Papa, you know I can! Just because you can't..."

"Don't lip off to me now." He practically flung me at the auto. "Run it behind the hacienda where the grove of olive trees is. Put some branches over it so they don't spot it at first glance. If we have to make a break for it, we'll go down that horsetrail over the mountain and onto the plain. Outrun the buggers."

Poor Patrick, machinery just wasn't his forte. He'd tried often to operate autos, but he was so impatient and clumsy that he was always jamming the wrong gears. So now he just wheeled onto his horse and went clattering off in the dust to search the hills that overlooked the hacienda. He was so lithe and vigorous, just plain tough, that it was sad for me to realize that he wasn't a young man anymore. He was sixty years old. The world he'd known was dying.

In the middle of that afternoon, I was taking a siesta when I heard a thud. Sometimes lost birds smacked against the adobe, but this wasn't any bird! Crack, crack, one of the shutters blew open in a shower of splinters. Stupidly, I ran to it and looked out. Beyond the hacienda wall, horsemen in black were galloping up and down, their guns spurting flame. I saw one of our vaqueros topple from his horse, and Conchita, our big fat cook, was wailing, lumbering across the courtyard, dragging her two children after her.

Roughly, Patrick pulled me away from the window and thrust a Winchester into my hand. "I taught you how to use it, Nora, so you remember. Fire it only to save yourself. On the floor with you, and stay there!"

He shoved me down, then raced out, slamming and locking the thick mesquite door. "But Papa," I screamed, "what about you? Please be careful!"

I don't know how many raiders there were. More than us, to be sure. From the roaring and thocking of their bullets into the hacienda, it seemed like an army was out there. And of course, I couldn't just stay cringing on the floor. There was a peep hole in the wall, used years ago to fire through during Apache attacks. I crawled to it and peered out.

I could see maddeningly little, but just the way our Mexicans were fighting back, I knew Patrick had to be with them. Then I saw him. He was crouching, moving slowly along the big adobe wall toward the main gate. I wanted to scream at him! Didn't he see there was smoke wisping up from the gate? Then, with a crash, half the gate ripped from its hinges and fell to the dust. Black-shirted horsemen had torn it off with their lariats, and others were running in, so close that I could see the crossed bandoliers of cartridges on their chests. Howling *"Viva Villa! Muerto a los gringoes!"* they were heaving away the tables and furniture blocking the gate. "Papa!" I screamed.

Oh, God, that instant was frozen in the sun. The Mexicans, with their big black hats, whipped their rifles toward him. But Papa was quicker, he'd surprised them. Firing his Winchester from his hip, he blazed right into them, cutting them down, and when his rifle was empty, he smashed its stock against the head of the last man. Then with revolvers in both hands, he kept firing at the more distant ones, dropping several of their horses, and they were running in panic.

I sobbed, pressing my head against the wall. Come back, Papa! But when I dared to look again, our other vaqueros, the few that were left, were standing shoulder to shoulder with him, their rifles crashing at the last scattering blackshirts, many of them limping and crawling away. One of them, on a far ridge, was gesturing excitedly at the sky.

In all the noise, I didn't hear it until then. First a whine, and then closer, a tinny little popping. A shadow flashed across the hacienda. I raced to the window and climbed out. Wobbling in the sun came a frail brown airplane with a white star on its lower wing.

U.S.? Oh God, was it one of ours?

By the time I'd rushed to Papa, he was slowly lowering his revolvers and watching in wonder as the air machine swept across the tawny hills. "Jesus and Mary," he whispered.

The plane, like a horseman in the sky, was diving, whining over the black shirts until they were galloping wildly across the hills toward the distant blue mountains. Guns popped far off, a few of the Mexicans daring to shoot at the thing, but the rest just fled.

"Will ya look at it!" Patrick breathed. "He's running them Mex like cattle!"

I was hugging him, sobbing, "Papa, you're bleeding!"

"Hell, a nick!" He slapped at his ear where the lobe was slightly torn and dripping blood onto his shirt. He seized my hand and we began to run. "He's comin' in, girl, gonna set her on the ground!"

In the hot wind, and buffeting air currents from the baking desert, the pathetic little plane was bobbing and bouncing toward us. I clapped my hand to my mouth. The plane was kiting up and down so crazily that I just knew it was going to spear its wing into the sand. "Careful, lads!" Patrick shouted. "Go easy there!" In a last angry roar, the quivering plane lifted, then plopped onto the earth. Its dinky wooden wheels were rattling and swerving, billowing up dust. We ran through it and stopped at the very tip of the frail wing. I'd never been this close to an air machine. The wonder of it overcame Patrick. Slowly he reached out and touched the taut, dusty fabric that covered the wing. Then he snapped his finger against it. "Why," he whispered, "she ain't nothing but canvas and wood, wires holding the flimsiness of it together. How in hell do they get her into the sky?" He shook his head.

By then, a short, stocky man raised the goggles on his helmet and pushed himself up out of the cockpit. The man in the rear seat was bareheaded and boyish-looking, his sandy hair swirled by the wind. Both of their faces were so smeared with oil that they could have been garage people.

"*Habla Ingles?*" the pilot said to Patrick, who was staring at him like he'd dropped in from the planets. "*Patron? You jefe?*" Patrick chuckled. "Save your Tex-Mex, lad. Yas, I'm *jefe*, what's left of it anyhow. Name is Kelly. Run the ranch for Hearst."

"Well, by God, that's a lucky shot." The pilot was wiping the oil from his eyes with his white scarf. "Intelligence told me that Hearst had something out this way, but hell, the only maps we have of this country were drawn by General Scott's troops in 1845. We're blind as bats. Lieutenant," he called to the other officer who seemed to be having difficulty extricating himself from the plane, "wooden blocks hanging in your cockpit. Grab 'em, set the wheels so that the machine stays put. Be careful now, if you kick that off switch, we'll never get the damn thing started again." When he turned back to us, he was shaking his head. "These liaison cavalrymen they give us don't know a spur from a joystick. But then again, I was one myself once. Well, Mr. Kelly, it looks like you had a sharp little fight. Casualties?"

"Ah, a few Mex cowboys nicked. I ain't counted how bad."

"You got off well. That band of Villistas has been raiding up and down the line stealing weapons. Mean as snakes. By the way, I'm Ben Foulois. Captain. Command the First Aero Squadron."

"Squadron?" Patrick echoed. "You ain't telling me that you got more of them things!"

"Damn few, sir, and by guess and by God at that. When the Army gets anything they don't know how to handle, they pass it off on the Signal Corps. Call it scientific experimentation. These kites here," Foulois squatted and grinned at the plane, "we had ten to start with and cut our teeth on. Martins, Sloans, Sturtevants. Well, only the Curtiss, this number 44, is worth a damn, and its magneto is shot. So now we're down to five that can fly, that's the total Signal Corps Air Service of the U.S. Army. If I don't get this one home in one piece, General Pershing will kick me from here to Washington."

"Pershing?" Patrick echoed, and dropped down beside Foulois.

By now the other young officer was standing above us, as if he didn't want to butt in. He glanced shyly at me, then began cleaning the goggles that were strapped to his peaked campaign hat. Unlike Captain Foulois, who wore a greasy, baggy flying suit, this young man was in khakis and riding boots, and I recognized the crossed sabers of the cavalry on his choke collar.

Slowly Patrick seemed to realize that I was there, and introduced me. "The daughter." We couldn't shake hands because theirs were so oily, but the young lieutenant had a gallant sort of manner. He

370

bowed slightly. "Apologies, Miss, our loss. Name is Ned Barrow, and you're...?"

His gray eyes had a lovely twinkle. "Nora," I said weakly.

He glanced toward the hacienda, where smoke was wisping up. "Quite a time you had here. Lucky we dropped by."

"Yes. I should say so."

"Why, hell," Patrick snorted, "just some ragpicker Mex, not the first and won't be the last." He looked at Captain Foulois. "Pershing, by God, he's General, is he, and down here, too? What in hell?"

They couldn't believe we hadn't heard, not realizing, I suppose, how remote we were from anything. It seems that after Villa's raid on Columbus, the entire nation had risen up in fury, and President Wilson ordered Pershing to take columns of troops into Mexico, trucks, planes, everything, and hunt Villa until they ran him down and punished him.

"Well, high time," Patrick said. "Daughter, the fellers is dry. Fetch the *cocinera, correle* now, bring cool water, tortillas, too." He grinned. "I got whiskey and tequila both, lads. Are you wanting to cut the dust?"

"Plenty," Foulois said, "but I'd never get this bird home if I did."

By the time I'd pattered the cook and houseboys back down from the hacienda, Patrick and the air officers were squatting under the shade of the wing. "Remarkable that you were with Pershing at Wounded Knee," Foulois said, as he took an olla of water. "You go back a ways, sir."

"Ain't that the truth! Cuba, too. Ah, the papers made T.R. the glory boy, but I'll tell you this, lad, we'd have never taken Kettle Hill if it hadn't been for Black Jack and his nagurs."

"Well, you'll be seeing him again, Mr. Kelly. We've headquartered at Colonia Dublan, the Mormon town. All American and foreign nationals in this area have been ordered into our camp, where we can keep your throats from being cut."

Patrick frowned. "Well, now, Cap, I don't mind seeing old Pershing, not a bit, for I like the man. But I'm hired to run this ranch for Hearst. If I take off from this place, them bandits will pick it clean. We've got valuable livestock here."

"I realize that, sir. In fact, we'll have them patrolled, and requisition some beef from you. We're that short of rations until our truck trains get operating. But for now, you'll have to come in. You're running too big a risk out here, particularly with your daughter."

"Risk, hell! Them Mex ain't trying us again." Patrick was scowling and muttering as he pushed up from under the wing, but Captain Foulois said, "I'll drop Lieutenant Barrow over at his troop. They're nearby. Can you make it this far by dark, Barrow?"

"Do our damndest, sir." The lieutenant was smiling, and had, I realized then, a quite charming Southern accent. "I don't blame yo'all, Mr. Kelly, for not wanting to trade this place for an army camp, but your daughter shouldn't mind. You'll be the only American girl in town, Miss, save for the Mormons, and their men are so stingy with 'em we can't catch a single one. Pleasure, sir." With a boyish grin, he snapped Papa a salute. "We'll get you there."

Patrick jammed his hands onto his hips and glowered as the officers climbed into the air machine. "Well, if that one ain't the cocky snot!"

"Oh, Papa, they're just trying to be accommodating. They know you don't want to leave."

"And I know them spiffs. Bars on 'em. Swaggers. Flirting with you, he is."

"Patrick! He never even noticed me!" My face went hot, I was blushing, trying to hide it.

As we started back to the hacienda, Patrick stared glumly up at the air machine, which was whining and popping off into the dying sun. "They can put wings on it all right," he grunted, "but down in the dirt it's still the same goddamn mucked-up Army. Tent streets, stinking latrines. If you got the idea of a Blackstone dancing party, girl, leave it in your dreams."

"I don't have any such notions, Patrick. Do you think that I haven't been around Army all my life?"

"Ah," he sighed, "I suppose you have. I'm tired, Nora, that's all. You just get working something fine, try to get settled someplace, and they blow you out of it. Well, go on now. Pack us up. Piss in the fire one more time. It ain't gonna be the last, that's for sure." He kicked his boot at the dirt, and went sluffing off toward the hacienda.

What happened then was really comic and quite wonderful, in a bittersweet sort of way. Patrick, I mean. The fight with the Villistas must have taken a lot out of him. He'd lost blood from his nicked ear, and looked drained and quite gaunt. When the cavalry came rattling into the patio just about dark, they were so dusty and white-faced that until they washed in the horse troughs, I didn't realize that they were actually black men. Negro troopers. That woke Patrick up all right. "Tenth Cavalry," he cried, "damn good men. Git in here, you kinky-headed buffaloes!" He was clapping his arm around some of them, whom he'd known in other wars.

But the last thing I needed, in the rush of packing, was to organize our Mexicans to feed at least 50 starving soldiers. Why, Patrick treated them as if I should have put Mr. Hearst's best crystal and lace on the long tables. "These is the boys that do the fightin'," he crowed. "*Correle,* girl. Git 'em *cerveza!*"

By then, the troop captain had come wheezing in. He was a red-faced old curmudgeon who looked terribly out of shape for such cavalry activities. "Damn butt polisher from some quartermaster

372

office," Patrick muttered to me. The captain, whose name I don't recall, was furious at Patrick for giving his men alcohol. "When they're in my house, mister," Patrick bellowed, "they git what I want. Here," he said, jerking open the antique armoire next to the sideboard, "Hearst's got some good brandy. Take a snift for your ticker. You're pantin' like a hog."

So while the Captain sulked, drinking alone by the hearth, the great, shadowy *sala* was filled with the noise and chuckling of these black men tearing into Mexican ribs, beans and tortillas. Patrick was laying the cupboard bare for them, and had me running around like a common waitress.

The worst, or the best, was to come. I was just having a Mexican houseboy carry in a tall iron candelabra when, through the flickering flames, I saw several truly horrid men squatting like animals by the front door. They were partly naked, with white or red headbands tied around their flowing black hair. At that moment, I heard Lieutenant Barrow's voice. I didn't even know he was there, and I'd missed him. "Captain," he said, "I've just located the scouts. Permission to feed them, sir."

Then I heard Patrick cry: "Scouts! Well, goddamn if they ain't still with us!" By then he was clattering into the hallway, the scouts pushing up from their squats, their dark, evil faces flashing with grins. I hadn't realized until then that these men were Apaches. Some of them wore khaki Army blouses, and Patrick of course had served with their kind, years ago.

In many ways, it was touching. Wouldn't you know, Patrick found one that he remembered, a squat, older Apache with wide cheekbones and wearing sergeant's stripes on his sleeve. At the sight of him, Patrick let out a howl. "Why, look at him, you worthless old sonofabitch! Dutchy!" The Apache was howling, too, they were hugging each other, dancing around just plain silly, with the other Indians clucking and whistling. "Why, Nora," Patrick shouted, "I ain't seen this heathen since Corralitos. He got drunk and ended me up in the clink, but we're getting even now!" Of course, none of it meant anything to me. I was embarrassed to glance at Lieutenant Barrow, but he was laughing, for Patrick and the Indian had started jabbering at each other in the native tongue, and we were all out of it.

That was the end of any order or military discipline. Like a red-eyed, bellowing bull, Patrick herded the Apaches into the great room, pushing the black troopers aside to make room for them.

"Ten minutes to water horses and mount," the captain was barking. "Move now, we have a long way to go." He grabbed Patrick by the shoulder. "Kelly, I need those scouts out front. They've had enough time here!"

"You'll get 'em, mister, when I says so."

Poor Lieutenant Barrow was caught right in the middle, trying to keep Patrick and his captain from a fist fight. As the black soldiers finally clanked away to get our column ready, Patrick was sitting on the big hearth, his arm around Dutchy, his Indian, and both of them slobbering tequila, passing the bottle back and forth. In English, Spanish and Apache, they were moaning about someone called Nati, and Patrick was cursing and weeping. It was awful. It came over him so quickly, he was a different man.

I was stunned to see him so drunk. Mother was always proud of how temperate he was, but in the sadness of losing her, and the uncertainty we'd lived with ever since, he must have needed some way to let it all out.

By the time the troop was formed, black shapes weary in their saddles, and horses stomping in the patio, our Mexicans were hugging me and weeping goodbyes. They practically worshipped Patrick, bowing so low when he passed down the line of them. He said to them in Spanish, "Take it all, you've earned it. *Dios cuidalos.*" He slurred the words, and with a clank, dropped a big sack of silver coins that burst when it struck the tile floor. The servants had too much pride to scramble for it. They just wept and watched us go.

When we came to our Dodge sedan, which we'd be traveling in, Patrick and his Dutchy were like a pair of India rubber men, arms around each other, stumbling, clanking their liquor bottles. It was tequila and whiskey now.

Lieutenant Barrow had escorted me to the auto, doing his best not to watch poor Papa. I was so ashamed, I grabbed his hand. "Please forgive him. I've never seen him like this."

"Don't worry about it, Nora. He's had a fight today, a lot of strain. He'll cool out, but you'd best not let him drive."

"Oh, he can't, doesn't know how. I do it."

There was a terrible scene then. Papa had heaped Dutchy into the back seat of the roadster and crawled in beside him. At that, the beefy captain spurred up on his horse. "You, sir!" he shouted, "get a hold of yourself! You gave my troops beer, I winked at it, but I'll not stand for you giving liquor to these Indians. Put that man out of the auto!" The Apache was rolling his eyes, trying to sit up. "You'll walk it off, Sergeant, and when you drop in your tracks, you're broken to private!"

"He'll walk like hell!" Patrick roared. "I was giving this Injun orders long before you ever seen one, you butt-polishin' poppycock!"

The captain whirled. "Lieutenant Barrow, do you command these scouts?"

"I thought I did, sir."

"Then get him out of there! Your responsibility!"

"Don't you lay a hand on him, sonny," Patrick roared at the poor young man. "He's my bunkie! God Almighty, fought and bled for us against his own people, and what do we give him? Medal, is it? My ass! Ten years in a Florida clink! Git your Army snots out of here, I had enough of you!"

It was useless trying to argue with Papa when he was in such fury. The only thing I could think of was to snatch up my skirts and leap behind the wheel of the Dodge. Get us started somehow.

Oh, dear me, what a stroke of fate!

Wouldn't you know it, the car wouldn't start! Not for me anyway. I clicked it and groaned it, but nothing. Finally, it was the dear young lieutenant who creaked up the hood and tinkered around, getting himself all greasy.

By then, both Papa and the captain had simmered down. When Ned Barrow finally got the auto roaring into life and belching out smelly exhaust, he looked over at the captain and said, "Permission to drive these people, sir. I can keep up with the column. We don't want them breaking down."

The captain growled off to lead his troops, and away we went. With Patrick and Dutchy sprawled in the back seat, Ned Barrow drove me, slow and jostling, through that beautiful night.

We talked about everything. He told me that he came from Mississippi, and had gone on to West Point. He was so young, had I been a year or two earlier at Vassar, we both would have been up the Hudson together, neither of us knowing. He laughed about how he'd been trying to find a proper young Vassar lady, to bring to his graduation ball.

I didn't think that Patrick had been conscious enough to butt in on our chatting, but at the mention of Mississippi, he thrust forward, with a terrible breath on him, and slurred, "Mississippi, is it? Didja ever hear of a place called Leatherton? Family by that name?"

Ned frowned. "Well, no sir, can't say I have. Those plantation towns with the family name on them are usually down in the Delta. Though I was born in Natchez, I grew up mostly in Memphis. My father was a surgeon, Baptist Hospital. Is there someone down there that you know, sir?"

"Not anymore," Papa whispered. "Maybe never was." He sagged back and wiped the tears from his eyes. After that, he left us alone.

Oh, but for me, it was anything but sad! I felt as if Ned had me on a heavenly chariot, sweeping me across the sweet cool desert, with the dry wind rustling our hair. I kept throwing back my head, wanting to pinch myself. Above us were nothing but giant, glistening stars, so close that I wanted to snatch them to my breast. Oh sure, I can hear you saying that they were in my eyes. I'd lost myself to this young man.

Well, what's wrong with that! I'm nineteen, aren't I? It's the best time, the only time I have! I hope the stars will be there forever. I'm the happiest girl on earth. Please God don't take it away...

Nora LIBERTY Kelly

P.S. Your patient no more! Cured!

WINNIN' A WAR, LOSIN' A WORLD

When we hit Colonia Dublan, Pershing was off elsewhere, and I wished to hell I was. The last time I'd seen this sleepy little Mormon burg, it was a prim and decent place, wide streets, brick houses with picket fences around them, and flowers in the window boxes. The whole outfit looked like the saints had ripped up an Illinois farm town and plunked her into the desert where they could do their praying in peace. Well, forget them days. The Army had swarmed it like a flock of crows in a cornfield. Reminded me of the mess down in Tampa during the Cuban War. Soldiers were falling all over each other, hammering up tent cities, digging latrines and dumps and sandbagging gun positions. The racket was fierce, cavalry troops rattling off after every dust devil that swirled up in the desert. Day and night, truck trains were growling in from the border, hauling supplies that nobody knew where to put or how to use. The air that was once desert-clear was rank with oily smoke and burning garbage. Even a few of the tinny little flying machines were whining like lost wasps, back and forth across the pale blue skies. Big, stocky Mormon men and their pinchy-faced dames were slamming the shutters of their tidy brick houses, and for all the world I wanted to be inside with them, lying in the coolness and quieting the hammers in my brain.

Ah, what a hell of a night I had with Dutchy. You damn old fool, I kept telling myself, you know better than this. But did I now?

Just the sight of Nora broke my heart, and no crying jag could heal it. What a pretty thing she was, the sun catching her coppery hair, lighting the freckles on her face, and her icy blue eyes. Daisy was gentle, soft, as female as a doe, slipping off through the forest. But not the daughter. Nora would come at you crashing, head on. My doing, I'm afraid. The damn feisty Irish blood had made a wiry tomboy. A long-limbed, gutty thing, she'd go anyplace a man would. All her life she'd taken to men more than little girl playmates. She wasn't shrinking behind any violets, not that one, and I was proud of her the way she behaved, when the Villistas plinked at us.

But the minute she got into the Army camp, spiffed up in a baresleeved Mexican shirt and her hair flaming loose, more than one of them khaki buggers were trying to look down her front and catch sight of her freckled bosom. Tall as Nora was, and her head held high, she let you know that she was around, and mister, you wasn't pushing her around neither. I says to her, warning, "I don't know what they taught you at your high and mighty Vassar university, but if

377

it was wearing low-cut frocks and smoking them dinky cigarettes, that's pure hussy to me. You're sending a signal to fellers to knock the chip off your shoulder, and sister, somebody's gonna take a whack at it."

"Well, what's so bad about that?" she snaps. "I can do anything boys can. I can handle them. Why waste time playing games?"

Well, that Barrow dandy caught on quick enough. South in his mouth, snapping his heels together cavalry style, ain't he the gallant one, though! He had poor Nora gulled into thinking that he could hang the goddamn moon. I says, "Girl, before we get out of this dump, you're going to see a hundred like him, so you just cool off. We got a whole new life to plan, with the Hearst business gone under in this damn war."

"Well, it's not we."

"Who then?"

She jammed her hands on her hips. "Papa, one of these days, you're going to realize that you simply have to make your life without Mum, and I've got to make mine. I have every right to."

"Ah, so now it's rights, is it? What have we got here, a barracks lawyer! Who the hell do you think raised you!"

"Papa! Don't you know how much I love you! God, our fabulous interlude on the ranch, why, I even had fantasies of living there with you for the rest of our lives. But girls grow up. Even with Irish fathers, someday they have to get loose."

"Well, you're that, you are! I'm a hair away from taking you over my knee!"

She sighed. "Please don't be so dense. You're a different generation, a whole different culture. This is 1916. Sure, girls smoke, they don't wear bustles, and sometimes they even let a boy kiss them without getting permission from the Pope or some clingy chaperone. Wake up. I'm nineteen. You can't just freeze me in amber like Daddy's pretty little butterfly. There's even a war coming on. Listen to the officers talk. Germany has spies down here. They're stirring up the people, hoping to lure us into a war with Mexico, so that we won't go to Europe and help the poor allies. Ned really believes that."

"Ned! Ned! Ned! Shavetail punk, don't know nothing!"

"He's on the inside, Patrick, and you're outside! You've had your wars. You shouldn't even be playing soldier down here. You're too old, Papa! Please, I don't want you to get shot...."

She began to weep, and maybe it was the whiskey still in me, but I was blubbering, too, so she hits me with her temperance lecture, Carrie Nation bustin' damn saloons. I should swear off, for Momma's sake if not for myself. Finally she had me saying, Ah, hell, maybe I would, feeling bad enough to die, the rotgut never having agreed with my belly.

378

But that very night, here comes Barrow in his military motor car. So swanky, bringing her a mittful of desert weeds with a ribbon on 'em, and skylarking her off to see the sights. Well, I seen mine, I did, swilling beer in a sloppy saloon with the common troopers, and a few Injuns tossed in for old time's sake.

Her words had hurt me. Sure and it was clear by then that all the glory marches of my young days had led me noplace at all, just back where I started. The bitter price I paid for it was losing my beloved Daisy to the damn fever of war, and now my girl, drifting to the very same thing, without a thought in her balmy head of what it was going to mean.

Because there wasn't no accommodations in camp for transients, the staff brass gave us a common wall tent, and a black orderly hangs an army blanket down the middle of it so's we wouldn't be seeing each other in the flesh. But sometimes in the nights, me in my cot on one side, and she in hers, on the other, I'd hear the little girl sigh in her sweet loving dreams, and damn, my heart like to break.

To get away from it, and kill time till Pershing got back, I talked a stable sergeant out of a couple of cavalry mounts. By damn, Barrow wasn't the only feller who could take her sightseeing, so off we'd canter along the irrigation ditches and Mormon cornfields in the green arroyo below town.

What chapped me, she was already making noises about going to work as a steno for Pershing's headquarters. Most of the dumb soldiers couldn't run a typewriting machine, but her high falutin' education had taught her how. The hell with that, I says, every officer on the post sniffing and swaggering around her, Barrow at the head of the pack.

Well, wouldn't it be my luck, one morning when we were trotting down a lane of willows along an irrigation ditch, an air machine whines over us. It acted like it had gone loco, the motor roaring, then cutting out and popping, the craft swooping up and down like a kite. I says to Nora, "I ain't never seen one flying like that!"

"Papa! He must be in trouble!"

He flashes right over our heads, khaki and stars shining and the wooden wheels spinning. Our guvmint horses give a squeal and buck, and I had to snatch Nora out of her saddle. At that, my own muleheaded bugger jumps fifteen feet in a shy, toppling the both of us off, smacking the hard dirt, me cradling her in my arms and my boots splashing into the irrigation ditch. "Them sonsofbitches!" I bellowed, shaking my fist at the sky. And then getting loose from Nora, dust all over her, "Are you hurt, darlin'?"

"Of course not! Patrick," she cried, "he's falling!"

The machine, upping and downing like a rolly-coaster, nosed straight at the fallow field. "There ain't room!" I shouted. "Pull up!"

He was going to smack a bank of dirt at the far end. Nora grabbed my hand, we leapt the irrigation ditch and pell-melled across that soft field. With a shatter like the breaking of a thousand box crates, the machine went slamming into the earth, wheels flying off, the double wings ripping and snapping the wires holding the contraption together. By the time we run up, the whole sorry mess lay ticking and smoking like a bomb about to go off. Nora screamed, "Ned!"

Damn if it wasn't him, his face covered with oil and bits of the machine sticking to his hair. He was trying to get loose of the rear seat, and the other skybird, a tall, blond feller, was pulling him out.

But the sound I heard sure wasn't the moaning of wounded men. Why, the pair of 'em were doubled over laughing, Barrow slapping the other man on the shoulder. "You read the book all right, George, but what about the chapter on how to land the damn thing?"

"Icarus and Daedalus, my boy. We got too near the sun." The blond feller grinned and kicked his boot through the wrecked wing. "Come on, quick now, we want no part of this."

He broke into a run, scrambling over the ditch bank. Nora was trying to get the slivers out of her precious Ned, but he was running, too. When I caught up to them, they were a half mile away, hunkered down in the rows of tall corn where an army couldn't have found them.

Damn skylarkers. The way it come out, the first looey, name of George Patton, was Pershing's aide. I'd seen him around the camp, a rangy, firebrandy sort, twinkling blue eyes and bushy blond eyebrows. The crazy devil had got the idea that he could teach himself and Barrow to fly, air machines being the career of the future. Zooming around sure beat hell out of polishing butt on a McClellan saddle. So Patton reads the instruction book that come with the crate, figures that's all there is to it and roars her into the sky. "The only problem," he says to me with a wink, "that machine we parked in the dirt is the last serviceable one in the command. The General is not going to be pleased. We appreciate your dropping in on us. But not only did you not see the mishap take place, but for the life of you, you have no idea who was in the machine. It could have been any of a thousand soldiers. You have never heard of these two." He had a cold sort of grin by then, hooking his fingers around the brace of pearl-handled Colt .44's that were dangling from his issue belt. "Do I have your word on that?"

"Mr. Kelly is old Army, George," Ned Barrow said lightly. "He knows how the game is played."

"And I do, too," Nora butted in. "Nobody's saying anything. I'm just so glad that you aren't hurt."

Patton gave me a hard look. "I'll take your word then. Sometime I hope to do you a favor in return." He was squinting toward the dis-

380

tant wreck, where I noticed now that a motorcycle and side car was wheeling in. "Ned, shuck that uniform, wash the oil off it yourself. Then put in for a patrol, get out in the desert for a few days until this thing cools off. Move now, time's a-wasting."

They lit out of there quick, but Nora and I had to take our mounts back to the stable. It was about noon before we showed up at headquarters where our tent was.

Standing at attention on the dusty parade ground were all the officers in the expedition. Poor buggers were stiff as ten pins, sweat running down their faces, and none of them daring to lift a finger to brush away the sand flies buzzing their ears.

With his riding quirt clenched in his fists, Black Jack Pershing was walking slowly down the line of them, staring into each face, his brown-gray moustache bristling and his eyes spitting sparks.

The thing was, Pershing had returned to camp just about the time that the air machine hit the dirt. He didn't see it, of course, but an old Injun fighter like him had a sixth sense about where every truck or gun or cavalry troop ought to be. And with the air machines, which were his favorite toys, and a lifeline both, he must have counted the damn things in his sleep. When one come up missing, hell was going to pay.

If I thought the man could cuss at Wounded Knee or in the river at Cuba, that was just warming up for the tongue-lashing he give his lads this time.

Who had done it? he was roaring. Which of the rotten sons of whores had taken the last operative air machine and junked it in a field? "Who! One of you is guilty! When that miserable cur steps forward, goddamn his hide, he'll wish he'd never left his mother's tit. I'll have his bars, his career, his ass!"

Not a muscle moved. Khaki ties ruffled in the wind, campaign hats were tilted down at the dirt. I whispered to Nora, "Git back in the tent, I ain't having you hear that man's turrible mouth."

"But Papa, if you say anything, if you peep...? Please, can I trust you...?"

I shoved her out of there and tried to get scarce myself. Pershing was still scowling from face to face. When I passed Patton, who was at the end of the line, he gave me a sly wink of his bushy eyebrow, then went back to staring at his boots. If there ever was a cat choked on an awful big canary, it was that scamp, standing up to the bombardment with nary a flinch. I liked the lad. He had some guts.

But he was going to pay for them, too, before very long. The thing simmered down finally. Time went by. Nobody must have coughed up who done it. Besides, Pershing had other troubles by then. The columns of cavalry that he was sending off goose-chasing hadn't turned up hide nor hair of Pancho Villa. There was a few fights with Mexican starvies out in the cactus, but the main problem now was coming from the Carranzista Federal troops. Our allies, they were supposed to be, but hell, when Americans go racing into Mexico, you can count on the buggers quitting their fight with each other and turning on you like rabid dogs. Instead of helping us, their Federal Generals were ordering Pershing to get out of Mexico, every damn one of us. If U.S. troops went anyplace south of Dublan, they'd be attacked by the Carranzistas and Villistas both.

But old hard rock Pershing was the wrong man to try to bluff. He shot back to Carranza: "I do not take orders except from my own government." Stuff that one in your tortilla, *senor jefe!*

One night, along about then, Pershing sends an orderly to fetch me. The soldiers had built him an adobe with a tent top on it, but the tall, stiff general was outside, cricked down on a blanket, Plains Injun style, beside the embers of a fire.

The man never smiled that you could count on, but his eyes twinkled in his leathery face and he shoved me a hard mitt. "Heard you were here, Sergeant. Wanted to see you. Long time it's been. A mite better than Kettle Hill, but not much. Sit down, Kelly."

I says yessir, but was struck at how old the man seemed. Eighteen years since the creek crossing in Cuba, and 26 since Wounded Knee. He still had the fire of command in him, but his face was deeper lined, and his eyes held a smoky bitterness.

I'd heard the talk around camp, of course. When Pershing got orders to take command of the Punitive Expedition, he left his wife and children behind at the cushy Army post of the Presidio, out in Frisco, weeping under the redwoods after Daisy had lost our child. Anyhow, Pershing must have figured his family would be more comfortable at the Presidio than chasing after him in the desert. I'd met his wife in Washington, a graceful lady and daughter of Wyoming's Senator Francis Warren. Not two days after he'd said goodbye to her at the Presidio, their quarters burned to the ground, the lovely lady and their kiddies dying in the flames.

Patton was sitting in Pershing's office in El Paso when the telly-gram come, bringing the horrible news. Pershing just stared at it and dropped it on his desk. God almighty, what a hard man, seeing his life burned up, but all he did was to brush at his eyes, and then without a word, turned back to the Army business at hand.

He'd been trying to get rid of the pesky Patton. That young turk was so determined to become Pershing's aide that he'd set for three days on the floor of the office, begging the General to take him on. But when the tellygram hit, the old soldier finally gave in, maybe like Patton was his last son to raise, now that the rest were gone.

As we sat by the fire, none of that come out, of course. Patton had strolled in and joined us. With a flinty look at him, Pershing says quietly, "Now here's a young man who doesn't get enough war. Says I'm not giving him combat assignments, so maybe he'd be better off transferring to another branch. Aviation section."

Pershing was scowling at him, but Patton just grinned. "Risk my life in one of those machines? Not a chance, sir. I'm happy as a clam doing staff work. This paper here, that paper there. Let somebody else smell the powder smoke."

"Lying sonofabitch," Pershing grunted, and jerked a map out of his dispatch case. "All right, you asked for it. Ranch house at San Miguelito, east of Lake Itascate. Sergeant Kelly, do you know that area?"

"I been through it, sir. They scrabble out a bit of maize, corn, down there. I bought some for Hearst not long ago."

Pershing squinted at me. "You've been Secret Service, and also a scout. We're short of that. I can use you. I want you to buy some corn for us. Requisition it, U.S. dollars. Have you got the stomach for it?"

"Well, I'll damn well give her a shot, Jack. Tired of sitting under canvas cutting my toenails. But I ain't saying that the Mex won't run us out of there, either. The way this thing is getting, we're enemies of the lot of 'em."

"You won't be alone, Kelly." Pershing flicked the map to Patton. "I had word tonight that a colonel or a general, whatever the hell they call him, Julio Cardenas, has been seen at San Miguelito. He's a big fish, Patton, chief of Villa's bodyguards, the Dorados. I want him hooked. I need something to stuff in Wilson's craw so that he'll stop pussyfooting and let us fight the war we came for."

He laid it out quick. Patton was to take three Dodge automobiles and six black riflemen. Pick the best shooters in the regiments. A Mormon cowboy named Lem Spilsbury would guide us to the place. Get out there and do it.

I grinned. "Sounds like there's more here than corn, General. Do I get in on the fight?"

"Corn's your excuse to be there, but I'll be needing some afterward." He glanced at Patton, "You shove this young pup's nose in it and show him that the only war isn't in the sky. Bring him back to me, Kelly, I don't want to have to break in another one of these goddamn restless heroes."

We left that night. Hell, I didn't even go back to our tent, risk waking Nora and getting another lecture about old men doing what they shouldn't. I helped Patton sort out six black boys, fine veteran troopers who'd tasted ball on the Plains, Cuba and the Philippines. We loaded 'em into the autos and picked Spilsbury out of his cow corral in Dublan. Hell of a lad, arms on him like fence posts and standing six foot eight in his big boots. He must have had Mex in him someplace, for he spoke pure Chihuahua, and just the way he

383

sniffed the country and spotted trail, I was glad to have him along.

In the first light of day, our Dodges come clunking up a hill. Patton lifts his arm and we stop in billowing dust. There in a tawny basin below us stands a rambling hacienda, built like a damn garrison, slit windows for firing at Apaches long ago, and behind the top battlements, a dark roof made out of ocotillo branches. The whole place was hunkered down behind a thick adobe wall, a square fortress that could have held way more Villistas than we needed.

But Patton was standing up in his auto seat, dust goggles on his khaki campaign hat. When he lowered his field glasses, he grinned. "Ideal," he said. "Mobilized, we can encircle the whole place before they even know what hit them. I'm going to tell you men," his eyes swept the dusty faces of the black shooters, "this is going to be the first automotive attack in the U.S. Army. Historic charge. Now, do it right, do it well. I don't want a single enemy to escape. Leave women and children unharmed, and under orders of our schoolteacher President, you are not to fire at an enemy until he fires at you first. Clear? Make me proud of you, boys."

They were nodding, yassuh, chuckling. Hell, to them stony-faced buffalos, one war was the same as the next, wheels or not. But maybe, at that, Patton had it right. We were doing something brand new, and I thrilled at it, the young turk jamming the gears on his auto and away we sped, me standing on the running board with the desert flying past. I thought of all the times I'd done it on a horse, but they were gone now, them glory days of bugles and thundering hooves. The motor cars were roaring and swerving, bucking down the long hill, two of the contraptions peeling away from us in spires of dust, swooping behind the hacienda to cut off any escape.

Patton slams us right up to the big gate in the adobe wall. Hell, we come in so fast the Mex didn't even have time to shut it. The Dodge careens to a stop, me leaping off the runner, Patton and the Spilsbury lad lurching in behind me.

I stopped dead in my tracks. Now, mind you, we didn't know if anybody was here, but what do I see, in the shadows of the adobe wall, but an old vaquero and a youngster in white cottons, bloody machetes in their hands. They had a beef hanging on the wall and were skinning it. I swung my Springfield at them, I know they seen me, but neither one give even a flinch. Like no noise had come, no dust, no gringoes, they just kept fleshing out their hide.

"Fishy," I says to Patton and Spilsbury. The Mormon lad nodded. "Likely more is waiting inside, sir. Leave the Judas goats out here like nothing was happening."

Patton, his pearly revolvers in both hands, starts running toward the thick mesquite doors of the hacienda, which were closed tight, an old iron latch on them. I grabbed him as we come into the shadows near the doorsteps.

"Slow down, lad. They seen us by now, and that door's got a latch from the inside, too." I shoved him off to one side of the door, Spilsbury already crouching against the adobe on the other side. I had it in my mind to leap the last two red tile steps and fling off that iron latch. I was close enough to see scars in the mesquite door, like bullets had made them. And maybe it was warning enough, something from the old days anyhow. I flung myself over on Patton's side, against the wall, just as the door flies open with a crash.

Two Mexicans, mounted, they had their damn horses in there, come leaping out, Winchesters at their hip, and they were levering them, blamming, spraying, not two yards from us, the bullets hissing, smacking plaster off the adobe wall.

The shock of it, or maybe instinct, knocked me down on all fours, groping for my rifle in the dust. But not Patton. He was standing widelegged in the sun, and cool as if he was on a target range, he fires both his Colts, crash-bang, crash-bang. Horses squeal, there's a scream from one Mex, hit in the back, blood streaming through his white shirt and the crisscrossed bandoliers of ammunition.

The other Mex, a tall bugger in a big black sombrero and tight vaquero trousers, had managed to get ten yards or so away from us, his horse on the dead run. Patton draws down on him. Boom! The horse, gutshot, buckles his knees and goes down in the dirt with the rider under him.

I throws up my rifle to fire at the bastard, but Patton knocks it aside. "Hold fire. He's pinned. Give him a chance."

Sure enough, the big bay horse had fallen square on top of the Mex, who was cursing and roaring, getting untangled, and when he crawls out and gets to his knees, I see his Winchester lifting.

"Patton!" I shouts, the cocky punk standing there grinning with his revolvers dangling by his legs. "Shoot the sonofabitch!"

"Not until he fires first."

Zwwiish! The first Winchester round screams between the both of us. Patton raises his right hand Colt, steadies it over his left forearm and fires. The greaser staggers, clutches at his left side, and falls on his face.

At maybe forty yards, Patton had shot him square through the left armpit. I heard later that he was the best pistol shot on the Expedition, and I believed it then.

By now, several of the black shooters had come racing into the patio. Others were supposed to be blocking escape from the back of the hacienda. "I want the roof!" Patton shouts. Spilsbury and the boys lugged over a big dead tree, and damn if Patton doesn't scale up the thing, hike over the battlement and leap onto the roof.

Crazy fool, I could have warned him how these adobes are built.

Nothing but ocotillo branches lying over rafters. Patton lets out a howl, and he falls through the roof. Not all the way, just treed on a rafter, with his feet dangling into the living room.

Spilsbury thought quicker than I did. He starts racing up the dead tree, followed by a black trooper, and shouting at me, "If there are people inside, they'll cut his legs off with machetes!"

It didn't happen, though. The black trooper and Patton were laughing like hell when they finally got him loose of the spiny ocotillo branches. One last Mex was hiding out along the south wall, pinging at Patton and his troopers as they approached him. Then he stood up, raised his left arm like he was surrendering. "Easy now," I says to Patton. We edged to within about five yards of him, damn if the sneaky bugger doesn't whip out a revolver with his right hand and blows it right into our faces.

But his aim was wrong. His knees had already buckled. When we came to him and Patton rolled his body over with his boot, blood was running out both corners of his mouth. He was stone dead, and the man we were after, General Julio Cardenas.

I says to Patton and Spilsbury, "Mop it up and git gone from here."

"I want these bodies for identification," Patton says, and beckons a black trooper. "Bring the motor cars, strap the bodies on the hoods."

The trooper grins. "You's meaning like dead deer, sah?"

Patton slaps him on the shoulder. "Good hunt, boy. Dead deer."

Inside the hacienda was a bunch of squealing, moaning women and kids. They was Madre de Diosing us, clinging to our bloody hands, sure they'd be next, but I says in Tex-Mex, "Senoras, just get yourselves back to where you come from. This war's over. We're burying the dead."

We had three bodies, the general, a captain on Villa's staff, and a poor damn private soldier who didn't know what hit him when Patton gave him the slam. Inside the gloomy old place, stacked with Villista arms, I found a threadbare telephone line and jerked it down. "Good thinking," Patton said. "We've got to go back through Rubio, don't we?"

"If they've already heard about this, we're in trouble," I says. Rubio was a huddly little pueblo, like thousands of others down here, different only because we knew that it was a hotbed of Villistas. Patton asks Spilsbury if there wasn't some other route to take, but the lad says, "No, sir. We've just got to bull our way through. No shooting back, though, or that whole countryside will be howling for our scalps."

It was about dusk when we come rumbling into the little dump, narrow, rutted main street of adobes, doors and shutters flying open. God almighty, the hate in those faces when they seen dead

Villistas on our hoods. First the mongrel dogs come out growling, baring their teeth. Then women, kids, old men swarmed us, screaming "Viva Villa!", beating on the sides of the Dodges with rocks and spitting in our faces. When they stuffed a burro cart in front of the lead Dodge, the black trooper driving just crashed it aside. I've got to hand it to them boys, being so cool. Here they was dark-skinned themselves, and we were killing dark skins. But just like the loyal Apache scouts before them, they were serving our flag, though the sadness of wiping out their own kind would long rankle, just as it had in Cuba and the Philippines.

When we got back to camp, officers and Pershing himself were milling around in the headlights of those Dodges, fingering the bodies on the hoods and slapping us on the back. "You can do something right, Patton," Pershing muttered. "First blood, and it's about time. Maybe put some backbone into Wilson." When he passed me, he glowered, "I don't send old men into fights like that, not on purpose. You're stretching your luck. Get out of here and go home, while you still can!"

"If I had a home, sir," I says, grinning.

But the end wasn't far off by then. I suppose Pershing seen it coming, because he was onto the political shenanigans. Our Carranza Federal allies, cocky, blow-harding buggers, were turning up the heat on Pershing. Nora give me some of it from her precious Ned. According to rumors among the cavalry officers, 10,000 Federal troops were now massing to the east of us along the Mexican National railway. Idea was to cut Pershing's communications on all sides so that we'd have no direction to go but home.

One night, Nora come rushing back to our tent from her stenoing at headquarters and cried, "Patrick, it's going to be war with Mexico! I'm sure of it!"

The poor thing was trembling, splashing water on her face and rubbing the dust off with a towel. When she turned to me, the color had risen in her cheeks and her blue eyes were dark and mournful. "Ned will have to go!"

Gently, I took her wet hands. "Now girl, you don't know who will have to do what, so quit worrying your head with it. Besides, the man's a soldier, or says he is. That's what they're here for, if it's got to be a war."

"But Papa, it's so criminally stupid. Ned says that the Germans are laughing at Pershing and all of us floundering around in the desert. If we can't even catch a bandit like Villa, their spies are telling them that we're a paper tiger. Our Army is so weak that we couldn't possibly help the Allies in France. So now the Germans are goading the Carranza troops to attack us. Patrick, if we get lured into a big war down here, Germany will have a free hand to do anything it wants in Europe. Overrun the place, rape even more of those poor Belgian nuns…"

"Nuns is it now? And I suppose they're stripping white women naked, too. Ah, girl, wake up, they're gullin' you with them tales! Didn't I see it in Cuba, rotten yellow newspapers and dandy correspondents firing people up to the bloodlust, until they're ready to go rip the throats out of the world."

"Well, you've done your share of it, I'd say!"

"Indeed so, and was sorry for most of it, too. Sick of it. Why, I was even thinking tonight, Pershing's telling me to get out. We can't stop their damn war, and I'm tired of trying. Hearst give me a job here, and I aim to finish it. Sell Hearst's beef to the Army, put some caretakers up there with a stand of rifles to protect his damn furniture, and skedaddle the hell north. That's best for the both of us, girl. I'm taking you out of here."

She whipped to me. "Just like that, is it?"

"If I says so, yas! I'm your father, Nora, didja forget!"

"Oh, Jesus Christ," she screamed. "Don't I wish I could! Well, you've pulled that string for the last time, Patrick. You go north, yes, I think you should. You're tiring, you look terrible, and still drinking, which you promised not to." She came over and gripped my shoulders. "You want it straight, Papa, well, this is it. You're going and I'm staying. Ned is here. I love him."

It wasn't two hours later when Ned wasn't there anymore. Gone with his troop, slipped out in the night, and Nora, grief-stricken. "'You're talking about loving a soldier. Get used to it, darlin,'" I says, and hugs the poor thing to me in her sobs.

What it come down to, Patton told me, Pershing was calling Carranza's bluff. He ordered a cavalry captain, Boyd, to take two black troops, including Ned as one of the shavetails, and march this handful of buffalo soldiers smack into the Mex garrison of 10,000. Not to fight, Patton said, just showing the flag, plunking our cards on the table. If our lads made it to the railroad, then Pershing would know that he hadn't been cut off, and the Mex were bark and no bite. If, on the other hand, they slammed the door, old Black Jack was going to make them pay dearly for the consequences.

A day passed, then a second, and as the hot dusty winds riffled through the camp, there was electricity in the air, like a thunderstorm building, far off. Nora was so jumpy she was like trying to catch a kite. I'd find her running down to the stables, begging common troopers for news of her soldier boy. My heart ached for her, and finally after she'd goaded me into it, I went to see Pershing.

On a bluff behind headquarters, I noticed a bonfire blazing

never been there before, so I strolls over to it. A few soldiers were heaping cardboard boxes into the flames, the papers inside curling black and wisping into the night. "Well, now," I says to one lad, "what are you dog robbers up to?"

He sniffs at me like, who the hell am I butting in? "Ah, come on, son," I says, "I ain't no civvy. I'm part of this outfit."

"Then watch it go up in smoke." He kicks another box into the fire. "Expedition records, orders and the like."

"Why would they be doing that?"

"Why anything in the goddamn Army, mister! The Man says it's so we don't got to lug 'em home." He pointed out across the fire, and I saw a tall, solitary figure half-lighted in the flames.

When I come up beside Pershing, he had his arms folded across his chest, and he was staring into the bonfire. His face was so grim, I had to wonder if he was seeing again that terrible night when he'd lost his missus and kiddies to the flames. Finally, I says gently, "I ain't trying to butt in, General, but this bonfire sure looks like the end of something. Heading home, are we?"

"If I knew the answer to that, Kelly..." Shaking his head, he moved past me a few paces, opened his pants and took a leak, trickling down the bluff below. When he was done, he grunted, "Have you time for a walk back to headquarters?"

"Yessir."

"Well, come on then."

We edged out into the darkness, walking in silence the long way around toward headquarters. When we got out to where the horse remuda was, he stopped and watched the guvmint animals chomping the miserable desert weeds. "I wonder how long they've got left," he murmured. "Or any of us."

"Sir?"

"The old ways of war. Forty miles a day on beans and hay. You had a mission back then, a clear-cut target, you charged it head on. No politicians telling you how to fight, and best of all, no goddamn machinery except a carbine!" He kicked wearily at the dirt. "Every aeroplane I've got is down, and the new ones are rotting in crates at Columbus, because nobody knows how to put them together. And these infernal telephone systems, jangling one order one minute and another diametrically opposed order the next. Don't they remember that we used to fight battles without this crap? But they've doped us with their modern wizardry, Kelly, they make us rely on it, and when it quits me, I'm down to having no eyes, no ears, and facing a goddamn hostile wilderness with green, spoiled troops who don't think that war is supposed to happen like this anymore."

I could see by then that the lonely, hardbitten man was trying to get it all off his chest, so I just nods and says, "Well, sir, I'm thinking that we had pretty much the same going into Rosebud. Nothing but hostile wilderness, not knowing where Custer was, or he us. But maybe that's what war has to be, blundering on the best you can."

He turned to me sharply. "Captain Boyd blundered. I have to think that."

"Sir?"

His pace began to quicken. The man had a real stride on him, particularly when his fury was rising. "I sent him out with two troops, two days ago. Gave him that Mormon boy, Patton's friend Spilsbury, as guide. Test the Federal garrison at Carrizal. A test, not a fight unless fired upon. I cannot remain here blind, Kelly. If they're massing a signifigant force against us...." He shook his head.

"Do you think they had a fight, sir?"

"I goddamn don't know! Just tonight, a Mexican rides in here, the bastards lie, but he was bragging about a U.S. force getting its butt kicked in the Carrizal region." He smacked his fist into his palm. "Now that has to be Boyd's people! The four other columns I have out are too far away. But if I respond to this rumor or outright lie, that could be just what the Mexicans want, suck out more of my command on a wild goosechase and leave us as sitting ducks."

We were closer to the headquarters tents now, and I could see shapes walking around the campfires. "Why not send out a patrol, sir?"

"Two have already left," he grunted. "If this rumor is a lie, they'll come back empty. But if it's true, they'll either have a fight or spend most of their time rounding up our stragglers. Goddammit, I need accurate information now! Wilson has been hounding me so much that I've shut off communication with him. What does he know up there? Damn naive foreign policy, he recognizes Carranza, thinking he can trust him because he's a fellow schoolteacher, and so when the sonofabitch spits in our face, we're supposed to cringe and send apologies. Wilson stonewalls us. Here's Freddy Funston in El Paso, veteran guerilla fighter in Cuba and the man who captured Aguinaldo for us in the Philippines, yet the White House kills every recommendation he makes. Same for Hugh Scott back at Army HQ. Those men are the best soldiers we have. Don't matter to Wilson. He's cut our balls off down here, and I'm not taking it!"

"General," I says, "I know that country around Carrizal. If I went alone, no troopers kicking up dust..."

Pershing glowered at me. "You're too goddamn old! I told you to get out of here while you still could."

"Yessir," I says, and grins, "but as long as your air machines is busted down, maybe you could still use a man on a horse. Besides, my daughter's got a feller riding with one of them troops. She wants to know what happened to him."

"You damn Army mule. Ah, maybe I'm lucky to have one left.

390

Get moving then, find out if the Carranza troops attacked my people, and how bad."

"And if they did, sir?"

Pershing took a deep breath. "Then by God, mister, they've drawn a line in the sand and dared me to step over. I'll hit them with every troop in my command, 10,000 men, trucks, artillery and a 100,000 National Guard backing us up. If Carranza wants it, or Villa either, they'll get it. We'll go to war with all of Mexico, regardless of which sides the bastards pretend to be on!" In fury, he strode away, then stopped short and walked back. He thrust out his hand and gripped mine. "Thanks, soldier. Make this your last fight, will you?"

"I hope like hell, sir," I says, but even then knowing it wouldn't be. We were too far into war now ever to get loose of it for a long, long time.

I slipped out of Dublan in the middle of that windy night. I'd picked myself a strapping guvmint mount, a long-legged bay with enough thoroughbred in him to eat up the sand and lonely miles.

That Chihuahua country west of Carrizal was such a miserable desert a jackrabbit couldn't make a living in it, so I wasn't much worried about Mex being out there. Hell, I didn't even see cattle, just rode on past occasional windmills, creaking ghostly, trying to pump water that had long ago gone dry.

By dawn, though, I started to get wary. In the pale sky, more buzzards were circling than ought to be there with such slim pickings. Ahead of me, shimmering in the first light, was a row of cottonwoods, and behind it, a single street of adobes, the pueblo of Carrizal.

Dismounting, I eased my way through the cover of mesquite until I dropped into a dry irrigation ditch that ran past the town. By then, I could smell it—stinking, sun-rotted, bird-torn human flesh.

I crawled to the first of the lads. Buffaloes, good boys, their faces puffed up like black balloons and their dead mouths gaping at the sky. A Mex Mauser machine gun lay shattered in the irrigation ditch. The troopers had tried to take it out, ran at it across an open field and were cut down like cornstalks. The damn Mex hadn't buried anybody. Even the rag-tag Federal troops were laying as they fell, and there were more of them by far than our lads. The black troopers of the 10th Cavalry went down all right, but not before they'd taught the Carranza gang a bitter lesson.

I crouched in the ditch, covering my nose from the stink. Bluebelly flies were swarming me like I was the next corpse to feed on. But then, just above me, I heard the tinkling of a bell. Peering out, I saw the furry gray legs of a burro, and beside them, the bare feet of a tattery little Mex girl. She was wearing a Pillsbury flour sack for a skirt.

At the sight of me, her mouth dropped open. *"Querida,"* I

391

whispered in Spanish. "I'm not going to hurt you. *Ven.* Come here."

She twisted around to look back at the adobes, her rope of black hair switching across her little butt. When she hesitated, I slid some U.S. coins onto the ditch bank. That got her attention. She scurried in and when she snatched them, I grabbed her arm. "*Digame.* Tell me, what happened, little sister?"

Ah, she was an angel, that one, black button eyes flashing with all the fire and courage of her race, and mostly the mourning. Tears streamed down her dusty cheeks.

"*Senor, senor, que barbara!*" she whimpered. How could *Dios* allow such horror to happen? I hugged her to me and finally wormed out all I needed to know. "The American officer," she pointed out Boyd, a swollen lump of khaki a few yards from us, "that man told mi General, el General Gomez that he was going to take his troops through this town. Those were his orders, and no Mexican soldiers were going to stop him. Oh senor, we did not want there to be this killing. We wanted only to run. Mi mama took us all to the church, we were praying in there, the doors locked, but too late, they begin the guns anyway, the terrible sound of the guns!"

By then, the pueblo had started to awaken, mongrels barking, and old crones shuffling out of the hovels to stoke their mesquite ovens. It was time for me to get scarce, so I kissed the little tyke on her forehead and folded a greenback into her palm. A few minutes later, I'd edged out of the ditch, with nobody seeing me, and figured that I'd found what I came for. There'd been a bad fight indeed, and Pershing was going to have to know about it quick.

Yet, as I swung onto my horse, something struck me fishy. I'd counted maybe 25 U.S. dead. But with two troops attacking, Boyd would have had 100 men anyway, and the guide Spilsbury, too. What the devil had happened to them? Even Nora's precious Ned Barrow? I saw no whites other than Boyd among the dead. Had the rest of them broken and run, maybe with the Federals pursuing? Whatever, there was more to this tragedy than I'd seen so far, and I'd best smoke it out.

I had water in my canteen and a pocket full of hardtack, but damn, as I sat there on my big guvmint bay, I felt glum, and hard used too. Old. Just plain too old for these long desert rides, and skulking around in a hostile land. One voice in me said, Lad, let the armies bury their own dead, it ain't your war, and you seen too many like it for too long now, with nary a tinker's damn for thanks. Yet the other voice says, Sure, just park your horse back in the barn and sit in a rocker swapping lies with the other old vets. Is that how you want to end your days?

In the sun, under the drooping mesquite tree where I was pondering, in trots a mangy jackrabbit, flopping his tall ears and munching his chops. "Ah, you scamp!" I says, dust in my throat, "what are you grinnin' at!" I flung him a bit of hardtack, knowing by then that I wasn't going to need all of it. Why play games with myself and pretend I was packing it in? I was a running man, I'd always been running square into the thick of it, and the day I stopped, I'd croak. So I was laughing there, feeling blessed that the good Lord was still giving me the chance to carry on.

Instead of heading back to Pershing, I made a wide circle of Carrizal and picked up a hot trail leading east to Villa Ahumada, and from there south down the Mexican National Railway track to Chihuahua City.

I took pains to steer clear of Federal troops, but once, along the track, a mounted patrol ran me down. They were ugly buggers, wanting to slap me around good, so I thinks quick and says, "Git your damn mitts offa me! Can't you see, I'm a *ganadero*, cattleman?" I give them a windy about buying beef for Presidente Carranza him-self, to feed their starving bellies. Any man who touched me would be shot. Growling like dogs, they backed off, and got a few pesos for their trouble. None of them were smart enough to notice that I was riding a horse with a U.S. brand.

By the time I hit big bustling Chihuahua City, I'd picked up enough gossip to send me galloping straight to the English consul, Thomas Beecham. He was a spindly lad I'd done business with for Hearst a few months back, so I busted right into his office and laid out the story I'd heard on the streets. Captain Boyd had gone down at Carrizal all right, but not before his troopers had killed General Gomez. That put the fat in the fire. In fury, the Federal garrison had swarmed our lads, took several dozen black troopers prisoners, and Lem Spilsbury with them. It turned out that Gomez's young widow had watched her husband get shot, and claimed that Spilsbury did it. She had the guards pin his arms while she beat him on the head with a rock until he was bleeding, almost out cold. Then she ordered the Federal troops to strip the prisoners naked and march them in the hot sun, first to Ahumada and finally to the Governor himself, at the palacio in Chihuahua. "So I'm figuring, Beecham," I says to the consul, "that they got to be here now, and that you'd know who and how many. What the hell we going to do about it?"

He was pleasant enough for a damn Englishman, sitting at a big desk, having his tea. But now, as he poured me a cup, his hand trembled. "I daresay it's a bloody mess, and we may be too late. The Governor and General Trevino have already tried the prisoners at the Palacio. They'll be shot this morning."

"Shot!" I bellowed. "Jesus, man, what in hell for? They were troops under fire!"

He sighed. "I'm just leaving to go over there. In light of the

393

news, I dread it. Did you hear? No, you couldn't have, you've been on the road." He stood up stiffly and lifted a dispatch from a spindle. "This came in moments ago from the U.S. command. Before dawn today, Pershing—he must have heard about Carrizal from some source other than you—he's begun to march out of Dublan with his entire command. He's launching a full-scale attack against the Federal forces. Do you have any idea what that means? War with all of Mexico."

"It figured to be," I said, thinking of Pershing staring at the flames in Dublan. "They bluffed the wrong man."

"Only it isn't going to happen."

"What?"

Beecham pushed the dispatch down on the spike. "In Pershing's attack force, there's a single radio receiver mounted in a wagon. Apparently it doesn't work properly, but this morning they managed to repair it. Less than an hour ago, on this radio, President Wilson managed to get a message through to Pershing, ordering him back to Dublan. 'Under no circumstances will your President involve the United States in a war with Mexico.' Thank God for the man's wisdom. Nothing would please the Boche more than to see your armies tied down in this cursed desert, and leaving us, the allied powers, to our fates in Europe." He grinned in his pale sort of way. "You surely must know by now, Mister Kelly, we sorely need you Yanks shoulder to shoulder with us in France."

"Ah, you and your damn British Empire," I muttered. "Sure, it's all you think of, across the ocean, saving your Queen, while right here under your nose, we got men shot at, killed, prisoners. Are we supposed to take that lyin' down?"

"All you can do, sir. There's far too much at stake here. The war is a long way from this desert."

"But them black troopers and the Mormon lad!" I blurted. "Maybe even my daughter's officer! Goddammit, I know these greasers. If they think they won't be punished, they'll put our lads up against the wall, Beecham!"

"It could be done by now. I'm afraid we're too late, sir!"

"Like hell!" I roared, and jerked him up out of his chair. "You're taking me to the Governor, and I'll thank you not to open your trap. I'll do the talking, that clear?"

"Well," he flustered, "I don't want to become persona non grata with the Carranza government. This is highly irregular…"

"So is war! Move now, get your motor car!"

Ten minutes later, we'd bumped through those dusty, crowded streets. Maybe I couldn't drive, but I could sure blow that klaxon horn, blaring burros and starvies out of our road. When we hit the Palacio, I stormed past the guards, flew up the marble steps and clattered into the Governor's office.

God help us, the first thing I see is a corpse, stripped naked and laying on a white sheet on the Governor's desk. General Gomez, it was, with two bloody holes in his chest big enough to put your fist through. "Dum-dum bullets!" the Governor roared at the sight of Beecham and me. "This is what you do to our people. Attack us without warning, disregard all conventions of war agreed upon by our nations. We shall not endure such treatment by Yankee invaders. The guilty will pay! See for yourself."

The Governor was a big man with flowing white hair and moustache, and beside him was General Trevino, the pockfaced Federal commander and a mean bastard at that. Together, they flung back the tall wooden shutters and daylight streamed in.

My heart rose in my throat. Below us, along the patio wall, stood about twenty black troopers, and Spilsbury, the only white man among them. The Federal firing squad had already formed. Soldiers were moving down the line, wrapping blindfolds across the eyes. A padre in a black hat was shuffling from man to man, mumbling his beads and asking for the poor devils' last confession.

"Jesus Christ!" I whirled to the Governor. "You can't do that!"

"Who are you telling me what I can do? Guard!" He shouted at the doorway, and Federal soldiers in mustard-colored uniforms came swarming toward me.

I swung on the buggers, and this time I had a Colt .45 service automatic drawn and aimed at the lead soldier. "One more step, *pendejo*," I said in Spanish, "and you die. After that, it's the Governor and the General, and then all the rest of you miserable bastards who will fall to Yanqui guns just like Gomez there. Back off," I swept the Colt over the Governor and Trevino. "I'm here to save your damn lives!"

"What are you talking about?" the Governor bellowed, face flaming red.

"General Pershing!" I cried, bluffing like hell that they didn't know that he'd turned back. "Right this minute, while you're getting ready to gun down innocent American soldiers, do you have any idea where Pershing is?"

Trevino frowned. "Well, of course we do! He's in garrison in Dublan where Presidente Carranza has ordered him to remain. Any movement of American forces except north, to your own country, will be regarded an act of war against Mexico!"

"Well, mister, you got it. Allies, are you? Oh, no. When you turned on our soldiers and gunned them down at Carrizal, you signed your death warrant." Beecham was cringing, trying to get me to back off, and Trevino thrusting toward me, but I bulled right on. "As I speak, Pershing is marching toward this city with 10,000 U.S.

troops, and 100,000 National Guard crossing the border behind them. That's what your treachery has brought you. Did you enjoy fighting the gringos at Carrizal? Do you like to look at the bodies of your dead generals?" I flung my arm at Gomez's corpse. "Well, Jefe, you have just started to look. Your corpse will be lying on that desk. Pershing will turn your tierra into a desert of blood, the slaughter of a thousand Carrizals will ring out up and down your cursed land!"

Trevino whirled to the Governor and both of their faces went ashen. "This cannot be possible!" the Governor cried. "He is not so foolhardy…"

"Say your prayers, burn your papers, flee now while you can, so you won't be tried as criminals of war."

"Criminals? We have done nothing!"

"What is that wall down there?" I cried. "Slaughterhouse. Mexican murder! Pershing will be here before the sun sets, and senor, I will personally show him the blood of innocent Americans reddening the dirt of your palacio!"

"They attacked us first!" Trevino raged. "They killed our people with illegal bullets! We have done nothing but what war demands!"

"Tell it to Pershing," I snapped, "and if he's the man I've served with all these years, I can tell you this, *cabron*. You and your mighty Gobernador will be the next ones standing at that wall and dead before dark!"

Their eyes darted back and forth. From the patio below trailed the command to the firing squad. "*Listo.*" Then, "*Apurete.*" I rushed to the window and stared down. The Federal troops had lifted their Mausers, glinting in the sun. The officer in charge raised his arm.

I whirled. "Hear it! Feel those bullets hitting you. Take your choice!"

The Governor hesitated, sweat gleaming on his pale forehead. Then with a moan and a lunge, he thrust past me. "No!" he bellowed out the window. "*Alto! Alto!*"

The faces below lifted to him. "*No tires!*" he screamed.

Slowly, the Mausers lowered, and now I was the one with sweat streaming out of me, my knees weak. When I turned to the Governor and Trevino, my voice was dry and hoarse. "You are wise men, senores. You have just saved your own lives and Mexico along with you. Release the prisoners."

The terrified Governor was more than happy to have it over with. In rapid Spanish, he began growling at Trevino for his stupidity in trying to bring the two nations to the edge of war. But Trevino was a hard nut, with his machismo badly gored.

"You let them do this, this provocation, Governor?" he cried. "I am no politician like you. I am a soldier. I have honor. Look at brave Gomez, my wife's cousin, and shot down with these vile

396

dum-dums of the Yanquis! Does Mexico now cringe before such dogs!"

"You're a lying bastard, Trevino! Look at this!" I jerked the sheet from Gomez's body. "Sure, the bullet holes are big, and I'll tell you why, because I've just come from Carrizal. Our troops and yours were only a few yards apart when they began shooting. That's what a Springfield slug does at point-blank range. Get me one of the captured rifles and a corpse and I'll blow the exact same holes in it."

Trevino scowled at the body. "I don't believe this and will not accept your insults!"

"Then start telling the truth, General." I drew the sheet back up over Gomez's body. "Ever since we've been in Mexico, and one of your people gets shot, you make up these lies about our ammunition. Well, that's going to stop, and I hope for your sake, right here and now." I turned to the Governor. "Bring the prisoners to this office and get the release papers signed. I'm taking them home."

Fifteen minutes later, the lads from the wall came trooping in. When they saw me, the darkies from the 10th were praising de Lawd and pumping my hand. Some of the poor buggers had crusted bandages on their arms and black faces. One had been shot through the throat and was leaking blood down his neck. Nobody had doctored him. Young Spilsbury's forehead was black and blue and deep scarred where Gomez's widow had pounded on him with rocks. He grinned at me in his broad-faced Mormon way. "Reckon I'll have these souvenirs the rest of my days. Will say this, though. I hope I ain't never that close again." He thrust out his hand. "Owe it to you, friend Kelly. Thank you, sir."

In truth, I was sagged out myself from the strain of it. I couldn't believe that I'd got the lads safe at last. But you can count on it, things in Mexico ain't never so easy. The Governor and Trevino were sulky and growly, now that they'd been shamed into backing down. Various flunkies come in, everybody complaining that there'd be extensive paperwork necessary before prisoners of war could be repatriated. Then, by that night, the roof fell in. They got word from their spies that Pershing wasn't attacking after all, the end result being that all of us, yours truly included, got dumped back into the stinking old Chihuahua City military jail.

One thing, though, I did find out from Spilsbury. When Boyd decided to bull through Carrizal, and Spilsbury warning him against it, Ned Barrow's troop got split off to go back for reinforcements. Chances are, Spilsbury thought, they might have made it to U.S. lines without being shot up too bad. At least, they didn't die there in the irrigation ditch.

"Well," I says, "the daughter will be pleased by that."

Spilsbury nodded with a grin. "On the patrol out, riding together, I got to talking to Lieutenant Barrow about your girl, Mr. Kelly.

Daresay he's quite smitten by her. Good reason, I'm thinking."

"We'll see about that, lad," I grunts. "First thing is to get us busted out of this clink." I stalked off and began rattling the cell bars until I got the guards paying enough attention to bring me the commandant.

By next morning, the Federales scurried around, polite as you please, and turned us loose. From what I could pick up, all hell had busted loose after Carrizal, and Pershing's near war with Mexico. By now, Beecham told me, the two nations had agreed on a peace conference, up someplace in cool New England. Funston and Scott would be going there, along with Wilson's striped-pants diplomats. Sit down with the Carranza generals and find a way for everybody to save face, and us go slinking home.

Pershing's Punitive Expedition was done for, that was the long and short of it. No Pancho Villa caught, nothing but some dead black lads face down in those lonely sands.

When we come up the Mex railway in a boxcar and hit El Paso, seemed like the whole town swarmed us, greeting the so-called heroes of Carrizal. Pretty girls were rushing out and giving us mittfuls of flowers, candies and smokes. The Texas papers were screaming bloody murder that this was the time to go in and wipe out all the damn greaser bandits that were left. Do it in one fell swoop, do it right this time, and carve out of that sorry country all we didn't snatch away in the war of 1845.

Me, though, I wanted none of it. Just to go home, wherever home was, find my Nora and get on with our normal lives again, if there could be such a thing anymore.

There wasn't, though. Not for Nora and me, and not for the US of A. I could feel it in my bones then, and how I mourned it.

For the rest of my days, my adopted land would never be the same precious place that I and all greenhorns and huddled masses had fled to. Fortress of freedom, was it? No kings, no slaves, an ordinary working stiff just as equal as the spiffiest nabob. Protected by our mighty oceans, sheltered in the bosom of Lady Liberty, we stood proud and alone like a rock of safety in a foul torrent, thumbing our noses at the old ways of the old lands that could never harm us again. Wasn't that why we'd come?

We had it, a fleeting moment of glory, but then, getting too soft, too greedy, too fearful, we let it slip through our fingers. Sold it for a pittance of coppers, I suppose, snatched at the glitter and mistook it for the gold. From that day in 1916 when our troopers thundered into the cursed Mexican desert, we buried not only the wilderness frontier but the grand, brawling nation I'd fled to as a lad. Instead of escaping from the Old World, we decided to let ourselves be sucked right back into it, swallowed by the Moloch of these dying empires beyond our shores.

Hell, I seen it coming in Cuba in '98, Specs Roosevelt and the jingo bunch steaming us out across the oceans with his Great White Fleet. Raise our starry flag, kill the kakiak ladrones, snatch the riches from the palmy isles. Imperialists we decided to become, just as ruthless as the damn English, and so it was natural that we'd throw in with the thrones on The Other Side, getting into the family spat between England, Germany and Russia, where all the kings were damn cousins, having a falling out that would cost millions of lives before it was done, and never done it would be. So don't stand clear of it as George Washington had warned. No, lads, not anymore. Play their bloody war games side by side with them until we'd be tramping our boots across muddy European nations that had been fighting each other for a thousand years, and nobody had won yet or ever would.

Isolationism, you say? Yes, by God, and it had worked, it had blossomed us into the greatest nation ever seen. So why lose it, why trade it away?

What had come over us, what kind of madness to make us give up the precious freedom we'd had, all those long years since we'd first had the guts to kick the redcoats out of our sacred land?

Ah, hell, how would a stiff like me know why? As my spidery little friend, Smedley Butler, used to say, "All my career in the Marine Corps, I've been nothing but a high-class muscleman, a racketeer for Wall Street or Standard Oil." He was talking the Boxer Rebellion days, Philippines and the Banana Wars too. Another officer I served with in Mexico said, "Get this straight, boys. If we have to go fight the Boche in Europe, we'll be doing it as bill collectors, to pull the House of Morgan's bad European loans out of the fire."

When we killed off the frontier and the poor reds along with it, did we think that Manifest Destiny had run its course and was done?

Ah, no, lads. We was just beginning to fight, beginning to sound the grand battle cries of freedom. Saving humanity from the beast, was we?

What we was saving, in truth, was the dirty money fingers of the principalities and powers that would be running the world and digging our graves for all of our new century that my eyes would ever see.

Glory, was it?

Not now. Never again for this old grayhead. My wars might not have been done yet, still no peace, but by 1916, my poor soul was wailing at the sham of it, the injustice, the loss of loves and lives, in a world that was mine no more.

Youth gone, middle age too. Old now. Turn the nag toward home, Patrick, and ride down that last long hill.

GO OUT FIGHTIN'

Just like young Matt before her, Nora had turned to her Dutch uncle, old Specs Roosevelt, to steer our lives again. He sent me the letters.

April 15, 1917
Aviation Section Flying Field
San Antonio, Texas

Dearest Cousin Teedie,

How sweet of you to write me congrats on my engagement to Ned. Oh, Teedie, he's such a darling. Can't wait for you to meet him. We will be coming your way soon, I know that, now that IT'S HAPPENED!

I've so admired you for your brave words and deeds in waking up the country, making us prepare ourselves for the war we've all known that we can't avoid. And now I read in the papers that not only are your boys already in uniform (of course, after Plattsburg!) but that young Ted has left for France for staff work, and Quentin, like my Ned, is training as an aviator. Wouldn't it be grand if the two of them could be in the same squadron, "Over There!"

What I write you about, though, is a dreadful imposition, particularly since your robust self has not been quite up to snuff lately. I pray for your health to improve.

Please, dear Teedie, can you help me with my father!

He respects you so much. You've had such a long friendship, not only serving together, but way back to the Wyoming mountains, when you became Cupid's angel for Mum and Patrick.

My problem is simply this. I'm on the outs with Papa! And I fear for him when he gets in one of his black Irish rages.

I dread even putting this on paper. I truly believe he's become so depressed, so violent in anger that he's decided to go to war with war. The Germans took Mum from him, and now Mexico and their new war has taken me.

All Patrick has left, and I know him too well, is to hurl himself into the fight in Europe and get himself killed. Suicide by battle. Put himself out of his misery.

Oh, Teedie, I want to weep. I'm so powerless to change him or save him from himself. It wasn't my fault that you got him down to Mexico for Mr. Hearst and I happened to meet Ned there and fall in love. Nor my fault that at the very moment General Pershing with-

400

drew the expedition from Mexico this January, the Boche apparently took it as a sign of weakness, because, as the newspapers claim, within hours, they resumed unrestricted submarine warfare. As more and more of our merchant ships were sunk, even our spineless President couldn't stand it. He finally did the right thing, that you urged him to. When he made the declaration of war two weeks ago, the rumor is that he went back to the White House and wept.

Well, I'm not weeping nor is Ned. He's so gallant and brave, and it doesn't hurt that General Pershing thinks the same of him. Do you realize that when Ned applied for Aviation Section, Pershing jumped him over hundreds of others, including George Patton, and let him go off to fly. Some of the officers were sore about it, but it was your keen judgement of character that put Pershing where he is, jumping him over 800 other officers to give him his stars, and now commanding the AEF.

You picked the right man, but please, Teedie, don't let Patrick hang onto his coattails. For goodness sakes, Papa is 61, a broken-down old horse soldier, and the thought of him plunging into the slaughter of modern war is obscene!

His suicidal bent started with Ned, of course. The night in January when the Expedition trooped back to Columbus, New Mexico, I had an awful showdown with Papa. He was waiting there for us like some vengeful hawk, ready to pounce. When I told him that not only was Ned going to aviation, but that I was going with him as his soon-to-be bride, Papa flew into diabolical rage. Really, that's all I can call it. You know him, he's old Irish, and their way is that damn clannish possessiveness. And yes, I feel for him. I'm all he has left in the world. But dammit, don't I have my own life, too!

What he really did was to cut me off, Teedie. Right then and there. It came down to: You go your way and I'll go mine.

How I hate that, how I mourn it! I love him, can't he see? But he's like dealing with a bull, blinded by the blood in his eyes.

Remember, he's clever, too. With me now so thoroughly cut out of his life, he's turned again to my half-brother Matt. I should say Major Matthew Kelly, whose Army career you birthed. I don't really know where Matt is, just someplace in Europe, but I'm sure Papa has contacted him, out of sheer loneliness if nothing else. I did hear a few months back that Matt had served or was serving as a military attache to the Czar's dreadful government in St. Petersburg, but the way Russia seems to be disintegrating, I have little hope of reaching Matt, and just pray that Papa doesn't get to him first and use him as an excuse to hurl himself into the war.

So please, Teedie, if there's anything you can do, either officially or sub rosa, to keep Papa from going to France and out of harm's way, I pray you to. I begged him to go back to Chicago, where he at least has the remnants of the Archibalds, and I'm sure they could get him into the civilian war effort there.

Don't you really think this is the wisest course?

God bless you and keep your family happy and safe. We're going to win, Teedie! Three cheers for us all, and to you, my sincerest thanks, and always, my love.

Nora

Sagamore Hill
Oyster Bay

May 2, 1917

My dear Nora,

The wisest course with men like your father is to get out of their way and let them run their flag up the hill. That's all they know, and thank God we have men like him.

I can't turn up your brother, Major Matt, either. They have him in secret work.

Quentin is making a peach of an aviator. I hope that he and your beau will soar our common sky to victory! Bully for your spirit, young lady!

Affectionately,

T.R.

Nora's damn meddlin' didn't work. I knew my own paper-shufflers in Washington and in the confusion, got 'em to stamp my ticket. Why, they'd send a monkey over there, just to fill the boats!

By the time I wangled my way to France, courtesy of the Secret Service, Pershing was living like a damn king in a castle. Chaumont was the name of the spiffy place, an elegant tree-shaded chateau north of Paris on the Metz road.

AEF headquarters it was, and when I hit there in February of 1918, all I could think of was Black Jack shivering beside us troopers in the frozen coulees of Wounded Knee, or sweating and dying with us in the cursed jungles of Cuba. Even Dublan, I had to chuckle, remembering his sorry little adobe, with a tent top over it.

But here, now, at Chaumont, he had a staff of flunkies, snapping

402

to in the big boomy rooms. You couldn't take a step but what you'd bump into some gorgeous antique, elegantly carved by the Frogs many hundreds of years before. The tall windows streamed with pale winter sun, and crystal chandeliers flickered the beams onto the tapestried walls.

The young captain who was leading me to Pershing had a real line of gab on him. His job, I gathered, was nursemaiding the press, polishing the lads up so that they'd write favorable stories about the AEF and Black Jack. "Why, Mr. Kelly," he says, "you're walking through history in these rooms. Napoleon led his troops from here, and after him, in 1870, the German, Von Moltke, did the same. The valley of the Marne," he says, and sweeps his arm out at the black trees and yellow rolling hills of winter. "Roman legions under Caesar marched here, sir. And if that's not exciting enough for you, some of us, when we get a rare day off, go over to Domremy. I trust you know what's there?"

"I do like hell."

He laughed. "Joan of Arc, man. We sit on the same wall under the same tree where she first heard heavenly voices commanding her to save France."

"Well, I'll be damned," I says, and not caring for it much. It was like walking into a grave.

"Permission to interrupt, General," he says, when he leads me into a giant parlor as big as a saloon. Flunkies were skittering around with dispatches and pinning tags on wall maps. Two leathery colonels, booted cavalrymen, were jabbering on telephones in a corner. Pershing himself was seated at a kingly desk, the legs carved with flowers and grapevines. The sun came through the tall windows behind him and warmed his back. When he glowers up at me, I grins and says, "Well, sir, I'd say that this is finally getting to be the right kind of Army, palaces and all."

"Goddamn mule," he grunts, and thrusts me a stern mitt. "How did you get here anyway?"

"Knocking some heads, I did. Them butt polishers in Washington hung so much red tape on me, I thought I'd never get loose. You'd think this was some kind of private war them yahoos is running. Never wore a uniform before, never heard a gun go off."

Pershing grunted, leaned back and put his cavalry boots up on the grand antique desk. "So you think this is an old people's home, do you? What in hell are you here for, Kelly? Worm something out of me, you and Patton!"

I chuckled. "Now then, where is the lad, sir? Did he come over with you?"

"Crazy as a tick, that's where he is. Now he's got the idea that the tank is the weapon of the future. I've stuck him off west of Paris and helped him get six little French Renaults. Tin cans they are, but leave the young idiot to his dreams." Pershing swung his boots onto the floor and scowled. "You want a job, I suppose?"

"Not shuffling paper, sir, or nursemaiding correspondents. If it's all the same to you, give me a Springfield or even one of them damn Enfields. Come this far, I want to fight."

"Not a chance! Fight, you say? Every American over here wants that, but the bastards don't let us at it. Marshal Foch and Sir Douglas Haig are trying to take my troops away from me, stuff my doughboys into their weakened, demoralized divisions. Well, they've got another think coming. I've told them and Wilson, too. I will not stand for my soldiers to serve under any flag but our own. While they're sorting that out, we'll build a damn fine Army. They'll see what Yanks can do!" Chomping his lips in anger, he barked across the office. "Marshall! Aren't there regulations to prevent these old warhorses from showing up on our doorstep?"

A young, apple-cheeked colonel strode over, took a glance at me and grinned. "Yes sir, I'm sure there are, but sometimes old mossbacks slip through, who know how to work the system."

"Well, find a hole in it, George," Pershing grunted, "give him something to do. Get out of here, Sergeant, and don't fall in love with a French mademoiselle, you might get more than cooties!"

Chuckling, he waved me aside and went back to work. I had to hand it to this young colonel, George Marshall, a southern lad but smart enough at that. Less than an hour later, he'd signed me on as a dispatch carrier for HQ, running messages between the commands in motorcycles or autos. I says, "George lad, I can't drive nothing but a horse." He grins and says, "I got a driver for you, Kelly." Used to run car races he did, young, dark-haired scamp name of Rickenbacker. Like Patton before him, he was one of these bloodthirsty comers who'd badgered Pershing until Black Jack finally made him his personal chauffeur.

As we walked down the steps of the Chaumont palace, Rickenbacker winked at me and said, "Well, old timer, I'm delighted to take you on a few of these errand-boy runs, but I'm asking you a favor in return."

"Do her if I can, lad."

"Fine. When I park us at an aerodrome, you just sit for a spell in the auto and go to sleep, all right? I'm learning to fly. I've got about two more weeks with a French squadron and the bacon's done. The old man doesn't know that yet, and doesn't have to. Do you get the idea?"

I chuckled, thinking of Patton pulling the same stunt. "What the brass don't know don't pass these lips, me boy," I says. He gives me a slap on the back and we go off in a damn khaki Dodge to

404

find ourselves a war.

One thing I did want to do was track down Matty. The lad had all but dropped out of my life ever since we seen him in Panama. He'd written me a long letter, grieving for Daisy, but when we was in the Mexican desert, nothing come through. Last I'd heard, he'd told Nora he was going to England, some sort of staff job that would put him next to the war, before we got in. Then word come, through the Secret Service, that they had him serving up in Russia where every day more of them bearded, scraggly troops was surrendering. I longed to have some kind of get-together with Matty. With Nora off on her high horse, and no kin of any kind, I was feeling the loneliness of old age. Often, I'd scan the officer rolls of the U.S. divisions, but Matty wasn't on 'em. That saddened me. Knowing how much he wanted to fight, and how important his career was to him, he'd best not miss out on this one. It worried me that maybe he'd done something wrong, or the brass were passing him by.

But mostly in those first months it was paper-shuffling. Pershing had a war on his hands all right, but he didn't have no army. Back home, Wilson was humping to get nearly 3,000,000 men into uniform, press-ganging them through these selective draft boards, something I'd never heard of before. Line the buggers up in all the cities and tank towns, pick the fittest lambs for slaughter, and you're in the Army now. But according to young Rickenbacker, the whole scheme was going pretty punk. A lot of bindlestiffs and bib-overall boys out in the tank towns soon discovered that they didn't have no personal fight with the Boche. Why, a quarter of a million of them, he tells me, just changed their names and ran off into the canebreaks where the law couldn't catch them. Other hundreds of thousands says to themselves, Hey, if I get myself a wife, they can't take marrieds, so the wedding bells get tinkling and the mattresses bouncing. It wasn't what you'd call a popular war like Cuba. Maybe the starvies had seen enough killing, and didn't want to get whipped up to hate some spike-helmeted Hun. Ah, the nabobs in Washington started beating the drums, throwing these flag-waving rallies where gauzy movie gals and pompadoured actor prigs stood up, begging the lads to enlist, and them that couldn't, at least buy War Bonds to pay for bullets and the like.

Come down to the fact, Rick said, finally the local drafting boards got so desperate that they rounded up all the misfits and half-wits in their burgs and dumped 'em on Uncle Sam as the best way to get rid of the buggers. As it turned out, only half of all the cannon fodder served up could even pass the tests to get into the Army, and only four percent of these had a high school diploma. Most of the poor clods had never gone beyond eighth grade.

Like the old Reb veteran had told me in '76 as we rattled west to the Sioux War, "It's a rich man's war and a poor man's fight." The game never changed, I suppose, and never would neither. But whether Black Jack could make an Army out of it would be the big trick.

Damn, he had a mess on his hands. Old frontier soldier that he was, he believed in the power of the rifle. He was a stickler on going in with a Springfield and bayonet and doing the job that way. But here in the muddy trenches of France were these Frogs and Tommies, huddling in their stinking holes and dying for years just sitting on their butts, waiting for a Big Bertha shell to splat 'em into pulp. If they ever did get out of a trench, they'd long ago given up on using a rifle. Grenades was what they loved, so here you had the comical of some Frenchy or Englisher running around tossing grenades at a Boche who was doing the same thing, tossing potato mashers. Ridiculous. Nobody shot nobody, finally just slogged back to their trenches and huddled in their holes like rain-soaked rats.

Supply was a shambles. Pershing couldn't find enough rifles for his lads, and no artillery. Not a single U.S.-made 75 mm field gun or 155 ever reached the front. What few we had, we bummed from the French or English. And field shoes, God almighty, two weeks in that wet mud, the things come apart, the soles fell off, and it seemed like more doughboys were down with bruised and bleeding puppies than from any other act of war.

How I felt for the lads. Even our fancy air pilots didn't have but a hundred U.S. planes, and them not till near the end. When Rick finally got his own squadron, the 94th Hat in the Ring, he chuckled to me that it ought to be the "tail in the crack" squadron. The only planes the Frenchies give him were their castoffs.

So we become an army of panhandlers, that was the truth of it. Yet at the same time, though Washington couldn't give us the tools of war, they could sure load us with tons of other crap. One day at Chaumont HQ, George Marshall showed me an angry dispatch he was firing off, to the effect, Stop sending us bathtubs, bookcases, cuspidors, floor wax, lawnmowers and window shades!

I had to hand it to Black Jack, though. Grim-faced, eating the butt polishers alive, he just kept bulling on, building himself an army. He was waiting for the right moment to bust it loose, and it came in June of '18.

I got into it pretty much by luck, being in the right place at the right time. Pershing had had me nursemaiding one of the newspaper correspondents, a lean-faced gutty feller named Floyd Gibbons. We hit it off right from the start. Gibbons had been down with us in Mexico, and though I seen him a few times at Dublan, we wasn't friends or nothing, other than him knowing I'd been with Patton on the auto charge, and later saving our marbles after Carrizal. "Sometime, Kelly," he says, "I'm going to do a story on you, but right now, the real war is going to be on this Metz road. We'd best attend it."

He made it sound like it was a dancing party or something.

But Gibbons was clever, too, and had been around wars enough to know how to duck the army discipline and get out with the troops, which was just swell with me. "It's the Marines, Kelly," he says, and we both heap into a side car, the motorcycle attached to it being driven by a lanky young devil dog with a mean lantern jaw. "If we're heading for the war, son," I says, "I'll thank you for a rifle and sidearm both."

"You'll get 'em, sir. Our colonel is Thomas Holcomb, and he knows how to fight."

That wasn't far from the truth. Bouncing up the Metz road, Gibbons tells me that of all the troops in the AEF, here were 40,000 Marines, and every damn one of them a sharpshooter marksman. Compare them, he says, to most of the poor Army doughboys who not only had been given no training but didn't even know which end of the rifle fired, if they had one.

"Then why ain't Pershing used the Marines?" I says.

"Old Army politics. He hates the cockiness of the Corps, and besides, they're competing for men and supplies that he wants himself. But right now, in this show, he doesn't have any choice. These hardboiled leathernecks are virtually all he's got."

Having served with Marines against the Boxers and the Filipinos, I had respect for them all right. They were professionals, riding the ships of the line all across the world, and in the damn banana jungles where nobody saw them die, or gave a damn. Most of them were tall, rangy men, tin hats jammed down over their eyes, and their putteed legs had a swagger when they marched. We run into the first of them, striding up the Metz road in the sunset, and I was glad to be in their midst.

The road was a pale white strip of gravel lined by poplar trees which, if they'd been human sentries, would have been weeping. What happened, Gibbons tells me, the Boche Field Marshal Ludendorff had busted through the French and English lines with an avalanche of fresh divisions, brawny storm troopers, elite guards, the toughest fighters the Heinies had. Right at that moment when we threw in with the Marines, the Boche had at least a third more soldiers than all the Allies in France. Facing them, we were a fart in a windstorm. First they blammed out an artillery barrage with their 77's and 88's, and it blew a hole in the world. When the smoke cleared, on they come, heading for Paris. End the war right here and now, they thinks. Hell, they were covering 30 or 40 miles a day, streaming through the wheat fields and the wooded hills, just like Pershing had been begging to do all along. Modern war, he'd told Foch, was mobility, not hunkering down in trenches. When those pot-helmeted Heinies struck the English, they were like a sea of gray beetles, 300,000 Tommies falling before the orange flashes of their minenwerfer mortars, Maxim machine guns and Mausers. Just yesterday, Gibbons says, the Boche took 60,000 prisoners out of the beaten and broken Poilus and Tommies.

So here now in the dusk come the pitiful survivors, streaming south down the road, and us passing them, going into the jaws of death. The Poilus, this late in the war, looked like the bottom of the French barrel, wispy, scared youngsters, limping along in their muddy, bloody blue overcoats. Ah, they'd try to grin at us, parley-vouzing cheers, but their voices were weak and their eyes flinchy, burned out with death.

Then, as we kept striding on into the dark, we passed the most pitiful beggars of all, French farmers and their families, running down the road for their lives, with all their possessions in the world clutched in their hands or clunking along in wheelbarrows or horse carts. Old men, women and kids mostly, the ancients clopping along in wooden sabots and dusty blue linen smocks. They was all weeping, little boys in black pinafores, and curly headed little girls, clutching each others' hands. When old Maman or Papa would come along, they'd be clinging to brass pots and pans, strings of garlic, bird cages and pet rabbits. Once in a while, some leathery Marine would bust out of our file and at least try to cheer the peasants up with a chaw of tobacco or hardtack. Then some Marine looey would bark, "Get your ass back in there," and we'd march on in the dark. We had a war to fight.

By now, the roar was as loud as I'd ever heard it, the night sky ahead of us rumbling and flashing with bursts of flame. It struck me then that the roar had been in my ears almost since my first day at Chaumont. This was the new thing to me about modern war. In all the fights of my life, it had been mostly empty silence, snapped by a few shots. But not in this lousy land. Here, the big guns were roaring day and night, heavy artillery from both sides, batteries trying to locate and blast each other out, blowing holes, rattling rocks, pocking the good earth with the steady roar of death. God Almighty, it was like spending your life under a waterfall of lead. I wondered if there'd ever be a day when I could get the sound of it out of my ears.

We were single file in the dark, moving through woods, each of us holding onto the pack of the Marine ahead, for we couldn't see our hands in front of us. No smokes, no lights. Presently, the woods begun to stink. The Marines didn't talk much, officers forbade it, just a grunt here and there. But then a youngster I was holding onto cracks in an Okie-like voice, "Horses been in here, mates, dead horses."

"That ain't horseflesh," grunts an old timer. Somebody was kicking a busted hand cart off of the trail. It had been carrying bread to the troops. An officer shines his light and long French loaves were scattered about the wreckage. Khaki lumps were lying there in a smoking shellhole, one Marine cut in two, and I felt the awful squish of him as I stepped into his guts.

Later we come to a huddle of Marines squatting down in a clearing in the woods. A faint strip of light was coming out of a dirt bank there, a mound all covered with leaves. Gibbons grabs me and pulls back the blanket they'd used to hide the opening. Inside was a huddle of grizzled Marine officers kneeling around a map that they'd spread in the dirt. The head honcho, I didn't get his name, was saying that this was the one and only map the division had, so the platoon leaders better sketch it if they couldn't commit it to their heads. Anyhow, it didn't matter much. Nobody knew anything about this Belleau Wood except that it had once been a private hunting park for rich Frenchies. Somewhere in the gloomy forest was a chateau for the huntsmen, and the rest of the terrain was mostly swatchy timbered hills, manicured into escape lanes where the stags could run out, and if no Frenchy was shooting at them, graze in the wheat fields below. "We aren't sure what Heinie has got in there," the head officer said, "but we think plenty, big trouble. It could be another Verdun, pillboxes, Maxims with interlocking fire."

Then he went on to say, "The objective is a patch of woods, a kilometer and a half northeast, about." He tapped the map. "Form your platoons in four waves, guide right, French troops will be on the left." He nodded, re-lit his pipe and it made a glow into his hard young eyes.

When we come outside of the hutch, Gibbons shook his head. "Attacking in four waves is the old way of trench warfare. It's all the Allies know, they've done it for years now. Jump up, move a few yards, spill over the wire and take the enemy trench. They concede that the first three waves will be wiped out but the fourth gets in. Stupid damn stalemate. Here, where we've got so much ground to cover, in open warfare, I've got an awful hunch that we're going to pay for following those lousy tactics."

I was thinking the same thing as we lay down in the wet leaves beside these youngsters. But then again, as I studied their hard faces in the darkness, I had to figure, from what I'd seen of leathernecks, these lads didn't swallow nobody's rotten orders very long. They were mostly mean loners who knew how to shoot and bayonet. They'd sort it out when the fat was in the fire.

But not soon enough, oh Lordy, no. Lying beside them, I spent the scant hours tossing in dreams. I was back in the roaring charge with Captain Bloxham at Crazy Woman Fork. Then we were marching up Rosebud creek, knowing the trap that was being set. And then I was in the river in Cuba, Pershing flogging the black troopers up Kettle Hill. Boxers, Mindanao, Vera Cruz, all the wars crashing over me like dying waves. Cold, shivering in fear, clutching my Daisy's limp body to me in the Irish Sea. What had it all been for? Why me, now, here? God help us, let me have some peace before I finally go down. Just a moment's silence. But there was none. Only the roaring sky and the groaning earth. Would the noise of the mad shelling ever cease?

In the first gray of dawn, I went along with the lads, wearing the khaki blouse of a dead Marine, tin hat, too. No gas mask, hell with it, not my kind of war. But I had a Colt .45 in my belt, the pistol General Chaffee had hoped would smash down the crazed juramentado Moros of Samar, and in my mitts a Browning automatic rifle. What else did a soldier need if he'd made up his mind to die?

Was that me, I wondered?

In some moments, yes, I'd let her go. Tired, old, the glory worn out. But if I was faced with going down hurt and shrieking pain in this lovely foreign land, with the birds just starting to chirp, would I give up the ghost so easy, or try to cling to the precious life I had left? How in hell did I know, and why worry about it anyhow?

A freckle-faced Marine wriggles up beside me and grins with the map of Ireland in his blue eyes. "Are you saying your prayers, Dad? Mumbling there?"

I chuckles. "Well, ain't I now, son. It's always worked before, and it'll work for the both of us here, I'm saying." I grabbed the canvas pack slung over his shoulders, and give it a shake to stiffen his heart.

"Thank you, sir," he whispers. "I'll be right beside you. I've got a chaut-chaut," and he holds up one of them Frog automatic rifles that they cobbled out of sardine cans or something. You couldn't get it to fire three rounds without jamming. "Throw that pipe away, lad. Take this." I gives my Colt to him.

Then the first peep of sun hit the far horizon, green rolling hills to the end of the world, and above them, what looked like gray clouds. But they wasn't. Fat Heine sausages of air balloons, with their officers peering down at us through glasses, and slamming their 88's crashing among us. The sun glowed over the wheat field in front of us, yellow as gold now, the tiny poppies bobbing their red heads like they were singing joy to the world.

Far down the line, some leatherneck shouts, "Come on, you sonsofbitches, do you want to live forever!" Then there was a roar from thousands of tight throats, and we were going.

Five yards into the charge, the Irisher lad was laying face down, cut in two by a Maxim. I knelt beside him, took the Colt back, and went on.

All day it was, that bright sunny day, crawling and running and cursing through those waving rows of wheat, with the Heinie lead cutting us down like scythes. I wonder what God Almighty thought, up in his throne of peace, looking down at his ants, dying. That's all we were, hiding in the yellow stalks, screaming for Jesus as the steel raked us hour after hour. I don't know how many writhing boys I stepped over, but one thing was sure. The old French way of attacking stunk, and the leathernecks knew it by now. Six thousand of them would die in that wheat until us that were left began doing the only kind of fighting we knew. Kill them with rifles and bayonets, man to man. Blow their guts away, one by one.

That's what turned the tide, scrambling through the last rows of wheat, and being close enough to the black woods to see in them now the pot helmets and gray tunics of the Boche, big square Dutch-heads, some of them flaming red with anger, and others pale in fear. The Marines weren't stopping. The angry roaring in our throats was for blood, for revenge, for buying our lives with theirs.

I don't know why I wasn't hit in that hail of lead. I kept running with the other lads toward the first Maxim pillboxes, cleverly hidden in the hunting woods of the Frog princes. With the powerful BAR, God's own terrible swift sword, I fair blew apart the logs and faces and flesh of the first nest until the Heinies were screaming, "*Liebe Gott, brandighe!*" First Aid, stretcher bearers, this way!

But the Marines were in the woods, and I could see Boche scattering back through the dark timber lanes. Smoke billowing up, the stink of cordite, cracking flashes of the Heinie mortars, and the slamming of BARs. But I was still in the wheat, and Maxim bullets from someplace to our left were chopping down the stalks, yellow chaff drifting into the air. I see a Marine pitch and fall, and then a man in khaki without a helmet beside him. Running over, I see that it's Floyd Gibbons, and he's taking a Springfield from the lad's dead hands.

"Goddammit, Gibbons," I flares, crouching beside him. "You got no business being up here on the front. Replacements is coming in. Hang with them until we get this hill secured."

He was grinning, breathing hard, down on all fours like a dog. "That's the point, Kelly. The hill there is what we call 142. Tough nut. It's going to be the symbol of Belleau Wood, what Marines can do, and by God I'm going to be on it with them! Come on," he cries, "cover me, Kelly!"

We hadn't but pushed up out of the wheat before there's a hissing of bullets all around us, the angry chopping of Mausers. I was running toward the dark woods, trying to pick out a target, but even over the blasting of my BAR I hear a scream. "Jesus!"

I whirled. Gibbons was standing, tall and swaying in the sun, his left hand pawing at his face. Then I see blood bubbling between his fingers. Matter of fact, he says, "They shot me in the eye. I'm blind."

I rushes to him, pulls him down into the cover of the wheat. His face was pale but he wasn't whimpering or nothing. The whole left side of his face was a smashed mess, yet he was coolly feeling with his bloody fingers into the hole where his eye had been. I didn't have bandage packs, but I starts swabbing his face with a handkerchief, only then realizing that he was kneeling there, chuckling. "I have it, Kelly. This!" Reaching into the dusty wheat chaff, he picks up the little white marble that had been his eye and holds it between his thumb and forefinger like a jewel. "Ah, goddammit!" I screams. "Medics!" It wasn't long before two of them came ducking in and put Floyd on a stretcher. Grinning, he grabbed my mitt. "With the help of God and a few Marines! That's Belleau Wood. That's my story, Kelly!"

By the time we hit the woods, and for all that awful day, there were fewer and fewer of us, and the help of God, I'm thinking, had better come quick or we'd be done for. The Heinies were in the heavy underbrush, and some of them up in trees like the sniper who had blowed Gibbons' eye. But the Marines were hunter-killers, fighting Injun style now, and when they saw a flash of gray, if they couldn't gun it down, they leapt on it and plunged in the bayonet. By late afternoon, we'd gone all the way up Hill 142 and started down the far slope, where there were wheat fields below and a crumbly white French village not far off. Then, crouching, I hear a shout. "Lordy!" somebody cries. "More of the bastards!"

I didn't see it at first, but on the road leading into the village, out of the shrubs appears a marching file of Boche. Goose-stepping they were, troop after troop, hundreds, and they were heading straight up the hill toward us. A cool young lieutenant flings himself down near me and hollers at the other Marines crouching on the slope. "Battle sight," he shouts, "take your windage, set your range."

The handful of us waited, watching in the gloom of dusk as the pot-helmeted Heinies kept trudging on toward us, packed like sardines in a can. When the flash of Springfields hit them like one ripping volley, gray sacks toppled all over each other. They were breaking and falling, some running, screaming *"Kamerad!"* But the Marine rifles kept crashing on until the first can of sardines lay wriggling and dying all along the slope of Hill 142.

Then the world started to end, for me at least. My eyes were scorched with smoke, I was so weak and dizzy I could hardly stay on my feet. None of us had eaten for more than twelve hours. Plumb wore out. Yet in the last light of dusk, here come hundreds more, even thousands of Boche, milling toward us like sheep. But the young lieutenant thought quick. He sent his runner to scare up a rattling battery of French 75s which he'd spotted behind us. These blue-coated Poilus came charging in, wheeling off their horses and caissons and sighting the guns straight at the gray mass rising up from below. There were four guns, and those Frenchies were good shooters, for they'd had so many sorrowful years of practice. This time, when they fired, it was like one gun, smash, boom! The whole world below blew into the sky, the shells flaming those tight, clotted Boche columns, arms and legs and helmets whirling through the air, the Marines cheering the awful slaughter of it until the Boche were broken again and slinking off to count their dead.

"Dig in along this line," the young lieutenant says. "They'll be back. They want this hill, but they're not going to get it."

At the moment he spoke, he was talking to a tall sergeant who wasn't but a few yards from where I crouched. The sergeant looks at me and says, "Get yourself a shovel, mate."

Then there was the whoosh and scream of a big Boche shell. Their batteries had found us. The sergeant was in the act of tossing me a shovel. It was in his hand, me staring at him, about to catch it. Jesus God, he had no head! He was still standing there, a spray of blood spouting up from his neck, and the shell that decapitated him screaming on to thunder a roar far behind us.

By the time his body fell, the lieutenant and others were clustering around him. But me, damn the shame of it, I was so stricken at the sight of that pitiful headless goblin, all I could do was to rock there on my knees, tears streaming down my face. Ah God, I kept sobbing, why do we do it, why?

A bearded one puts his arm around me and says, "Don't weep, old man. That don't help."

"But I got to weep, lads," I whimpers. "I seen so many like you, so long now, blowed away. What's it for…?"

The young lieutenant stares at me. "For knowing that we never let each other down. That's all we've got." He turns to the others, crouching with us. "Get this man to the rear."

"The hell you do!" I roared, catching onto myself by then.

He looks at me and shrugs. "Suit yourself, sir. It's going to be a long night."

Then he smiles at me, pats my shoulder and strides off to get his boys dug in on the line. "Who's that shavetail?" I asks one of the lads.

"Lieutenant Cates. Clifton Cates," an old timer answers, watching the lad ducking through a hail of fire to reach his flankers. "Him's the kind that will run the Corps someday, if he lives that long."

I heard that he did live all right, and got a Congressional Medal for holding that worthless hill.

The night was all flash and roar, the hissing, ripping steel so terrible on us that some of the boys were whimpering prayers between the bursts, and others cackling foul curses, exposing themselves to death just to get it over with. By then, the Boche must have realized that the tide of the war had turned on this hill. Always before, they'd scoffed at us Yanks, never believed we was worth a damn as fighters. But by the end of Belleau Wood, and it took weeks, their thousands of prisoners and dead showed them that we was a different breed, and the war would never be the same again. For all the Marines who died in the bloody wheat and forest of Bois de Belleau, stopping the Germans in their tracks on their run to Paris, the Frenchies took the old name off, and from then on called it Bois de Marine.

But the flag waving hadn't happened yet, and none of us knew if it ever would. I lasted out the first night with the lads, and by dawn, when the fires of hell started roaring again, I says to myself, Patrick, give it up, you done what you had to do.

Yet here was brave young Cates saying that we never let each other down, that was all that counted. Sonsofbitches, did we want to live forever? That was the cry that bound us. I couldn't quit my bunkies, never had in all the fights, and too old to start now so I hung on.

Streaming down the hill in the dawn, we passed through the smashed white buildings of a little town. I even wanted to linger there, for these broken hutches and thatch roofs wasn't all that different from what I used to live in back in County Mayo. But there was no stopping. We had to charge up the next hill ahead, into more woods and Maxim nests which the Heinies had reinforced during the night. Maybe I done it wrong, I don't know, because this kind of war was so strange to me. But always before, every fight I'd been in, I went for the high ground. I was running with a handful of Marines up to a ridge top, a clearing in the trees, telling the lads that we had to take this and kill off a Maxim that was lacing us from somewhere.

I'd no sooner spoke the words than whiss, crash, there wasn't no hilltop. I was flying through the air, slamming into a tree that was cut and ripped by slashes of 88 steel. I patted around, seen I wasn't hit, not that I could feel. But all there was in the clearing was two giant, smoking shell holes, and in the bleeding mud lay hunks of flesh and khaki that had been my buddies.

Ah God, I groans, fumbling around, couldn't even find my Springfield. But then from someplace, the Maxim finds me, bullets chuffing, racing up the dirt, stinging pebbles into me. I flung myself at the nearest shellhole, slid into it head first beside the torn bodies of my lads. I was clawing to get deeper because the Maxim was still striping the place. They seen me, they knew they had me.

I feel a rock rubbing against my left leg. But it wasn't a rock, it was going numb. I turned over to look and there's blood running down into my boot. Damn, I couldn't move. I was lying there, belly up like a turtle on its back, and I couldn't for the life of me draw my legs down from the lip of the hole.

So the hissing bees come and stung me, the calf, the thigh,

once, twice, I don't know how many times. Chattering machine gun. Jesus and Mary, I whimpers. The sun blows into a great orange cloud and then for awhile, I couldn't even hear the roar.

I don't know how much later, maybe a minute, maybe an hour, I come to enough to hear something that makes me drag my eyelids open. Strange grunting voice, was it Sioux, even Apache?

But no, it was tall and gray, a stiff choke collar with silver braid on it, and a soft hat. A stern man with a blond moustache was standing on the lip of the hole and looking down at me sprawled on my back. The orange sun caught a glint in his hand, and I knew too well that black, beastly thing. Mauser, the Boche officer's automatic.

He's staring at me, sniffing whether I'm as dead as the lumps of my buddies. Hell, I was too blood-drained to move, had no weapon anyhow, not even a knife. Play dead was all that was left. I quivered my eyes shut and moved nary a muscle.

Blam, my foot flamed. The bastard had shot me, but he was shooting down and all he blasted was my sole, screaming a ramrod of pain up through it and into my ankle.

All I could remember after that was hunching in a ball like a baby, waiting for the one that would blow my head. But it never come. Maybe the Boche figured that he'd done his job, or the roar killed him before he could finish it. Whatever, the Good Lord let me lie there in peace, dead to the wars, and finally, to this last cursed one that was supposed to end them all.

TAPS

U.S. Naval Training Station,
Great Lakes, Illinois, September 2, 1918.

Patrick Kelly, Esq.
Base Hospital AEF,
Lucy en Bocage, France.

Oh Papa, Papa, darling Patrick!

I've just found out! It's so beastly, there's no communication!
Poor dear Papa, why did you have to do it! Five wounds in your legs,
they've told me, and all these months, I never knew! Couldn't you
have written anyway? Just once, just said, I'm alive!

But that's not fair. You didn't know where I was or I you. If I
could only have known and helped and sent you Red Cross food
and smokes, anything!

Are you all right? Please let me know the minute you get this. Are
you healing? I'm praying for you, dropping tears on this very page.

It never should have happened, dammit. I'm furious at you for
storming over there in the first place. I tried to pull every string to
keep you out of it. Why in God's name did you have to get into the
fight and try to destroy yourself?

I know that you want nothing to do with me after Ned, but
please, can't you let me help you sometime? Ned's father is a surgeon attached to the Navy at Bethesda. These people all know each
other and he says he can find you the best the Army has over there.
You just can't become a cripple, please!

Damn General Pershing! What right did he have to let you go
off to that terrible slaughter at Belleau Wood? Oh, they make so
much of it now. I read Mr. Gibbons still writing about it here in the
Chicago Tribune. I don't know what the Marines did, or if they're
twenty feet tall like he says. Maybe they did turn the tide, but why
did you have to be there, Papa? Haven't you seen enough? I'm not
writing you to scold you. I just love you. And then to hear of your
wounds! I've been sending you letters for months now, trying to
hook you up with Ned, who's in the 96th Pursuit Squadron at someplace called Triaucourt. Anyway, all the letters I wrote to you at AEF
HQ Chaumont just came back, "not known to this command." But
then, today, the shock! A Colonel named George Marshall scribbled
me a note atop my last one, telling me what had happened to you
and the hospital where you were.

416

I had thought all these months that Teedie could help me find you, but perhaps you don't know that poor Quentin was shot down. The papers are calling it an epochal, gallant death, a symbol for us, all that stuff, and now the doughboys come and put flowers on his grave. Poor Teedie is devastated. I don't think he'll ever get over it.

What dreadful times these are! If I'm not praying for you, I'm weeping for my darling Ned. But he's terribly happy, Papa. He loves the sky. He hasn't shot down a Hun yet, and maybe will be transferred to a heavy bombing squadron, which doesn't please him. But he's just fine, we're so much in love! Won't it end one of these days soon? Please let it!

Can you believe where I am? Great Lakes, just a few miles up the lakeshore from our old house on the Archibald place? When I look out at the gray stormy lake, I think of our fond times there, dear Papa. Yes, they were taken away, but the memory lingers.

Young Emory Archibald, Uncle Em, has been quite nice to me. He knows admirals, you can trust, and pulled some strings to get me a steno job at Great Lakes HQ. At first, I thought I'd do hospital work, but to see these wards filled with broken and legless or armless wretches, really, I don't mean to sound cruel, but I'm just not cut out to be Florence Nightingale!

So I have good interesting work, and I'm counting the days when you and my Ned come home. Please, Papa, when you heal, God willing, do see Ned. He doesn't want any feud or break with you. And most of all, I want to hug you again. Please write how you are! I promise not to scold you. Your loving, always,

 Nora.

It wasn't till October 20 of 1918 that they sprung me out of their damn hospital coop. The legs had healed. They give me two canes, and I says, "What the hell is this? A tin cup comes next, does it, and I can panhandle all the way home."

The doc says, "You're 62 years old, Mr. Kelly, and your system has had a shock that few younger men could even endure. I advise you to go easy, build your weight back up. I've recommended you for medical transfer to New York on the first hospital ship passage available."

He hands me a slip of paper that I was supposed to take to some damn French port. No sooner had I got out of the Army hospital, and hitched a ride on a Frog camion, I tore the paper to bits, and with it the medical prescriptions the sawbones had give me. There was a couple of bearded old Poilus in the back of the camion with me, and damn if they didn't have a bottle of champagne. Between us, we parley-vouzed pretty good about wars and madamoiselles.

The next thing I knew, the champagne was gone and I was sitting on a park bench in Paris, watching them gorgeous French pretties switching their butts past me. One winks and says, "*Vous etes adorable, mon vieux.*" She strokes my face, and I pops her on my knee. We set there cuddling and giggling until night come, watching the world stream past. When I waked up in her pension the next morning, I had one hell of a champagne head, but my legs had quit hurting for a spell, and even the roar, though it was still there, far to the north, didn't seem as loud or maddening as before.

I stayed soused for maybe a week, I don't know how long, but the old wheels with the silvery scars in them were improving every day. One thing I says to myself is this, Old is in your head, Patrick, it ain't in your legs. My dear Momma on the other side used to tell me that we make our own suffering and inflict it on our flesh. So I thinks that I can unmake the pains that throb my legs and burn my foot in the night. Every time one of them hurt places would ouch me, I'd concentrate on it and say, I'm sending you help, little lad. You're gonna heal. You ain't about to turn me into a crippled old man.

Along about then, I lit out from Paris. A lucky deal was, one day on the sunny Champs Elysee, who do I bump into but a swaggery little spider with a hook nose, and on the chest of his Marine blouse, a deck of medals from the Boxers on up, including the blue, starry ones of his two Congressional Medals of Honor.

Smedley Butler, the hero of all the Marines, and I cries, "Why in hell wasn't you with us at Belleau Wood?"

"That, son," he says, "is a long, sad story, and we'd better get it on the table!" He claps his arm around me, and in his staff car, we trundle off to the base camp where Washington had sent him.

I suppose it had to happen, Smedley being such a cranky loner that he rubbed a lot of the high muckety-mucks wrong. For years now, he'd been lipping off on what he called "political matters", such as calling himself nothing but a hired gunman for the nabobs of Wall Street. The truth smarted all right, and finally the White House slapped him down. Here he was, one of the greatest scrappers the Marines ever had, and the pussyfoots finished him off by making him run a rear-area supply base. He never did see a Boche or get a shot fired at him.

Such a waste of a true leader, but so it was with the pantywaists back in Washington trying to run this damn stupid war.

One feller who come out of it pretty good, though, was my other old pal, Douglas MacArthur. Of course, he was Army, and it was their war, Marines to them being just pesky hornets swarming in on the glory. I'd heard that MacArthur had organized what they called the Rainbow Division, lads from every state, so I went up to their sector of the front, hoping that the lanky cuss and I could spin a few windies about how we skulked through the Mex lines at Vera Cruz.

Damn if he wasn't at it again! The night I hit the Rainbow's trenches, rain and mud and the roaring of shelling going on crazy as hell, his aide tells me that Colonel MacArthur was out on a personal prisoner-catching patrol. Imagine, doing a wild thing like that when he could have sent any number of yardbirds.

But risk was in his blood. About two in the morning, I was sleeping in a trench when a soldier shakes me and says, "Colonel's coming in."

I look up, and across no man's land, in the flashes and flares, here slogs a couple of doughboys, and behind them, a tall figure in a flapping greatcoat, and not even wearing a tin hat. Doug had his prisoner all right, a grizzled old Boche that he was leading in by the lobe of his ear.

"MacArthur," I says, "you look like a schoolteacher punishing a naughty kid."

He grins, his long face wet with rain. "If I'd have known you were coming, Kelly, I would have brought two!" We had a chuckle then and some hot rum down in his dugout. The story about him earing in a Boche spread quick across the AEF. Some said that it wasn't true, just MacArthur propaganda, but I seen it happen.

When I got ready to leave, Doug, in that kingly way of his, orders a bespectacled artillery captain to billet me for the night, and then haul me where I wanted to go in the morning. The captain wasn't pleased about it. When we left the dugout, he began cussing MacArthur like a teamster. He had a gun battery to run, and that didn't include nursemaiding Prince Doug's uninvited cronies. The captain was a hot-tongued kid from Missouri name of Harry Truman.

Visiting wears out, though. The boys in the trenches had a job to do, and I wasn't part of it. Like old Crookie, I'd turned into a bump on a log. Old soldiers' dreams of glory wasn't needed in young men's wars.

Right about then, thinking of my Nora, I set out to find her damn precious Ned for her, at least look in on the lad, for by then I was feeling even more lonely and useless, the action sweeping on past me. With my wounds and my age, I'd never talk 'em into lettin' me fight again.

The roads was jammed with camions and artillery, division after division of doughboys streaming north. This was the time of the Meuse Argonne, biggest battle the Yanks had ever fought, 1,200,000 doughboys in combat, and 120,000 of them would bite the dust, dead or wounded. No wonder that by now, the roar was louder than I ever heard it, our heavy artillery blasting the Boche day and night. They were breaking and running. Plodding past us were thousands of Heinie prisoners, not goosestepping anymore, just shuffling along sullen and sad, with their hands atop their heads.

I found Rickenbacker's aviation field all right, hoping that he could locate Ned in the paperwork of the various outfits. But Rick was a hero by then, blasting Hun after Hun out of the sky, and with the brass parading him around, he didn't have time for me.

Finally, late one afternoon, I come into another airdrome over near the coast. This one had big heavy bombing machines with English colors on the wings, but U.S. boys was flying them. I grabs hold of one lad in a heavy leather air suit and starts asking him the whereabouts of a Lieutenant Barrow. He frowns and says, "You better talk to the C.O., sir," and leads me into a little shack with maps on the walls.

Seated at a deskful of papers is a puffy-faced little pilot with twinkling eyes and a shock of black hair. I states my business, and the pilot major breaks into a grin. "By God," he says, "I know you, Mr. Kelly! Are you still throwing people off of ships?"

"I what?"

"That transport, the Yucatan. Remember the day I was trying to ship out with you Rough Riders for Cuba, and you told me that I was too young to be a correspondent? Fiorello LaGuardia," he chuckles and slaps me his mitt.

"Well, I'll be damned, son! And you running a squadron now?"

"Trying to." Then he tells me, sit down, sit down, and about five minutes later, his face darkening, he hands me a dispatch paper he'd pulled out of a stack.

"It was Barrow's first flight with us. He'd been transferred out of Pursuit. Got into a scrape with too many Boche. All we know, via Red Cross, he crashed inside the German lines. He had some injuries, we're not sure how bad. Unfortunately, there was a gas attack underway at the time of his crash, and he took some. He's in a German hospital."

"Ah, God in heaven!" I stares at the paper and groans.

"They treat them pretty decently," La Guardia answered. "The best we can hope, get this war over and get him home. Your daughter's husband, is he?"

"Is or was. Poor little girl, how'm I going to tell her?"

LaGuardia shrugged. "Maybe you shouldn't. That's up to you."

The sun was going down by then, and LaGuardia was busy. He had a bombing flight to lead, and after it, his air machines would be based at a whole different airdrome, closer to the Boche. So he didn't even have a bed to offer me, with trucks hauling his outfit away.

By then, another air pilot had eased into the room. He was a barrel-chested man with twinkly blue eyes and close-shaved blond hair. When he heard that I'd been with the lads at Belleau Wood, he snorted, "I wish to hell they'd given me a rifle. I'm tired of being an aerial messenger boy." Turned out that he was a Marine himself, Major Roy Geiger, commanding the leatherneck bombing machines.

"Kelly?" he asks, with a wink at LaGuardia, "have you ever been up?"

"Only in my dreams, lad."

"We'll fix that, and I'll also give you a sack for the night."

Ten minutes later, Geiger dresses me like a doll in an oily leather air suit, and straps me into the rear cockpit of his machine which was a DeHavilland crate bummed from the English.

Just as the sun was dying, off we roar into the flaming sky. God in heaven, what a thrill I felt when the dinky wheels rattle up off the grass and we're whining and soaring over rows of trees, and files of doughboys plodding in the mud below.

Then the stars start popping out around us and we rise through skimmy little clouds, heading toward the coast of France. The noise of the machine, spitting oil and clunking us along, managed to wipe out the roar of the guns.

Geiger in the front seat turns his goggled face to me and shouts, "Are you liking it?"

In the screaming air, I could hardly hear what he said, so I just hollers back that it's a hell of a way to go, all right, and as close to heaven as this old plug would ever get.

At that, the crazy devil fusses around in the floor of his cockpit, and a moment later jokes me by holding up the control stick he's been flying the contraption with. "You got it!" He points down in my own cockpit.

Sure enough, I see the same kind of stick wobbling between my legs and banging me in the knees. "Grab it! Fly the damn thing!"

"Me?"

"Take over!"

God help me, when I grab the stick and give her a jerk, up we go soaring, my belly lifting into my throat. "Easy, damn you," Geiger shouts. "This isn't a horse!" Then he motions me to push the thing forward, gentle like, but I was so tightened up and freezing, when I shoves the stick down, here come the black earth screaming up toward us. "All right, wreck us if you want!" Geiger roars, and hunkers down into his seat with his shoulders shaking in mirth.

Maybe the big bruiser might not have been scared, but I sure was. Finally, though, with enough rolly-coastering, I gets the idea that the flying contraption was as skittery as a mare in heat. Instead of throttling the stick like I was going to choke it, I begins touching it light-fingered, and our wild gyrations start smoothing out. Then Geiger points to the pedals on the floor, and as I push them with my boots, I catch on that these are the controls that swish the contraption left or right. By then, I was having a grand old time, feeling the power of the throbbing thing, and me skidding her back and forth across the sky.

Presently, Geiger hooks up his own stick again, and swoops us down onto the dark, wet grass of his airdrome. After he'd shut off the fire-spitting monster, he comes around and gets me untangled from my seat. My legs were pretty rubbery by then, so I hits the ground with a thump, Geiger chuckling, "I suppose you want to kiss the earth, old boy, that how you feel?"

"I do like hell." I shook my head and began stroking the dark, wet bones of the flimsy machine. "I been to a lot of places, lad, and done a lot of things, but this here flying beats them all. Do you figure I could learn how?"

"Hell, you already did. You flew!"

"Quit joshing me, Geiger. You know damn well that I was only rolly-coastering her way up high where I couldn't hurt nothing. I mean, learning the whole racket, how to get her off the ground and back down again. Do you figure I could learn someday?"

"Nothing to it, Kelly. I was as green as you my first flight, but you get the hang of it. Come on, we'll warm up." He claps his arm around me and took me across the field to the mess hall. Inside the long bare hut, the leatherneck pilots had a fire roaring, and one of them was tinkling a piano, singing:

"If he can fight like he can love,
oh, what a soldier boy he'll be.
If he's half as good in a trench
as he is in a park on a bench...
If he can fight like he can love,
then it's good-bye Germany!"

I ate like a damn horse, and after it, the lads give me some brandy to wash it down. I could see right off that these boys played hard, after the flying was done, and we had high jinks, swapping tales of old wars and banana wars, and all the far-flung lands we'd seen.

I was a curio to them, an old Indian fighter pretending to be young. Yet I was busting out with hope that night. Flying was the new thing, wasn't it? A whole new life waiting for me, if I could just learn how. By God I would, and when I told the lads that, they cheered.

Then we got to toasting the war to end wars, but Geiger wasn't smiling when his turn came. His blue eyes were cold as steel. "Here's to what's not done yet, boys. We've got a lot of miles left to fly. The best that we can hope for is that we're all together at the end."

The way he said it sent a shiver through me. What end? I wondered, and where, and with who? Hell, the man was a total stranger to me, all of them were. Yet that very night, I had the same ghostly feeling I remembered with Pershing when I'd left him at Wounded Knee.

No, our wars weren't done yet. We'd be together someplace else, in some other lifetime that only God himself could know about. Eerie. It was like Crazy Horse seeing the future before it happened.

By then, my face was flaming red, and I had the shakes real bad. Geiger gives me a hard look, then barks at a medical officer. "Is it or isn't it, Doc?"

The sawbones felt of my scorching head, and nodded. "I'm afraid so. Come on, sir." Next thing I knew, they'd led me into a sick-bay hut, past the bodies of two khaki stiffs on litters with U.S. blankets covering their faces.

The Boche couldn't beat us, but the bugs sure did. Influenza, the great epidemic of 1918. God knows how many thousands of lads went down before it, and from the front in France, the ravaging plague spread on troopships going home until the whole US of A was racking and dying with the fever that nobody seemed to know how to cure.

Well, I ain't going down to the damn curse, I tells myself. I'll beat it somehow. But even Geiger, strong as a bear, fell prey to it that very night. The damn thing made him go loco. He flung his medicines away, they wasn't worth a fart anyhow, and tried to treat it with whiskey. Kept flying, bulling on. Finally he comandeered a staff car to take him to the front where he could grab a rifle and fight alongside the other leathernecks. I learned later that the MPs ran him down, and when they hauled him back to the hospital, they took away his uniform and his shoes. I believe they would have chained him to the bed if he wasn't so damn strong.

But he beat it and I beat it. I don't know which of us first. God in heaven, I was loony with such a high fever that it sent me kiting off into leprechaun land. I was soaring through the clouds, time uncounted anymore, days, weeks, who knew? There were nurses around us, and faces of strangers floating above me like moons. Every day they'd haul out more dead, until the days were all nights, streaming together in the shivering sweats that took us to the edge, and dangled us there, waiting for the Maker to pluck us away.

But one morning, I knew it was morning because sun was streaming in, I sits up in my bed, weak, dizzy, and my ears as empty as if I was deaf. "Why ain't I hearing?" I screamed.

But then I knew that I was hearing just fine. The roar that I'd lived with so long was gone.

Silence!

Not a shot, not a shellburst nor the distant growling of cannon.

Instead, far off, faint bugles and bands were starting to play. A moment later, closer, hundreds of voices, struck dumb at first by the silence, broke out into a thunder of rejoicing and cheering.

I leapt from bed and grabbed a brown haired nurse. "What is it, damn ye!"

"All over, soldier," she says and smiles. "They signed the Armistice this morning, November 11th."

I hugs her and twirls her. "Gimme a kiss, darlin'! We're still alive! We're the ones who got away!"

The end come quick then. All over France, pandemonium broke out. The lads who had been spared were carousing, kissing every mademoiselle in sight, and scrambling to get home to their own lassies. That's all I wanted, for I had gorgeous dreams by then. Maybe the flu had burned a new kind of hole in my brain, and in it I was seeing blue sky out there and oceans, too, far-off palmy isles. It was almost like the joy I'd felt with Daisy, living in the green of Hawaii, loving our young days away, as close as we'd ever get to paradise.

Damn if I wouldn't do it again! Follow the sun to the west, be young again, run on so far that the wars could never find me. Curl up my toes in the warm sand, listening to the silence that was finally peace.

But the old Army racket wasn't quite done with this warhorse, not yet. One afternoon, a lanky MP strides into the hospital and shoves me a fistful of papers. Embarkation orders, only there was a hitch to it. The MP hikes me into an Army Dodge and hauls me down to Pershing's old headquarters at Chaumont.

They were breaking up the place now, lugging out all the Army desks, tellyphones and crates of paperwork, garbage of war that we'd never need again.

When I come trooping into the palace, somebody says Pershing wasn't around, but in the confusion, a red-faced colonel catches sight of me. "Kelly, damn your hide, you're harder to turn up than a bad penny! Did you think we'd just let you off so easy?" It was George Marshall, and he snaps to the MP. "Put this man in the guardroom."

"God in heaven, Marshall, what have I done now?"

"Being in the wrong place at the wrong time, soldier." He nodded at the MP who leads me off like a damn malingerer, and takes me into one of the palatial rooms where there wasn't nothing but tapestries on the wall and a long table. "Get yourself in uniform, soldier."

Well, hell, I was already wearing my rumpled hospital khakis, what else did the bugger want? But then slowly, I turns to the sun. Lying like a corpse on the far end of the table is a blue U.S. blouse, and blue pants too, with the yellow cavalry stripe down the sides.

My eyes filled with tears. I liked to choke, fingering it. The old-fashioned blouse had crossed cavalry sabers on the collar, and sergeant stripes on the sleeves.

I swung back to the doorway. George Marshall was standing

there grinning. "Fortunately, Kelly, the QM had a few of these relics left. The General made you a sergeant, didn't he? Now start looking like one. Your Army isn't done with you yet."

He turned on his heel and left me blubbering, holding the old cloth. Before I knew it—and I don't know what possessed me—I'd dropped to my knees, my face buried in the musty uniform and my tears soaking it. To feel the cavalry blue again hurtled me back to that graveyard at Wounded Knee when I handed my duds to an old Injun and vowed to give up war. Give it up for Walks Outside, lying in her frozen grave. And for Matty, too, my little half-breed, driving the wagon "like a man," he says, and off we go toward the setting sun, far, anyplace far, to begin again.

So what did I give up? No, not the fight, not the senseless wars. Love was what I give up. That was the price I paid for the glory, burying my two blessed wives, and losing a daughter as well, now. So goddamn alone! I blurted into the dark cloth. Matt? Matty, where are you, boy? You're all that's left!

Rocking on my knees, sobbing, I was praying to the Maker to take my pain away. In the dream of it, the darkness, a voice says, "Don't cry. Be proud."

I jerked the old uniform away from my eyes and staggered to my feet. A tall, powerfully-built major was standing in the open door, doughboy khakis on him and ribbons on his chest. His face was dark, his eyes smouldering. He lifts his hand to his peaked campaign hat. "Time for a salute, isn't it?"

"Ah, Christ," I whimpered. "Matt! Matty!"

"Return my salute, Sergeant."

Did I ever, my hand lifting shakin' to my brow, and him snapping his down like a knife! We rushed together, gripping each other, me blubbering but not him, never him. His wide Sioux lips curled in a hard smile, "I've waited a long time for this, Papa. We've both won a war, haven't we?"

"Ah, God yes! Look at you! Major and all that, ribbons, too! Where did you go, lad? I've been searching all over France for you!"

He laughed and sat down on the bare table where they'd laid out my uniform. "You can thank General Pershing for rigging it. He never forgets his old non-coms. As for me, I've been a few places, but not Belleau Wood. That was a brave thing you did."

"Stupid, son."

"No. Probably necessary, now that Daisy's gone. Nora, too, you might say. She's written me, said you've cut her off. That's too bad."

"Dammit, Matt, I been tryin' to find her feller, this Ned. He was shot down."

"I know. But she'll get him back any day now. They're repatriating prisoners quite rapidly. In fact, I've been trying to have our staff

425

people locate him."

"You ain't here, are you? Chaumont, this HQ?"

He shook his head and his eyes went dark in the old Indian way. "I'm not anyplace in this war. They've managed to keep me out of it."

I frowned. "The hell you say. Are you on the wrong side of somebody?"

"I don't know. Could be, but it's probably just the roulette wheel of Army assignments. They pick you for certain skills. My years down at the Canal got me pigeon-holed into engineering. Damn paperwork. I've tried like hell to get combat assignments. All these years I've dreamed of nothing but fighting. It's my career, dammit. You've got to have the battles to get the stars."

"Matty," I says, and put my hand on his shoulder, "there's lads layin' in the mud out there that ain't never gonna see their stars. Count yourself lucky that you missed this fight."

"Well, it hasn't been all bad," he said, and smiled. "You know, Papa, growing up, I used to envy you. In fact, I hated your guts. Here you'd had all your damn wars, with no more training than blundering and bullheading your way through them. Made me mad. I was smarter than that. I had a better future than you, because I understood what modern war has to be. 'Smarty shavetail snot' you used to call me. Do you know something? It's taken all these years on the shelf to prove to me you were right. I'd learned everything I needed to be a top soldier, except the most important thing. Humility. You had it. You were a simple man, you took your orders and did a brave job. I'm in your debt, Papa, for what your life has shown me."

Tears filled my eyes. I drew him to me. "Damn ye, got me snifflin'. There ain't even a handkerchief in these old rags."

He laughed. "Well, put 'em on, Sergeant. The best is still to come."

"What are you talking about?"

"You'll see." He walked over to the window, tapped on the glass and beckoned toward the patio. "While you're getting decent," he said, and I was stripping down to pull on the old duds, "prepare yourself for a shock. A couple of 'em, actually. Did you ever hear of General James Harbord?"

I frowned. "Ain't he Pershing's chief of staff?"

"More than that. What he's done in supply and getting these troops and materiel to the front has made Pershing a hero and won his war. Harbord is the smartest man in the Army. I've heard Pershing say it. So I've had a real break. While I was stuck in staff work, I came to Harbord's attention. He wants me to stay on with him in some peacetime capacity, I don't know what yet, but it's a pretty fine star to hang onto, wouldn't you think?"

426

"Sure sounds like it, Matt. That's the way the game is played. If it hadn't been for old Crook taking a shine to me, I'd be in a coffin out at Ft. Bowie with no name on it."

He smiled. "We're both shot with luck. You see, it was Harbord who assigned me to St. Petersburg when Russia was starting to fall apart. He's a man who looks way beyond the present wars. That great landmass of Russia, those millions of desperate people are going to have to be reckoned with."

"But son, they's reds now, ain't they? Long-haired agitator bastards. Them raggedies couldn't fight nobody."

"Don't count on it. I was there when they took over in the Revolution. Mobs of them, but God, the energy, the anger, the spirit. They're going to make something out of Russia. And so am I. In fact, I already have."

Smiling, he turned and opened the door to the patio. A slim young woman was standing there in the sunlight. Like Matt himself, she had high cheekbones and slanty, pale eyes. But she was blonde, her hair done up in a bun, and wearing a simple, gray dress. Her right hand and forearm were bandaged, and my first thought was: here's another poor French gal who got caught in the war.

"Aleka," Matt says quietly. "My father, Sergeant Patrick Kelly."

She came forward shyly, took my left hand in hers, drew it to her mouth and kissed it. "Enchantee." Then she laughed. "Forgive me, please. My English is not as good as my French. We lost our British nanny some years ago."

Matt drew himself up and grinned. "Papa, this is Aleka. Aleka Usipov. We were married last week."

"Married?" I echoed. "Lord, Matty, if it ain't about time! Here you come bustin' in after all these years, never said nothin'." I was shaking my head, plumb stunned, Aleka snatching my hand again.

"Father," she cries, "we did not know where you were! So much we wanted you to stand up in the church. My mother was there, young brother, too. But now we have you, we never let you go!"

Then we all hugged, and I felt like dancing around with the two of 'em, so much in love were they. "Damn," I cried, "Pershing ought to have some cognac in this dump. Break it out, drink to ye both!"

"He's got more than that," Matt laughed. He glanced out the chateau window. "They're forming the colors. Time for front and center, Sergeant."

"Meanin' what?"

"Don't fight it. Aleka and I will be out there with you. Just stand tall, shoulders back."

I scowled. "What in hell kind of joke you two playin' on this old fool!"

Matt smiled. "I told you I had a shock for you. But that's what life is, nothing you can ever count on. When this little Injun went up to the frozen steppes of Russia, who'd ever have dreamed that he'd come back, bringing a princess?"

"A what?" I bellers, lookin' at the plain-dressed little gal.

"Princess Alexandra Usipov, cousin of the Romanoffs and of the English queen."

"Ah, God, you're twittin' me, boy!" I grabs Aleka and turns her. "Is he tellin' the truth?"

She nodded and flicked a wisp of blonde hair across her forehead. "One doesn't say these things nowadays. But yes, we had the wrong kind of names for the Revolution. Only because of him, your noble son, am I here."

Then, quickly, Matt told me how it happened. He'd met Aleka at a military hospital where she was working as a nurse. They were both smitten. When the roof fell in on the Tsar, Matt knew the old way was doomed. He hurried to Aleka's family dacha out in the country someplace. Through his Army connections, he'd arranged to smuggle her and her family out of Russia. They'd go in freight cars, dressed as peasants. Matt took her small hand and turned over the palm. "I thought it would be a good idea to toughen their hands in saltwater and lye. Then when the Red guards examined them, they'd think they were only serfs."

"So!" Aleka held up her bandaged arm. "Look what your Dr. Pasteur did to me. Infection. But it is nothing. A war wound I'm proud of!"

"Well, it must have worked. You're here, ain't you, darlin'?"

Her eyes flickered. "Almost not," she said quietly. "Matthew had it fixed with his diplomatic papers."

"And some U.S. dollars," he cut in.

"There was one train we would go on," Aleka said. "Out at the dacha, we pack all the bags, the silver, my Mother's things. Just when we were getting into the sleighs to go to the train, my mother screamed. Her wedding ring was missing, could not find it. 'I will not go,' she cries. 'This is a bad omen!' Poor Matthew, he was standing in the snow pleading with her. He even told Mother that the red Indians he descended from believed in omens, but it was all rot. Mother just says, 'No, we stay here.'"

Matt put his arm around her, and his eyes lifted to mine. "That night, the train they were supposed to take was stopped by the Red Guards. I don't think there was a single Russian of noble birth on it, but the troops had been alerted somehow. They took the passengers out in the snow and machine-gunned every last one."

"Ah, you poor gal," I says, gripping her hands.

She laughed. "Yes, poor, Father Kelly. But I have your son, too, and this..." she held up her small hand and touched the gold ring on her third finger. "Mother prayed very much. A few days later, she found her ring, right in her laundry box where she had placed it. But I tell you, it was not there the first day we were to leave. Superstitious Russians, yes! So Matthew finally got us another train. We crossed the German border. They were very suspicious, but..."

"Luck again," Matt said quietly. "The crossing point was totally disorganized with Hindenburg about to surrender. Nobody knew where anyone was supposed to be. I found a German colonel who'd spent a year at Sandhurst. I played on the West Point tie. He even knew about General Harbord. That, my diplomatic visa and a bottle of wine got us through."

"Bully for you, lad!" I cries. "I can't think of a better man to wriggle out of a tight place."

"And who do you suppose I learned it from?"

"Ah, you damn Injun!" I grips his strong hand and hugs her to me as well. "God speed the both of you!"

But Matt wasn't listening. He'd turned to the door where two MPs were standing at attention. "Your prisoner," he grins. "Don't let him run out on you."

"Snap to, Sergeant," one said, and with Matt and Aleka following, they led me out into the big garden behind the chateau.

I felt like I was walking on air, floating in this miracle where a greenhorn lad who'd only turned soldier to cure his clap, was now gliding down a path of elegant shrubbery and old trees of French kings. Ahead of me, several dozen doughboys, Marines and aviators come filing in to stand at attention. The MPs placed me at the far end of the rank. The drums roll. Then a band strikes up the Star Spangled Banner.

Pershing, stiff as a Springfield, but gray and tired, comes slowly down the line. A colonel beside him had a boxful of medals. One by one, Pershing shook the men's hands, and draped their necks with the glory they'd won. Just behind Pershing limped a bearded French General, and his flunkies had their own boxful of Croix de Guerres.

When Pershing reached me, at the far end, his face flickered into a trace of a grin. "Damn Army mule," he grunted. "What does it take to kill you?"

I was so choked, I couldn't answer. He whirls, beckoning to Matt and Aleka. "Get in here, Major, stand close. You, too, Mrs. Kelly. I want a photo of this." A doughboy with a Kodak scurries up. Then Pershing leans forward and drapes a bobbin around my neck, the Colonel behind him reading, "For his 42 years in combat, in U.S. campaigns from the Sioux Wars to the Great War, the nation honors Sergeant Patrick M. Kelly, Third U.S. Cavalry, retired, with the Distinguished Service Cross."

"General," I blubbers, "there ain't no need for this..."

His voice lowered. "Wounded Knee, Kettle Hill, Carrizal. You old bastard, I tell you what the need was!"

He whirled and strode on to the next man, his face set hard like he was squinting down tears. By then, the French general had busted in and gave me a beardy kiss on both cheeks. He was parley-vouzing about Bois de Marine, and hung his Croix de Guerre on top of the blood red one of the US of A.

The bugler played "Taps." The party broke up, the heroes drifted away into the dark shadows and leafless trees of that November afternoon. I felt like I was saying goodbye to Crook again out on the Arizona desert, the train clanking the poor Apache devils off to their captivity.

I wanted to run out someplace and celebrate with Matt and Aleka. "Hell, lad," I cries, "it ain't every day that I get kissed so many times, and a new daughter to boot."

"And a son back," he says, hugging me. "I've picked up a lift for Aleka and me, not an easy thing nowdays. She's never seen Paris, and it's a helluva place for the honeymoon we never had."

"Well, off with you," I said. "Go, sure!"

"You, too, Papa. Grab your embarkation orders and good sailing. We have to go on to England for awhile, wrapping up Army business. And," he smiled, "other unfinished business. Aleka has never met her cousin, the Queen. She's helped many of her relatives get out of Russia, bought their jewels, that sort of thing. So we have a date at Buckingham Palace, red carpet, if you can believe it."

"The Queen, the royal biddy herself! Ah, son," I whispers, "I'm beyond believing this day."

Then Aleka kissed me warmly, a laughing, gentle thing. I watched them stride away, Matt with his West Point shoulders squared and his dark Injun hand sneaking around her lovely waist. Damn, I thinks, a princess in a family that come from a pigsty. What wonders would the Good Lord bring me next!

After they'd gone rattling off in an Army Ford—somebody had hung ribbons on it for 'em—I figured to set and visit a while with old Pershing, for I had the idea that I'd never see the man again, and I'd miss him.

But hell, he was on center stage right then. I was in the crowd that cheered him into his khaki limousine. As I swung open the door so's he could get in, I said, "Well, Black Jack, looks like we come to the end of a hard, old trail here. Just want to say thank you."

His jaw tightened, his eyes swept across the men. "Kelly," he said, with a quiet sigh, just for my ears, "I wish it were the end. I tried like hell to do that. I wanted to take the surrender of the German Army on their turf in Berlin, dismantle them for all time. But the politicians want the quick gain, the cheers of the crowds back home.

430

They sold us out too cheap. We're not done yet, Sergeant. Sometime, sooner than I want to believe, we'll have to do this all over again."

His hand snapped to the visor of his campaign hat. He shot a salute to the troops, mounted the car like a horse and banged the tinny door. I watched him driving away with his shoulders sagged and his head slumped forward.

All over again? I thinks. It was like a lead ball had struck me in the chest. Here was a man who knew what lay ahead, and lay behind us, too, all the campaigns of bleeding and dying. What for? Just to breed more of the same?

The auto trailed down a long white road, through the lines of poplar trees. And my road? I wonders.

More wars was it, Jack? No, not for this lad. Crossed the wilderness, we had, and then the oceans. All that was left was the world, and out there someplace beyond the sun, there'd be freedom, I knew, and peace at last.

While I still had life in my bones and breath in my damn soul, if there was one, from this moment on, I'd be soaring so far off, maybe in an air machine, that the snarling dogs of war would never track me down again.

Do you hear me, Daisy? Ain't that what we had once? Gentle waves lapping on the shore, and our young love lifting to the stars? Well, I'm closing in on you, darlin'. Wait up for me. I'll be along, any day now.

PATRICK

THIRD FRONTIER:
THE WORLD
1923-1944

DARK CLOUDS GATHERIN'

Honolulu, Hawaii (Special to the *Chicago Tribune*)
January 30, 1923

HORSEMAN IN THE SKY

Indian Fighting Cavalryman Stars in Hickam Field Air Show

by Floyd Gibbons
Tribune Worldwide Correspondent

In the sunny skies over Pearl Harbor today, an old man and an old plane wobbled off into history—and gave me a lump in my throat.

We were relics of the American past, he and I. We'd campaigned together in the wars to end wars. Yet now, in the Hickam Field Air Show, we found ourselves hurled together again, to stare dumbstruck at the terrifying future that was roaring over our heads.

A world we never made.

Thousands of spectators had gathered for the aerial fireworks. The grassy runways were thronged with Hawaiians in bright colored mumus, and haoles, local whites, in linen suits and straw hats. Family groups were the order of the day, picnic lunches and kiddies scampering off to finger the wondrous, gleaming planes.

When they roared skyward, all eyes followed them until they were specks, careening across the cliffs of sun-tinged Hawaiian clouds.

Then the specks became hunters and killers. In ear-splitting dogfights, our Army pursuit pilots zoomed through the aerobatics that had made them heroes in France, and now, without doubt, the finest airmen in the world. They thrilled the home folks with screaming dives and twisting Immelmans, chasing each other in a combat so vicious that it seemed incongruous, even offensive, in this timeless, balmy land, where the green jungled peaks of paradise rise up from the Ocean of Peace.

On the heels of the dogfighters came a black flock of deadly vultures, General Billy Mitchell's bomber squadrons, droning in awesome precision through a pass in the mountains. Hawaiians call this sacred place the Pali, shrouded with rainbows like the tears of ancient lovers who sacrificed themselves here. But now the powerful engines of the bombers blew the rainbows away, the attackers thundering relentlessly on toward the white, peaceful cities on the shore.

434

Though Pearl Harbor bristled with ships of the fleet and extensive gun batteries, after what we saw today, observers doubt that the great base could protect itself against such an aerial onslaught.

Alighting from his bomber this afternoon, General Mitchell described his test attack on obsolete battleships, which caused such furor in the Navy. "When we bombed the *New Jersey* and the *Virginia* over on the East Coast, both of those so-called impregnable battle wagons sunk like stones. Doesn't that prove it to the Admirals! The battleship is finished, and so are these fixed bases that suckle them!"

So air power had its day here, mapped its future trails in the sky. By now, the assembled crowd thought the show was over. Some were even picking up their baskets and kiddies to go home.

Yet one surprise remained, for this old war-horse at least.

When the last roar of engines had faded across the cane fields, and ukeleles began plinking again at the Aloha Clock tower, here came a lone aircraft, whining in from the gleaming Pacific. In contrast to the other new engines, this one sounded like something on a sewing machine. As for speed, it was barely hanging in the sky. An albatross in a hurry could have beaten it to shore.

Kiting on the air currents, the dogged biplane made a slow turn over Pearl Harbor, and then, quite inauspiciously, slipped into the shadows and landed on Hickam's grass.

By then, most of the crowd was trailing away. But I stayed. I had to. I owed it to the memories I'd shared with the old man who was piloting that ancient plane.

Threadbare in the sun, it was a Curtiss JN-4, identical to those flying coffins that I'd watched crash in the Mexican desert when I was down there with General Pershing during the Pancho Villa chase of 1916.

How Black Jack used to curse the cranky, fragile machines! He had only six of them in his command. They were his precious eyes, and when they were smashed into rubble by pilot or mechanical error, he was left blind in a hostile, dust blown land.

But the JN-4 didn't die there, far from it. Those first six craft of Pershing's were the primitive granddaddies of the now vaunted Army Air Corps, and the powerful portent that they showed us today!

I said this to the two men who stepped out of the plane. One, youthful and confident, was Major General Benjamin Foulois. He'd commanded Pershing's first six planes in Mexico, then all U.S. aircraft in France, and, some say, will soon be chief of the Air Corps.

But as he grinned to me, wiping the oil from his face, the lump rose in my throat. "I wasn't flying this one, Gibbons. Sergeant Kelly was at the controls."

He turned to a tall, rangy oldtimer, his face as leathery as his jacket, a shock of white hair wild from the wind, a hook nose and hard blue eyes.

At first sight, he looked like somebody's grandfather, who should have been on the porch in a rocking chair. But not that man. The Patrick Kelly who grabbed me in a vigorous bear hug, and then tapped the white patch over my eye, said, "While they was at it, lad, they should have closed the both of 'em, to keep you from snooping around other people's wars!"

Patrick Kelly, 67 years young now, a brawling Irishman growling in his brogue, had been beside me in the wheat field at Belleau Wood the day I lost my eye. In fact, after I'd plucked my eyeball out of the dirt, he helped pack me out on a litter.

Pershing used to call him an old Army mule that you couldn't kill, and just about every American enemy had tried to. Patrick Kelly, Sergeant, Third U.S. Cavalry, might have been wearing a khaki flying suit for now, but that didn't hide all the years before, when his eyes had seen the glory, and his big tough body riddled by the wounds of our wars. From arrows to juramentado bolo knives to Mauser slugs, he was the Ancient Mariner who couldn't be blown away.

As a greenhorn Irish recruit, he'd started his military career on the Plains against the Sioux chief, Crazy Horse. He'd ridden with General Crook into the fastness of Mexico's Sierra Madre, conquering the Apache chief, Geronimo. Add Kettle Hill in Cuba, Boxer Rebellion, Philippines, Mexican Intervention and the Great War— Patrick Kelly is his own powder-burned and tattered battle flag. Believe me, he still waves it proudly.

Not only did this old cavalry trooper learn to fly shortly after the Armistice, but he used the plane to chase a new kind of rainbow.

After suffering five machine gun wounds at Belleau Wood, Army doctors advised him to seek a mild climate. He had settled, as much as he'd ever light anyplace, in Santa Monica, California, to become a pioneer in locating schools of yellowtail tuna from the air, and then directing his fishing boat to them.

"My father," Kelly told me with a wink, "used to sneak a fish or two from his Lordship's pampered salmon streams in County Mayo. Wouldn't he be chuckling at his lad now, herding his fish from the sky, in a pond of his own, half the size of the world!"

Patrick Kelly's story makes you proud to be an American. Fleeing to our shores as a penniless immigrant, he dedicated his life to our flag, and we remembered. We thanked him.

Shortly after the Armistice, General Pershing personally awarded him the Distinguished Service Cross for his 42 years of courageous combat in American wars.

And the future now? Will it be peace?

"Out there it is, lad," Patrick Kelly said to me tonight. We were sitting at his familiar table at the Moana Hotel, under the gigantic banyan tree. Mark Twain, in his Hawaiian days, had watered himself in this exact place. And there was a look about Patrick Kelly in his planter's linen suit and unconquered shock of white hair that reminded me of the indomitable Twain. He flung his arm west, toward the sun that was dying in the distant waves beyond Waikiki. "That big pond is where the frontier is going to end, Gibbons. Manifest Destiny lies on the Asian shore. But whether it will be ours or theirs, who knows? The ocean of peace," he sniffed. "God Almighty, lad, let's pray that it is!"

In the shadows, several half-naked Hawaiian children came to him. They were giggling shyly as he tousled their hair. "Ah, you worthless little sea slugs," he said, taking nickels from his pocket and pasting them into the brown hands. The prettiest tyke, with her shower of black hair, he put on his lap and joggled her like she was playing horsie.

That's how I left him, riding out his memories in the sunset.

I have a hunch that Sergeant Patrick Kelly, soldier of the flag, will be there when I get back. His long long trail to the wars has finally led him home.

⟶⟶⟶⟶⟶

> 18 E. Scott St.
> Chicago, Ill.

Dearest Papa,

This was in today's *Tribune,* smack on the front page! I don't know if you even get papers out there, or give a damn, but I'm so proud of you, and grateful to Mr. Gibbons for writing you such a flowery l'envoi!

I'm also quite sad, Patrick. I don't know if I'm just tired, but I'm low, feeling punk. Life is cruel.

I enclose a snapshot of your grandson, your namesake, John Patrick Kelly Barrow, nearly a year now, and you haven't laid eyes on him. Yes, thank you for the bouquet of flowers you sent, four months after his birth. But I can't eat flowers, Papa. Dammit, I'm not trying to be ungrateful, just human!

Isn't it understandable that your daughter would want to hear something from you all these months and years? Do you realize, I had to phone Mr. Gibbons to find out how I could even reach you at the Moana Hotel?

I'm going to be very frank, Papa. You and I are all the flesh and blood we have left in this family. Yes, Ned, too, and now our little John Patrick. But sometimes I feel so alone in a stormy sea that I just can't stand it. I want you, I need you. I want to show off my son, my life. But all that comes back is the roar of the waves, wherever you're wandering now.

Yes, we had a feud over Ned. We had a break, and I chose it. But isn't it ever over?

As long as I've found out how to reach you, I want you to know this. Ned and I have had a hard go. Not personally. I love and respect him. But we're poor, Papa. We're scrimping and saving just to get by.

Ned has never recovered from his gassing in France. Poor dear, the war really shell-shocked him, which of course was why he turned to medicine like his father. His hope to heal others.

But it's not been all peaches and cream. He's doing well at Rush Medical School. He'll be out to interning next year. The studies are hard, they're costly, with no guarantee of anything better very soon. Doctors and teachers are the most underpaid people in our society, and it's a pity. It galls me. I see Chicago and Lake Forest acquaintances, these buddies of the Archibald boys. Why, they're all brokers on LaSalle Street, pushing around their dumb stocks and bonds, driving the latest classy car, or whacking their golf sticks, and they make more in a day than we do in six months. Things are upside down, Papa! Are riches everything? You never thought so, and poor Mama would shriek out from her grave at the greediness of this Flapper Age!

I've had to go to work to support us. Ned's father's inheritance was peanuts. We'd hoped for more, but his mother is in a nursing home. I answered an ad in the *Trib* and became a salesgirl in Fine Frocks at Marshall Fields. Many of the women I serve are from Lake Forest, and if they're not Archibald friends of relatives, they're girls I knew in school. But how they snub me—with exceptions. The Swift girls are nice, and one of the Pullmans.

Anyhow, when I began to show too much with John Patrick, Fields let me go, so I went to the Girls Latin School around the corner from where we live, and they hired me to teach part-time Spanish. You made me get good at the language when we were in Mexico, and I'm proud of that.

We have met one nice couple about our ages, Roger and Mary Castle. You may remember from Mum that the Castles go as far back in Lake Forest as the Archibalds, Armours or any of the lot. But Roger is so gentle, and quite brilliant as an investment banker with the family firm of Castle, Dawes. They're going lickety-split now with everybody buying stocks. Roger thinks that when Ned gets his M.D., he should put up his shingle in Lake Forest. They need a good town doctor because the one they've got now is ancient and on the way out. I don't know what Mary thinks about the scheme, she's terribly quiet. But we do party once in a while at a speakeasy where Roger has a key. Ned doesn't drink anything because, as I say, his lungs aren't so strong.

But the baby, Papa, is a joy! I even think he looks like you. He has your black hair (I guess you had!) and those warm blue eyes that never met a stranger. When I take him to Lincoln Park, some of the working men's wives are there with their little Slovenian or Polish punks, and John Patrick charms, and bosses, the lot of them! You'll love him!

Please, sometimes I have a fantasy. I'll win a contest or something and whisk all of us off to see you on the sands of Waikiki. Or even California. It's closer, if you go back there much.

Roger Castle heard from somebody in Los Angeles, a business connection—maybe this is not a true story, but he said, they told him that a few years ago, an Army veteran named Kelly took a motor car out west of Los Angeles city and found himself driving through miles of empty orange groves or forsaken goat pastures. Then, boom, right in the middle of this wasteland, up rises a splendid pink hotel. Kelly is supposed to have said, "Is somebody out of his mind, building this palace way out in the middle of noplace? Who'll ever come here? Call it the Beverly Hills Hotel, do they? Why, they'll be lucky to get bats to live in the damn mausoleum!"

Now Papa, that sounds awfully much like you. Was it?

But anyhow, as Roger's story goes, this Kelly soon found some old war comrades or somebody with money, and began buying lots around the hotel. This happened shortly after the war's end, and now I hear that the place is booming. The *Trib* did a story the other day on "The California Explosion," and said real estate prices are dizzying, particularly in that new area of Beverly Hills.

I hope that's your land, Patrick. Maybe it even bought you your fishing boats, and really, do you have a plane? *Verdad?*

Papa, please. Take wings, come see us. We miss you terribly. And we need your help now! Could you, possibly? Ned sends love. He does love you still, and I always will.

Your Nora.

The living was grand in Hawaii, and much to my liking. But then again, a man can only drink so much rum and stare at the palmy stars so long. After the fooferaw of meeting old Gibbons out there, I began to get tired of curling up my toes in the warm sands.

The sea beyond beckoned me. I believe my Momma said that one of her Riley uncles had shipped out and sailed his own bark around the dark continent of Africa, and then to the islands of

439

spice, wherever they was, and never come back.

So perhaps I had it in my blood, this lusting to see the far shore.

The Good Lord had blessed me in California, no doubt. From selling a few pieces of land my old bunkies and I had owned, I got into the air and fish business, and in debt too, I finds, when the longshoremen and a crooked cannery throws a strike against us. So then a rich Armenian comes down from Los Angeles City, and my last surviving bunkie and I unloaded the rigamarole on him, plane, fishing ship and the scrubby desert lots in Beverly Hills. God in Heaven, I never seen so much money in my mitt, a quarter of a million dollars, my share. Of it, I had the Armenian's bank send a hundred thousand to Nora and my grandson, no name attached. The rest I pocketed, and sailed out on the Lurline to the palmy isles.

I loved the sky indeed, but Foulois and the pilots at Hickam soon talked me out of exploring west in an air machine. They said that the cussed things needed enough motors to travel the vast distances, which made them too costly and also untried. Leave it for the air pioneers, the young lads. Anyhow, I didn't have the skills to do much in the sky other than bouncing around the local, windy fields of the islands.

Fine with me, because by then, a real bargain had come on the market, something I figured I could handle. During the Great War, the Germans had held the island of Ponape in the Carolines. But when the British shelled them out of there, one of the trophies captured was a fine Boche-made patrol boat. Not too big, only a harbor craft with one bow gun.

Now that the Japanese had grabbed the islands out of the Versailles treaty, the ship ends up for sale or salvage in Honolulu Harbor. A kanaka friend I'd known from the old days says, "Buy her, brah, her engines hum like bees."

They did that all right, Mercedes diesels from the old country, and though the bridge and main cabin was tinked up somewhat by gunfire, I got that cobbled thing back together quick. A new coat of white paint, I signs the check over to the War Production Board, and the sleek sea chariot is mine. My kanaka lad, Barnabas, says, "Whatcha gonna name her, brah?" He starts feeding me names of fish or Hawaiian goddesses. I says, hell with that. I got my own mystic man to name her after. I scrawls it on a scrap of paper: "Crazy Horse."

He wrinkles his big, fuzzy brow. "You talkin' some God here, brah, loco guy?"

"Crazy like a fox, lad. He was a God to my Injun friends, their hides as black as yours, and so he'll be to me." I'd sail this ship down to the end of my days, and I almost did.

I took to living aboard the Crazy Horse, and why not? My stateroom was a lovely big coop, just under the bridge, portholes on both sides to let the sun stream in. Maybe it still stunk of Boche, but I was smoking a pipe by now, sea dog style, and with that and the rum, I soon marked my lodgings with my own scent, like a dog lifting his leg on new territory.

The pipe was a corncob, not the Irish clay kind that my Poppa sucked. Doug MacArthur, who'd come through the islands, inspecting this or that, give it to me. He'd just finished up a tour running West Point, trying to change the hidebound old place, and he said that the pipe made him look like a professor.

Be that as it may, it was cheaper living afloat than on the beach, and besides, I'd put together a fine kanaka crew to spoil hell out of this old horse. Barnabas, my skipper, was a strapping native Hawaiian, too missionaried up for my tastes. He had rosaries hanging on his neck, and would plop his big bare feet around the deck, always humming hymns or talking direct to the Maker. But the lad was a hell of a seaman. He'd shipped out of Hilo as a youth, piloting for a Japanese trawler that took him the length and breadth of the Pacific. He could keep the engines humming, and that wasn't my strong suit.

Working under him was a giant named Dismus. If you ever dreamed of being cast adrift on a cannibal isle, Dismus would be the devil stirring the pot to cook you in. I never seen a man who cared less about danger. He'd swim with the sharks, that one. He had a Polynesian face that looked like a Mack truck had backed into it and squashed his nose, lips and ears into a flat pancake. Topping it off was a gigantic ball of black, kinky hair. That was the Fijian in him, and he had Tongan on his Momma's side. Cannibals all, him with a fishbone through his nose and two more in his ears, he'd scare the pants off you on a dark night.

But ah, how the lad knew the ocean. He could sniff the air or the stars and give you a straight track to any speck of coral you wanted to find. He could read what the kanakas called "sea life," the way the tides moved, or the plankton glowed in the sun, or how the birds behaved. He was so far from civilization that he still remembered how these spirit forces worked. If he hadn't been so damn ugly, he would have reminded me of Crazy Horse. They were cut from the same smoky past, carrying on the lore and glory of his people, handed down father to son since the beginning of time.

Dismus had his woman along to cook for me. Big Fella Cap, she called me, and her chocolate skin had as many tattoos on it as a carnival contortionist. A woman from the isles of Palau, she was, a chief's daughter, according to her, and if you ever seen an ape, she was it, her arms so long they almost reached her knees. But she had a good heart behind her swelling breasts. Sometimes when I'd be eating what she'd served up, she'd hug me and stroke my face. I says to her, "Why, you old harridan, you're spoiling my digestion." She'd just chuckle, "Big Fella Cap, we go far off islands, I get you young Palau girl. Sweet meat. She cook your balls good."

"We'll see about that," I says, but damn, about now, I was indeed hankering for a young brown-skinned gal. There wasn't anything in the world like them patient lovelies to comfort a man, particularly since this old cob didn't have much else left in a whiter shade.

So it was a good crew. We sailed west out of Honolulu to shake down the boat—Johnston Island, Canton, down through the Samoas. I wasn't heading anyplace in particular, for in truth, I loved all of it, the salt smell, the sun, the porpoise herds leaping from the sea, blowing their noses and grinning at us. And then the darkening skies, flashing with lightning and scorching us with white sizzling rain. In the days in the Pacific you lazed off to sleep, and in the nights, the squalls lashed you, ripped you from the womb of darkness, and when you were born again in the dawn, you were young and clean.

No cares. No business to do. Noplace to get. Barnabas, the smart one, kept working on me to become a trader. The island folk were begging for civilized goods, and the Crazy Horse had room enough in its hold to carry to the brown brethren all the junk and finery of the Sears Roebuck catalogue.

"By'em'by," I says to Barnabas. "Maybe we'll get to trading one day."

I never dreamed that it was going to be so soon, and no picnic either.

One night, shortly after we'd re-docked back in Honolulu, I was strolling along Kalakaua Avenue, looking to buy a new straw lid, when who do I bump into but the airman, General Ben Foulois. I hadn't seen him since the Hickam air show. He was searching the stalls, hoping to pick up touristy geegaws that he'd bring home to the wife and kiddies back in Washington, D.C.

We fell to talking about the old days down in Mexico, particularly the afternoon him and young Ned Barrow had swooped in on us at Hearst's ranch. Foulois inquired after Ned, knowing his health was bad after the war, and what about my pretty daughter, too? How were they doing?

I shrugged. "I hear from the girl now and then, give me a grandson, she did. They'll get by. Anyhow, lad, I ain't one for living in the past. It wears a man down too much, thinking of what might have been. All we really got, Foulois, is this lovely night here under the stars, and waking up to an even better one tomorrow."

He grins and claps his arm around me. "Kelly, the boys are tossing a goodbye party for me tonight out at Fort Shafter. You might see some old pals, or some that you'd have been better off not knowing. One thing for sure, these young bucks will get a kick out of you. They haven't an idea how it was in the old horse Army, and it's high time they started learning."

Up at Shafter they had a fancy Officers Club, bamboo and thatched native style, white pikaki leis and pink and purple ones too, hanging like rainbows on the roof posts, and gardenias in the womens' hair. These officers wives and girlfriends were swishing around in snaky Hawaiian mumus, their various perfumeries stuffing my nose. Beautiful American ladies, dainty flesh indeed, and though I'd squeeze one here and there, I knew better than to hang on. They were as off limits to this old common trooper as poor Leah had been. A chapter closed, and mourned still.

The girl I left behind me. Girls, now, remembering my Daisy, looking like these here, soft and gentle, tinkling with laughter, that day we'd danced at the Iolani Palace.

Sentiment is the curse of the Irish, I says to myself, so I was glad when the young turks hauled me into the saloon part of the club. Filipino messmen were pattering in and out with enough rum drinks to float the Navy. The officers at the tables were bronzed and smart-looking in their dress whites, handsome buggers. In their clear eyes and hard-jawed faces, I saw glimpses of Emmet Crawford, way back, or Maus or Bourke.

They sits me down at a noisy table where a young major named Ike Eisenhower was holding forth. He was an open-faced lad with a twinkle in his eye, smoking one cigarette after another, and pounding the rum pretty good, too. When they introduce me to him, he pushes up and grips my hand. "I've been waiting to meet you, sir. We have a friend in common. Your son, Major Matt Kelly."

"Well, I'll be damned. Served with him, did you?"

He laughed. "If you can call staff duty service. We pushed some desks around back at the War Department. My plebe year at the Point was his last year there, and he made it hell. This Kelly guy," he turned to the others, "was one rough hunk of Indian. Half Sioux—" he glanced at me, "I suppose it's no secret?"

I chuckles. "Hell, you can look at him and see it."

"The warrior part of him was still alive and kicking," Ike continued. "Damn he was tough on us! He peppered me with demerits all of my plebe year, but as I got to know him more, I regarded him as one pretty crafty hombre. He's sure proved that lately, hasn't he, Mr. Kelly?"

I frowned. "Well, now, lad, I don't know. We ain't in much contact, me way out here. The boy's wife, she's Russian—wrote me a while back and says she's teaching him her language. Last I heard, he was still with Harbord in Washington."

Ike shook his head. "The General is out, sir." He pushed back in his chair and said to the others, "Boys, here's a story to inspire us. A by-passed officer in the War—like me, Matt never got to the front—well, he hung in with Harbord in staff, took his lumps. You know the rest of it from the newspapers." He turned to me. "Mr. Kelly, a couple of months ago, an inventor named David Sarnoff in New York hired General Harbord to set up a radio network. Your son is right up there with the old man, trying to figure out how to send National Broadcasting Company radio signals world-wide."

"By damn," I whispered. "Radio, is it?"

"I saw Matt in New York maybe three weeks ago. Your son is riding a tall horse, all right. He says if we capture the airwaves, we capture the mind of the world. It sure beats wearing the khaki."

I was dumbstruck. "He's out of the Army then, turned in his suit?"

"All the way, sir. He and Aleka just moved into a nice little apartment overlooking Central Park. We had supper up there. Anybody envy him?" he chuckled to the others.

Another officer said, "Well, for an Indian—and I knew him, too, Ike—it sure beats sending smoke signals."

They laughed, and while we was drinking a toast to Matty, a tall officer in whites strode to the table and clapped his hand on Ike's shoulder. "Damn fool, you never should have left Kansas!"

Ike swung to him with a grin. "It takes a Jayhawker to know one, doesn't it? Long time, Pete!" Sliding out a chair for the newcomer, Ike turned to Foulois. "One question, General. How in hell did a Marine get invited here?"

"Because he's a stinking spy!" Foulois laughed in his grizzled way, and shook the man's hand. "Glad you could come, Ellis. I've been wanting to catch up with you." Then he turned to the others. "We let Marines in when they've been at Belleau Wood."

From the deck of medals on Ellis's lean chest, I could see that he'd been to a lot of wars, that boy. He had quick gray eyes that showed brains, and a stubborn jaw that let you know that he wasn't a feller to be pushed around. The story was, said one of the officers, when General LeJeune, commanding the Marines in France, had run into a stalemate in the trenches, he sent for Ellis to bust it open. One of the General's flunkies said, "But sir, Colonel Ellis is sleeping off a hangover." At which, LeJeune barks, "Bring him to me! Ellis, drunk, is smarter than any man on this staff!"

So now, while Ellis was swilling the first of many whiskies, Foulois gave him a hard look. "When's the next war, Pete?"

Ellis shrugged. "Whenever the enemy wants it, wouldn't you think?"

"Quit stalling," Foulois snapped. "You're among friends, and it's common knowledge at the War Department that LeJeune had you draw up something called Operations Plan 712. I want to know what's in it."

Ellis smiled coldly. "Thirty thousand well-chosen words, Ben."

"Meaning?"

"Our next war will be against Japan."

"Talk sense, man!" Foulois cried. "Did you ever hear of a place called Germany? What about the Huns?"

"Sure, they're a possibility. But Germany is so distraught and broken right now, strapped by punitive reparations, they're going to have to create a strong leader to rally them. Japan is not in that situation. Japan is unified, aggressive, ultimately dangerous."

The officers looked at each other. "The Japanese as a threat? Oh, for God's sake, Ellis, you can't expect us to believe that! What kind of alky are you Marines drinking?"

"We'll be fighting Japan," Ellis retorted, "within fifteen or twenty years. Mark my words."

"The hell I will!" snorted a Colonel. "I don't know where you staff planners get your lunacy, but Japan is nothing, zero. They could barely beat a pitiful Russian army twenty years ago, and now, when we own the seas around that isolated, backward island, we can choke them to death. They have no industrial capacity, no oil unless they beg it from us. Why, those little banty cocks, they can't even see well enough to fight a war. I was attached to the legation in Tokyo. I studied their troops. Every other man in the ranks wears eyeglasses. Clever imitators, that's all they are, bow-legged toymakers, not worth wasting powder on!"

"Well, Colonel, you'd better keep some of yours dry," Ellis answered. "For two years now, I've heard exactly your kind of gibberish from General Staff and the War Colleges. You people have your heads in the sand. You're staring down the hole of the last war, and still fighting it, thinking that the next one is bound to be the same. It won't!"

"But Japan has no Navy!"

"Wait."

"Okay, Pete," Foulois cut in, "you wrote some plans for LeJeune, and maybe you do have some sixth sense that we lesser mortals don't possess. Fine, we're listening, we give you the benefit of the doubt. Now when does Cassandra say that the next war is going to happen? Where? How?"

Ellis smiled and slowly tapped his whiskey glass on the table. "Right where you're sitting, Ben."

"What?"

"Pearl Harbor. All of this, forts, airfields, guns pointed in the wrong direction for yesterday's war. The Japanese have only one chance against us. They'll do it swift and sudden, hit us right here, blow our fleet, our troops, our retaliation capacity into a cocked hat."

"And then?" Foulois said.

"We'll take the only course left to us." Ellis drained his whiskey, and slowly moved the empty glass across the wet table. "Counterattack. Inch by inch. Here, here, here, we'll have to blast them out of one fortified rock to the next, storm our way across a hundred different coral reefs until we finally bring the war to the Empire's shores. That's the only way we can beat them."

The bombshell of it left the officers staring at him in disbelief. A few were trying to make jokes of it. Some were downright surly. There was no love lost between Army and Marines anyhow, let alone a stubborn one trying to cram something down their proud throats. As I listened, I thought about Teddy Roosevelt, warning about the Japanese as the next threat. But I didn't say nothing. This was officer-fighting, Ellis finally flaring, "You don't have to believe me, nobody else does, except your own bad penny Billy Mitchell. Ask him what he thinks!"

"Billy Mitchell," Foulois grunted, "has made himself so obnoxious to the Congress with his bombardment theories that he's within an inch of being courtmartialed. I've warned him. I like the man, admire him. So does MacArthur. God, they were schoolmates in Milwaukee, that must mean something. But at this point, read the papers, Ellis, our armed services are being decimated every day on Capitol Hill. Neither the politicians nor the people at large are going to spend another red cent on preparations for war, when we've just finished the one that's supposed to end them all. Even a brilliant man like Mitchell can't cram that bitter pill down America's throat. You're swimming up a long, muddy stream, Ellis, and though I might agree with some of your doomsday predictions, I wouldn't bet much on your ability to survive, let alone be listened to."

By then, it broke up into little arguments among the others. Ellis didn't say anything more. He poured himself another whiskey and with his jaw clamped tight, sat staring at it. Soon Foulois pushed up, saying that he had an early departure. Then the other officers drifted off, some dancing to jazz tunes with their pretty ladies. In the end it was just Eisenhower, Pete Ellis and this old cob, sitting at a wet table, wisping with dead cigarettes.

Ellis and I got to swapping tales about me being dinked at Belleau Wood. It turned out that he'd been adjutant of our battalion that day, and was decorated for it and for the Soissons fight after it.

I liked the lad and young Ike, too, maybe because they had a quick way of cutting through the old Army bull. Many of the high officers never listened to a common trooper like me, but these lads seemed to have a bit of Crookie in them. They were interested in getting it straight from the poor stiffs that had been shot at.

I was getting a little rubbery in the lips by then, and when the lads asked me about my future plans, I says, Hell, I didn't have none exactly, just lazing around the islands in my boat.

Ellis' gray eyes narrowed, and he glanced at Eisenhower. The young major smiled. "Now there's a coincidence for you, Pete. The man happens to have a sailing ship. Let's take a walk out in the grass and piss on some palm trees."

Outside we went, where it was quiet and private, and before the long night was done, I'd pretty much heard the story of Colonel Ellis' life, and the life that he was willing to give for his country, if it come to that.

In the Armistice Treaty, Ellis told me, the Japanese had picked up all the former German possessions in the Pacific. The Marianas islands, except for our base on Guam, the Palaus, and the giant chain of the Carolines, fortresses like Truk and Ponape, now had the Rising Sun proudly waving above them.

"What's that got to do with me?" I says.

"At this point, Kelly," Ellis answered quietly, "nobody knows what's going on in these future bases. The Treaty permits the Japanese to colonize them, but for commercial purposes only. Phosphate mining, copra production, fishing. Yet, from what I read in the Tokyo press, a hell of a lot of settlers are being hauled from the Homeland down to these islands. They don't pretend to be military units, but how do you know their armament or the amount of construction equipment they're bringing in? I've got to find that out, because if I don't—you've heard the reaction here tonight, and the staff is even more blind—nobody will ever believe that Japan is fortifying those islands as bases from which to attack us."

"Kelly," Eisenhower glanced at me, his sunny smile gone, "does your ship have sea range and capability of say, a thousand or two thousand miles?"

"It does, lad. Them Boche tars sailed her all the way from Germany to Ponape, before they lost her."

"Does your boat have armament?" Ellis asked.

"One old Mauser bow gun. I ain't never fired the thing, no reason to."

Ellis nodded and looked at Eisenhower. "With the capacity of a trader, using that as the cover, with enough cargo on the decks, what do you think, Ike? Can we pull if off?"

Before he could answer, I says, "Now boys, whoa. I ain't never done no trading from my Crazy Horse. Got a good crew of kanakas, they're pushing me toward it, but hell, I ain't cut out for playing storekeeper. A feller gets to a time in life where he'd just as soon dangle his toes in the warm sea and let the rest of the world float by."

Ike frowned at Ellis. "Well, Pete, maybe we've got the wrong man here. Sergeant Kelly has earned his stripes in too many wars. I don't blame him for being sick of it. I am too, sometimes."

"It ain't the shooting that scares me, lad. It's just the why of it. Why do we have to keep playing these killing games, fight for some worthless island that some nabob wants for his own power or profit? I been to these rocks, boys, I bled on 'em. Why again?"

"Because if we don't, Kelly, nobody else will, and the next war is going to happen just like I said." Ellis leaned his lanky form against a palm tree and stared at me. "I don't want any favors from you, Kelly, and I won't put you at risk either. All I'm asking is that you let me ship aboard with you, and I'll pay you for your trouble. Here," he took a paper from his blouse pocket and let me look at it. Typewritten on it, with seals and geegaws, was "Earl Hancock Ellis. Civilian. U.S. Commercial Traveler."

"But you's a Colonel," I says.

"Retired. Just like you, my friend. No more wars."

"You ain't telling me straight, Ellis."

"My family has been informed that if I don't come back, they are not to make inquiries with the Marine Corps or anyone else. Let's put it this way. You and Ike here know what I'm about, but beyond that, I'm off the world, I'm over."

"You're making a pretty big bet."

"It's the only hand I've got left to play, Kelly." His eyes smouldered. "The Japanese are fortifying those mandated islands, harbors, airfields, interlocking pillbox defenses that someday American boys, footsoldiers like you, are going to have to buy with blood. If I can prove that, we might head it off."

"You're talking about going in there?"

"Absolutely. I need maps, photographs, garrison strengths. If these people are breaking the Treaty, and I suspect they are, we've got to start preparing now, or better yet, expose their treachery to the World Court. Are we so asleep that we can't do that? Are we so lacking in balls that we don't dare even try? I was hoping to find a man who'd been in enough fights to know that the best wars are those that you can head off before anybody gets shot."

"Ah lads," I grunts, "you're a pair of slick shysters you are, conning this old horse. Sure and I've heard the glory talk before, and the bugles blowing. But I've never headed off no war yet, and I doubt you can either. You got a bad dream, Ellis, you're blinded by it, but I'm saying, suppose it don't happen? Ain't you just pissing in the wind?"

He grabbed my arm tight. "It *will* happen, and exactly like this, Kelly! Once the Japanese have fortified those islands, those stepping stones of coral, they'll be poised to knock us out, take control of the Pacific Ocean and Asia. And do you know how they'll do it? One sunny day, they'll roar right into our impregnable fortress of Hawaii

448

and blow our fleet away. Air attack. They're already building the carriers to do it. But not just any old day. My studies of Japanese tactics show that, historically, they always rely on surprise attack. And when are we the most vulnerable to surprise? On a Sunday morning, just like tomorrow morning, when all of us have been sotting ourselves for all of Saturday night, and in the daybreak we're lying in our bunks, sleeping it off. Take your choice, Sergeant. It's going to happen just like that—unless somebody risks his life to stop it. I'm putting mine up. What about yours?"

Maybe it was the rum in my brain, or the anger in my eyes, thinking of them sneaky little Japs, trying such a monstrosity, but when Ellis thrusts out his mitt to me, I grabs it. "Loco bastard," I says, "you ain't the first I been with, riding off to some wildgoose-chasing war. Damn ye, git your gear, git aboard. When's we sailing?"

Ellis smiled. "Tomorrow daybreak, Kelly. The tides will be right."

The bugger had it all figured out down to the minute. He had me in his mitt, and maybe knew all along that I wouldn't refuse him. Ike chuckled and give me a slap on the back. "Bring us some souvenirs, Kelly. You won't regret it."

"Hey, Ike lad," I says, "will you do me a favor and tell Matt where I'm goin'?"

"No. He's a civilian now. We don't want it on the radio. You're on your own, sir, but you've been there before."

That's all there was to it, an old saddle soldier and a young rummy dreamer, galloping off together to find the next war.

I says to Ellis, after our first week of plowing west across the ocean, "Leave them bottles alone, son. If you're playin' drunk to fool the Japs, I ain't puttin' up with it."

Lordy, how the man could drink! At first it worried me, and then I pitied him. He'd been straining for so many years, trying to get his visions across to them hardheads at the top that now, when they wasn't listening, he'd plunge the mad of it into his bottle. In the long pitching nights under the stars, he'd be pacing the deck, staring at the blackness of the western horizon.

By the time we made landfall at Ponape, a jungly cone of island rising up into rain clouds, I pitched the last bottle into the sea and grabbed Ellis by his khaki shirt. "Now look, lad," I says, "across that reef, we're going into Injun country. Stand straight there, Colonel, shave your face, and when I send the skiff in with you, look like somebody that might have his wits about him."

Ellis ripped away from me and lurched down into the skiff rocking beside us. "You run your ship, I'll run mine, Sergeant!"

Before they pushed off, him and my skipper Barnabas, I

grabbed Dismus with his black heathen knife gleaming in his lava-lava. "You stay next to Mister Ellis every step he takes on that rock. Keep him out of saloons, and if you've got to kill somebody to get him back here, do it!"

Dismus' eyes gleamed. "All come back, Big Fella Cap. Dismus eat Japan man for breakfast!"

We got off to a pretty ugly start. All that flaming day, with an umbrella over me, I sat in my bosun's chair and stared at the shore. By late afternoon, madder than hell, I thundered ashore and had to spring Colonel Earl Ellis out of the mossy old Ponape jail. He'd had a drunken fight in a saloon. Dismus and I got him staggered to the skiff all right, but just as we were about to pull away, a tall Japanese civilian, wearing a neat khaki suit, strode up to the naval officer who'd arrested Earl. The civilian rattled a string of Japanese, but three English words come through loud and clear: "Colonel Earl Ellis."

When we pulled away, Ellis was heaped in the stern like a sack of oats. His lean face was bloodied from a cut over the eye, and his aloha shirt half ripped in two. He smelled like he'd been soaked in beer. I gripped his shoulder. "Now come out of it, lad, and answer me straight. Did you give them buggers your name? Or your papers?"

With a sly smile, he pulled off his boot, and his commercial paper was lying in the bottom, wet and wrinkled. "They never knew what hit them," he slurred.

"Goddammit, son, they do know! They got your name somehow."

He slumped back with a faint grin. "That was here, Kelly. But we aren't going to be here. We're moving on, to where they don't know me."

I had to hand it to the lad, and I don't know till this day whether his drunk act was posed or real. But by the time we boarded the Crazy Horse and pulled the hook in darkness, Ellis was already in the wheelhouse cabin with charts and papers spread out in front of him. The man's mind was too quick for me. He was scribbling numbers and impressions of what he seen. He winked at me. "The best way to evaluate military force is to get them to arrest you."

"You seen something, did you, Earl?"

"Enough. A start anyway."

Much as I pumped him, he never told me a word beyond that.

Funny bugger. When he was sober, he'd never let you through the wall of his tight lips and squinted eyes, and when he was drunk, you didn't want to be around him anyway.

From the night we left Ponape, he took over running the ship. He knew sea charts and the lay of the islands. He had Barnabas steer us due west, plowing through empty seas and flaming sunsets until I didn't think there was a landfall left in the world. Nothing out there but towering clouds in the day, and the whistling wake of the Crazy Horse in the nights. Finally, in the middle of one night, he shook me awake. "We're going into Truk, Kelly. I've got to run that reef."

Barnabas, Dismus and Lourdes were standing by the wheel when I come up on deck. "No good place, Big Fella Cap," Barnabas snapped, and flung his arm at a white line several hundred yards from us. Hell, I knew what it was, the sea crashing onto an awful shelf of coral.

"There's a pass through that reef," Ellis said, tapping his chart.

"Kapu! Japan man make kapu!!" Dismus seized my arm. "Cap, one time, ship take me here, Tonga ship. Jap come with gun, he got plenty gun, big boom boom, inside islands there."

"We're going in," Ellis said, and folded the chart. "Tell them to quit stalling and steer the pass."

The night was inky black and whipping with rain squalls. Much as I didn't want to risk my ship, maybe Ellis was right. This was the best chance we'd have to tiptoe in unseen.

Slowly, Barnabas steered us toward the gap in the reef where big ocean swells were roaring between heads of coral that could slice us like a tin can. I give Ellis a torch, and he and Dismus crouched on the pitching bow, the torch stabbing the water, and Ellis waving hand signals for Barnaby to steer by. We inched into the dark pass, so close to the waves crashing on the coral that the spray drenched my face. We had maybe fifty black yards to cover before we'd get free and into the lagoon.

Then Dismus shouts, the ship lurching in a thunk, and Barnaby clanging the screws into reverse. Too late. I runs to the bow and Ellis' torch flames the water. Bobbing right beside us is a giant black ball that we'd hit. It had steel spines sticking out of it, wet, ugly monster. "Jesus God, man!" I cries, gripping Ellis's shoulder, "that's a mine!"

He lifted the torch from it and grinned. "A dud, Kelly. You must have said your prayers." He shouted back at Barnabas. "Speed ahead, move past it!"

I peers over the side, the mine still clunking against our bow plates. "Ellis, no, goddammit! If there's one in here, there's more!"

No sooner than I'd said it, the Crazy Horse gives a groan, and there's a gnashing of steel. Barnabas thought quick. He shut off the power. There we were, pitching in the narrow trough with a Jap submarine net screeching and tearing at our screws.

I didn't have to holler at Dismus. He's already plunged over the side and came spluttering up, holding the barnacled, oozy wire netting that was trapping us. The way the tides were sucking us into that awful lagoon, we didn't have time to waste. Barnabas left me holding the tiller, him leaping into the water with a pair of giant steel shears he'd brought from the engine room. Him and Dismus, diving repeatedly like they done as lads after pearls, managed to cut holes in the net to set free our screws. Dismus, like some maniac giant, was flailing the water, drawing the net away from us, Barnabas at the same time flopping back aboard and racing to the wheel. "Got to rip it," he cried, "maybe is rusty enough, let us loose!" He jammed the engine telegraphs into full reverse, the big Mercedes churning the sea, the net squealing across our steel hull plates until finally, by God, the monster snapped, someplace far down in the depths, and we lurched back out of the pass, loose and free.

"Ellis, you crazy sonofabitch!" I roared, "we ain't doing that again!"

He stood in the wheelhouse, wiping the sea spray from his face. "Kelly," he said quietly, "this is Truk. If the mines and the nets don't prove to you that it's valuable to the enemy, then I'm going to prove it." He took a mug of coffee from Lourdes, and bit a hot gulp out of it. His eyes met mine. "I'll get in there, Kelly, if I have to swim."

Right then, I had to ask myself, What in hell am I doing out in this dark sea with such a crazy bastard! But he never backed off an inch. He'd get in there, get into Truk, even if he never came back.

After we'd steered the Crazy Horse out into the big open sea waves, Ellis talks Dismus into running the pass with him in our skiff. But the frail thing had only an inboard putt-putt, never too strong under the best of circumstances. "You ain't wrecking my skiff, Ellis!" I cries, and he answers, with that wild leer, "Then drive it yourself, old man, if you've got the guts to!"

Clever sonofabitch, he knew how to bait me. With Dismus in the bow, me at the tiller, the three of us make another run at the dark, awful gap between the coral heads. But it was no use. The broken Jap net was writhing all around us like a sea snake. We were clunking stuff that could have been mines, until finally I wheels us the hell out of there.

Ellis had tied an old life raft to the stern of the skiff. It wasn't nothing but a rim of cork with canvas webbing on the bottom. I'd seen similar flimsy things in the water the morning the *Lusitania* went down, and my Daisy was snatched away from me. But here was Ellis, climbing into it. "I'm running the reef myself, Kelly. It's the only way. See that?" He pointed off through the darkness, beyond the roaring surf. "Island just beyond the reef. You can pick me up there after daybreak, when you can see."

I don't know whether it was remembering Daisy, or wanting to go out like she had, but I jerked the flimsy raft up amidships and dumped myself into it alongside him.

"Don' go, Cap! No, no!" Dismus wailed.

"Take the skiff back, Dismus. If there's an island like the crazy fool says, pick us up there in the dawn." Then I grab one tin oar and Ellis the other, and we plow into the giant waves that were crashing over the reef.

Of all the bad rides I'd had, in all the wars, there never was a rollycoaster quite like this one. Hell, we wasn't fighting humans now, we was fighting God almighty, and I ain't never seen him so close and so fierce as when the sea lifted us and flung us like a cork into hell and damnation. The waves must have been twenty feet high, the roar was all the noise of creation, smashing against the coral, flinging geysers of spray into the dark night, and us, poor human specks, lifting and falling and tumbling end over end in the violence of God's mighty hands, until we were spluttering and gasping and floating like corpses in the stillness beyond.

Then I feel sand under my fingers, and Earl Ellis, Colonel of the Marines, is dragging me by my shirt until we're both lying face down on the beach.

He was kneeling beside me, breathing hard, but smiling, too. "I had to see the war, Kelly. This is what it's going to be like, crossing these damn reefs. We'd better learn how to fight it."

When daylight finally come, I was lying in a grove of palm trees on a fringe of island that wasn't 50 feet wide. The big ocean was still smashing on the reef we'd run, and beyond, the Crazy Horse was lolling safe in the swells of dawn. But as I looked through the fringe of palm trees to the other side of the island, I saw a magnificent sight. It was Truk lagoon, largest in the world, Ellis had said, and now, with the rising sun burning a copper stripe across it, it shimmered like a giant, glassy lake, as peaceful as a millpond, and stretching to the horizon. Closer to me in the lagoon, tufty islands poked up like green pincushions.

Ellis was sitting cross-legged on the beach, chewing the meat of a coconut. As I walked across the sandspit to him, he lifted his glasses and stared at the islands. "Welcome to paradise, Kelly."

In the crystal sky, sea birds were drifting, cawing, tilting their beady eyes downward to peer at us, like who the hell were we, butting in here? Smelling the salt, the sweet sour of rotting coconuts, watching the silvers and golds and scarlets of the sun warming the corals in the lagoon, I felt like Adam himself flung down in God's lonely creation, and longing for an Eve to share it with me.

"Well, Earl, lad," I says, bumming a chaw of his coconut, "it's a long way from your damn war. If we had fresh water on this rock, we could lay back and cool our heels forever, I'm thinking."

He shook his head and handed me the glasses. "They'll spot us soon enough, Kelly. That big island, second one over there, note the flat area just above the mangrove swamp. Airfield."

With the glasses to my eyes, and shading them from the fierce sun, I could see a white ribbon of coral running along the shore of the next island. Like rusty ants, machinery was working here, a steamroller and dinky trucks, wisping up dust. Looking closer, I picked out several low, hulking concrete buildings. They had dark holes in them, gunports no doubt, hidden by the jungle, and draped with camoflauge netting for good measure. "Ain't them the clever little buggers! Damn sneaks."

He nodded. "A million miles from noplace, and nobody will ever know."

But it wasn't good enough for him. He had to know more. Against my protests, we paddled close enough to the nearest island to snap shots of the airfield with his Kodak.

When we came back, I said, "Ellis, I'm going to let you keep your war."

His hair was tousled with salt, his gray eyes hardening. "The trip's not over, Kelly, and neither are you." He thrust out his hand and pulled me up.

"Damn ye, Ellis. You risked our necks, you got your photos. What the hell else do you need?"

"The same thing that they do. A battle plan. If Truk's their Pearl Harbor, and I'm sure they'll make it into that, then where do they go from here? It's got to be the Philippines, and the Marianas and Palaus to protect the seas to the east."

That night, after we'd run the reef out to the Crazy Horse, I told Ellis that we were turning east. I'd take him back to Pearl Harbor if he wanted, but I'd had enough of this endless sailing with no goal in sight.

We were standing together at the bow, watching the sea slipping past. Ellis didn't answer. He was leaning with his forearms on the rail, and his hands knotted tight. Finally he muttered, "You don't believe me, is that it?"

"My momma on the Other Side used to read the tea leaves. Ah, she had leprechaun in her, no doubt, but it's not a bad gift, and perhaps she passed it on to me, who knows? If you quiet your brain long enough, lad, you can hear voices from the dark powers. I seen it often with the heathen. They're ahead of us in their listening. And do you know why? Because they ain't got no clock running them like you have. You're running so fast, Ellis, you're catching up to your own shadow."

"What in hell does that mean?" he snapped.

"You ain't coming back."

His sniffed. "What is it, too much sun?"

"Yas, maybe. Seein' these lovely islands and them gentle native people we've passed by all these weeks, it gripped my heart, Earl.

454

Here's them, paddlin' their canoes like they been doin' for a thousand years, not a care in the world, and here's you, medals and grim lips. Ambitions, ah, how swell! Patriot, are you? And sure you'd die for it, God love you. Give up the ghost for your country. What's a country but a piece of rag with blood on it? It ain't life, like what God made. Hear Mister Dooley writing back in Chicago, 'Look at them stars, Paddy,' he cries. 'Don't they think they're grand! Don't they think they're raising hell!'" I turned him slowly to me. "Earl, today, lying in that sand, when all the noise of your world was gone, I seen you floating face down in this cursed sea."

"So what?"

"That all you got to say?"

He whirled on me, his eyes blazing. "If it has to be, it has to be!"

"But lad, it don't! I've come to know you, these weeks afloat. To hate your mean miserable heart sometimes, most of the time. But what's left over, I love you, too, for your sheer insolent guts."

"Don't give me old man gibberish! You want to quit, quit. Take my photos and charts back to Pearl. If Eisenhower's gone, I'll give you another name at Marine Base."

"Damn you, Ellis, you ain't listening to me, but you will, by God. I've been fighting wars for two lifetimes that you ain't had yet. And the only decent thing that's come out of them is the comrades I've made. And buried, most of 'em. When I see you, I see Crawford in the Sierra. I see Captain Bloxham in the red clay of Wyoming. Even brave dumb Fish, staring at the Cuban sun."

"I don't know what you're talking about, Kelly. The islands are rotting your brain."

"You bet they are, son, and I wish to hell it had been sooner. Don't be a goddamn fool, Earl! Yes your country, yes your bravery, it don't mean a fart to the kind of life we saw today. Letting it all go, that's what I'm saying, living the precious time you got left, every second of it. But you won't, I'm knowing that now. The only chance you got is for me to haul you back from your goosechase, your holy grail. So you predict the next war, who the hell will listen, who the hell will care?"

He was facing me with his fists clenched at his side. "I care, Kelly. That's the difference between a leader and a follower."

"You damn snot!" I gripped his arms and they were hard as steel. "I don't want you killed! I seen it happening. They'll do it, them Japs, and you and an army of you's ain't gonna stop 'em! Quit with what you got! Let the Lord do the rest."

He jerked his arms away from me. "If I wanted a chaplain, I would have signed one on. Dismissed, Sergeant. Thanks for the boat ride."

The following morning, maybe it was two mornings later, I crossed the freighter lane going east to west. Two stacks were smearing the horizon, belching coal. It was a rusty Norwegian freighter making way from Lima to Yokohama. I hailed her, we tied on, and Earl Ellis climbed up the ladder they dropped. It took him a long time in the cabin, making arrangements, the Norwegian tars and us rocking in the sea, grinning at each other. Then they fling back the hawser rope onto our deck. Barnabas, Dismus and Lourdes were standing beside me, looking up at that black cliff of a hull. Dismus scowled. "Tall mister, he go from us?"

"He go from us."

The last I seen of Colonel Earl Ellis, he was a ramrod of khaki, bent in the middle, his forearms on the rail, and his eyes staring west toward the rising sun. I waved at him, the kanakas waved, but he never let on that we was even in his world.

Maybe we weren't, and never had been.

Earl went on west all right, not only to Yokohama and Tokyo, but finally wangled his way down to the Palau Islands, where Lourdes was from. According to a relative of hers who was living with him by then, Ellis had figured out that when the Japs seized the Philippines from us, they'd have to grab Palau as well, to protect their eastern sea frontier. While he was sniffing out whatever they were doing on Palau, the Kempetai, Jap secret police, caught up to him. They claimed that he'd drunk himself to death, but years later, a big old Palau woman sobbed to me the truth of it. She'd been with him the night they'd put cyanide in his beer.

His body never came home to us and, as far as I could tell, neither did his warnings. By the time I'd got back to Pearl Harbor, MacArthur had latched onto Ike Eisenhower and made him his aide in the Philippines. I tried to interest some Marine and Navy muckety-mucks in Ellis' few charts and snapshots, but when the brass hats wasn't off playing golf or the stock market, they'd finger the stuff and say they were forwarding it to Washington. I could tell by the way they humored this old fart that they thought Earl's evidence was fake. Hell, they almost said as much, easing me out the door.

After that, the officers I knew clammed up, and everybody pretended that they'd just as leave forget a burned out Marine named Ellis. Died in disgrace, in the bottom of a bottle.

But I'd never forget him. For all the long voyages in the next years, I carried him with me like an albatross, perched on my shoulder, whispering doom.

He wasn't the first to see what was coming, and he wasn't going to be the last. His sin was being right, and having the guts to die for what he believed. But who the hell was listening back in the Twenties? The US of A was giddying itself with the jazzy flapper times and the booming of stocks and bonds. Get rich quick, that was all anybody cared about. The dance of greed would never end, so they figured, until it curled up like a boiled stuffed shirt and smacked them in the face.

Even in the far off Pacific, we felt the aftershocks of the Crash of '29. The occasional papers I'd get from Honolulu showed breadlines in the streets of the big, dingy mainland cities. Crippled old vets, who never got their bonus money, were down to selling apples, and bums warming themselves around flame-lit barrels through all the long winters of the Depression.

Once in a while I'd get a letter from Nora telling me how tough things were. She and Ned had moved from Chicago to the swanky suburb of Lake Forest, where he was the town doc. But even here, among the great manicured estates, money was tight, and fear was setting in. The big booming myth of free enterprise had gone belly up, and nobody knew why. Didn't the American Dream work anymore?

Nora was still teaching Spanish to help support the doc and keep my grandson, Jake, they called him, in fancy schools. I could tell from her letters that the strain was wearing her down. In 1931, she lost a child at birth, and that set her back even more. Then, by '33, what was left of the Archibald empire got pissed away by the oldest son, Eben. One morning, he stepped out his office window and splatted on LaSalle street, twenty stories below.

Last of my brother-in-laws gone, like Daisy before them. End of the old rich ways.

I wrote Nora and said, Wake up, girl, the past is gone and never coming back. So why in hell are you and Ned still trying to chase it, living like swells in a costly place where you have to scrape to get by? What's it worth? All for show, ain't it? Putting on the dog.

She lashed back, giving me this lecture about how young Jake, my grandson, deserved to have the best education possible, and by God she'd get it for him, one way or the other. I gathered by then that a friend of hers named Castle, a nabob she often mentioned, was helping pay the lad's freight. I wasn't keen on the notion of begging anybody, but hell, it was their life back there, and a long way from me. Once and awhile, when I'd make a good haul, trading, I'd send her a postal order with a few funds to help out.

Back in New York, Matt and Aleka were also feeling the pinch. They had a little boy whom they named Brendan after my Papa, then a girl with the Russian moniker, Turia. Matt had risen high in the new radio world, so I was puzzled when he writes me a short, sad letter. "Even in this giant corporation, even in the great future of the airwaves, the real power isn't here. It's moving to Washington. Under Roosevelt's schemes, and some have worked, the U.S. is being centralized into Federal control. The people who are running things more and more come out of the big Wall Street law firms. Or, they're investment bankers. I have no use for that field, but the law does interest me. Aleka and I have made a mutual decision that I get a law degree, and follow it hopefully into the government. I've started at Columbia Law School. There'll be years of this, with a tight belt, too, but I'm confident it will pay off."

Well, that was Matty for you. He had the guts to begin again, and was so Injun-proud like his mother, such a loner that he'd never accept help from me. When I wrote him back, I says I had little use for them honchos on Wall Street, for when they started meddling in politics, it seemed like we'd always end up in a war that was profiting somebody's bank. As for lawyers, I'd had a bellyful of 'em when they looted Daisy's estate.

While I was writing Matt, I remembered that last afternoon in '90 when the little tyke and I were driving our wagon away from Wounded Knee. Freeman McTighe's warning still rang in my ears: high on the top of the heap, men without faces, money men we never knew were running the world. They didn't care who died in the wars or who ran the nations. We all worked for them, somehow, we common ones did the paying and the dying, and never knew why.

It saddened me that Matty must have seen the same thing, and decided to get in on the power. Divvy up the spoils like his warrior ancestors used to.

But, hell, why write that to him? He was a grown man and wouldn't listen, maybe shouldn't. He had to make his own way and find out for himself. All I said was, "These are tough times in the US of A, but you'll come out on your feet, I know that." Maybe in answer, Aleka sent me snaps of the kids, and a Victrola record of all of 'em singing a Russian song to me. One night in a Tahiti saloon, I played the scratchy thing for a bunch of drunks and outcasts. We all had a laugh and a drink to the health of 'em, which was about all I could do, being so far out of things.

It suited me fine, though. I kept drifting through the islands, further and further from the noise back home. In them turrible '30's, banks were failing, lives being shattered. Fear had gripped the nation, and I seen it in my own flesh and blood. They were hiding, trembling in their cozy apartments or houses, clutching their things, their trappings of riches, against the mob howling in the streets, threatening to snatch them away. No wonder they couldn't hear the wailing of banshees in far-off lands. Waving the banner of our Manifest Destiny, we'd tamed two giant frontiers all right, leaping the wilderness and then the oceans until we'd seized the rich isles of the heathen, trying to make markets for the goods that clanked out of our industrial machine. But even at that, we'd gone broke. Horn of plenty, was it? Ah no, a sham, this free enterprise capitalism that had buried so many boys in distant lands. Our grand dream was dry as a widow's tit now, and nobody knew how to fill it up again. In our glory cry, our masters had sent us plundering all that lay before us, luring us with the riches we'd get. But it was on the blood of poor men dying that we'd swept across the western sea, only to strike rock on the far shore.

That was the sound I was hearing—the roar of a giant tsunami tidal wave rising in the east. To me, it was the nightmare I'd had in Havana Bay after the *Maine* blew me out of my senses. Black and brown and yellow devils dancing around the fires of vengeance on far off palmy isles. Make the white men pay for our centuries of arrogance and our greed.

So pay we would, and one day soon. Even sailing to the ends of the earth, burying my head in the sand, I couldn't outrun it. That giant tidal wave from the east was going to sweep away my last dreams of a peaceful old age.

Like the warning of the Sioux war I seen coming long ago, or the fraud of Cuba, why try anymore? I'd said my piece to a world that wasn't listening, and never did care. They had to do it their way. Swell. Go to it! The blind buggers, leave 'em to God, I'm saying, but just leave me be, stay out of my road, byes, for the precious time I've got left no man is going to take away.

A BROTH OF A BOY

In them last years of the '30's, I'd just about quit writing things down. Hell, I was nearing 80, and drifting through them lazy island lagoons, I seemed so far away from the world that there wasn't no sense in trying to remember how I'd got there, or what used to matter. Time now just to go fishin'.

But then, by God, if the past don't curl up and hit me in the kisser. Years later, Nora give me the lad's letter. It was on account of him that I begun my writing again, putting down the life I had left, like maybe this young one might care to know what it had all been for.

Aboard the freighter Loire,
Cie. Francais/Pacifique

August 27, 1939

Dearest Mother and Father,

Well, it's finally over! Stanley has met Livingston and survived! Bertie and I boarded this rusty French bucket in Papeete yesterday, and when we looked back toward the reefs of Tahiti, Bertie said, "I still can't believe that we're loose of that old bastard." But just now, when we passed the Tuamotus and Grandpa still didn't come screaming after us like a frigate bird, I do believe that our hide-and-seek is over. We're "olly-olly-ottsen free!"

Please don't misunderstand. We've had the experience of our lives, but oh, Mother, your Poppa is one hard case! They broke the mold with him, Bertie says, and I'm afraid it's true. He just about scared the pants off us, but in the end, as I hope to show, it was worth it, just knowing such a guy.

So here I am, sitting on a hot deck with the smokestack roaring behind me, and trying to put down what this trip has meant. Since Uncle Roger Castle paid for it, please show him the letter, too, because his son Bertie has turned into such a beach bum he won't even do a postcard!

Speaking of writing, Pop, I know you consider me such a jock I'll never get into med school—well, really, this trip has given me a glimmer of a career that's anything but medicine.

I'll say it. Writing. I'm considering being a writer. I know that sounds crazy, and compared to the wooden stuff I used to put down at Hotchkiss, and I'm sure more of it ahead at Yale this fall, dull damn themes—but out here in these islands, it's so exotic, so

460

fragrant, so totally *bizarre* compared to Lake Forest, something just snapped in me. I saw those palm trees, and they *are* just like the postcards, the girls *are* "Mutiny on the Bounty", only better, with less on! Overwhelming. From the first night in Papeete, I couldn't wait to run back to my *fale* (thatch hut) and start scribbling. Who knows, maybe I can use some of it at Yale, and maybe I never will be a real writer, I can hear you saying there's no money in it. But brother, for now, am I having fun letting all this wonderment out of me! This is the first time I've ever seen anything except our treadmill of schools and deb parties and chasing hockey pucks or whacking baseballs.

What I'm saying, this is *life*, Mom and Pop, and Patrick Kelly is right out of Somerset Maugham. Barefoot, a native lava-lava wrapped around him, and a straw hat that looks like a mule ate it. What you can see of his skin has been sunburned into old leather, and his white beard so wild and matted you expect butterflies to whir out of it. Robinson Crusoe, I swear, cranky, bullheaded, you can't make a simple statement to him that he doesn't contradict it, just to be on the fight. A really horrible man when you rub him wrong (and did Bertie ever!). But when you drill through that cliff of his face, when you don't let his hawky eyes and nasty beak terrify you, there's a heart underneath his bony chest that's awful big and tender.

I know you don't agree, Mom, but he really loves you, and Pop, too. One day when I told him how sad you were that he seemed to have no interest in us, he barked, "Why, you snot, what are you expecting me to do, wipe your fancy butts? Who done it for me? Make your own way, that's all there is, yesterday gone and good riddance! Today is what counts, and if there ain't enough today for you, start looking at tomorrow. Put the look of eagles in your eyes! There's always something thrilling across the horizon, lad. Go to it, chase it down!"

Do you know, Mom, your father will not talk about death. He will not wear a shred of black, will not go to funerals, which are a big thing out here, the natives wailing and mourning for days. Not Patrick Kelly. He'll walk a mile to avoid a cemetery, turns his back on anybody who tries to tell him about ill health, and won't even glance at the obituaries in the Tahiti newspaper. "The Irish Sport Page," he sneers, even though they're written in French.

Yet it must work. He hasn't been in a hospital since his war wounds years ago. Rx for a long life, Pop. Chase tomorrow. Maybe you and your colleagues should bottle up the juices old Patrick has!

So Mom, stop worrying about how lonely he is in his old age. What a laugh. Bertie called him a randy billy goat, and that's not far wrong. These women in Tahiti are different, okay? They do a lot of hugging and kissing, and your father can't get enough. He spends half his days sitting under a palm tree, joggling naked urchins on

461

his knees, and some not so little maidens, too. Gleam in his eye. "Fanny pincher," Bertie whispered to me our first night ashore. Patrick overheard and collared him. "Why, you sissified little fart," he cried, "you wouldn't know where it was or what to do with it if you had it!"

Then later that night, he caught Bertie trying to neck with a native girl, and he literally threw him off the dock into the lagoon. Turned out the girl was Patrick's wife's daughter, and engaged to a local bigshot. How to screw up race relations on the islands.

Did you hear me right, Mom? I said, "Patrick's wife." I wish you'd warned me, but probably you didn't know. Your indomitable old father took himself a bride several years ago, either "before or after Amelia," he dates everything, which I'll explain later.

Anyhow, his wife has a long rippling Tuamotu name, Tehaare something-something LeGoupil, but for short, he just calls her Pearlie. Did he ever fall into it and come out with a new suit! Pearlie is some kind of Tuamotu queen. Out here, all property is apparently owned by the maternal side, and Pearlie ended up with her own beautiful little island named Tehaare. It's out in the middle of noplace, a lagoon in the center, mangrove swamps and coconut groves, but the cherry on top, the lagoon shells have black pearls in them (like Pearlie, I suppose), and Patrick says that someday, people are going to pay good money for these "geegaws."

When Patrick is around, and not wandering off to explore the far horizon, he keeps his Crazy Horse boat parked in the lagoon. It's about a day's run to Papeete where he picked us up. But upon arrival, we didn't go right back to Tehaare. In his threadbare white linen suit, Patrick caroused us through a succession of wharf saloons in Papeete, picking up drifters, windbags and gamey Tahitian women at every stop. He's the local character, everybody hugging him and the gals draping him with leis. Getting away from Tehaare was, I suppose, his excuse for a lovely bender, rum at every stop, and shamelessly relieving himself on the boulevard trees whenever he felt the urge. To his seedy pals, he'd introduce me as "the daughter's son." Or, next stop I'd be "*le gamin*," or "*l'enfant terrible*." By the time we'd made it out to Mr. Nordhoff and Mr. Hall's beachhouse, I'd become "The Crown Prince," or sometimes, "Clown Prince." And how he'd guffaw at my discomfort. Boy! I thought, this guy is going to wear awfully thin!

Nordhoff and Hall are who you've guessed, the famous authors. They get a big kick out of Grandpa, entertaining him with rum and Polynesian women loading us with pork, poi and squirmy little shellfish, all steamed in pandanus leaves. The stuff was so rich, Bertie upchucked it on the beach, but I pretty much coasted, knowing that I couldn't go drink for drink with the old geezer. The party lasted all night, Patrick, Nordhoff and Hall lying in hammocks on the veranda and swapping stories about what Patrick calls "The World's War." From what I gathered, Nordhoff and Hall had been pilots Over There, and Patrick claims that a Marine squadron commander had taught him how to fly.

Days later, we wore out Papeete, a feat in itself, the people so hospitable that they'd party with you until they killed you.

As we pitched and tossed back to Tehaare, Patrick sweated out his hangover by fishing. He did it native style, using their primitive bone hooks, and boated a big tuna and some mahimahi. Typical of him, though his kanaka crewmen wanted to help, the stubborn old fool insisted on handlining in his own heavy fish. He was wheezing so with the tuna that I thought he'd have a coronary, but Bertie said, "No such luck, buster. You couldn't kill that old fart with a pole axe."

Coming ashore at Tehaare, it was a moonlight night, silver palms and crystal water. Really heaven. Patrick stumped ahead of us in the sand, up toward the one building on the island. "Tiptoeing home, byes," he grunted, "we'll catch our penance now, hell to pay."

What he calls home is a shack of driftwood, up on stilts to keep it from floating away in a hurricane. It's like something L'il Abner would live in (he's the hillbilly in the new *Tribune* comic strip.) The veranda was draped with fishing nets, the whole place stinking of seashells and rotting coconuts. Inside, a lantern flamed on, the moldy screen door banged open and out roared an apparition who sure wasn't L'il Abner's curvy Daisy Mae. This amazon stood at least as tall as Patrick, who has to be six-four. With her mumu flapping like a sail on a ship, she flew at him, swooped him up and swung him in a circle. She had a mane of gray hair down to her waist, and Patrick, with a roar, grabbed a handful of it and jerked her off him. "Damn ye, hussy, behave yourself! I brung ye the bye, and the little squirt too, his friend."

Paying no attention to Bertie and me, she flung Grandpa against the rickety porch, seized his face with her giant hands, and when she smelled the breath on him, began howling in Tahitian. Chuckling, he stuffed a wad of francs down the front of her mumu. "Put that in your boobies," he chuckled with a wink at me. "Yer Grandma is a costly female, but a queen for all that, and worth it, ain't you, dearie, all cuddles and beer?" He patted her fanny, drew her to him and kissed her. "Tell her, lad, I never so much as winked at another woman over at Papeete, and every draught of rum was toasting my Pearlie, now ain't that the truth?"

"Scout's honor, Grandpa."

She scowled at us and said in perfect English, "You're lying son-sofbitches, it must run in the family. But," she sighed, "grass widows have to take whatever washes up on the beach." She gripped my shoulders, murmured something in Tahitian, and kissed me on both cheeks. "You are welcome on Tehaare in spite of your lunatic grandfather, so don't just stand out here giving me pneumonia. *Entrez, faites-toi comfortable, mon petit.*"

Several Tuamotu boys came pattering up to take our luggage, and when we got settled in the smoky parlor, it reeked of rum and beer, despite Pearlie's temperance lecture. A pretty Tuamotu girl with a rope of black hair knelt gracefully and began putting wooden dinner plates on a straw mat on the floor. When she leaned toward us, her mumu draped down to reveal her ample charms, which Bertie was ogling. "Run through those barefoot," he whispered. Grandpa whirled on him. "Mind your tongue, you horny little bugger. You're in a queenly house and that don't mean tampering with the help."

Pearlie chuckled, "Ah, you old rounder, let boys be boys. Terita is my niece. We're all one family here, Polynesian style." Pearlie heaped down cross-legged beside me and patted my leg. "Turn up the lamp, Terita. I want to see what the tide brought in." When the glow rose and crossed our faces, Pearlie's dark eyes gleamed. She stroked her fingers across my cheek and my lips. "Ah, handsome, but not too much. Lovely eyes, *mon petit,* but surely they couldn't have come from this old buzzard who claims you. Perhaps you favor your mother...?"

By then, her scrutiny was making me quite uncomfortable. I suppose it's the frank, Polynesian way, and with the lamp flickering over her high cheekbones, I was struck by her imperious, stately beauty, though faded now.

She was scowling at me. "Well, come on, talk. Are you afraid to be among natives?"

"Gosh no, ma'am," I stammered, "I mean, Pearlie. I love it out here, just wish my French weren't so lousy so I could understand more. Of course with you, knowing English...."

"English, do you hear!" She tossed back her head and roared. "Little man, before you were a seed running down your father's leg, I was making love to the most handsome guards officer at Buckingham Palace. He had me dancing for the Queen at the Court of St. James."

"Ah, so now it's queens, is it!" Patrick snorted. He was sitting across the mat from us, his lips greasy with pork. "Look who's putting on the dog."

"You know it's true," she said, her eyes going sad. "I gave him a son who was killed at the Somme."

"I take it you were a dancer then?" Bertie said, glancing at some old photographs on the walls.

"Then, you say! Do you think I forget? I was the lead dancer in *La Companie Tahitienne,* Europe, America, China, everywhere we went. *Fameuse, incroyable!* Terita, the Victrola!" Unsteadily, a beer in her hand, she pushed up like a mountain moving, as the girl pattered over to wind a phonograph in the corner. Squealing from an ancient needle came the quick drum beats, rattles and chants of Tahitian music. Pearlie, barefoot, kicked Bertie and me back to make room. Her eyes closed, her arms outstretched, she began throbbing her pelvis not in the slow hula style but in triphammer bumps and grinds so rapid that the whole creaky floor began quivering. Bertie and I looked at each other, unable to believe this sudden wild orgy, her hands fluttering like little birds and her lips whispering faint smiles. She was lost in it for a few really tragic seconds. Then abruptly, the Victrola gave a groan and stopped.

"*Merde!*" she shouted, and kicked at Patrick. "You were to fix it in Papeete! What are you good for? Tell me what you're good for!"

"Loving you, darlin'." Patrick chuckled, and pulled her gently out of the dance to sit on his lap. Tears began running down her dark cheeks, and he brushed them away. "Now, ain't she grand, lads," he said to Bertie and me. "The best in the world she was. I'll brag on you, you old thing, shaking your ass to the four corners of the earth and the crowned heads indeed."

She sniffled something in Tahitian and wiped at her eyes.

"What do you mean, nobody cares?" Patrick growled. "I care. Ain't I somebody? A champion she still is, byes, but there's a time for all things. I'll get the machine fixed in the morning, dearie, and we'll give 'em a show, just like you used to."

"Eat your dinners," she said gruffly. "I'm an old woman, and I'm not waiting up all night to entertain babies and a cadaver!" She hooked her thumbnail under her front teeth and flicked it at us, then pushed up unsteadily and hulked away.

The next morning on the beach, while Patrick was tinkering with the Victrola, he sighed. "Ah, she's a moody one, boy. Polynesians are like the sun, one minute all smiles, and the next, ducking behind a cloud, and pissing down rain squalls. But she heals quick. She's a good old bat."

"Good for you, I'd say, this island and all."

"A fine port in the storm, indeed. But don't think that it was always so. Why, when I come on Pearlie, she was about dead. Broken heart."

"You mean, when she got too old for dancing with her troupe?"

"Ah, sure that was part of it, but mostly..." he glanced through the shadows of the palms behind us..."mum's the word, lad. Pearlie, poor old dear, never said no to a man."

"I don't follow you?"

"Lovers. She had 'em worldwide. Come by it rightly, I suppose. Her father was a whoremaster Frenchman, planter in New Caledonia, and he must have had fifteen Tonkinese gals in his bed. Her mother was Tuamotu, dignified princess, Catholic to the beads. But maybe the girl got her wild side from the old man. She went at it good. A looker like her, shaking her ass, men swarmed her like bees to honey. She had that Britisher, then a German count, no-account, I says, and after him a French richie. I don't know how many, even a A-rab sheik, sporting her to the ritziest spas. Every time she'd bed down, she'd get a baby. Then she'd drop the stud and find a new one. She's got eight kiddies that she tells me of, some drowned in the sea, some dead in the war. The last one is out of a Tonga sire, boy named Andre, and what did the bugger do with a whore for a mother? He become a Catholic priest, praying for her poor soul, I suppose."

He sighed, and slammed the lid on the Victrola. "The bitterest woman in the world is one that relies on and then loses her beauty and her charms, and the men discard her like an old rag. When I come on her, she'd been lying in that shack, drunk for months, fevers and DTs, and trying to kill herself with knives when the booze didn't." His bushy eyebrows beetled down and his blue eyes danced. "D'ye know how I brung her back, lad?"

"Got her off the booze?"

"Hell, no! Just loving her back to life. Making her feel the beauty that's in her soul. It took years, but by damn, it's been worth it. She's an angel taking wing, and if I ever done one decent thing in my life, maybe she's it."

A giant shadow crossed us. I whirled to see Pearlie standing in the sand, hands on her hips. "So this is where you hide the poor boy! Talk him to death. Doesn't he have better things to do? Come on now, *mon petit* Jake." She said it 'sjaik', "I love that silly name. Terita will take you to the reef, if you can swim."

"You bet I can," I said, trying not to look at Terita, who was only wearing the tight bottom of her yellow pareu, and the beautiful rest of her gleaming in the sun.

(As I read this back, it sounds like the *Police Gazette* or something, but honestly, Mother and Pop, it's so natural and shameless out here, I shudder to remember our prim Lake Forest girls, practically wearing chastity belts just to lie beside the Onwentsia Club pool!)

During the weeks on Tehaare, Patrick asked me many questions about our life at home. I'm not sure that he could understand much of it, our ways being so totally different from his. Once I caught him leafing the Hotchkiss year book that Bertie had lugged out, why I don't know. Grandpa would flick the pages, photos of one team after the next, then he'd poke his finger at me in the middle of a hockey or baseball lineup. "So it's games now!" he snorted. "Is that what your folks pay a fortune for, teach you to whack little balls?"

I tried to tell him that games would prepare us for the dog-eat-dog competition we'd have to face in our careers.

"So what will you be when you grow up? A nabob in a spiffy suit? Some butt-polishing shyster in a bank, I suppose?"

I tried to tell him that I wasn't sure yet. Sometimes I even dreamed of becoming a writer. "Ah," he growled, "stuff your dreams in your barracks bag, lad, and your pasture games along with them. You'll be in the real game soon enough."

"The real game?"

"Killing men. That's what the damn richies have in mind for you. Cannon fodder, one more time, poor man's fight."

He flung the yearbook down and wouldn't talk about it anymore. In moments like that, I thought he was just a bitter old man, poisoning youth against any hope for the future. But then something happened to change my entire view of him.

I stumbled on his diary.

I'm sure you don't know, Mother and Pop, that Patrick has been keeping a record of his life ever since he fled County Mayo in 1875. As Bertie put it, "Now you know where the horsethieves and murderers are in your family!"

His story is awesome, and I came on it totally by chance. Pearlie had some business to attend to over at Rangiroa, more or less the capital of the Tuamotu chain. While they were gone, and Terita and the staff with them, Bertie took it on himself to prowl through the shack looking for cold beer. In the shambles of their bedroom, he discovered a rusty old safe that Patrick had salvaged from a sunken German ship. Because Bert is a born snoop, and the combination door was ajar, he peered inside and saw a bunch of copybooks, the kind schoolkids use. Some of them were very old, one covered in leather and tooled with Indian signs. Another was stenciled "Property U.S. Government". When I discovered Bertie sitting on the floor, dropping cigarette ashes on the old pages, I said, "Damn it, you shouldn't be messing with Grandpa's personal stuff."

"Personal, hell, it's got your mother and father all over it, grandmother, too, even you. A real chore to read. Looks like the old boy did it with goose quills or fingerpainting in mud. However," he said and grinned, "he's also got a copy of it. Look at this." He handed me a brown paper sack. Inside, wrapped in oilskin to keep it from getting wet was a large notebook filled with typewritten pages. Apparently, and quite recently, a stenographer in Tahiti had transcribed the entire diary. Skimming it, I could see that it wasn't the world's greatest translation, a lot of Frenchified English crept in, but boy, did the story sock me!

Bertie and I kept passing it back and forth all that hot afternoon and into the night. Sometimes Bertie would say, "The old fart has got to be a liar in the class of Paul Bunyan. Jake, you know damn well he couldn't have done all these things, been in all those wars. And who the hell is going to care anyway? Why does he bother to put it down?"

"Well, I damn well care, Bert." Honestly, it was like opening a grave. Eerie, thrilling. Not only were the adventures so gripping, but the span of history that Patrick had lived really opened my eyes. We'd never been taught these things in school. Patrick had a way of cutting through the bullshit our teachers gave us. The so-called glory of war, forget it. On these pages was the dirt, the suffering and sham of it, which he cursed often enough.

"But dammit, Jake," Bert said, "the guy is practically illiterate. He even writes in an Irish brogue."

"Well, what do you expect? Hotchkiss, Yale and LaSalle Street, like your father and grandfather! This is real life, Bertie!"

"Yeah, it is, if you want to lie down with dogs and get up with fleas."

I don't know why the diary got to Bert. I even wondered if he were jealous that I had such an exciting grandpa, and him stuck with the old school tie. Anyhow, we didn't have long to argue. Sometime in the night, a wet Tuamotu urchin slipped into the bedroom and caught us reading the stuff. Quick as hell, we put it all back where it came from and ran outside. The lights of the Crazy Horse streamed across the lagoon, and Patrick, Pearlie and the hangers-on were plodding up the sand toward us.

They were tired and mildly soused, so nothing was said. But the next morning, just as I was starting toward the reef to go out spearing fish with Terita, Patrick barked at me. He was sitting in the shade of his favorite palm tree, having a mug of coffee. He took his corncob from his lips and aimed it at me. "All right, you sneaky bugger, stand to. Which of youse done it, you or the squirt?"

"Done what, Grandpa?"

"You know damn well!" He jerked the spear from me and spiked it into the sand. "Robbing a man's private books, you was, the boat boy caught youse!"

My face went hot, I wanted to cringe, but that didn't work with him. Finally I just looked him in the eye and said, "Yes, sir. We were in there, we shouldn't have done it. But Grandpa, I didn't think I was robbing anything either. Reading your story meant more to me than anything in my life."

His white brows beetled down. "You're a lying snot, that was gibberish you read."

"But it's not! Patrick, don't you see, you gave me an education with what you wrote. I mean, all that stuff about the old days, and Mom and her mother, and what you went through. I only had a chance to skim it, but can't you understand that it hit me in the heart. Goddamn it, I'm so proud of you I want to..." I was going to say, "weep", but I couldn't get the word out. I sure choked up, though, Terita standing shyly in the shadows, wondering why.

Patrick flicked his hand at her. "G'wan, cherie. Play with the other squirt if you gotta have a mate. Leave me this one."

When she was gone, Patrick jerked me over to him, and with his pipe wisping smoke, he put his arm around my shoulders and hugged me.

"Jesus and Mary," he muttered, "how long I've waited for a touch of my own. You're a good lad, Jake, broth of a boy. You've got the truth in you, I see that now. As for filching the silly book, maybe I would have let you do it anyhow, but I'm glad you done it on your own. All them years, scribbling rot for nobody but God himself to see. I keep saying, Why? I keep looking for hope, out of the raging storms of life. Is there a meaning to any of it? But maybe I'm knowing now. Passing it along to my own flesh and blood, showing them a road that I pray they don't have to travel."

"Grandpa," I said suddenly, "if Mother and Pop could see what you've written, it would explain so much to them about the old days. I know that it would make them happy. You have a copy of the diary now. I thought, if I could just take it with me, show it to them...?"

He shook his head, drew his arm down from my shoulder, and sat staring at his knotted hands. "No, lad," he said quietly, "you ain't taking nothing, because if you did, my life would be done. Ah," he growled, "I'm sick of the thing, the world I've seen, all the warnings they don't heed. Before you come here, yes, I'd quit it all right, give up the writing. The thing never would have been put in the typing machine if Charlie Nordhoff and Hall too hadn't been beating on me. Sure, they got bigshots printing their words, they says, why not mine, earn me a copper or two. Ah, no. My words, I tells 'em, is just for me, all I got left of my miserable soul, and until I get a spade flinging dirt in my face, that's the way it will stay."

"Well, at least, Grandpa, I'm glad that I saw it. Maybe someday, you'll agree to put it in print."

"Someday," he murmured, "is coming sooner than you think, lad. War is heading toward these very isles. Like the tea leaves, the clouds are," and he nodded toward a darkening cumulus rising over the reef. "Coming for us both, lad. Me, I don't care how. But for you, ah, how I grieve. All the storybooks in the world aren't going to keep you from it, or spare you from the horror. But maybe it's God's way, making these turrible things happen. At least, an old man has to figure that, for he can't do nothing else to head it off. That's what I told White Eyelashes anyhow."

"Who?"

He smiled. "The lady in the sky. Two years back now, it was. I come on her at Lae, over in New Guinea. Amelia. Amelia Earhart. Kissed her hand, I did, clung to her, she was such a brave one, but I couldn't stop her. Ah," he tapped out his pipe and spat in the sand, "all the good ones go, that's the hell of getting old."

As we walked together along the beach, he told me an incredible story about how Amelia Earhart was lost. It was certainly nothing we ever read in our papers at home, and I have no way to know if it were true.

Apparently, Grandpa had known her over the years, when she was flying in and out of Hawaii. He used to kid her about her eyelashes, burned white by the sun in her goggles when she was searching for some far-off horizon. She was his kind of pioneer, and he had a fatherly protectiveness toward her. But when he stumbled onto her in New Guinea, his concern became angry fear.

"You're pulling a goddamn crazy stunt, girl," he bellowed, "and I don't care if Roosevelt and them navies sweet-talked you into it, when you're out there in that lonely sky over the Carolines, there ain't no coming back, and there ain't a one of the high and mighty that will lift a finger to help you."

Then he told her how they'd chopped off a Colonel Ellis of the Marines, and let him die. She'd be next. A spy that nobody wanted to claim, or believe, even if her flight were a success.

What angered Patrick was that he surprised Earhart when she, her navigator Fred Noonan, and a naval intelligence officer were secretly changing the engines on her Lockheed airplane. He told me the model numbers of the engines, which meant nothing to me, except that they hadn't shown up in Lae by accident. "The purpose was clear, lad, and could only mean one thing. With them giant Wasp motors, Amelia could fly all across Truk and the other Carolines, see what the Japs was up to, maybe take photos, and still have range enough to make it to Baker or Howland, U.S. islands."

In Patrick's opinion, and maybe Amelia admitted it, either the Navy or FDR had put her up to this dangerous mission. The big new engines simply weren't needed for her normal around-the-world flight. To make matters worse, Fred Noonan had been drinking heavily on the rainy night when they roared north out of Lae. Patrick warned him that to navigate across those uncharted Carolines was going to be a big challenge even for a sober man.

"When I seen her go," Patrick muttered, "I knew she wasn't coming back. In the years since I'd been at Truk with Earl Ellis, I'd heard stories about it from kanaka fishermen. The Japs was fortifying the place heavy now, radios, airplanes, and they'd paid off Trukese natives to rat on any intruders. Let her and Noonan drift too far, run onto the wrong headwinds or get lost, they'd go down on the reefs, and them yellow monkeys would hand 'em their heads on a samurai sword."

Patrick sailed north out of Lae that same night, monitoring Earhart's radio signals until they faded away. By the time he reached Howland Island, he was sure that she'd crashed. "Then it turned into a boat race," Patrick said, "them Japs churning the seas looking for her, and our navies doing the same. But hell, lad, as an Admiral told me, FDR didn't want to risk running our battlewagons into the Carolines. Run onto a Jap, there'd be a shootout and a war, and we wasn't ready for it. So," he sighed, "it was just like I told that brave gal. We'd cut and run from her, let her go."

"Do you think she's dead, Patrick?"

His lips curled and he spat in the sand. "Hell, yes, she is. But we ain't never gonna know where or how until we take them rocks back in the next war. Your war, lad, God help ye."

"Boy," I said, "you really make it sound depressing, Grandpa."

He smiled and gripped my arm. "You're a good lad. I've been into war with worse, I'll tell you. So enjoy your young days, Jake. I've got a hunch that our paths will cross, someplace, before this is done."

"I sure hope so, Grandpa."

Then it was over, and several days later, when we sailed out of Tehaare, I had tears in my eyes. They all came to Papeete to put us aboard this freighter. Pearlie, in her gruff way, loaded us down with shell necklaces she'd had the Tuamotu people make, plus a special gift for you, Mother, that I'll deliver shortly. As we started down the gangplank for the last time, Terita began to weep. "*Quand tu retournez,*" she whispered, "*ca c'est pour vous.*" The innocent wonderful child took my hand and laid it on her breast.

Patrick collared me in his rough way and grunted, "Keep the look of eagles in your eyes, me bye."

"I'll try, Grandpa."

"And you," he roared, grabbing Bertie by the hair, "you impudent little squirt, grow up a notch or two and keep me bye out of trouble, or I'll whale you!"

Patrick shoved us down the gangplank and stormed back to his cabin. I like to think that he had tears in his eyes, but the old shellback would never give me the satisfaction of seeing the softness in his heart.

So now it's done. It's a watershed in my life. Thank you, Mother and Pop, and particularly Uncle Roger. Thomas Wolfe said, "You can't go home again." But in Patrick, I've found a home I never knew I had.

With love and see you soon,

Jake

SECOND TIME AROUND

The lad hadn't been gone a week from Tehaare before I was sitting in the wheelhouse of the Crazy Horse, tuning the crackles and squeals of the radio until I had her set on the Papeete station.

Pearlie, the Terita lass and my kanaka crew were crowding around me in the darkness when the sharp-tongued Frenchman began spitting out the words:

"*Commencait ajourd'hui la guerre! La deuxieme guerre mondiale!*"

The Boche, damn their gray pot helmets, had thundered across their borders and grabbed Europe by the throat! All I could think of was Black Jack Pershing, that last day at Chaumont, saying that unless we destroyed the Heinie war machine then and there, we'd end up having to fight them all over again.

Pearlie was wailing, Would they take Tahiti? Would their ships come? I says, "Hell no, woman! They've got to lick Europe first, bust through the Frenchies Maginot Line, and that won't happen overnight, maybe never. The world ain't gonna stand for another slaughter like we had in '18."

But Pearlie kept sobbing. "I know the French better than you, old goat. I have their blood from my father. They're greedy, they're soft. They want no more wars. They lost the flower of their nation the first time. They'll sell out rather than fight."

It took months to learn what was happening so far from us. But in the end, Pearlie was right. The Frenchies gave up and collapsed like a pricked balloon, leaving the English and Russians slogging the muddy trenches. It made me sick watching the same old death dance, and praying that this time, the US of A would have the sense and the guts to stand clear. Let the rotten empires of Europe kill each other off, drench their own turf in blood. It wasn't no cause of ours whether the Boche won, or the English, even the damn Eyeties. But as the months dragged on, in the crackling of the radio, I heard the sound that T.R. had feared, and Ellis, and Amelia. It was the thumping boots of the Rising Sun, Jap troops screaming banzais, their planes whining down, machine-gunning port cities and rice-paddy hamlets. The bandy-leggers were flaming their way across China, just as Ellis had predicted. From there they'd lash on to the Philippines, Indo-China and Malaysia. They'd need rubber, tin and oil to carry on their bloody war, and, knowing full well that neither we nor the British or Dutch would let them grab it, they'd have to knock us out first. When I says to an old Tahitian Chinaman, "Why, them Japs would be mad to try such a thing," he smiles. "*Mon ami,* what seems madness to the narrow western mind is to the Oriental supremely logical. Strike when your enemy least expects it."

So, little by little, I seen it happening. By the time the Japs dropped their mask, signed a damn treaty and threw in with the Axis powers, I says to Pearlie, "Start packing your things, dearie."

Little did I dream how quick we'd be doing just that.

One bright morning in June 1941, almost two years after Jake had left us, a Frenchy patrol boat come churning into Tehaare. The Vichy skipper hands me a cablegram.

Pop killed himself. Awful here. Mother shattered, we all need you. Won't you please come home?

    Jake

The Vichy skipper hands me a pen and paper. "*Voulez-vous responder, mon vieux?*"

I scribbled, "Next boat."

Three weeks later, Pearlie and I rumbled into the city of Chicago on the big U.P. train. God in heaven, I couldn't believe the hundreds of passenger cars snaking into the boomy depot, clanking and fouling the sky with smoke, the giant buildings towering over us, and the streets milling with worker ants. What a different town that I left on the U.P. back in the Christmas of 1875, lonely, scared greenhorn, off to fight the Sioux. "Where did the years go?" I says to Pearlie, and she chuckles, patting my cheek. "You're wearing them, *mon amour.* A wrinkle for every memory. Stop feeling sorry for yourself. You're lucky to have lived so long."

"I suppose," I says, and brightened when Jake come running down the platform to us. He had a tweed coat on and flannel pants, grown into a handsome, rangy lad now, taller than me, black hair and blue eyes smoldering with a sadness he didn't have back on Tehaare.

In his Ford roadster with the top down, he jockeyed us out of the Loop and down mournful streets of dingy worker houses until he struck a wide boulevard heading north. I could hardly remember the lay of the land anymore. What used to be farm fields was now cluttered with little white cities, suburbs Jake called them, one after the other, crusting along the shore of Lake Michigan until they reached the big oaks and quiet lanes of Lake Forest. On the way, we passed Fort Sheridan, and it give me a chuckle. I tells Pearlie about dandy pouter-pigeon General Phil, and how the bigshots of Chicago built him his own private fort so's he could protect 'em from the mobs howling in the streets. Jake says, "Did you know the General, Grandpa?" and I says, "Why, lad, I shod that bugger's horse when I was still driving Armour's meat wagon." Jake just sighed, and sometimes I wondered if he believed me, or if I even believed myself anymore. My bluebelly bunkies were long gone from the fort. Now it was a booming Army post, sandstone towers, rows of barracks, rifle ranges popping as the poor khaki-clad doughboys got themselves ready for the next war our masters had in store for us. Why, even the roads were so superior that they were hurtling me faster than I could catch up with. It only took us an hour or so to reach Lake Forest. Driving along, I kept remembering the night Nora was begging me to let her beau drive her three hours to the Blackstone dance. And me fearing that she could break down on that terrible motor trip, and suppose the feller started messing with her?

"Ah, God, Jake," I says, "this old cob don't belong here no more. I ain't up to the speed of things."

The lad was driving fast, but even at that, other autos were whining past us, more of the damn machines than I could ever believe possible. Where did all the people come from, where did they get so rich? I shook my head, but Jake was gripping the wheel tight, his face pained.

"Maybe rich is the trouble," he murmured. "Before we see Mother, you better know it all, Grandpa." Talking slow and kind of disjointed, he went on to tell how Bertie Castle and him had been friends ever since they was boys, and Uncle Roger Castle, the squirt's dad, had been helping out Nora and Ned for a long time. He had the money, and they was struggling to get by. Growing up, Jake seen nothing wrong in it. In that swanky, clicky set in Lake Forest, kids often had Dutch uncles and aunts, making their road easier. But in Nora's case, with Uncle Roger—Jake shook his head and his voice cracked—"It went too damn far! Do you want the truth! She'd been having an affair with him for years. I guess people in town knew. Bertie wisecracked about it one time but I never believed it. Wouldn't. Then, a few months ago, Aunt Mary Castle died, almost like she was getting out of their way. I don't know why Mother did it, but Pop, you know, his health has been bad, that lung thing from the war just got worse. He kept working himself to death in his practice. And then, last week, Mother was off shopping in Chicago, she was always in there once or twice a week. But this time, Pop got called to some kind of emergency medical meeting at the Blackstone. Down in the elevator comes Mother and Uncle Roger. Pop caught them red-handed. I don't know what was said, but two nights later, at home in his study, he took a shotgun and blew his brains out."

We'd stopped at a traffic light. Jake leaned forward and pressed his head against the wheel. Pearlie, in the back seat, gripped him by the shoulders and started sweet-talking him in French, but the lad wasn't hearing.

"Respectability and being rich, that's all Mother wants," he murmured. "She's got it now. Oh, Jesus, Grandpa, what a mess we make of our lives. I loved Pop, goddamn it. Oh, maybe he was hard to be close to, just quiet and sort of worn out, but he was great to me. I really respected him. I don't see why it had to happen. I love her, too, that's what's so tough..."

A few minutes later, Jake rolled us up to Nora's house, the tires ticking on the gravel, and in the shrubs, bees buzzing and all the flowers of June bobbing their lovely heads. It reminded me of the morning Daisy brought me to the Archibalds when she was carrying little Nora in her belly, the whole world rejoicing in the beauty of this place.

Where Nora and Ned lived was in the cheaper housing over west of the lake, a New England style cottage, its white shingles heavy with vines and big oaks shading the dark windows. We hadn't but got out of the car, Pearlie in her flowered mumu and ropes of shells, before the front door creaked open and a shadow was standing there.

I couldn't believe my Nora. Ah, she was still tall and erect, a handsome woman even in her middle age, but her freckled face was wan, and the fire had gone from her eyes. When she moved toward me, the sunlight flamed her reddish hair which was swept up in some fancy coiffure that didn't hide the streaks of gray. "Ah God, darlin'," I says, and she run to me, hugging me and tears wetting both our faces.

"Thank you, Poppa," she sobbed. "I have no way to tell you how much this means."

Then Pearlie barges in Polynesian style and hugs the three of us. "Meet the wife, Nora! Ain't she a grand ticket for an old fart!"

"Oh, Pearlie," Nora cried, laughing now, "I always dreamed of Papa finding a queen. Thank you for taking him in. You poor thing, he's not easy, he's never been easy, but he's worth it, isn't he?"

They starts chattering and making up over each other like females do, Pearlie lifting off her shell necklaces and draping them on Nora, and she admiring the mumu on the big old thing, like it was the finest gown out of Saks Fifth Avenue.

"Ah, the both of you hens," I says, "you'll get Pearlie so excited, next thing she'll start shaking her ass in her damn Tahitian tamure. It's their kind of hula."

"I want to see," Nora cried. "Jake says you showed him, you're such a wonderful artist, I always did want to learn it. I could surely use a dance right about now."

When she got us settled, and the girl kept a tasteful house, I will admit, I asked her for a rum, the trip having dried me. Then Jake took Pearlie out to wander through the garden and sniff the flowers.

475

Nora still had her old guts, all right. Damn if she didn't lead me smack into Ned Barrow's study, where the poor man had given up his ghost. Silently we stood there, looking at the walls hung with his medical documents, and faded photos of the young pair of them, lovey-dovey way back in Dublan, him in his khakis and cavalry boots. There was other photos of Ned, grinning beside his air machine in France. Handsome daredevil, so much confidence in his eyes. On Ned's desk was a lineup of silver framed snaps, him and Nora christening young Jake, Halloweening the lad in his clown suit, and later, standing proudly beside him in this team uniform or that and holding trophies from his various ball games.

My eyes swung to the chair at the desk. It had been cleaned up, of course, but the leather was still red as blood. "He come a long way, girl, to die here," I murmurs. "Didn't seem like it was in the cards for you, such a grand and blessed family shot to pieces." I gripped her hands. "I pray you didn't have to find him yourself."

She sighed. "No, thank God. He wanted to spare me, I'm sure. Knew when the cleaning woman came, and did it just before. I never thought I'd step into this room again, Papa, but you give me strength. I'll say it, I'll say it to you," she whispered. "It's my fault. I'm responsible for all this." Turning her face from me, she clutched her arms across her breast and stared out into the garden. The sun came over her face and lit the tears that were streaming down her cheeks. "You always told me how headstrong I was. And I got away with it for years. But life has a way of evening the score. When I married Ned, I escaped from you. I wanted to build something so strong and wonderful, so free. But we were babies, naive, idealistic. Then the war, it burned up all the dreams, Patrick. Ned never really recovered."

"None of us do, gal."

"But I mean here, coming back into such a competitive life. You have to be tough, you have to win, and that just wasn't Ned's way. Didn't care about anything monetary. Damn it, Papa, I tried to be a good wife. I slaved for him, but the world crowds in, reality crowds in. We drifted off toward different goals. The older Jake got, the less we seemed to share. Ned loaded himself with too much work, and each patient he failed with galled him into more depression and distance between us. But I'm lying. Don't let me lie! I could have helped save him. Sure, he'd lost his luster. But we swore for better or for worse, didn't we, in sickness and in health! Oh, Papa," she turned to me and lay her face on my shoulder, "I've let you all down, poor Ned, Mama and you. Mostly Jake. Can I ever be forgiven?"

I gripped her tight. "I ain't playing God on you, not now, not ever, so don't look for that. I love you the way you are, Nora, from the first carabao ride I trotted you on in the Walled City, to fighting

476

them Mex in the hacienda. All them years, darlin', I've been riding with you in my heart. Sure with me wandering, maybe I didn't look in enough on you and the family. But it was because I believed in you, knew you had the starch. Nora, it's just going on, that's the ticket for life, and it don't end with death neither. It ain't judging, it ain't hating ourselves, it's only doing our best with the sorry souls we've been given. Moving on, not quitting, is all that counts."

"But you don't know what I did, Papa! How long I've lived a lie."

"Yas, I know. The lad told me, and I'm saying, so what? You wanted the rich life, Nora, all them geegaws. You always have. When Ned couldn't give it to you, you went to where the honey is."

"Patrick! I did it for Jake. Roger wanted to help us. He's been doing it for years. We just weren't getting by..."

"And so who gives a damn? These richies out here, this swanky living? Is that what you're saying? Is that the price you paid to join it?"

"I suppose it is. Yes."

"No suppose. Face it, gal. Your reasons ain't mine, never was mine, but nobody can live your life for you. All I'm asking now, remember, you're a classy dame, always have been. Throw back your shoulders, admit what you done, and go on. If there is a God Almighty, and I'm thinking that it ain't poppycock, there's something out there, some great spirit like the Injuns say, well, by my lights, that grand creation ain't keeping score on any of us, or punishing us like some hedge priest mumbling beads on the Other Side. Ah, no, we punish ourselves, gal. We go to hell seconds at a time in this life of ours. So take it, pay the price and get on with tomorrow."

She took my old grizzled face in her hands and kissed me on the lips. "You're giving me that chance, Papa. I've always longed for you to care, but now, touching you, having you here, I know that you do. Oh, thank you, darling, thank you...."

About then, Pearlie and the lad drifted in. "God in heaven," I says, "I didn't come half way around the world for a wake."

"We're not going to let you!" Nora cried. "Papa, tonight there's a debut party at the Onwentsia Club. The little Addison girl is coming out. Of course, I can't possibly go, being in mourning. But I'll call Sarah Addison and include you and Pearlie. Sarah would love to snare Jake for her daughter."

"That'll be the day!" The lad was grinning. "I'll show you and Pearlie how the other half lives, Grandpa, and you show 'em where the real world is, out on Tehaare!"

All old Pearlie needed was an invite to go prance with the swells. She got herself tricked out in the best mumu she had, and I come in a Papeete linen suit, hula shirt and Jap leather sandals. "Really, Papa," Nora scolded, "you must wear a tie, and please, socks. Jake will give you some."

I chuckled, thinking of Daisy and them Archibald boys, dressing me up like a doll to pass muster with the swells. "Girl, before you was born, people tried to make a silk purse out of this old sow's ear. It didn't work then and ain't now either. I'm going to your fancy club the way I is, and them that don't like it can lump it."

When we hit the party that night, the Onwentsia Club was lit up like a Polish cathederal, a big brick masoleum it was, surrounded by parklands for the golf players and lines of wire cages where the tennisers popped away. Ah, such splendor in the June night, Japanese lanterns winking in the oak trees, flunkies carting in wines and liquors by the buckets after we'd swum like salmon up what they called a receiving line. Here stood the Mister and Missus, so proud of their plump and primpy little gal that they was all grinny and shaking our mitts like they was dying to peddle her off to the first gent who asked. Everywhere I looked, slick-faced, pampered snots, pals of Jakes, were sucking down booze or wisping cigarettes like they was the cat's meow and the sun rose and set on their precious butts. The little gals, what they called de-butantes, were tricked out in the fanciest gowns, nattering and skittering around the young fellers like fillies in a breeding pasture. Their parents was standing on the sidelines like they was judging a livestock fair in Mayo. I heard one old biddy whispering to another, "Oh, isn't that so-and-so girl just lovely!" Another crone says, "What an unattractive boy, can't so-and-so do anything for his acne?" I bulled on through them to get out in the night air again. I never seen so many stuffed shirts in one place, with their white tuxedo coats and patent leather dancing shoes. When the music starts, I grabs Pearlie and says, "We'll show 'em a dance, you old bat."

As we started creaking around, I seen some of the swells eyeing us, like who in hell let them fogies in? But by and large, they was hospitable enough in their starchy way. One grand female with a pointy nose begins fingering Pearlie's mumu. "Oh my dear, that's just lovely. So unusual, so native. Do you suppose I can get one at Fields?"

Pearlie had had a rum shot or two by then, and she rears back with a toss of her gray mane. "Madame, my barefoot grandmother made this for me in a thatch hut. A native, of course, in fact, the queen of the Tuamotus, which is why neither you nor your Fields would ever have enough money to insult us by trying to buy it. *Bonne nuit, cherie.*"

While the grand dame was choking down that one, the squirt, Bertie, runs over to the band and says, "How about it, guys? Can you play a hula for the queen of Tehaare?"

Old Pearlie chuckled, raring like a fire horse, but when the band boys start moaning out some kind of drowsy island song, she bellows, *"Merde!* Hollywood shit music! Give me the Hawaiian war chant, if you haven't anything closer to my people."

They managed to start throbbing it out, banging their drum and wailing their horns. Pearlie tore loose her hair, kicked off her sandals and went at it, her big hips pumping like a piston. I heard one of the prissy snots saying, "Oh my God, Dorothy Lamour! Do we have to put up with this all night?"

I collars him. "Better than putting up with you, you little bugger. Mind your mouth or I'll close it."

Surprisingly, Pearlie was a big hit. These folks was so set in their ways, they got a kick out of watching something so wild and strange. When a kindly old lady whispered to me that Pearlie was quite a professional, I says, "Dearie, she's been worldwide, shaking her ass, crowned heads and all."

"My, my!" the lady exclaimed. As she drifted away, I heard her whisper to her husband, "How in the world would the Addisons even know such a dreadful old creature?"

"Roger Castle's new in-laws, I hear," and he grinned her a wink.

Well, Pearlie and I had our dance and some more rum, but by then I was wearing down, sour on the whole deal. The lads, Jake the leader of them, stood up by the bandstand and began singing a song to the fat little de-butante girl. In their tuxedos, frilly shirts and tiny ties, they was a handsome enough lot, young sunburned faces and athletic bodies. The flower of sassiety, I'm thinking, pampered, finely educated at the great universities, superior game players, trained to win the riches, get the top office jobs and end up living in the big mansions of this place. Drinking and golf playing and, like my Nora, swapping mates when it suited them. The cocky looks in their eyes said, We're the new generation, born out of World War I, survived the Depression, and now we're ready to harvest the riches, feed ourselves with the silver spoons our old daddies and mummies handed us.

Well, lads, I thinks, if you're the flower of the US of A, then this old cob and all my bluebelly bunkies are the manure that made it grow. You ain't standing there on your own, byes. You're standing on the bones of Injuns we slaughtered for you, the wilderness we tamed for you. You dance on the graves of the stiffs who went down in Cuba, the Philippines and Belleau Wood. Stole half the world for you, we did, ripped it away from the dark skins so's your machines could keep clanking out dollars, and stuffing your banks to pay your help. So's you could be safe to dance under these big oaks, and when the sun comes up tomorrow, to whack your golf balls across the green turf. Laughing, taking it for granted, like it would be there forever.

Play your games well, lads, enjoy 'em while you can. I flicked Jake a salute when him and the snots finished their ditty, but he never seen me in the crowd. Then, the band starts playing this noisy, brassy music called Dixieland, stole from the nagurs, I suppose. The crowd went wild, winging into their dancing, lads whirling the silly girls and jostling the old folks aside. First song was the Reb battle cry, "Dixie." I thought of Leah. The poor dead South, and her with it. Next was "Bye Bye Blackbirds," the lads singing, "No one here can love or understand me, oh what hard luck stories they all hand me. Make my bed and light the light, I'll be home late tonight, blackbirds, bye bye."

By the time they come to the last song, the lads and frilly gals were stomping and marching around in a line, roaring, "Mine eyes have seen the glory of the coming of the Lord. He has trampled out the vineyards where the grapes of wrath are stored...."

Tears in my eyes and my belly full of rum, I turned away from the sound. I'd heard it too long now. In the darkness, I couldn't pick my way into the clubhouse to find the proper can, so I just drifts off through the towering oaks until I was out in the parking lot, lined with shiny cars. With the glory song fading in the background, I opens my pants and starts to drain it all out.

Beside me, the front door of a limousine clangs open, and a flunky in a uniform and cap hollers, "Stop that, damn it. What do you think you're doing!"

"What does it look like? Pissing!"

"Not here you don't! This is Mrs. J. Ogden Armour's car!"

I hadn't noticed, but maybe I was leaking water onto the shiny wheel of the damn thing. "So, it's the grand lady's, is it?" I buttons up and taps the flunky on the chest. "Sonny, before you was born, I was killing steers in the Yards for Armour, and driving his meat wagon to the swells, and even brung him buffalo to Melody Farm!"

"So what?" he cries.

"So I'll piss on her tire any damn time I likes, that's what. Tell the queen it was just one of the family dogs, finally come home."

When I stalked away, the lowly bugger was mopping his handkerchief over the wet I'd left on his precious wheel.

Three days later, I'd had a bellyful of the high-falutin'. "I was glad to come," I says to Nora, "but I'll be gladder still to get the hell out and back to being what I am."

She nodded sadly. "I know, Papa. But we miss you so much. Can't there be some other time soon?"

Saying goodbye to her turned a knife in my heart, and Jake seemed to take it even harder. So I says, not thinking, "Maybe next summer, when it's cool on Tehaare, you get your rich Castle man and we'll show him the shack your father lives in."

They all said, Oh, that would be great fun, of course they'd come. But even as I spoke, I knew it didn't have a snowball's chance in hell of happening.

As Pearlie and I clanked out of Chicago—we were on the S.P. train this time, heading southwest—I says to her, "The summer of 1942 ain't gonna come, dearie. Just now, we've said goodbye to them and this old life with it. No coming back."

"*Merde!* What are you, Jesus Christ telling us what will come to pass?"

"Use your eyes," I says, and taps a front-page story in the morning paper. It was the *Chicago Tribune,* Floyd Gibbons' old sheet, and where that gutty devil was I didn't know, maybe croaked. But the story told how FDR had just declared an embargo against Japan, shut off all their oil and steel that day. "Don't he see, Pearlie, that he's going to force them into fighting us? They ain't gonna give up what they've clawed out of China. They're just going to keep rolling on, and we're in their way, trying to choke 'em off."

"Oh, bah. What do you know about it, old man?"

"Enough to know Roosevelt." I tells her about that morning Daisy and I sailed on the *Lusitania,* FDR having champagne with us in the stateroom. "Shirttail relative of Daisy's, she called him a charming young man, and maybe he was. But all of them, him, T.R. and the eastern nabob bunch, they got this view that the world belongs to them, and they're quick buggers to pick a fight. It's no skin off their ass. They got a million starvies out there to hurl over the top in some foreign land and save the banks in Noo Yawk and the richies on Wall Street. World War I was to bail out the House of Morgan, and this one will bail out somebody, you can bet. They're empire boys like the English, all in the same bed. Ask Smedley Butler, a great Marine, two Congressionals hung on him, and for what? Being a hired gun for the capitalists, he said it in public and they slapped him down."

Pearlie sniffed. "Ah, your American politics is vile, I care nothing about it. But your family, that's different. I like your daughter and grandson very much, and I'll not have you stopping me if I want to entertain them on Tehaare."

"In your dreams, dearie," I says, and hugs the big old thing to me. Down the long track we sped, and when she got noticing that we was coming into strange country, deserts and quartzy mountains with no trees, she pouts, Why, where are you taking me?

To yesterday, it was. I've never been one for looking back, trying to cling to it, but now, something in me said, you'd best let your eyes see it one more time, old lad. So on we rumbled along the border. When we come to Columbus, New Mexico, there was nary a shred left of Pershing's war town. Just a forlorn whistle stop, gathering dust. Even Colonia Dublan, when I plowed Pearlie down there in a rickety Mex truck, there wasn't a trace of anything familiar. The square-face

Mormons were still in their brick houses, and peacefully farming their fields, like there'd never been a Villa or a Pershing. I did learn that old Lem Spilsbury was still hale and hearty, working as a ranch hand someplace in Arizona. I missed seeing him, and re-living a few tales about Patton, Carrizal and the like. But when I told Lem's grandson that I wanted to have a look at the country where I served with Captain Crawford and the Apache scouts, damn if the lad didn't put us on pack horses and we went into that turrible Sierra. Not an Apache was left, all imprisoned long ago. I couldn't even find the trails where my little Nati had led me to Geronimo. In the pueblo towns, the Mex were still as sorry and shoeless as they'd been back in my day. I'd ask, What did the Revolution do for you? And they'd shrug, "Nada, senor. Mismo." The same. Our long bloody fights and their wars too had done nothing to better the lot of anybody.

I couldn't even find where we'd buried poor Crawford under three boards. A mine had dug it up and was now abandoned. Heading north, following the exact trail over which Tom Moore had hauled me to justice, we crossed the line into Arizona. Nothing here either but rock and cactus. Late one afternoon, Pearlie and I banged an old ranch Ford truck into the red-spined basin where Ft. Bowie lay. I tried to point out what used to be Crook's house, and the guardhouse where they had me, and the office where Crookie and Bourke set me free of my crimes.

"Why, you old cadaver," she scoffs, "you're seeing ghosts. Here it is nothing. Dust, pouf, blown away!"

All that remained of Bowie were crumbled adobe foundations. There wasn't no sign, no momument to the brave men who rode out of this post. A rancher's bony Hereford cows were picking at weeds in the red dirt. Their dry hard balls of manure littered the forgotten cemetery, and calves were rubbing on the last standing wooden slabs. The names of soldiers who died here and why had been sandpapered away by the sun and howling desert winds.

When we come to Ft. Huahuachua, where so many black troopers had staged from in the Injun wars, Cuba and the Philippines, ah, the Armies had the post humming full speed now. I seen batteries of French 75's firing, just like 1918, and some dinky tanks were churning up the desert sand. I wondered if George Patton was playing in them tanks, but when I asked about him, nobody seemed to know his name. Dusty and hungry, I finally pulls Pearlie into a hash house just beyond the Post gate. We sits down, looks at the greasy menu. Just as I gives my order to a narrow-eyed blonde waitress, she puts her hands on her hips and minces, "Boss's orders. We don't serve niggers. If you gotta eat, I'll bring you plates out back."

"And stuff 'em up your ass, dame!" I bellers. "Black troopers from this post died for you, so you could run your damn slop house!"

When we drove away, cranky as hell, Pearlie says, "What is the matter with your country? I see every kind of skins, but to you, only the white ones count. Oh, we're natives on Tahiti, cannibals, *bien sur,* but we are all colors, aren't we? No one is ever turned away. *Merde!* You are crazy Americans. You are going to learn someday. I am sick of bad food and terrible manners. Vile customs. Take me home, Patrick."

We did just that, as soon as the train could get us to Los Angeles and the sea. By then I'd burned out the past and longed only for the comforts of my shack, and dangling my tootsies in the peaceful sea.

We got to Tehaare on the fifth day of December 1941. The ship that hauled us was a Danish merchantman, going direct from Los Angeles to Pago Pago, Samoa, and from there on down to Papeete. So it was that we'd bypassed Hawaii. I always felt that if I could have touched that balmy place just once more, I might have been able to sense the doom that lay ahead.

As it was, Pearlie and I were laying in our bunks on the Crazy Horse, night of December 8th, Pacific time. A crackling and squealing in the wheel house awakened her. "Ah, stupid old fool," she growled, "why do you leave that cursed thing on when we try to sleep?"

When I come back down to her, I says, "We were all asleep, Pearlie. The Japs have hit Pearl Harbor. Sent the goddamn fleet to the bottom of the ocean."

She reared up in bed. "You joke! Come now, this is not serious!"

"It's worse than that, dearie. They ain't giving many details yet, maybe don't know. But it's panic, what the radio says, the brass hats in Washington and London running in circles, even talk that the Japs are going to hit California, maybe already have. Nobody can believe that they pulled it off. God help us," I stared through the black porthole beyond her bunk, "they done it just like Earl said, roared in at dawn when the troops was sleeping off Saturday night, or having chow. No ammo in the guns, planes all parked, sitting ducks, row on row. Surprise attack, Earl warned us, so did Billy Mitchell, but nobody was listening. Caught us asleep at the switch. When in the name of God are we going to learn!?"

"It must be war now, no?"

"Ah, sure. If there's anything left to fight with. I seen it, Pearlie. Damn ye, you laughed at me! Seen it, only not this way, so quick, never dreaming that they could blow us all down."

"But what do we do?"

"Pray."

As she began to sob, I sat down on the bunk and took her in my arms. This far from the storming world, so forgotten by it, these two old relics would be safe enough, at least for the present. Yet I knew in my heart that the time we had left was being counted out now.

The sands were trickling through the hourglass. Knowing war, having spent my life chasing the folly of it, the whore of death and her dancing devils were reaching their bloody arms toward me. I couldn't outrun them forever. I'd used up more lives than a cat. The paths of glory lead but to the grave, some wise man said. And mine, God help me, was yawning there, somewhere out across this dark and fearful sea.

Like the Marine sergeant had bawled out at Belleau Wood, "Come on, you sonsofbitches, do you want to live forever!"

Sure they did, who wouldn't, but they were gunned down anyhow, and me with them.

It had to be sometime.

There was worse ways to go.

On, I'd said to Nora. On is all there is.

A MISERABLE PLACE TO DIE

I never thought it would be God Almighty steering my course from then on, but the Old Bird sure did. Ah, it was comical, me, never setting foot in church, a miserable sinner, yet on a July night of 1942, here I come trumpeting like the angel Gabriel, carrying the Lord's work to the very gates of hell.

Solomon Islands, it was, steering the Crazy Horse through those perilous seas on a mission of mercy. Pearlie give me no out. If I loved her, I had to do it, and I did love that grand old thing who had so brightened my fading days.

Her last surviving son, out of wedlock like all the rest, was Father Andre of the Marist priests. I used to twit him that he was atoning for his wild mama's sins of the flesh. Well, now, he'd have his chance all right. The doddery French bishop of Bougainville had been murdered by kanakas and Andre's order in New Caledonia had sent him north to replace the fallen dignitary.

But, by July of 1942, Andre had more to worry about than man-eating heathen. Bougainville was a gigantic wilderness the size of Noo Yawk's Long Island. Volcanos towered thousands of feet up into the rain clouds, lighting the darkness with smoke and fire. Running down the slopes were hundreds of square miles of rain forest, unexplored, the devil's own playground of enormous trees, dangled with vines as thick as a man, and a canopy of humid, weeping foliage so heavy that it shut off daylight.

Andre had barely arrived on this island of mud, malaria and death before the Japs decided to seize it. In they swept, destroyers and assault craft churning through the gray surf, Army, Navy and Air Force troops spearing their Rising Sun into the beaches. The bandy-leggers began ripping the jungle, building airfields and Army bases at the ends of the island, Buka Passage to the west, Ballale and Buin to the east. In those days of chaos, nobody knew for sure what the enemy plans were, but one thing seemed certain. From the tips of the island, Jap patrols would begin crawling down the coasts like maggots, raiding native gardens, setting up gun positions and coconut log bunkers along the beaches. It was just a matter of time before they'd slice their way into Father Andre's unprotected coastal mission at Karoka.

"They'll kill him, *bien sur!*" Pearlie wailed. "They'll take my last boy. Look at the barbarous things they've done already, killing patients in a Hong Kong hospital, shooting priests and nuns in the Philippines."

By the spring of 1942, the Pacific skies were raining death on

485

the white man. Andre had gotten one letter through to his mother on Tehaare, but after that, no word. As Pearlie's fears grew, we sailed to Papeete. Nobody knew anything beyond the horrible tales of Japs looting, raping, bayonetting their way across the Orient. We went on to Noumea, New Caledonia, where Pearlie pleaded with the Marist order to do something about her boy, but hell, the sour old French priests had their hands full with another kind of attack. U.S. troops were piling onto the island day and night, footsoldiers, sailors, airmen. Homesick, confused buggers, they behaved like soldiers always do, tearing around in their jeep cars looking for booze or whores. The tight-lipped colonial French slammed their shutters and kept their daughters inside. All over the lovely, peaceful island, bulldozers were ripping up the red earth, making airfields and bases for an army of defenders that was supposed to come. The rumor was, once the Japs gobbled the Solomons, they'd hit New Cal, New Zealand, Australia. Noumea Bay was filling up with the few ships our Navy had left, old four-stack destroyers from '18, and some pitiful harbor craft.

The noisy, furious panic reminded me of Tampa, Florida when we were setting up to invade Cuba in '98. Here come giant crates of supplies, everything from toilet paper to movie screens that nobody knew where to put. When the fighting troops got ashore, the lucky ones who had rifles couldn't find their tanks or artillery, for it was still floating someplace between here and California. The officers were as grim as the cavalry commanders after Little Big Horn. Pearl Harbor had taken the heart out of them. Any day now, the Jap fleet could attack us. Hell, they could land on California, we were so demoralized and unprepared. The only ships we had left were a few old buckets that wasn't bellied up in the muck of Oahu. Any planes that we sent out were either too few, or the wrong, slow types that the Japs laughed at and blew out of the skies. With a war so big and disastrous, the Philippines, Singapore and Java gone, nobody gave a damn about Pearlie's stranded missionary son, and how in hell could you blame them?

I asked a Navy brass hat if we were going to try to save the Solomons, fish out the few white men still up there. "Solomons?" he snorted. "We don't even have charts of that lousy place. We're using old *National Geographics!*"

I would have given up on poor Andre if it hadn't been for Pearlie's father, Le Colonel Louis Napoleon LeGoupil, he was proud to tell you, bedecked in his ribbons. Louis was typical of them French planters, hard-bitten, law unto himself. He'd been crippled at Verdun, come home to collect a harem of indentured Tonkinese, the men tilling his soil and the women his bed. The new war was a bonanza to the miserly bugger. He'd leased his plantation at

486

Tontouta to the Marines, where they were making a giant airfield and camp. Due to the old man's dealings with Americans, the high brass were always hanging out at his mansion house in Noumea. It was a hulking gray stone barn, shaded by palm trees and walled in by an iron fence.

One night, when Pearlie and I come by for dinner, Louis points his cane at two visitors and says in French, "Daughter, these officers can help you."

He introduces us to a blond, stocky man wearing khaki shorts, and the insignia of the Dutch navy on his shirt. Commander Ter Porten, he was, and the other, a tall, balding Australian with hard, narrow eyes. "MacQuarrie, mate," he says, gripping my mitt, "here by the grace of God and a Catalina."

The two had been flown into Noumea that day on a U.S. patrol plane. Ter Porten was being shipped back to Washington to meet with our high muckety-mucks. MacQuarrie had been an English District Officer and plantation manager on Bougainville. "They've volunteered me to go back," he says, "only this time not to plant copra."

What MacQuarrie and Ter Porten said chilled me. Until then, I'd only heard dire radio tales of how we were losing the war, even though government flunkies were trying to hide the truth from us poor suckers by secrecy and official bragging. When Doug MacArthur's name come up, I said that I'd served with him, and a brave devil he was. MacQuarrie sniffed. "The jury hasn't yet made up its mind on Dugout Doug, mate."

"How is that now?"

He launches into a tirade. Maybe it wasn't MacArthur's fault, but FDR had cut him off in the Philippines, sent him no support, hung him out to flap in the wind. MacArthur needed three more months to get his troops ready, but all Roosevelt and Churchill wanted to fight was the war in Europe. The Pacific would have to wait. Eyes blazing, he muttered, "Wait? D'you know what it meant, man? MacArthur, booming with boasts, is sent fleeing out of Corrigedor, leaving behind 76,000 troops, Fil-Americans, to suffer, starve and die, and when enough had done so, to surrender to the murdering monkeys. Roosevelt and MacArthur kept howling, Never surrender, you must stem the tide, brave boys, buy us time. But surrender they did because the poor devils were down to one ration a day, and out of ammunition and hope. Largest surrender in the history of the United States. Tail between your damn legs, and the poor blokes marched until they dropped, to be butchered, beheaded by the Nips. They say 12,000 were murdered in General Homma's Death March out of Bataan, and how many of the abandoned wretches are still dying in the bush, nobody knows."

"*Incroyable!*" Pearlie breathed, and glowered at me. "Your famous friend, your General friend, leading a nation of quitters."

"*Tais-toi,*" I snaps. "That ain't so."

"But you do wonder why I'm going back, of course you would." MacQuarrie gulps his glass of wine. "Well, it's not over. There are more defeats ahead, yet we dare not give up. Even a worn-out cobber has to do what he can."

The Dutchman, Ter Porten, had been silent, but now he banged his fist on the table, and the plates shook. "Avoidable!" he bellowed. "Criminally avoidable, all this."

Speaking slowly, his eyes burning our faces, he told of his escape from Java after the British fleet had abandoned the Dutch, and the pitiful handful of U.S. sailors and airmen had been shredded apart in the Sula sea. "Why?" he muttered. "Why such incredible slaughter to be permitted? Two men. Churchill, Roosevelt. They are the true war criminals."

"I ain't following you, mister."

"They knew!" he banged the table. "Look, old man, I am Dutch Naval Intelligence. In Surabaya, eight, nine days before Pearl Harbor, my admiral and I are reading codes from the Japanese. Our Catalinas identified their invasion fleet heading south into the Gulf of Siam. We actually fired on these ships a day before Pearl Harbor! But the point is, that was not the main attack. Our intercepts show us that the real Japanese fleet is moving northeast, toward Pearl Harbor. When we flash this to the Naval Department in Washington, they say, 'No, it cannot be true.' My Gott, man, we message them again and again the coordinates of the enemy fleet, every hour their carriers drawing closer to Hawaii. But even our highest admirals, communicating direct to Roosevelt, can get no answer. Then we try with the British. We give them the same urgent information. A fleet nearing Pearl Harbor. More than this, we have intercepts from Japanese agents there marking the exact berthing of your capital ships. Is this not an attack, we plead? Silence. Did you know that the English read the Japanese codes? It is broken, partly by the Americans, but mostly the English. They have all the codes, diplomatic, Army, Navy, which the Americans don't. Churchill is reading them daily, I know this from my admiral. He thinks that Churchill purposely refused to give this information to Washington."

"Ah come on, man," I growled, "spare me the fairy tales. I ain't no English lover, that's for sure, and FDR, I run onto him a few times, shirttail relative of the wife. In the first war, he helped save the Marines, which I thank him for. Hell, I even got a son, working for his lash-up in Washington. As for this Churchill, why, I met the pudgy bugger when he was a shavetail, and me off to fight in Cuba. Right then, I knew he'd be a fine one for shedding other men's

488

blood. So'd Roosevelt. Ain't nothing as dangerous as them high and mighty aristocrats. But, still, I'll need more proof to think they done something this bad."

"Realists. They made it happen."

"But if that's true," I cried, "if they were warned, Ter Porten, why in hell didn't they pass it on to them that was about to die? At least alert the poor bastards."

Ter Porten smiled grimly. "Had they been warned, there would have been no 'stab in the back', as your FDR says. No emotional incident to inflame the American people against an enemy. And least of all, my friend, there would have been no reason for your isolationist citizens to plunge in and join your English kinsmen in the destruction of Hitler."

I shook my head bitterly. "Are you saying, mister, that Roosevelt and Churchill had to have Pearl Harbor? Stand by and let it happen?"

He nodded. "One or both did. History may show which one."

"But dammit, man, to leave our people sitting ducks all over the Orient. How could anybody sentence men to die like that?"

"They didn't dream that it would be so bad, so total," Ter Porten said quietly. "Who respects the Japanese military? Not the Dutch, not you. Why, the English in Singapore even left their guns turned the wrong way and then had tea. They never dreamed that these stupid little people would ever attack by land and sink the unsinkable island. No, my friend, our blind old-school commanders felt, Let the Japanese strike at Pearl or Hong Kong or Singapore. We may take small losses for an hour or two, but in the end we'll blow them out of the skies and seas. No one could conceive of entire fleets being destroyed in one strike. Personally, I suspect that Churchill had this attitude. By withholding the Japanese code from Roosevelt, he trapped your President in a blind alley. But not hopeless, they think. This class of leaders regard war as a prize fight. Let the weak little fellow jab you in the nose, shrug it off, a moment later, you knock him out. I have served in the British Navy and know the thinking of their politicians. They have more duplicity in them than you innocent Americans. From their days of empire, they're more skilled at manipulating their unsophisticated cousins across the sea. I think they did just that." He shrugged. "I ask no one to believe me. What I have on my conscience is between me and my Maker. I'm sure the urgency to get me to Washington is to seal my lips. Put me in some backwater where I make no waves, and harm nothing in our noble allied war effort. Be that as it may, I know what I know, my friend. Someday truth will out, I pray."

"Too damn late," I growled, "to save the thousands that have already gone down, and more to come, you can bet."

"You have been in war?"

"All me life, Dutchman. Dreams of empire. Send the starvies over the top to drench the flags in blood. It ain't never gonna change, I suppose."

"Unless," MacQuarrie said, "a few men try to stop it. Yes, fight back."

"A fart in a windstorm," I says.

Pearlie gripped my hand "You could, though. We could. Listen to these men, please, I beg you."

Ah hell, the talk went on for hours that night. Ter Porten was a smart square-head all right, and MacQuarrie a cold-blooded island hand. There wasn't fleets, wasn't troops to take on the Japs, not yet anyhow. But where the bandy-legged Japanese Army was weak was against enemies at their back. Armed natives, friendly to the old white colonial powers. "Jungle constables, mate," MacQuarrie says. "Those are my kinky-headed lads, leather issue belts with the English crest on the brass buckles, and long silent knives in their lava-lavas. My constables beg me, 'Kiap, make killing Japan fella. We do something good for our King.'"

Ter Porten agreed. Resistance was building, Malaysia, Java, Indo-China. In the Philippines, a few American officers were training guerrilla commands of Moros and Igorots, sabotaging, fighting back, bleeding the Japs. From what they said, the Solomons was going to be the death trail down which the enemy would roar to seize New Cal, New Zealand and Australia. "We either hit them a-cropper there, or the Pacific is lost."

Before we left the house that night, MacQuarrie, and mostly Pearlie, had sold me on this last wild gamble. There wasn't no military craft daring to enter the Solomons anymore. But MacQuarrie had begged and stolen a few radios, some old British Enfield rifles, and medical supplies. If I could put him ashore on Bougainville, hook him into the network of a few other white planters or officers scattered through the Solomons, we might be able to harry the Japs long enough to get some help. At the very least, I could put into the mission, whisk Andre away, and any other survivors he'd gathered. "Go home then if you like, Captain Kelly, but you can leave me, and I'll buy some time, you can trust."

Quietly, I tells him the truth of it. The only home I had left was pretty much with this old Tahitian bat, and the seas that spawned her. We'd slip on north when he got his gear aboard. Shades of Earl Ellis, only this time there was shootin' going on.

We had to cross 1500 miles of dangerous ocean to reach Bougainville, and never would have made it had it not been for MacQuarrie. The waters north of New Caledonia were a no-man's land roamed by Jap subs and Kawanishi flying boats lumbering across the sky like black albatrosses. Many's the night we ducked into rain squalls to stay out of their road. It was rare to see any friendly plane. Once, high up, a Flying Fortress limped past us, engines streaming smoke from being shot up on a lonely raid. MacQuarrie shook his head sadly. "There is no American fleet, mate, or air either. The further we go, the more we're on our own." After we'd left the protection of Efate and the New Hebrides islands, we slid north, away from the Solomons, and hugged the coastline of wild Malaita. To avoid being spotted by a Jap snooper plane or patrol boat, we'd run at night, and in the days, tie up against some cliffy shore where the jungle trees would cover us. Dismus, my only kanaka left from the original crew, would take his rifle and search the jungle for Malaita men who might be lurking there. I chuckled at this fierce giant with bones in his ears and nose, yet his eyes rolled white in fear of the Malaita men whom he said were the worst cannibals in the Solomons. Missionaries and the English D.O.'s tried to tame them, but the devils still slipped off to butcher a "long pig" whenever they could catch one.

Early in the dawn of August 7th, we were running for cover down a channel in the Russell Islands, Pearlie and I still in our bunks in the half light, when distant thunder waked us. But it didn't sound right. There was too much of it, hammering on, and the sky lighting up with flashes. I run up on deck, MacQuarrie crouching with glasses to his eyes. "Guadalcanal!" he roared. "Can you believe it, mate? They're hitting the beaches at Lunga Point!" He hands me the glasses, and, looking south, I see the long green mound of Guadalcanal, smoke wisping up from the palm groves along the shore, and out to sea, the gray hulks of a pitiful few transports and old destroyers. Above them screamed several stubby little planes, guns puffing smoke, and on their blue wings, white stars gleaming.

"God in heaven," I says, "we ain't got a pot to piss in, but the lads are going in there anyway."

Maybe the Japs got caught with their pants down. MacQuarrie pointed out the rocky island of Tulagi, across the strait from Guadalcanal. Bombs were striking it, buildings burning, the old British colonial headquarters. "Hurrah!" MacQuarrie cried, with our radio headset clamped to his ears. "I've got their ship frequency, Kelly. It's your Marines attacking, First Marine Division."

"Sonsofbitches," I says, and tears come to my eyes. "They couldn't blow you out of Belleau Wood, lads, and maybe not here neither."

MacQuarrie shook his head. "If I know the Jap, he'll not take this counterthrust in his belly, Why, up there northwest, it's only 250 miles to Rabaul. Major base, capital ships, airfleets. We're going to run, Kelly, daylight run. Order your kanaka."

"Risky, ain't it?"

"Not like here. I want to be off this target and onto Bougainville quick. It's a big hiding place. My radio has to be on net with the other coastwatchers. I have a hunch, my friend, that we're going to earn our jolly sixpences from this day on."

Hugging the north shores, avoiding the jungled lumps of New Georgia, Kolombangara, Choiseul and the Shortlands, we finally turned through low clouds and rain toward the coast of Bougainville. Looming up in the oily green water, how fierce it was, like a continent the size of a giant corpse, lying face down in the sea, green barnacles of jungle on its back, and the mountains shearing up like broken bones. Humid steam was rising from the heavy underbrush, the whole place a pyre of mourning. Even the damn beaches were black sand.

"Well, Pearlie," I says, "pray that your lad is still on his feet."

When we edged into the mouth of a jungle river to hide the boat, down he comes, his black robe flapping. Pearlie fair leapt off the bow to seize him in her arms, the two of them twirling around, hugging and kissing, native way. Andre was a slim, frail youth, and he showed the Tonga and Fiji in him because he had kinky hair, different from the Tahitians. Pearlie kept rubbing his top and was already breaking out crackers and tinned New Zealand goat from the Crazy Horse supplies.

MacQuarrie had the boat boys slash foliage to cover the ship's foredeck. Then in the dusk, we hurried up the jungle trail to Andre's mission.

It sure wasn't much, a scatter of thatch huts, the biggest of which was the church. His flock of Bougainville kanakas gaggled around us, the women in nothing but grass skirts and anklets and the fellers, black and scowly as sin, their faces drilled with horrible tattoos, and bones in their ears and noses. Proud as Punch, Andre was showing his mother the gardens they'd planted, little hacked-out plots of red earth where green shoots were sticking up. MacQuarrie had two of his own kanakas on shipboard, and with Dismus and my lads, we lugged up a few cases of supplies. When the natives started fingering them right off, Andre says, No, no, we must spread these among the various parishes.

I had to chuckle at that. "Lad," I says, "you mean you got believers all over this island?"

His teeth flashed in a dark, thin smile. "More than you could imagine, Bon Papa. They are most devout. Right now, when you came, we were practicing for the Mass tomorrow. You will see many of my people then, in from the bush."

He leads me over to the little church, a long thatch hut with a gnarly Cross of vines and flowers perched on the top. By God, inside, if they don't have a creaky, battered old organ. A native girl, black tits jiggling, was proudly pressing the moldy keys. Some little

492

naked buggers scurried into line, Andre's choir they was, and, white teeth flashing in their red gums, they begin singing: "O Kiap, him fella heaven bokis, hittem teeth, make 'im sing."

I looks at Andre. "What in hell, lad?"

He smiled, translating. "Our Father who art in heaven—O Kiap, him fella heaven bokis—hallowed be thy name—hittem teeth make 'im sing. They're used to hymns being done with an organ, and the teeth, of course, are the keys."

"God help us," I says, "you priests are the same the world over. You ain't but smashed down the heathens' idols before you got the buggers singing to yours." Shaking my head, I stooped to get out of the smelly place, taking precaution to Sign the Cross with Holy Water out of a tin cup. Pleasing to my mama, I suppose. In the gloom under the heavy trees, I see MacQuarrie taking a black radio transmitter out of a small crate. When Andre came up, MacQuarrie said, "Do you have a boy here, of some intelligence, whom you can train on radio?"

Andre frowned. "Why would I do that, sir?"

"Because we need a watcher on this coast. You'll be gone, Father Andre. Captain Kelly has orders to take you back to Noumea."

The lad's cheeks went white. He looked at his mother, then me, and covered his face with his hands. "They're mine," he whispered. "They depend on me, they need the sacraments. I can't abandon them!"

Pearlie was hugging him, trying to plead some sense, but he kept wailing, "Our Lord wants me here!"

"But does He now? Look, lad," I says, and puts my arm around him, "you got this priestly training, and that's a grand thing. But it ain't no Ghost Shirt like the Sioux used to wear, thinking that no bullet could penetrate it. I buried dozens of 'em, Andre, there in the frozen earth. I ain't burying you here when a Jap Mauser cuts you apart. Leave your God and your trappings behind for your people, and when this war is over, come back, all the better for it, and them too. My mother used to say, The Lord ain't no murderer, and I believe that. You dassent give him the chance, boy."

His eyes lifted to me, wet with tears. "If I'm martyred, I knew that possibility. The Church is built on martyrs. I welcome my chance to join them!"

"Ah, you poor fool," I says, "look what you're doing to your Ma." Pearlie was plopping out big tears, wailing at him in Tahitian and French that didn't do nothing but make him more stubborn. Finally I sighs, "You're a hard-headed bugger, but a man's got a right to choose his own death. Let him stay, then, but I ain't. I done what I promised you, Pearlie. Now I got your sweet ass to protect, and my own and my ship." I turned to MacQuarrie. "When your gear is unloaded, I'm pulling hook here, Mac, under cover of dark."

Though I meant what I said about Andre having the choice, maybe the reality of it sunk in on the lad, that and Pearlie's caterwauling. In the end we struck a compromise. If I'd hold the Crazy Horse hidden here for just a few days, then Andre would go by foot to his various parishes, bringing the heathen such food and medicines as he had, and mostly, the religious trappings, Bibles, vestments and the sacred Hosts for communion. "I have deacons now in most of my villages," he said sadly. "God willing, they'll keep the faith alive until I return."

I nods. "A wise choice, but be quick, lad." Even as we talked, the jungle darkened, parrots shrieking and God knows what kind of lizards licking their forked tongues at us. The tree trunks were as big as an auto at their base, and cut with folds and caves. In every one I was seeing a Jap. Wasn't no reason that they couldn't be there. MacQuarrie told me that the enemy was already bribing natives to turn in any white man.

Squatting on banana leaves, the heathen treated us to a feast, roast pig that I hoped wasn't human, taro, yams, poi and squirmy bowls of creatures that I didn't care to know. The heat was so heavy and oppressive I like to sweat out any waters I had left. Down at the Crazy Horse, I had a stash of rum, so after the feast was over and the heathen had hymned us and wailed over Andre's leaving, I slipped alone down the trail to the river mouth. Eerie, it was, tangling into vines as big as my arm, thinking every one was a boa constrictor, and maybe some was. Everything in the jungle was wet and mossy, the smell of flowers sicky sweet, and insects clicking and junebugging around my ears. Warm rain would begin pattering in little squalls, and my sandals were gumming and sliding in the mud. I hadn't but reached the shore before I hears a sound behind me. Whirling, I couldn't see it, just felt it. The hot, wet skin of a native lad, black as the very night. "You friend," he whispers sing-song. "Name Simon Called Peter, fella Bible."

"You sneak, you could have slit my throat, fella Bible." I chuckles and the lad helps me get aboard. Not thinking, I struck up the kerosene lamp in my cabin, but Simon called Peter scurried to the porthole blinds and shut them. "Japan man, big eyes."

"I'm sure. Any come here, you ever see?"

He tapped his ears. "Listen drums, say close."

"How close?"

He grinned his beteled gums and touched his palms together in the praying position. "O Kiap in heaven bokis know. Good Lord."

"You believe, do you?"

"Ah sir, yes! I give my life for Lord."

I patted his hard little shoulder and shared the rum with him.

Glad to have the company. I must have fallen asleep with him sitting there like a faithful black dog. When I stirred, MacQuarrie was standing in the cabin with Dismus beside him. MacQuarrie took off his Aussie bush hat, wiped his brow and lit a cigarette. "We may have company before long."

"Nips?"

He nodded. "With the radio I brought to the mission, I patched into the coastwatcher net." He mumbled a few names that didn't mean anything to me, English, Aussies or New Zealanders, brave buggers hiding out on these rocks. "The enemy radio is aflame with anger at the Lunga Point landing. There are fleets on the way, Army detachments. They intend to push your Marines into the sea. Extermination, they're talking."

"In a pig's eye. Those lads will go out feet first before they run."

"Whatever," he sighed, "the watcher, Endicott, is on a hill south of us, near Buin. He reports Japanese landing craft beginning reconnaissance of beaches between him and us here."

"How long we got?"

"No way to tell, mate. The best luck is that the Guadal landing will keep them so occupied that they won't be prowling much way up here. On the other hand, Commander Feldt, our watcher on Guadal, told me tonight that he thinks he's compromised and must move position. However, D.C. Kennedy, he's on Segi, south of here, Kennedy's a wild cobber who's already trained his bush boys as guer-rillas. They slip out in war canoes, hit Japanese positions and behead every man they find. It's a strong lesson, and must be supported."

He looked at me strangely, and I says, "So what's that got to do with me, Mister?"

He tapped his foot on the teak floor of the cabin. "Big engines, speed, Kelly. The armaments I brought aren't going to be any use to most of the coastwatchers, but Kennedy's bush army can sure use 'em. How's a proposition, mate? Give me your Dismus, I've got my own boat boys, let me run your ship down to Segi, support Kennedy. I'll be back in maybe three, four days. By that time, the priest will have contacted his parishes, be ready to leave, he agreed to that. Then you can all head south."

"God Almighty, Mac...." I stared around at the cabin, my rum, pipes, all the books and geegaws Pearlie and I had accumulated over the years. "Unload what you need here," MacQuarrie said, reading my mind, "I know that you'll be safe for a few days at least. And when you leave, you'll know that you left a dagger in the Jap's heart. Don't that make sense?"

"You're a wild looney, MacQuarrie," I grunted, "and I ain't in love with risking this craft, but you did get us here, and maybe that's good enough. Take the damn thing, lad. I'll have our outfit packed and stomping at the dock when you come home."

He grabbed my hand in his rough one and clapped his arm around my shoulder. "Kelly, you've been in more wars than I ever hope to see. One brave Yank you are, God bless you."

When the Crazy Horse edged out of the slip an hour later, I stood on the wet shore with all the belongings I could think of to protect. "Good hunting," I cries to MacQuarrie, and he flicks me a salute, the screening branches of the river trees squealing across the plates of the deck, and then rustling and finally letting her go out into the dark, lapping waves of the Solomon Sea.

"Goddamn this place!" I roared five days later when MacQuarrie hadn't returned. With Father Andre still off tracking down his flock, the black lad, Simon Called Peter, must have got a drum message from his Lord, for he moves me, Pearlie and our trappings out of the empty mission. For an hour or two, we slogged up a wet trail until we were on the top of a peaky little mountain. The soil was dry, the trees a scrubby kind that made a lacy canopy above us and protected us from the sky. On the crest was an old thatch hut, well hidden in an abandoned kanaka garden. From here, we could not only look down on the mission and river mouth where the Crazy Horse would put back in, but we could see the long spine of Bougainville and the squally, angry skies above it. The greeny, oily ocean lay far below us, and we were above the fierce jungle heat, too, just gentle breezes wisping Pearlie's hair over her eyes. I grins. "Well, darlin', you've finally made it to the Garden of Eden. Adam and Eve, ain't we?"

She smiled softly and lay me down beside her, the both of us staring at the clouds running overhead. "I used to think," she murmured, "to go dancing everywhere, chasing the excitement, was all life meant. But do you know, just being here these few days with my son, doing what one can to help these black children of the Stone Age, ah no, *mon Patrice*, you have brought me to real joy. Someone needs us, do you see that?" She laughed, "Oh, pouf, I am tired of you cranky old one. When the boat comes, let me stay here and be a nurse to these people."

Slowly she sat up and peeled off her pareu, the sun through the leaves playing a glimmery pattern over her tawny skin and her enormous breasts. I touched them fondly and says, "Go nurse the world, you Tahitian darlin', but just now, leave some for this old lad, eh?"

I don't know where Simon Called Peter was, and neither of us cared. Like Adam and Eve, we rolled in the garden and made love in the dying sun.

That night, we were still sleeping in the dry leaves when, from inside the hut, comes a crackling. Simon Called Peter had lugged the radio up here, and before MacQuarrie left, he'd told me how to

496

run the thing, crank the dial onto the coastwatcher frequency, and moving through the snapping static, I could pick up hissing, clicking Jap voices as well.

Dialing in, standing naked except for the earphones, I hear the crackle of a Limey voice. D.C. Kennedy on Segi. "To all stations, bad luck, chaps." He was using code words for much of it, but the gist come through and I like to weep.

MacQuarrie had sneaked down and delivered his guns, but on the way out of Onodonga Channel, he goes to the rescue of a downed New Zealand pilot. Bobbing in his lifejacket, the lad was, with Zero fighter planes screaming over him, trying to machine gun him in the water.

Brave MacQuarrie not only ran the ship through the chattering bullets, but under cover of a rain squall, got the lad to safety back on the Segi shore. Trouble was, the Japs had seen the Crazy Horse. About dark, when MacQuarrie was running north, in whined a flight of Zeros. Blasting .50 cals and cannon shells, they blew it up, and my loyal Dismus and MacQuarrie's boat boys sunk bloody into the dark sea. It was only luck and guts that let MacQuarrie cling to some wreckage and swim many miles to shore. Kennedy had him, badly shot up, and was hoping for a U.S. sub or Catalina to slip in and take him to medical before he croaked.

I sits there on the dirt of the hut, cursing that my beloved craft was no more, all the miles on her, the memories come to this. A big part of my life had sunk, and for what? A war I never wanted to be in. The ghost of Earl Ellis went down on her, almost like he'd doomed the both of us for not listening to him. "Ah, don't grieve, *mon amour*," Pearlie whispered. "What is a ship but a coffin of iron? Let it go. I have other boats on Tehaare."

"Tehaare! If it wasn't for you, we never would have left. And now, stranded here, we ain't getting back!"

"So?" she shrugged. "Perhaps it is God's will."

"What in hell is this?" I cried, whirling her to me. "You whore for all your life and now beg God's will to save ye! That's a laugh, dearie."

"It is not," she said, her eyes lowering. "I have come to believe. I have come to be ready, just as my son is. I am only sorry that it took so long."

I stormed away from her and went outside. The stars were gone, the night had closed in. For the first time in my life, I thought, You have bit the wrong coin here, lad. You've grown old and weak and soft in the head. There is no escaping this time. Bougainville, the corpse floating in the sea, will bury you face down in its black sand.

It was over two weeks before Andre and his kanaka deacons returned from the bush. The lad was wan and hollow eyed, must have lost twenty pounds slogging the jungle trails, and weeping at every village where he said goodbye to his flock. He hadn't seen any Jap patrols, but the kanaka log drums were thumping rumors that they were coming. "We ain't staying to greet 'em," I growls.

"Look at him tremble," Pearlie cried. "My boy has malaria. Use the quinine we brought, cure him. We stay until he is ready!"

"And then what? Wait for the Angel Gabriel to pluck us off of this rock?"

Andre pushed up from his straw mat. "Men in the next village, my parishioners, have canoes. They are sea-faring. We will go south." He nodded at the radio. "Ask your English people where we go?"

That night, when I hooked onto the coastwatcher net, I never dreamed it would trap me like a fly in a spider web. MacQuarrie must have told Kennedy about me, for he crackled, "Welcome back, chap, You've got beautiful reception wherever you are. High, I trust, so you can see the sky. My line is open for your reports day and night. For God's sake, be diligent."

"Reports?" I echoes.

"Aircraft passing your station, time, numbers and types."

"How in hell do I know what them things is? Just air machines."

"Look, man, there have been two major sea battles near Guadalcanal. This is a massacre going on. Your poor blokes at Henderson Field are stranded and being shelled round the clock. There is virtually no Allied opposition, most of your planes blown apart right on the field. For the few that can get airborne, urgent you flash us Jap formations heading south so that your pilots can have advance warning to get above them, break them up. If you can observe the sea, I also demand time, type and description of Japan sea forces heading our station."

"You're asking for the moon, mate."

"And I expect you to give it! The entire Pacific is at stake right here in this Solomons Slot. You can save lives. You must. Get to it!"

"God save the Queen," I mutters, never thinking that it would be me, serving Limeys. But as the radio crackled on day after day, I seen that it was way bigger than English, Aussies, New Zealands. Brave sentinels they were, but the fighters catching the real pasting were U.S. lads.

Poor devils, they hardly had rations except rotten rice the Japs had left behind. Most of them were shot through with malaria and dysentery. I'd hear them screaming in the nights, thousands of them burrowing into the slime of Henderson Field while the Jap fleet stood just off shore, blowing them apart point blank with the heaviest guns of battlewagons and cruisers. There wasn't no Navy left. The Japs had sunk it at Savo island. And the few fliers that creaked aloft, fevered, crapping in their jeans with dysentery, were fighting at odds of a hundred to one. I'd hear their gutty screams in the radio, "Get that bastard. On your tail! Turn! Jesus, man, pull up! Got him!" Then more roaring and chattering guns, and some poor lad wailing, "Ah, mama, Christ. I'm hit. On fire, can't get out." And a last dying scream as he flamed down into the sea.

It didn't take many days of this before I clung to that radio, my teeth gritted in fury. Simon Called Peter was a sharp-eyed bugger, and I had him up in a tree most of the time, spotting Jap planes. They were swarming like wasps off the fields of Buka Passage, north of us, and Buin-Ballale below. I soon got handy at thinking of the sky as a compass. When Simon and Pearlie spotted the specks heading over us, I'd crank in Kennedy, spit him the time over us, compass course, and numbers. Some of the flights had hundreds in them, lumbering green bombers with silver Zeros flitting above, darting in and out of clouds, waiting to bushwhack our lads. "Relaying to Henderson," Kennedy would grunt. "You'll save some lives today, Mister Robinson Crusoe."

That was the code moniker they'd hung on me, and I sure looked the part of a derelict swept up on the beach. My Tahitian hat was long gone. Simon had woven me a lid of green palm fronds, but hell, my hair was so shaggy, and beard too, I could hardly cram it over my ears. What was left of my pants I'd sliced off at the knees, didn't wear no shirt because of the heat, but sometimes the kanaka gals would drape me with leis of sweet jungly flowers to tickle my sun-black skin.

As the months dragged on, the battle for Guadalcanal got bloody awful. So busy was I with air and ship reports, I lost track of the dates. And maybe, in the fury of it, the Japs had lost track of us, or just didn't care. Andre slowly came back to health. He and Pearlie would go down to the mission in the days, where she was nursing sick kanakas and pickaninnies that seemed to be trooping in from all over the island.

I never seen Pearlie happier in my life, and that pleased me. And I suppose, too, that I was getting my last sniff of shot and shell by helping the brave lads on Guadalcanal. Still though, I wanted to get Pearlie and the boy off of this place. Our luck couldn't hold forever.

Then, one dusk, the skies above us began blasting and shrieking with a great air battle. When the Jap squadrons did their fighting to the south, we never seen it. But now, with glasses, I could see blue planes with the U.S. star screaming into the swarming Nips. Ah, God, it was so lopsided, just a handful of us against squadrons of theirs. Almost as night fell, I see a streak of flame in the sky, and directly above us, a gleam of white.

"Parachute!" I cries. By God it was, a black doll figure swaying back and forth in it, and then tumbling out of sight into a grove just below the peaky hill. With Simon and some nimble mission boys, down we slide, stumble and hack through the foliage until we hit a tiny clearing. Writhing like a crippled lion in a net is a young pilot, his face and red hair blackened with oil and smoke. Seeing us, and still trapped in his parachute lines, he trembles up a .45 Colt and points it at my face.

"Friend," he croaks hoarsely. "American friend."

I chuckles. "Well, ain't you now, lad. Put the damn piece down, bye. I'm one of you."

"Holy cow," he whispers. "Way out here. I thought I was finished. Bought the farm."

Gently, the boys and I cut him loose from his shrouds. He was bleeding from his left leg, couldn't but hobble, so the kanakas knotted hands and we lugged him up the hill.

In the dark hut in the garden, we give him some native beer, and what taro, yams and pork we had. The lad couldn't have been more than in his early twenties, and he ate ravenous, laughing all the time, the grease smearing his cheeks. By then, Pearlie and Andre had taken charge of him, ripping his flying suit up to his privates and swabbing clean the bullet wound in his thigh. He kept staring at us in amazement, his blue eyes sparkling. "I fell into it, didn't I? Who are you, coastwatchers?"

When I told him that we were stranded here just like him, he frowned. "But I've got to get back, sir. Isn't there any way to get me to the Canal, to my outfit?"

I glanced at Andre and Pearlie. "If there's a way, we'll find it. But you had a long float down from the sky, lad. You need resting a few days."

"I need being back on my ship," he said glumly, "but I don't suppose that's going to happen." Then he tells me that his name is Ensign Franklin McCoy. Naval flier, come off the Lexington, and not long before that, graduated the Naval Academy. "Hell, sir, this was my first combat. Not only blew away a precious Wildcat, but if I don't make it home, old Stone Face is going to have me for lunch."

"You're meaning your skipper?"

"Well, not exactly. Any orphans, Army, Navy or Marine that stagger into Henderson Field like we did, this guy commands. Marine General he is, running all the air we've got. Rough bastard, that Geiger, but if it wasn't for him, we'd be shit out of luck."

I was sitting in the darkness, staring at him. "Geiger, you said?"

"Yes, sir. You heard of him?"

"Heard!" I bellows. "Pearlie, Andre, you too lad, this here Roy Geiger taught me to fly in France in the war of '18! God help us, don't things come full circle. Why, it just seems yesterday, but I'm still seeing Geiger in his Marine squadron mess, drinking a toast of

500

brandy to all of us being together again, someplace down the road."

"That's incredible," the lad breathes, but Pearlie growls, "Ah, my old husband remembers things that nobody in the world cares about. Of course you want to go back to your people, *mon petit*. Andre, can this be done?"

"When your leg is better, to be sure there's no infection," Andre said, "I have natives with sea-faring canoes. I will talk to them about paddling you in the nights at least as far as Segi, where the coast-watcher is. We hear on the radio now that American planes and submarines can sometimes return fallen airmen."

"We will leave you now to sleep, *mon brave*," Pearlie said, and eased the lad back on the straw mat. She plucked my arm. "*Va te,* you old parrot, he doesn't need to be talked to death."

Three nights later, we took the lad to the river mouth and bedded him down in a big log canoe. Six strong kanakas were the paddlers, and before they shoved off, they showed how they'd bury him under a mound of copra husks and straw mats so that the Japs would think the canoe was just innocent natives off on a trading voyage.

The lad hugged Pearlie and Andre, who was signing the Cross on him. "I can never thank you," he blubbered, "never forget you." Then, brightening, he clutches my hand. "Sir, if I make it to the Canal, I know I'll be seeing Geiger. He personally interrogates everybody who's shot down. Can I tell him about you? Hell, sir, I don't even know your name."

I chuckles. "Patrick Kelly, Marines of '18. Tell that old bear, if I had a kite like he taught me in, I'd swoop down there and blow his damn hat off!"

Then they were gone, slipping into the dark waves like MacQuarrie. Andre was mumbling prayers in Latin, but I just says, "Lord, get that good lad home."

About two weeks later Kennedy flashed me. "Sea bird back in Cactus. (Guadalcanal code name.) Air boss sends thanks Semper Fi."

Always faithful. Ah, it tickled me, thinking of stern old Geiger, and the tricks life played on the both of us. If he hadn't got the fight he wanted in France, he sure had his hands full of it now. Sometimes in the nights, I'd hear that Jap dame, Tokyo Rose, mouthing at us on the radio, cooing and sweet-talking. Always she'd be telling how many Guadalcanal planes they'd shot down, and that the island was ready to fall. Shouldn't we just quit and go home to our wives and girlfriends who were twitching in their beds waiting to be loved, and if we weren't there, maybe they'd be taking in a black man.

Ah, it was comical, because Tokyo Rose only give the side of it she wanted to. I knew the other, from my plane reports I was chattering daily to Kennedy. The tide was turning at the Canal. The Jap airfleets were growing smaller, and often our lads, more of them all the time, were blasting apart bombers and Zeroes way up in the Shortlands and Bougainville. "We're blowing the buggers away, Pearlie," I says, "and our work here is almost done. Time to pull up stakes, I'm thinking."

She didn't favor the idea, nor did Andre, but I could tell from the bald-faced lying of Tokyo Rose and the cursing of the Japanese pilots that they were turning into sore losers. Sometimes they'd scream at the American pilots in English: "Come here fight. We no fear you. Babu Rusu eat shit!"

I had to chuckle. Here the little buggers figured that Babe Ruth was our God or something, our Emperor, and if they could insult him enough, we'd give up and go home.

By March of '43, I was picking up on radio that the Japs had abandoned Guadalcanal, and with the Yanks striking north and west up through the Russells and New Georgia, the bandy-leggers were going to dig in and fight on Bougainville. Their destroyers and troop transports were piling into Buin below us and Buka Passage above.

Lying with Pearlie in the hut on the hill on the night of March 18, I had a wild and angry dream. Freezing in the snow I was, then thundering on a horse with Cap Bloxham huffing beside me, screaming and howling into the teepees of the reds. March 18th out here was March 17th back home. Saint Paddy's day, hurling this scared greenhorn into the awful fight at Crazy Woman Fork. Sixty-seven years ago, would you believe, and waking up from the nightmare of it, sweat in my eyes, I takes Pearlie to me and says, "We're pulling stakes here now, dearie, I seen the signs of a fight."

By the time dawn come, she'd agreed, and Andre, too. He sent Simon Called Peter down the trail to arrange for an ocean canoe the next night, taking us south to Kennedy at Segi.

But because it was a rare sunny day, one of the few without rain, Pearlie says, "Let's go to the sea, old one. We never dared before, but if we're leaving, who cares?" Her idea was to fish a little point we could see below us. A reef it was, jutting into the ocean, and Pearlie had often observed that the coral pools were churning with sardine-like bait fish. As a girl on the Tuamotus, she used to net the things and bring them to her mother, the Queen, for a feast. "Tonight I cook them for you, *mon Patrice*, and we say *bon adieu* to our *jardin d'Eden*."

When Pearlie got a notion, she was like a big, strong-headed mare charging for the barn, so I just humors her and says, Yas, Queenie, we'd go. Besides, I was interested in looking at a sandstone cliff that sheered up out of the jungle not far from the rocky point. Simon, whom I'd trained to replace me on the radio, had suggested that if we put kerosene and a lamp on this cliff, he could flash signals from here to Yank subs or patrol planes, which were

502

cruising closer every day. If the lad happened to pick up any more shot-down airmen, he could send them home quick this way.

So off we starts, St. Pat's day picnic, me lugging the lamp, kerosene can and an old canvas folding chair that English planters must have left behind. Pearlie and Andre were wearing their flowery Tahitian pareus, naked from the waist up, and she, giggling like an island girl again, with her gleaming throw net over her shoulder.

Ah, how grand and fresh it was along the beach. The three of us stripped off and took a swim in the coral pools before Pearlie started her netting. Showers of bright-colored fish skittered between our legs. With a thrust of her strong arms, she surfaced beside me like a giant shark, her gray hair plastered around her head and her dark eyes sparkling with salt. "See, see what we have missed!" she cried. "Beauty, life right in our fingers, not your damn wars. Andre, your Polynesian grandmother used to command me, Every day, daughter, go to the sea. Sit in it, play in it, and you will be healed."

"But I am healed already, Maman, thanks to you and *Le Bon Dieu*." Andre smiled and kissed the wet black rosary that dangled around his neck.

"Pouf, you and praying!" Pearlie flicked the beads with her finger. "The real God swims with the fish. When I get you home to Tehaare, I'll build you a fine church right on the shore, and every day we take the sea back into our blood. *Promettez?*"

"*Absolument, Maman,*" Andre said with a wink at me, "provided that you're the one who begs permission from my Bishop."

"Ah, that silly old fool, I let him pat my ass and wrap him around my finger!"

While they were laughing and playing in dreams of tomorrow, I walked across the hot sand, pulled on my jeans, and strapped my belt that had a scabbard for my machete, and a holster with a Colt .45. Earl Ellis had given me this 1918 model, and I'd packed it all these years, remembering him. The cliff wasn't far, maybe a half mile through the jungle, but the going was tough. I had to chop my way through vines and mangroves. In the scrubby stuff, the heat was choking, and by the time I'd scaled the cliff, lugging the kerosene and lamp, I was tuckered.

The place was ideal for a signal station, wide open ocean to the right. Below and to the left, I could see the bronzy point of coral, Andre a tiny brown figure swimming around, and the sun glistening on Pearlie's net as she flung it into the pools. The only area I couldn't see was to the far left of the point where the long beach veered back and was hidden.

After settting up the lamp and cleaning the dead brush in the lookout, I lay down and took me a doze on a hot limestone rock. I don't know how long I catnapped, maybe five minutes, maybe half hour, but too damn long!

Jesus and Mary, a scream chills my heart! Far off, even over the crash of the surf, I could hear the terror in it, wailing, pleading. Pearlie! Ripping back the foliage, I see Japs, mustard-colored uniforms, shiny pot helmets, and they were squealing and splashing into the tide pools where Pearlie and Andre had been.

There had to be twenty of them or more; their rifles black sticks with bayonets sparkling in the sun. Ah, God, I sobbed, how did the bastards get in here and trap us? The shapes that they were dragging out of the tide pools were Pearlie and Andre. They'd already ripped off her pareu, it was floating flowery in the waves, and they were shoving and kicking her gleaming nakedness back onto the sand where she fell face down and I couldn't hear her screams anymore.

God help me, I had one Colt, maybe six cartridges against three times the number of the buggers, and besides, I was way out of range. Fight back, blast 'em, slash 'em with my machete, Jesus yes, but how! And maybe it was cursing my Maker, and begging Him too that flashed the thought into my head.

Fire!

Touch off the rubbish in the lookout! Flames rising from the exposed cliff might bring somebody snooping the coast, probably Jap, but I prayed the longshot. Couldn't it be a Yank, this once?

Whirling, I flung kerosene on the dry rubbish in the roost, threw in the can and camp chair, too, and touched her off with a roar. The top of the cliff burst into flame, smoke rising into the pale sky, and me, hurtling down the cliff, corals bruising and slicing my bare legs. Who the hell cared? I was dead anyhow, we were all dead.

When I hit the jungle, I run until tears were streaming down my face and breath scorching my lungs. Finally close enough to hear the foul laughing and cackling of the fiends, I flings back the jungle leaves and sees to my horror what had happened.

On the beach which had been hidden from my view sits a Jap landing boat, its brown tongue spilled open onto the sand. The buggers had run up from here, an entire patrol of them, catching Pearlie and Andre before they knew what hit them.

Not fifty yards from where I crouched, the Japs were dancing around, bandy-legged, naked. They'd stripped off their tawny pants, puttees and two-toed rubber shoes, and were shoving in for their shot at the lump of flesh lying on the sand. God in heaven, they had the poor thing spread-eagled, the fiendish buggers pinning her arms and pulling her legs apart.

The sight of her body, the writhing, screaming, helpless pain cut into my heart. Christ Almighty, the bravery of her, trying to fight them off.

"Sonsofbitches!" I howled, leaping from the jungle, but the

flesh-crazed devils never even turned to me. I fired, the Colt booming out the first round, too far, maybe I hit one, a bugger slumped. Then, racing closer, my legs water and my arm bouncing up and down, I fires the second and third rounds, heard them thock flesh. The bandy leggers were dancing squeals, but one of them was still wrestling with Pearlie. "I'm coming!" I screamed at her, then hollered for Andre, but I couldn't pick him out. The Japs were running toward me now, so close I could see their skinny ribs.

I flung myself belly first in the hot sand, fired again and again, with hisses of Mauser bullets snapping all around me and singing into the jungle. "Well, hit me you monkeys!" I roars, "Get it done!" Rising, I blew my last two slugs into Japs who were twenty yards from me, firing from the hip.

I leapt over them as they fell, flung my empty Colt into the face of the next one and snatched his rifle. Now I had a bayonet, maybe a full clip too. I wasn't thinking clear by then, only knowing that if I had to die, I would die beside her, and quick now, please God!

The back of my head exploded, flinging me forward with stars of pain in my eyes and screaming in my ears. Above me stands a gold-toothed Jap, hissing curses and whirling his rifle over his head. He'd clubbed me with it, and now swung the bayonet point to me, stomping his foot onto my chest. With the last strength I had, I slashed my machete across his legs, blood spraying out onto my face.

But his tunic and bare chest were bleeding, too, a stripe of holes, his body twitching and falling. The sand was exploding, the sky screaming, a chattering of bullets, and a shadow flashing over us, then a second. I felt the whoosh of their wings, the roaring of the engines. The Japs were breaking, running, some falling like bloody sacks, to be slammed again and again by bullets chopping up the sand.

When I twists to the sky, two strange blue planes were thundering upward, then peeling back down to lace us again. "Jesus God!" I cries. "White stars! Do it, lads, kill every one of the bastards!"

I never seen whistling planes of this type. New, probably, some kind of miracle just arrived. They had bent wings like a gull, and when they come back the second time, they blew the Jap landing boat into a splintery roar of matchsticks. Mustard bodies were bobbing in the water, and if anybody else was alive on the beach, they must have hightailed it to the safety of the jungle.

In a final long roar, the planes lifted away and left me on my face, sobbing.

When I finally dared look, crawling on all fours across the hot sand, I come to my lover, my queen, and covered her from the sun with myself, our two bodies joined again.

I knew she was dead, blood all over her. Gleaming beside her was a samurai—she was still clutched in the hands of the dead Jap who'd been butchering her. In my sobs, I heard something, Mother Mary, I felt it! A moan down deep, then the shudder of her breasts against me. "Pearlie?" I whispered. She was wailing in Tahitian and French, her bloody fingers clawing her shoulder where the samurai had ripped her, trying to cut off her head.

"I'm with you, darlin'," I says. "Stop this blood, get you out of here."

"*Mon fils,*" she groaned, and tried to turn her head.

A few yards away, Andre was writhing naked in the sand. He was gagging. They'd stuffed his rosary down his thoat, and the lower parts of him, the male parts, they'd tried to slice with bayonets. I could hardly look at the wretchedness of him, cursing God for letting this happen, and the fiends for doing it.

Pearlie was reaching out for me, and Andre, scratching toward me like a wounded crab. "Hold on now," I says. "I'll wash you in the sea. It'll sting, but it'll clean."

I don't know how long it took, half-dragging their ripped bodies into the surf. Andre was begging to let him die, but I roared back, "Like hell! I'm takin' you home!" I stood up, tottering. My skull, where the rifle butt had whacked me was screaming pain that I could only begin to feel now when the shock had worn off. I swayed and fell, stood up again, roaring curses. "Why not me instead of them! Ain't it time! Let me go!"

But when the scare and anger finally burned out, I knelt beside them and tried to ease their pain. God help us, alone, I couldn't doctor the awful rips in their flesh, couldn't lug 'em anyplace, and we sure dassent stay out here in the sun for more Japs to find. Then I sees Jap rifles lying close. I cocks one, lifts it to the sky and fires the only cartridge in it. "*Non, non! Mon Dieu!*" Pearlie screamed, "you will bring them back!"

"We got to take the chance. The jungle has big ears, Pearlie. Say your prayers, lass."

While she was protesting and tugging at my leg, I stood above her and spacing the shots into volleys of three, the distress call in any language, I fired the full magazine into the sky. Then I snatched up the rest of the Jap rifles, dug a hole in the sand and eased my loved ones into it. "If more of 'em come back, you still got fingers. Shoot and kill! Save the last bullets for yourselves. I'm going for help."

Tears were running down Pearlie's cheeks. When she tried to wipe them, blood smeared her. "*Je n'ai pas peur,*" she whispered. "But kiss me."

When I did, she clung so hard I couldn't get loose. Finally I just broke away and ran. I hadn't gone an hour up the jungle trail before I stumbled onto Simon Called Peter and three kanaka boys.

Sharp lads. They'd heard the signal I sent by slow-firing the rifles.

It was after dark before we'd made litters and got Pearlie and Andre off the beach. I was so weak that I robbed a dead Jap and shared with Pearlie the crackers and rice he had in his pack. Andre was unconscious by then.

When we finally reached the dark little peak, I was sure we'd lose him, but Simon had already sent one of the kanakas off to find a witch. When the old crone come, she set right to work with her herbs and voodoo moaning. She even had leeches to suck the blood. I couldn't bear to watch her mumbo-jumbo, but God in heaven, it was all we had until Simon dug up a little morphine from a kit McQuarrie had buried. With it, I put my dear ones to sleep.

I ain't never wanted to look at death or touch the damn thing. How many wars, I'd watched my bunkies drop beside me, and when I seen that they'd given up the ghost and couldn't be helped, I'd just step over 'em and charge on.

Not so with my poor Walks Outside at Wounded Knee, and valiant little Daisy on the *Lusitania*. I could still hear their last words to me. All the running away and trying to forget wouldn't ever silence their cries in my heart. So here now was death's whore again, eh? Foul hag staring me in the face, shrieking for vengeance! Not this time, I cries! Out with ye, cursed banshee! By God, seeing my last lover fighting for her life, I'd be damned if I'd let the precious thing go!

I eased out of the hut and squatted in the darkness with Simon. "Can you keep 'em alive, boy?"

He nodded darkly. "If Kiap in heaven-bokis say."

"That ain't good enough. They got to have medical treatment. The morphine will soon be gone."

He murmured that the witch crone would stop the bleeding. Then he shrugged and blessed himself.

I rubbed my fists into my eyes. Why say it? He knew. We were cut off on this little peak. You couldn't scratch yourself in the jungle but what you weren't infected. They either got doctored quick or they were goners. What a hell of a choice. As much blood as they'd lost, they'd be lucky to live to the beach, let alone lie moaning through several nights in native canoes, and hiding out in hot jungle in the days. Whatever I did had to be fast. "Japan man see us," I grunted. "Know where we are. Probably come back."

He grinned. "Japan-man all die."

"Not by a longshot." I pushed wearily to my feet, for the pain in my noggin was like an axe still sticking in it. "Simon, you got fine next top boy, you make him kiap here along with spirit-woman. Right now, trail," I pointed. "Simon take me, fast-run, find war canoe belonga strong paddle men."

His eyes gleamed. "Like pilot-man night?"

"Same. You get me to Kennedy on Segi. Belonga PBY big bird or sub sea-fish, come back, take all long pigs off, home-go."

"No pig. Christian you, Kiap."

"Yes, yes."

"Leave wife-Mary?"

I nodded, tight in the throat. I beckoned the old crone outside and had Simon explain it to her. She would care for wife-Mary until old Kiap come back and make her well. Then I eased again into the hut. Pearlie was lying face down on a straw mat like she was dead. But her wounds were bandaged in pandanus leaves and her breath still warm on my cheek. "Wait for me, darlin'," I whispers, kissed her and then signed a Cross on Andre's feverish forehead.

In truth, what the hell else was left? Turning, sniffling like a goddamn baby, I goes back outside into the stars and follows Simon down the trail.

TWILIGHT'S LAST GLEAMING

Rotten luck! We couldn't find a war canoe to take us south to Segi. Hearing that we'd been attacked, the natives along our shore sulked in terror. If Japanmen dared to butcher white priests and mission women, no telling what kind of torture they'd give poor lowly bush boys who'd helped us.

The best Simon could scrape up was a mossy, abandoned log dugout. "I take you place belonga Segi," he said, "but much far, Master, many paddling. Stay in bush night, Jap eye no see. One danger big."

"Sure, it's danger," I snapped. "Get on with it."

He shook his head. "Master no savvy. Jap eye see, you white man. Blue eye, white hairs. They kill you, say you coast radio fella. But no kill if you priest fella."

"Like hell! Look what they did to Andre."

"Is why, Master," Simon grinned slyly. "They no see he priest. No wearing robe. You got robe, carry Big Book, many Cross for Jesus. Japanman scare Cross. Afraid touch."

A Cross for Jesus, was it? For the old sinner's penance, make him play the part of a priest. "Comical," I says to Simon, "my dear mother and her saints would be howling in their graves." He didn't know what I was talking about, yet the pious little bugger was right, too. If I had one snowball's chance in hell, hiding in the Cloth might be it. My mind reeled back to Father Craft at Wounded Knee. If he'd been wearing his robes that turrible morning, the Injuns would have spared him. Hurrying to beat it out of there before the Japs come back, I had Simon bury his radio in the jungle. I'd thought of trying to contact Kennedy with it, and let him send a boat or plane for us, but the risk was just too great. I was certain the Japs knew our location, and any signal from us would bring 'em howling down on Pearlie and Andre. Besides, there was the future to think about. After dumping me, Simon was planning to return here, move to a different location and carry on the coastwatching.

Taking a hard look at the dugout canoe, I saw the next problem. The pitiful craft was only as wide as my butt. I couldn't pack much with me except the few sorry possesions I had left, two sour corncobs, native tobacco, a flask of rum, and, for the decoy of it, Andre's priestly satchel of holy robes and sacred chalices.

One thing I sure didn't want to leave behind was my diary book, with all these years squashed into it. But Simon insisted that I had to take the Big Book, the Bible, so I figured out something keen. Maybe the apostles would have winced, but with a razor blade,

Simon and I cut out the center pages of the Good Book, and slipped into the hole, wrapped in oil-skin, the ancient bundle of my life. There was some blank pages at the end of it. I prayed I could fill 'em with hope this time, and finally get us home.

We set out on a dark, stormy night, me a black mummy in Andre's robes, and hogtied with a Crucifix and ropes of rosaries as pious as the Pope in Rome.

I helped the lad paddle, but in the storm it was hard going, waves crashing over us, sogging the canoe. As the dark mass of Bougainville slips behind, Simon starts huffing toward a leeward shore where we'd strike some calm.

As we eased into the slick, black water, the wind chop died. It was so still I was nodding off.

Whoosh! A roar, a shower of spray, not twenty yards from us, a monster broaching. Whale! Had to be! But water was running off dull black steel, and a deck gun spiked up through the foam. I see the outline of a conning tower, heads bobbing up to look over it, and on its side, a white flag with a red meatball dripping like blood.

The sub's engines roared, stirring the sea, the snout of it slicing toward us. Already, Jap sailors in white caps and shorts were spilling down and running to the deck gun. One bugger squatted by the conning tower and ripped a burst of a Nambu machine gun across in front of us.

"No shoot!" I howled. Then, in the little Jap I knew, I cried, "Friend. Man of God, Priest. Red Cross."

The firing stopped. Several officers had scrambled down onto the wet deck. One called: "Who you person? English, Mellican? Who kanaka?"

"My helper!"

Somebody on deck cursed the kanaka, the machine gun pupping, blasting holes in the stern where Simon was.

I seized his hand and wrenched him over the side. "Swim, lad!" I cries. "God be with you!"

By then, a searchlight knifed over me, like to blind me. "Where you kanaka?"

"Dead. You shot him!"

I took one last glance at the blackness outside the light, a faint splash in the water like a rising fish. Then Simon ducked under again, and as strong a swimmer as he was, I figured he'd make it. "You bastards," I growled at the sub, "that lad will be back to haunt you."

By then, the sub had bumped against the dugout. They threw a hawser line on me and roped me in, priestly luggage and all.

Cackling, shoving me with their guns, they dragged me up the conning tower and down the hatch into the control room where they had their periscope and walls of gauges and levers for shooting their torpedoes. I felt like Jonah inside the damn hot whale. Most of the sailors wore breechclouts and banzai bandanas around their foreheads. They were hissing, clicking, fingering me and my holy paraphernalia. One bugger snapped up a knife and was going to slice the Crucifix thong, but an officer in a cloth cap and white jacket knocked him aside.

"You speak. Talk quick, come captain." The officer snapped some commands and pointed at a dark row of batteries. I got the idea that they were surface-cruising now to charge their electric. The conning tower hatch was open, lookouts on watch, but hell, as I glanced up though it at the faint stars, I knew that I was a thousand miles away from getting loose, and probably never would again.

They led me down through gleaming tubes lined with pipes, the valves and steel ladders tiny as hell to fit these little monkeys' hands and feet. The sailor shoving me grins. "Big for Mellican, yes?"

"Goddamn small," I grunts, by now stooping like a hunchback just to get through the next hatch. Then my face went hot. A Jap officer stood there frowning at me like he'd heard me taking the Lord's name in vain. Jesus and Mary, I thinks, mind your tongue, lad. Priest, ain't ye?

The captain's cabin was a tiny steel box, yellow walls, dim red lights, and himself sitting like a Buddha on the deck. All he wore was a red and white kimono, his fat, crossed legs sticking out sweating. He was a mean-looking bastard, shaveheaded, and eyelids so heavy I couldn't see no human behind them.

One of the flunkies shoves me down facing him, then rips off my sandals like I was soiling the holy place.

Slowly, the Buddha bugger picks up his samurai sword and flicks it at my Cross, tocking it back and forth. Having been around Japs for years in the Pacific, I knew their haughtiness, and wouldn't flinch before it. Lifting my head and staring him in the face, I never let on that I felt what he was doing.

With a roar, he whacked me across the shoulder. Another flunky pushed me down. I got the idea that they wanted me to bow, and I did so.

The Captain's eyes jerked open, hot, brown. "Salute Japanese Imperial Navy! Honor!"

"I don't know how to salute," I said. "That is for military men."

"Honor, honor!" he screamed. I did a couple more stoopdowns. Then he spat: "Priest! Why priest Bougainville?"

"Because I have a flock there. My people."

"Not you peopre! Japan peopre!"

"They pray to God. I'm there to help them." I run my fingers up and down my beads, and he blew up, cursing. I knew enough Jap to catch that he sure wasn't swallowing my act.

By then, another officer had crawled up the tube behind him. Hissing angrily, the Captain shoved the newcomer forward until he sat in front of me and bowed. "I am Lieutenant Sato Ohmae, Japanese Imperial Navy. Intelligence officer this ship. To whom am I speaking, please?"

"Patrick Kelly," I blurts, then gulps. "Meaning, Father Patrick. Marist Order."

"Yes, of course." His narrow eyes flickered, and there was almost a smile in them. By now, I got a good look at the lad, handsome he was, fine, thin features and hair slicked back. There was something different about him than the others. His white naval shirt had several ribbons on it, and the shoes that he'd taken off, I noticed now, were not zori thong sandals or rubber two-toed frog feet like the others wore. His shoes were brown leather moccasins, the kind that I'd seen on my grandson, Jake. Trying to open up the lad, I says, "Glad there's somebody here savvies English."

"I ought to. I was educated in the States. University." He started to say something else, friendly, but the Captain slapped his arm in warning. "My Commander must know your nationality. You are…?"

"Irish!"

"Oh? An Irish priest?"

"That's right. Marist Order."

Ohmae frowned. "I have known some of the Catholic Orders. We have Jesuits in the Homeland. I didn't realize that the Marists had Irish priests."

"They do now," I blurts, then went on to windy him about my long years ministering the heathen in many parts of the Pacific. He kept nodding and passing it back to the fat boss. Finally his face tightened. "My commander believes that you are an English speaker like Kennedy on Segi, Endicott, Feldt, these other spies who send radio reports of Japanese planes."

"Radio?" I cries. "Look, lad, lieutenant, a man of God has no part of war. You should know that if you've studied the orders of our Holy Mother Church. I could no more run a radio than you could preach the Holy Mass."

"You are American."

"No, no," I said, "Irish. Listen to the brogue on me, will you! Irish are neutrals in this cursed war."

"We understand that. However, it does not explain where you were going when we picked you up. What purpose?"

"Why, down the shore to another village." I fumbled out a name. "Fever there. My parishioners dying. You wouldn't stop an old man from giving them last rites, would you?"

When we got that translated back, I seen that we struck a stone

512

wall. The Captain was hissing about shooting me then and there and dumping me over the side after they'd charged their batteries. But young Ohmae was begging permission of his Excellency to inquire whether the staff, possibly even Admiral Yamamoto, might want to interrogate me at Rabaul regarding native cooperation on Bougainville. This could be most important in the fighting ahead.

The Captain hissed and huffed, finally growling that they didn't have food to waste on me. Right there, I seen a last chance to persuade the buggers. "Lieutenant," I says, piously blessing myself, "a priest needs no food. Often we fast for days at a time, serving our Lord, praying for the sins of the world."

At that, the Captain roared. Sick of me, out of his sight! Ohmae motioned, and I did my double-bowing, picked up my holy sandals and followed the lad down into a lower coop where the junior officers lived. On a straw mat that I took as Ohmae's bed stood my black, priestly valise. I seen to my horror that it had already been opened and rummaged through. Ohmae smiled thinly. "Well, Father, since we are pagans on this boat, I trust that you'll have no more need for your religious appliances."

"Well," I says, thinking quick, "I got my rosaries hanging on me, of course, but the Bible, that's something else, Lieutenant. Can't part with that."

"Actually," he said, "I studied the Bible in a course of English literature. They may teach it differently in America than you do in Ireland. Still and all, I'll enjoy reacquainting myself with the apostles' tales. We've been on patrol a long time and our books have all been read cover to cover."

"Sure and I love reading myself, lad," I blurts, trying to hide my terror that he'd stumble on my diary, "but you've got to understand how it is with priests. Our Order forbids us from letting the Bible out of our sight. I have to say my Holy Office every day, twice a day, surely you wouldn't keep me from that."

"Don't worry," he said, and snapped the valise shut. "You'll have all the time in the world for your prayers."

Yes, time. The time of a lifer.

Ah, sure, I played God in the submarine, and I played Him on Rabaul. A priest, was I? Who the hell cared? Once they'd stuck me and their other prisoners in their dank concrete tunnel lined with prisoner cages, it didn't matter the color of a man's skin or the flag he'd served, and least of all what his role had been when he was alive. We wasn't human anymore. We was naked dogs, cringing, whining to a God who'd forgot the lot of us. The only way out was to starve and die, and we tried that, too, maggot wretches, trying to burrow into the bodies of our comrades that the Japs hauled off every day to feed to the sharks in Rabaul Harbor.

I can't write about the time because I lost track of it. Months is all, dragging into years.

The bandy-legged bastards divvied us into groups of ten stiffs per cage, made us sit naked on the wet dirt floor all the long day, staring at the wall. Tracking ants that trailed down the wet stone. Tracking dreams of glory, remembered times when there was love and the laughter of humans in the world. If we as much as turned our eyes or whispered to the poor devil next to us, guards would howl in and beat us with clubs. They made us scream in Japanese: "Prisoners will salute Nipponese soldiers and corps. The penalty for attempting riot or escape will be death by shooting. Violations of any regulations will be death by shooting."

Every day, without any rhyme or reason, the guards would drag two or three prisoners outside. They never came back. They were beheaded, for what crime no one knew, and we never even knew their names.

Animals.

For food, we had one bowl of rice and water a day, dead bugs floating in the swill, and a stinking hole in the rock in the corner, to pass our bloody, dying stool.

Outside, the world of Rabaul was booming and blasting with Yank shells, but we never seen it, never got no sun or air. If any man among the ten of us in our cage tried to escape, even knowing that there wasn't any way out, the remaining nine of us would be shot. If some crazed devil would totter up and strike at a guard, he'd be shot, and on the second offense, all of us that was left.

Skin and bones, fevers, madness. Jesus God, how many times I begged the Good Lord to put me out of it.

Instead, He put me into a place that I'd never been before. The wild, weeping, lonely land of my own deepest soul. I'd never have survived the battles I'd fought if I hadn't lived by my wits, controlling my life in every waking moment. But it had slipped through my fingers now. I couldn't control nothing, even my bowels. In my hallucinations, staring at the cursed wall, I got to hear Him talking to me, and saying, so gentle-like, Patrick lad, all your years of running are over now. Don't you see, can't you feel it happening? Let go. Rest in me. Have no fear. I'm finally taking you home.

With that comfort alone, or the endless penance of not being able to give up the ghost, I more or less closed my eyes to time, and floated in God. All the fights and the glory were gone. Meaningless. I'd served my time. I was ready when He was.

When it ended, I was tottering in the sun outside the tunnel. I couldn't have weighed a hundred pounds, my eyes dizzying, my hear-

514

ing all but gone. But a Japanese sailor lifts me into the front seat of a Naval staff car. In the back seat, spiffed in the gold braid of a commander sits Sato Ohmae. He smiled. "Welcome to the Greater Eastern Co-Prosperity Sphere. Second World War, Sergeant Kelly."

"Sergeant? Sir...?" I stammers.

"Ingenious, really, how you masqueraded as a Holy One."

"How...how was that?" I was trembling, hoarse, my voice cracking after so much silence.

"Come now, Sergeant, truth only. No one will punish you for it. In fact, the only reason you're alive is because I read your diary. I started reading it the night we picked you up. I was suspicious then about the cock and bull story you told us, but had I revealed it, my commander would have shot you. Now, however, I find it utterly fascinating, your wars of glory, traveling the world with you in the pages of your Bible." He smiled. "We shall talk about these things, of course, but my God, man, you look like death itself." He reached forward and gripped my bony shoulder. "You need the sea air, Sergeant Kelly. An ocean voyage. Quite possibly, our last."

That very night, he put me aboard his submarine. He had his own boat now, the big-bellied old skipper long ago sent to the bottom by U.S. planes.

When we reached Ohmae's private cabin, he said, "Sit down, be comfortable. You are here as my prisoner, an important and quite remarkable spy whom I'm bringing to the Homeland, because the Admiralty will want to interrogate you in detail. For now, the crew accepts that." He stripped off his jacket of rank, tossed it on his straw mat, put on a white navy cap and field glasses. "Wait. I must steer us out of the harbor. Your aviators have mined the place."

Then he clapped his hands and a Jap sailor, who couldn't have been fifteen, scurried in and brought me tea.

Seated there alone, as the sub began to thrum and move, I saw my priestly satchel, and the Bible in it, protruding out of Sato's wall locker. With the tea hot in my throat, the first decent drink I'd had in God knows how long, I reached out and touched the book, tears flooding my eyes.

All this nonsense I'd put down, a life that nobody cared about but me, and yet, the years hurtled me back. Crookie had read it, and the damn words had saved me from a firing squad. Will it be the same again, Lord, I asks? Can a man's humble words, the gift of his life, be the very prayer that could save him one last time?

At any moment, as we slid through the dark depths, I expected to feel the blast, the roar of a U.S. mine that we'd blundered into in the harbor. Yet even then, I thinks, if that's how you want me to go, Lord. You couldn't do me in that night on the *Maine,* but I wasn't ready then. I am now. Thy will be done.

Food, Holy smoke, once we were safe of U.S. planes and running north, submerged, Sato's cabin boy brung us a fine dinner of pork, bamboo shoots and even some Jap sake to wash it down. The stuff was so rich I had to swallow hard to keep from puking.

Because of the heat in the boat, Sato had stripped to his kimono, and sitting there cross-legged, I sees his moccasin shoes. I chuckled, telling him about Jake, my grandson, going to Yale college and wearing the same damn things.

Sato laughed. "Ah, it's the uniform, of course. The well-bred cream of American youth, educated in the Ivy League. Snappy dressers, weren't we? Gentlemen songsters off on a spree. And those same boys, some of them came all the way round the world to die here. Or were flamed down in their Corsairs to be captured and executed on Rabaul."

I nods. "Where I would have croaked, lad, if it hadn't been for you. Why, I'm asking?"

He stretched out on his mat, arms behind his head. "Because you see, old grandfather, I was one of those boys once. Do you know the college of Dartmouth?"

I shook my head. "Can't say I do."

"Well, it's up in the beautiful green mountains of New England. I spent four of the happiest years of my life at Dartmouth. Oh, not from the start. What was I but a scared, skinny little Japanese kid, desperately homesick. Yes, I could ski well. That's why I went. But I was so afraid being in your vast country. I felt as abandoned as you do with us. I was always burning up the telephones, calling down to Princeton where my friend and cousin, Fumitaka Konoye, son of our former Premier, was an upperclassman, very smooth and accepted. Then I'd call the Tsubaki brothers who were at Yale and Cornell, and they told me to buck up, I'd get used to it. You say, why did I save you?" He smiled and shook his head. "Because, grandfather, so many of your young Americans saved me, in those years. Truly remarkable generosity, hospitality. They opened their hearts and their homes to me. Why," he pushed up suddenly, and fumbled into the steel locker beside us, "there was even a girl. Julie. Julia Lockhart." Out spilled a stack of snaps. As he ran his fingers over them, like a deck of cards, I seen glimpses of him in snow on skis, playing tennis, visiting the city of Noo Yawk. And then, a girl, kind of plumpy in a bathing suit, but a lovely laughing look as he hugged her beside a merry-go-round. "Atlantic City," he said. "Do you know, I proposed to her that night, and she said yes."

"Married her, did ye?"

He shook his head and brushed the photos aside. "Her father was in your government. They were a fine, prominent family in Washington. In those days, people of wealth could check out through

516

their banks similar people all over the world. What came back to the Lockharts from Japan was, yes, Sato Ohmae has the proper blood qualifications, it seems. Diplomatic family, related to the Premier. Sufficient funds to educate him abroad as a diplomat. But only one thing wrong, Mr. Lockhart said. Slant eyes, yellow skin. Jap. Enemy to Americans. Too soon we would be killing each other, instead of lying in the marriage bed. Mr. Lockhart forbade me to see Julie again."

I shook my head. "Bad luck, lad, but I been there myself, them rich families, walling out the outsider."

"I still love Julie. Do you know, she writes me, and sometimes the letter gets through. She says that she's waiting. We all wait, eh, wait to die, despising each other. What is it all for, old man?"

"Glory, they tell you."

He sat up sharply. "But I know different. I read your words. All your wars, your destroying of races, bah! What have you proved except that we are all the same? Ah, your stories of the American Indians. At Dartmouth, we proudly called ourselves Indians, wore their beautiful faces on our hockey shirts. Look what your guns have done to them. Are they all gone now?"

"A few still live. Pathetic buggers, festering on reservations. And to get themselves free, some of 'em are surely out on these jungle islands, fighting you to the death, fighting for the very stars and stripes that wrapped 'em in chains."

"Tragic, really. As a boy, how I thrilled at stories of your frontier. Your Crazy Horse, your Geronimo. To think that you actually knew them, fought and killed them. Were they as fierce as I've been led to believe?"

"Ah," I sighed, "so long ago now, lad, the truth gets lost. Yes, I suppose they was fierce, cruel, but fighting for their turf, they were, and not a whit worse in their black hearts than your Nippon troops I seen butchering my wife, and them devilish guards of yours, slaughtering prisoners in the Rabaul tunnel."

He sat up slowly and rubbed his fingers into his eyes. "Your Indians came from our same Asiatic root, traveling across the Bering Strait. We are the same stock, only we are not white. Why must white rule the world?" he cried. "Are you the only superior race?"

"I never said that, son, nor do I believe it. I've bedded with other bloods, from native queens to Injun spitfires, and loved every hair on their heads. A body and a soul ain't got a color to me. Fact is, I've learned more from the dusky races than I ever did from my own kind. If we was so smart, how come we didn't see this last war storming toward us? How come we needed it? Ain't it greed, lad? Ain't that what pulls the triggers?"

He nodded. "That and being different. The terror of the stranger stalking toward our cave. Kill or be killed. Will we ever get beyond that ghastly reflex?"

"Someday," I murmurs, "we'll make the killing so bad, so God-awful, we'll blow the very heavens down on ourselves. Maybe then, I'm thinking, what's left of us will give the damn thing up."

"You blame Japan for this war?"

"Not any more than us, lad. Greed done it on both sides, always does. Ain't that the truth?"

He sighed. "Yes, probably, yet it is hard to see when we're in the midst of it." He smiled. "Patrick. May I call you that?"

"Father Patrick," I chuckled and gripped his hand. "Bless ye, lad, for what you done."

"I think you would have done the same for an enemy. Your words said that you even married one." Then his face darkened. "Anyhow, it's not over, one never knows how things end in war. You must rest and feed yourself. If anyone comes to you while I am not in this cabin, say nothing, answer no questions."

"You're saying it's dangerous for me? Your crew, I'm meaning."

"It could be a problem. There is so much anger toward Americans, our morale is so low. Japanese commanders have total authority. I can sever an enlisted man's hand if he refuses to salute. I can shoot him on the spot for any disobedience. But now," he sighed, "when we are all dying so fast, Yamamoto is gone, shot down by your planes, our garrisons bypassed, men starving, our fleets sunk, in times like this, my dear Patrick, no one is safe from the dying agonies of bushido. Say your prayers, grandfather. My hope is to put you ashore on the Homeland. Prison, of course, but I have enough friends in high places. I will try to keep you alive."

Then he put on his uniform and went back to his duties on the bridge. I lay in the dark, thrumming cabin, pondering what he'd said. More prison if I was lucky, quick death if I wasn't. Who knew now, except the Good Lord. Again, I gave the choice back to Him, and for the first time in years, slept on a rich, full belly like I'd already gone to heaven.

Maybe five, six days later, and cooped up below, I couldn't tell day from night, I hear alarm bells ringing and feel the boat thundering up and rising. The cabin lad patters in, thrusts me a black rubber raincoat, and hauls out my valise from the Commander's locker. When he wasn't going to give it to me, I grabbed it away from him. He shakes his head, and with a hiss, motions to go up top.

In the tight torpedo room where the periscope was, radios were crackling and sailors scurrying about. From the tightness of their faces, the angry looks they give me, I had a feeling that something had changed fast, and not for the better. One mean-faced junior officer again tried to snatch away my valise, and when I jerked it back, he spat, "You go Saipan, Japan corps kill you Saipan!"

It was Greek to me until they shoved me out onto the deck. A black rubber raft was bobbing beside the hull. Two Jap sailors, Nambu pistols belted around their rain suits, reached up from their tin oars and hauled me aboard. Only then did I see Sato Ohmae seated in the stern. He was dressed the same way, armed, with night field glasses around his neck. He pulled me down beside him. As we shoved off from the sub and dug into the heavy swells, Sato's dark eyes glinted angrily. He growled something to the sailors in the boat and others shouted at him from the conning tower. When I asked what they were saying, he grunted, "Get rid of the American pig quickly, this is dangerous water."

I was stunned at the change in him. When I tried to fumble something out, he snapped in Japanese, "Be quiet!"

Off to the north, there was a flash in the sky, naval guns, I figured. The sailors on the oars looked in terror at the rumbling flashes. Then one of them kicked me sharply on the leg.

"Commander," I whispered, "Sato, lad, what have I done now?"

"June 15, yesterday morning, your fleet struck Saipan. More of your ships are laying off behind us." He flung his arm at the dark sea beyond the sub. "Your Marines are on Saipan. They'll be on top of us soon. How do you think we feel, pig, seeing the Empire barrier broken!"

One of the Jap sailors must have savvied some English, because he was hissing strong now, kicking my leg again like it was my fault.

Everything had changed so fast, my heart was in my mouth. I couldn't figure the way Sato was behaving, unless something in him had snapped. By then, though, I seen where we were heading. The sub had laid off in a small harbor, very near a giant island. All I could make out were tall, white cliffs, surf crashing into the base of them. But God Almighty, even scared, I had to suck in the sweetness of the air, the scent of trees, flowers, and a damp warm rain.

When the surf crashed us up on the beach, the sailors jumped out, dragging me with them harshly. Pulling the raft in between two big rocks, Sato flashed his torch across the black sand and illuminated a narrow trail up through mangroves.

Hurrying, he snapped orders to the Jap sailors, pointing, quick, up there to the top. I gathered something about an Excellency waiting.

One of the sailors didn't like the idea, for he growled something, and Sato slapped him with his pistol. Go!

The sailor stood wide-legged and shouted in English. "Spy pig! First kill pig! We see!"

"Go!" Sato roared, "I take care of this one!" He shoved me ahead of him so hard I fell into the surf. Then he swung to the sailors and cocked his pistol. "Follow my orders or you die with him!" Sulking, their eyes smoldering, they turned and began moving slowly toward the path in the mangroves.

Sato kept watching them. They must have stopped, for he shouted again, Go! I was just getting to my feet when he seized me and dragged me into the rocks. He flashed on his torch to show them that I was lying there beneath him.

Lowering his Nambu automatic, he blasted into the sand beside my head, once, twice, the grains biting my face, my ears ringing. Then he snapped off the torch and looked toward the jungle.

Still lying face down, I could just make out the last Jap, the surly one, finally turning and slogging up the trail.

Sato knelt beside me, his teeth gleaming in the darkness. "You've come a long way to die on American soil, Sergeant Patrick. This is Guam."

The words smashed into my brain. "Guam? God in heaven, lad, can it be! Can I be back?!" I was blubbering, remembering loving Daisy on the warm sands of Inajaran beach. Where did it all go?

Sato was nodding, having no idea what I meant. "Apologies for the way it had to be done. I'll never make a living as an actor, but it was the only way to save you."

"Lad, you give me a scare."

"All of us," he breathed, "mostly me. When the crew heard of the landings at Saipan, they went wild with rage. They wanted to kill you on the boat, but fortunately I had an excuse. At sea, I received a message from the Guam command. There's a visiting Excellency here, Admiral Nakagawa, who's ill and must be evacuated to the Homeland. That's where those sailors have gone, to bring him down and put him on my boat. But of course he's not there. I know that, they don't. A second message told me he committed hara-kiri yesterday, in the shame of having the Marianas barrier broken. So hurry now," he said, "get up into these rocks." Scrambling ahead of me, he picked his way onto a ledge trail that ran up the limestone cliffs. Then he squatted, breathing hard. "We've intercepted American plans for landing on Guam, Patrick. They'll do it as soon as they beat down Saipan. Already, they have cruisers and a destroyer screen shelling this coast. The landing beaches will be somewhere to the north of here, probably Asan and Agat, if their bombardment is any indication. Yet my charts show that in these cliffs there are caves. Probably Japanese gun positions. They may have been shelled already, but be careful."

I seized the lad's arm. "You're letting me go, Sato?"

"Why, of course. How could I do anything else after what your people did for me? You're a dead spy whose body has been carried out to sea. That's what my sailors will find when they return empty-handed. So, my friend," he smiled, "we have bought you a little time. Perhaps even a life, where we may meet again, if not here, in the next one."

I gripped him to me. "Damn ye, lad, if God put men like you on this world, there's hope, ain't there? Look now," my voice was hoarse, "sure and someday this madness has got to end. How do I find ye, to shake your mitt and thank ye? Maybe even your Julie lass in the States...?"

He was sitting on the trail, shaking his head. "Julia Lockhart in Washington. Tell her I waited, too."

"But you can tell her that! It's going to end, lad!"

"Tonight," he said, wiping at his eyes and pushing up, "we have orders to proceed westerly and encounter the American fleet. Our entire air arm, the majority of our capital ships, are going to attack your fleet. The last defense of the Empire. Lure you out to destroy you!" He laughed harshly. "Go for broke, you have the saying. We go against them, the tonnage you have, the giant air fleets, well, we are broke. The last dying banzai of bushido. I wait for my dear one at the bottom of the sea."

"God Almighty," I cried, "if you know you're doomed, and you will be, tell the bastards to go to hell. Sink your ship. Come ashore here. Stay with me. I can keep you alive, lad!"

He gripped me to him and patted my back. "Some day we will know better, but it is not yet, my friend. As your God would say, Speed thee, keep thee in peace." Then he laughed and gave me a shove up the trail. "Pretend you are hiding again from the Indians, Patrick. As you say, we are all one. You beat us before, why not now?"

Then the pebbles began to slide as he hurried down the narrow trail. "A cave, remember," he cried. "Quick now, hide!"

It wasn't a moment too soon. By the time he'd struck the beach, his light had flashed on. The two Jap sailors were running angrily toward him down the trail. Sato was cool, pointing at the dark waves with his pistol. Both of the sailors began splashing around in the shallows, searching for my corpse.

They jabbered back and forth a few moments, and finally seemed to give it up. Sato shoved them into the raft, and they dug their oars into the black sea, where he'd lie for all time, remembering the love that he'd had, and the part of it that he'd given back to me, God rest his soul.

In that dying night on Guam, I seen that love was all that life was about, strong enough even to spare this old sinner. All the glory I'd seen meant nothing compared to the peace God was granting me at last, finally bringing me home.

———————

Up the cliff in the dawn, I found my cave. Made to order by the Japs, and their damn coffin too.

I couldn't believe it when I stumbled blinking out of the sunlight, beholding a sandstone cavern carved by ages of wind and rain. But the clever little bandy-leggers had improved on it all right, sandbagging part of the entrance, and behind it, spiking down a twin-barreled Bofors anti-aircraft gun. But they didn't get to shoot much. A few empty shells lay littered on the cave floor, and then behind them, I caught the stink. Lying grotesque and shattered against the rear wall were the torn mustard-yellow sacks of three Japs. Their faces were swollen black in death, blue-bottle flies swarming over the flesh they had left, and maggots crawling over their stiff, dead hands.

I covered my nose, and weak as I was, I drags each of the bodies to the lip in front of the cave, kicks them over, and watches them spin downward like dolls to splash in the angry waves, pounding the rocks below.

With the poor buggers gone, I seen that their fate was going to be this old lad's salvation. In a tunnel at the rear of the cave were the straw mats the gun crew had been sleeping on until U.S. bullets riddled their piece and put them down. The walls were pocked and burned with exploding shells, yet the real treasure was untouched. I fair danced for joy, kicking through tin Jap ammunition boxes to canteens of water, and best of all, in a wooden locker with wiggly Jap writing on it, tins of fish and sacks of rice. Hell, in an old metal canister, they even had three tall green bottles of sake. Now I could drink and feed to the end of time. Nothing could get at me here, unless of course more of the buggers decided to come back.

The one thing that worried me, at the rear of the cavern was a steel ladder that led upward. For the first few days, I was too weak and tired even to try scaling it. But finally, when my ribs were filled with enough fish, rice and sake, I pulled myself up the rusty rungs, maybe 30 feet upward, where I felt of a steel lid.

Wary, I creaked it open and pulled myself out into a patch of bristly green sea plants. The top of the bluff looked as empty and wind-howled as the moors of my boyhood in Mayo. Yet inland, further beyond, rose a dark wall of jungly trees. Though I couldn't pick up nothing in them, I see red rips in the earth that I knew were bomb holes. The Yank gunners in their ships and planes must have thought that there were targets here, but I sure wasn't going to snoop around and find out.

Lowering the lid and wriggling down into my cave, I felt free as a bird, knowing that it was only a matter of time now until our lads come back. After the years in prison and the years of running, I was gaining on that day when I'd be resting safe, and rejoicing. I even had dreams of hugging Pearlie again. God keep her alive, I prayed.

Scrambling to the lip of the cave, where I could see the green-blue ocean and the long shoreline to my right, I began re-living my time with Daisy here, little Nora and Matty. Where had the war swept my youngsters? Would they live through it so I could see 'em again? Then the old fear come to me. I was seeing the transport, hauling us back from the Philippines in '92, Daisy, Nora and me, clutching the rail and mourning the poor infant that the sister had pushed through the porthole. Ah, these cursed Guam waters, the omen of it, Daisy at the Presidio soon losing the last child we'd ever have.

Crazy as I was, I begun whispering for Nora, missing her so bad, wanting to make it all up to her if I ever seen her again. Maybe it would be all of us, Pearlie and Matt, too, and I'd be howling: Did you ever dream I'd be adrift again in this Guam sea? And what about Earl Ellis, too? He and I in the Crazy Horse had put into Guam, and from here, he sailed on to die at Palau. Well, Earl, I thinks, it ain't been in vain. Now they're listening to you, now we're back, by God!!

Lying on my belly, squinting against the sun, I tried to get my bearings and recall what I remembered about Guam. The long dark shoreline swept north, then veered seaward in an ugly jungled thumb with a harbor beyond. This was Orote Point, I remembered, and the harbor beside it, Apra. We'd dropped the hook here and gone ashore to the frame green and white buildings that were the Marine Barracks. Poor lambs, no guns, no protection after Churchill and FDR had let Pearl Harbor happen. Stab in the back, was it? Ah, Christ, did them liars know? Was the rumors true that they were reading the Jap codes showing the enemy fleet steaming toward Oahu? So why did they turn a deaf ear? Would the world ever know if it was exactly what they wanted, their stab in the back to shock us with anger and fling us us pell-melling into their war? As for the Marines trapped here, probably they were dead, or at best prisoners in some Jap hole. I couldn't see nothing at this distance but scrubby trees. Yet there were trucks churning up dust, and on Orote, the stripe of an airfield. As I watched, two silvery Jap planes came whining in to land.

Well, enjoy it, you devils, I thinks, because you ain't going to have it long. Clearly, from the dust I seen, the occasional movements of troops, black little ants filing in and out of underbrush, the Japs were getting ready to die on this rock, and we were going to oblige them.

Manifest Destiny, wasn't it? I howled at the thought. Here, we'd swept across our mountains and deserts, hit the sea and ran on west, drenching our starry flag in blood until we had the Philippines and Guam. And now, hadn't it come full circle? MacArthur had lost the Philippines, but knowing the man, and that the tides of war had turned our way, old Doug would soon be storming ashore on Luzon. But first, to protect his flank, we'd have to break the Marianas barrier, as Sato Ohmae had said, and we were doing that indeed, landing on Saipan. Guam had to be next, and with a vengeance! For this island, where America's day begins, we used to say, would be our first star-spangled turf to take back from the Japanese.

As the days and nights dragged on, I was so excited I could hardly sleep. Just the waiting. When would it be? Ah, byes, make it soon!

Sometimes in the nights, there'd be the far-off booming of fleet guns, over to the west. I dreaded thinking of that noble lad, Sato, going down in his punctured tin can.

But it must have been happening. More and more in the days now, crouching, hidden, I'd see Yank planes, whining overhead, leaving smoke trails. God in heaven, what a change from those miserable skies over Bougainville, where there was just a lonely handful of our airmen. Here, they come rat-tat-tatting, lacing Guam, one blue swarm of 'em after the other. I marveled that we could ever build so many air machines. All this had started with Pershing's six toys, less one that Patton wrecked.

In the next pounding night, Orote Peninsula exploded in fire. When dawn come, all I could make out was smoking bomb holes on the strip, and scattered in the mangroves and coral revetments, the shiny wreckage of Jap planes.

Day after day the noise of it grew. At first the ships were far off. I heard the throbs of heavy naval shells rocking Guam, blowing trees and turf sky high. For a time, the Jap batteries barked back, and sometimes the firefight reminded me of the constant roar in France during the first Great War. But now, instead of cursing the noise in my ears, I was laughing at it. My time has come! Trampling out the vineyards where the grapes of wrath are stored.

Slowly the Jap counter-fire faded away. They were hiding like rats in their holes, because now, cutting the seas below me and slicing up and down the landing coast, were the gray streaks of destroyers, then bigger ships, cruisers, battlewagons. Remember the *Maine!* God in heaven, here she comes, our giant dreadnoughts lying right off the reef, blamming their massive guns, puffing smoke-rings at the sky. What has happened to war? I thinks, remembering when it was just a charging guvmint mount between my legs and a clumsy Springfield carbine jamming in my mitts. Have I seen all this, these swarming planes and naval guns firing by wizardry from the far horizon, tools of the devil that man's fiendish brain had evolved, all the better to blow away our fellow man. And what for, what for?

The island was shaking and flashing day and night, and I knew from the frenzy of it that my waiting was almost done.

Dawn broke, sun streamed in, and the roaring blasted just below my cave. "You're here, byes!" I cried, "you're here!"

Tears were running down my face. Rocking in the swells just

524

beyond the reef were transports. I couldn't believe the number of ships, a miracle it was, compared to the old days in the Solomons, when all we had left was a few battered hulks.

What great power had done this? Maybe FDR was right, flaming us with anger to destroy this enemy, until we were burying him now with all the men and iron and guts that the great US of A could rip out of its soil.

Like little black piglets, wriggling across the sea, here come row after row of camouflauged landing craft, shiny huddles of scared men, crouching behind the armor. How far we'd come from that morning at Daiquiri, Cuba, when our frail boats were floundering and swamping. But not these steel monsters, roaring through shot and shell. Hadn't Earl Ellis begged for craft like these? Was they Marines aboard? Wouldn't they have to be, not only making this landing that was too big for Army soldiers, but hitting the beach to avenge our Marines the Japs had killed here.

Belleau Wood was ringing in my ears. Come on, you sonsof-bitches, the old sarge had cried, do you want to live forever! On they come, hitting the beach north of Orote, then more waves of 'em thundering onto the shore to the south. Leaping out of their boats were jungly camouflauged riflemen, the first squads digging a foothold in the sand, and the next squads rushing past 'em, lacing the jungle with a hail of bullets. Their field guns began blasting bar-rages at the enemy dug in on the cliffs. But it wasn't no cakewalk. I happened to be watching one of the landing craft when a Jap shell struck it in a white geyser, and when the smoke cleared, bodies were floating face down in the surf.

Dammit, lads, keep moving, scatter, take 'em off of that high ground! Right then, I was seeing all my comrades gone down all these years. I wanted to lead 'em again, win it this time. "I'm with you, byes!" I shouts. "I got a box seat for your war!"

Out I rushes onto the lip of my cave, out in the bright sun, no need to hide anymore. I was waving my shirt at 'em, cheerin'. Then I thinks: Write it down, damn ye! You'll only see this once! I crouched in the rocks, scribbling. Here come the planes, white stars on their blue bodies, glittering, flashing in from the sea. Then one splits off, gull wings on it, rushing toward me with a whistling sound. By God, if it ain't the same kind that saved me on the Bougainville beach. Now he's slicing toward the cliffs, streaks of fire flashing from his wings. Bullets? Hell, no! Strange white sticks trailin' smoke. God help me, what is them things? Rockets, could they be? Sure, rockets, smashing the cliffs off to my left! Dance and howl, "rockets red glare, the bombs bursting in air!" God help me, ain't this what it's all been for! Now that one plane is roaring up into the sky. Gone? No! Turnin', comin' back dead at me he

525

"~~KILROY~~ KELLY WAS HERE!"

Battle cry of American troops, scrawled across the world they'd won.

EPILOGUE

JAKE

Then to Now

I stared at Patrick's last word on his last page. "He." He what? A moment of horror, a life chopped, unfinished. The ancient paper was seared with the rocket's flame, and the dried brown stains on it were his blood. I could almost hear him groan, "Is this where it ends, Jake lad?"

No, by God! I wanted him to be shouting again, "Fight on, byes!" Prevail!

Like a man coming out of a trance, I lay down his copybook, and in the shadows of my office, I wept.

Who could see me? Nobody that I cared about. Nobody there at all. Just me, alone with him, saying goodbye.

Thirty floors below, outside the blackened windows, Chicago was silent except for the occasional wail of a distant siren. The day was long gone. In the world I'd traveled with Patrick, there'd been no beepers, no faxes or call-waitings. Nobody was running to catch the last commuter train. It hadn't mattered back then, not with a wilderness to tame, and the dream he'd fought for to make America great. But in the world I'd returned to, only our skeletons remained, dark skyscrapers gleaming wet with a storm that had come and gone without my knowing. A few lights were on in the buildings, cleaning women gathering trash bags of crumpled buy-sell orders, ripped and failed spreadsheets, empty Gelusil wrappers—the spent ammo of today's war that had to be swept up before we could begin tomorrow's.

And my war, Patrick? What have I been fighting for all these years? Not by bread alone, was it? No, we'd long ago buried that quaint notion, drifted so far from the spirit of your little Indian Matthew at Wounded Knee that we didn't even discuss it in polite conversation. Our rainbows had turned to rust. We'd chased our lives away—mine, anyhow—pursuing the golden calf of image, status, possessions, the

526

safe, the comfortable. Security the god. As T.S. Eliot said, "Distracted from distraction by distractions." I could almost hear Patrick snarling in disgust at our surrender. He'd seen it coming, and wrote it down so bitterly that summer of '41. Our last hurrah of peace before our old world would be shattered, all the king's horses and all the king's men never able to put Humpty-Dumpty back together again. Gentlemen songsters off on a spree. Yes, we *were* those pampered snots he'd called us, "flowers of sassity," mindless that the bones of men like him on all their perilous frontiers had been the seedbed from whence we sprung. But we had no way of knowing it then. We were running too fast to pause and honor the Patrick Kellys who'd won us such riches. So it was no wonder that we'd be standing up that night at the Onwentsia Club dance, proud and cocky in our tuxedos, and chortling out our toast to a long-forgotten debutante: "Make my bed and light my light, I'll be home, late tonight, blackbirds, bye bye."

Are they all gone now, Patrick? Is it all over, your life and mine?

I switched off my reading lamp and sat in darkness. I dreaded letting him go, unheard and unremembered. He was still so close to us in time. Just a wink of the clock, you might say, just yesterday his struggles had been ours, the arc of his life a rocket's red glare, still illuminating what we were, because of him, and in the afterglow of what he'd left us, maybe we could still find the hope and strength needed to carry us home and complete our dream.

In a rush of emotion, I longed for my three children and seven grandchildren to know him as I had. There wasn't much time left to hold onto him. Doesn't it always happen that when the old ones go, we feel a sadness that we were too busy or too bored to listen to what they might have told us? At my age and generation, most of us were fading away. My Adelaide, mother of our two daughters and one son, had died in 1991. I'd finally accepted coming home to an empty house. But there was no rush getting there, certainly not tonight. Now was the time to gather us together and put it all down before it was lost. Impulsively, I hurried to my desk, and snapped on the tiny Japanese recorder I use for correspondence. "Dear Ones," I said, startled by the sound of my voice in the ghostly silence, "I've just this moment finished reading my grandfather's diary. Your great and great-great grandfather, whom you never knew. He's a name to you, that's all. But it's so incredible, the way he came back into our lives, I must tell you how it happened, hoping you'll treasure him as I did. And learn from him, God willing. His life really isn't in the history books yet, not the truth of it, anyhow. If we fail to learn from the tragedies that he and our nation lived through, we might, as someone said, be doomed to repeat them."

Fifty years ago, I continued, almost to this very day, my mother Nora—your Gomma Nora as you used to call her—was sitting at her breakfast table in Lake Forest. She'd married Roger Castle by that time, and they were living in his house down by the Lake, no longer in the family, but it was then.

Roger's custom was faithfully to read the *Chicago Tribune* at breakfast, then leave it for Nora as he hurried off to the eight o'clock train. Imagine her in that sun-filled breakfast room, peacefully having her dry toast and coffee, when suddenly she cried out.

On the *Tribune* page of news from the war-fronts, she saw an astonishing headline: "Indian Fighting Cavalryman Rescued by U.S. Marines on Guam."

She almost fainted, gripping that paper, and reading about a recent July morning when a badly wounded, white-bearded American had tottered into the U.S. lines. Hoarsely, in an Irish brogue, he shouted, "Lay down your pieces, byes! Damn ye, I'm one of ye!"

One indeed. He was Sergent Patrick Kelly, eighty-nine years old, and a veteran of all the campaigns of Manifest Destiny, from the Sioux wars to the recapture of Guam.

Seeing that he was badly wounded in the head and chest, ironically by a rocket from a U.S. plane, the Marines rushed him to an aid station on the beach. En route, and apparently quite delirious, Patrick had blurted something about serving with the Marines, and knowing many of its officers. In fact, he claimed that one of them had been a Marine major named Roy Geiger, who'd taught him to fly in France during the first World War.

As Patrick's lucky shamrock would have it, the man who was leading the Guam invasion was none other than Roy Geiger, now major-general USMC, commanding half the Marines in the Pacific.

It wasn't clear from the *Trib* story whether the Navy doctors ever permitted Patrick to meet with Geiger, the old man's condition being so grave, and the general so totally occupied in the Guam battle which, for the first few days, was a bloodbath. We took several thousand casualties just getting off the beach.

But my mother Nora, as you recall, was one determined lady. General Geiger struck a bell with her, as of course it would, for she knew I'd been with him many months as co-pilot and navigator on his private aircraft. So Mother had her foot in the door. Ever since Pearl Harbor, she'd lost track of her father. He and his Tahitian wife, Pearlie, seemed to have been swallowed up by the Pacific war. Her frantic letters and cables to him on Tehaare came back, "*pas de forward.*" She even feared that Patrick was dead. With the hard life he'd had, he couldn't live forever. But now, not only had she found him—she was devoted to him in her crusty way—but more important, my connection with Geiger could only help him.

I forget the Commandant's name at Great Lakes Naval Station, some Admiral, but he'd been a golf partner of Roger Castle's, and Mother had entertained him often. Lake Foresters in the war years were wonderfully hospitable to the high brass from Great Lakes and Fort Sheridan.

The social connection was enough to send Mother storming into the Admiral's office like she owned the place. She begged him to find out all details about her father's condition, and inform me at once because I'd certainly be on Guam with Geiger.

Poor Mother, she was so imperious, and had been around Army/Navy highest circles from girlhood on, she expected the brass to drop everything and move heaven and earth for her.

I pity that Admiral. He did try to explain to her, Mother admitted later, that there was a time lag in these stories from the war zones, in addition to censorship clearances and circuits jammed with military traffic. But she'd have none of it. I can just see her badgering the old sea dog until he finally promised that he'd try to break through to Geiger via Admiral Nimitz at Pearl, in the hope of getting Patrick top medical treatment, and rejoining him to his kin.

What Mother didn't realize, by the time all this happened, days had passed since Patrick had come into the lines. After much hard fighting, Geiger declared Guam secure, and we flew him, via Eniwetok, the long way around, about 1500 miles back to his headquarters on Guadalcanal.

Now, mind you, I had no idea Patrick was even alive, let alone on Guam. Mother tried to write and tell me, but we were island hopping, and V-mail letters took weeks to catch up. But then a strange thing happened, one of those random shots so typical of war.

When we landed Geiger on Guadalcanal, all of us worn out from the battle on Guam and long flights after it, Geiger hulked up to the cockpit. He put his hand on Dick Penniman's shoulder. Dick was a captain, Geiger's aide and first pilot. "Boys, I'm sending you back to Guam. Gas up, get moving. Fly to Emirau, then through the Carolines tonight. Up one night, back the next. The short way," he winked.

We were dumbfounded. The Carolines, which included the Jap fortress of Truk, struck fear in the heart of any American aviator. You needed a task force to go anyplace near those bristling islands, yet here we'd be blundering in fat, dumb and happy, unarmed and unescorted, tiptoeing a thousand miles through enemy air space. Hell, our only weapons were two Thompson sub-machine guns!

But you didn't talk back to Geiger, a grizzled warhorse who'd been fighting and flying since before we were born. What was the urgency? we wondered, why such risk, but again, you didn't ask things like that, just followed orders.

After rushing north to Emirau, we found that the Navy base commander refused to clear us out without escort, and his fighter aircraft didn't have the range to accompany us. Only a stern TWX from Geiger made him back off. "Send them alone, as directed," Geiger answered, and we went. To sneak through the Carolines, we'd have to fly a tricky dog-leg and hit a 60 mile slot between two Jap islands, Puluwat and Lamotrek, both with airfields on them. Drift too close to either one, they'd pick us up on radar and blast us out of the sky.

It was dicey, as you can imagine, but by using celestial navigation and drift sights, we must have hit the deadly slot between the two islands. Nobody came up after us. We landed at dawn on Orote strip at Guam, totally exhausted.

I hurried into a wrecked building to catch some sleep, and died for most of that day. Just about dusk, a Navy ensign shook me awake and hurried me down to our plane. He said that CincPac, on Nimitz's orders, had a passenger for our flight back to the Canal. I thought nothing of it, really, because we already had a very curious cargo that night. A half dozen Marine officers were waiting by the plane, supervising the loading of several big, flat wooden crates. I knew that the officers were on Geiger's staff, but none of them would give us a clue as to what was in those crates.

Just as we were getting ready to leave, a hospital jeep swerved up to the hatch. I was pre-flighting the plane for Dick Penniman, so all I noticed were corpsmen lifting a stretcher aboard and lashing it to the cabin bulkheads. One corpsman remained with the stretcher, and when I passed through the cabin to go to the cockpit, he was busy hooking up a plasma bottle.

Ordinarily, you'd think that I might have at least glanced at our latest passenger, but frankly that night, the tension and the haste was too great. Peering out the cockpit windows, we saw a fierce, black wall of storm driving down on Guam. Rain was already pattering on the fuselage, and distant flashes of lightning snapped across our faces.

It meant just one thing. We were going to be in serious weather, possibly even flying into the teeth of a hurricane. Faced with this, unable to use stars or drift sights, we didn't have a snowball's chance in hell of even finding our 60 mile slot of safety in the Carolines, let alone creeping through it. All we could hope was that the violent weather would keep any Jap planes on the deck.

The storm was horrendous. We hadn't even leveled off at 8000 feet, our cruising altitude, before we struck towering thunderheads, lightning crashing around us, the plane pitching like a cork in the terrible sky. The clouds were layered so heavily that we could see no stars to steer by, no ocean below for a drift sight. The turbulence was so great that even putting the landing gear down for stability, cutting off all power, both of us pushing the control yokes full forward, we'd scream upward 2000 feet a minute, 95 knots. At the top of the roller coaster, the plane would groan in anguish, and we'd ram on full power, but even at that, we'd go screaming down at 250 knots, far above the red-line speed for which our twin-engine Douglas DC-3 was designed for. The rain was so heavy the windshield wipers froze and gave up. The rubber window seals began leaking until the squalls were spraying into the cockpit and soaking us.

At any moment I was sure we'd come apart. As the first hour dragged into the second, the storm only worsened. Finally Dick Penniman told me to go back aft, check on the passengers and the condition of the aircraft. As I picked my way into the darkened, lurching cabin, hand-over-handing on the cabin bulkheads to stay on my feet, I was confronted by a half dozen ashen-faced Marine officers. Some were sitting rigid, gripping the bucket seats. Others were throwing up. These Marines were ground fighters, pavement pounders we used to call them, and they certainly wanted no part of this chaotic, powerless combat with the sky, where you didn't have a foxhole to pull over your head. I tried to comfort them, but I was scared myself. Frankly, I'd never seen it this bad.

When I finally reached the back of the cabin, checking to see that the rear hatch was still tight, I started crawling my way forward again, and this time I paused beside the terrified corpsman kid and his litter patient. I think I asked him if the poor guy was doing all right. He was strapped in, huddled in Navy blankets, but the litter was pitching terribly, the plasma bottle whacking the plane ribs with every thermal jolt.

But just as I was getting up from my squat, a long, bony arm reached out. The patient's face turned, tousled white hair protruding from his bandaged head, a wild beard, a fierce hook nose, and blue eyes like gunsights. A hoarse voice rose from deep within him. "Lad?" he whispered. He seized my leg in a death grip. "Lad, it's ye! It's Jake, ain't it?"

I fell on my knees beside him. "Oh, Christ," I sobbed. "Grandpa! It can't be you, not way out here! What's happened! Why are you here!"

I was holding his hot, dry face, gripping his shoulders, our tears splashing each other. The pent-up emotion of that awful night, and now, finding him not only alive after all these years, but with me, his life in my hands, oh my God, it was almost more than I could handle.

"Grandpa, are you badly hurt?"

At first he shook it off, but finally nodded. "Yas, lad," he whispered, "close to the heart this time. But with you, me bye, can you fly this damn thing, can you get us there?"

"I hope so, Patrick." I wanted to tell him that with him aboard, I had new strength now. I had his courage. But in war there's no time to say things like that. Only in movies.

I couldn't linger beside him. The radioman came sliding back to us, saying that I was needed in the cockpit. When I stumbled back up and strapped in, I told Dick, for God's sake, my grandfather was aboard, the wounded man in the litter! I couldn't believe it!

He glanced at me with a weary smile. "Son, I'll believe anything after tonight. Let's hope God and your old boy get us out of this."

Then, gripping the yokes, we plunged back into the war against the sky. We had no idea where we were. Our only navigation was dead reckoning, for we were constantly twisting and turning, trying to avoid the monstrous lightning-flashed thunderheads. Knowing that we must be nearing the deadly slot between the two islands, we turned off all radios, running lights and electrical, so the enemy radar wouldn't have a signal to hook onto.

Then the radioman cried out. He was peering through the navigation bubble on the top of the fuselage. He was jabbing his finger to our left and above. When I scrambled up for a look, silhouetted in the next lightning flash was a green, twin-engine Japanese Betty bomber. We never knew if he'd seen us or not, but for that fraction of a second, he was virtually flying wing on us!

As I flung myself back to the cockpit, Dick had already wheeled the plane into a violent diving turn. Below us was a heavy black cloud, rattling us with its hail, but at least it wasn't bullets from the Betty. Making a wide turn and plunging into one hiding place after another, we finally managed to lose ourselves completely. By the time we resumed course for Emirau, no more than a speck of coral in that vast blackness, we knew that we could easily be several hundred miles from where we hoped we were.

I wanted so badly to go back to Patrick, but I couldn't leave the cockpit. We began following a radio beam that we were certain came from Emirau. Then, in a moment of horror, the radioman rushed to the cockpit. Suppose the signal was false? He almost sobbed. Though it had the right frequency, couldn't it be possible the beam had hit the cloud cover and skipped down to us? If so, instead of heading us to Emirau, what we were actually picking up was Townsville, Australia. And at that instant, its vector was guiding us directly to smash into the 14,000 foot Owen Stanley mountains of New Guinea!

With a curse and a howl, we made a violent turn and picked up another beam. Surely this had to be Emirau, the true signal. But as we followed it endlessly, the dark slamming hours droning on, the signal was crackling and never seeming to gain strength. Lost! Finally, in desperation, we broke radio silence. In plain language, not code, we begged Emirau that if they heard us, aim a searchlight at the sky.

After more uncounted minutes of staring at our taut faces in the dark windshield, somewhere out in the clouds was a touch of light. Then a flicker. Then the stab of a powerful beam.

We rejoiced, shouting, slapping each other on the backs. Twisting, screaming down through the blackness, we finally saw the wet green lights of a runway, lowered the gear, swept through the rain, and rattled onto the Emirau mat.

Trembling, I looked at our gas gauges. They were ticking on empty. We had maybe ten or fifteen minutes left.

EPILOGUE

While the plane was taxiing, I ripped off my seat belt and rushed back through the cabin. When I slid to a stop beside Patrick, I knelt and gripped his hands. "Grandpa, Grandpa," I cried, "we made it! We're home free."

But his hands were cold, his eyes barely flickering. Slowly, trembling in the effort, he lifted his head slightly and held his hand against my cheek. "Yas, lad," he whispered. "Home. The wars all done. God bless ye...peace, ain't it...peace at last..."

Slowly, his hand fell from my face. His body gave a shiver and went still. The corpsman thrust in, pressing his bony chest, pumping his heart. But no more, there was no need.

"Gone?" I echoed. I was sure of it, and how much it might have spared him! That's what I had to learn, a few dark moments later when a Navy ambulance came swerving up the the hatch. Working fast, the doctor was administering something to Patrick. Maybe adrenalin or oxygen. I couldn't see because they were all crowded in front of me in the neon-lit ambulance. Only when the doctor, a young Navy lieutenant, took me outside in the rain did he say, "He's still alive. Maybe he's got five minutes more, maybe five years. No way to tell. My suspicion is, he's had a stroke. He's started paralysis."

I gripped his arm. "We've just flown him through a hell of a night. Could that have caused it?"

He shrugged. "Anything, my friend. His chart shows H-E, high-explosive head wounds. Your flying him at altitude couldn't have helped, but I guess you had to."

"We couldn't get down on the water," I almost sobbed. "Too much storm."

"Well, he's in luck, sort of. We've got the hospital ship they used for the Guam landing. It's offshore and will pull the hook tomorrow for Pearl. I know a fine brain surgeon who's on it. They've got the facilities to do the job. We'll hope."

"Can I see him again!" I cried, but he'd already turned, hopped into the ambulance beside Patrick and slammed the door.

It's painful for me to remember what happened after that, or to try to fill the hole he'd left in my life.

Just because we'd reached Emirau safely that cursed night didn't mean for a minute that we were home free. We'd no sooner taken off at 2:30 A.M. for Guadalcanal before the radioman rushed into the cockpit. Our IFF, he cried, had gone out. This was the identification-friend-or-foe signal that kept our own planes from shooting us down. Without it, we were appearing as a Japanese bogey to every trigger-happy night fighter squadron, all the way down the 500 miles to Guadalcanal. I told the radioman to contact the fighter-directors at every base and convince them we were a friendly. With the bad weather affecting communications, there was certainly no guarantee. Somebody could fail to get the word. They'd roar up, unable to identify us in the darkness, and blow us away. Then I went back into the cockpit and sat beside Dick Penniman. With our shoulders hunched up, we waited. Interminably, it seemed. When the sky was just turning gray, we came out of a cloud and saw the green mound of Guadalcanal, shining wet in the dawn. Dick smiled. "Maybe your old boy got us through. Something did, anyhow." We glanced at each other, pulled back the power and went on in to land.

I wanted desperately to talk to General Geiger about Patrick. Thank him for what he'd done, and mostly, what could we do next to help him? In a jeep I went racing from Henderson Field to our jungle tent camp at Tetere. The soggy old place was almost deserted. What Geiger hadn't told us, and it wasn't our business, he'd boarded his command ship that morning, he and his First Marine Division leaving for the new landing at Peleliu, less than 2 weeks away.

The strange wooden crates we'd carried down, along with poor Patrick, were filled with the operation charts for the Peleliu invasion. That was the urgency of our flights through the Carolines, and perhaps the irony. All I could think of was Patrick and his friend, the Marine Colonel Earl Ellis, daring to penetrate those islands 20 years before us. For predicting what would happen in the Palaus, the Japanese murdered Ellis. And his earlier predictions about Pearl Harbor—possibly we wouldn't even have been out in that Pacific, had anyone listened to him.

Geiger took Peleliu all right, in an operation that neither he nor Admiral Halsey wanted. They felt it was unnecessary to protect MacArthur's landing in the Philippines, because he was already ashore on Leyte. But the high brass disagreed, insisting that Peleliu had already been planned and couldn't be called off.

And so, for a worthless piece of coral, five miles long by three miles wide, twenty-two thousand human beings, Americans and Japanese, were slaughtered, all the Japanese dead except for a pitiful handful who kept crawling out of their caves and surrendering for the next twenty years. For the Americans, the dead were in the thousands, and the wounded limped on home, cursing a useless fight that the rest of the world had long forgotten.

But Bertie Castle wouldn't ever forget it. My wild childhood chum, the son of our benefactor, Roger Castle, my mother's husband and before that her lover—the cause of my father's suicide—maybe it all ended on Peleliu. Bertie, the crazy bastard, wouldn't work hard enough to be an officer. He'd just buck-ass enlisted as a Marine rifleman. He'd risen to corporal a couple of hours before a Japanese sniper shot him through the head.

What's it all been for? Patrick would ask? We had no answer. I didn't anyhow.

And Patrick couldn't tell us anymore. He did have a stroke some-

EPILOGUE

where in our awful night going through the Carolines. The words he said to me, "peace at last," were indeed his last. He never spoke again.

In his silence, so much lay buried. I know now that though agonizingly wounded, he'd obviously managed to stuff his copy books into a Japanese ammunition tin and hide them in a crevice in his cave. It would be 50 years before his old enemies would finally dig up his words and return him to us.

I don't like writing about Patrick's end. On the hospital ship, the Navy surgeons did an exploratory operation. It proved to be a mistake. A tiny sliver of the rocket was imbedded in a critical part of his brain, affecting both speech and motor skills.

Just before we'd flown Geiger off to his next and final battle, the bloodbath of Okinawa, Mother wrote that my uncle, Brigadier General Matthew Kelly, had flown out to see Patrick at Pearl Harbor. Uncle Matt was furious at his lack of progress. He went over everybody's heads, and with his powerful Washington connections, had Patrick shipped back stateside to the finest medical skills we had. At Bethesda Naval Hospital, the surgeons concluded that they couldn't remove the fragment. All that could be done for Patrick was extensive therapy to get his limbs working, and beyond that, the care and love of his own family.

The night Matthew Kelly took charge of his father's life was important, in a way that none of us knew. Uncle Matt had been in civilian clothes, literally sneaking into Patrick's hospital room at Pearl. After visiting an hour or so, and knocking some heads, Matt hurried out to Hickam Field and caught an Air Corps transport for Guam. He probably never told Patrick why his mission was so secret. Five days later, as a military observer for President Harry Truman, Matt crouched in the cockpit of the Enola Gay, and witnessed the awesome orange cloud of the first atomic bomb.

Our world would never be the same. Nobody had expected it, nobody had known. Even General Geiger, for all his rank, wasn't in on the secret. By now, after three years of constant fighting from Guadalcanal up through Okinawa, he seemed to be wearing out. The last time I saw him in his sun-lit office at Pearl Harbor, he had a dead cigar clamped grimly in his teeth. He and his staff were working on the charts of the invasion of Japan, having no idea that it would never come.

When I told him that after my two years with him, I'd had enough war and wanted to go home, he grunted that I was a damn fool kid. Stay in the Marine Corps, he said. He'd help me if he could. There'd be plenty of wars to go around for everybody. But when I refused, he shrugged and began talking warmly about Patrick. "When you see that relic," he said, "tell him Semper Fi. He knows what it means." Then gruffly, Geiger barked to his adjutant, "Write up orders for Barrow, get him the hell out of here." Only

535

that night did I realize that his way of saying thanks had been to get me a berth on a Pan Am clipper, a luxurious privilege reserved only for officers of flag rank, surely not a lowly captain.

Two mornings later, I was lying on a beach in LaJolla, California with a girl I'd picked up the night before. We were hung over and spent, and when a newsboy ran down the beach, waving his paper and shouting, "Atom Bomb! Atom Bomb! It's Over!," we looked at each other, dumbfounded. We'd never heard of such a thing. We had no idea of what it would mean, this cloud that would darken the rest of our days.

But it was over, indeed. We'd won the world. And so we came pell-melling home, trying to forget the friends, faces and lives that we'd left shattered in the coral rocks and seas of the Pacific.

And then, unexpectedly, on a Sunday in June, 1946, Patrick returned to us. Uncle Matt, back in uniform again, brought him to Mother and Roger Castle's house in Lake Forest. The moment was almost too much for me to process. We were all out on the lawn overlooking the lake. Slowly, Patrick came pegging toward us, walking on two canes, and when Matt or Mother would try to help him, he'd grunt and fling off their arms.

Then came a howl, and here was Pearlie, flapping like a shrieking sea bird in her giant mumu. Typical of Mother, she'd fixed it all, finally locating Pearlie in a hospital on New Caledonia. She'd been there, healing her considerable wounds, ever since being evacuated from the Bougainville jungle after V-J Day. Her son, Father Andre, had died on the island, but old Pearlie was very much alive, crippled in the shoulder yet wrapping herself around Patrick like she'd love him to death.

We all wept, hours it seemed, laughing, then weeping, trying to put it all back together. But I worried about Patrick. His big frame was now just bones, his face shrunken and hollowed like a skeleton head. Yet his blue eyes were sharp. Though he couldn't communicate with us, he didn't miss much. He'd keep grabbing me by the arm, or punching his fist at me. "Go to it, lad," he seemed to be saying. "We got more of this fight left!"

And he hadn't lost sight of the pretty girls, either. Aleka, Uncle Matt's Russian wife, was a beautiful woman. She always wore silky things and Patrick's gnarled hand would unfailingly slip around her and pat her in restricted places. Though Aleka would just laugh, Mother would tell him to grow up, and Pearlie would roar in French, "I'll take care you, *mon vieux*. Old goat or cadaver, what does it matter anymore! *Nous sommes ici, la triomphe!*"

Only Roger Castle's face seemed sad. When he'd glance at me, I know he was seeing Bertie, never to return. Perhaps I'd be his son from then on.

The re-adjustments of post-war life crashed over us. At first,

Mother put Patrick and Pearlie into her guestroom. Then a wing was added for them, turning Bertie Castle's old room into a kitchenette. It didn't work too well. Patrick was immobilized much of the time. Pearlie was difficult anyway, and found prim Lake Forest too confining for a reef princess from Polynesia. When Roger Castle's health began to fail, Pearlie took the cue, and against Mother's protests, hauled Patrick with her back to Tehaare. "Pouf!" she sniffed. "He feels nothing anyhow. Why not let him feel it there, in the place he loves best?"

I hated to see him go. I thought it would be the last time. But now, unfortunately, like all of us returned from the war, we were scrambling back into the competitive business world, trying to make up for the precious young years we'd lost. And we were vowing, never again, a madness like this war.

But too soon, we were shockingly disabused of our idealism. Korea exploded overnight, and certainly not for any reason we'd foreseen or thought mattered. To my dismay—maybe I purposely hadn't married because I sensed something was in the wind—the Marine Corps tapped me to go back and fly in Korea. It would be jets this time. God, I dreaded it, but I didn't duck it. I did a six month combat tour over there before Mother, and mainly Matt in Washington, pulled the military strings and got me home and out. Mother even said that when she'd written Patrick that I'd had to fight again, Pearlie had answered from Tehaare and said he'd thrown a fit. I sensed I knew why, and I loved him even more for wanting to spare me from another senseless war.

But Korea was only the muddled beginning. Our masters in Washington were telling us that the world had been cut in two now. We had to stand and fight for our half. And so we'd blundered into an interminable war. Oh, I bought the Pentagon party line, but I know Patrick would have seen through it. Again and again, we'd be hurled off to fight the next enemies our government had chosen for us to destroy. Rich man's war, poor man's fight, Patrick would be snorting, and it had never changed from his day to ours. A country made by war, weren't we? But who listened then? Instead, meekly, because it gave us jobs, kept our factories pumping out our Good Life, we permitted our leaders to turn our beloved free land into a permanent, oppressive warfare state. For the next fifty years, we, and the clients we'd armed world-wide, good guys versus bad guys, we went over the top to do the paying and the dying for our obscene slaughter, and in the process, God being on Our Side, and the Devil on the Evil Side, between us, we managed to massacre more human beings than had been killed in both World War I and World War II combined.

Peace, Patrick had breathed as his last word. I think he knew what we, in our century, have forgotten. Love, wasn't it? Healing ourselves. Wasn't that the only going home?

None of this was clear to me, really, in the years that followed.

Our culture makes us live a certain way. We're swept up in it, it buys us off, and we're too fearful to break with the past and risk the new. Our lives became sterile punches out of our commuter tickets, and lost golf balls in the country club grass.

In 1951, Mother received word from Tahiti that Pearlie had drowned in a launch that had sunk between Tehaare and Papeete. I was at a banking convention in London at the time, so Mother didn't wait for me. She flew out to the islands and brought Patrick home.

He was never the same after losing Pearlie. I was shocked at how he'd failed. Roger Castle had died, too, so now it was just father and daughter alone in the big house overlooking the lake. By then I'd met your mother, Adelaide, and was madly courting her, as well as trying to better myself in investment banking. So I had less time than I wanted to be with Mother, and Patrick, too.

He seemed to be longing for death to take him. He'd sleep a lot in the days when Mother was off golfing or doing her charity work. He was fascinated by the new wonder of TV, particularly the cowboy and Indian shows. By this time, his moods were such that he'd either be sulking restlessly, or exploding into manic, uncontrollable fits of laughter, at what we didn't know.

Then he got to wandering, and Mother begged me to help with him, which wasn't easy when I was working a hard nine hours downtown at a brokerage firm, and stealing off with Adelaide every night we could. But on weekends, when I wasn't playing golf or squash, I'd go hunt up Patrick. His favorite hiding place was down the bluff overlooking the lake and I found him several times sitting in the tangled thickets.

Now that I've read his diary, I know he must have been remembering my grandmother Daisy here, for his secret get away had been hers, just below the old Archibald house, now wrecked and gone. At other times, Mother had me take him for long drives. He'd be grunting and jabbing at me when we passed Fort Sheridan. Once, I had to take him all the way into Chicago, and on the dingy West Side, locate the site of the Haymarket bombing. There was a monument here, and he leaned against it and wept.

Once, about then, Uncle Matt came back from Washington and sat with Patrick for a long visit. When it was over, Matt strode outside the house and said to me, "Somebody ought to put a bullet in his brain." Mother sobbed, How could he say such a thing! When Matt turned back to us, there were tears in his dark Sioux eyes. "I love him so much, I don't want to see him like this, nor does he want to be this way. Let him out of it!"

I married Adelaide October 25th, 1952. Patrick had attended, but during the ceremony—she was Episcopal, not Catholic, and I went along—I began hearing whoops from the back of the church.

Patrick had a laughing fit, and nobody could shut him up. The ushers carted him outside so he wouldn't wreck things. Then Laidy and I sped off to Jamaica for a two week honeymoon.

We were down there on the night General Eisenhower was elected President. Some of Mother's group, the movers and shakers of Chicago, had given a party at the Racquet Club, all the rock-ribbed Republicans clustered around the big TV screen, watching their white hope win a landslide.

To cheer up Patrick, she'd taken him with her to the party, and it must have worked. When Ike appeared on the screen, flashing his now-famous grin, and jabbing his fingers into the air, V for victory, Patrick fairly danced in joy. Ike had been his friend long ago. Mother knew that. Even if he couldn't say it to her, his exuberance seemed to be triggered by having a good man finally up there to save the nation he loved. Strong hands at the controls, and more than this, during the TV coverage, when Ike was pledging to end the war in Korea, the man he turned to and introduced was Uncle Matthew Kelly, a major-general, and Ike's first national security adviser.

I can only imagine the pride Patrick felt, seeing his little half-breed Injun from Wounded Knee now at the side of the most powerful man of the most powerful nation in the world.

Maybe it was time to let it go.

One of the guests had given Patrick a drink and a cigar. Mother hadn't seen him break her rules, but when she found out, she raced around searching, and finally discovered him standing outside on the Racquet Club balcony. With his hands gripping the concrete balustrade, his old eyes were sweeping the vastness of Chicago. God knows what he saw out there, the muddy streets of his youth, the carriages, the stockyard stink of Back of the Yards. Or the thunder of the Haymarket bomb.

But now the city was exploding in another way. Parties, shouts of "We Like Ike!" Bands were booming his songs, *Battle Hymn of the Republic, Caissons Rolling Along.* From *It's a Grand Old Flag* to *Lili Marlene*, echoes of the last war gone down. *I'm Dreaming of a White Christmas.*

It would be again, now, with Ike.

As Mother ran toward Patrick to bring him in out of the cold, he flicked his cigar away, then creaked to his knees as if he were praying. Not really his habit, but maybe it was that night.

By the time she'd taken him in her arms, his blue eyes were still open, but they saw no more. The smile on his lips was perhaps the peace he'd found, after a lifetime of fighting for it.

Maybe it was better that Laidy and I were lying as lovers on the warm sands of Jamaica when we heard the news. "Let him slip away," she said. "He'd want it like that."

Now that I've read his diary, I think his last smile was his irrepressible optimism. Things could only get better on The Other Side.

We buried him with full military honors in the Lake Forest cemetery overlooking the lake. Though alone, Mother lived out her last years pleasantly and comfortably with her friends and her assured social status. She'd gotten what she wanted. When she died—on the Onwentsia golf course, actually, the day was too damn hot for her to be out there—we buried her beside her father.

In 1964, General Matt Kelly had gone to Vietnam, trouble-shooting for the newly-elected and badly worried Lyndon B. Johnson. The Pentagon had now decided to fight the nasty war with helicopters, but the untried machines were crashing right and left. Uncle Matt ended his life in one, but we didn't bring him home to us. At his request, he was buried beside his mother, Walks Outside, in the common massacre grave at Wounded Knee.

So, my dear ones, they all go. It's life, and we survivors try to live on. Roger Castle did make me his son, in his way, and his generosity added my name to the door of his firm. I've had many good years here, the Castle money insulating you, and certainly me, from any financial strains.

We've played it safe, haven't we, and it's paid off. But I say in closing, and beg you to remember, Patrick gave us that luxury. We are only consuming what he won for us. By his living the glory of our last great adventure, his daring the unknown wilderness, he's handed down to us finally now a blending of all the races and all the frontiers into a single humanity.

If you don't dream, me byes, you die!

God help me, that dream is our story! Sure, we writhe, we groan right now, we're torn apart, conflicted and blitzed by media, lost, our poets and our gods apparently dead. But are they? Isn't our story and Patrick's echoing on? He knew and we must know that we've endured far worse before, and still prevailed!

We *are* there. It *is* better on his Other Side. For now after the millennia of savagery, it's no longer Us versus Them. What a moment of hope! We dare not take it for granted. In our new world—jet-spanned, electronically linked—there are no backwaters left, no strangers, no senseless wars possible, not with all peoples huddling under the prospect of instant death from satellite-glittering skies.

We're all becoming Us. We've had to. One die, all die. Patrick Kelly's wars have brought us this awesome and terrifying peace.

God bless you, dear ones. Keep it.

With love,

Father

540